Domain 105: Shells, Scripting, and Data Management

Objective	Chapter
105.1 Customize and use the shell environment	7
105.2 Customize or write simple scripts	7
105.3 SQL data management	13

Domain 106: User Interfaces and Desktops

Objective	Chapter
106.1 Install and configure X11	2, 6, 8, 14
106.2 Setup a display manager	8
106.3 Accessibility	14

Domain 107: Administrative Tasks

Objective	Chapter
107.1 Manage user and group accounts and related system files	10
107.2 Automate system administration tasks by scheduling jobs	9
107.3 Localization and internationalization	2, 13

Domain 108: Essential System Services

Objective	Chapter
108.1 Maintain system time	2, 13
108.2 System logging	10, 14
108.3 Mail Transfer Agent (MTA) basics	1, 13
108.4 Manage printers and printing	10

Domain 109: Networking Fundamentals

Objective	Chapter
109.1 Fundamentals of Internet protocols	12
109.2 Basic network configuration	12
109.3 Basic network troubleshooting	12
109.4 Configure client side DNS	12

Domain 110: Security

Objective	Chapter
110.1 Perform security administration tasks	4, 10, 12, 14
110.2 Set up host security	10, 12, 14
110.3 Securing data with encryption	12, 14

CompTIA Linux+ Guide to Linux Certification

CompTIA Linux+ Guide to Linux Certification

Fourth Edition

Jason W. Eckert
triOS College

CENGAGE
Learning·

Australia • Brazil • Mexico • Singapore • United Kingdom • United States

CENGAGE Learning®

CompTIA Linux+ Guide to Linux Certification, Fourth Edition
Jason W. Eckert and triOS College

SVP, GM Skills & Global Product Management: Dawn Gerrain

Product Development Manager: Leigh Hefferon

Managing Content Developer: Emma Newsom

Senior Content Developer: Natalie Pashoukos

Development Editors: Ann Shaffer, Kent Williams

Product Assistant: Scott Finger

Vice President, Marketing Services: Jennifer Ann Baker

Senior Marketing Manager: Eric La Scola

Production Director: Patty Stephan

Senior Content Project Manager: Brooke Greenhouse

Managing Art Director: Jack Pendleton

Software Development Manager: Pavan Ethakota

Technical Edit/Quality Assurance: Serge Palladino, Danielle Shaw

Cover Image: © HunThomas/Shutterstock.com

Source: Fedora

For product information and technology assistance, contact us at
Cengage Learning Customer & Sales Support, 1-800-354-9706

For permission to use material from this text or product, submit all requests online at **www.cengage.com/permissions**
Further permissions questions can be e-mailed to **permissionrequest@cengage.com**

Library of Congress Control Number: 2014958602

ISBN: 978-1-305-10714-4

Package ISBN: 978-1-305-10716-8

Cengage Learning
20 Channel Center Street
Boston, MA 02210
USA

Cengage Learning is a leading provider of customized learning solutions with office locations around the globe, including Singapore, the United Kingdom, Australia, Mexico, Brazil, and Japan. Locate your local office at: **www.cengage.com/global**

Cengage Learning products are represented in Canada by Nelson Education, Ltd.

To learn more about Cengage Learning, visit **www.cengage.com**

Purchase any of our products at your local college store or at our preferred online store **www.cengagebrain.com**

Notice to the Reader

Printed in the United States of America
Print Number: 06   Print Year: 2018

Brief Table of Contents

vii

Table of Contents

Introduction

"In a future that includes competition from open source, we can expect that the eventual destiny of any software technology will be to either die or become part of the open infrastructure itself."

Eric S. Raymond, *The Cathedral & the Bazaar: Musings on Linux and Open Source by an Accidental Revolutionary*

As Eric S. Raymond reminds us, open source software will continue to shape the dynamics of the computer software industry for the next long while, just as it has for the last decade. Coined and perpetuated by hackers, the term "open source software" refers to software in which the source code is freely available to anyone who wishes to improve it (usually through collaboration). And, of course, at the heart of the open source software movement lies Linux—an operating system whose rapid growth has shocked the world by demonstrating the nature and power of the open source model.

However, as Linux continues to grow, so must the number of Linux-educated users, administrators, developers, and advocates. Thus we find ourselves in a time where Linux education is of great importance to the information technology industry. Key to demonstrating Linux ability is the certification process. This book, *CompTIA Linux+ Guide to Linux Certification*, uses carefully constructed examples, questions, and practical exercises to prepare readers with the necessary information to achieve the sought-after Linux+ Powered by LPI certification from CompTIA. Whatever your ultimate goal, you can be assured that reading this book in combination with study, creativity, and practice will make the open source world come alive for you as it has for many others.

The Intended Audience

Simply put, this book is intended for those who wish to learn the Linux operating system and master the Linux+ certification exam from CompTIA. It does not assume any prior knowledge of Linux. Also, the topics introduced in this book and the certification exam are geared towards systems administration, yet they are also well suited for those who will use or develop programs for Linux systems.

Chapter Descriptions

Chapter 1, "Introduction to Linux," introduces operating systems as well as the features, benefits, and uses of the Linux operating system. This chapter also discusses the history and development of Linux and open source software.

Chapter 2, "Linux Installation and Usage," outlines the procedures necessary to prepare for and install Linux on a typical computer system. This chapter also describes how to interact with a Linux system via a terminal and enter basic commands into a Linux shell, such as those used to obtain help and properly shut down the system.

Chapter 3, "Exploring Linux Filesystems," outlines the Linux filesystem structure and the types of files that can be found within it. This chapter also discusses commands that can be used to view and edit the content of those files.

Chapter 4, "Linux Filesystem Management," covers the commands you can use to locate and manage files and directories on a Linux filesystem. Furthermore, this chapter outlines the different methods used to link files as well as how to interpret and set file and directory permissions.

Chapter 5, "Linux Filesystem Administration," discusses how to create, mount, and manage filesystems in Linux. This chapter also discusses the various filesystems available for Linux systems and the device files that are used to refer to the devices that may contain these filesystems.

Chapter 6, "Linux Server Deployment," introduces the types of configurations and installation considerations that may prove useful when installing Linux in a server environment. This chapter also discusses common problems that may occur during installation, system rescue, and the ZFS distributed filesystem commonly used on large-scale Linux server systems.

Chapter 7, "Working with the BASH Shell," covers the major features of the BASH shell, including redirection, piping, variables, aliases, and environment files. Also, this chapter details the syntax of basic shell scripts.

Chapter 8, "System Initialization and X Windows," covers the different bootloaders that may be used to start the Linux kernel. This chapter also discusses how daemons are started during system initialization as well as how to start and stop them afterwards. Finally, this chapter discusses the structure of Linux graphical user interfaces as well as their configuration and management.

Chapter 9, "Managing Linux Processes," covers the different types of processes as well as how to view their attributes, change their priority, and kill them. Furthermore, this chapter discusses how to schedule processes to occur in the future using various utilities.

Chapter 10, "Common Administrative Tasks," details three important areas of system administration: printer administration, log file administration, and user administration.

Chapter 11, "Compression, System Backup, and Software Installation," describes utilities that are commonly used to compress and back up files on a Linux filesystem. This chapter also discusses how to install software from source code as well as how to use the Red Hat Package Manager and the Debian Package Manager.

Chapter 12, "Network Configuration," introduces networks, network utilities, and the TCP/IP protocol as well as how to configure the TCP/IP protocol on a NIC or PPP interface. In addition, this chapter details the configuration of name resolution and common networking services and discusses the technologies you can use to administer Linux servers remotely.

Chapter 13, "Configuring Network Services," explores the detailed configuration of key infrastructure, Web, file sharing, e-mail, and database network services. More specifically, this chapter examines the structure and configuration of DHCP, DNS, NTP, NIS, FTP, NFS, Samba, Apache Web server, Postfix, and PostgreSQL services.

Chapter 14, "Troubleshooting, Performance, and Security," discusses the system maintenance cycle as well as good troubleshooting procedures for solving hardware and software problems. This chapter also describes utilities you can use to monitor and pinpoint the cause of performance problems as well as utilities and procedures you can use to secure the Linux system against unauthorized access.

Additional information is contained in the appendices at the rear of the book. Appendix A discusses the certification process, with emphasis on the Linux+ Powered by LPI certification. It also explains how the objective list for the Linux+ Powered by LPI certification matches each chapter in the textbook. Appendix B provides a copy of the GNU Public License. Appendix C explains how to find Linux resources on the Internet and lists some common resources by category.

Features

To ensure a successful learning experience, this book includes the following pedagogical features:

- *Chapter objectives*—Each chapter in this book begins with a detailed list of the concepts to be mastered within that chapter. This list provides you with a quick reference to the contents of that chapter as well as a useful study aid.

- *Illustrations and tables*—Numerous illustrations of server screens and components aid you in the visualization of common setup steps, theories, and concepts. In addition, many tables provide details and comparisons of both practical and theoretical information and can be used for a quick review of topics.

- *End-of-chapter material*—The end of each chapter includes the following features to reinforce the material covered in the chapter:
  - ○ *Summary*—A bulleted list is provided that gives a brief but complete summary of the chapter.
  - ○ *Key Terms list*—A list of all new terms and their definitions.
  - ○ *Review Questions*—A list of review questions tests your knowledge of the most important concepts covered in the chapter.
  - ○ *Hands-on Projects*—Hands-on Projects help you to apply the knowledge gained in the chapter. These projects are designed to be completed in consecutive order, to allow students to build on their knowledge throughout the book.
  - ○ *Discovery Exercises*—Additional projects that guide you through real-world scenarios and advanced topics.

New to This Edition

This edition has been updated to include the concepts and procedures tested on the latest CompTIA Linux+ Powered by LPI certification. More specifically, this edition contains:

- Updated information pertinent to the latest Linux distributions

- New and expanded coverage of distribution-specific topics, such as package managers, with Hands-on Projects designed for both Fedora Linux and Ubuntu Server Linux installed on the same computer.

- New material on Linux technologies such as Systemd, firewalld, ZFS, and AppArmor.

- Updated material on key job-related networking services, including FTP, NFS, Samba, Apache, DNS, DHCP, NTP, Postfix, SSH, VNC, and SQL.

- New and expanded material on security practices and technologies, with a focus on managing server-based Linux systems.

Text and Graphic Conventions

Wherever appropriate, additional information and exercises have been added to this book to help you better understand what is being discussed in the chapter. Icons throughout the text alert you to additional materials. The icons used in this textbook are as follows:

The Note icon is used to present additional helpful material related to the subject being described.

Each Hands-on Project in this book is preceded by the Activity icon and a description of the exercise that follows.

Textbook DVD

The DVD that accompanies this textbook contains the ISO images for Fedora 20 Linux (64-bit) and Ubuntu Server 14.04 Linux (64-bit). You can use these ISO images to install each Linux operating system within a virtual machine on your PC in order to complete the exercises within each chapter.

CertBlaster Test Prep Resources

CompTIA Linux+ Guide to Linux Certification, Fourth Edition includes CertBlaster test preparation questions that mirror the look and feel of the CompTIA Linux+ (Powered by LPI) certification exam.

To log in and access the CertBlaster test preparation questions for *CompTIA Linux+ Guide to Linux Certification, Fourth Edition*, go to *www.certblaster.com/login/*.

Activate your CertBlaster license by entering your name, e-mail address, and access code (found on the card bound in this book) in their fields, and then click Submit.

The CertBlaster user's online manual describes features and gives navigation instructions. CertBlaster offers three practice modes and all the types of questions required to simulate the exams:

- *Assessment mode*—Used to determine the student's baseline level. In this mode, the timer is on, answers are not available, and the student gets a list of questions answered incorrectly, along with a Personal Training Plan.

- *Study mode*—Helps the student understand questions and the logic behind answers by giving immediate feedback both during and after the test. Answers and explanations are available. The timer is optional, and the student gets a list of questions answered incorrectly, along with a Personal Training Plan.

- *Certification mode*—A simulation of the actual exam environment. The timer as well as the number and format of questions from the exam objectives are set according to the exam's format.

For more information about dti test prep products, visit the website at *www.dtipublishing.com*.

Instructor Resources

Instructor Companion Site

Everything you need for your course in one place! This collection of book-specific lecture and class tools is available online at *www.cengage.com/login*. Access and download Power-Point presentations, images, instructor's manual, test banks, and more.

Instructor's Manual—The Instructor's Manual that accompanies this book includes additional material to assist in class preparation, including suggestions for classroom activities, discussion topics, and additional activities.

Solutions—The instructor resources include solutions to all end-of-chapter material, including review questions, projects, and discovery exercises.

Figure Files—Figure files allow instructors to create their own presentations using figures taken from the text.

PowerPoint Presentations—This book comes with Microsoft PowerPoint slides for each chapter. These slides are included as a teaching aid to be used for classroom presentation, to be made available to students on the network for chapter review, or to be printed for classroom distribution. Instructors can add their own slides for additional topics they introduce to the class.

Cognero—Cengage Learning Testing Powered by Cognero is a flexible, online system that allows you to:

- Author, edit, and manage test bank content from multiple Cengage Learning solutions
- Create multiple test versions in an instant
- Deliver tests from your LMS, your classroom, or wherever you want
- Instructor Companion Site (ISBN 978-1-30510-492-1)

ExamConnection

ExamConnection is an online testing system that automatically grades students and keeps class and student records. ExamConnection tests against Cengage's textbook, as well as against the CompTIA Linux+ (Powered by LPI) certification exam, including a quiz for each chapter in the book along with a mid-term and final exam. ExamConnection is managed by the classroom instructor who has 100 percent of the control, 100 percent of the time.

- ExamConnection (ISBN 978-1-30510-507-2)

LabConnection

With powerful computer-based exercises, video demonstrations, lab simulations, and in-depth remediation capabilities, LabConnection provides a uniquely integrated supplement to hands-on networking courses and can be used both as a virtual lab and homework assignment tool. LabConnection supports Cengage Learning's textbooks, the corresponding certification exam, and offers remediation towards both. It includes the following features:

Enhanced Comprehension—Through the LabConnection labs and guidance, while in the virtual lab environment, the student develops skills that are accurate and consistently effective.

Exercises—Includes dozens of exercises that assess and prepare the learner for the virtual labs, establishing and solidifying the skills and knowledge required to complete the lab.

Virtual Labs—Labs consist of end-to-end procedures performed in a simulated environment where the student can practice the skills required of professionals.

Guided Learning—LabConnection allows learners to make mistakes, but alerts them to errors made before they can move on to the next step, sometimes offering demonstration as well.

Video demonstrations—Instructor-led video demonstrations guide the learners step by step through the labs while providing additional insights to solidify the concepts.

SCORM Compliant Grading and Record Keeping—LabConnection will grade the exercises and record the completion status of the lab Portion, easily porting to and compatible with distance learning platforms.

To get started with LabConnection, login at *https://login.cengage.com*. If you do not have a Cengage faculty account, go to "New Faculty User" to create an account.

- LabConnection online (ISBN 978-1-30510-797-7)
- LabConnection on DVD (ISBN 978-1-30510-801-1)

Total Solutions for CompTIA Linux+

To access additional materials, please visit *www.cengagebrain.com*. At the *CengageBrain .com* home page, search for the ISBN of your title (from the back cover of your book), using the search box at the top of the page. This will take you to the product page where these resources can be found. Additional resources include a Lab Manual, CourseNotes, assessment, and digital labs.

Companion Lab Manual

The Lab Manual provides you with the hands-on instruction necessary to prepare for the certification exam. Designed for classroom-led or self-paced study, labs complement main text content and offer a unique, practical approach to learning that is a key component to the exams. The Lab Manual includes lab activities, objectives, materials lists, step-by-step procedures, illustrations, and review questions.

- Lab Manual (ISBN 978-1-30510-757-1)

CourseNotes

This six-panel quick reference card reinforces the critical knowledge related to CompTIA Linux+ and the CompTIA Linux+ (Powered by LPI) certification exam in a visual and user-friendly format. CourseNotes will serve as a great reference tool during and after you complete the course.

- CourseNotes (ISBN 978-1-30510-504-1)

Becoming a CompTIA Certified IT Professional is Easy

It's also the best way to reach greater professional opportunities and rewards.

Why Get CompTIA Certified?

Growing Demand

Labor estimates predict some technology fields will experience growth of over 20% by the year 2020.* CompTIA certification qualifies the skills required to join this workforce.

Higher Salaries

IT professionals with certifications on their resume command better jobs, earn higher salaries and have more doors open to new multi-industry opportunities.

Verified Strengths

91% of hiring managers indicate CompTIA certifications are valuable in validating IT expertise, making certification the best way to demonstrate your competency and knowledge to employers.**

Universal Skills

CompTIA certifications are vendor neutral—which means that certified professionals can proficiently work with an extensive variety of hardware and software found in most organizations.

Learn > **Certify** > **Work**

Learn more about what the exam covers by reviewing the following:

- Exam objectives for key study points.
- Sample questions for a general overview of what to expect on the exam and examples of question format.
- Visit online forums, like LinkedIn, to see what other IT professionals say about CompTIA exams.

Purchase a voucher at a Pearson VUE testing center or at CompTIAstore.com.

- Register for your exam at a Pearson VUE testing center:
- Visit pearsonvue.com/CompTIA to find the closest testing center to you.
- Schedule the exam online. You will be required to enter your voucher number or provide payment information at registration.
- Take your certification exam.

Congratulations on your CompTIA certification!

- Make sure to add your certification to your resume.
- Check out the CompTIA Certification Roadmap to plan your next career move.

Learn more: Certification.CompTIA.org/linuxplus

* Source: CompTIA 9th Annual Information Security Trends study: 500 U.S. IT and Business Executives Responsible for Security
** Source: CompTIA Employer Perceptions of IT Training and Certification
*** Source: 2013 IT Skills and Salary Report by CompTIA Authorized Partner

Author Biography

Jason W. Eckert is an experienced technical trainer, consultant, and best-selling author in the information technology (IT) industry. With over 20 IT certifications, 25 years of IT experience, 4 published apps, and 22 published textbooks covering topics such as UNIX, Linux, Apache, MySQL, Windows Server, Security, Microsoft Exchange, PowerShell, Black-Berry Enterprise Server, and video game development, Mr. Eckert brings his expertise to every class that he teaches at triOS College. He is also the dean of technology at triOS College, where he continues to refine and improve college technology programs. For more information about Mr. Eckert, visit *about.me/jasoneckert*.

Acknowledgments

First, I would like to thank the staff at Cengage for an overall enjoyable experience writing a textbook on Linux that takes a fundamentally different approach than traditional textbooks. Additionally, I wish to thank Natalie Pashoukos, Brooke Greenhouse, Sumathy Kumaran, Ann Shaffer, and Kent Williams for working extremely hard to pull everything together and ensure that the book provides a magnificent Linux experience. I'm also very grateful to our technical reviewers, Serge Palladino and Danielle Shaw, who checked every chapter top to bottom for errors. Finally, I wish to thank Frank Gerencser of triOS College for freeing me up to write this book, the Starbucks Coffee Company for keeping me on schedule, and my dog Pepper for continually reminding me that taking a break is always a good idea.

Readers are encouraged to e-mail comments, questions, and suggestions regarding *CompTIA Linux+ Guide to Linux Certification, Fourth Edition,* to Jason W. Eckert: jason.eckert@ trios.com.

Before You Begin

Linux can be a large and intimidating topic if studied in a haphazard way. So, as you begin your study of Linux, keep in mind that each chapter in this book builds on the preceding one. To ensure that you gain a solid understanding of core Linux concepts, read the chapters in consecutive order. You should also participate in a local Linux Users Group (LUG) and explore the Internet for websites, FAQs, HOWTOs, and newsgroups that will expand your knowledge of Linux.

Lab Requirements

The following hardware is required at minimum for the Hands-on Projects at the end of each chapter:

- A 64-bit CPU
- 4 GB RAM
- 80 GB hard disk

Linux technical expertise is essential in today's computer workplace as more and more companies switch to Linux to meet their computing needs. Thus, it is important to understand how Linux can be used, what benefits Linux offers to a company, and how Linux has developed and continues to develop. In the first half of this chapter, you learn about operating system terminology and features of the Linux operating system, as well as the history and development of Linux. Later in this chapter, you learn about the various types of Linux and about the situations in which Linux is used.

Operating Systems

Every computer has two fundamental types of components: hardware and software. You are probably familiar with these terms, but it's helpful to review their meanings so you can more easily understand how Linux helps them work together.

Hardware consists of the physical components inside a computer that are electrical in nature; they contain a series of circuits that are used to manipulate the flow of information. A computer can contain many different pieces of hardware, including the following:

- A processor (also known as the central processing unit or CPU), which computes information
- Physical memory (also known as random access memory or RAM), which stores information needed by the processor
- Hard disk and solid state disk drives, which store most of the information that you use
- CD and DVD drives, which read and write information to and from CD and DVD discs
- Flash memory card readers, which read and write information to and from removable memory cards, such as Secure Digital (SD) cards
- Sound cards, which provide sound to external speakers
- Video cards, which display results to the computer monitor
- Circuit boards (also known as mainboards or motherboards), which hold and provide electrical connections between various hardware components

Software, on the other hand, refers to the sets of instructions or **programs** that allow the various hardware components to manipulate data (or files). When a bank teller types information into the computer behind the counter at a bank, for example, that bank teller is using a program that understands what to do with your bank records. Programs and data are usually stored on hardware media, such as hard disks or solid state disks, although they can also be stored on removable media or even embedded in computer chips. These programs are loaded into various parts of your computer hardware (such as your computer's memory and processor) when you first turn on your computer, and when you start additional software, such as word processors or Internet browsers. After a program is executed on your computer's hardware, that program is referred to as a **process**. In other words, a program is a file stored on your computer, whereas a process is that file in action, performing a certain task.

There are two types of programs. The first type, **applications** (or **apps**), includes those programs designed for a specific use and with which you commonly interact, such as word processors, computer games, graphical manipulation programs, and computer system utilities. The second type, **operating system (OS)** software, consists of a series of software components used to control the hardware of your computer. Without an operating system, you would not be able to use your computer. Turning on a computer loads the operating system into computer hardware, which then loads and centrally controls all other application software in the background. At this point, the **user** (the person using the computer) is free to interact with the applications, perhaps by typing on the keyboard or clicking a mouse. Applications then take the information supplied by the user and relay it to the operating system. The operating system then uses the computer hardware to carry out the requests. The relationship between users, application software, operating system software, and computer hardware is illustrated in Figure 1-1.

The operating system carries out many different tasks by interacting with many different types of computer hardware. For the operating system to accomplish this, it must contain the appropriate device driver software for every hardware device in your computer. Each **device driver** tells the operating system how to use that specific device. The operating system also provides a **user interface**, which is a program that accepts user input indicating what is to be done, forwards this input to the operating system for completion, and, after it is completed, gives the results back to the user. The user interface can be a command-line prompt, in which the user types commands, or it can be a **graphical user interface (GUI)**, which consists of menus, dialog boxes and symbols (known as icons) that the user can interact with via the keyboard or the mouse. A typical Linux GUI is shown in Figure 1-2.

Finally, operating systems offer **system services**, which are applications that handle system-related tasks, such as printing, scheduling programs, and network access. These system services determine most of the functionality that is seen in an operating system. Different operating systems offer different system services, and many operating systems allow users to customize the services they offer. A **server** is a computer with an operating system that is configured to allow other computers to connect to it from across a network.

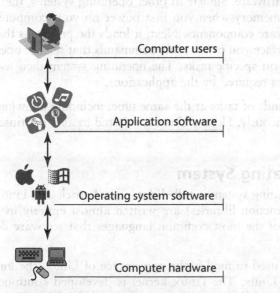

Computer users

Application software

Operating system software

Computer hardware

Figure 1-1 The role of operating system software

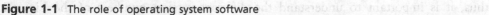

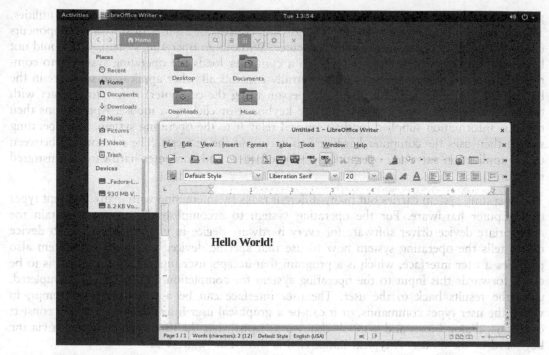

Figure 1-2   A Linux graphical user interface

The Linux Operating System

Linux (pronounced "lih-nucks") is an operating system that is used today to run a variety of applications on a variety of different hardware. Similar to other operating systems, the Linux operating system loads into computer memory when you first power on your computer and initializes (or activates) all of the hardware components. Next, it loads the programs that display the interface. From within the interface you can execute commands that tell the operating system and other applications to perform specific tasks. The operating system then uses the computer hardware to perform the tasks required by the applications.

Linux has the ability to manage thousands of tasks at the same time, including allowing multiple users to access the system simultaneously. Hence, Linux is referred to as a **multiuser** and **multitasking** operating system.

Versions of the Linux Operating System

The core component of the Linux operating system is called the Linux **kernel**. The Linux kernel and supporting software (called function libraries) are written almost entirely in the C programming language, which is one of the most common languages that software developers use when creating programs.

Although a variety of software can be used to modify the appearance of Linux, the underlying kernel is common to all types of Linux. The Linux kernel is developed continuously;, thus, it is important to understand the different version numbers of the Linux kernel to decide which kernel version is appropriate for your needs. Because the Linux kernel is directly responsible for controlling the computer's hardware (via device drivers), you might sometimes need to upgrade the Linux kernel after installing Linux, in order to take advantage of new technologies or to fix problems (also known as bugs) related to your computer's hardware. Consequently, a good understanding of your system's hardware is important in deciding which kernel to use.

A complete list of kernels, kernel versions, and their improvements can be found on the Internet at *www.kernel.org*.

In some cases, updates in the form of a kernel module or a kernel patch can be used to provide or fix hardware supported by the kernel. Kernel modules and kernel patches are discussed later in this book.

Identifying Kernel Versions

Linux kernel versions are made up of the following three components:

- Major number
- Minor number
- Revision number

Let's look at a sample Linux kernel version, 3.15.9. In this example, the **major number** is the number 3, which indicates the major revision to the Linux kernel. The **minor number**, represented by the number 15, indicates the minor revision and stability of the Linux kernel. An odd minor number indicates a developmental kernel, whereas an even minor number indicates a production kernel. **Developmental kernels** are not fully tested and imply instability; they are tested for vulnerabilities by people who develop Linux software. **Production kernels** are developmental kernels that have been thoroughly tested by several Linux developers and are declared to be stable. In the previous example, the kernel has a major number of 3 and a minor number of 15. Because the minor number is odd, you know that this is a developmental kernel. This kernel will eventually be improved by Linux developers, tested, and declared stable. When this happens, the version of this kernel will change to 3.16 (indicating a production kernel).

Linux kernel changes occur frequently. Those changes that are very minor are represented by a **revision number** indicating the most current changes to the version of the particular kernel that is being released. For example, a 3.16.12 kernel has a major number of 3, a minor number of 16, and a revision number of 12. This kernel is the 12th release of the 3.16 kernel. Some kernels might have over 100 different revisions, as a result of developers making constant improvements to the kernel code.

When choosing a kernel for a mission-critical computer such as an e-mail server, ensure that the minor number is even. This reduces the chance that you will encounter a bug in the kernel and, hence, saves you the time needed to change kernels.

Table 1-1 shows the latest revisions of each key major and minor kernel released since the initial release of Linux.

Kernel Version	Date Released	Type
0.01	September 1991	First Linux kernel
0.12	January 1992	Production (stable)
0.95	March 1992	Developmental
0.98.6	December 1992	Production (stable)
0.99.15	March 1994	Developmental
1.0.8	April 1994	Production (stable)
1.1.95	March 1995	Developmental
1.2.12	July 1995	Production (stable)
1.3.100	May 1996	Developmental
2.0.36	November 1998	Production (stable)
2.1.132	December 1998	Developmental
2.2.26	February 2004 (latest release; was developed concurrently with newer kernels)	Production (stable)
2.3.99	May 2000	Developmental
2.4.17	December 2001	Production (stable)
2.5.75	July 2003	Developmental
2.6.35	August 2010	Production (stable)
3.2.62	January 2012	Production (stable)
3.4.103	May 2012	Production (stable)
3.10.54	June 2013	Production (stable)
3.12.28	November 2013	Production (stable)
3.14.18	March 2014	Production (stable)
3.15.10	March 2014	Developmental
3.16.2	September 2014	Production (stable)

Table 1-1 Latest revisions of common Linux kernels

Licensing Linux

Companies often choose Linux as their operating system because of the rules governing Linux licensing. Unlike most other operating systems, Linux is freely developed and continuously improved by a large community of software developers. For this reason, it is referred to as **Open Source Software (OSS)**.

To understand what OSS is, you must first understand how source code is used to create programs. **Source code** refers to the list of instructions that a software developer writes to make up a program; an example of source code is depicted in Figure 1-3.

```
#define MODULE
#include <linux/module.h>
int init_module(void){
        printk("My module has been activated.\n");
        return 0;
}
void cleanup_module(void){
        printk("My module has been deactivated.");
}
```

Figure 1-3 Source code

After the software developer finishes writing the instructions, the source code is compiled into a format (called machine language) that only your computer's processor can understand and execute. To edit an existing program, the software developer must edit the source code and then recompile it.

The format and structure of source code follows certain rules defined by the **programming language** in which it was written. Programmers write Linux source code in many different programming languages. After being compiled into machine language, all programs look the same to the computer operating system, regardless of the programming language in which they were written. As a result, software developers choose a programming language to create source code based on ease of use, functionality, and comfort level.

The fact that Linux is an OSS operating system means that software developers can read other developers' source code, modify that source code to make the software better, and redistribute that source code to other developers who might improve it further. Like all OSS, Linux source code must be distributed free of charge, regardless of the number of modifications made to it. People who develop OSS commonly use the Internet to share their source code, manage software projects, and submit comments and fixes for bugs (flaws). In this way, the Internet acts as the glue that binds together Linux developers in particular and OSS developers in general.

 The complete open source definition can be found at *www.opensource.org.*

Here are some implications of the OSS way of developing software:

- Software is developed very rapidly through widespread collaboration.
- Software bugs (errors) are noted and promptly fixed.
- Software features evolve very quickly, based on users' needs.
- The perceived value of the software increases because it is based on usefulness and not on price.

As you can imagine, the ability to share ideas and source code is beneficial to software developers. However, a company's business model changes drastically when OSS enters the picture. The main issue is this: How can a product that is distributed freely generate revenue? After all, without revenue any company will go out of business.

The OSS process of software development was never intended to generate revenue directly. Its goal was to help people design better software by eliminating many of the problems associated with traditional software development, which is typically driven by predefined corporate plans and rigid schedules. By contrast, OSS development assumes that software creation is an art in which a particular problem can be solved in many different ways. One software developer might create a program that measures widgets using four pages of source code, while another developer might create a program that does the same task in one page of source code. You might think that this openness to multiple ways of solving a problem would result in a haphazard software development process, but the sharing of ideas that is the heart of OSS development keeps developers focused on the best possible solutions. Also, while OSS developers contribute their strengths to a project, they learn new techniques from other developers at the same time.

Because the selling of software for profit discourages the free sharing of source code, OSS generates revenue indirectly. Companies usually make money by selling computer hardware that runs OSS, by selling customer support for OSS, or by creating **closed source software** programs that run on open source products such as Linux.

The OSS development process is, of course, not the only way to develop and license software. Table 1-2 summarizes the types of software you are likely to encounter. The following section explains these types in more detail.

Types of Open Source Licenses

Linux adheres to the **GNU General Public License (GPL)**, which was developed by the **Free Software Foundation (FSF)**. The GPL stipulates that the source code of any software published under its license must be freely available. If someone modifies that source code, that person must also redistribute that source code freely, thereby keeping the source code free forever.

GNU stands for "GNU's Not UNIX."

The GPL is freely available at *www.gnu.org* and in this book's Appendix B, "GNU General Public License."

Type	Description
Open source	Software in which the source code and software can be obtained free of charge and can be modified
Closed source	Software in which the source code is not available; although this type of software might be distributed free of charge, it is usually quite costly
Freeware	Closed source software that is given out free of charge
Shareware	Closed source software that is initially given out free of charge but that requires payment after a certain period of use

Table 1-2   Software types

Another type of open source license is the **artistic license,** which ensures that the source code of the program is freely available yet allows the original author of the source code some control over the changes made to it. Thus, if one developer obtains and improves the source code of a program, the original author has the right to reject those improvements. As a result of this restriction, artistic licenses are rarely used because many developers do not want to work on potentially futile projects.

In addition to the two different open source licenses mentioned, many types of open source licenses are available that differ only slightly from one another. Those licenses must adhere to the open source definition but might contain extra conditions that the open source definition does not.

A list of approved open source licenses can be found at *www.open source.org.*

Types of Closed Source Licenses Closed source software can be distributed for free or for a cost; either way, the source code for the software is unavailable from the original developers. The majority of closed source software is sold commercially and bears the label of its manufacturer. Each of these software packages can contain a separate license that restricts free distribution of the program and its source code in many different ways.

Examples of closed source software are software created by companies such as Microsoft, Apple, or Electronic Arts (EA).

Another type of closed source software is **freeware,** in which the software program is distributed free of charge, yet the source code is unavailable. Freeware might also contain licenses that restrict the distribution of source code. Another approach to this style of closed source licensing is **shareware,** which is distributed free of charge, yet after a certain number of hours of usage, or to gain certain features of the program, payment is required. Although freeware and shareware do not commonly distribute their source code under an open source license, some people incorrectly refer to freeware as OSS, assuming that the source code is free as well.

Linux Advantages

Many operating systems are in use today; the main ones include Linux, Microsoft Windows, UNIX, and Mac OS X. Notably, Linux is the fastest growing operating system released to date. Although Linux was only created in 1991, the number of Linux users estimated by Red Hat in 1998 was 7.5 million, and the number of Linux users estimated by Google in 2010 was over 40 million (including the number of Linux-based Android smartphone and device users). In 2013, *LinuxCounter.net* (*http://linuxcounter.net*) estimated that the number of Linux users was over 70 million, and Google estimated that over 900 million Linux-based Android devices had shipped to date. Since 1998, many large companies, including

IBM, Hewlett-Packard, Intel, and Dell, have announced support for Linux and OSS. In the year 2000, IBM announced plans to spend one billion dollars on Linux and Linux development alone.

There are a multitude of reasons that so many people have begun using Linux. The following advantages are examined in the sections that follow:

- Risk reduction
- Meeting business needs
- Stability and security
- Flexibility for different hardware platforms
- Ease of customization
- Ease of obtaining support
- Cost reduction

Risk Reduction Companies need software to perform mission-critical tasks, such as database tracking, Internet business (e-commerce), and data manipulation. However, changes in customer needs and market competition can cause the software a company uses to change frequently. This can be very costly and time-consuming, but is a risk that companies must take. Imagine that a fictitious company, ABC, Inc., buys a piece of software from a fictitious software vendor, ACME, Inc., to integrate its sales and accounting information with customers via the Internet. What would happen if ACME went out of business or stopped supporting the software due to lack of sales? In either case, ABC would be using a product that had no software support, and any problems that ABC had with the software after that time would go unsolved and could result in lost revenue. In addition, all closed source software is eventually retired some time after it is purchased, forcing companies to buy new software every so often to obtain new features and maintain software support.

If ABC instead chose to use an OSS product and the original developers became unavailable to maintain it, then ABC would be free to take the source code, add features to it, and maintain it themselves provided the source code was redistributed free of charge. Also, most OSS does not retire after a short period of time because collaborative open source development results in constant software improvement geared to the needs of the users.

Meeting Business Needs Recall that Linux is merely one product of open source development. Many thousands of OSS programs are in existence, and new ones are created daily by software developers worldwide. Most open source Internet tools have been developed for quite some time now, and the focus in the Linux community in the past few years has been on developing application software for Linux, such as databases and office productivity suites. Almost all of this software is open source and freely available, compared to other operating systems, in which most software is closed source and costly.

OSS is easy to locate on the Web, at sites such as SourceForge (*www.sourceforge.net*) and GNU Savannah (*http://savannah.gnu.org*). New software is published to these sites daily. SourceForge alone hosts over 430,000 different software developments.

Common software available for Linux includes but is not limited to the following:

- Scientific and engineering software
- Software emulators
- Web servers, Web browsers, and e-commerce suites
- Desktop productivity software (e.g., word processors, presentation software, spreadsheets)
- Graphics manipulation software
- Database software
- Security software

In addition, companies that run the UNIX operating system might find it easy to migrate to Linux. For those companies, Linux supports most UNIX commands and standards, which makes transitioning to Linux very easy because the company likely would not need to purchase additional software or retrain staff. For example, suppose a company that tests scientific products has spent much time and energy developing custom software that runs on the UNIX operating system. If this company transitions to another operating system, its staff would need to be retrained or hired, and much of the custom software would need to be rewritten and retested, which could result in a loss of customer confidence. If, however, that company transitions to Linux, the staff would require little retraining, and little of the custom software would need to be rewritten and retested, hence saving money and minimizing impact on consumer confidence.

For companies that need to train staff on Linux usage and administration, several educational resources and certification exams exist for various Linux skill levels. Certification benefits and the CompTIA Linux+ Powered by LPI certification are discussed in this book's Appendix A, "Certification."

In addition, for companies that require a certain development environment or need to support custom software developed in the past, Linux provides support for most programming languages.

Stability and Security OSS is developed by those people who have a use for it. This collaboration among several developers with a common need speeds up software creation, and when bugs in the software are found by these users, bug fixes are created very quickly. Often, the users who identify the bugs can fix the problem because they have the source code, or they can provide detailed descriptions of their problems so that other developers can fix them.

By contrast, customers using closed source operating systems must rely on the operating system vendor to fix any bugs. Users of closed source operating systems must report the bug to the manufacturer and wait for the manufacturer to develop, test, and release a solution to the problem, known as a **hot fix**. This process might take weeks or even months to occur. For most companies and individuals, this process is slow and costly. The thorough and collaborative open source approach to testing software and fixing software bugs increases the stability of Linux; it is not uncommon to find a Linux system that has been running continuously for months or even years without being turned off.

In addition, several Internet newsgroups allow Linux users to post messages and reply to previously posted messages. If someone has a specific problem with Linux, that person can simply post her problem on an Internet newsgroup and receive help from those who know the solution to the problem. Linux newsgroups are posted to frequently; thus, you can usually expect a solution to a problem within hours. A list of common Linux newsgroups can be found at *http://groups.google.com.*

Appendix C, "Finding Linux Resources on the Internet," describes how to navigate Internet resources and lists some common resources useful throughout this book.

Although online support is the most common method of getting help, other methods are available. Most Linux distributions provide professional telephone support services for a modest fee, and many organizations exist to give free support to those who ask. The most common of these groups are referred to as **Linux User Groups (LUGs)**, and most large cities across the globe have at least one. LUGs are groups of Linux users who meet regularly to discuss Linux-related issues and problems. An average LUG meeting consists of several new Linux users (also known as Linux newbies), administrators, developers, and experts (also known as Linux gurus). LUG meetings are a place to solve problems as well as learn about the local Linux community. Most LUGs host Internet Web sites that contain a multitude of Linux resources, including summaries of past meetings and discussions. One common activity seen at a LUG meeting is referred to as an Installfest; several members bring in their computer equipment to install Linux and other Linux-related software. This approach to transferring knowledge is very valuable to LUG members because concepts can be demonstrated and the solutions to problems can be modeled by more experienced Linux users.

 To find a list of available LUGs in your region, search for the words "LUG cityname" on an Internet search engine such as *www.google.com* (substituting your city's name for "*cityname*"). When searching for a LUG, keep in mind that LUGs might go by several different names; for example, the LUG in Hamilton, Ontario, Canada is known as HLUG (Hamilton Linux Users Group). Many LUGs today are managed using Facebook groups or meeting sites such as *www.meetup.com.*

Cost Reduction Linux is less expensive than other operating systems, such as Windows, because there is no cost associated with acquiring the software. In addition, a wealth of OSS can run on a variety of different hardware platforms running Linux, and a large community of developers is available to diagnose and fix bugs in a short period of time for free. However, although Linux and the Linux source code are distributed freely, implementing Linux is not cost free. Costs include purchasing the computer hardware necessary for the computers hosting Linux, hiring people to install and maintain Linux, and training users of Linux software.

The largest costs associated with Linux are the costs associated with hiring people to maintain the Linux system. However, closed source operating systems have this cost in addition to the cost of the operating system itself. The overall cost of using a particular operating system is known as the **total cost of ownership (TCO)**. Table 1-3 shows an example of the factors involved in calculating the TCO for operating systems.

Operating System	Linux	Closed Source Operating System
Operating system cost	$0	Greater than $0
Cost of administration	Low: Stability is high and bugs are fixed quickly by open source developers.	Moderate/high: Bug fixes are created by the vendor of the operating system, which could result in costly downtime.
Cost of additional software	Low/none: Most software available for Linux is also open source.	High: Most software available for closed source operating systems is also closed source.
Cost of software upgrades	Low/none	Moderate/high: Closed source software is eventually retired, and companies must buy upgrades or new products to gain functionality and stay competitive.

Table 1-3   **Calculating the total cost of ownership**

The History of Linux

Linux is based on the UNIX operating system developed by Ken Thompson and Dennis Ritchie of AT&T Bell Laboratories in 1969 and was developed through the efforts of many people as a result of the hacker culture that formed in the 1980s. Therefore, to understand how and why Linux emerged on the operating system market, you must first understand UNIX and the hacker culture. Figure 1-4 illustrates a timeline representing the history of the UNIX and Linux operating systems.

UNIX

The UNIX operating system has roots running back to 1965, when the Massachusetts Institute of Technology (MIT), General Electric, and AT&T Bell Laboratories began development of an operating system called **Multiplexed Information and Computing Service (MULTICS)**. MULTICS was a test project intended to reveal better ways of developing time-sharing operating systems, in which the operating system regulates the amount of time each process has to use the processor. The project was abandoned in 1969. However, Ken Thompson, who had worked on the MULTICS operating system, continued to experiment with operating systems after the project was abandoned. In 1969, he developed an operating system called **UNIX** that ran on the DEC (Digital Equipment Corporation) PDP-7 computer.

Shortly thereafter, Dennis Ritchie invented the C programming language that was used on Ken Thompson's UNIX operating system. The C programming language was a revolutionary language. Most programs at the time needed to be written specifically for the hardware of the computer, which involved referencing volumes of information regarding the hardware in order to write a simple program. However, the C programming language was much easier to use to write programs, and it was possible to run a program on several different machines without having to rewrite the code. The UNIX operating system was rewritten in the C programming language, and by the late-1970s, the UNIX operating system ran on different

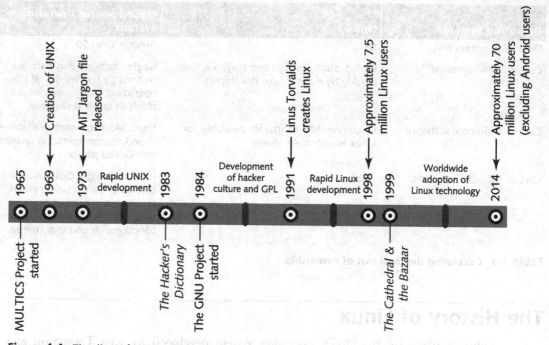

Figure 1-4 Timeline of UNIX and Linux development

hardware platforms, something that the computing world had never seen until that time. Hence, people called UNIX a portable operating system.

Unfortunately, the company Ken Thompson and Dennis Ritchie worked for (AT&T) was restricted by a federal court order from marketing UNIX. In an attempt to keep UNIX viable, AT&T sold the UNIX source code to several different companies, encouraging them to agree to standards among them. Each of these companies developed its own variety, or **flavor**, of UNIX yet adhered to standards agreed upon by all. AT&T also gave free copies of the UNIX source code to certain universities to promote widespread development of UNIX. One result of this was a UNIX version developed at the University of California, Berkeley, in the early 1980s known as **BSD (Berkeley Software Distribution)**. In 1982, one of the companies to whom AT&T sold UNIX source code (Sun Microsystems) marketed UNIX on relatively cheaper hardware and sold thousands of computers that ran UNIX to various companies and universities.

Throughout the 1980s, UNIX found its place primarily in large corporations that had enough money to purchase the expensive computing equipment needed to run UNIX (usually a DEC PDP-11, VAX, or Sun Microsystems computer). A typical UNIX system in the 1980s could cost over $100,000, yet it performed thousands of tasks for client computers (also known as dumb terminals). Today, UNIX still functions in that environment; most large companies employ different flavors of UNIX for their heavy-duty, mission-critical tasks, such as e-commerce and database hosting. Common flavors of UNIX today include Oracle's **Solaris** (formerly SUN Microsystem's Solaris), Hewlett-Packard's **HP-UX**, IBM's **AIX**, as well as Apple's **Macintosh OS X** and **iOS** operating systems.

The Hacker Culture

The term **hacker** refers to a person who attempts to expand his knowledge of computing through experimentation. It should not be confused with the term **cracker**, which refers to someone who illegally uses computers for personal benefit or to cause damage.

In the early days of UNIX, hackers came primarily from engineering or scientific backgrounds, because those were the fields in which most UNIX development occurred. Fundamental to hacking was the idea of sharing knowledge. A famous hacker, Richard Stallman, promoted the free sharing of ideas while he worked at the Artificial Intelligence Laboratory at MIT. He believed that free sharing of all knowledge in the computing industry would promote development. In the mid-1980s, Stallman formed the Free Software Foundation (FSF) to encourage free software development. This movement was quickly accepted by the academic community in universities around the world, and many university students and other hackers participated in making free software, most of which ran on UNIX. As a result, the hacker culture was commonly associated with the UNIX operating system.

Unfortunately, UNIX was not free software, and by the mid-1980s some of the collaboration seen earlier by different UNIX vendors diminished and UNIX development fragmented into different streams. As a result, UNIX did not represent the ideals of the FSF, and so Stallman founded the **GNU Project** in 1984 to promote free development for a free operating system that was not UNIX.

A description of the FSF and GNU can be found at *www.gnu.org*.

This development eventually led to the publication of the GNU Public License (GPL), which legalized free distribution of source code and encouraged collaborative development. Any software published under this license must be freely available with its source code; any modifications made to the source code must then be redistributed free as well, keeping the software development free forever.

As more and more hackers worked together developing software, a hacker culture developed with its own implied rules and conventions. Most developers worked together without ever meeting each other; they communicated primarily via newsgroups and e-mail. *The Hacker's Dictionary*, published by MIT in 1983, detailed the terminology regarding computing and computing culture that had appeared since the mid-1970s; it, along with the FSF, GNU, GPL, served to codify the goals and ideals of the hacker culture. But it wasn't until the publication of Eric S. Raymond's *The Cathedral and the Bazaar*, in 1999, that the larger world was introduced to this thriving culture. Raymond, a hacker himself, described several aspects of the hacker culture:

- Software users are treated as codevelopers.
- Software is developed primarily for peer recognition and not for money.
- The original author of a piece of software is regarded as the owner of that software and coordinates the cooperative software development.
- The use of a particular piece of software determines its value, not its cost.

- Attacking the author of source code is never done. Instead, bug fixes are either made or recommended.
- Developers must understand the implied rules of the hacker culture before being accepted into it.

This hacker culture proved to be very productive, with several thousand free tools and applications created in the 1980s, including the famous Emacs editor, which is a common tool used in Linux today. During this time, many programming function libraries and UNIX-like commands also appeared as a result of the work on the GNU Project. Hackers became accustomed to working together via newsgroup and e-mail correspondence. In short, this hacker culture, which supported free sharing of source code and collaborative development, set the stage for Linux.

Linux

Although Richard Stallman started the GNU Project to make a free operating system, the GNU operating system never took off. Much of the experience gained by hackers developing the GNU Project was later pooled into Linux. A Finnish student named **Linus Torvalds** first developed Linux in 1991 when he was experimenting with improving **MINIX** (Mini-UNIX, a small educational version of UNIX developed by Andrew Tannenbaum) for the Intel x86 platform. The Intel x86 platform was fast becoming standard in homes and businesses around the world and was a good choice for any free development at the time. The key feature of the Linux operating system that attracted the development efforts of the hacker culture was the fact that Torvalds had published Linux under the GNU Public License.

Since 1991, when the source code for Linux was released, the number of software developers dedicated to improving Linux has increased each year. The Linux kernel was developed collaboratively and was centrally managed; however, many Linux add-on packages were developed freely worldwide by those members of the hacker culture who were interested in their release. Linux was a convenient focal point for free software developers. During the early- to mid-1990s, Linux development proceeded at full speed, with hackers contributing large amounts of their time to what turned into a large-scale development project. All of this effort resulted in several distributions of Linux. A **distribution** of Linux is a collection or bundle of software containing the commonly developed Linux operating system kernel and libraries, combined with add-on software specific to a certain use. Well-known distributions of Linux include **Red Hat, Ubuntu,** and **OpenSUSE.**

This branding of Linux did not imply the fragmentation that UNIX experienced in the late 1980s. All distributions of Linux had a common kernel and utilities; the fact that they contained different add-on packages simply made them look different on the surface. Linux still derived its usefulness from collaborative development.

Linux development continued to expand throughout the late 1990s as more and more developers grew familiar with the form of collaborative software development advocated by the hacker culture. By 1998, when the term "OSS" first came into use, there were already many thousands of OSS developers worldwide. Many small companies that offered Linux solutions for business were formed. People invested in these companies by buying stock in them. Unfortunately, this trend was short-lived. By the year 2000, most of these companies had vanished. At the same time, the OSS movement caught the attention and support of many large companies (such as IBM, Compaq, Dell, and Hewlett-Packard), and there was a shift in Linux development over the following decade to support the larger computing environments and mobile devices.

It is important to note that Linux is a by-product of OSS development. Recall that the OSS developers are still members of the hacker culture and, as such, are intrinsically motivated to develop software that has an important use. Thus, OSS development has changed over time; in the 1980s, the hacker culture concentrated on developing Internet and programming tools, whereas in the 1990s, it focused on developing the Linux operating system. Since 2000, there has been great interest in embedded Linux (Linux OSes that run on smaller hardware devices, such as mobile devices) and developing application programs for use on the Linux operating system. Graphics programs, games, and custom business tools are only some of the popular developments that OSS developers have released in the past couple of years. Because Linux is currently very well developed, more application development can be expected from the OSS community in the next decade.

For more information on the free software movement and the development of Linux, watch the 2001 television documentary *Revolution OS* (available on YouTube). It features interviews with Linus Torvalds, Richard Stallman, and Eric S. Raymond.

Linux Distributions

It is time-consuming and inefficient to obtain Linux by first downloading and installing the Linux kernel and then adding desired OSS packages. Instead, it's more common to download a distribution of Linux containing the Linux kernel, common function libraries, and a series of OSS packages.

Remember that although different Linux distributions appear different on the surface, they run the same kernel and contain many of the same packages.

Despite the fact that varied distributions of Linux are essentially the same under the surface, they do have important differences. Different distributions might support different hardware platforms. Also, Linux distributions include predefined sets of software; some Linux distributions include a large number of server-related tools, such as Web servers and database servers, whereas others include numerous workstation and development software applications. Still others might include a complete set of open source tools that you can use to customize a Linux system to perform specific functions. In that case, you simply choose the open source tools you want to install. For example, you might choose to install a database server.

Linux distributions that include many specialized tools might not contain a graphical user interface (GUI); an example of this is a Linux distribution that fits on a floppy and can be used as a **router**. Most distributions, however, do include a GUI that can be further customized to suit the needs of the user.

The core component of the GUI in Linux is referred to as **X Windows**. There are two implementations of X Windows: XFree86 and *X.org*. XFree86 is the traditional implementation of

X Windows, and *X.org* is the latest implementation of X Windows based on the original MIT X Windows project that was released as OSS in 2004. In addition to X Windows, several Linux window managers and desktop environments are available, which together affect the look and feel of the Linux GUI. X Windows in combination with a window manager and desktop environment is referred to as a **GUI environment**. The two main competing GUI environments available in Linux are the **GNU Network Object Model Environment (GNOME)** and the **K Desktop Environment (KDE)**. These two GUI environments are more or less comparable in functionality, although users might have a personal preference for one desktop over the other. This is often the case when a company wants to do a great deal of software development in the GUI environment; the GNOME desktop, written in the C programming language, uses the widely available gtk toolkit, whereas the KDE desktop, written in the C++ programming language, uses the qt toolkit. Which language and toolkit best fits the need will be the one preferred at that time. Most common Linux distributions ship with both GNOME and KDE GUI environments, whereas others offer support for both so that either GUI environment can be easily downloaded and installed. A comparison of these two GUI environments can be seen in Figures 1-5 and 1-6.

In addition to GNOME and KDE, there are several other desktop environments available to Linux systems. One example is XFCE, which is a lightweight desktop environment designed for Linux systems with few CPU and RAM resources.

Figure 1-5   The GNOME desktop

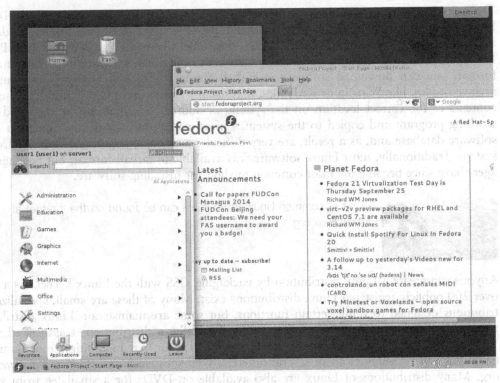

Figure 1-6 The KDE desktop

Another difference between Linux distributions is language support, with some distributions offering more support for certain languages than others. One example of this is TurboLinux, which has increased support for Japanese and Chinese. Consequently, TurboLinux is far more common in Asia than in North America. Many Linux distributions are specialized for different languages, and most Linux documentation, such as HOWTO documents, is available in many different languages.

Although these differences between Linux distributions can help narrow the choice of Linux distributions to install, one of the most profound reasons companies choose one distribution over another is support for package managers. A **package manager** is a software system that installs and maintains software. It keeps track of installed software, requires a standard format and documentation, and can manage and remove software from a system by recording all relevant software information in a central software database on your computer.

A package manager in Linux is similar to the Add/Remove Programs or Programs and Features applet within the Windows Control Panel.

The most widely supported package manager is the Red Hat Package Manager (RPM). Most Linux software is available in RPM format, and the RPM is standard on many Linux distributions. The Debian Package Manager offers the same advantages as the Red Hat Package Manager, yet few distributions offer it. In addition to obtaining software in package manager format, you can download software in tarball format. A **tarball** is merely a compressed archive of files, like WinZip or RAR files, that usually contain scripts that install the software contents to the correct location on the system, or source code that can be compiled into a working program and copied to the system. Unfortunately, tarballs do not update a central software database and, as a result, are very difficult to manage, upgrade, or remove from the system. Traditionally, most Linux software was available in tarball format, but package managers have since become the most common method for installing software.

A list of common Linux distributions can be found on the Internet at *www.linux.org*.

Anyone can create a Linux distribution by packaging OSS with the Linux kernel. As a result, over 200 publicly registered Linux distributions exist. Many of these are small, specialized distributions designed to fulfill certain functions, but some are mainstream Linux distributions used widely throughout the computing world. Typically, a distribution is associated with a Web site from which the distribution can be downloaded for free. In addition, most Linux distributions can be obtained from several different Web sites, such as *http://iso.linuxquestions. org*. Many distributions of Linux are also available on DVDs for a small fee from various computer stores and Web sites; however, downloading from the Internet is the most common method of obtaining Linux.

Table 1-4 briefly describes some mainstream Linux distributions, their features, and where to find them on the Internet.

Common Uses of Linux

As discussed earlier, an important feature of Linux is its versatility. Linux can provide services meeting the needs of differing companies in a variety of situations. Furthermore, configuring these services is straightforward given the wide range of documentation freely available on the Internet; you can simply choose the services that are required and then customize Linux to provide those services. These services can be used on a local computer **workstation**, or you can configure a service to allow other computers to connect to it across a network. Services that are used on the local computer are referred to as **workstation services**, whereas services that are made available for other computers across a network are known as **server services**.

A computer that hosts a server service is commonly referred to as a server.

Distribution	Features	Platforms	Location
Red Hat Linux	One of the earliest Linux distributions, and one that is commonly used within organizations today. Two distributions of Red Hat are available: the Enterprise distribution geared for enterprise environments and the Fedora distribution geared for all environments (servers, desktops, laptops, etc.). Both editions ship with GNOME as the default desktop environment, and with the RPM package manager.	x86/x64 PPC Mainframe ARM	*www.redhat.com* *www.fedoraproject.org*
SUSE Linux	Originally developed primarily in Europe, SUSE is the oldest business-focused Linux distribution. Novell purchased SUSE Linux to replace its NetWare OS and distributes enterprise versions of SUSE packaged with Novell software. The current distribution of SUSE Linux is called OpenSUSE; it ships with the KDE desktop environment by default and with the RPM package manager.	x86/x64	*www.opensuse.org* *www.suse.com*
Slackware Linux	The oldest Linux distribution that is currently maintained (it was the basis for many other Linux distributions in the 1990s, including SUSE). It has its own package manager, ships with GNOME and KDE desktops, boasts many features similar to UNIX, and has always been focused on multiprocessor environments.	x86/x64 Mainframe ARM	*www.slackware.com*
Debian Linux	Offering the largest number of packages of all Linux distributions, Debian Linux contains software packages for any use and ships with GNOME, KDE, and the Debian Package Manager.	x86/x64 UltraSPARC Mainframe ARM PPC MIPS ARM	*www.debian.org*
Ubuntu Linux	A Debian-based distribution that is widely used in all environments. It is designed to be easy to use and supports nearly all hardware, including mobile computing devices. It typically ships with GNOME and the Debian Package Manager.	x86/x64 UltraSPARC PPC MIPS ARM	*www.ubuntu.com*
Linux Mint	A relatively new and easy-to-use Linux distribution that is focused on providing desktop and mobile user capabilities. It uses the Debian Package Manager and ships with GNOME, KDE, and Cinnamon (based on GNOME) desktop environments.	x86/x64	*www.linuxmint.com*
TurboLinux	A very common distribution of Linux in Asia that is famous for its clustering abilities. It ships with the GNOME and KDE desktop environments, as well as with the RPM package manager.	x86/x64	*www.turbolinux.com*

Table 1-4 Common Linux distributions

Although thousands of different server and workstation services are available that you can use to customize Linux, Linux configurations commonly used today include:

- Internet servers
- File and print servers
- Application servers
- Cloud systems
- Supercomputers
- Scientific workstations
- Office/personal workstations
- Mobile devices

Internet Servers

Linux hosts a wide range of Internet services, and it was from these services that Linux gained much popularity in the 1990s. All of these services are available free of charge and, like all OSS, undergo constant improvement, which makes Linux an attractive choice when planning for the use of Internet services in a company. Companies that use services on a computer to serve client computers are said to have an Internet server. Linux contains hundreds of network services that provide the framework for an Internet server; the most common of these services include:

- Mail services
- Routing services
- FTP services
- Firewalls and proxy services
- Web services
- News services
- DNS services

Many of these applications are discussed in more detail later in this book.

Mail Services In the 1980s and early 1990s, e-mail was a service that was found primarily in universities. Today, almost every Internet user has an e-mail account and uses e-mail on a regular basis. E-mail addresses are easy to acquire and can be obtained free of charge.

E-mail is distributed via a network of e-mail servers, also known as **Mail Transfer Agents** (**MTAs**). Many MTAs are freely available for Linux, including sendmail, postfix, smail, and exim. Before the user can access his e-mail, it must be downloaded from a MTA; the service that provides this is known as a **Mail Delivery Agent** (**MDA**). Linux also provides several of these services; procmail and fetchmail are two of the most common. Finally, the user views her e-mail using a program known as a **Mail User Agent** (**MUA**). Common MUAs available for Linux include mutt, pine, printmail, elm, mail, Netscape, and Eudora.

Routing Routing is a core service that is necessary for the Internet to function. The Internet is merely a large network of interconnected networks; in other words, it connects company networks, home networks, and institutional networks so that they can communicate with each other. A router is a computer or special hardware device that provides this interconnection; it contains information regarding the structure of the Internet and sends information from one network to another. Companies can use routers to connect their internal networks to the Internet as well as to connect their networks together inside the company. Linux is a good choice for this, as it provides support for routing and is easily customizable; many Linux distributions, each of which can fit on a small USB flash drive, provide routing capabilities.

FTP Services The most common and efficient method for transferring files over the Internet is by using the File Transfer Protocol (FTP). In addition, FTP is commonplace when transferring files on an internal company network because it is very quick and robust. A user simply starts the FTP service on her computer (now known as an FTP server) and allows users to connect; users on other computers then connect to this server using an FTP client program and download any desired files. Most FTP servers available on the Internet allow any user to connect and are, hence, called anonymous FTP servers. Furthermore, most operating systems, such as Linux, UNIX, Microsoft Windows, and Macintosh, are distributed with an FTP client program, making it easy for users to connect to these FTP servers.

Although several FTP service software programs are available for Linux, the most commonly used is the Very Secure FTP Server, which can be downloaded at *https://security.appspot.com/vsftpd.html.*

Firewalls and Proxy Services The term "firewall" describes the structures that prevent a fire from spreading. In the automobile industry, a firewall protects the passengers in a car if a fire breaks out in the engine compartment. Just as an automobile firewall protects passengers, a computer firewall protects companies from outside intruders on the Internet. Most firewalls are computers that are placed between the company network and the company's connection to the Internet; all traffic must then pass through this firewall, allowing the company to control traffic at this firewall, based on a complex set of rules. Linux has firewall support built directly into the kernel. Utilities such as ipchains and netfilter/iptables, which are included with most distributions, can be used to configure the rules necessary to make a system a firewall.

You can find out more about using netfilter/iptables to configure Linux firewalls at *www.netfilter.org.*

Because firewalls are usually located between a company's internal network and the Internet, they often provide other services that allow computers inside the company easy access to the Internet. The most common of these services are known as proxy services. A **proxy server** requests Internet resources, such as Web sites and FTP sites, on behalf of the computer inside the company. In other words, a workstation computer inside the company simply sends a request to the proxy server connected to the Internet. The proxy server then obtains and returns the requested information to the workstation computer. One proxy server can allow thousands of company workstation computers access to the Internet simultaneously without lengthy configuration of the workstation computers; proxy servers keep track of the information passed to each client by maintaining a Network Address Translation (NAT) table. Although ipchains and netfilter/iptables can both perform some proxy server functions, the most common proxy server used on Linux is Squid. Squid retains a copy of any requested Internet resources (via a process known as caching) so that it can respond quicker to future requests for the same resources.

To obtain or find information regarding the Squid proxy server, visit *www.squid-cache.org*.

Web Services Although many Internet tools and services are available, the most popular is the Internet browser, which can connect client computers to servers worldwide hosting information of many types: text, pictures, music, binary data, video, and much more. The community of servers that hosts this information is known as the World Wide Web (WWW), and a server hosting information is known as a Web server. On a basic level, a Web server is just a server using Hypertext Transfer Protocol (HTTP) to provide information to requesting Web browsers running on client computers; however, Web servers can also process programs known as Common Gateway Interface (CGI) scripts and provide secure connections such as Secure Sockets Layer (SSL) or Transport Layer Security (TLS). A CGI is a program that runs on the Web server and enables connection to a resource running on another server on the network not connected to the Internet such as a database. This is very useful, as not all information provided over the Internet needs to reside on Web servers. CGIs can be written in several programming languages, including C and C++, making them readily compatible with Linux. SSL and TLS are secure methods of communicating with a Web server in which the information passing between the client computer and the Web server is encrypted to keep it secure. This form of transmission is widely used any time confidentiality is required, such as in Internet banking or in transferring a client's credit card information in e-commerce. You can tell SSL/TLS is in use when the http:// in the browser's address bar changes to https://.

To better understand how SSL/TLS works, visit *www.gmail.com* and note the change in the browser's address bar immediately after the page has loaded.

Many open source Web server software packages are available for Linux. The most widely used is the Apache Web Server, comprising more than 55 percent of all Web servers in the world during 2013.

For more information about the Apache Web Server, visit *httpd.apache.org*.

News Services Web servers host valuable information, but most do not provide any means for users to communicate with each other. This functionality is provided by a news server, which allows users to post messages in forums called **newsgroups** and allows other users to read and reply to those messages. Newsgroups are sometimes referred to as computer bulletin boards and are similar to bulletin boards seen around a school campus and in other public places; persons having or requiring information or services post a notice that others see and respond to. Newsgroup forums are grouped according to topic. Posting to a newsgroup is often a very quick way to find the solution to a problem because people who read the posting are likely to have had the same problem and found the solution. In addition, newsgroup forums can be moderated, in that a person or group responsible for the forum edits messages before they are posted to ensure they fit the forum's theme. This ensures proper newsgroup etiquette, which dictates that before posting a question you search previous postings to ensure that the question has not already been asked and answered and that only messages relevant to the newsgroup topic are posted.

Many OSS developers use newsgroups to exchange information and coordinate software creation. As with e-mails, a special program called a newsreader is necessary to access newsgroups and read postings hosted on news servers. Common Linux newsreaders include Gnews, PAN, Gnus, Thunderbird, and pine. The most popular open source news server software available for Linux is called InterNetworkNews (INN); it is included with most common Linux distributions and is maintained by an open source organization called the Internet Systems Consortium, which continually develops and improves several open source Internet technologies.

For more information on how to subscribe to newsgroups, visit *groups.google.com*.

DNS Services Each computer on a network needs a unique way to indentify itself and to refer to other computers. This is accomplished by assigning each computer a number called an **Internet Protocol (IP) address**. An IP address is a long string of numbers that would be very hard for the typical person to remember. Thus, IP addresses are often associated with more user-friendly names. In particular, servers are identified by names like *www.linux.org*, which are known as **fully qualified domain names (FQDNs)**. When you use a Web browser such as Internet Explorer or Netscape Navigator to request information from a Web server, you typically type the Web server's FQDN (e.g., *www.linux.org*) into your browser's address bar. However, FQDNs exist only for the convenience of the human beings who use computer networks. The computers themselves rely on IP addresses. Thus, before your browser can retrieve the requested information from the Web server, it needs to know the IP address associated with the FQDN you typed into the address bar. Your browser gets this information by contacting a server hosting the Domain Name System (DNS). The DNS server maintains a list of the proper FQDN to IP mappings and quickly returns the requested IP address to your browser. Your browser can then use this IP address to connect to the target Web site.

For companies wanting to create a DNS server, Linux is an inexpensive solution, as many distributions of Linux ship with a Domain Name System known as BIND (Berkeley Internet Name Domain).

Each computer participating on the Internet must have an IP address.

However, to a data architect, the term "cloud" refers to a large system of computers that work together to provide a wide set of services to users and organizations across the Internet. Facebook, Amazon, Twitter, Gmail, Office365, PayPal, and eBay are all good examples of cloud systems; each one consists of thousands of different servers that host specialized software that store and retrieve large amounts of information using specialized server applications and provide mechanisms that prevent data loss.

Most cloud systems on the Internet run Linux in a cloud-based configuration using cloud software (collectively called a **cloud platform**). OpenStack is one of the most popular open source cloud platforms available and is supported by nearly all major Linux distributions.

 You can find more information about OpenStack at *www.openstack.org.*

Supercomputers

Many companies and institutions use computers to perform extraordinarily large calculations for which most computers would be unsuitable. To accomplish these tasks, companies either buy computers with multiple processors or use specialized services to combine several smaller computers in a way that allows them to function as one large supercomputer. Combining several smaller computers is called **clustering**. Companies and individuals requiring this type of computing make up the supercomputing community, which is growing quickly today as technology advances in new directions.

Although it might seem logical to purchase computers that have a large number of processors, the performance of a computer relative to the number of processors decreases as you add processors to a computer. In other words, a computer with 64 processors does not handle 64 times as much work as one processor because of physical limitations within the computer hardware itself; a computer with 64 processors might only perform 50 times as much work as a single processor. The ability for a computer to increase workload as the number of processors increases is known as **scalability**, and most computers, regardless of the operating system used, do not scale well when there are more than 32 processors. As a result of this limitation, many people in the supercomputing community **cluster** several smaller computers together to work as one large computer. This approach results in much better scalability; 64 computers with one processor each working toward a common goal can handle close to 64 times as much as a single processor.

Most of the supercomputing community has focused on Linux when developing clustering technology; the most common method of Linux clustering is known as **Beowulf clustering**, which is easy to configure and well documented. Although there are many different ways to implement a Beowulf cluster, the most common method is to have one master computer send instructions to several slave computers, which compute parts of the calculation concurrently and send their results back to the master computer using a **Message Passing Interface (MPI)** software framework such as OpenMPI. This type of supercomputing breaks tasks down into smaller units of execution and executes them in parallel on many machines at once; thus, it is commonly referred to as parallel supercomputing, and many free programs are available that are written to run on parallelized computers. Beowulf parallel supercomputer technology has been aggressively developed since the mid-1990s and has been tested in various environments; currently, thousands of Beowulf clusters exist worldwide in various institutions, companies, and universities.

You can find more information about OpenMPI at *www.open-mpi.org.*

Scientific/Engineering Workstation

Many of the developers from Richard Stallman's Free Software Foundation came from the scientific and engineering community, which needed to develop many programs to run analyses. In the 1980s and early-1990s, this scientific and engineering community largely developed software for the UNIX operating system that was common in universities around the world; today, this community is focusing on developing software for Linux. Any software previously made for UNIX can be ported to Linux easily. Scientists and engineers often use parallel supercomputers to compute large tasks, and OSS developers, with a background in scientific computing, have done much of the development on Beowulf technology. One example of this is SHARCnet (Shared Hierarchical Academic Research Computing Network) in Ontario, Canada, in which several universities have developed and tested supercomputing technology and parallel programs for use in the scientific and engineering fields.

You can find more information about SHARCnet at *www.sharcnet.ca.*

Often, the programs that are required by the scientific and engineering community must be custom developed to suit the needs of the people involved; however, many OSS programs, which you can use or modify, are freely available in many different scientific and engineering fields, including, but not limited to, the following list:

- Physics, Astrophysics, and Biophysics
- Fluid Dynamics and Geophysics
- Biocomputation
- Materials and Polymer Chemistry
- General Mathematics and Optimization
- Data Mining
- Number Theory
- Computer/Linear/Array Algebra
- Mathematical Visualization and Modeling
- Statistics and Regression Analysis

Key Terms

AIX   A version of UNIX developed by IBM.

Android   A mobile Linux-based operating system currently developed by Google's Open Handset Alliance.

application (app)   The software that runs on an operating system and provides the user with specific functionality (such as word processing or financial calculation). Applications are commonly referred to as apps today.

artistic license   An open source license that allows source code to be distributed freely but changed at the discretion of the original author.

Beowulf clustering   A popular and widespread method of clustering computers together to perform useful tasks using Linux.

BSD (Berkeley Software Distribution)   A version of UNIX developed out of the original UNIX source code and given free to the University of California, Berkeley by AT&T.

closed source software   The software whose source code is not freely available from the original author; Windows 98 is an example.

cloud   Another term for the Internet.

cloud platform   A series of software components that are installed on servers distributed across the Internet and provide services to a large number of Internet users.

cluster   A grouping of several smaller computers that function as one large supercomputer.

clustering   The act of making a cluster; see also *cluster*.

cracker   A person who uses computer software maliciously for personal profit.

database   An organized set of data.

Database Management System (DBMS)   Software that manages databases.

developmental kernel   A Linux kernel whose minor number is odd and has been recently developed yet not thoroughly tested.

device driver   A piece of software containing instructions that the kernel of an operating system uses to control and interact with a specific type of computer hardware.

distribution   A complete set of operating system software, including the Linux kernel, supporting function libraries, and a variety of OSS packages that can be downloaded from the Internet free of charge. These OSS packages are what differentiate the various distributions of Linux.

flavor   A term that refers to a specific type of UNIX operating system. For example, Solaris and BSD are two different flavors of UNIX.

Free Software Foundation (FSF)   An organization started by Richard Stallman that promotes and encourages the collaboration of software developers worldwide to allow the free sharing of source code and software programs.

freeware   Software distributed by the developer at no cost to the user.

frequently asked questions (FAQs)   An area on a Web site where answers to commonly posed questions can be found.

fully qualified domain name (FQDN)   A string of words identifying a server on the Internet.

GNU   An acronym that stands for "GNU's Not Unix."

GNU General Public License (GPL)   A software license, ensuring that the source code for any OSS will remain freely available to anyone who wants to examine, build on, or improve upon it.

GNU Network Object Model Environment (GNOME)   One of the two competing graphical user interface (GUI) environments for Linux.

GNU Project   A free operating system project started by Richard Stallman.

graphical user interface (GUI)   The component of an operating system that provides a user-friendly interface comprising graphics or icons to represent desired tasks. Users can point and click to execute a command rather than having to know and use proper command-line syntax.

GUI environment   A GUI core component such as X Windows, combined with a window manager and desktop environment that provides the look and feel of the GUI. Although functionality might be similar among GUI environments, users might prefer one environment to another due to its ease of use.

hacker   A person who explores computer science to gain knowledge—not to be confused with "cracker."

hardware   The tangible parts of a computer, such as the network boards, video card, hard disk drives, printers, and keyboards.

hardware platform   A particular configuration and grouping of computer hardware, normally centered on and determined by processor type and architecture.

hot fix   A solution for a software bug made by a closed source vendor.

HOWTO   A task-specific instruction guide to performing any of a wide variety of tasks; it is freely available from the Linux Documentation Project at *www.linuxdoc.org*.

HP-UX   A version of UNIX developed by Hewlett-Packard.

Internet Protocol (IP) address   A unique string of numbers assigned to a computer to uniquely identify it on the Internet.

iOS   A mobile version of UNIX developed by Apple for use on iPhone, iPod and iPad devices.

K Desktop Environment (KDE)   One of the two competing graphical user interfaces (GUIs) available for Linux.

kernel   The central, core program of the operating system. The shared commonality of the kernel is what defines Linux; the differing OSS applications that can interact with the common kernel are what differentiates Linux distributions.

Linus Torvalds   A Finnish graduate student who coded and created the first version of Linux and subsequently distributed it under the GNU Public License.

Linux   A software operating system originated by Linus Torvalds. The common core, or kernel, continues to evolve and be revised. Differing OSS bundled with the Linux kernel is what defines the wide variety of distributions now available.

Linux Documentation Project (LDP)   A large collection of Linux resources, information, and help files supplied free of charge and maintained by the Linux community.

Linux User Group (LUG)   The open forums of Linux users who discuss and assist each other in using and modifying the Linux operating system and the OSS run on it. There are LUGs worldwide.

Macintosh OS X   A version of UNIX developed by Apple for use on Apple desktop computers and servers.

Mail Delivery Agent (MDA)   The service that downloads e-mail from a mail transfer agent.

Mail Transfer Agent (MTA)   An e-mail server.

Mail User Agent (MUA)   A program that allows e-mail to be read by a user.

major number   The number preceding the first dot in the number used to identify a Linux kernel version. It is used to denote a major change or modification.

Message Passing Interface (MPI)   A system that is used on Beowulf clusters to pass information to several separate computers in a parallel fashion.

MINIX   Mini-UNIX created by Andrew Tannenbaum. Instructions on how to code the kernel for this version of the Unix operating system were publicly available. Using this as a starting point, Linus Torvalds improved this version of UNIX for the Intel platform and created the first version of Linux.

minor number   The number following the first dot in the number used to identify a Linux kernel version, denoting a minor modification. If odd, it is a version under development and not yet fully tested. See also *developmental kernel* and *production kernel*.

Multiplexed Information and Computing Service (MULTICS)   A prototype time-sharing operating system that was developed in the late-1960s by AT&T Bell Laboratories.

multitasking   A type of operating system that is able to manage multiple tasks simultaneously.

multiuser   A type of operating system that is able to provide access to multiple users simultaneously.

newsgroup   An Internet protocol service accessed via an application program called a newsreader. This service allows access to postings (e-mails in a central place accessible by all newsgroup users) normally organized along specific themes. Users with questions on specific topics can post messages, which can be answered by other users.

Open Source Software (OSS)   The programs distributed and licensed so that the source code making up the program is freely available to anyone who wants to examine, utilize, or improve upon it.

OpenSUSE   One of the most popular and prevalent distributions of Linux, originally developed in Europe.

operating system (OS)   The software used to control and directly interact with the computer hardware components.

package manager   The software used to install, maintain, and remove other software programs by storing all relevant software information in a central software database on the computer.

process   A program loaded into memory and running on the processor performing a specific task.

production kernel   A Linux kernel whose minor number (the number after the dot in the version number) is even, therefore deemed stable for use through widespread testing.

program   The sets of instructions that know how to interact with the operating system and computer hardware to perform specific tasks; stored as a file on some media (e.g., a hard disk drive).

programming language   The syntax used for developing a program. Different programming languages use different syntaxes.

proxy server   A server or hardware device that requests Internet resources on behalf of other computers.

Red Hat   One of the most popular and prevalent distributions of Linux in North America, distributed and supported by Red Hat, Inc. Fedora is a Red Hat-based Linux distribution.

revision number   The number after the second dot in the version number of a Linux kernel that identifies the release number of a kernel.

router   A computer running routing software or a special function hardware device that provides interconnection between networks; it contains information regarding the structure of the networks and sends information from one component network to another.

scalability   The capability of computers to increase workload as the number of processors increases.

search engine   An Internet Web site, such as *www.google.com*, where you simply enter a phrase representing your search item and receive a list of Web sites that contain relevant material.

server   A computer configured to allow other computers to connect to it from across a network.

server services   The services that are made available for other computers across a network.

shareware   The programs developed and provided at minimal cost to the end user. These programs are initially free but require payment after a period of time or usage.

software   The programs stored on a storage device in a computer, which provide a certain function when executed.

Solaris   A version of UNIX developed by Sun Microsystems from AT&T source code.

source code   The sets of organized instructions on how to function and perform tasks that define or constitute a program.

system service   The additional functionality provided by a program that has been incorporated into and started as part of the operating system.

tarball   A compressed archive of files containing scripts that install Linux software to the correct locations on a computer system.

total cost of ownership (TCO)   The full sum of all accumulated costs, over and above the simple purchase price of utilizing a product. Includes training, maintenance, additional hardware, and downtime.

Ubuntu   A major Linux distribution that is widely used in North America.

UNIX   The first true multitasking, multiuser operating system, developed by Ken Thompson and Dennis Ritchie, and from which Linux was originated.

user   A person who uses a computer.

user interface   The interface the user sees and uses to interact with the operating system and application programs.

workstation   A computer used to connect to services on a server.

workstation services   The services that are used to access shared resources on a network server.

X Windows   The core component of the GUI in Linux.

Review Questions

1. Every computer consists of physical components and nonphysical components. The nonphysical components of a computer that understand how to work with the physical components are referred to as _____.

   a. hardware

   b. records

   c. software

   d. processors

2. The operating system software is necessary for a computer to function. True or False?

3. Linux is a _____ and _____ operating system.

   a. production, stable

   b. multiuser, multitasking

   c. processing, closed source

   d. large, useful

4. The core component of the Linux operating system is the Linux kernel. If you were a Linux systems administrator for a company, when would you need to upgrade your Linux kernel? (Choose all that apply.)

   a. when you need support in Linux for new hardware

   b. when you need another user interface

   c. when you need to increase the stability of Linux

   d. when you need to use kernel modules

5. Which of the following kernels are developmental kernels? (Choose all that apply.)

   a. 3.3.4

   b. 3.5.5

   c. 3.2.7

   d. 3.4.4

6. A production kernel refers to a kernel whose_____.

   a. revision number is even

   b. minor number is odd

   c. major number is odd

   d. minor number is even

7. Many types of software are available today. Which type of software does Linux represent?

   a. Open Source Software

   b. closed source software

   c. freeware

   d. shareware

8. Which of the following are characteristics of Open Source Software? (Choose all that apply.)

   a. The value of the software is directly related to its price.

   b. The software is developed collaboratively.

   c. The source code for software is available for a small fee.

   d. Any bugs are fixed quickly.

9. To which license does Linux adhere?

   a. open license

   b. artistic license

   c. GNU General Public License

   d. free source license

10. What are some good reasons for using Linux in a corporate environment? (Choose all that apply.)

    a. Linux software is unlikely to be abandoned by its developers.

    b. Linux is secure and has a lower total cost of ownership than other operating systems.

    c. Linux is widely available for many platforms and supports many programming languages.

    d. Most Linux software is closed source.

11. Which of the following are common methods for gaining support for Linux?

    a. HOWTO documents at *www.linuxdoc.org*

    b. a local Linux User Group

    c. Internet newsgroups

    d. all the above

12. Which two people are credited with creating the UNIX operating system? (Choose two answers.)

    a. Dennis Ritchie

    b. Richard Stallman

    c. Linus Torvalds

    d. Ken Thompson

13. Who formed the Free Software Foundation to promote open development?
    a. Dennis Ritchie
    b. Richard Stallman
    c. Linus Torvalds
    d. Ken Thompson

14. Which culture embraced the term "GNU" (GNU's Not UNIX) and laid the free software groundwork for Linux?
    a. the hacker culture
    b. the MIT culture
    c. the cracker culture
    d. the Artificial Intelligence culture

15. Linus was developed by _____ to resemble the _____ operating system.
    a. Linus Torvalds, MINIX
    b. Linus Torvalds, GNU
    c. Richard Stallman, GNU
    d. Richard Stallman, MINIX

16. When the core components of the Linux operating system are packaged together with other Open Source Software, it is called a _____.
    a. new kernel
    b. new platform
    c. Linux distribution
    d. GNU Project

17. Which common GUI environments are available in most Linux distributions? (Choose all that apply.)
    a. GNOME
    b. CDE
    c. KDE
    d. RPM

18. Which of the following are factors that determine which Linux distribution a user will use? (Choose all that apply.)
    a. package manager support
    b. hardware platform
    c. kernel features
    d. language support

1

19. What is the most common open source Web server available for Linux?
   a. Samba
   b. Apache
   c. Squid
   d. pine

20. Which of the following can be used on Linux to provide file and print services?
   a. Samba
   b. Apache
   c. Squid
   d. pine

Discovery Exercises

1. You work for a large manufacturing company that is considering Linux as a solution for some or all servers in its IT Department. The company hosts an Oracle database on UNIX, and the UNIX servers that host this database contain several small programs that were custom-made. Furthermore, Windows 8 is currently used on desktops throughout the company, and users store their data on Windows Server 2012 file servers. What considerations must you keep in mind before migrating your company's servers to Linux? Which distribution(s) and Open Source Software would you choose to accomplish this? If you need to create a report detailing the benefits of moving to an open source solution using Linux, what benefits would you list in the report to persuade others in the company that Linux lowers the total cost of ownership?

2. At a local Linux User Group (LUG) meeting, some people who are unfamiliar with Linux ask you to explain what the GPL is and how it relates to OSS. These people also don't understand how OSS generates profit and are under the impression that the quality of OSS is poor compared to commercial software. They suggest that the potential for OSS in the future might be limited. How do you reply? Include examples to demonstrate your points. To which Web sites can you direct them for further information?

3. As a software developer working for a large clothing store chain, you are responsible for creating software used to connect retail store computers to a central database at the head office. Recently, some friends of yours suggested that you publish your software under the GPL. What are some direct benefits to publishing your software under the GPL? To publish software made for a company under the GPL, you need the company's permission because the company owns any software that it pays developers to create. When you approach people in your company regarding OSS and explain how companies benefit from releasing software as open source, you are asked what benefits the company will receive from funding an open source project over time. Your company also wants to know what the procedure is for releasing and maintaining OSS. What benefits will you offer them? Where could you send them to gain more information on procedures involved in the open source community?

4. You are a network administrator who is in charge of a medium-sized Linux network. The company you work for asks you to implement routing in the network, a topic with which you are unfamiliar. Where could you go to learn what you must obtain to enable routing on your Linux network? Provided that you have a functional Web browser and an Internet connection, explore this topic on the Internet and list the Web sites that you used to obtain the information required. This information might range from broad descriptions of what you need to do to accomplish a certain task to detailed guides and instructions on putting your plan into action. From these sources of information, devise a report outlining the major steps necessary to implement routing on your network.

5. At a company function, a top executive corners you and complains that your department is wasting too much money. The executive demands to know why the company must spend so much money on computers and software, especially operating systems and related licenses (for closed source programs and operating systems). Write a report that defends your department by explaining the nature of hardware, software, and operating systems. In the report, be sure to explain how OSS and the Linux operating system can be used to reduce these costs in the long term.

6. You are contacted by a project organizer for a university computer science fair. The project organizer asks you to hold a forum that discusses the origins of the Linux operating system, including how it has evolved and continues to develop. The main focus of this forum is to encourage university students toward participating in the open source community; therefore, it should detail the philosophy, major features, and methods of the hacker culture. Prepare a bulleted list of the major topics that you will discuss, and write down some sample questions that you anticipate from the participants as well as your responses.

7. Research three different distributions of Linux on the Internet. Record where you went to obtain your information. Compare and contrast the different distributions with regard to their strengths and the packages available for each. After you finish, locate and visit two Linux newsgroups. How did you locate them and where did you obtain the information? What are the topics specific to each? Find two questions per newsgroup posted by a user in need of a solution to a problem, and follow the thread of responses suggested by others to solve that problem.

Linux Installation and Usage

After completing this chapter, you will be able to:

- Prepare for and install Fedora Linux using good practices
- Outline the structure of the Linux interface
- Enter basic shell commands and find command documentation
- Properly shut down the Linux operating system

Figure 2-1 The Fedora LiveUSB Creator program

After the imagining process is complete, you can simply insert your USB flash drive into a free USB slot, turn on your computer, use the appropriate key for your computer to select the target boot device (e.g., F12), and then choose the option to boot from your USB flash drive.

Many server and workstation computers today have the ability to run multiple operating systems concurrently using **virtualization software.** There are several virtualization software products available on the market today, including:

- Microsoft Hyper-V
- VMware
- Oracle VM VirtualBox

Each operating system that is run within virtualization software is called a **virtual machine,** and the underlying operating system running the virtualization software is called the **virtual machine host.** Figure 2-2 shows a Fedora Linux virtual machine running on the Windows 8 operating system using the Microsoft Hyper-V virtualization software.

Most enterprise environments today take advantage of virtualization software to run multiple server operating systems concurrently on the same computer hardware. This allows organizations to better utilize their server hardware and reduce costs.

To install Linux as a virtual machine, you simply need to download the standard DVD or live media DVD ISO image to a directory on your virtual machine host (e.g., Windows). When you open the virtualization software and choose to create a new virtual machine, you

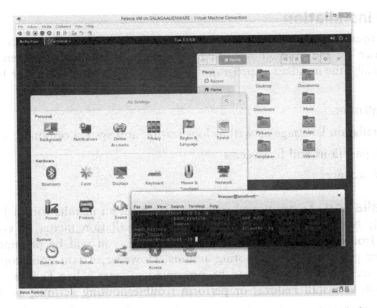

Figure 2-2 Fedora Linux running as a virtual machine on the Windows 8 operating system

can specify the file location of the appropriate ISO image, and the virtualization software will boot from the ISO image directly, without the need to write the ISO image to a DVD or USB flash drive. Figure 2-3 shows the section of the Hyper-V New Virtual Machine Wizard that allows you to specify the location of an ISO image that contains the Fedora 20 installation media.

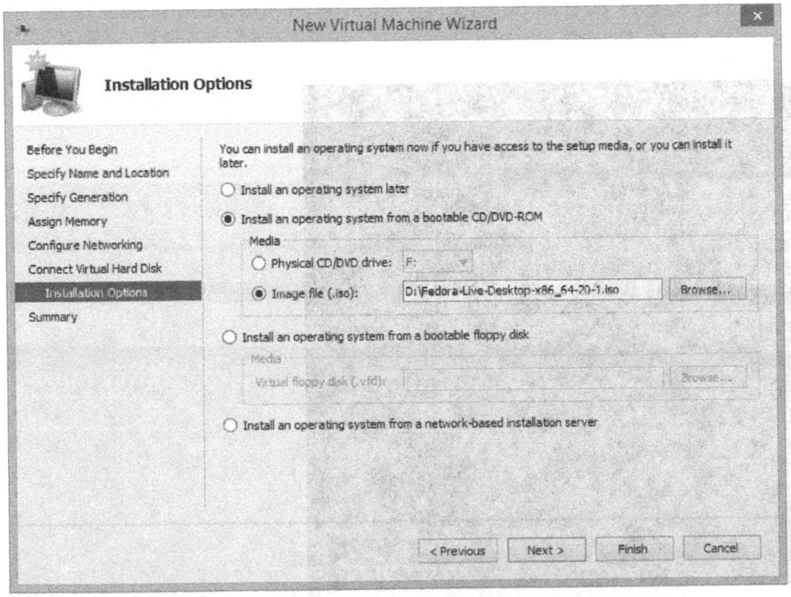

Figure 2-3 Selecting installation media within the Hyper-V New Virtual Machine Wizard

Figure 2-7 The Fedora Live welcome screen

or continue using the live Fedora system loaded from your installation media, as shown in Figure 2-7.

If you choose *Install to Hard Drive* in Figure 2-7, the Fedora installation program will start. Alternatively, if you choose *Try Fedora*, you will be able to explore the desktop of a live Fedora system and can later select *Install to Hard Drive* from the Activities menu in the upper-left corner of the desktop to start the Fedora installation program.

Choosing an Installation Language as Well as Localization and System Options
After you start a Fedora installation, you will be prompted to select a language that is used during the installation program, as shown in Figure 2-8. If you press *Continue*, you will be prompted to configure the date and time, keyboard layout, installation destination (e.g., hard disk, SSD), and network configuration, as shown in Figure 2-9.

You can click on each of the localization and system option icons in Figure 2-9 to modify its configuration. By default, your keyboard layout is automatically detected, your network interface is set to obtain network configuration automatically using the DHCP protocol, and the date and time are automatically obtained from the Internet if your network has Internet connectivity. However, you must manually select an installation destination before the installation can continue (hence the warning shown in Figure 2-9). The installation destination is a permanent storage device that will contain the Linux operating system; it is often a hard disk or SSD.

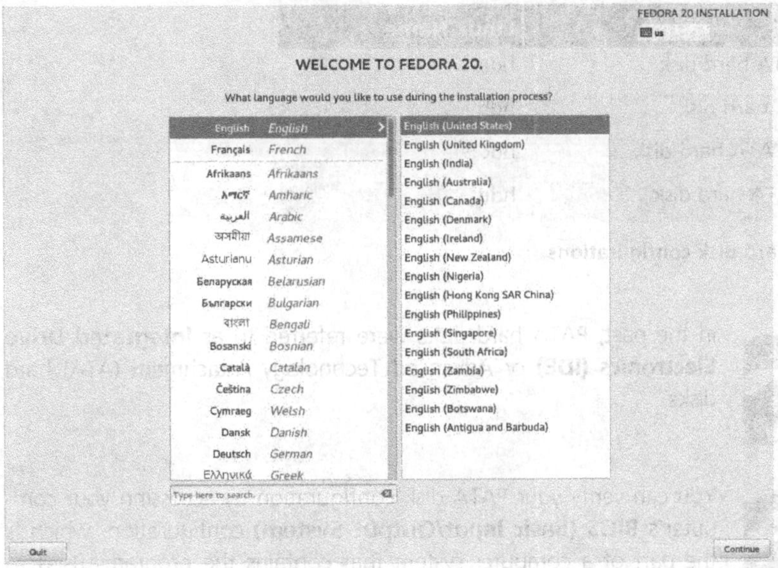

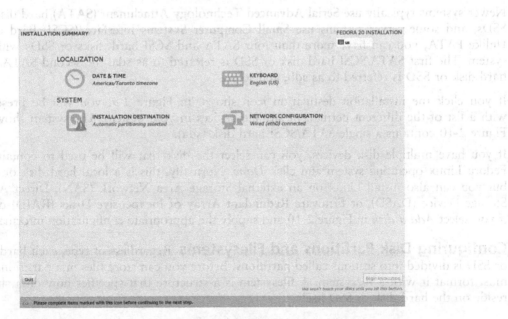

Figure 2-8 Selecting an installation language

Figure 2-9 Configuring localization and system options

Older systems often use **Parallel Advanced Technology Attachment (PATA)** hard disks that physically connect to the computer in one of four different configurations. As shown in Table 2-2, Linux refers to each of these disks according to its configuration on your computer.

Description	Linux Name
Primary master PATA hard disk	hda
Primary slave PATA hard disk	hdb
Secondary master PATA hard disk	hdc
Secondary slave PATA hard disk	hdd

Table 2-2   PATA hard disk configurations

In the past, PATA hard disks were referred to as **Integrated Drive Electronics (IDE)** or Advanced Technology Attachment (ATA) hard disks.

You can verify your PATA disk configuration by accessing your computer's **BIOS (Basic Input/Output System)** configuration, which is the part of a computer system that contains the programs used to initialize hardware components at boot time. You can access your BIOS configuration by pressing the appropriate manufacturer-specific key, such as F10, during system startup.

Newer systems typically use **Serial Advanced Technology Attachment (SATA)** hard disks or SSDs, and some server systems use **Small Computer Systems Interface (SCSI)** hard disks. Unlike PATA, you can have more than four SATA and SCSI hard disks or SSDs within a system. The first SATA/SCSI hard disk or SSD is referred to as sda, the second SATA/SCSI hard disk or SSD is referred to as sdb, and so on.

If you click the installation destination icon shown in Figure 2-9, you will be presented with a list of the different permanent storage devices in your system. The system shown in Figure 2-10 contains a single SATA/SCSI hard disk (sda).

If you have multiple disk devices, you can select the disk that will be used to contain the Fedora Linux operating system and click *Done*. Normally, this is a local hard disk or SSD, but you can also install Linux on an external Storage Area Network (SAN), Direct Access Storage Device (DASD), or firmware **Redundant Array of Inexpensive Disks (RAID)** device if you select *Add a disk* in Figure 2-10 and supply the appropriate configuration information.

Configuring Disk Partitions and Filesystems   Regardless of type, each hard disk or SSD is divided into sections called **partitions**. Before you can store files in a partition, you must format it with a filesystem. A **filesystem** is a structure that specifies how data should reside on the hard disk or SSD itself.

In the Windows operating system, each drive letter (e.g., C:, D:, E:) can correspond to a separate filesystem that resides on a partition on your hard disk or SSD.

There are limits to the number and types of partitions into which a hard disk or SSD can be divided. By default, you can create a maximum of four major partitions (called **primary**

INSTALLATION DESTINATION   FEDORA 20 INSTALLATION

Done   us

Select the device(s) you'd like to install to. They will be left untouched until you click on the main menu's "Begin Installation" button.

Local Standard Disks

20.48 GB

Msft Virtual Disk
sda / 20.48 GB free

Disks left unselected here will not be touched.

Specialized & Network Disks

Add a disk...

Disks left unselected here will not be touched.

Full disk summary and bootloader...

1 disk selected; 20.48 GB capacity; 20.48 GB free

Figure 2-10 Configuring an installation destination

partitions). To overcome this limitation, you can optionally label one of these primary partitions as "extended"; this **extended partition** can then contain an unlimited number of smaller partitions called **logical drives**. Each logical drive within the extended partition and all other primary partitions can contain a filesystem and be used to store data. The table of all partition information for a certain hard disk or SSD is stored in the first readable sector outside all partitions; it is called the **Master Boot Record (MBR)**.

The MBR is limited to hard disks that are less than 2TB in size. Newer hard disks and hard disks larger than 2TB use a **GUID Partition Table (GPT)** instead of an MBR. The MBR and GPT are functionally equivalent.

Recall that, in Linux, the first SATA/SCSI device in your system is referred to as sda, the first primary partition on this device is labeled sda1, the second sda2, and so on. Because there are only four primary partitions allowed, logical drives inside the extended partition are labeled sda5, sda6, and so on. An example of this partition strategy is listed in Table 2-3.

For the primary master PATA hard disk device, simply replace sda with hda in Table 2-3.

Partitioning divides a hard disk into sections, each of which can contain a separate filesystem used to store data. Each of these filesystems can then be accessed by Linux if it is attached (or mounted) to a certain directory. When data is stored in that particular directory, it is physically stored on the respective filesystem on the hard disk. The Fedora installation program

Description	Linux Name	Windows Name
First primary partition on the first SATA/SCSI device	sda1	C:
Second primary partition on the first SATA/SCSI device	sda2	D:
Third primary partition on the first SATA/SCSI device	sda3	E:
Fourth primary partition on the first SATA/SCSI device (EXTENDED)	sda4	F:
First logical drive in the extended partition on the first SATA/SCSI device	sda5	G:
Second logical drive in the extended partition on the first SATA/SCSI device	sda6	H:
Third logical drive in the extended partition on the first SATA/SCSI device	sda7	I:

Table 2-3   Example partitioning scheme for the first SATA/SCSI device

can automatically create partitions based on common configurations; however, it is generally good practice to manually partition to suit the needs of the specific Linux system.

At minimum, Linux typically requires only two partitions to be created: a partition that is mounted to the root directory in Linux (/) and that can contain all of the files used by the operating system, applications, and users, and a partition used for **virtual memory** (also known as **swap memory**). Virtual memory consists of an area on the hard disk or SSD that can be used to store information that would normally reside in physical memory (RAM) if the physical memory was being used excessively. When programs are executed that require a great deal of resources on the computer, information is continuously swapped from physical memory to virtual memory, and vice versa. Traditionally, Linux swap partitions were made to be at least the size of the physical RAM in the computer; however, they can be much larger if the Linux system is intended to run large applications. A swap partition does not contain a filesystem and is never mounted to a directory because the Linux operating system is ultimately responsible for swapping information.

Although you might choose to create only root and swap partitions, extra partitions make Linux more robust against filesystem errors. For example, if the filesystem on one partition encounters an error, only data on one part of the system is affected and not the entire system (i.e., other filesystems). Because there are some common directories in Linux that are used vigorously and as a result are more prone to failure, it is good practice to mount these directories to their own filesystems. Table 2-4 lists directories that are commonly mounted to separate partitions as well as their recommended sizes.

Each of these filesystems can be of different types. The most common types used today are the **ext2**, **ext3**, **ext4**, **VFAT**, and **REISER** filesystems, although Linux can support upward of 50 different filesystems. Each filesystem essentially performs the same function, which is to store files on a partition; however, each filesystem offers different features and is specialized for different uses. The ext2 filesystem is the traditional filesystem, and the Virtual File Allocation Table (VFAT) filesystem is compatible with the FAT and FAT32 filesystems in Windows. The ext3, ext4, and REISER filesystems, however, are much more robust than the ext2 and VFAT filesystems, as they perform a function called journaling. A **journaling** filesystem keeps track of the information written to the hard disk in a journal. If you copy a file on the hard disk from one directory to another, that file must pass into RAM and then be written to the new location

Directory	Description	Recommended Size
/	Contains all directories not present on other filesystems	Depends on the size and number of other filesystems present, but is typically 10GB or more
/boot	Contains the Linux kernel and boot files	500MB
/home	Default location for user home directories	200MB per user
/usr	System commands and utilities	Depends on the packages installed—typically 20GB or more
/usr/local	Location for most additional programs	Depends on the packages installed—typically 20GB or more
/opt	An alternate location for additional programs	Depends on the packages installed—typically 20GB or more
/var	Contains log files and spools	Depends on whether the Linux system is used as a print server (which contains a large spool). For print servers, 10GB or more is typical. For other systems, 2GB or more is usually sufficient.
/tmp	Holds temporary files created by programs	500MB

Table 2-4   **Common Linux filesystems and sizes**

on the hard disk. If the power to the computer is turned off during this process, information might not be transmitted as expected and data might be lost or corrupted. With a journaling filesystem, each step required to copy the file to the new location is first written to a journal; this means the system can retrace the steps the system took prior to a power outage and complete the file copy. These filesystems also host a variety of additional improvements compared to ext2 and VFAT, including faster data transfer and indexing, which makes them common choices for Linux servers today.

Once you have selected the appropriate hard disk or SSD as an installation destination during the Fedora Linux installation, the installation program will prompt you to choose the partitioning scheme, whether the number and type of disk partitions should be configured automatically, and if partition contents should be automatically encrypted, as shown in Figure 2-11.

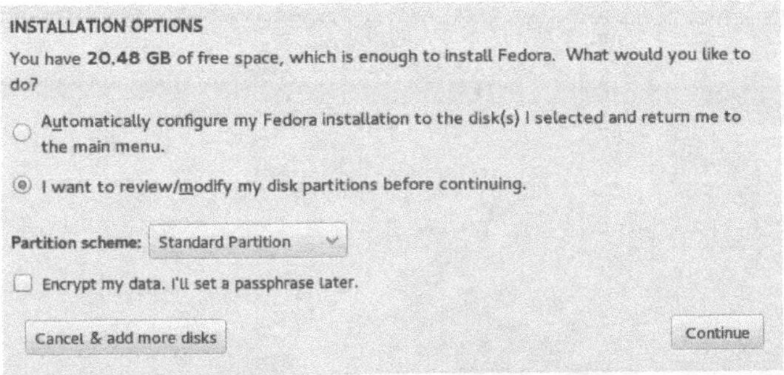

INSTALLATION OPTIONS

You have **20.48 GB** of free space, which is enough to install Fedora. What would you like to do?

○ Automatically configure my Fedora installation to the disk(s) I selected and return me to the main menu.

◉ I want to review/modify my disk partitions before continuing.

Partition scheme: [Standard Partition ▾]

☐ Encrypt my data. I'll set a passphrase later.

[Cancel & add more disks]   [Continue]

Figure 2-11   Selecting disk partitioning options

In addition to the standard partitions that we have discussed already, you can instead choose a partition scheme that creates logical volumes for your Linux filesystems using the **Logical Volume Manager (LVM)** or partitions that support the new **B-tree Filesystem (BTRFS)**. LVM and BTRFS are discussed in Chapter 5.

To allow for easier system recovery, it is good form to choose a standard partition scheme and ensure that contents of disk partitions are not encrypted.

If you select the *I want to review/modify my disk partitions before continuing* option in Figure 2-11 and click *Continue*, you will be prompted to create a default partition layout that you can modify to suit your needs, as shown in Figure 2-12. This layout will consist of a /boot and a / partition with an ext4 filesystem, as well as a swap partition that is the same size as the RAM in your computer.

If your system has a hard disk or SSD that uses a GPT instead of an MBR and does not contain an EFI BIOS on the motherboard, the installation program may create a small BIOS Boot partition to store GPT-related information.

Once you are satisfied with your partition and filesystem configuration, you can click *Done* in Figure 2-12, confirm your changes in the dialog window that appears, and return to the localization and system options configuration screen shown in Figure 2-9. If you click the *Begin Installation* button in Figure 2-9, partition changes will be written to your storage device and the Fedora system packages will be installed from the installation media to the appropriate filesystems. This process will take some time to complete.

Configuring User Accounts All Linux systems require secure access, which means that each user must log in with a valid user name and password before gaining access to a user interface. This process is called **authentication**. During installation, you need to

Figure 2-12 Configuring disk partitions and filesystems

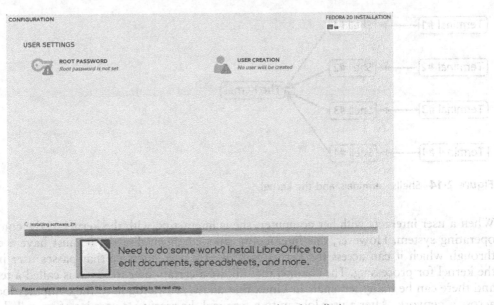

Figure 2-13 Configuring user accounts during a Fedora installation

configure two user accounts: the administrator account (root), which has full rights to the system, as well as a regular user account, since the root user account should only be used when performing system administration tasks.

While the Fedora system packages are being installed, the Fedora installation program prompts you to configure the password for the root user as well as create a new user account (with a name of your choice) by selecting the associated icons shown in Figure 2-13.

One you have configured a new user account and specified a password for the root user, you can click the *Quit* button that appears to exit the installation program. Next, you can shut down your live Fedora system, remove the installation media from your computer, and boot your computer into your new Fedora system.

Basic Linux Usage

After the Linux operating system has been installed, you must log in to the system with a valid user name and password and interact with the user interface to perform useful tasks. To do this, it is essential to understand the different types of user interface that exist, as well as basic tasks, such as command execution, obtaining online help, and shutting down the Linux system.

Shells, Terminals, and the Kernel

Recall that an operating system is merely a collection of software that allows you to use your computer hardware in a meaningful fashion. Every operating system has a core component, which loads all other components and serves to centrally control the activities of the computer. This component is known as the kernel, and in Linux it is simply a file, usually called vmlinuz, that is located on the hard disk and loaded when you first turn on your computer.

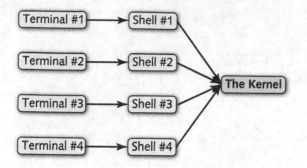

Figure 2-14 Shells, terminals, and the kernel

When a user interacts with her computer, she is interacting with the kernel of the computer's operating system. However, this interaction cannot happen directly; it must have a channel through which it can access the kernel as well as a user interface that passes user input to the kernel for processing. The channel that allows a certain user to log in is called a **terminal**, and there can be many terminals in Linux that allow you to log in to the computer locally or across a network. After a user logs in to a terminal, he receives a user interface called a **shell**, which then accepts input from the user and passes this input to the kernel for processing. The shell that is used by default in Linux is the **BASH shell** (short for Bourne Again Shell), which is an improved version of the Bourne shell from AT&T and is the shell that is used throughout this book. The whole process looks similar to what is shown in Figure 2-14.

As mentioned earlier, Linux is a multiuser and multitasking operating system and, as such, can allow for thousands of terminals. Each terminal could represent a separate logged-in user that has its own shell. The four different "channels" shown in Figure 2-14 could be different users logged in to the same Linux computer. Two users could be logged in locally to the server (seated at the server itself), and the other two could be logged in across a network, such as the Internet.

By default, when you log in to a terminal, you receive a command-line shell (BASH shell), which prompts you to type in commands to tell the Linux kernel what to do. However, in this computing age, most people prefer to use a graphical interface in which they can use a computer mouse to navigate and start tasks. In this case, you can simply choose to start a graphical user interface (GUI) environment on top of your BASH shell after you are logged in to a command-line terminal, or you can switch to a graphical terminal, which allows users to log in and immediately receive a GUI environment. A typical command-line terminal login prompt looks like the following:

```
Fedora release 20 (Heisenbug)
Kernel 3.11.10-301.fc20.x86_64 on an x86_64 (tty2)

server1 login:
```

A typical graphical terminal login for Fedora Linux (called the GNOME Display Manager or gdm) is depicted in Figure 2-15.

To access a terminal device at the local server, you can press a combination of keys, such as Ctrl+Alt+F2, to change to a separate terminal. If you are logging in across the network, you

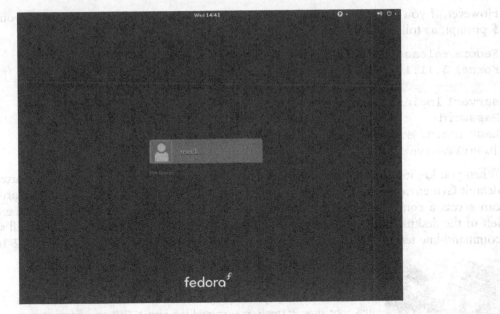

Figure 2-15 The GNOME Display Manager (gdm)

Terminal Name	Key Combination	Login Type
tty1 (:0)	Ctrl+Alt+F1	graphical
tty2	Ctrl+Alt+F2	command-line
tty3	Ctrl+Alt+F3	command-line
tty4	Ctrl+Alt+F4	command-line
tty5	Ctrl+Alt+F5	command-line
tty6	Ctrl+Alt+F6	command-line

Table 2-5 Common Linux terminals

can use a variety of programs that connect to a terminal on the Linux computer. A list of local Linux terminals, along with their names and types, is shown in Table 2-5.

After you are logged in to a command-line terminal, you receive a prompt where you can enter commands. The following example shows the user logging in as the root (administrator) user. As you can see in this example, after you log in as the root user, you see a # prompt:

```
Fedora release 20 (Heisenbug)
Kernel 3.11.10-301.fc20.x86_64 on an x86_64 (tty2)

server1 login: root
Password:
Last login: Mon Aug 16 09:45:42 from tty2
[root@server1 ~]#_
```

However, if you log in as a regular user to a command-line terminal (e.g., user1), you see a $ prompt, as follows:

```
Fedora release 20 (Heisenbug)
Kernel 3.11.10-301.fc20.x86_64 on an x86_64 (tty2)

server1 login: user1
Password:
Last login: Mon Aug 16 09:45:42 from tty2
[user1@server1 ~]$_
```

When you log in to a graphical terminal, the GUI environment of your choice is started; the default GUI environment in Fedora Linux is GNOME. After the GUI environment starts, you can access a command-line Terminal window by accessing the Activites menu in the upper left of the desktop and navigating to Show Applications, Utilities, Terminal. This will start a command-line terminal window within your GNOME desktop, as shown in Figure 2-16.

By default, Fedora 20 allows the root user to log into the GNOME desktop. However, this practice is not recommended for security reasons, as several graphical programs are not designed to be run as the root user. Instead, you should log into a GUI environment as a regular user. When you run a graphical administrative utility as a regular user, the GUI environment prompts you for the root user password in order to continue.

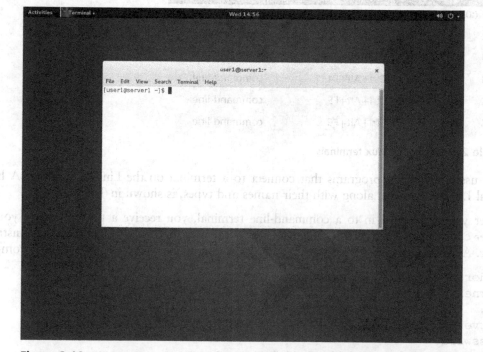

Figure 2-16 Using a command-line terminal within the GNOME desktop

Basic Shell Commands

When using a command-line terminal, the shell ultimately interprets all information the user enters onto the command line. This information includes the command itself, as well as options and arguments. **Commands** indicate the name of the program to execute and are case sensitive. **Options** are specific letters that start with a dash "-" and appear after the command name to alter the way the command works. Options are specific to the command in question; the persons who developed the command determined which options to allow for that command.

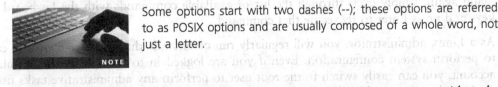

Some options start with two dashes (--); these options are referred to as POSIX options and are usually composed of a whole word, not just a letter.

Arguments also appear after the command name, yet they do not start with a dash. They specify the specific parameters that tailor the command to your particular needs. Suppose, for example, that you want to list all of the files in the /etc/rpm directory on the hard disk. You could use the `ls` command with the `-a` option (which tells the `ls` command to list all files) and the `/etc/rpm` argument (which tells `ls` to look in the /etc/rpm directory), as shown in the following example:

```
[root@server1 root]# ls -a /etc/rpm
.   macros.color  macros.fjava   macros.imgcreate
..  macros.dist   macros.gconf2  macros.jpackage
[root@server1 root]#_
```

After you type the command and press Enter in the preceding output, the `ls` command shows us that there are six files in the /etc/rpm directory. The command prompt then reappears, so that you can enter another command.

Commands, options, and arguments are case sensitive; an uppercase letter (A), for instance, is treated differently than a lowercase letter (a).

Always put a space between the command name, options, and arguments; otherwise, the shell does not understand that they are separate, and your command might not work as expected.

Although you can pass options and arguments to commands, not all commands need to have arguments or options supplied on the command line to work properly. The `date` command, which simply prints the current date and time, is an example:

```
[root@server1 root]# date
Sun Aug 19 08:46:57 EDT 2015
[root@server1 root]#_
```

Table 2-6 lists some common commands that you can use without specifying any options or arguments.

If the output of a certain command is too large to fit on the terminal screen, simply use the Shift and Page Up keys simultaneously to view previous screens of information. Also, Shift and Page Down, when pressed simultaneously, can be used to navigate in the opposite direction.

You can recall commands previously entered in the BASH shell using the keyboard cursor keys (the up, down, right, and left arrow keys). Thus, if you want to enter the same command again, simply cycle through the list of available commands with the keyboard cursor keys and press Enter to reexecute that command.

As a Linux administrator, you will regularly run commands that only the root user can run to perform system configuration. Even if you are logged in to the system as a regular user account, you can easily switch to the root user to perform any administrative tasks using the su (switch user) command. To switch to the root user and load the root user's environment variables, you can run the su command with the – option and supply the root user's password when prompted:

```
[user1@server1 ~]$ su - root
Password:
Last login: Mon Aug 16 09:45:42 EDT 2015 from tty2
[root@server1 root]#_
```

Alternatively, to run a single command as the root only, you can run the su -c "command" root and specify the root user's password when prompted.

Command	Description
clear	Clears the terminal screen
reset	Resets your terminal to use default terminal settings
who	Displays currently logged-in users
w	Displays currently logged-in users and their tasks
whoami	Displays your login name
id	Displays the numbers associated with your user account name and group names; these are commonly referred to as User IDs (UIDs) and Group IDs (GIDs)
date	Displays the current date and time
cal	Displays the calendar for the current month
exit	Exits out of your current shell
uname	Displays system information

Table 2-6 Some common Linux commands

If you do not specify the user name when using the su command, the root user is assumed. Additionally, the root user can use the su command to switch to any other user account without specifying a password:

```
[root@server1 root]# su - user1
Last login: Mon Aug 16 10:22:21 EDT 2015 from tty2
[user1@server1 ~]$_
```

Shell Metacharacters

Another important part of the shell are shell **metacharacters**, which are keyboard characters that have special meaning. One of the most commonly used metacharacters is the $ character, which tells the shell that the following text refers to a variable. A variable is simply a piece of information that is stored in memory; variable names are typically uppercase words, and most variables are set by the Linux system automatically when you log in. An example of how you might use the $ metacharacter to refer to a variable is by using the echo command (which prints text to the terminal screen):

```
[root@server1 root]# echo Hi There!
Hi There!
[root@server1 root]# echo My Shell is $SHELL
My Shell is /bin/bash
[root@server1 root]#_
```

Notice from the preceding output that $SHELL was translated into its appropriate value from memory (/bin/bash, the BASH shell). The shell recognized SHELL as a variable because it was prefixed by the $ metacharacter. Table 2-7 presents a list of common BASH shell metacharacters that are discussed throughout this book.

It is good practice to avoid metacharacters when typing commands unless you need to take advantage of their special functionality, as the shell readily interprets them, which might lead to unexpected results.

Metacharacter(s)	Description
$	Shell variable
~	Special home directory variable
&	Background command execution
;	Command termination
< << > >>	Input/Output redirection
|	Command piping
* ? [ ]	Shell wildcards
' " \	Metacharacter quotes
`	Command substitution
( ) { }	Command grouping

Table 2-7 Common BASH shell metacharacters

If you accidentally use one of these characters and your shell does not return you to the normal prompt, simply press the Ctrl and c keys in combination and your current command is canceled.

There are some circumstances in which you might need to use a metacharacter in a command and prevent the shell from interpreting its special meaning. To do this, simply enclose the metacharacters in single quotation marks ´ ´. Single quotation marks protect those metacharacters from being interpreted specially by the shell (that is, a $ is interpreted as a $ character and not a variable identifier). You can also use double quotation marks " " to perform the same task; however, double quotation marks do not protect $, \, and ` characters. If only one character needs to be protected from shell interpretation, you can precede that character by a \ rather than enclosing it within quotation marks. An example of this type of quoting follows:

```
[root@server1 root]# echo My Shell is $SHELL
My Shell is /bin/bash
[root@server1 root]# echo 'My Shell is $SHELL'
My Shell is $SHELL
[root@server1 root]# echo "My Shell is $SHELL"
My Shell is /bin/bash
[root@server1 root]# echo My Shell is \$SHELL
My Shell is $SHELL
[root@server1 root]#_
```

As shown in Table 2-7, not all quote characters protect characters from the shell. The back quote characters ` ` can be used to perform command substitution; anything between back quotes is treated as another command by the shell, and its output is substituted in place of the back quotes. Take the expression `date` as an example:

```
[root@server1 root]# echo Today is `date`
Today is Tue Mar 29 09:28:11 EST 2015
[root@server1 root]#_
```

Getting Command Help

Most distributions of Linux contain more than 1000 different Linux commands in their standard configurations, and thus it is impractical to memorize the syntax and use of each command. Fortunately, Linux stores documentation for each command in central locations so that it can be accessed easily. The most common form of documentation for Linux commands is **manual pages** (commonly referred to as **man pages**). Simply type the man command followed by a command name, and extensive information about that Linux command is displayed page-by-page on the terminal screen. This information includes a description of the command and its syntax, as well as available options, related files, and related commands. For example, to receive information on the format and usage of the whoami command, you can use the following command:

```
[root@server1 root]# man whoami
```

The manual page is then displayed page by page on the terminal screen. You can use the cursor (arrow) keys on the keyboard to scroll though the information or press q to quit. The manual page for whoami is similar to the following:

```
WHOAMI(1)                     User Commands                     WHOAMI(1)


NAME
whoami - print effective userid

SYNOPSIS
whoami [OPTION]…

DESCRIPTION
Print the user name associated with the current effective
user id. Same as id -un.

       --help    display this help and exit

       --version
              output version information and exit

AUTHOR
       Written by Richard Mlynarik.

REPORTING BUGS
       Report bugs to <bug-coreutils@gnu.org>.
       GNU coreutils home page: <http://www.gnu.org/software/coreutils/>
       General help using GNU software: <http://www.gnu.org/gethelp/>
       Report whoami translation bugs to <http://translationproject.org/>

COPYRIGHT
       Copyright©2013 Free Software Foundation, Inc. License GPLv3+: GNU
       GPL version 3 or later <http://gnu.org/licenses/gpl.html>.
       This is free software: you are free to change and redistribute it.
       There is NO WARRANTY, to the extent permitted by law.

SEE ALSO
       The full documentation is maintained as a Texinfo manual.
       If the info and whoami programs are installed at your site,
       the command

           info coreutils 'whoami invocation'

       should give you access to the complete manual.

GNU coreutils 8.21          August 2013
[root@server1 root]#_
```

Manual Page Section	Description
1	Commands that any user can execute
2	Linux system calls
3	Library routines
4	Special device files
5	File formats
6	Games
7	Miscellaneous
8	Commands that only the root user can execute
9	Linux kernel routines
n	New commands not categorized yet

Table 2-8 Manual page section numbers

Notice that the whoami command is displayed as WHOAMI(1) at the top of the preceding manual page output. The (1) denotes a section of the manual pages; section (1) means that whoami is a command that can be executed by any user. All manual pages contain certain section numbers that describe the category of the command in the manual page database; you can find a list of the different manual page section numbers in Table 2-8.

Sometimes, there is more than one command, library routine, or file that has the same name. If you run the man command with that name as an argument, Linux returns the manual page with the lowest section number. For example, if there is a file called whoami as well as a command named whoami and you type man whoami, the manual page for the whoami command (section 1 of the manual pages) is displayed. To display the manual page for the whoami file format instead, you simply type man 5 whoami to display the whoami file format (section 5 of the manual pages).

Recall that many commands are available to the Linux user; thus, it might be cumbersome to find the command that you need to perform a certain task without using a Linux command dictionary. Fortunately, you have the ability to search the manual pages by keyword. To find all of the commands that have the word "usb" in their names or descriptions, type the following:

```
[root@server1 root] # man -k usb
```

This command produces the following output:

```
fxload              (8) - Firmware download to EZ-USB devices
lsusb               (8) - list USB devices
sane-canon630u      (5) - SANE backend for the Canon 630u USB flatbed
                          scanner
sane-cardscan       (5) - SANE backend for Corex CardScan usb
                          scanners
sane-epjitsu        (5) - SANE backend for Epson-based Fujitsu USB
                          scanners.
```

sane-find-scanner	(1) -	find SCSI and USB scanners and their device files
sane-genesys	(5) -	SANE backend for GL646, GL841, GL843, GL847 and GL124 based USB flatbed scanners
sane-gt68xx	(5) -	SANE backend for GT-68XX based USB flatbed scanners
sane-kvs1025	(5) -	SANE backend for Panasonic KV-S102xC USB ADF scanners.
sane-kvs20xx	(5) -	SANE backend for Panasonic KV-S20xxC USB/SCSI ADF scanners.
sane-kvs40xx	(5) -	SANE backend for Panasonic KV-S40xxC USB/SCSI ADF scanners.
sane-ma1509	(5) -	SANE backend for Mustek BearPaw 1200F USB scanner
sane-mustek_usb	(5) -	SANE backend for Mustek USB flatbed scanners
sane-mustek_usb2	(5) -	SANE backend for SQ113 based USB flatbed scanners
sane-plustek	(5) -	SANE backend for LM983[1/2/3] based USB flatbed scanners
sane-sm3600	(5) -	SANE backend for Microtek scanners with M011 USB chip
sane-sm3840	(5) -	SANE backend for Microtek scanners with SCAN08 USB chip
sane-u12	(5) -	SANE backend for Plustek USB flatbed scanners, based on older parport designs
sane-usb	(5) -	USB configuration tips for SANE
usb-devices	(1) -	print USB device details
usb_modeswitch	(1) -	switch mode of "multi-state" USB devices
usb_modeswitch_dispatcher	(1) -	dispatcher not intended for direct invocation.
usbhid-dump	(8) -	dump USB HID device report descriptors and streams

```
[root@server1 root]#_
```

After you find the command needed, you can simply run the man command on that command without the –k option to find out detailed information about the command.

You can also use the apropos usb command to perform the same function as the man –k usb command. Both commands yield the exact same output on the terminal screen.

If you do not see any output from the man –k or apropos command following a Linux installation, you might need to run the mandb command to index the manual page database.

Another utility, originally intended to replace the man command in Linux, is the GNU **info pages**. You can access this utility by typing the info command followed by the name of the command in question. The info command returns an easy-to-read description of each command and also contains links to other information pages (called hyperlinks). Today, however, both the info pages and the manual pages are used to find documentation because manual pages have been utilized in Linux since its conception, and for over two decades in the UNIX operating system. An example of using the info utility to find information about the whoami command follows:

[root@server1 root]# **info whoami**

The info page is then displayed interactively:

```
File: coreutils.info, Node: who invocation, Prev: users invocation,
Up: User information

20.6 'who': Print who is currently logged in
============================================

'who' prints information about users who are currently logged on.
Synopsis:

    who [OPTION] [FILE] [am i]

    If given no non-option arguments, 'who' prints the following
information for each user currently logged on: login name, terminal line,
login time, and remote hostname or X display.

If given one non-option argument, 'who' uses that instead of a default
system-maintained file (often '/var/run/utmp' or '/var/run/utmp') as the
name of the file containing the record of users logged on. '/var/log/wtmp'
is commonly given as an argument to 'who' to look at who has previously
logged on.

If given two non-option arguments, 'who' prints only the entry for * bash:
(bash). The Bourne Again Shell. the hostname. Traditionally, the two
arguments given are 'am i', as in 'who am i'.

Time stamps are listed according to the time zone rules specified by the
'TZ' environment variable, or by the system default rules if 'TZ' is not
set. *Note Specifying the Time Zone with 'TZ': (libc)TZ Variable.

The program accepts the following options. Also see *note Common
options::.

'-a'
'--all'
    Same as '-b -d --login -p -r -t -T -u'.

'-b'
'--boot'
    Print the date and time of last system boot.

--zz-Info: (coreutils.info.gz)who invocation, 103 lines --Top------
[root@server1 root]#_
```

While in the info utility, press the ? key or Ctrl+h key combination to display a help screen that describes the usage of info. As with the man command, you can use the q key to quit.

2

Some commands do not have manual pages or info pages. These commands are usually functions that are built into the BASH shell itself. To find help on these commands, you must use the help command, as follows:

```
[root@server1 root]# help echo
echo: echo [-neE] [arg ...]
    Write arguments to the standard output.

    Display the ARGs on the standard output followed by a newline.

    Options:
     -n     do not append a newline
     -e     enable interpretation of the following backslash escapes
     -E     explicitly suppress interpretation of backslash escapes

    `echo' interprets the following backslash-escaped characters:
     \a     alert (bell)
     \b     backspace
     \c     suppress further output
     \e     escape character
     \f     form feed
     \n     new line
     \r     carriage return
     \t     horizontal tab
     \v     vertical tab
     \\     backslash
     \0nnn the character whose ASCII code is NNN (octal). NNN can be
     0 to 3 octal digits
     \xHH  the eight-bit character whose value is HH (hexadecimal). HH
     can be one or two hex digits

    Exit Status:
    Returns success unless a write error occurs.
[root@server1 root]#_
```

Shutting Down the Linux System

Because the operating system handles writing data from computer memory to the disk drives in a computer, simply turning off the power to the computer might result in damaged user and system files. Thus, it is important to prepare the operating system for shutdown before turning off the power to the hardware components of the computer. To do this, you can

Command	Description
`shutdown -H +4`	Halts your system in four minutes
`shutdown -r +4`	Reboots your system in four minutes
`shutdown -H now`	Halts your system immediately
`shutdown -r now`	Reboots your system immediately
`shutdown -c`	Cancels a scheduled shutdown
`halt`	Halts your system immediately
`poweroff`	Halts your system immediately and powers down the computer
`reboot`	Reboots your system immediately

Table 2-9 Commands to halt and reboot the Linux operating system

issue the `shutdown` command, which can halt or reboot (restart) your computer after a certain period of time. To halt your system in 15 minutes, for example, you could type:

[root@server1 root] # **shutdown -H +15**

This produces output similar to the following:

Broadcast message from root@server1 (Wed 2014-09-17 15:36:48 EDT):

The system is going down for power-off at Wed 2014-09-17 15:51:48 EDT!

Shutdown scheduled for Wed 2014-09-17 15:51:48 EDT, use 'shutdown -c' to cancel.

Notice from the preceding output that you do not receive the command prompt back again after the `shutdown` command has started. Thus, to stop the shutdown, simply press the Ctrl and c keys in combination to return to a command prompt and then issue the command `shutdown -c` to cancel the shutdown.

To halt your system now, you could type:

[root@server1 root] # **poweroff**

Other examples of the `shutdown` command and their descriptions are shown in Table 2-9.

Chapter Summary

- Prior to installation, you should verify hardware requirements using the HCL.

- You can obtain Linux installation media by downloading an ISO image from the Internet that can be written to a DVD or USB flash drive or can be used directly by virtualization software.

- A typical Linux installation prompts the user for information, such as language, date, time zone, keyboard layout, network configuration, user account configuration, and permanent storage configuration.

- Users must log in to a terminal and receive a shell before they are able to interact with the Linux system and kernel. A single user can log in several different times simultaneously to several different terminals locally or across a network.

- Regardless of the type of terminal that you use (graphical or command-line), you are able to enter commands, options, and arguments at a shell prompt to perform system tasks, obtain command help, or shut down the Linux system. The shell is case sensitive and understands a variety of special characters called shell metacharacters, which should be protected if their special meaning is not required.

Key Terms

Advanced Technology Attachment (ATA)   See *Parallel Advanced Technology Attachment*.

arguments   The text that appears after a command name, does not start with a dash (the - character), and specifies information that the command requires to work properly.

authentication   The process whereby each user must log in with a valid user name and password before gaining access to the user interface of a system.

B-tree Filesystem (BTRFS)   An experimental Linux filesystem that contains advanced features such as storage pools and filesystem snapshots.

BASH shell   Also known as the Bourne Again Shell, this is the default command-line interface in Linux.

BIOS (Basic Input/Output System)   The part of a computer system that contains the programs used to initialize hardware components at boot time.

command   A program that exists on the filesystem and is executed when typed on the command line.

ext2   A nonjournaling Linux filesystem.

ext3   A journaling Linux filesystem.

ext4   An improved version of the ext3 filesystem, with an extended feature set and better performance.

extended partition   A partition on a hard disk or SSD that can be further subdivided into components called logical drives.

filesystem   The way in which a hard disk or SSD partition is formatted to allow data to reside on the physical media; common Linux filesystems include ext2, ext3, ext4, REISERFS, and VFAT.

GUID Partition Table (GPT)   The area of a large hard disk (> 2TB) outside a partition that stores partition information and boot loaders.

Hardware Compatibility List (HCL)   A list of hardware components that have been tested and deemed compatible with a given operating system.

info pages   A set of local, easy-to-read command syntax documentation available by typing the info command-line utility.

Integrated Drive Electronics (IDE)   See *Parallel Advanced Technology Attachment*.

ISO image A file that contains the content of a DVD. ISO images of Linux installation media can be downloaded from the Internet.

journaling A filesystem function that keeps track of the information that needs to be written to the hard disk or SSD in a journal; common Linux journaling filesystems include ext3, ext4, and REISER.

live media Linux installation media that provides a fully functional Linux operating system in RAM prior to installation on permanent storage.

logical drives The smaller partitions contained within an extended partition on a hard disk.

Logical Volume Manager (LVM) A set of services that are used to manage logical volumes stored on one or more hard disks.

manual pages The most common set of local command syntax documentation, available by typing the man command-line utility. Also known as man pages.

man pages See *manual pages*.

Master Boot Record (MBR) The area of a typical hard disk (< 2TB) outside a partition that stores partition information and boot loaders.

memtest86 A common RAM-checking utility.

metacharacters The key combinations that have special meaning in the Linux operating system.

options The specific letters that start with a dash (the - character) or two and appear after the command name to alter the way the command works.

Parallel Advanced Technology Attachment (PATA) A legacy hard disk technology that uses ribbon cables to typically attach up to four hard disk devices to a single computer.

partitions A section of a hard disk or SSD. Partitions can be primary or extended.

primary partitions The separate divisions into which a hard disk or SSD can be divided (up to four are allowed per hard disk).

Redundant Array of Inexpensive Disks (RAID) A type of storage that can be used to combine hard disks together for performance and/or fault tolerance.

REISER A journaling filesystem used in Linux.

Serial Advanced Technology Attachment (SATA) A technology that allows for fast data transfer along a serial cable for hard disks and SSDs. It is commonly used in newer workstation and server-class computers.

shell A user interface that accepts input from the user and passes the input to the kernel for processing.

Small Computer Systems Interface (SCSI) A high-performance hard disk technology that is commonly used in server-class computers.

solid-state drive (SSD) A type of disk drive that functions within a computer like a hard disk drive but instead uses fast flash memory chips to store data.

swap memory See *virtual memory*.

terminal The channel that allows a certain user to log in and communicate with the kernel via a user interface.

VFAT (Virtual File Allocation Table)   A non-journaling filesystem that might be used in Linux.

virtual machine   An operating system that is running within virtualization software.

virtual machine host   An operating system that runs virtualization software.

virtual memory   An area on a hard disk or SSD (swap partition) that can be used to store information that normally resides in physical memory (RAM), if the physical memory is being used excessively.

virtualization software   A set of programs that can be used to run an operating system within an existing operating system concurrently.

Review Questions

1. What is the default shell in Linux called?
   a. SH
   b. BSH
   c. CSH
   d. BASH

2. What equivalent to the man command generally provides an easier-to-read description of the queried command and also contains links to other related information?
   a. who
   b. man help
   c. man -descriptive
   d. info

3. What command can you use to safely shut down the Linux system immediately?
   a. shutdown -c
   b. shutdown -r
   c. down
   d. halt

4. What command is equivalent to the man –k *keyword* command?
   a. find *keyword*
   b. man *keyword*
   c. apropos *keyword*
   d. appaloosa *keyword*

5. Which of the following is not a piece of information that the Fedora installation program prompts you for?

    a. time zone

    b. installation destination

    c. firewall settings

    d. keyboard layout

6. Linux commands entered via the command line are not case sensitive. True or False?

7. Which command blanks the terminal screen, erasing previously displayed output?

    a. `erase`

    b. `clean`

    c. `blank`

    d. `clear`

8. When sitting at a computer running Linux, what key combination is pressed to open the graphical terminal?

    a. Ctrl+Alt+G

    b. Ctrl+Alt+F4

    c. Ctrl+Alt+F1

    d. Ctrl+7

9. To install Linux within a virtual machine, you can specify the path to an ISO image that contains the Linux installation media within virtualization software without having to first write the ISO image to a DVD or USB flash drive. True or False?

10. After you log in to a terminal, you receive a user interface called a _____.

    a. GUID

    b. shell

    c. text box

    d. command screen

11. Users enter commands directly to the kernel of the Linux operating system. True or False?

12. How can you protect a metacharacter (such as the $ character) from shell interpretation?

    a. Precede it with a /.

    b. Follow it with a \.

    c. Precede it with a $.

    d. It cannot be done because metacharacters are essential.

    e. Precede it with a \.

13. You know a Linux command will perform a desired function for you, but you cannot remember the full name of the command. You do remember it will flush a variable from your system. Which command typed at a command prompt displays a list of commands that would likely contain the command you desire?

    a. `man -k flush`

    b. `man -k find all`

    c. `man flush`

    d. `man -key flush`

14. Which command displays the users who are currently logged in to the Linux system?

    a. `finger`

    b. `who`

    c. `id`

    d. `date`

15. Which prompt does the root user receive when logged in to the system?

    a. `$`

    b. `@`

    c. `#`

    d. `!`

16. Which prompt do regular users receive when logged in to the system?

    a. `$`

    b. `@`

    c. `#`

    d. `!`

17. Which of the following refers to the third primary partition on the second SCSI hard disk within Linux?

    a. `hdb2`

    b. `sda3`

    c. `hdb3`

    d. `sdb3`

18. Which two partitions do you typically create at minimum during a Fedora Linux installation? (Choose two answers.)

    a. `/`

    b. `/boot`

    c. `swap`

    d. `/home`

19. If you boot your computer from Linux live media, you will be able to use a fully functional Linux system prior to installing Linux on permanent storage. True or False?

20. Which of the following is not an example of virtualization software that can be used to install Linux within another operating system?

    a. Oracle VirtualBox

    b. Microsoft Hyper-V

    c. Spiceworks

    d. VMware

Hands-on Projects

These projects should be completed in the order given and should take a total of three hours to complete. The software and hardware requirements for these projects include the following:

- A 64-bit computer with at least 4GB of RAM, 80GB of permanent disk storage, and a DVD drive
- A Windows operating system that contains a virtualization software product, a Web browser, and an Internet connection
- The ISO image for Fedora 20 live media (Fedora-Live-Desktop-x86_64-20-1.iso)

Project 2-1

In this hands-on project, you install Fedora 20 Linux within a virtual machine on a Windows computer.

1. In your virtualization software, create a new virtual machine called **Fedora Linux** that has the following characteristics:

    a. 2GB of memory

    b. an Internet connection via your PC's network card (preferably using bridged mode)

    c. a 20GB virtual hard disk

    d. the virtual machine DVD drive attached to the ISO file for Fedora 20 live media (Fedora-Live-Desktop-x86_64-20-1.iso)

2. Start and then connect to your Fedora Linux virtual machine using your virtualization software.

3. At the Fedora Live welcome screen, press **Enter** to boot Fedora Live.

4. Once the graphical desktop and Welcome to Fedora screen has loaded, select the option **Install to Hard Drive** to start the Fedora installation program.

5. At the Welcome to Fedora 20 screen, select **English (United States)** if necessary, and press **Continue**.

6. On the Installation Summary page, click **Date & Time**, ensure that your time zone is selected, and press **Done**.

7. On the Installation Summary page, click **Installation Destination**. You should see that your 20GB virtual disk is already selected and called sda. Press **Done** when finished.

8. When the Installation Options screen appears, select **I want to review/modify my disk partitions before continuing**, choose a partition scheme of **Standard Partition**, and press **Continue**.

9. At the Manual Partitioning screen, select the link **Click here to create them automatically**. This will create several partitions.

   a. Highlight the / (sda3) partition, reduce the Desired Capacity to **12 GB**, and click **Update Settings**. This will leave some free unpartitioned space on our first disk for a later exercise.

   b. Press **Done** and then click **Accept Changes** when prompted.

10. At the Installation Summary page, click **Begin Installation**.

11. During the installation process, click **Root Password**, supply a password of **LNXrocks!**, and press **Done**. Next, click User Creation and create a user with a name and description of **user1** and password of **LNXrocks!**. Ensure that you select the option to make this user an administrator user, then press **Done**.

12. When the installation has finished, click **Quit**. This will return you to your Fedora live desktop.

13. Click the power icon in the upper-right corner, select the power icon that appears, and click **Power Off** to shut down your Fedora Live installation image.

14. In the Settings for your virtual machine in your virtualization software, ensure that the DVD drive is no longer attached to the Fedora ISO image.

15. Finally, start your Fedora Linux virtual machine using your virtualization software to boot into your new Fedora Linux OS.

Project 2-2

In this hands-on project, you explore some command-line terminals on a Linux system and enter some basic commands into the BASH shell.

1. After your Linux system has been loaded, you are placed at a graphical terminal (tty1). Instead of logging in to this graphical terminal, press **Ctrl+Alt+F2** to switch to a command-line terminal (tty2) and then log in to the terminal using the user name of **root** and the password of **LNXrocks!**. Which prompt did you receive and why?

2. At the command prompt, type **date** and press **Enter** to view the current date and time. Now, type **Date** and press **Enter**. Why did you receive an error message? Can you tell which shell gave you the error message?

3. Switch to a different command-line terminal (tty5) by pressing **Ctrl+Alt+F5** and log in to the terminal using the user name of **user1** and the password of **LNXrocks!**. Which prompt did you receive and why?

4. At the command prompt, type **who** and press **Enter** to view the users logged in to the system. Who is logged in and on which terminal?

5. Switch back to the terminal tty2 by pressing **Ctrl+Alt+F2**. Did you need to log in? Are the outputs from the date and Date commands still visible?

6. Try typing in each command listed in Table 2-6 in order (pressing **Enter** after each) and observe the output. What did the last command (exit) do?

7. Switch to the terminal tty5 by pressing **Ctrl+Alt+F5** and type **exit** to log out of your shell.

Project 2-3

In this hands-on project, you log in to a graphical terminal in Fedora Linux and interact with the GNOME and KDE desktops.

1. Switch to the graphical terminal (tty1) by pressing **Ctrl+Alt+F1**, click **user1**, supply the password of **LNXrocks!**, and click **Sign In**. Which desktop is started and why?

2. The first time you log into the desktop, you will be prompted to select desktop preferences.

   a. At the Welcome screen, ensure that **English (United States)** is selected and click **Next**.

   b. At the Input Sources screen, ensure that the **English (US)** keyboard layout is selected and click **Next**.

   c. At the Online Accounts screen, click **Next** to bypass personal account configuration.

   d. On the Thank You screen, click **Start using Fedora**.

3. Observe the GNOME desktop. Use your mouse to select the **Activities** menu in the upper-left corner of your screen, select the **Show Applications** icon (at the bottom of the application panel), and then navigate to **Utilities, Terminal** to open a BASH shell prompt. What prompt do you receive and why?

4. At the command prompt, type **who** and press **Enter** to view the users logged in to the system. Note that tty1 is listed as running on port 0 (:0) and that your Terminal application is running as a pseudo-terminal session (pts/0) within your GUI environment.

5. At the command prompt, type **su -** and press **Enter** to switch to the root user. Supply the root user password (**LNXrocks!**) when prompted.

6. By default, the KDE desktop is not installed in Fedora 20. To download and install the KDE desktop from the Internet, type **yum groupinstall "KDE Plasma Workspaces"** and press **Enter**. Press y when prompted to download and install the software packages for the KDE desktop. This may take several minutes, depending on your Internet speed. The yum command will be discussed in more detail in Chapter 11.

7. By default, the log out option is not enabled in Fedora 20 (it is useful if you are going to switch desktops). Type **gsettings set org.gnome.shell always-show-log-out true** to enable the log out option, and press **Enter** when finished.

8. Type **reboot** to restart Fedora Linux. After the system has rebooted, log into the GNOME desktop as **user1** with the password **LNXrocks!**.

9. Click the power icon in the upper-right of the GNOME desktop and note that there is now a section that lists the currently logged-in user (user1). Click **user1, Log Out,** and then click **Log Out** again to log out of the GNOME desktop.

10. At the Fedora login screen, click **user1** and then click the cog wheel icon next to the Sign In button. Select **KDE Plasma Workspace**, supply the password for user1 (**LNXrocks!**), and click **Sign In**.

11. Click the Fedora start button in the lower left of the desktop and navigate to **Applications, System, Terminal** to start a command-line shell. How does application navigation in the KDE desktop differ from the GNOME desktop?

12. At the command prompt, type **echo $SHELL** and press **Enter** to view your current shell. Is this shell the same shell used for command-line terminals?

13. Click the Fedora start button, navigate to **Leave, Log out**, and click **Logout** to exit the KDE desktop.

Project 2-4

In this hands-on project, you use and protect shell metacharacters.

1. Switch to a command-line terminal (tty2) by pressing **Ctrl+Alt+F2** and log in to the terminal using the user name of **root** and the password of **LNXrocks!**.

2. At the command prompt, type **date;who** and press **Enter** to run the date command immediately followed by the who command. Use the information in Table 2-7 to describe the purpose of the ; metacharacter.

3. At the command prompt, type **echo This is OK** and press **Enter** to display a message on the terminal screen.

4. At the command prompt, type **echo Don't do this** and press **Enter**. Which character needs to be protected in the previous command? Press the **Ctrl** and **c** keys together to cancel your command and return to a BASH shell prompt.

5. At the command prompt, type **echo "Don't do this"** and press **Enter**. What is displayed on the terminal screen?

6. At the command prompt, type **echo Don\'t do this** and press **Enter**. What is displayed on the terminal screen?

7. At the command prompt, type **echo $SHELL** and press **Enter** to view the expansion of a variable using a shell metacharacter. What is displayed on the terminal screen? Next, type **echo $TEST** and press **Enter** to find out what happens when a variable that does not exist is used in a command. What is displayed?

8. At the command prompt, type **echo You have $4.50** and press **Enter**. What is displayed? Why? Which character needs to be protected in the previous command? What are two different ways that you can protect this character from interpretation by the shell?

9. At the command prompt, type **echo 'You have $4.50'** and press **Enter**. What is displayed on the terminal screen? Did the single quotation marks protect this metacharacter from shell interpretation?

10. At the command prompt, type **echo "You have $4.50"** and press **Enter**. What is displayed on the terminal screen? Did the double quotation marks protect this metacharacter from shell interpretation?

11. At the command prompt, type **echo You have \\$4.50** and press **Enter**. What is displayed on the terminal screen? Did the backslash protect this metacharacter from shell interpretation?

12. At the command prompt, type **echo My name is `whoami`** and press **Enter**. What function do back quotes perform?

13. Type **exit** and press **Enter** to log out of your shell.

Project 2-5

In this hands-on project, you find information about commands using help utilities.

1. Press **Ctrl+Alt+F2** to switch to a command-line terminal (tty2), and then log in to the terminal using the user name of **root** and the password of **LNXrocks!**.

2. At the command prompt, type **man –k cron** and press **Enter** to view a list of manual pages that have the word "cron" in the name or description. Use Table 2-8 to determine what type of manual pages are displayed. How many manual pages are there for crontab? Are they different types of manual pages?

 If you do not see any output from the man –k command, run the mandb command to generate the manual pages index.

3. At the command prompt, type **man crontab** and press **Enter** to view the manual page for the crontab command. Observe the syntax of the crontab command and press **q** when finished to quit the manual page and return to your command prompt.

4. At the command prompt, type **man 5 crontab** and press **Enter** to view the manual page for the crontab file format. Observe the syntax of the crontab file format and press **q** when finished to quit the manual page and return to your command prompt.

5. At the command prompt, type **info** and press **Enter** to view a list of available GNU info pages. When finished, press **q** to quit the info utility.

6. At the command prompt, type **info date** and press **Enter** to view syntax information regarding the date command, and press **q** to quit the info utility when finished.

7. At the command prompt, type **help** to view a list of BASH shell functions that have documentation. If the list is too long for your terminal, press the **Shift** and **Page Up** keys simultaneously to shift one page up to view the top of the list. Then press the **Shift** and **Page Down** keys simultaneously to shift one page down to view your command prompt again.

8. At the command prompt, type **help exit** to view information on the exit command, a function of your BASH shell.

9. Type **exit** and press **Enter** to log out of your shell.

Project 2-6

In this hands-on project, you properly shut down your Linux system.

1. Press **Ctrl+Alt+F2** to switch to a command-line terminal (tty2), and then log in to the terminal using the user name of **root** and the password of **LNXrocks!**.

2. At the command prompt, type **poweroff** to shut down your Linux system immediately. Which commands from Table 2-9 can also be used to shut down your Linux system?

Discovery Exercises

1. You are the network administrator for Slimjim, a peripheral device company. The network uses Linux, and you need information on some commands to perform your job. Open the manual pages and find all the commands that have the word "copy" in their name or description. What command did you use to accomplish this task? Are there any commands in this list that only a root user can execute? How are they indicated? Select any two of them and compare their info and manual pages. Access and read the manual pages on three other commands that interest you either by using the command name or searching for them by related keyword (try using `apropos`).

2. Identify the errors with the following commands and indicate possible solutions. (*Hint:* Try typing them at a shell prompt to view the error message.)

```
Echo "This command does not work properly"
date -z
apropos man -k
help date
shutdown -c now
echo "I would like lots of $$$"
man 8 date
```

Project 2-6

In this hands-on project, you properly shut down your Linux system.

1. Press Ctrl+Alt+F2 to switch to a command-line terminal (tty2), and then log in to the terminal using the user name of root and the password of LNXrocks!

2. At the command prompt, type poweroff to shut down your Linux system immediately. Which commands from Table 2-5 can also be used to shut down your Linux system?

Discovery Exercises

1. You are the network administrator for Shaing, a peripheral device company. Your network uses lamps and you need information on some commands to perform your job. Open the manual pages and find all the commands that have the word "copy" in their name or description. What command did you use to accomplish this task? Are there any commands in this list that only a root user can execute? If how are they indicated? Select any two of them and compare their info and manual pages. Access and read the manual pages on three other commands that interest you either by using the command name or searching for them by related keyword (try using apropos).

2. Identify the errors with the following commands and indicate possible solutions. (Hint: Try typing them at a shell prompt to view the error messages.)

echo "This command does not work properly!"
date -z
apropos man -k
help date
shutdown -c now
echo "I won't Like Jota to", <<-
man 5 date

chapter **3**

Exploring Linux Filesystems

After completing this chapter, you will be able to:

- Understand and navigate the Linux directory structure using relative and absolute pathnames
- Describe the various types of Linux files
- View filenames and file types
- Use shell wildcards to specify multiple filenames
- Display the contents of text files and binary files
- Search text files for regular expressions using grep
- Use the vi editor to manipulate text files
- Identify common alternatives to the vi text editor used today

An understanding of the structure and commands surrounding the Linux filesystem is essential for effectively using Linux to manipulate data. In the first part of this chapter, you explore the Linux filesystem hierarchy by changing your position in the filesystem tree and listing filenames of various types. Next, you examine the shell wildcard metacharacters used to specify multiple filenames as well as view the contents of files using standard Linux commands. You then learn about the regular expression metacharacters used when searching for text within files and are introduced to the vi text editor and its equivalents.

The Linux Directory Structure

Fundamental to using the Linux operating system is an understanding of how Linux stores files on the filesystem. Typical Linux systems could have thousands of data and program files; thus, a structure that organizes those files is necessary to make it easier to find and manipulate data and run programs. Recall from the previous chapter that Linux uses a logical directory tree to organize files into different directories (also known as folders). When a user stores files in a certain **directory**, the files are physically stored in the filesystem of a certain partition on a hard disk or SSD inside the computer. Most people are familiar with the Windows operating system directory tree structure as depicted in Figure 3-1; each filesystem on a hard drive partition is referred to by a drive letter (such as C: or D:) and has a root directory (indicated by the \ character) containing subdirectories that together form a hierarchical tree.

It is important to describe directories in the directory tree properly; the **absolute pathname** to a file or directory is the full pathname of a certain file or directory starting from the root directory. In Figure 3-1, the absolute pathname for the color directory is C:\windows\color and the absolute pathname for the sue directory is D:\home\sue. In other words, we refer to C:\windows\color as the color directory below the windows directory below the root of C drive. Similarly, we refer to D:\home\sue as the sue directory below the home directory below the root of D drive.

Linux uses a similar directory structure, but with no drive letters. The structure contains a single root (referred to using the / character), with different filesystems on hard drive partitions mounted (or attached) to different directories on this directory tree. The directories that each filesystem is mounted to are transparent to the user. An example of a sample Linux directory tree equivalent to the Windows sample directory tree shown in Figure 3-1 is depicted in Figure 3-2. Note that the subdirectory named "root" in Figure 3-2 is different from the root (/) directory. You'll learn more about the root subdirectory in the next section.

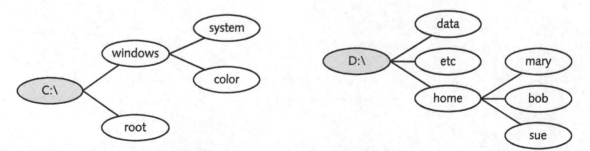

Figure 3-1 The Windows filesystem structure

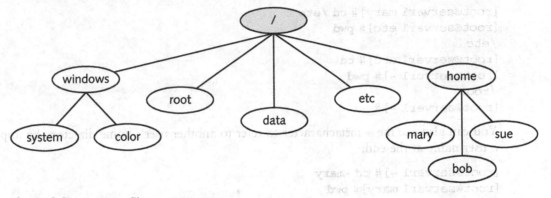

Figure 3-2 The Linux filesystem structure

In Figure 3-2, the absolute pathname for the color directory is /windows/color and the absolute pathname for the sue directory is /home/sue. In other words, we refer to the /windows/color directory as the color directory below the windows directory below the root of the system (the / character). Similarly, we refer to the /home/sue directory as the sue directory below the home directory below the root of the system.

Changing Directories

When you log into a Linux system, you are placed in your **home directory**, which is a place unique to your user account for storing personal files. Regular users usually have a home directory named after their user account under the /home directory, as in /home/sue. The root user, however, has a home directory called root under the root directory of the system (/root), as shown in Figure 3-2. Regardless of your user name, you can always refer to your own home directory using the ~ **metacharacter.**

To confirm the system directory that you are currently in, simply observe the name at the end of the shell prompt or run the **pwd** (**print working directory**) **command** at a command-line prompt. If you are logged in as the root user, the following output is displayed on the terminal screen:

```
[root@server1 ~]# pwd
/root
[root@server1 ~]#_
```

However, if you are logged in as the user sue, you see the following output:

```
[sue@server1 ~]$ pwd
/home/sue
[sue@server1 ~]$_
```

To change directories, you can issue the **cd** (**change directory**) **command** with an argument specifying the destination directory. If you do not specify a destination directory, the cd command returns you to your home directory:

```
[root@server1 ~]# cd /home/mary
[root@server1 mary]# pwd
/home/mary
```

```
[root@server1 mary]# cd /etc
[root@server1 etc]# pwd
/etc
[root@server1 etc]# cd
[root@server1 ~]# pwd
/root
[root@server1 ~]#_
```

You can also use the ~ metacharacter to refer to another user's home directory by appending a user name at the end:

```
[root@server1 ~]# cd ~mary
[root@server1 mary]# pwd
/home/mary
[root@server1 mary]# cd ~
[root@server1 ~]# pwd
/root
[root@server1 ~]#_
```

In many of the examples discussed earlier, the argument specified after the cd command is an absolute pathname to a directory, meaning that the system has all the information it needs to find the destination directory because the pathname starts from the root (/) of the system. However, in most Linux commands, you can also use a relative pathname in place of an absolute pathname to reduce typing. A **relative pathname** is the pathname of a target file or directory relative to your current directory in the tree. To specify a directory underneath your current directory, simply refer to that directory by name (do not start the pathname with a / character). To refer to a directory one step closer to the root of the tree (also known as a **parent directory**), simply use two dots (..). An example of using relative pathnames to move around the directory tree is shown next:

```
[root@server1 ~]# cd /home/mary
[root@server1 mary]# pwd
/home/mary
[root@server1 mary]# cd ..
[root@server1 home]# pwd
/home
[root@server1 home]# cd mary
[root@server1 mary]# pwd
/home/mary
[root@server1 mary]#_
```

In the preceding example, we used ".." to move up one parent directory and then used the word "mary" to specify the mary **subdirectory** relative to our current location in the tree; however, you can also move more than one level up or down the directory tree:

```
[root@server1 ~]# cd /home/mary
[root@server1 mary]# pwd
/home/mary
[root@server1 mary]# cd ../..
[root@server1 /]# pwd
/
```

```
[root@server1 /]# cd home/mary
[root@server1 mary]# pwd
/home/mary
[root@server1 mary]#_
```

You can also use one dot (.) to refer to the current directory. Although this is not useful when using the cd command, you do use one dot later in this book.

Although absolute pathnames are straightforward to use as arguments to commands when specifying the location of a certain file or directory, relative pathnames can save you a great deal of typing and reduce the potential for error if your current directory is far away from the root directory. Suppose, for example, that the current directory is /home/sue/projects/acme/ plans and you need to change to the /home/sue/projects/acme directory. Using an absolute pathname, you would type cd /home/sue/projects/acme; however, using a relative pathname, you only need to type cd .. to perform the same task because the /home/sue/ projects/acme directory is one parent directory above the current location in the directory tree.

An alternate method for saving time when typing pathnames as arguments to commands is to use the **Tab-completion feature** of the BASH shell. To do this, type enough unique letters of a directory and press the Tab key to allow the BASH shell to find the intended file or directory being specified and fill in the appropriate information. If there is more than one possible match, the Tab-completion feature alerts you with a beep; pressing the Tab key again after this beep presents you with a list of possible files or directories.

Observe the directory structure in Figure 3-2. To use the Tab-completion feature to change the current directory to /home/sue, you simply type cd /h and then press the Tab key. This changes the previous characters on the terminal screen to display cd /home/ (the BASH shell was able to fill in the appropriate information because the /home directory is the only directory underneath the / directory that starts with the letter "h"). Then, you could add an s character to the command, so that the command line displays cd /home/s, and press the Tab key once again to allow the shell to fill in the remaining letters. This results in the command cd /home/sue/ being displayed on the terminal screen (the sue directory is the only directory that begins with the s character underneath the /home directory). At this point, you can press Enter to execute the command and change the current directory to /home/sue.

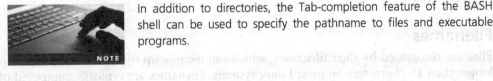

In addition to directories, the Tab-completion feature of the BASH shell can be used to specify the pathname to files and executable programs.

Viewing Files and Directories

The point of a directory structure is to organize files into an easy-to-use format. In order to locate the file you need to execute, view, or edit, you need to be able to display a list of the contents of a particular directory. You'll learn how to do that shortly, but first you need to learn about the various types of files and filenames, as well as the different commands used to select filenames for viewing.

File Types

Fundamental to viewing files and directories is a solid understanding of the various types of files present on most Linux systems. Several different types of files can exist on a Linux system; the most common include the following:

- Text files
- Binary data files
- Executable program files
- Directory files
- Linked files
- Special device files
- Named pipes and sockets

Most files on a Linux system that contain configuration information are **text files**. Another type of files are programs that exist on the hard drive before they are executed in memory to become processes. A program is typically associated with several supporting **binary data files** that store information such as common functions and graphics. In addition, directories themselves are actually files; they are special files that serve as placeholders to organize other files. When you create a directory, a file is placed on the hard drive to represent that directory.

Linked files are files that have an association with one another; they can represent the same data or they can point to another file (also known as a shortcut file). **Special device files** are less common than the other file types that have been mentioned, yet they are important for systems administrators because they represent different devices on the system, such as hard disks and serial ports. These device files are used in conjunction with commands that manipulate devices on the system; special device files are typically found only in the /dev directory and are discussed in later chapters of this book. As with special device files, **named pipe files** are uncommon and used primarily by administrators. Named pipes identify a channel that passes information from one process in memory to another, and in some cases they can be mediated by files on the hard drive. Writes to the file are processed while another process reads from it to achieve this passing of information. Another variant of a named pipe file is a **socket file**, which allows a process on another computer to write to a file on the local computer while another process reads from that file.

Filenames

Files are recognized by their **filenames**, which can include up to 255 characters yet are rarely longer than 20 characters on most Linux systems. Filenames are typically composed of alphanumeric characters, the underscore (_) character, the dash (—) character, and the period (.) character.

It is important to avoid using the shell metacharacters discussed in the previous chapter when naming files. Using a filename that contains a shell metacharacter as an argument to a Linux command might produce unexpected results.

Filenames that start with a period (.) are referred to as hidden files. You need to use a special command to display them in a file list. This command is discussed later in this chapter.

Filenames used by the Windows operating system typically end with a period and three characters that indentify the file type—for example, document.txt (a text file) and server.exe (an **executable program** file). However, most files on the hard drive of a Linux system do not follow this pattern, although some files on the Linux filesystem do contain characters at the end of the filename that indicate the file type. These characters are commonly referred to as **filename extensions**. Table 3-1 lists common examples of filename extensions and their associated file types.

Listing Files

Linux hosts a variety of commands that can be used to display files and their types in various directories on hard drive partitions. By far, the most common method for displaying files is to use the **ls command**. Following is an example of a file listing in the root user's home directory:

```
[root@server1 ~]# pwd
/root
[root@server1 ~]# ls
current myprogram project project12 project2 project4
Desktop myscript project1 project13 project3 project5
[root@server1 ~]#_
```

Metacharacter	Description
.c	C programming language source code files
.cc .cpp	C++ programming language source code files
.html .htm	HTML (Hypertext Markup Language) files
.ps	Files formatted for printing with postscript
.txt	Text files
.tar	Archived files (contain other files within)
.gz .bz2 .Z	Compressed files
.tar .gz .tgz .tar .bz2 .tar .Z	Compressed archived files
.conf .cfg	Configuration files (contain text)
.so	Shared object (programming library) files
.o	Compiled object files
.pl	PERL (Practical Extraction and Report Language) programs
.tcl	Tcl (Tool Command Language) programs
.jpg .jpeg .png .tiff .xpm .gif	Binary files that contain graphical images
.sh	Shell scripts (contain text that is executed by the shell)

Table 3-1 Common filename extensions

The files listed previously and discussed throughout this chapter are for example purposes only. The Hands-on Projects use different files.

The `ls` command displays all the files in the current directory in columnar format; however, you can also pass an argument to the `ls` command indicating the directory to be listed if the current directory listing is not required. In the following example, the files are listed underneath the /home/bob directory without changing the current directory.

```
[root@server1 ~]# pwd
/root
[root@server1 ~]# ls /home/bob
assignment1 file1 letter letter2 project1
[root@server1 ~]#_
```

When running the `ls` command, you will notice that files of different types are often represented as different colors; however, the specific colors used to represent files of certain types might vary from terminal to terminal and distribution to distribution. As a result, do not assume color alone indicates the file type.

Windows uses the `dir` command to list files and directories; to simplify the learning of Linux for Windows users, there is a `dir` command in Linux, which is simply a pointer or shortcut to the `ls` command.

Recall from the previous chapter that you can use switches to alter the behavior of commands. To view a list of files and their type, use the `-F` switch to the `ls` command:

```
[root@server1 ~]# pwd
/root
[root@server1 ~]# ls -F
current@ myprogram*  project    project12  project2  project4
Desktop/ myscript*   project1   project13  project3  project5
[root@server1 ~]#_
```

The `ls -F` command appends a special character at the end of each filename displayed to indicate the type of file. In the preceding output, note that the filenames current, Desktop, myprogram, and myscript have special characters appended to their names. The @ symbol indicates a linked file, the * symbol indicates an executable file, the / indicates a subdirectory, the = character indicates a socket, and the | character indicates a named pipe. All other file types do not have a special character appended to them and could be text files, binary data files, or special device files.

It is common convention to name directories starting with an uppercase letter, such as the D in the Desktop directory shown in the preceding output. This allows you to quickly determine which names refer to directories when running the `ls` command without any options that specify file type.

Although the `ls –F` command is a quick way of getting file type information in an easy-to-read format, at times you need to obtain more detailed information about each file. The `ls –l` command can be used to provide a long listing for each file in a certain directory.

```
[root@server1 ~]# pwd
/root
[root@server1 ~]# ls -l
total 548
lrwxrwxrwx    1 root   root         9 Apr  7  09:56  current -> project12
drwx-----    3 root   root      4096 Mar 29  10:01  Desktop
-rwxr-xr-x    1 root   root    519964 Apr  7  09:59  myprogram
-rwxr-xr-x    1 root   root        20 Apr  7  09:58  myscript
-rw-r--r--    1 root   root        71 Apr  7  09:58  project
-rw-r--r--    1 root   root        71 Apr  7  09:59  project1
-rw-r--r--    1 root   root        71 Apr  7  09:59  project12
-rw-r--r--    1 root   root         0 Apr  7  09:56  project13
-rw-r--r--    1 root   root        71 Apr  7  09:59  project2
-rw-r--r--    1 root   root        90 Apr  7  10:01  project3
-rw-r--r--    1 root   root        99 Apr  7  10:01  project4
-rw-r--r--    1 root   root       108 Apr  7  10:01  project5
[root@server1 ~]#_
```

Each file listed in the preceding example has eight components of information listed in columns from left to right:

1. A file type character
   - The d character represents a directory.
   - The l character represents a symbolically linked file (discussed in Chapter 4).
   - The b or c characters represent special device files (discussed in Chapter 5).
   - The n character represents a named pipe.
   - The s character represents a socket.
   - The – character represents all other file types (text files, binary data files).
2. A list of permissions on the file (also called the mode of the file)
3. A hard link count (discussed in Chapter 5)
4. The owner of the file (discussed in Chapter 5)
5. The group owner of the file (discussed in Chapter 5)
6. The file size
7. The most recent modification time of the file
8. The filename (Some files are shortcuts or pointers to other files and indicated with an arrow ->, as with the file called "current" in the preceding output; these are known as symbolic links and are discussed in Chapter 5.)

For the file named "project" in the previous example, you can see that this file is a regular file because the long listing of it begins with a – character, the permissions on the file are rw-r--r--, the hard link count is 1, the owner of the file is the root user, the group owner of the file is the root group, the size of the file is 71 bytes, and the file was modified last on April 7th at 9:58 a.m.

If SELinux is enabled on your system, you may also notice a period (.) immediately following the permissions on a file or directory that is managed by SELinux. SELinux will be discussed later in Chapter 14.

On most Linux systems, a shortcut to the `ls` command can be used to display the same columns of information as the `ls -l` command. Some users prefer to use this shortcut, commonly known as an alias, which is invoked when a user types `ll` at a command prompt. This is known as the **ll command**.

The `ls -F` and `ls -l` commands are valuable to a user who wants to display file types; however, neither of these commands can display all file types using special characters. To display the file type of any file, you can use the **file command**; simply give the `file` command an argument specifying what file to analyze. You can also pass multiple files as arguments or use the * metacharacter to refer to all files in the current directory. An example of using the `file` command in the root user's home directory is:

```
[root@server1 ~]# pwd
/root
[root@server1 ~]# ls
current    myprogram  project    project12  project2   project4
Desktop    myscript   project1   project13  project3   project5
[root@server1 ~]# file Desktop
Desktop:   directory
[root@server1 ~]# file project Desktop
project:   ASCII text
Desktop:   directory
[root@server1 ~]# file *
Desktop:   directory
current:   symbolic link to project12
myprogram: ELF 32-bit LSB executable, Intel 80386, version 1, dynamically
linked (uses shared libs), stripped
myscript:  Bourne-Again shell script text executable
project:   ASCII text
project1:  ASCII text
project12: ASCII text
project13: empty
project2:  ASCII text
project3:  ASCII text
project4:  ASCII text
project5:  ASCII text
[root@server1 ~]#_
```

As shown in the preceding example, the `file` command can also identify the differences between types of executable files. The myscript file is a text file that contains executable commands (also known as a shell script), whereas the myprogram file is a 32-bit executable compiled program. The `file` command also identifies empty files such as project13 in the previous example.

Some filenames inside each user's home directory represent important configuration files or program directories. Because these files are rarely edited by the user and can clutter up the listing of files, they are normally hidden from view when using the `ls` and `file` commands. Recall that filenames for hidden files start with a period character (.). To view them, simply pass the –a option to the `ls` command. Some hidden files that are commonly seen in the root user's home directory are shown next:

```
[root@server1 ~]# ls
current   myprogram   project    project12   project2   project4
Desktop   myscript    project1   project13   project3   project5
[root@server1 ~]# ls -a
.                       .gimp-2.8          project
..                      .gnome             project1
.bash_history           .gnome-desktop     project12
.bash_logout            .gnome_private     project13
.bash_profile           .gtkrc             project2
.bashrc                 .ICEauthority      project3
.cshrc                  .kde               project4
current                 .mcop              project5
.DCOPserver_server1_0   .MCOP-random-seed  .sane
Desktop                 .mcoprc            .sawfish
.first_start_kde        .mozilla           .tcshrc
.galeon                 myprogram          .Xauthority
.gconf                  myscript           .Xresources
.gconfd                 .nautilus          .xsession-errors
[root@server1 ~]#_
```

As discussed earlier, the (.) character refers to the current working directory and the (..) character refers to the parent directory relative to your current location in the directory tree. Each of these pointers is seen as a special (or fictitious) file when using the `ls –a` command, as each starts with a period.

You can also specify several options simultaneously for most commands on the command line and receive the combined functionality of all the options. For example, to view all hidden files and their file types, you could type:

```
[root@server1 ~]# ls -aF
./                       .gimp-2.8/         project
../                      .gnome/            project1
.bash_history            .gnome-desktop/    project12
.bash_logout             .gnome_private/    project13
.bash_profile            .gtkrc             project2
.bashrc                  .ICEauthority      project3
.cshrc                   .kde/              project4
current@                 .mcop/             project5
.DCOPserver_server1_0@   .MCOP-random-seed  .sane/
Desktop/                 .mcoprc            .sawfish/
```

```
.first_start_kde              .mozilla/    .tcshrc
.galeon/                      myprogram    .Xauthority
.gconf/                       myscript     .Xresources
.gconfd/                      .nautilus/   .xsession-errors
[root@server1 ~]#_
```

The aforementioned options to the ls command (-l, -F, -a) are the most common options you would use when navigating the Linux directory tree; however, many options are available in the ls command that alter the listing of files on the filesystem. Table 3-2 depicts the most common of these options and their descriptions.

Option	Description
-a --all	Lists all filenames
-A --almost-all	Lists most filenames (excludes the . and .. special files)
-C	Lists filenames in column format
--color=n	Lists filenames without color
-d --directory	Lists directory names instead of their contents
-f	Lists all filenames without sorting
-F --classify	Lists filenames classified by file type
--full-time	Lists filenames in long format and displays the full modification time
-l	Lists filenames in long format
-lh -l --human-readable	Lists filenames in long format with human-readable (easy-to-read) file sizes
-lG -l --no-group -o	Lists filenames in long format but omits the group information
-r --reverse	Lists filenames reverse sorted
-R --recursive	Lists filenames in the specified directory and all subdirectories
-s	Lists filenames and their associated sizes in kilobytes (KB)
-S	Lists filenames sorted by file size
-t	Lists filenames sorted by modification time
-U	Lists filenames without sorting
-x	Lists filenames in rows rather than in columns

Table 3-2 Common options to the ls command

Metacharacter	Description
*	Matches 0 or more characters in a filename
?	Matches 1 character in a filename
[aegh]	Matches 1 character in a filename—provided this character is either an a, e, g, or h
[a-e]	Matches 1 character in a filename—provided this character is either an a, b, c, d, or e
[!a-e]	Matches 1 character in a filename—provided this character is NOT an a, b, c, d, or e

Table 3-3 Wildcard metacharacters

Wildcard Metacharacters

In the previous section, you saw that the * metacharacter stands for all the files in the current directory, much like a wildcard stands for, or matches, certain cards in a card game. As a result, the * metacharacter is called a **wildcard metacharacter**. Wildcard metacharacters can simplify commands that specify more than one filename on the command line, as you saw with the file command earlier. They match certain portions of filenames or the entire filename itself. Since they are interpreted by the shell, they can be used with most common Linux filesystem commands, including a few that have already been mentioned (ls, file, and cd). Table 3-3 displays a list of wildcard metacharacters and their descriptions.

Wildcards can be demonstrated using the ls command. Examples of using wildcard metacharacters to narrow the listing produced by the ls command are shown next.

```
[root@server1 ~]# ls
current myprogram  project   project12  project2  project4
Desktop myscript   project1  project13  project3  project5
[root@server1 ~]# ls project*
project project1  project12  project13  project2  project3  project4
   project5
[root@server1 ~]# ls project?
project1  project2  project3  project4  project5
[root@server1 ~]# ls project??
project12  project13
[root@server1 ~]# ls project[135]
project1  project3  project5
[root@server1 ~]# ls project[!135]
project2  project4
[root@server1 ~]# _
```

Displaying the Contents of Text Files

So far, this chapter has discussed commands that can be used to navigate the Linux directory structure and view filenames and file types; it is usual now to display the contents of these files. By far, the most common file type that users display is text files. These files are usually small and contain configuration information or instructions that the shell interprets (called a shell script) but can also contain other forms of text, as in e-mail letters. To view an entire text file on the terminal screen (also referred to as **concatenation**), you can use the **cat** command. The following is an example of using the cat command to display the contents of an e-mail message (in the fictitious file project4):

```
[root@server1 ~]# ls
current  myprogram  project   project12  project2  project4
Desktop  myscript   project1  project13  project3  project5
[root@server1 ~]# cat project4

Hi there, I hope this day finds you well.

Unfortunately we were not able to make it to your dining
room this year while vacationing in Algonquin Park - I
especially wished to see the model of the Highland Inn
and the train station in the dining room.

I have been reading on the history of Algonquin Park but
no where could I find a description of where the Highland
Inn was originally located on Cache lake.

If it is no trouble, could you kindly let me know such that
I need not wait until next year when I visit your lodge?

Regards,
Mackenzie Elizabeth
[root@server1 ~]#
```

You can also use the cat command to display the line number of each line in the file in addition to the contents by passing the −n option to the cat command. In the following example, the number of each line in the project4 file is displayed:

```
[root@server1 ~]# cat -n project4
     1  Hi there, I hope this day finds you well.
     2
     3  Unfortunately we were not able to make it to your dining
     4  room this year while vacationing in Algonquin Park - I
     5  especially wished to see the model of the Highland Inn
     6  and the train station in the dining room.
     7
     8  I have been reading on the history of Algonquin Park but
     9  no where could I find a description of where the Highland
    10  Inn was originally located on Cache lake.
    11
    12  If it is no trouble, could you kindly let me know such that
    13  I need not wait until next year when I visit your lodge?
    14
    15  Regards,
    16  Mackenzie Elizabeth
[root@server1 ~]#
```

In some cases, you might want to display the contents of a certain text file in reverse order, which is useful when displaying files that have text appended to them continuously by system services. These files, also known as **log files**, contain the most recent entries at the bottom of the file. To display a file in reverse order, use the **tac command** (tac is cat spelled backwards), as shown next with the file project4:

```
[root@server1 ~]# tac project4
Mackenzie Elizabeth
Regards,

I need not wait until next year when I visit your lodge?
If it is no trouble, could you kindly let me know such that

Inn was originally located on Cache lake.
no where could I find a description of where the Highland
I have been reading on the history of Algonquin Park but

and the train station in the dining room.
especially wished to see the model of the Highland Inn
room this year while vacationing in Algonquin Park - I
Unfortunately we were not able to make it to your dining

Hi there, I hope this day finds you well.
[root@server1 ~]#_
```

If the file displayed is very large and you only want to view the first few lines of it, you can use the **head command**. The head command displays the first 10 lines (including blank lines) of a text file to the terminal screen but can also take a numeric option specifying a different number of lines to display. The following shows an example of using the head command to view the top of the project4 file:

```
[root@server1 ~]# head project4
Hi there, I hope this day finds you well.

Unfortunately we were not able to make it to your dining
room this year while vacationing in Algonquin Park - I
especially wished to see the model of the Highland Inn
and the train station in the dining room.

I have been reading on the history of Algonquin Park but
no where could I find a description of where the Highland
Inn was originally located on Cache lake.
[root@server1 ~]# head -3 project4
Hi there, I hope this day finds you well.

Unfortunately we were not able to make it to your dining
[root@server1 ~]#_
```

Just as the head command displays the beginning of text files, the **tail command** can be used to display the end of text files. By default, the tail command displays the final

10 lines of a file, but it can also take a numeric option specifying the number of lines to display on the terminal screen, as shown in the following example with the project4 file:

```
[root@server1 ~]# tail project4

I have been reading on the history of Algonquin Park but
no where could I find a description of where the Highland
Inn was originally located on Cache lake.

If it is no trouble, could you kindly let me know such that
I need not wait until next year when I visit your lodge?

Regards,
Mackenzie Elizabeth
[root@server1 ~]# tail -2 project4

Regards,
Mackenzie Elizabeth
[root@server1 ~]#_
```

Although some text files are small enough to be displayed completely on the terminal screen, you might encounter text files that are too large to fit in a single screen. In this case, the cat command sends the entire file contents to the terminal screen; however, the screen only displays as much of the text as it has room for. To display a large text file in a page-by-page fashion, you need to use the more and less commands.

The **more command** gets its name from the pg command once used on UNIX systems. The pg command displayed a text file page by page on the terminal screen, starting at the beginning of the file; pressing the spacebar or Enter key displays the next page, and so on. The more command does more than pg did, because it displays the next complete page of a text file if you press the spacebar but displays only the next line of a text file if you press Enter. In that way, you can browse the contents of a text file page by page or line by line. The fictitious file project5 is an excerpt from Shakespeare's tragedy *Macbeth* and is too large to be displayed fully on the terminal screen using the cat command. Using the more command to view its contents results in the following output:

```
[root@server1 ~]# more project5
Go bid thy mistress, when my drink is ready,
She strike upon the bell. Get thee to bed.
Is this a dagger which I see before me,
The handle toward my hand? Come, let me clutch thee.
I have thee not, and yet I see thee still.
Art thou not, fatal vision, sensible
To feeling as to sight? or art thou but
A dagger of the mind, a false creation,
Proceeding from the heat-oppressed brain?
I see thee yet, in form as palpable
As this which now I draw.
Thou marshall'st me the way that I was going;
```

```
And such an instrument I was to use.
Mine eyes are made the fools o' the other senses,
Or else worth all the rest; I see thee still,
And on thy blade and dudgeon gouts of blood,
Which was not so before. There's no such thing:
It is the bloody business which informs
Thus to mine eyes. Now o'er the one halfworld
Nature seems dead, and wicked dreams abuse
The curtain'd sleep; witchcraft celebrates
Pale Hecate's offerings, and wither'd murder,
Alarum'd by his sentinel, the wolf,
--More--(71%)
```

As you can see in the preceding output, the more command displays the first page without returning you to the shell prompt. Instead, the more command displays a prompt at the bottom of the terminal screen that indicates how much of the file is displayed on the screen as a percentage of the total file size. In the preceding example, 71 percent of the project5 file is displayed. At this prompt, you can press the spacebar to advance one whole page, or you can press the Enter key to advance to the next line. In addition, the more command allows other user interactions at this prompt. Pressing the h character at the prompt displays a help screen, which is shown in the following output, and pressing the q character quits the more command completely without viewing the remainder of the file.

```
--More--(71%)
Most commands optionally preceded by integer argument k. Defaults in brack-
ets. Star (*) indicates argument becomes new default.
-------------------------------------------------------------------
<space>                   Display next k lines of text [current screen size]
z                         Display next k lines of text [current screen size]
<return>                  Display next k lines of text [1]
d or ctrl-D               Scroll k lines [current scroll size, initially 11]
q or Q or <interrupt>     Exit from more
s                         Skip forward k lines of text [1]
f                         Skip forward k screenfuls of text [1]
b or ctrl-B               Skip backward k screenfuls of text [1]
'                         Go to place where previous search started
=                         Display current line number
/<regular expression>     Search for kth occurrence of regular expression[1]
n                         Search for kth occurrence of last r.e [1]
!<cmd> or :!<cmd>         Execute <cmd> in a subshell
v                         Start up /usr/bin/vi at current line
ctrl-L                    Redraw screen
:n                        Go to kth next file [1]
:p                        Go to kth previous file [1]
:f                        Display current filename and line number
.                         Repeat previous command
-------------------------------------------------------------------
--More--(71%)
```

Just as the more command was named as a result of allowing more user functionality, the **less command** is named for doing more than the more command (remember that "less is more," more or less). Like the more command, the less command can browse the contents of a text file page by page by pressing the spacebar and line by line by pressing the Enter key; however, you can also use the cursor keys on the keyboard to scroll up and down the contents of the file. The output of the less command, when used to view the project5 file, is as follows:

```
[root@server1 ~]# less project5
Go bid thy mistress, when my drink is ready,
She strike upon the bell. Get thee to bed.
Is this a dagger which I see before me,
The handle toward my hand? Come, let me clutch thee.
I have thee not, and yet I see thee still.
Art thou not, fatal vision, sensible
To feeling as to sight? or art thou but
A dagger of the mind, a false creation,
Proceeding from the heat-oppressed brain?
I see thee yet, in form as palpable
As this which now I draw.
Thou marshall'st me the way that I was going;
And such an instrument I was to use.
Mine eyes are made the fools o' the other senses,
Or else worth all the rest; I see thee still,
And on thy blade and dudgeon gouts of blood,
Which was not so before. There's no such thing:
It is the bloody business which informs
Thus to mine eyes. Now o'er the one halfworld
Nature seems dead, and wicked dreams abuse
The curtain'd sleep; witchcraft celebrates
Pale Hecate's offerings, and wither'd murder,
Alarum'd by his sentinel, the wolf,
Whose howl's his watch, thus with his stealthy pace.
project5
```

Like the more command, the less command displays a prompt at the bottom of the file using the : character or the filename of the file being viewed (project5 in our example), yet the less command contains more keyboard shortcuts for searching out text within files. At the prompt, you can press the h key to obtain a help screen or the q key to quit. The first help screen for the less command is shown next:

SUMMARY OF LESS COMMANDS

```
     Commands marked with * may be preceded by a number, N.
     Notes in parentheses indicate the behavior if N is given.
     A key preceded by a caret indicates the Ctrl key; thus ^K is ctrl-K.


h  H                    Display this help.
q  :q  Q  :Q  ZZ        Exit.
---------------------------------------------------------------------------
```

```
                          MOVING
  e  ^E  j  ^N  CR       * Forward one line (or N lines).
  y  ^Y  k  ^K  ^P       * Backward one line or N lines).
  f  ^F  ^V  SPACE       * Forward one window (or N lines).
  b  ^B  ESC-v           * Backward one window (or N lines).
  z                      * Forward one window (and set window to N).
  w                      * Backward one window (and set window to N).
  ESC-SPACE              * Forward one window, but don't stop at end-of-file.
  d  ^D                  * Forward one half-window (and set half-window to N)
  u  ^U                  * Backward one half-window (and set half window to N)
  ESC-(  RightArrow      * Left 8 character positions (or N positions).
  ESC-)  LeftArrow       * Right 8 character positions (or N positions).
  F                        Forward forever; like "tail -f".

HELP -- Press RETURN for more, or q when done
```

The more and less commands can also be used in conjunction with the output of commands if that output is too large to fit on the terminal screen. To do this, simply use the | metacharacter after the command, followed by either the more or less command, as follows:

```
[root@server1 ~]# cd /etc
[root@server1 etc]# ls -l | more
total 3688
-rw-r--r--  1 root     root     15276 Mar 22 12:20 a2ps.cfg
-rw-r--r--  1 root     root      2562 Mar 22 12:20 a2ps-site.cfg
drwxr-xr-x  4 root     root      4096 Jun 11 08:45 acpi
-rw-r--r--  1 root     root        46 Jun 16 16:42 adjtime
drwxr-xr-x  2 root     root      4096 Jun 11 08:47 aep
-rw-r--r--  1 root     root       688 Feb 17 00:35 aep.conf
-rw-r--r--  1 root     root       703 Feb 17 00:35 aeplog.conf
drwxr-xr-x  4 root     root      4096 Jun 11 08:47 alchemist
-rw-r--r--  1 root     root      1419 Jan 26 10:14 aliases
-rw-r-----  1 root     smmsp    12288 Jun 17 13:17 aliases.db
drwxr-xr-x  2 root     root      4096 Jun 11 11:11 alternatives
drwxr-xr-x  3 amanda   disk      4096 Jun 11 10:16 amanda
-rw-r--r--  1 amanda   disk         0 Mar 22 12:28 amandates
-rw-------  1 root     root       688 Mar  4 22:34 amd.conf
-rw-r-----  1 root     root       105 Mar  4 22:34 amd.net
-rw-r--r--  1 root     root       317 Feb 15 14:33 anacrontab
-rw-r--r--  1 root     root       331 May  5 08:07 ant.conf
-rw-r--r--  1 root     root      6200 Jun 16 16:42 asound.state
drwxr-xr-x  3 root     root      4096 Jun 11 10:37 atalk
-rw-------  1 root     root         1 May  5 13:39 at.deny
-rw-r--r--  1 root     root       325 Apr 14 13:39 auto.master
-rw-r--r--  1 root     root       581 Apr 14 13:39 auto.misc
--More--
```

In the preceding example, the output of the ls –l command was redirected to the more command, which displays the first page of output on the terminal. You can then advance through the output page by page or line by line. This type of redirection is discussed in Chapter 7.

Displaying the Contents of Binary Files

It is important to employ text file commands, such as cat, tac, head, tail, more, and less, only on files that contain text; otherwise, you might find yourself with random output on the terminal screen or even a dysfunctional terminal. To view the contents of binary files, you typically use the program that was used to create the file. However, some commands can be used to safely display the contents of most binary files. The **strings command** searches for text characters in a binary file and outputs them to the screen. In many cases, these text characters might indicate what the binary file is used for. For example, to find the text characters inside the /bin/echo binary executable program page by page, you could use the following command:

```
[root@server1 ~]# strings /bin/echo | more
/lib/ld-linux.so.2
PTRh|
<nt7<e
|[^_]
[^_]
[^_]
Try '%s --help' for more information.
Usage: %s [OPTION]... [STRING]...
Echo the STRING(s) to standard output.
  -n            do not output the trailing newline
  -e            enable interpretation of the backslash-
                   escaped characters listed below
  -E            disable interpretation of those sequences in STRINGs
    --help      display this help and exit
    --version   output version information and exit
Without -E, the following sequences are recognized and interpolated:
\NNN    the character whose ASCII code is NNN (octal)
\\      backslash
\a      alert (BEL)
\b      backspace
\c      suppress trailing newline
\f      form feed
\n      new line
--More--
```

Although this output might not be easy to read, it does contain portions of text that can point a user in the right direction to find out more about the /bin/echo command. Another command that is safe to use on binary files and text files is the **od command**, which displays the contents of the file in octal format (numeric base 8 format). An example of using the od command to display the first five lines of the file project4 is shown in the following example:

```
[root@server1 ~]# od project4 | head -5
0000000   064510   072040   062550   062562   020054   020111   067550   062560
0000020   072040   064550   020163   060544   020171   064546   062156   020163
0000040   067571   020165   062567   066154   006456   006412   052412   063156
0000060   071157   072564   060556   062564   074554   073440   020145   062567
0000100   062562   067040   072157   060440   066142   020145   067564   066440
[root@server1 ~]#_
```

You can use the **-x** option to the **od** command to display a file in hexadecimal format (numeric base 16 format).

Searching for Text Within Files

Recall that Linux was modeled after the UNIX operating system. The UNIX operating system is often referred to as the "grandfather" of all operating systems because it is over 40 years old and has formed the basis for most advances in computing technology. The major use of the UNIX operating system in the past 40 years involved simplifying business and scientific management through database applications. As a result, many commands (referred to as **text tools**) were developed for the UNIX operating system that could search for and manipulate text, such as database information, in many different and advantageous ways. A set of text wildcards was also developed to ease the searching of specific text information. These text wildcards are called **regular expressions (regexp)** and are recognized by several text tools and programming languages, including, but not limited to, the following:

- grep
- awk
- sed
- vi
- Emacs
- ex
- ed
- C++
- PERL
- Tcl

Because Linux is a close relative of the UNIX operating system, these text tools and regular expressions are available to Linux as well. By combining text tools, a typical Linux system can search for and manipulate data in almost every way possible (as you will see later). As a result, regular expressions and the text tools that use them are commonly used in business today.

Regular Expressions

As mentioned earlier, regular expressions allow you to specify a certain pattern of text within a text document. They work similarly to wildcard metacharacters in that they are used to match characters, yet they have many differences:

- Wildcard metacharacters are interpreted by the shell, whereas regular expressions are interpreted by a text tool program.

- Wildcard metacharacters match characters in filenames (or directory names) on a Linux filesystem, whereas regular expressions match characters *within* text files on a Linux filesystem.

- Wildcard metacharacters typically have different definitions than regular expression metacharacters.

- More regular expression metacharacters are available than wildcard metacharacters.

In addition, regular expression metacharacters are divided into two different categories: common regular expressions and extended regular expressions. Common regular expressions are available to most text tools; however, extended regular expressions are less common and available in only certain text tools. Table 3-4 shows definitions and examples of some common and extended regular expressions.

The grep Command

The most common way to search for information using regular expressions is the grep command. The **grep command** (the command name is short for global regular expression print) is used to display lines in a text file that match a certain common regular expression. To display lines of text that match extended regular expressions, you must use the **egrep command** (or the −E option to the grep command). In addition, the **fgrep command** (or the −F option to the grep command) does not interpret any regular expressions and consequently returns results much faster. Take, for example, the project4 file shown earlier:

```
[root@server1 ~]# cat project4
Hi there, I hope this day finds you well.

Unfortunately we were not able to make it to your dining
room this year while vacationing in Algonquin Park - I
especially wished to see the model of the Highland Inn
and the train station in the dining room.

I have been reading on the history of Algonquin Park but
no where could I find a description of where the Highland
Inn was originally located on Cache lake.

If it is no trouble, could you kindly let me know such that
I need not wait until next year when I visit your lodge?

Regards,
Mackenzie Elizabeth
[root@server1 ~]#_
```

Regular Expression	Description	Example	Type
*	Matches 0 or more occurrences of the previous character	letter* matches lette, letter, letterr, letterrrr, letterrrrr, and so on	Common
?	Matches 0 or 1 occurrences of the previous character	letter? matches lette, letter	Extended
+	Matches 1 or more occurrences of the previous character	letter+ matches letter, letterr, letterrrr, letterrrrr, and so on	Extended
. (period)	Matches 1 character of any type	letter. matches lettera, letterb, letterc, letter1, letter2, letter3, and so on	Common
[...]	Matches one character from the range specified within the braces	letter[1238] matches letter1, letter2, letter3, and letter8;letter[a-c] matches lettera, letterb, and letter	Common
[^...]	Matches one character NOT from the range specified within the braces	letter[^1238] matches letter4, letter5, letter6, lettera , letterb, and so on (any character except 1, 2, 3, or 8)	Common
{ }	Matches a specific number or range of the previous character	letter{3} matches letterrr letter, whereas letter {2,4} matches letterr, letterrr, and letterrrr	Extended
^	Matches the following characters if they are the first characters on the line	^letter matches letter if letter is the first set of characters in the line	Common
$	Matches the previous characters if they are the last characters on the line	letter$ matches letter if letter is the last set of characters in the line	Common
(... | ...)	Matches either of two sets of characters	(mother|father) matches the word "mother" or "father"	Extended

Table 3-4 Regular expressions

The grep command requires two arguments at minimum, the first argument specifies which text to search for, and the remaining arguments specify the files to search. If a pattern of text is matched, the grep command displays the entire line on the terminal screen. For example, to list only those lines in the file project4 that contain the words "Algonquin Park," enter the following command:

```
[root@server1 ~]# grep "Algonquin Park" project4
room this year while vacationing in Algonquin Park - I
I have been reading on the history of Algonquin Park but
[root@server1 ~]#_
```

To return the lines that do not contain the text "Algonquin Park," you can use the -v option of the grep command to reverse the meaning of the previous command:

```
[root@server1 ~]# grep -v "Algonquin Park" project4
Hi there, I hope this day finds you well.
```

Unfortunately we were not able to make it to your dining
especially wished to see the model of the Highland Inn
and the train station in the dining room.

```
no where could I find a description of where the Highland
Inn was originally located on Cache lake.

If it is no trouble, could you kindly let me know such that
I need not wait until next year when I visit your lodge?

Regards,
Mackenzie Elizabeth
[root@server1 ~]#_
```

Keep in mind that the text being searched is case sensitive; to perform a case-insensitive search, use the -i option to the grep command:

```
[root@server1 ~]# grep "algonquin park" project4
[root@server1 ~]#_
[root@server1 ~]# grep -i "algonquin park" project4
room this year while vacationing in Algonquin Park - I
I have been reading on the history of Algonquin Park but
[root@server1 ~]#_
```

Another important note to keep in mind regarding text tools such as grep is that they match only patterns of text; they are unable to discern words or phrases unless they are specified. For example, if you want to search for the lines that contain the word "we," you can use the following grep command:

```
[root@server1 ~]# grep "we" project4
Hi there, I hope this day finds you well.
Unfortunately we were not able to make it to your dining
[root@server1 ~]#_
```

However, notice from the preceding output that the first line displayed does not contain the word "we"; the word "well" contains the text pattern "we" and is displayed as a result. To display only lines that contain the word "we," you can type the following to match the letters "we" surrounded by space characters:

```
[root@server1 ~]# grep "we" project4
Unfortunately we were not able to make it to your dining
[root@server1 ~]#_
```

All of the previous grep examples did not use regular expression metacharacters to search for text in the project4 file. Some examples of using regular expressions (see Table 3-4) when searching this file are shown throughout the remainder of this section.

To view lines that contain the word "toe" or "the" or "tie," you can enter the following command:

```
[root@server1 ~]# grep "t.e" project4
especially wished to see the model of the Highland Inn
and the train station in the dining room.
I have been reading on the history of Algonquin Park but
no where could I find a description of where the Highland
[root@server1 ~]#_
```

To view lines that start with the word "I," you can enter the following command:

```
[root@server1 ~]# grep "^I" project4
I have been reading on the history of Algonquin Park but
I need not wait until next year when I visit your lodge?
[root@server1 ~]#_
```

To view lines that contain the text "lodge" or "lake," you need to use an extended regular expression and the egrep command, as follows:

```
[root@server1 ~]# egrep "(lodge|lake)" project4
Inn was originally located on Cache lake.
I need not wait until next year when I visit your lodge?
[root@server1 ~]#_
```

Editing Text Files

Recall that text files are the most common type of file modified by Linux users and administrators. Most system configuration is stored in text files, as is commonly accessed information such as e-mail and program source code. Consequently, most Linux distributions come with an assortment of text editors, and many more are available for Linux systems via the Internet. Text editors come in two varieties: editors that can be used on the command line, including vi (vim), nano, and Emacs, and editors that can be used in a GUI environment, including Emacs (graphical version) and gedit.

The vi Editor

The **vi editor** (pronounced "vee eye") is one of the oldest and most popular visual text editors available for UNIX operating systems. Its Linux equivalent (known as vim, which is short for "vi improved") is therefore standard on almost every Linux distribution. Although the vi editor is not the easiest of the editors to use when editing text files, it has the advantage of portability. A Fedora Linux user who is proficient in using the vi editor will find editing files on all other UNIX and Linux systems easy because the interface and features of the vi editor are nearly identical across Linux and UNIX systems. In addition, the vi editor supports regular expressions and can perform over 1000 different functions for the user.

To open an existing text file for editing, you can type vi *filename* (or vim *filename*), where *filename* specifies the file to be edited. To open a new file for editing, simply type vi or vim at the command line:

```
[root@server1 ~]# vi
```

The vi editor then runs interactively and replaces the command-line interface with the following output:

```
~
~
~
~
~
~
~                            VIM - Vi IMproved
```

```
~
~                              version 7.4.27
~                          by Bram Moolenaar et al.
~                     Modified by <bugzilla@redhat.com>
~                   Vim is open source and freely distributable
~
~                      Become a registered Vim user!
~         type     :help register<Enter>        for information
~
~         type     :q<Enter>                     to exit
~         type     :help <Enter> or <F1>         for on-line help
~         type     :help version7<Enter>         for version info
~
~
~
~
~
~
~
```

The tilde ~ characters on the left indicate the end of the file; they are pushed further down the screen as you enter text. The vi editor is called a bimodal editor because it functions in one of two modes: **command mode** and **insert mode**. The vi editor opens command mode, in which you must use the keyboard to perform functions, such as deleting text, copying text, saving changes to a file, and exiting the vi editor. To insert text into the document, you must enter insert mode by typing one of the characters listed in Table 3-5. One such method to enter insert mode is to type the i key on the keyboard while in command mode; the vi editor then displays --INSERT-- at the bottom of the screen and allows the user to enter a sentence such as the following:

This is a sample sentence.

Key	Description
i	Changes to insert mode and places the cursor before the current character for entering text
a	Changes to insert mode and places the cursor after the current character for entering text
o	Changes to insert mode and opens a new line underneath the current line for entering text
I	Changes to insert mode and places the cursor at the beginning of the current line for entering text
A	Changes to insert mode and places the cursor at the end of the current line for entering text
O	Changes to insert mode and opens a new line above the current line for entering text
Esc	Changes back to command mode while in insert mode

Table 3-5 Common keyboard keys used to change to and from insert mode

~
~
~
~

-- INSERT --

When in insert mode, you can use the keyboard to type text as required, but when finished you must press the Esc key to return to command mode to perform other functions via keys on the keyboard. Table 3-6 provides a list of keys useful in command mode and their associated functions. After you are in command mode, to save the text in a file called samplefile in the current directory, you need to press the : character (by pressing the Shift and ; keys simultaneously) to reach a : prompt where you can enter a command to save the contents of the current document to a file, as shown in the following example and in Table 3-7.

This is a sample sentence.
~
~
~
~
~
~
~

:w samplefile

As shown in Table 3-7, you can quit the vi editor by pressing the : character and entering q!, which then returns the user to the shell prompt:

This is a sample sentence.
~
~
~
~
~
~
~

:q!
[root@server1 ~]# _

The vi editor also offers some advanced features to Linux users, as explained in Table 3-7. Examples of some of these features are discussed next, using the project4 file shown earlier in this chapter. To edit the project4 file, simply type vi project4 and view the following screen:

Hi there, I hope this day finds you well.

Unfortunately we were not able to make it to your dining
room this year while vacationing in Algonquin Park - I

Key	Description
w, W	Moves the cursor forward one word to the beginning of the next word
e, E	Moves the cursor forward one word to the end of the next word
b, B	Moves the cursor backward one word
53G	Moves the cursor to line 53
G	Moves the cursor to the last line in the document
0, ^	Moves the cursor to the beginning of the line
$	Moves the cursor to the end of the line
X	Deletes the character the cursor is on
3x	Deletes three characters starting from the character the cursor is on
dw	Deletes one word starting from the character the cursor is on
d3w, 3dw	Deletes three words starting from the character the cursor is on
dd	Deletes one whole line starting from the line the cursor is on
d3d, 3dd	Deletes three whole lines starting from the line the cursor is on
d$	Deletes from cursor character to the end of the current line
d^, d0	Deletes from cursor character to the beginning of the current line
yw	Copies one word (starting from the character the cursor is on) into a temporary buffer in memory for later use
y3w, 3yw	Copies three words (starting from the character the cursor is on) into a temporary buffer in memory for later use
yy	Copies the current line into a temporary buffer in memory for later use
y3y, 3yy	Copies three lines (starting from the current line) into a temporary buffer in memory for later use
y$	Copies the current line from the cursor to the end of the line into a temporary buffer in memory for later use
y^, y0	Copies the current line from the cursor to the beginning of the line into a temporary buffer in memory for later use
p	Pastes the contents of the temporary memory buffer underneath the current line
P	Pastes the contents of the temporary memory buffer above the current line
J	Joins the line underneath the current line to the current line
Ctrl+g	Displays current line statistics
u	Undoes the last function (undo)
.	Repeats the last function (repeat)
/pattern	Searches for the first occurrence of pattern in the forward direction
?pattern	Searches for the first occurrence of pattern in the reverse direction
n	Repeats the previous search in the forward direction
N	Repeats the previous search in the reverse direction

Table 3-6 Key combinations commonly used in command mode

Function	Description
:q	Quits from the vi editor if no changes were made
:q!	Quits from the vi editor and does not save any changes
:wq	Saves any changes to the file and quits from the vi editor
:w filename	Saves the current document to a file called filename
:!date	Executes the date command using a BASH shell
:r !date	Reads the output of the date command into the document under the current line
:r filename	Reads the contents of the text file called filename into the document under the current line
:set all	Displays all vi environment settings
:set	Sets a vi environment setting to a certain value
:s/the/THE/g	Searches for the regular expression "the" and replaces each occurrence globally throughout the current line with the word "THE"
:1,$ s/the/THE/g	Searches for the regular expression "the" and replaces each occurrence globally from line 1 to the end of the document with the word "THE"

Table 3-7   Key combinations commonly used at the command mode : prompt

```
especially wished to see the model of the Highland Inn
and the train station in the dining room.

I have been reading on the history of Algonquin Park but
no where could I find a description of where the Highland
Inn was originally located on Cache lake.

If it is no trouble, could you kindly let me know such that
I need not wait until next year when I visit your lodge?

Regards,
Mackenzie Elizabeth
~
~
~
~
~
~
~
"project4" 17L, 583C
```

Note that the name of the file as well as the number of lines and characters in total are displayed at the bottom of the screen (project4 has 17 lines and 583 characters in this example). To insert the current date and time at the bottom of the file, you can simply move the cursor to the final line in the file and type the following at the : prompt while in command mode:

```
Hi there, I hope this day finds you well.
```

```
Unfortunately we were not able to make it to your dining
room this year while vacationing in Algonquin Park - I
especially wished to see the model of the Highland Inn
and the train station in the dining room.

I have been reading on the history of Algonquin Park but
no where could I find a description of where the Highland
Inn was originally located on Cache lake.

If it is no trouble, could you kindly let me know such that
I need not wait until next year when I visit your lodge?

Regards,
Mackenzie Elizabeth
~
~
~
~
~
~
~
:r !date
```

When you press Enter, the output of the date command is inserted below the current line:

```
Hi there, I hope this day finds you well.

Unfortunately we were not able to make it to your dining
room this year while vacationing in Algonquin Park - I
especially wished to see the model of the Highland Inn
and the train station in the dining room.

I have been reading on the history of Algonquin Park but
no where could I find a description of where the Highland
Inn was originally located on Cache lake.

If it is no trouble, could you kindly let me know such that
I need not wait until next year when I visit your lodge?

Regards,
Mackenzie Elizabeth
Sat Aug 7 18:33:10 EDT 2015
~
~
~
~
~
~
```

To change all occurrences of the word "Algonquin" to "ALGONQUIN," you can simply type the following at the : prompt while in command mode:

```
Hi there, I hope this day finds you well.

Unfortunately we were not able to make it to your dining
room this year while vacationing in Algonquin Park - I
especially wished to see the model of the Highland Inn
and the train station in the dining room.

I have been reading on the history of Algonquin Park but
no where could I find a description of where the Highland
Inn was originally located on Cache lake.

If it is no trouble, could you kindly let me know such that
I need not wait until next year when I visit your lodge?

Regards,
Mackenzie Elizabeth
Sat Aug 7 18:33:10 EDT 2015
~
~
~
~
~
~
```

:1,$ s/Algonquin/ALGONQUIN/g

The output changes to the following:

```
Hi there, I hope this day finds you well.

Unfortunately we were not able to make it to your dining
room this year while vacationing in ALGONQUIN Park - I
especially wished to see the model of the Highland Inn
and the train station in the dining room.

I have been reading on the history of ALGONQUIN Park but
no where could I find a description of where the Highland
Inn was originally located on Cache lake.

If it is no trouble, could you kindly let me know such that
I need not wait until next year when I visit your lodge?

Regards,
Mackenzie Elizabeth
Sat Aug 7 18:33:10 EDT 2015
```

```
~
~
~
~
~
~
~
```

Another attractive feature of the vi editor is its ability to customize the user environment through settings that can be altered at the : prompt while in command mode. Simply type set all at this prompt to observe the list of available settings and their current values:

```
:set all
--- Options ---
   aleph=224           fileencoding=        menuitems=25         swapsync=fsync
noarabic               fileformat=unix      modeline             switchbuf=
   arabicshape         filetype=            modelines=5          syntax=
noallowrevins       nofkmap                 modifiable           tabstop=8
noaltkeymap            foldclose=           modified             tagbsearch
   ambiwidth=single    foldcolumn=0         more                 taglength=0
noautoindent           foldenable           mouse=               tagrelative
noautoread             foldexpr=0           mousemodel=          tagstack
                                              extend
noautowrite            foldignore=#         mousetime=500        term=xterm
noautowriteall         foldlevel=0        nonumber              notermbidi
   background=light    foldlevelstart=-1  nopaste                termencoding=
   backspace=2         foldmethod= manual pastetoggle=          noterse
nobackup               foldminlines=1     patchexpr=            textauto
   backupcopy=auto     foldnestmax=20     patchmode=            notextmode
   backupext=~         formatoptions=tcq nopreserveindent       textwidth=0
   backupskip=/tmp/*   formatprg=           previewheight=12    thesaurus=
nobinary            nogdefault            nopreviewwindow       notildeop
nobomb                 helpheight=20        printdevice=          timeout
   bufhidden=          helplang=en          printencoding=      timeoutlen=1000
   buflisted        nohidden               printfont=            notitle
                                            courier
   buftype=            history=50           printoptions=        titlelen=85
-- More --
```

Note in the preceding output that most settings are set to either on or off; those that are turned off are prefixed with a "no." In the preceding example, line numbering is turned off (nonumber in the preceding output); however, you can turn it on by typing set number at the : prompt while in command mode. This results in the following output in vi:

```
1 Hi there, I hope this day finds you well.
2
3 Unfortunately we were not able to make it to your dining
4 room this year while vacationing in ALGONQUIN Park - I
```

```
 5 especially wished to see the model of the Highland Inn
 6 and the train station in the dining room.
 7
 8 I have been reading on the history of ALGONQUIN Park but
 9 no where could I find a description of where the Highland
10 Inn was originally located on Cache lake.
11
12 If it is no trouble, could you kindly let me know such that
13 I need not wait until next year when I visit your lodge?
14
15 Regards,
16 Mackenzie Elizabeth
17 Sat Aug 7 18:33:10 EDT 2010
18
~
~
~
~
~
~
~
~
```

:set number

Conversely, to turn off line numbering, you could simply type set nonumber at the : prompt while in command mode.

Other Common Text Editors

Although the vi editor is the most common text editor used on Linux and UNIX systems, there are other text editors that are easier to use.

An alternative to the vi editor that offers an equal set of functionality is the GNU **Emacs (Editor MACroS)** editor. Emacs is not installed by default in Fedora 20. To install it, you can run the command yum install emacs at a command prompt to obtain Emacs from a free software repository on the Internet. Next, to open the project4 file in the Emacs editor in a command-line terminal, simply type emacs project4 and the following is displayed on the terminal screen:

```
File Edit Options Buffers Tools Help
Hi there, I hope this day finds you well.

Unfortunately we were not able to make it to your dining
room this year while vacationing in Algonquin Park - I
especially wished to see the model of the Highland Inn
and the train station in the dining room.

I have been reading on the history of Algonquin Park but
no where could I find a description of where the Highland
Inn was originally located on Cache lake.
```

If it is no trouble, could you kindly let me know such that
I need not wait until next year when I visit your lodge?

Regards,
Mackenzie Elizabeth

```
-UU-:----F1 project4 All L1 (Fundamental)----------------------
```
For information about the GNU Emacs and the GNU system, type C-h C-a.

The Emacs editor uses the Ctrl key in combination with certain letters to perform special functions, can be used with the LISP (LISt Processing) artificial intelligence programming language, and supports hundreds of keyboard functions, such as the vi editor. Table 3-8 shows a list of some common keyboard functions used in the Emacs editor.

Unfortunately, the Emacs editor is not an easy-to-use editor because the user must memorize several key combinations to work effectively or use advanced features. If you run Emacs within a GUI environment, a graphical version of the Emacs editor is started. The graphical Emacs editor is much easier to use because the command-line key combinations are replaced by graphical icons, menus, and optional sidebars for many features. If you type emacs project4 at a terminal within a GUI environment, you will start a graphical Emacs session, as shown in Figure 3-3.

Another text editor that uses Ctrl key combinations for performing functions is the **nano editor** (based on the Pine UNIX editor). Unlike vi or Emacs, nano is a very basic and easy-to-use editor that many Linux administrators use to quickly modify configuration files if they don't need advanced functionality. As with Emacs, the nano editor is not installed by default in Fedora 20. However, you can run the command yum install nano at a

Key	Description
Ctrl+a	Moves the cursor to the beginning of the line
Ctrl+e	Moves the cursor to the end of the line
Ctrl+h	Displays Emacs documentation
Ctrl+d	Deletes the current character
Ctrl+k	Deletes all characters between the cursor and the end of the line
Esc+d	Deletes the current word
Ctrl+x + Ctrl+c	Exits the Emacs editor
Ctrl+x + Ctrl+s	Saves the current document
Ctrl+x + Ctrl+w	Saves the current document as a new filename
Ctrl+x + u	Undoes the last change

Table 3-8 Keyboard functions commonly used in the GNU Emacs editor

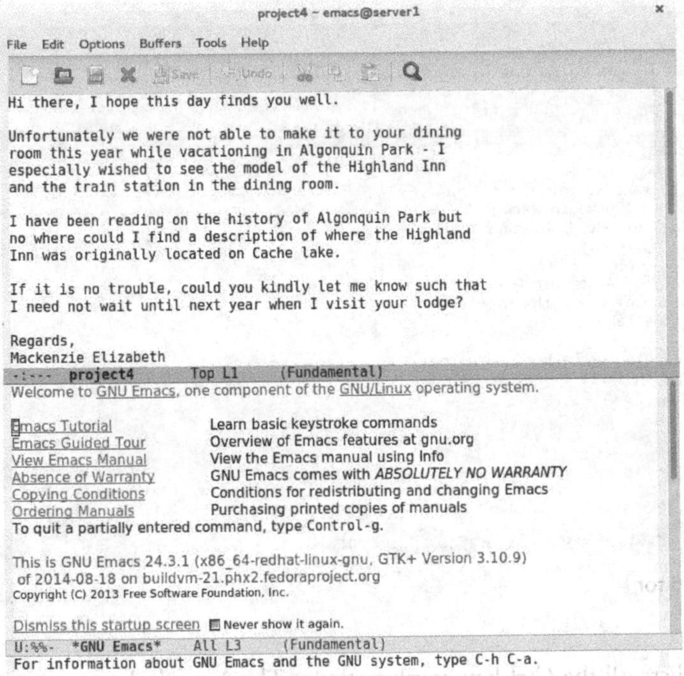

Figure 3-3 A graphical emacs session

command prompt to obtain nano from a free software repository on the Internet. If you type nano project4, you will see the following displayed on the terminal screen:

```
GNU nano 2.3.2                          File: project4.txt
Hi there, I hope this day finds you well.

Unfortunately we were not able to make it to your dining
room this year while vacationing in Algonquin Park - I
especially wished to see the model of the Highland Inn
and the train station in the dining room.

I have been reading on the history of Algonquin Park but
no where could I find a description of where the Highland
Inn was originally located on Cache lake.

If it is no trouble, could you kindly let me know such that
I need not wait until next year when I visit your lodge?

Regards,
Mackenzie Elizabeth

                         [ Read 16 lines ]
^G Get Help  ^O WriteOut  ^R Read File  ^Y Prev Page  ^K Cut Text   ^C CurPos
^X Exit      ^J Justify   ^W Where Is   ^V Next Page  ^U UnCut Txt  ^T Spell
```

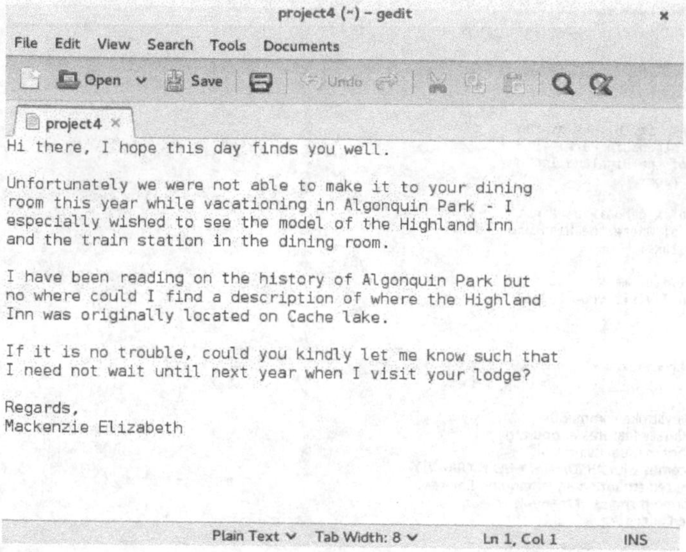

Figure 3-4 The gedit text editor

The bottom of the screen lists all the Ctrl key combinations. The ^ symbol represents the Ctrl key. This means that, to exit nano, you can press Ctrl+X (^X = Ctrl+X).

If you are using a GUI environment, you can instead use the **gedit editor** to quickly edit text files. Although the gedit editor does not have the advanced functionality that vi or Emacs has, it is the easiest editor to use as it is functionally analogous to the Windows Wordpad and Notepad editors. If you type `gedit project4` in a GUI environment, you will see the screen shown in Figure 3-4.

Chapter Summary

- The Linux filesystem is arranged hierarchically using a series of directories to store files. The location of these directories and files can be described using a relative or absolute pathname. The Linux filesystem can contain many types of files, such as text files, binary data, executable programs, directories, linked files, and special device files.

- The `ls` command can be used to view filenames and offers a wide range of options to modify this view.

- Wildcard metacharacters are special keyboard characters. They can be used to simplify the selection of several files when using common Linux file commands.

- Text files are the most common file type whose contents can be viewed by several utilities, such as `head`, `tail`, `cat`, `tac`, `more`, and `less`.

- Regular expression metacharacters can be used to specify certain patterns of text when used with certain programming languages and text tool utilities, such as `grep`.

- Although many command-line and graphical text editors exist, vi (vim) is a powerful, bimodal text editor that is standard on most UNIX and Linux systems.

Key Terms

~ metacharacter   A metacharacter used to represent a user's home directory.

absolute pathname   The full pathname to a certain file or directory starting from the root directory.

binary data file   A file that contains machine language (binary 1s and 0s) and stores information (such as common functions and graphics) used by binary compiled programs.

cat command   A Linux command used to display (or concatenate) the entire contents of a text file to the screen.

cd (change directory) command   A Linux command used to change the current directory in the directory tree.

command mode   One of the two modes in vi; it allows a user to perform any available text-editing task that is not related to inserting text into the document.

concatenation   The joining of text together to make one larger whole. In Linux, words and strings of text are joined together to form a displayed file.

directory   A special file on the filesystem used to organize other files into a logical tree structure.

egrep command   A variant of the grep command used to search files for patterns, using extended regular expressions.

Emacs (Editor MACroS) editor   A popular and widespread text editor more conducive to word processing than vi. It was originally developed by Richard Stallman.

executable program   A file that can be executed by the Linux operating system to run in memory as a process and perform a useful function.

fgrep command   A variant of the grep command that does not allow the use of regular expressions.

file command   A Linux command that displays the file type of a specified filename.

filename   The user-friendly identifier given to a file.

filename extension   A series of identifiers following a dot (.) at the end of a filename, used to denote the type of the file; the filename extention .txt denotes a text file.

gedit editor   A common text editor used within GUI environments.

grep command   A Linux command that searches files for patterns of characters using regular expression metacharacters. The command name is short for "global regular expression print."

head command   A Linux command that displays the first set of lines of a text file; by default, the head command displays the first 10 lines.

home directory   A directory on the filesystem set aside for users to store personal files and information.

insert mode   One of the two modes in vi; it allows the user to insert text into the document but does not allow any other functionality.

less command   A Linux command used to display a text file page-by-page on the terminal screen; users can then use the cursor keys to navigate the file.

linked file   The files that represent the same data as other files.

ll command   An alias for the `ls -l` command; it gives a long file listing.

log file   A file that contains past system events.

ls command   A Linux command used to list the files in a given directory.

more command   A Linux command used to display a text file page by page and line by line on the terminal screen.

named pipe file   A temporary connection that sends information from one command or process in memory to another; it can also be represented by a file on the filesystem.

nano editor   A user-friendly terminal text editor that uses Ctrl key combinations to perform basic functions.

od command   A Linux command used to display the contents of a file in octal format.

parent directory   The directory that is one level closer to the root directory in the directory tree relative to your current directory.

pwd (print working directory) command   A Linux command used to display the current directory in the directory tree.

regexp   See *regular expressions*.

regular expressions   The special metacharacters used to match patterns of text within text files; they are commonly used by text tool commands, including `grep`.

relative pathname   The pathname of a target directory relative to your current directory in the tree.

socket file   A named pipe connecting processes on two different computers; it can also be represented by a file on the filesystem.

special device file   A file used to identify hardware devices such as hard disks and serial ports.

strings command   A Linux command used to search for and display text characters in a binary file.

subdirectory   A directory that resides within another directory in the directory tree.

Tab-completion feature   A feature of the BASH shell that fills in the remaining characters of a unique filename or directory name when the user presses the Tab key.

tac command   A Linux command that displays a file on the screen, beginning with the last line of the file and ending with the first line of the file.

tail command   A Linux command used to display lines of text at the end of a file; by default, the `tail` command displays the last 10 lines of the file.

text file   A file that stores information in a readable text format.

text tools   The programs that allow for the creation, modification, and searching of text files.

vi editor   A powerful command-line text editor available on most UNIX and Linux systems.

wildcard metacharacters   The metacharacters used to match certain characters in a file or directory name; they are often used to specify multiple files.

Review Questions

1. A directory is a type of file. True or False?

2. Which command would a user type on the command line to find out which directory in the directory tree he is currently located in?

   a. pd

   b. cd

   c. where

   d. pwd

3. Which of the following is an absolute pathname? (Choose all that apply.)

   a. Home/resume

   b. C:\myfolder\resume

   c. resume

   d. /home/resume

   e. C:home/resume

4. A special device file is used to _____.

   a. enable proprietary custom-built devices to work with Linux

   b. represent hardware devices such as hard disk drives and ports

   c. keep a list of device settings specific to each individual user

   d. do nothing in Linux

5. If a user's current directory is /home/mary/project1, which command could she use to move to the etc directory directly under the root?

   a. cd ..

   b. cd /home/mary/etc

   c. cd etc

   d. cd /etc

   e. cd \etc

6. After typing the ls -a command, you notice that there is a file whose filename begins with a dot (.). What does this mean?

   a. It is a binary file.

   b. It is a system file.

   c. It is a file in the current directory.

   d. It is a hidden file.

7. After typing the `ls -F` command, you notice a filename that ends with an * (asterisk) character. What does this mean?

   a. It is a hidden file.

   b. It is a linked file.

   c. It is a special device file.

   d. It is an executable file.

8. The vi editor can function in which two of the following modes? (Choose both that apply.)

   a. text

   b. command

   c. input

   d. interactive

   e. insert

9. The `less` command offers less functionality than the `more` command. True or False?

10. Which command searches for and displays any text contents of a binary file?

    a. text

    b. strings

    c. od

    d. less

11. How can a user switch from insert mode to command mode when using the vi editor?

    a. Press the Ctrl+Alt+Del keys simultaneously.

    b. Press the Del key.

    c. Type in a : character.

    d. Press the Esc key.

12. If "resume" is the name of a file in the home directory off the root of the filesystem and your present working directory is home, what is the relative name for the file named resume?

    a. /home/resume

    b. /resume

    c. resume

    d. \home\resume

13. What will the following wildcard regular expression return: `file[a-c]`?

    a. filea-c

    b. filea, filec

    c. filea, fileb, filec

    d. fileabc

14. What will typing q! at the : prompt in command mode do when using the vi editor?

    a. quit because no changes were made

    b. quit after saving any changes

    c. nothing because the ! is a metacharacter

    d. quit without saving any changes

15. A user types in the command head /poems/mary. What will be displayed on the terminal screen?

    a. the first line of the file mary

    b. the header for the file mary

    c. the first 20 lines of the file mary

    d. the last 10 lines of the file mary

    e. the first 10 lines of the file mary

16. The tac command _____.

    a. is not a valid Linux command

    b. displays the contents of hidden files

    c. displays the contents of a file in reverse order, last word on the line first and first word on the line last

    d. displays the contents of a file in reverse order, last line first and first line last

17. How can you specify a text pattern that must be at the beginning of a line of text using a regular expression?

    a. Precede the string with a /.

    b. Follow the string with a \.

    c. Precede the string with a $.

    d. Precede the string with a ^.

18. Linux has only one root directory per directory tree. True or False?

19. Using wildcard metacharacters, how can you indicate a character that is NOT a or b or c or d?

    a. [^abcd]

    b. not [a-d]

    c. [!a-d]

    d. !a-d

20. A user typed in the command pwd and saw the output: /home/jim/sales/pending. How could that user navigate to the /home/jim directory?

    a. cd ..

    b. cd /jim

    c. cd ../..

    d. cd ./.

Hands-on Projects

These projects should be completed in the order given. The hands-on projects presented in this chapter should take a total of three hours to complete. The requirements for this lab include:

- A computer with Fedora Linux installed according to Hands-on Project 2-1.

Project 3-1

In this hands-on project, you log in to the computer and navigate the file structure.

1. Boot your Fedora Linux virtual machine. After your Linux system has been loaded, switch to a command-line terminal (tty2) by pressing **Ctrl+Alt+F2** and log in to the terminal using the user name of **root** and the password of **LNXrocks!**.

2. At the command prompt, type **pwd** and press **Enter** to view the current working directory. What is your current working directory?

3. At the command prompt, type **cd** and press **Enter**. At the command prompt, type **pwd** and press **Enter** to view the current working directory. Did your current working directory change? Why or why not?

4. At the command prompt, type **cd .** and press **Enter**. At the command prompt, type **pwd** and press **Enter** to view the current working directory. Did your current working directory change? Why or why not?

5. At the command prompt, type **cd ..** and press **Enter**. At the command prompt, type **pwd** and press **Enter** to view the current working directory. Did your current working directory change? Why or why not?

6. At the command prompt, type **cd root** and press **Enter**. At the command prompt, type **pwd** and press **Enter** to view the current working directory. Did your current working directory change? Where are you now? Did you specify a relative or absolute pathname to your home directory when you used the **cd root** command?

7. At the command prompt, type **cd etc** and press **Enter**. What error message did you receive and why?

8. At the command prompt, type **cd /etc** and press **Enter**. At the command prompt, type **pwd** and press **Enter** to view the current working directory. Did your current working directory change? Did you specify a relative or absolute pathname to the /etc directory when you used the **cd /etc** command?

9. At the command prompt, type **cd /** and press **Enter**. At the command prompt, type **pwd** and press **Enter** to view the current working directory. Did your current working directory change? Did you specify a relative or absolute pathname to the / directory when you used the **cd /** command?

10. At the command prompt, type **cd ~user1** and then press **Enter**. At the command prompt, type **pwd** and press **Enter** to view the current working directory. Did your current working directory change? Which command discussed earlier performs the same function as the **cd ~** command?

11. At the command prompt, type **cd Desktop** and press **Enter** (be certain to use a capital D). At the command prompt, type **pwd** and press **Enter** to view the current working directory. Did your current working directory change? Where are you now? What kind of pathname did you use here (absolute or relative)?

12. Currently, you are in a subdirectory of user1's home folder, three levels below the root. To go up three parent directories to the / directory, type **cd ../../..** and press **Enter** at the command prompt. Next, type **pwd** and press **Enter** to ensure that you are in the / directory.

13. At the command prompt, type **cd /etc/samba** and press **Enter** to change the current working directory using an absolute pathname. Next, type **pwd** and press **Enter** at the command prompt to ensure that you have changed to the /etc/samba directory. Now, type in the command **cd ../sysconfig** at the command prompt and press **Enter**. Type **pwd** and press **Enter** to view your current location. Explain how the relative pathname seen in the **cd ../sysconfig** command specified your current working directory.

14. At the command prompt, type **cd ../../home/user1/Desktop** and press **Enter** to change your current working directory to the Desktop directory underneath user1's home directory. Verify that you are in the target directory by typing the **pwd** command at a command prompt and press **Enter**. Would it have been more advantageous to use an absolute pathname to change to this directory instead of the relative pathname that you used?

15. Type **exit** and press **Enter** to log out of your shell.

Project 3-2

In this hands-on project, you navigate the Linux filesystem using the Tab-completion feature of the BASH shell.

1. Switch to a command-line terminal (tty2) by pressing **Ctrl+Alt+F2** and log in to the terminal using the user name of **root** and the password of **LNXrocks!**.

2. At the command prompt, type **cd /** and press **Enter**.

3. Next, type **cd ro** at the command prompt and press **Tab**. What is displayed on the screen and why? How many subdirectories under the root begin with "ro"?

4. Press the **Ctrl** and **c** keys simultaneously to cancel the command and return to an empty command prompt.

5. At the command prompt, type **cd b** and press **Tab**. Did the display change?

6. Press the **Tab** key again. How many subdirectories under the root begin with "b"?

7. Type the letter i. Notice that the command now reads "cd bi." Press the **Tab** key again. Which directory did it expand to? Why? Press the **Ctrl** and **c** keys simultaneously to cancel the command and return to an empty command prompt.

8. At the command prompt, type **cd m** and press **Tab**. Press **Tab** once again after hearing the beep. How many subdirectories under the root begin with "m"?

9. Type the letter **i**. Notice that the command now reads "cd me." Press **Tab**.

10. Press **Enter** to execute the command at the command prompt. Next, type the **pwd** command and press **Enter** to verify that you are in the /media directory.

11. Type **exit** and press **Enter** to log out of your shell.

Project 3-3

In this hands-on project, you examine files and file types using the `ls` and `file` commands.

1. Switch to a command-line terminal (tty2) by pressing **Ctrl+Alt+F2** and log in to the terminal using the user name of **root** and the password of **LNXrocks!**.

2. At the command prompt, type **cd /etc** and press **Enter**. Verify that you are in the /etc directory by typing **pwd** at the command prompt and press **Enter**.

3. At the command prompt, type **ls** and press **Enter**. What do you see listed in the four columns? Do any of the files have extensions? What is the most common extension you see and what does it indicate? Is the list you are viewing on the screen the entire contents of /etc?

4. At the command prompt, type **ls | more** and then press **Enter** (the | symbol is usually near the Enter key on the keyboard and is obtained by pressing the Shift and \ keys in combination). What does the display show? Notice the highlighted --More-- prompt at the bottom of the screen. Press **Enter**. Press **Enter** again. Press **Enter** once more. Notice that each time you press Enter, you advance one line further into the file. Now, press the **spacebar**. Press the **spacebar** again. Notice that with each press of the spacebar, you advance one full page into the displayed directory contents. Press the **h** key to get a help screen. Examine the command options.

5. Press the **q** key to quit the `more` command and return to an empty command prompt.

6. At the command prompt, type **ls | less** and then press **Enter**. What does the display show? Notice the : at the bottom of the screen. Press **Enter**. Press **Enter** again. Press **Enter** once more. Notice that each time you press Enter, you advance one line further into the file. Now press the **spacebar**. Press the **spacebar** again. Notice that with each press of the spacebar, you advance one full page into the displayed directory contents. Press the **h** key to get a help screen. Examine the command options, and then press **q** to return to the command output.

7. Press the ↑ (up arrow) key. Press ↑ again. Press ↑ once more. Notice that each time you press the ↑ key, you go up one line in the file display toward the beginning of the file. Now, press the ↓ (down arrow) key. Press ↓ again. Press ↓ once more. Notice that each time you press the ↓ key, you move forward into the file display.

8. Press the **q** key to quit the `less` command and return to a shell command prompt.

9. At the command prompt, type **cd** and press **Enter**. At the command prompt, type **pwd** and press **Enter**. What is your current working directory? At the command prompt, type **ls** and press **Enter**.

10. At the command prompt, type **ls /etc** and press **Enter**. How does this output compare with what you saw in Step 9? Has your current directory changed? Verify your answer by typing **pwd** at the command prompt and press **Enter**. Notice that you were able to list the contents of another directory by giving the absolute name of it as an argument to the `ls` command without leaving the directory in which you are currently located.

11. At the command prompt, type **ls /etc/skel** and press **Enter**. Did you see a listing of any files? At the command prompt, type **ls -a /etc/skel** and press **Enter**. What is special about these files? What do the first two entries in the list (. and ..) represent?

12. At the command prompt, type **ls -aF /etc/skel** and press **Enter**. Which file types are available in the /etc/skel directory?

13. At the command prompt, type **ls /bin** and press **Enter**. Did you see a listing of any files? At the command prompt, type **ls -F /bin** and press **Enter**. What file types are present in the /bin directory?

14. At the command prompt, type **ls /boot** and press **Enter**. Next, type **ls –l /boot** and press **Enter**. What additional information is available on the screen? What types of files are available in the /boot directory? At the command prompt, type **ll /boot** and press **Enter**. Is the output any different from that of the **ls –l /boot** command you just entered? Why or why not?

15. At the command prompt, type **file /etc** and press **Enter**. What kind of file is etc?

16. At the command prompt, type **file /etc/inittab** and press **Enter**. What type of file is /etc/inittab?

17. At the command prompt, type **file /boot/*** to see the types of files in the /boot directory. Is this information more specific than the information you gathered in Step 14?

18. Type **exit** and press **Enter** to log out of your shell.

Project 3-4

In this hands-on project, you display file contents using the cat, tac, head, tail, strings, and od commands.

1. Switch to a command-line terminal (tty2) by pressing **Ctrl+Alt+F2,** and then log in to the terminal using the user name of **root** and the password of **LNXrocks!.**

2. At the command prompt, type **cat /etc/hosts** and press **Enter** to view the contents of the file hosts, which reside in the directory /etc. Next, type **cat –n /etc/hosts** and press **Enter**. How many lines does the file have? At the command prompt, type **tac /etc/hosts** and press **Enter** to view the same file in reverse order. The output of both commands should be visible on the same screen. Compare them.

3. To see the contents of the same file in octal format instead of ASCII text, type **od /etc/hosts** at the command prompt and press **Enter**.

4. At the command prompt, type **cat /etc/inittab** and press **Enter**.

5. At the command prompt, type **head /etc/inittab** and press **Enter**. What is displayed on the screen? How many lines are displayed, which ones are they, and why?

6. At the command prompt, type **head -5 /etc/inittab** and press **Enter**. How many lines are displayed and why? Next, type **head -3 /etc/inittab** and press **Enter**. How many lines are displayed and why?

7. At the command prompt, type **tail /etc/inittab** and press **Enter**. What is displayed on the screen? How many lines are displayed; which ones are they and why?

8. At the command prompt, type **tail -5 /etc/inittab** and press **Enter**. How many lines are displayed and why? Type the **cat –n /etc/inittab** command at a command prompt and press **Enter** to justify your answer.

9. At the command prompt, type **file /bin/nice** and press **Enter**. What type of file is it? Should you use a text tool command on this file?

10. At the command prompt, type **strings /bin/nice** and press **Enter**. Notice that you are able to see some text within this binary file. Next, type **strings /bin/nice |** **more** to view the same content page-by-page. When finished, press **q** to quit the more command.

11. Type **exit** and press **Enter** to log out of your shell.

Project 3-5

In this hands-on project, you create and edit text files using the vi editor.

1. Switch to a command-line terminal (tty2) by pressing **Ctrl+Alt+F2** and log in to the terminal using the user name of **root** and the password of **LNXrocks!**.

2. At the command prompt, type **pwd**, press **Enter**, and ensure that /root is displayed, showing that you are in the root user's home folder. At the command prompt, type **vi** **sample1** and press **Enter** to open the vi editor and create a new text file called sample1. Notice that this name appears at the bottom of the screen along with the indication that it is a new file.

3. At the command prompt, type **My letter** and press **Enter**. Why was nothing displayed on the screen? To switch from command mode to insert mode to allow the typing of text, press **i**. Notice that the word Insert appears at the bottom of the screen. Next, type **My letter** and notice that this text is displayed on the screen. What types of tasks can be accomplished in insert mode?

4. Press **Esc**. Did the cursor move? What mode are you in now? Press ← two times until the cursor is under the last t in letter. Press the **x** key. What happened? Next, type i to enter insert mode, then type the letter "h." Did the letter "h" get inserted before or after the cursor?

5. Press **Esc** to switch back to command mode and then move your cursor to the end of the line. Next, type the letter "o" to open a line underneath the current line and enter insert mode.

6. Type the following:

   It might look like I am doing nothing, but at the cellular level **I can assure you that I am quite busy. And to a typical cell, it may** **seem like they are doing all the work!**

   Notice that the line wraps to the next line partway through the sentence. Though displayed over two lines on the screen, this sentence is treated as one continuous line of text in vi. Press **Esc** to return to command mode, and then press ↑. Where does the cursor move? Use the cursor keys to navigate to the letter "l" at the beginning of the word "level," and then press the **i** key to enter insert mode. Press the **Enter** key while in insert mode. Next, press **Esc** to return to command mode, and then press ↑. Where does the cursor move?

7. Type **dd** three times to delete all lines in the file.

8. Type **i** to enter insert mode, and then type:

   Hi there, I hope this day finds you well.

   and press **Enter**. Press **Enter** again. Type:

   Unfortunately we were not able to make it to your dining

and press **Enter**. Type:

    `room this year while vacationing in Algonquin Park - I`

and press **Enter**. Type:

    `especially wished to see the model of the Highland Inn`

and press **Enter**. Type:

    `and the train station in the dining room.`

and press **Enter**. Press **Enter** again. Type:

    `I have been reading on the history of Algonquin Park but`

and press **Enter**. Type:

    `no where could I find a description of where the Highland`

and press **Enter**. Type:

    `Inn was originally located on Cache lake.`

and press **Enter**. Press **Enter** again. Type:

    `If it is no trouble, could you kindly let me know such that`

and press **Enter**. Type:

    `I need not wait until next year when I visit your lodge?`

and press **Enter**. Press **Enter** again. Type:

    `Regards,`

and press **Enter**. Type:

    `Mackenzie Elizabeth`

and press **Enter**. You should now have the sample letter used in this chapter on your screen. It should resemble the letter in Figure 3-4.

9. Press **Esc** to switch to command mode. Next press the **Shift** and ; keys simultaneously to open the : prompt at the bottom of the screen. At this prompt, type **w** and press **Enter** to save the changes you have made to the file. What is displayed at the bottom of the file when you are finished?

10. Press the **Shift** and ; keys simultaneously to open the : prompt at the bottom of the screen again, type **q**, and then press **Enter** to exit the vi editor.

11. At the command prompt, type **ls** and press **Enter** to view the contents of your current directory. Notice that there is now a file called sample1 listed.

12. Next, type **file sample1** and press **Enter**. What type of file is sample1? At the command prompt, type **cat sample1** and press **Enter**.

13. At the command prompt, type **vi sample1** and press **Enter** to open the letter again in the vi editor. What is displayed at the bottom of the screen? How does this compare with Step 9?

14. Use the cursor keys to navigate to the bottom of the document. Press the **Shift** and ; keys simultaneously to open the : prompt at the bottom of the screen again, type **!date** and press **Enter**. The current system date and time appear at the bottom of the screen. As indicated, press **Enter** to return to the document.

15. Press the **Shift** and ; keys simultaneously again to open the : prompt at the bottom of the screen again, type **r !date** and press **Enter**. What happened and why?

16. Use the cursor keys to position your cursor on the line in the document that displays the current date and time, and type **yy** to copy it to the buffer in memory. Next, use the cursor keys to position your cursor on the first line in the document, and type **P** (capitalized) to paste the contents of the memory buffer above your current line. Does the original line remain at the bottom of the document?

17. Use the cursor keys to position your cursor on the line at the end of the document that displays the current date and time, and type **dd** to delete it.

18. Use the cursor keys to position your cursor on the **t** in the word "there" on the second line of the file that reads **Hi there, I hope this day finds you well.**, and press **dw** to delete the word. Next, type i to enter insert mode, type the word **Bob**, and then press Esc to switch back to command mode.

19. Press the **Shift** and ; keys simultaneously to open the : prompt at the bottom of the screen again, type **w sample2** and press **Enter**. What happened and why?

20. Press **i** to enter insert mode, and type the word **test**. Next, press Esc to switch to command mode. Press the **Shift** and ; keys simultaneously to open the : prompt at the bottom of the screen again, type **q**, and press **Enter** to quit the vi editor. Were you able quit? Why not?

21. Press the **Shift** and ; keys simultaneously to open the : prompt at the bottom of the screen again, type **q!**, and press **Enter** to quit the vi editor and discard any changes since the last save.

22. At the command prompt, type **ls** and press **Enter** to view the contents of your current directory. Notice that there is now a file called sample2, which was created in Step 19.

23. At the command prompt, type **vi sample2** and press **Enter** to open the letter again in the vi editor.

24. Use the cursor keys to position your cursor on the line that reads **Hi Bob, I hope this day finds you well.**

25. Press the **Shift** and ; keys simultaneously to open the : prompt at the bottom of the screen, type **s/Bob/Barb/g**, and press **Enter** to change all occurrences of "Bob" to "Barb" on the current line.

26. Press the **Shift** and ; keys simultaneously to open the : prompt at the bottom of the screen again, type **1,$ s/to/TO/g**, and press **Enter** to change all occurrences of the word "to" to "TO" for the entire file.

27. Press the **u** key to undo the last function performed. What happened and why?

28. Press the **Shift** and ; keys simultaneously to open the : prompt at the bottom of the screen again, type **wq**, and press **Enter** to save your document and quit the vi editor.

29. At the command prompt, type **vi sample3** and press **Enter** to open a new file called sample3 in the vi editor. Type i to enter insert mode. Next, type **P.S. How were the flies this year?** Press the Esc key when finished.

30. Press the **Shift** and **;** keys simultaneously to open the **:** prompt at the bottom of the screen again, type **wq**, and press **Enter** to save your document and quit the vi editor.

31. At the command prompt, type **vi sample1**, press **Enter** to open the file sample1 again, and use the cursor keys to position your cursor on the line that reads "Mackenzie Elizabeth."

32. Press the **Shift** and **;** keys simultaneously to open the **:** prompt at the bottom of the screen again, type **r sample3**, and press **Enter** to insert the contents of the file sample3 below your current line.

33. Press the **Shift** and **;** keys simultaneously to open the **:** prompt at the bottom of the screen, type **s/flies/flies and bears/g** and press **Enter**. What happened and why?

34. Press the **Shift** and **;** keys simultaneously to open the **:** prompt at the bottom of the screen again, type **set number**, and press **Enter** to turn on line numbering.

35. Press the **Shift** and **;** keys simultaneously to open the **:** prompt at the bottom of the screen again, type **set nonumber**, and press **Enter** to turn off line numbering.

36. Press the **Shift** and **;** keys simultaneously to open the **:** prompt at the bottom of the screen again, type **set all**, and press **Enter** to view all vi parameters. Press **Enter** to advance through the list, and press **q** when finished to return to the vi editor.

37. Press the **Shift** and **;** keys simultaneously to open the **:** prompt at the bottom of the screen again, type **wq**, and press **Enter** to save your document and quit the vi editor.

38. Type **exit** and press **Enter** to log out of your shell.

Project 3-6

In this hands-on project, you use the **ls** command alongside wildcard metacharacters in your shell to explore the contents of your home directory.

1. Switch to a command-line terminal (tty2) by pressing **Ctrl+Alt+F2** and log in to the terminal using the user name of **root** and the password of **LNXrocks!**.

2. At the command prompt, type **pwd**, press **Enter**, and ensure /root is displayed showing that you are in the root user's home folder. At the command prompt, type **ls**. How many files with a name beginning with the word "sample" exist in **/root**?

3. At the command prompt, type **ls *** and press **Enter**. What is listed and why?

4. At the command prompt, type **ls sample** and press **Enter**. What is listed and why?

5. At the command prompt, type **ls sample?** and press **Enter**. What is listed and why?

6. At the command prompt, type **ls sample??** and press **Enter**. What is listed and why?

7. At the command prompt, type **ls sample[13]** and press **Enter**. What is listed and why?

8. At the command prompt, type **ls sample[!13]** and press **Enter**. What is listed and why? How does this compare to the results from Step 7?

9. At the command prompt, type **ls sample[1-3]** and press **Enter**. What is listed and why?

10. At the command prompt, type **ls sample[!1-3]** and press **Enter**. What is listed and why? How does this compare to the results from Step 9?

11. Type **exit** and press **Enter** to log out of your shell.

Project 3-7

In this hands-on project, you use the grep and egrep commands alongside regular expression metacharacters to explore the contents of text files.

1. Switch to a command-line terminal (tty2) by pressing **Ctrl+Alt+F2** and log in to the terminal using the user name of **root** and the password of **LNXrocks!**.

2. At the command prompt, type **grep "Inn" sample1** and press **Enter**. What is displayed and why?

3. At the command prompt, type **grep -v "Inn" sample1** and press **Enter**. What is displayed and why? How does this compare to the results from Step 2?

4. At the command prompt, type **grep "inn" sample1** and press **Enter**. What is displayed and why?

5. At the command prompt, type **grep -i "inn" sample1** and press **Enter**. What is displayed and why? How does this compare to the results from Steps 2 and 4?

6. At the command prompt, type **grep "I" sample1** and press **Enter**. What is displayed and why?

7. At the command prompt, type **grep " I " sample1** and press **Enter**. What is displayed and why? How does it differ from the results from Step 6 and why?

8. At the command prompt, type **grep "t.e" sample1** and press **Enter**. What is displayed and why?

9. At the command prompt, type **grep "w...e" sample1** and press **Enter**. What is displayed and why?

10. At the command prompt, type **grep " ^I" sample1** and press **Enter**. What is displayed and why?

11. At the command prompt, type **grep "^I" sample1** and press **Enter**. What is displayed and why? How does this differ from the results in Step 10 and why?

12. At the command prompt, type **grep "(we|next)" sample1** and press **Enter**. Is anything displayed? Why?

13. At the command prompt, type **egrep "(we|next)" sample1** and press **Enter**. What is displayed and why?

14. At the command prompt, type **grep "Inn$" sample1** and press **Enter**. What is displayed and why?

15. At the command prompt, type **grep "?$" sample1** and press **Enter**. What is displayed and why? Does the ? metacharacter have special meaning here? Why?

16. At the command prompt, type **grep "^$" sample1** and press **Enter**. Is anything displayed? (*Hint:* Be certain to look closely!) Can you explain the output?

17. Type **exit** and press **Enter** to log out of your shell.

Discovery Exercises

1. You are the systems administrator for a scientific research company that employs over 100 scientists who write and run Linux programs to analyze their work. All of these programs are stored in each scientist's home directory on the Linux system. One scientist has left the company, and you are instructed to retrieve any work from that scientist's home directory. When you enter the home directory for that user, you notice that there are very few files and only two directories (one named Projects and one named Lab). List the commands that you would use to navigate through this user's home directory and view filenames and file types. If there are any text files, what commands could you use to view their contents?

2. When you type the pwd command, you notice that your current location on the Linux filesystem is the /usr/local directory. Answer the following questions, assuming that your current directory is /usr/local for each question.

    a. Which command could you use to change to the /usr directory using an absolute pathname?

    b. Which command could you use to change to the /usr directory using a relative pathname?

    c. Which command could you use to change to the /usr/local/share/info directory using an absolute pathname?

    d. Which command could you use to change to the /usr/local/share/info directory using a relative pathname?

    e. Which command could you use to change to the /etc directory using an absolute pathname?

    f. Which command could you use to change to the /etc directory using a relative pathname?

3. Using wildcard metacharacters and options to the ls command, view the following

    a. All the files that end with .cfg under the /etc directory

    b. All hidden files in the /home/user1 directory

    c. The directory names that exist under the /var directory

    d. All the files that start with the letter "a" underneath the /bin directory

    e. All the files that have exactly three letters in their filename in the /bin directory

    f. All files that have exactly three letters in their filename and end with either the letter "t" or the letter "h" in the /bin directory

4. Explore the manual pages for the ls, grep, cat, od, tac, head, tail, pwd, cd, strings, and vi commands. Experiment with what you learn using the file sample1 that you created earlier.

5. The famous quote "To be or not to be" (from Shakespeare's *Hamlet*) can be represented by the following regular expression:

    (2b|[^b]{2})

If you used this expression when searching a text file using the `egrep` command (`egrep "(2b|[^b]{2})" filename`), what would be displayed? Try this command on a file that you have created. Why does it display what it does? That is the question.

6. By default, a minimal version of the vi editor is installed on Fedora 20. Run the command **yum update vim-minimal** to update this editor to the latest version from software repositories on the Internet and then type **yum install vim** to install the full vi editor package. The full vi editor package comes with a short 30-minute tutorial on its usage. Start this tutorial by typing **vimtutor** at a command prompt and then follow the directions. Provided you have a functional Web browser and an Internet connection, explore the resources available at *www.vim.org*.

7. Enter the following text into a new document called question7 using the vi editor. Next, use the vi editor to fix the mistakes in the file using the information in Table 3-5, Table 3-6, and Table 3-7 as well as the examples provided in this chapter.

```
Hi there,
Unfortunately we were not able to make it to your dining room
Unfortunately we were not able to make it to your dining room
this year while vacationing in Algonuin Park - I especially wished
to see the model of the highland inn and the train station in the
        dining rooms.
I have been readng on the history of Algonuin Park but
no where could I find a description of where the Highland Inn was
originally located on Cache lake.

If it is not trouble, could you kindly let me that I need
not wait until next year when we visit Lodge?

I hope this day finds you well.
Regard
Elizabeth Mackenzie
```

8. The knowledge gained from using the vi editor can be transferred easily to the Emacs editor. Perform Question 7 using the Emacs editor instead of the vi editor.

9. When you use the vi editor and change environment settings at the : prompt, such as : set number to enable line numbering, those changes are lost when you exit the vi editor. To continuously apply the same environment settings, you can choose to put the set commands in a special hidden file in their home directory called .exrc; this .exrc file is then applied each time you open the vi editor. Enter the vi editor and find three environment settings that you want to change in addition to line numbering. Then create a new file called .exrc in your home directory and enter the four lines changing these vi environment settings (do not start each line with a : character, just enter the set command—e.g., set number). When finished, open the vi editor to edit a new file and test to see whether the settings were applied automatically.

Linux Filesystem Management

After completing this chapter, you will be able to:

- Find files and directories on the filesystem
- Understand and create linked files
- Explain the function of the Filesystem Hierarchy Standard
- Use standard Linux commands to manage files and directories
- Modify file and directory ownership
- Define and change Linux file and directory permissions
- Identify the default permissions created on files and directories
- Apply special file and directory permissions
- Modify the default access control list (ACL)
- View and set filesystem attributes

In the previous chapter, you learned about navigating the Linux filesystem as well as viewing and editing files. This chapter focuses on the organization of files on the Linux filesystem as well as their linking and security. First, you explore standard Linux directories using the Filesystem Hierarchy Standard. Next, you explore common commands used to manage files and directories as well as learn methods that are used to find files and directories on the filesystems. Finally, you learn about file and directory linking, permissions, special permissions, and attributes.

The Filesystem Hierarchy Standard

The many thousands of files on a typical Linux system are organized into directories in the Linux directory tree. It's a complex system, made even more complex in the past by the fact that different Linux distributions were free to place files in different locations. This meant that you could waste a great deal of time searching for a configuration file on a Linux system with which you were unfamiliar. To simplify the task of finding specific files, the **Filesystem Hierarchy Standard (FHS)** was created.

FHS defines a standard set of directories for use by all Linux and UNIX systems as well as the file and subdirectory contents of each directory. This ensures that, because the filename and location follow a standard convention, a Fedora Linux user will find the correct configuration file on a SuSE Linux or Hewlett-Packard UNIX computer with little difficulty. The FHS also gives Linux software developers the ability to locate files on a Linux system regardless of the distribution, allowing them to create software that is not distribution-specific.

A comprehensive understanding of the standard types of directories found on Linux systems is valuable when locating and managing files and directories; some standard UNIX and Linux directories defined by FHS and their descriptions are found in Table 4-1. These directories are discussed throughout this chapter and subsequent chapters.

To read the complete Filesystem Hierarchy Standard definition, go to *http://refspecs.linuxfoundation.org/fhs.shtml*.

Managing Files and Directories

As mentioned earlier, using a Linux system involves navigating several directories and manipulating the files inside them. Thus, an efficient Linux user must understand how to create directories as needed, copy or move files from one directory to another, and delete files and directories. These tasks are commonly referred to as file management tasks.

Following is an example of a directory listing displayed by a user who is logged in as the root user:

```
[root@server1 ~]# pwd
/root
[root@server1 ~]# ls -F
current@ myprogram* project    project12 project2 project4
Desktop/ myscript   project1   project13 project3 project5
[root@server1 ~]#_
```

Directory	Description
/bin	Contains binary commands for use by all users
/boot	Contains the Linux kernel and files used by the boot loader
/dev	Contains device files
/etc	Contains system-specific configuration files
/home	Is the default location for user home directories
/lib	Contains shared program libraries (used by the commands in /bin and /sbin) as well as kernel modules
/media	A directory that contains subdirectories used for accessing (mounting) filesystems on removable media devices such as floppy disks, DVDs, and USB flash drives
/mnt	An empty directory used for temporarily accessing filesystems on removable media devices
/opt	Stores additional software programs
/proc	Contains process and kernel information
/root	Is the root user's home directory
/sbin	Contains system binary commands (used for administration)
/tmp	Holds temporary files created by programs
/usr	Contains most system commands and utilities—contains the following directories: /usr/bin—User binary commands /usr/games—Educational programs and games /usr/include—C program header files /usr/lib—Libraries/usr/local—Local programs /usr/sbin—System binary commands /usr/share—Files that are architecture independent /usr/src—Source code /usr/X11R6—The X Window system (sometimes replaced by /etc/X11)
/usr/local	Is the location for most additional programs
/var	Contains log files and spools

Table 4-1 Linux directories defined by the Filesystem Hierarchy Standard

As shown in the preceding output, only one directory (Desktop), two executable files (myprogram and myscript), and several project-related files (project) exist on this example system. Although this directory structure is not cluttered and appears in an easy-to-read format on the terminal screen, typical home directories on a Linux system contain many more files; typical Linux users might have over 100 files in their home directories. As a result, it is good practice to organize these files into subdirectories based on file purpose. Because several project files are in the root user's home directory in the preceding output, you could create a subdirectory called proj_files to contain the project-related files and decrease the size of the directory listing. To do this, you use the **mkdir** (make directory) command, which takes arguments specifying the absolute or relative pathnames of the directories to create. To create a proj_files directory underneath the current directory, you can use the mkdir command with a relative pathname:

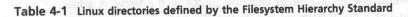

```
[root@server1 ~]# mkdir proj_files
[root@server1 ~]# ls -F
```

```
current@ myprogram* project   project12   project2   project4 proj_files/
Desktop/ myscript*  project1  project13   project3   project5
[root@server1 ~]#_
```

Now, you can move the project files into the proj_files subdirectory by using the **mv** (move) command. The mv command requires two arguments at minimum: the **source file/directory** and the **target file/directory**. For example, to move the /etc/sample1 file to the /root directory, you could use the command mv /etc/sample1 /root.

If you want to move several files, you include one source argument for each file you want to move and then include the target directory as the last argument. For example, to move the /etc/sample1 and /etc/sample2 files to the /root directory, you could use the command mv /etc/sample1 /etc/sample2 /root.

Note that both the source (or sources) and the destination can be absolute or relative pathnames and the source can contain wildcards if several files are to be moved. For example, to move all of the project files to the proj_files directory, you could type mv with the source argument project* (to match all files starting with the letters "project") and the target argument proj_files (relative pathname to the destination directory), as shown in the following output:

```
[root@server1 ~]# mv project*  proj_files
[root@server1 ~]# ls -F
current@ Desktop/  myprogram*  myscript*  proj_files/
[root@server1 ~]# ls -F proj_files
project project1 project12 project13 project2 project3 project4
project5
[root@server1 ~]#_
```

In the preceding output, the current directory listing does not show the project files anymore, yet the listing of the proj_files subdirectory indicates that they were moved successfully.

If the target is the name of a directory, the mv command moves those files to that directory. If the target is a filename of an existing file in a certain directory and there is one source file, the mv command overwrites the target with the source. If the target is a filename of a nonexistent file in a certain directory, the mv command creates a new file with that filename in the target directory and moves the source file to that file.

Another important use of the mv command is to rename files, which is simply moving a file to the same directory but with a different filename. To rename the myscript file from earlier examples to myscript2, you can use the following mv command:

```
[root@server1 ~]# ls -F
current@ Desktop/ myprogram* myscript*  proj_files/
[root@server1 ~]# mv myscript myscript2
[root@server1 ~]# ls -F
current@ Desktop/ myprogram* myscript2*  proj_files/
[root@server1 ~]#_
```

Similarly, the mv command can rename directories. If the source is the name of an existing directory, it is renamed to whatever directory name is specified as the target.

The mv command works similarly to a cut-and-paste operation in which the file is copied to a new directory and deleted from the source directory. In some cases, however, you might want to keep the file in the source directory and instead insert a copy of the file in the target directory. You can do this using the **cp (copy) command**. Much like the mv command, the cp command takes two arguments at minimum. The first argument specifies the source file/directory to be copied and the second argument specifies the target file/directory. If several files need to be copied to a destination directory, simply specify several source arguments, with the final argument on the command line serving as the target directory. Each argument can be an absolute or relative pathname and can contain wildcards or the special metacharacters "." (which specifies the current directory) and ".." (which specifies the parent directory). For example, to make a copy of the file /etc/hosts in the current directory (/root), you can specify the absolute pathname to the /etc/hosts file (/etc/hosts) and the relative pathname indicating the current directory (.):

```
[root@server1 ~]# cp /etc/hosts .
[root@server1 ~]# ls -F
current@ Desktop/  hosts  myprogram*  myscript2*  proj_files/
[root@server1 ~]#_
```

You can also make copies of files in the same directory. To make a copy of the hosts file called hosts2 in the current directory and view the results, type the following commands:

```
[root@server1 ~]# cp hosts hosts2
[root@server1 ~]# ls -F
current@ Desktop/  hosts  hosts2  myprogram*  myscript2*  proj_files/
[root@server1 ~]#_
```

Despite their similarities, the mv and cp commands work on directories differently. The mv command renames a directory, whereas the cp command creates a whole new copy of the directory and its contents. To copy a directory full of files in Linux, you must tell the cp command that the copy will be **recursive** (involve files and subdirectories too) by using the -R option. The following example demonstrates copying the proj_files directory and all of its contents to the /home/user1 directory without and with the -R option:

```
[root@server1 ~]# ls -F
current@ Desktop/  hosts  myprogram*  myscript2*  proj_files/
[root@server1 ~]# ls -F /home/user1
Desktop/
[root@server1 ~]# cp proj_files /home/user1
cp: omitting directory 'proj_files'
[root@server1 ~]# ls -F /home/user1
Desktop/
[root@server1 ~]# cp -R proj_files /home/user1
[root@server1 ~]# ls -F /home/user1
Desktop/  proj_files/
[root@server1 ~]#_
```

If the target is a file that exists, both the mv and cp commands warn the user that the target file will be overwritten and will ask whether to continue. This is not a feature of the command as normally invoked, but it is a feature of the default configuration in Fedora Linux because the BASH shell in Fedora Linux contains aliases to the cp and mv commands.

Aliases are special variables in memory that point to commands; they are fully discussed in Chapter 7.

When you type mv, you are actually running the mv command with the −i option without realizing it. If the target file already exists, both the mv command and the mv command with the −i option interactively prompt the user to choose whether to overwrite the existing file. Similarly, when you type the cp command, the cp −i command is actually run to prevent the accidental overwriting of files. To see the aliases present in your current shell, simply type alias, as shown in the following output:

```
[root@server1 ~]# alias
alias cp='cp -i'
alias egrep='egrep --color=auto'
alias fgrep='fgrep --color=auto'
alias grep='grep --color=auto'
alias l.='ls -d .* --color=auto'
alias ll='ls -l --color=auto'
alias ls='ls --color=auto'
alias mv='mv -i'
alias rm='rm -i'
alias which='alias | /usr/bin/which --tty-only --read-alias --show-dot
--show-tilde'
[root@server1 ~]#_
```

If you want to override this interactive option, which is known as **interactive mode**, use the −f (force) option to override the choice, as shown in the following example. In this example, the root user tries to rename the hosts file using the name "hosts2," a name already assigned to an existing file. The example shows the user attempting this task both without and with the −f option to the mv command:

```
[root@server1 ~]# ls -F
current@ Desktop/ hosts hosts2 myprogram* myscript2* proj_files/
[root@server1 ~]# mv hosts hosts2
mv: overwrite 'hosts2'? n
[root@server1 ~]# mv -f hosts hosts2
[root@server1 ~]# ls -F
current@ Desktop/ hosts2 myprogram* myscript2* proj_files/
[root@server1 ~]#_
```

Creating directories, copying, and moving files are file management tasks that preserve or create data on the hard disk. To remove files or directories, you must use either the rm command or the rmdir command.

The **rm (remove) command** takes a list of arguments specifying the absolute or relative pathnames of files to remove. As with most commands, wildcards can be used to simplify the process of removing multiple files. After a file has been removed from the filesystem, it cannot be recovered. As a result, the rm command is aliased in Fedora Linux to the rm command with the -i option, which interactively prompts the user to choose whether to continue with the deletion. Like the cp and mv commands, the rm command accepts the -f option to override this choice and immediately delete the file. An example demonstrating the use of the rm and rm -f commands to remove the current and hosts2 files is shown here:

```
[root@server1 ~]# ls -F
current@ Desktop/ hosts2 myprogram* myscript2* proj_files/
[root@server1 ~]# rm current
rm: remove 'current'? y
[root@server1 ~]# rm -f hosts2
[root@server1 ~]# ls -F
Desktop/ myprogram* myscript2* proj_files/
[root@server1 ~]# _
```

To remove a directory, you can use the **rmdir (remove directory) command**; however, the rmdir command only removes a directory if it contains no files. To remove a directory and the files inside, you must use the rm command and specify that a directory full of files should be removed. As explained earlier in this chapter, you need to use the recursive option (-R) with the cp command to copy directories; to remove a directory full of files, you can also use a recursive option (-R) with the rm command. If, for example, the root user wants to remove the proj_files subdirectory and all of the files within it without being prompted to confirm each file deletion, the command she must use is rm -Rf proj_files, as shown in the following example:

```
[root@server1 ~]# ls -F
Desktop/ myprogram* myscript2* proj_files/
[root@server1 ~]# rmdir proj_files
rmdir: 'proj_files': Directory not empty
[root@server1 ~]# rm -Rf proj_files
[root@server1 ~]# ls -F
Desktop/ myprogram* myscript2*
[root@server1 ~]# _
```

In many commands, such as rm and cp, both the -r and the -R options have the same meaning (recursive).

The -R option to the rm command is dangerous if you are not certain which files exist in the directory to be deleted recursively. As a result, the -R option to the rm command is commonly referred to as the -résumé option; if you use it incorrectly in a production server environment, you might need to prepare your résumé.

It is important to note that the aforementioned file management commands are commonly used by Linux users, developers, and administrators alike. Table 4-2 shows a summary of these common file management commands.

Command	Description
mkdir	Creates directories
rmdir	Removes empty directories
mv	Moves/renames files and directories
cp	Copies files and directories full of files (with the −R option)
alias	Displays BASH shell aliases
rm	Removes files and directories full of files (with the −R option)

Table 4-2 Common Linux file management commands

Finding Files

Before using the file management commands mentioned in the preceding section, you must know the locations of the files involved. The fastest method to search for files in the Linux directory tree is to use the **locate command**. For example, to view all of the files underneath the root directory with the file name "inittab" or with "inittab" as part of the filename, you can simply type locate inittab at a command prompt, which produces the following output:

```
[root@server1 ~]# locate inittab
/etc/inittab
/usr/share/vim/vim74/syntax/inittab.vim
[root@server1 ~]# _
```

The locate command looks in a premade database that contains a list of all the files on the system. This database is indexed much like a textbook for fast searching, yet can become outdated as files are added and removed from the system, which happens on a regular basis. As a result, the database used for the locate command (/var/lib/mlocate/mlocate.db) is updated each day automatically and can be updated manually by running the updatedb command at a command prompt. You can configure the directories that are searched by the updatedb command by editing the /etc/updatedb.conf file.

As the locate command searches all files on the filesystem, it returns too much information to display on the screen. To make the output easier to read, you can use the more (or less) command to pause the output, as in locate inittab | more. To prevent the problem entirely, you can do more specific searches.

A slower yet more versatile method for locating files on the filesystem is to use the **find command**. The find command does not use a premade index of files; instead, it searches the directory tree recursively, starting from a certain directory for files that meet a certain criterion. The format of the find command is find <start directory> -criteria <what to find>

For example, to find any files named "inittab" underneath the /etc directory, you can use the command find /etc -name inittab and receive the following output:

```
[root@server1 ~]# find /etc -name inittab
/etc/inittab
[root@server1 ~]# _
```

You can also use wildcard metacharacters with the find command; however, these wildcards must be protected from shell interpretation, as they must only be interpreted by the find command. To do this, ensure that any wildcard metacharacters are enclosed within quote characters. An example of using the find command with wildcard metacharacters to find all files that start with the letters "host" underneath the /etc directory is shown in the following output:

```
[root@server1 ~]# find /etc -name "host*"
/etc/hosts
/etc/hosts.allow
/etc/host.conf
/etc/selinux/targeted/modules/active/modules/hostname.pp
/etc/avahi/hosts
/etc/hostname
/etc/hosts.deny
[root@server1 ~]# _
```

Although searching by name is the most common criteria used with the find command, many other criteria can be used with the find command as well. To find all files starting from the /var directory that have a size greater than 4096K (kilobytes), you can use the following command:

```
[root@server1 ~]# find /var -size +4096k
/var/lib/rpm/Packages
/var/lib/rpm/Basenames
/var/lib/PackageKit/system.package-list
/var/log/journal/034ec8ccdf4642f7a2493195e11d7df6/user-1000.journal
/var/log/journal/034ec8ccdf4642f7a2493195e11d7df6/user-42.journal
/var/log/journal/034ec8ccdf4642f7a2493195e11d7df6/system.journal
/var/cache/yum/x86_64/20/updates/gen/prestodelta.xml
/var/cache/yum/x86_64/20/updates/gen/primary_db.sqlite
/var/cache/yum/x86_64/20/updates/gen/filelists_db.sqlite
/var/cache/yum/x86_64/20/updates/gen/updateinfo.xml
/var/cache/yum/x86_64/20/updates/gen/other_db.sqlite
/var/cache/dnf/x86_64/20/fedora-filenames.solvx
/var/cache/dnf/x86_64/20/fedora.solv
/var/cache/dnf/x86_64/20/updates-filenames.solvx
/var/tmp/kdecache-user1/plasma_theme_internal-system-colors.kcache
/var/tmp/kdecache-user1/plasma_theme_Heisenbug_v19.90.2.kcache
/var/tmp/kdecache-user1/icon-cache.kcache
[root@server1 ~]# _
```

As well, if you want to find all the directories only underneath the /boot directory, you can type the following command:

```
[root@server1 ~]# find /boot -type d
/boot
/boot/lost+found
/boot/grub2
/boot/grub2/locale
/boot/grub2/themes
/boot/grub2/themes/system
```

```
/boot/grub2/i386-pc
/boot/grub2/fonts
/boot/extlinux
/boot/efi
/boot/efi/EFI
/boot/efi/EFI/BOOT
/boot/efi/EFI/fedora
/boot/efi/EFI/fedora/fonts
/boot/efi/System
/boot/efi/System/Library
/boot/efi/System/Library/CoreServices
[root@server1 ~]# _
```

Table 4-3 provides a list of some common criteria used with the find command.

Although the find command can be used to search for files based on many criteria, it might take several minutes to complete the search if the number of directories and files being searched is large. To reduce the time needed to search, narrow down the directories searched by specifying a subdirectory when possible. It takes less time to search the /usr/local/bin directory and its subdirectories, compared to searching the /usr directory and all of its subdirectories. As well, if the filename that you are searching for is an executable file, that file can likely be found in less time using the **which command**. The which command only searches directories that are listed in a special variable called the **PATH variable** in the current BASH shell. Before exploring the which command, you must understand the usage of PATH.

Executable files can be stored in directories scattered around the directory tree. Recall from FHS that most executable files are stored in directories named bin or sbin, yet there are over 20 bin and sbin directories scattered around the directory tree after a typical Fedora Linux installation. To ensure that users do not need to specify the full pathname to commands such as ls (which is the executable file /usr/bin/ls), there exists a special variable called PATH that is placed into memory each time a user logs in to the Linux system. Recall that you can see the contents of a certain variable in memory by using the $ metacharacter with the echo command:

```
[root@server1 ~]# echo $PATH
/usr/local/sbin:/usr/local/bin:/usr/sbin:/usr/bin:/root/bin
[root@server1 ~]# _
```

The PATH variable lists directories that are searched for executable files if a relative or absolute pathname was not specified when executing a command on the command line. In the preceding output, when a user types the ls command on the command line and presses Enter, the system recognizes that the command was not an absolute pathname (e.g., /usr/bin/ls) or relative pathname (e.g., ../../usr/bin/ls) and then proceeds to look for the ls executable file in the /usr/local/sbin directory, then the /usr/local/bin directory, then the /usr/sbin directory, and so on. If all the directories in the PATH variable are searched and no ls command is found, the shell gives an error message to the user stating that the command was not found. In the preceding output, the /usr/bin directory is in the PATH variable and, thus, the ls command is found and executed, but not until the previous directories in the PATH variable are searched first.

Criteria	Description
-amin -x	Searches for files that were accessed less than *x* minutes ago
-amin +x	Searches for files that were accessed more than *x* minutes ago
-atime -x	Searches for files that were accessed less than *x* days ago
-atime +x	Searches for files that were accessed more than *x* days ago
-empty	Searches for empty files or directories
-fstype x	Searches for files if they are on a certain filesystem *x* (where n could be ext2, ext3, and so on)
-group x	Searches for files that are owned by a certain group or GID (*x*)
-inum x	Searches for files that have an inode number of *x*
-mmin -x	Searches for files that were modified less than *x* minutes ago
-mmin +x	Searches for files that were modified more than *x* minutes ago
-mtime -x	Searches for files that were modified less than *x* days ago
-mtime +x	Searches for files that were modified more than *x* days ago
-name x	Searches for a certain filename *x* (*x* can contain wildcards)
-regex x	Searches for certain filenames using regular expressions instead of wildcard metacharacters
-size -x	Searches for files with a size less than *x*
-size x	Searches for files with a size of *x*
-size +x	Searches for files with a size greater than *x*
-type x	Searches for files of type *x* where *x* is: • b for block files • c for character files • d for directory files • p for named pipes • f for regular files • l for symbolic links (shortcuts) • s for sockets
-user x	Searches for files owned by a certain user or UID (*x*)

Table 4-3 Common criteria used with the `find` command

To search the directories in the PATH variable for the file called "grep," you could use the word "grep" as an argument for the `which` command and receive the following output:

```
[root@server1 ~]# which grep
alias grep='grep --color=auto'
        /usr/bin/grep
[root@server1 ~]# _
```

As shown in the previous output, the `which` command will also list any command aliases for a particular command. In our example, the `grep` command has the path /usr/bin/grep, but it also has an alias that ensures that each time the user runs the `grep` command, it runs it using the `--color=auto` option.

If the file being searched does not exist in the PATH variable directories, the `which` command lets you know in which directories it was not found, as shown in the following output:

```
[root@server1 ~]# which grepper
/usr/bin/which: no grepper in
(/usr/local/sbin:/usr/local/bin:/usr/sbin:/usr/bin:/root/bin)
[root@server1 ~]# _
```

In addition to `locate`, `find`, and `which`, many different commands can be used to search for files on the filesystem. For example, `whereis` is a simpler version of `find`.

Linking Files

Files can be linked to one another in two ways. In a **symbolic link,** or symlink, one file is a pointer, or shortcut, to another file. In a **hard link,** two files share the same data.

To better understand how files are linked, you must understand how files are stored on a filesystem. On a structural level, a filesystem has three main sections: superblock, inode table and data blocks.

The **superblock** is the section that contains information about the filesystem in general, such as the number of inodes and data blocks, as well as how much data a data block stores, in kilobytes. The **inode table** consists of several **inodes** (information nodes); each inode describes one file or directory on the filesystem, and contains a unique inode number for identification. What is more important, the inode stores information such as the file size, data block locations, last date modified, permissions, and ownership. When a file is deleted, only its inode (which serves as a pointer to the actual data) is deleted. The data that makes up the contents of the file as well as the filename are stored in **data blocks,** which are referenced by the inode. In filesystem-neutral terminology, blocks are known as allocation units because they are the unit by which disk space is allocated for storage.

Each file and directory must have an inode. All files except for special device files also have data blocks associated with the inode. Special device files are discussed in Chapter 5.

Recall that directories are simply files that are used to organize other files; they too have an inode and data blocks, but their data blocks contain a list of filenames that are located within the directory.

Hard-linked files share the same inode. As a result, they share the same inode number and data blocks, but the data blocks allow for multiple filenames. Thus, when one hard-linked file is modified, the other hard-linked files are updated as well. This relationship between

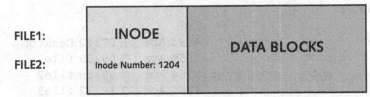

FILE1:

FILE2:

Figure 4-1 The structure of hard-linked files

hard-linked files can be seen in Figure 4-1. You can hard-link a file an unlimited number of times; however, the hard-linked files must reside on the same filesystem.

To create a hard link, you must use the **ln (link) command** and specify two arguments: the existing file to hard-link and the target file that will be created as a hard link to the existing file. Each argument can be the absolute or relative pathname to a file. Take, for example, the following contents of the root user's home directory:

```
[root@server1 ~]# ls -l
total 520
drwx------    3 root     root          4096 Apr  8 07:12 Desktop
-rwxr-xr-x    1 root     root        519964 Apr  7 09:59 file1
-rwxr-xr-x    1 root     root          1244 Apr 27 18:17 file3
[root@server1 ~]# _
```

Suppose you want to make a hard link to file1 and call the new hard link file2, as shown in Figure 4-1. To accomplish this, you issue the command ln file1 file2 at the command prompt; a file called file2 is created and hard-linked to file1. To view the hard-linked file-names after creation, you can use the ls –l command:

```
[root@server1 ~]# ln file1 file2
[root@server1 ~]# ls -l
total 1032
drwx------    3 root     root          4096 Apr  8 07:12 Desktop
-rwxr-xr-x    2 root     root        519964 Apr  7 09:59 file1
-rwxr-xr-x    2 root     root        519964 Apr  7 09:59 file2
-rwxr-xr-x    1 root     root          1244 Apr 27 18:17 file3
[root@server1 ~]# _
```

Notice from the preceding long listing that file1 and file2 share the same inode and data section, as they have the same size, permissions, ownership, modification date, and so on. Also note that the link count (the number after the permission set) for file1 has increased from the number one to the number two in the preceding output. A link count of one indicates that only one inode is shared by the file. A file that is hard-linked to another file shares two inodes and, thus, has a link count of two. Similarly, a file that is hard-linked to three other files shares four inodes and, thus, has a link count of four.

Although hard links share the same inode and data section, deleting a hard-linked file does not delete all the other hard-linked files; it simply removes one filename reference. Removing a hard link can be achieved by removing one of the files, which then lowers the link count.

To view the inode number of hard-linked files to verify that they are identical, you can use the –i option to the ls command in addition to any other options. The inode number is placed on the left of the directory listing on each line, as shown in the following output:

```
[root@server1 ~]# ls -li
total 1032
 37595 drwx------   3 root    root        4096 Apr  8 07:12 Desktop
  1204 -rwxr-xr-x   2 root    root      519964 Apr  7 09:59 file1
  1204 -rwxr-xr-x   2 root    root      519964 Apr  7 09:59 file2
 17440 -rwxr-xr-x   1 root    root        1244 Apr 27 18:17 file3
[root@server1 ~]# _
```

Directory files are not normally hard-linked, as the result would consist of two directories that contain the same contents. However, the root user has the ability to hard-link directories in some cases, using the −F or −d option to the ln command. Only directories that have files regularly added and need to maintain identical file contents are typically hard-linked. For example, on Fedora 20, the /etc/init.d directory is symbolically linked to the /etc/rc.d/init.d directory.

Symbolic links (shown in Figure 4-2) are different from hard links because they do not share the same inode and data blocks with their target file; one is merely a pointer to the other, thus both files have different sizes. The data blocks in a symbolically linked file contain only the pathname to the target file. When a user edits a symbolically linked file, he is actually editing the target file. Thus, if the target file is deleted, the symbolic link serves no function, as it points to a nonexistent file.

Symbolic links are sometimes referred to as "soft links" or "symlinks."

To create a symbolic link, you use the −s option to the ln command. To create a symbolic link to file3 called file4, as in Figure 4-2, you can type ln −s file3 file4 at the command prompt. As with hard links, the arguments specified can be absolute or relative

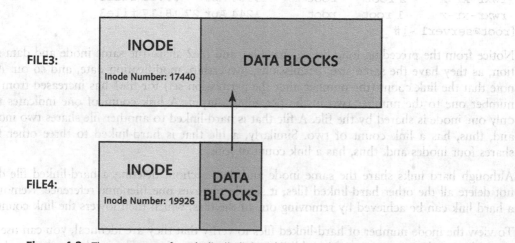

Figure 4-2 The structure of symbolically linked files

pathnames. To view the symbolically linked filenames after creation, you can use the
ls -l command, as shown in the following example:

```
[root@server1 ~]# ln -s file3 file4
[root@server1 ~]# ls -l
total 1032
drwx------  3 root   root     4096 Apr  8 07:12 Desktop
-rwxr-xr-x  2 root   root   519964 Apr  7 09:59 file1
-rwxr-xr-x  2 root   root   519964 Apr  7 09:59 file2
-rwxr-xr-x  1 root   root     1244 Apr 27 18:17 file3
lrwxrwxrwx  1 root   root        5 Apr 27 19:05 file4 -> file3
[root@server1 ~]# _
```

Notice from the preceding output that file4 does not share the same inode, because the permissions, size, and modification date are different from file3. In addition, symbolic links are easier to identify than hard links; the file type character (before the permissions) is l, which indicates a symbolic link, and the filename points to the target using an arrow. The ls -F command also indicates symbolic links by appending an @ symbol, as shown in the following output:

```
[root@server1 ~]# ls -F
Desktop/  file1*  file2*  file3*  file4@
[root@server1 ~]# _
```

Another difference between hard links and symbolic links is that symbolic links need not reside on the same filesystem as their target. Instead, they point to the target filename and do not require the same inode, as shown in the following output:

```
[root@server1 ~]# ls -li
total 1032
37595 drwx------  3 root   root     4096 Apr  8 07:12 Desktop
 1204 -rwxr-xr-x  2 root   root   519964 Apr  7 09:59 file1
 1204 -rwxr-xr-x  2 root   root   519964 Apr  7 09:59 file2
17440 -rwxr-xr-x  1 root   root     1244 Apr 27 18:17 file3
19926 lrwxrwxrwx  1 root   root        5 Apr 27 19:05 file4 -> file3
[root@server1 ~]# _
```

 Unlike hard links, symbolic links are commonly made to directories to simplify navigating the filesystem tree. Also, symbolic links made to directories are typically used to maintain compatibility with other UNIX and Linux systems. For example, on Fedora 20, the /usr/tmp directory is symbolically linked to the /var/tmp directory for this reason.

File and Directory Permissions

Recall that all users must log in with a user name and password to gain access to a Linux system. After logging in, a user is identified by her user name and group memberships; all access to resources depends on whether the user name and group memberships have the required **permission**. Thus, a firm understanding of ownership and permissions is necessary to operate a Linux system in a secure manner and to prevent unauthorized users from having access to sensitive files, directories, and commands.

File and Directory Ownership

When a user creates a file or directory, that user's name and **primary group** become the owner and group owner of the file, respectively. This affects the permission structure, as you see in the next section; however, it also determines who has the ability to modify file and directory permissions and ownership. Only two users on a Linux system can modify permissions on a file or directory or change its ownership: the owner of the file or directory and the root user.

To view your current user name, you can use the whoami command. To view your group memberships and primary group, you can use the groups command. An example of these two commands when logged in as the root user is shown in the following output:

```
[root@server1 ~]# whoami
root
[root@server1 ~]# groups
root bin daemon sys adm disk wheel
[root@server1 ~]# _
```

Notice from the preceding output that the root user is a member of seven groups, yet the root user's primary group is also called "root," as it is the first group mentioned in the output of the group's command.

On Fedora 20, the root user is only a member of one group by default (the "root" group).

If the root user creates a file, the owner is "root" and the group owner is also "root." To quickly create an empty file, you can use the **touch command**:

```
[root@server1 ~]# touch file1
[root@server1 ~]# ls -l
total 4
drwx------   3 root     root         4096 Apr  8 07:12 Desktop
-rw-r--r--   1 root     root            0 Apr 29 15:40 file1
[root@server1 ~]# _
```

Notice from the preceding output that the owner of file1 is "root," and the group owner is the "root" group. To change the ownership of a file or directory, you can use the **chown (change owner) command**, which takes two arguments at minimum: the new owner and the files or directories to change. Both arguments can be absolute or relative pathnames, and you can also change permissions recursively throughout the directory tree using the -R option to the chown command. To change the ownership of file1 to the user user1 and the ownership of the directory Desktop and all of its contents to user1 as well, you can enter the following commands:

```
[root@server1 ~]# chown user1 file1
[root@server1 ~]# chown -R user1 Desktop
[root@server1 ~]# ls -l
total 4
drwx------   3 user1    root   4096 Apr  8 07:12 Desktop
-rw-r--r--   1 user1    root      0 Apr 29 15:40 file1
```

```
[root@server1 ~]# ls -l Desktop
total 16
-rw-------    1 user1    root       163 Mar 29 09:58 Floppy
-rw-r--r--    1 user1    root      3578 Mar 29 09:58 Home
-rw-r--r--    1 user1    root      1791 Mar 29 09:58 Start Here
drwx------    2 user1    root      4096 Mar 29 09:58 Trash
[root@server1 ~]# _
```

Recall that the owner of a file or directory and the root user have the ability to change ownership of a particular file or directory. If a regular user changes the ownership of a file or directory that he owns, that user cannot gain back the ownership. Instead, the new owner of that file or directory must change it to the original user. However, the root user always has the ability to regain the ownership:

```
[root@server1 ~]# chown root file1
[root@server1 ~]# chown -R root Desktop
[root@server1 ~]# ls -l
total 4
drwx------    3 root     root      4096 Apr  8 07:12 Desktop
-rw-r--r--    1 root     root         0 Apr 29 15:40 file1
[root@server1 ~]# ls -l Desktop
total 16
-rw-------    1 root     root       163 Mar 29 09:58 Floppy
-rw-r--r--    1 root     root      3578 Mar 29 09:58 Home
-rw-r--r--    1 root     root      1791 Mar 29 09:58 Start Here
drwx------    2 root     root      4096 Mar 29 09:58 Trash
[root@server1 ~]# _
```

Just as the chown (change owner) command can be used to change the owner of a file or directory, you can use the **chgrp (change group) command** to change the group owner of a file or directory. The chgrp command takes two arguments at minimum: the new group owner and the files or directories to change. As with the chown command, the chgrp command also accepts the –R option to change group ownership recursively throughout the directory tree. To change the group owner of file1 and the Desktop directory recursively throughout the directory tree, you can execute the following commands:

```
[root@server1 ~]# chgrp sys file1
[root@server1 ~]# chgrp -R sys Desktop
[root@server1 ~]# ls -l
total 4
drwx------    3 root     sys       4096 Apr  8 07:12 Desktop
-rw-r--r--    1 root     sys          0 Apr 29 15:40 file1
[root@server1 ~]# ls -l Desktop
total 16
-rw-------    1 root     sys        163 Mar 29 09:58 Floppy
-rw-r--r--    1 root     sys       3578 Mar 29 09:58 Home
-rw-r--r--    1 root     sys       1791 Mar 29 09:58 Start Here
drwx------    2 root     sys       4096 Mar 29 09:58 Trash
[root@server1 ~]# _
```

Regular users can change the group of a file or directory only to a group to which they belong.

Normally, you change both the ownership and group ownership on a file when that file needs to be maintained by someone else. As a result, you can change both the owner and the group owner at the same time using the chown command. To change the owner to user1 and the group owner to root for file1 and the directory Desktop recursively, you can enter the following commands:

```
[root@server1 ~]# chown user1.root file1
[root@server1 ~]# chown -R user1.root Desktop
[root@server1 ~]# ls -l
total 4
drwx------    3 user1    root     4096 Apr  8 07:12 Desktop
-rw-r--r--    1 user1    root        0 Apr 29 15:40 file1
[root@server1 ~]# ls -l Desktop
total 16
-rw-------    1 user1    root      163 Mar 29 09:58 Floppy
-rw-r--r--    1 user1    root     3578 Mar 29 09:58 Home
-rw-r--r--    1 user1    root     1791 Mar 29 09:58 Start Here
drwx------    2 user1    root     4096 Mar 29 09:58 Trash
[root@server1 ~]# _
```

Note that there must be no spaces before and after the . character in the chown commands shown in the preceding output.

You can also use the : character instead of the . character in the chown command to change both the owner and group ownership (e.g., chown -R user1:root Desktop).

To protect your system's security, you should ensure that most files residing in a user's home directory are owned by that user; some files in a user's home directory (especially the hidden files and directories) require this to function properly. To change the ownership back to the root user for file1 and the Desktop directory to avoid future problems, you can type the following:

```
[root@server1 ~]# chown root.root file1
[root@server1 ~]# chown -R root.root Desktop
[root@server1 ~]# ls -l
total 4
drwx------    3 root     root     4096 Apr  8 07:12 Desktop
-rw-r--r--    1 root     root        0 Apr 29 15:40 file1
[root@server1 root]# ls -l Desktop
total 16
-rw-------    1 root     root      163 Mar 29 09:58 Floppy
-rw-r--r--    1 root     root     3578 Mar 29 09:58 Home
```

```
-rw-r--r--    1 root    root    1791 Mar 29 09:58 Start Here
drwx------    2 root    root    4096 Mar 29 09:58 Trash
[root@server1 ~]# _
```

You can override who is allowed to change ownership and permissions using a system setting. Many Linux distributions, including Fedora 20 Linux, use this system setting by default to restrict regular (non-root) users from changing the ownership and group ownership of files and directories. This prevents these users from bypassing disk quota restrictions, which rely on the ownership of files and directories to function properly. Disk quotas are discussed in Chapter 5.

4

Managing File and Directory Permissions

Every file and directory file on a Linux filesystem contains information regarding permissions in its inode. The section of the inode that stores permissions is called the **mode** of the file and is divided into three sections based on the user(s) who receive(s) the permissions to that file or directory:

- User (owner) permissions
- Group (group owner) permissions
- Other (everyone else on the Linux system) permissions

Furthermore, you can assign to each of these users the following regular permissions:

- Read
- Write
- Execute

Interpreting the Mode Recall that the three sections of the mode and the permissions that you can assign to each section are viewed when you perform an ls -l command; a detailed depiction of this is shown in Figure 4-3. It is important to note that the root user supersedes all file and directory permissions; in other words, the root user has all permissions to every file and directory regardless of what the mode of the file or directory indicates.

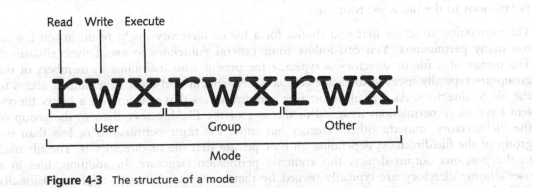

Figure 4-3 The structure of a mode

Consider the root user's home directory listing, shown in the following example:

```
[root@server1 ~]# ls -l
total 28
drwx------   3 root    root    4096 Apr  8 07:12 Desktop
-r---w---x   1 bob     proj     282 Apr 29 22:06 file1
-------rwx   1 root    root     282 Apr 29 22:06 file2
-rwxrwxrwx   1 root    root     282 Apr 29 22:06 file3
----------   1 root    root     282 Apr 29 22:06 file4
-rw-r--r--   1 root    root     282 Apr 29 22:06 file5
-rw-r--r--   1 user1   sys      282 Apr 29 22:06 file6
[root@server1 ~]# _
```

Note from the preceding output that all permissions (as shown in Figure 4-3) need not be on a file or directory; if the permission is unavailable, a dash (the hyphen character on your keyboard, -) replaces its position in the mode. Be certain not to confuse the character to the left of the mode (which determines the file type) with the mode, as it is unrelated to the permissions on the file or directory. From the preceding output, the Desktop directory gives the **user** or **owner** of the directory (the root user) read, write, and execute permission, yet members of the **group** (the root group) do not receive any permissions to the directory. Note that **other** (everyone on the system) does not receive permissions to this directory either.

Permissions are not additive; the system assigns the first set of permissions that are matched in the mode order: user, group, other. Let us assume that the bob user is a member of the proj group. In this case, the file called file1 in the preceding output gives the user or owner of the file (the bob user) read permission, gives members of the group (the proj group) write permission, and gives other (everyone else on the system) execute permission only. Because permissions are not additive, the bob user will only receive read to file1 from the system.

Linux permissions should not be assigned to other only. Although file2 in our example does not give the user or group any permissions, all other users receive read, write, and execute permission via the other category. Thus, file2 should not contain sensitive data because many users have full access to it. For the same reason, it is bad form to assign all permissions to a file that contains sensitive data, as shown with file3 in the preceding example.

On the contrary, it is also possible to have a file that has no permissions assigned to it, as shown in the preceding example with respect to file4. In this case, the only user who has permissions to the file is the root user.

The permission structure that you choose for a file or directory might result in too few or too many permissions. You can follow some general guidelines to avoid these situations. The owner of a file or directory is typically the person who maintains it; members of the group are typically users in the same company department and must have limited access to the file or directory. As a result, most files and directories that you find on a Linux filesystem have more permissions assigned to the user of the file/directory than to the group of the file/directory, and the other category has either the same permissions or less than the group of the file/directory, depending on how private that file or directory is. The file file5 in the previous output depicts this common permission structure. In addition, files in a user's home directory are typically owned by that user; however, you might occasionally find files that are not. For these files, their permission definition changes, as shown in the previous example with respect to file1 and file6. The user or owner of file6 is user1, who has read and write permissions to the file. The group owner of file6 is the sys group; thus, any members of the sys group have read permission to the file. Finally, everyone on the system receives read permission to the file via the other category. Regardless of the mode, the root user receives all permissions to this file.

Interpreting Permissions After you understand how to identify the permissions that are applied to user, group, and other on a certain file or directory, you can then interpret the function of those permissions. Permissions for files are interpreted differently from those for directories. Also, if a user has a certain permission on a directory, that user does not have the same permission for all files or subdirectories within that directory; file and directory permissions are treated separately by the Linux system. Table 4-4 shows a summary of the different permissions and their definitions.

The implications of the permission definitions described in Table 4-4 are important to understand. If a user has the read permission to a text file, that user can use, among others, the cat, more, head, tail, less, strings, and od commands to view its contents. That same user can also open that file with a text editor such as vi; however, the user does not have the ability to save any changes to the document unless that user has the write permission to the file as well.

Recall from earlier that some text files contain instructions for the shell to execute and are called shell scripts. Shell scripts can be executed in much the same way that binary compiled programs are; the user who executes the shell script must then have execute permission to that file to execute it as a program.

It is important to avoid giving execute permission to files that are not programs or shell scripts. This ensures that these files will not be executed accidentally, causing the shell to interpret the contents.

Remember that directories are simply special files that have an inode and a data section but what the data section contains is a list of that directory's contents. If you want to read that list (using the ls command for example), then you require the read permission to the directory. To modify that list, by adding or removing files, you require the write permission to the directory. Thus, if you want to create a new file in a directory with a text editor such as vi, you must have the write permission to that directory. Similarly, when a source file is copied to a target directory with the cp command, a new file is created in the target

Permission	Definition for Files	Definition for Directories
Read	Allows a user to open and read the contents of a file	Allows a user to list the contents of the directory (if she has also been given execute permission)
Write	Allows a user to open, read, and edit the contents of a file	Allows a user to add or remove files to and from the directory (if she has also been given execute permission)
Execute	Allows a user to execute the file in memory (if it is a program file or script)	Allows a user to enter the directory and work with directory contents

Table 4-4 Linux permissions

directory and you must have the write permission to the target directory for the copy to be successful. Conversely, to delete a certain file, you must have the write permission to the directory that contains that file. It is also important to note that a user who has the write permission to a directory has the ability to delete all files and subdirectories within it.

The execute permission on a directory is sometimes referred to as the search permission, and it works similarly to a light switch. When a light switch is turned on, you can navigate a room and use the objects within it. However, when a light switch is turned off, you cannot see the objects in the room, nor can you walk around and view them. A user who does not have the execute permission to a directory is prevented from listing the directory's contents, adding and removing files, and working with files and subdirectories inside that directory, regardless of what permissions the user has to them. In short, a quick way to deny a user from accessing a directory and all of its contents in Linux is to take away the execute permission on that directory. Because the execute permission on a directory is crucial for user access, it is commonly given to all users via the other category, unless the directory must be private.

Changing Permissions To change the permissions for a certain file or directory, you can use the **chmod** (change mode) command. The chmod command takes two arguments at minimum; the first argument specifies the criteria used to change the permissions (Table 4-5), and the remaining arguments indicate the filenames to change.

Take, for example, the directory list used earlier:

```
[root@server1 ~]# ls -l
total 28
drwx------  3 root   root   4096 Apr  8 07:12 Desktop
-r---w---x  1 bob    proj    282 Apr 29 22:06 file1
-------rwx  1 root   root    282 Apr 29 22:06 file2
-rwxrwxrwx  1 root   root    282 Apr 29 22:06 file3
----------  1 root   root    282 Apr 29 22:06 file4
-rw-r--r--  1 root   root    282 Apr 29 22:06 file5
-rw-r--r--  1 user1  sys     282 Apr 29 22:06 file6
[root@server1 ~]# _
```

To change the mode of file1 to rw-r--r--, you must add the write permission to the user of the file, add the read permission and take away the write permission for the group of the file, and add the read permission and take away the execute permission for other.

Category	Operation	Permission
u (user)	+ (adds a permission)	r (read)
g (group)	- (removes a permission)	w (write)
o (other)	= (makes a permission equal to)	x (execute)
a (all categories)		

Table 4-5 Criteria used within the **chmod** command

From the information listed in Table 4-5, you can use the following command:

```
[root@server1 ~]# chmod u+w,g+r-w,o+r-x file1
[root@server1 ~]# ls -l
total 28
drwx------      3 root    root    4096 Apr  8 07:12 Desktop
-rw-r--r--      1 bob     proj     282 Apr 29 22:06 file1
-----r--rwx     1 root    root     282 Apr 29 22:06 file2
-rwxrwxrwx      1 root    root     282 Apr 29 22:06 file3
----------      1 root    root     282 Apr 29 22:06 file4
-rw-r--r--      1 root    root     282 Apr 29 22:06 file5
-rw-r--r--      1 user1   sys      282 Apr 29 22:06 file6
[root@server1 ~]#
```

 You should ensure that there are no spaces between any criteria used in the chmod command because all criteria make up the first argument only.

You can also use the = criteria from Table 4-5 to specify the exact permissions to change. To change the mode on file2 in the preceding output to the same as file1 (rw-r--r--), you can use the following chmod command:

```
[root@server1 ~]# chmod u=rw,g=r,o=r file2
[root@server1 ~]# ls -l
total 28
drwx------      3 root    root    4096 Apr  8 07:12 Desktop
-rw-r--r--      1 bob     proj     282 Apr 29 22:06 file1
-rw-r--r--      1 root    root     282 Apr 29 22:06 file2
-rwxrwxrwx      1 root    root     282 Apr 29 22:06 file3
----------      1 root    root     282 Apr 29 22:06 file4
-rw-r--r--      1 root    root     282 Apr 29 22:06 file5
-rw-r--r--      1 user1   sys      282 Apr 29 22:06 file6
[root@server1 ~]# _
```

If the permissions to be changed are identical for the user, group, and other categories, you can use the "a" character to refer to all categories, as shown in Table 4-5 and in the following example, when adding the execute permission to user, group, and other for file1:

```
[root@server1 ~]# chmod a+x file1
[root@server1 ~]# ls -l
total 28
drwx------      3 root    root    4096 Apr  8 07:12 Desktop
-rwxr-xr-x      1 bob     proj     282 Apr 29 22:06 file1
-rw-r--r--      1 root    root     282 Apr 29 22:06 file2
-rwxrwxrwx      1 root    root     282 Apr 29 22:06 file3
----------      1 root    root     282 Apr 29 22:06 file4
-rw-r--r--      1 root    root     282 Apr 29 22:06 file5
-rw-r--r--      1 user1   sys      282 Apr 29 22:06 file6
[root@server1 ~]# _
```

However, if there is no character specifying the category of user to affect, all users are assumed, as shown in the following example when adding the execute permission to user, group, and other for file2:

```
[root@server1 ~]# chmod +x file2
[root@server1 ~]# ls -l
total 28
drwx------     3 root    root    4096 Apr  8 07:12 Desktop
-rwxr-xr-x     1 bob     proj     282 Apr 29 22:06 file1
-rwxr-xr-x     1 root    root     282 Apr 29 22:06 file2
-rwxrwxrwx     1 root    root     282 Apr 29 22:06 file3
----------     1 root    root     282 Apr 29 22:06 file4
-rw-r--r--     1 root    root     282 Apr 29 22:06 file5
-rw-r--r--     1 user1   sys      282 Apr 29 22:06 file6
[root@server1 ~]# _
```

All of the aforementioned chmod examples use the symbols listed in Table 4-5 as the criteria used to change the permissions on a file or directory. You might instead choose to use numeric criteria with the chmod command to change permissions. All permissions are stored in the inode of a file or directory as binary powers of two:

- read = 2^2 = 4
- write = 2^1 = 2
- execute = 2^0 = 1

Thus, the mode of a file or directory can be represented using the numbers 421421421 instead of rwxrwxrwx. Because permissions are grouped into the categories user, group, and other, you can then simplify this further by using only three numbers, one for each category that represents the sum of the permissions, as depicted in Figure 4-4.

Similarly, to represent the mode rw-r--r--, you can use the numbers 644 because user has read and write (4 + 2 = 6), group has read (4), and other has read (4). The mode rwxr-x--- can also be represented by 750 because user has read, write, and execute (4 + 2 + 1 = 7), group has read and execute (4 + 1 = 5), and other has nothing (0). Table 4-6 provides a list of the different permissions and their corresponding numbers.

To change the mode of the file1 file used earlier to r-xr-----, you can use the command chmod 540 file1, as shown in the following example:

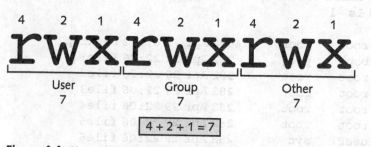

Figure 4-4 Numeric representation of the mode

Mode (One Section Only)	Corresponding Number
rwx	4 + 2 + 1 = 7
rw-	4 + 2 = 6
r-x	4 + 1 = 5
r--	4
-wx	2 + 1 = 3
-w-	2
--x	1
---	0

Table 4-6 Numeric representations of the permissions in a mode

```
[root@server1 ~]# chmod 540 file1
[root@server1 ~]# ls -l
total 28
drwx------    3 root     root     4096 Apr  8 07:12 Desktop
-r-xr-----    1 bob      proj      282 Apr 29 22:06 file1
-rwxr-xr-x    1 root     root      282 Apr 29 22:06 file2
-rwxrwxrwx    1 root     root      282 Apr 29 22:06 file3
----------    1 root     root      282 Apr 29 22:06 file4
-rw-r--r--    1 root     root      282 Apr 29 22:06 file5
-rw-r--r--    1 user1    sys       282 Apr 29 22:06 file6
[root@server1 ~]# _
```

Similarly, to change the mode of all files in the directory that start with the word "file" to 644 (which is common permissions for files), you can use the following command:

```
[root@server1 ~]# chmod 644 file*
[root@server1 ~]# ls -l
total 28
drwx------    3 root     root     4096 Apr  8 07:12 Desktop
-rw-r--r--    1 bob      proj      282 Apr 29 22:06 file1
-rw-r--r--    1 root     root      282 Apr 29 22:06 file2
-rw-r--r--    1 root     root      282 Apr 29 22:06 file3
-rw-r--r--    1 root     root      282 Apr 29 22:06 file4
-rw-r--r--    1 root     root      282 Apr 29 22:06 file5
-rw-r--r--    1 user1    sys       282 Apr 29 22:06 file6
[root@server1 ~]# _
```

Like the chown and chgrp commands, the chmod command can be used to change the permission on a directory and all of its contents recursively by using the −R option, as shown in the following example when changing the mode of the Desktop directory:

```
[root@server1 ~]# chmod -R 755 Desktop
[root@server1 ~]# ls -l
total 28
drwxr-xr-x    3 root     root     4096 Apr  8 07:12 Desktop
```

```
-rw-r--r--    1 bob      proj      282 Apr 29 22:06 file1
-rw-r--r--    1 root     root      282 Apr 29 22:06 file2
-rw-r--r--    1 root     root      282 Apr 29 22:06 file3
-rw-r--r--    1 root     root      282 Apr 29 22:06 file4
-rw-r--r--    1 root     root      282 Apr 29 22:06 file5
-rw-r--r--    1 user1    sys       282 Apr 29 22:06 file6
[root@server1 ~]# ls -l Desktop
total 16
-rwxr-xr-x    1 root     root      163 Mar 29 09:58 Floppy
-rw-r-xr-x    1 root     root     3578 Mar 29 09:58 Home
-rw-r-xr-x    1 root     root     1791 Mar 29 09:58 Start Here
drwxr-xr-x    2 root     root     4096 Mar 29 09:58 Trash
[root@server1 ~]# _
```

Default Permissions

Recall that permissions provide security for files and directories by allowing only certain users access and that there are common guidelines for setting permissions on files and directories so that permissions are not too strict or too permissive. Also important to maintaining security are the permissions that are given to new files and directories after they are created. New files are given rw-rw-rw- by the system when they are created (because execute should not be given unless necessary), and new directories are given rwxrwxrwx by the system when they are created. These default permissions are too permissive for most files, as they allow other full access to directories and nearly full access to files. Hence, a special variable on the system called the **umask** (user mask) takes away permissions on new files and directories immediately after they are created. The most common umask that you will find is 022, which specifies that nothing (0) is taken away from the user, write permission (2) is taken away from members of the group, and write permission (2) is taken away from other on new files and directories when they are first created and given permissions by the system.

Keep in mind that the umask applies only to newly created files and directories; it is never used to modify the permissions of existing files and directories. You must use the chmod command to modify existing permissions.

An example of how a umask of 022 can be used to alter the permissions of a new file or directory after creation is shown in Figure 4-5.

	New Files	New Directories
Permissions assigned by system	rw-rw-rw-	rwxrwxrwx
- umask	0 2 2	0 2 2
= resulting permissions	rw-r--r--	rwxr-xr-x

Figure 4-5   Performing a umask 022 calculation

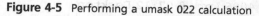

To verify the umask used, you can use the **umask command** and note the final three digits in the output. To ensure that the umask functions as shown in Figure 4-5, simply create a new file using the touch command and a new directory using the mkdir command, as shown in the following output:

```
[root@server1 ~]# ls -l
total 28
drwx------    3 root    root      4096 Apr  8 07:12 Desktop
[root@server1 ~]# umask
0022
[root@server1 ~]# mkdir dir1
[root@server1 ~]# touch file1
[root@server1 ~]# ls -l
total 8
drwx------    3 root    root      4096 Apr  8 07:12 Desktop
drwxr-xr-x    2 root    root      4096 May  3 21:39 dir1
-rw-r--r--    1 root    root         0 May  3 21:40 file1
[root@server1 ~]# _
```

Because the umask is a variable stored in memory, it can be changed. To change the current umask, you can specify the new umask as an argument to the umask command. Suppose, for example, you want to change the umask to 007; the resulting permissions on new files and directories is calculated in Figure 4-6.

To change the umask to 007 and view its effect, you can type the following commands on the command line:

```
[root@server1 ~]# ls -l
total 8
drwx------    3 root    root      4096 Apr  8 07:12 Desktop
drwxr-xr-x    2 root    root      4096 May  3 21:39 dir1
-rw-r--r--    1 root    root         0 May  3 21:40 file1
[root@server1 ~]# umask 007
[root@server1 ~]# umask
0007
[root@server1 ~]# mkdir dir2
[root@server1 ~]# touch file2
```

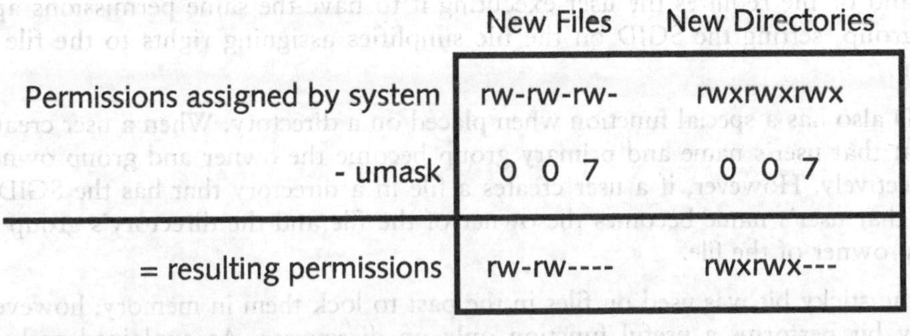

	New Files	New Directories
Permissions assigned by system	rw-rw-rw-	rwxrwxrwx
- umask	0 0 7	0 0 7
= resulting permissions	rw-rw----	rwxrwx---

Figure 4-6 Performing a umask 007 calculation

```
[root@server1 ~]# ls -l
total 12
drwx------   3 root    root    4096 Apr  8 07:12 Desktop
drwxr-xr-x   2 root    root    4096 May  3 21:39 dir1
drwxrwx---   2 root    root    4096 May  3 21:41 dir2
-rw-r--r--   1 root    root       0 May  3 21:40 file1
-rw-rw----   1 root    root       0 May  3 21:41 file2
[root@server1 ~]# _
```

Special Permissions

Read, write, and execute are the regular file permissions that you would use to assign security to files; however, you can optionally use three more special permissions on files and directories:

- SUID (Set User ID)
- SGID (Set Group ID)
- Sticky bit

Defining Special Permissions The SUID has no special function when set on a directory; however, if the SUID is set on a file and that file is executed, the person who executed the file temporarily becomes the owner of the file while it is executing. Many commands on a typical Linux system have this special permission set; the passwd command (/usr/bin/passwd) that is used to change your password is one such file. Because this file is owned by the root user, when a regular user executes the passwd command to change his own password, that user temporarily becomes the root user while the passwd command is executing in memory. This ensures that any user can change his own password since the default setting on Linux systems only allows the root user to change passwords. Furthermore, the SUID can only be applied to binary compiled programs. The Linux kernel does not let you apply the SUID to a shell script because shell scripts are easy to edit and thus pose a security hazard to the system.

Contrary to the SUID, the SGID has a function when applied to both files and directories. Just as the SUID allows regular users to execute a binary compiled program and become the owner of the file for the duration of execution, the SGID allows regular users to execute a binary compiled program and become a member of the group that is attached to the file. Thus, if a file is owned by the group "sys" and also has the SGID permission, any user who executes that file will be a member of the group "sys" during execution. If a command or file requires the user executing it to have the same permissions applied to the sys group, setting the SGID on the file simplifies assigning rights to the file for user execution.

The SGID also has a special function when placed on a directory. When a user creates a file, recall that that user's name and primary group become the owner and group owner of the file, respectively. However, if a user creates a file in a directory that has the SGID permission set, that user's name becomes the owner of the file and the directory's group becomes the group owner of the file.

Finally, the sticky bit was used on files in the past to lock them in memory; however, today the sticky bit performs a useful function only on directories. As explained earlier in this chapter, the write permission applied to a directory allows you to add and remove any file to and from that directory. Thus, if you have the write permission to a certain directory but no permission to files within it, you could delete all of those files. Consider a company that requires a common directory that gives all employees the ability to add files; this directory must give everyone the write permission. Unfortunately, the write permission also gives all employees the ability to delete all files and directories within, including the ones that others have added to the directory. If the sticky bit is applied to this common directory in addition to the write permission, employees can add files to the directory but only delete those files that they have added and not others.

 Note that all special permissions also require the execute permission to work properly; the SUID and SGID work on executable files, and the SGID and sticky bit work on directories (which must have execute permission for access).

Setting Special Permissions The mode of a file that is displayed using the `ls -l` command does not have a section for special permissions. However, because special permissions require execute, they mask the execute permission when displayed using the `ls -l` command, as shown in Figure 4-7.

The system allows you to set special permissions even if the file or directory does not have execute permission. However, the special permissions will not perform their function. If the special permissions are set on a file or directory without execute permissions, then the ineffective special permissions are capitalized as seen in Figure 4-8.

To set the special permissions, you can visualize them to the left of the mode, as shown in Figure 4-9.

Thus, to set all of the special permissions on a certain file or directory, you can use the command `chmod 7777 name`, as indicated from Figure 4-9. However, the SUID and SGID bits are typically set on files. To change the permissions on the file1 file used earlier such that

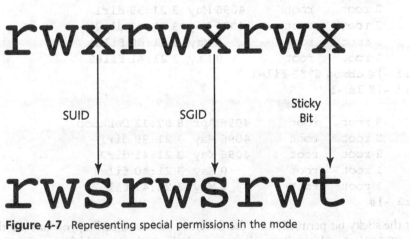

Figure 4-7 Representing special permissions in the mode

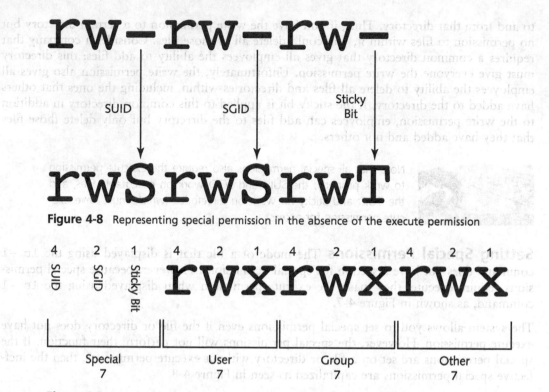

Figure 4-8 Representing special permission in the absence of the execute permission

Figure 4-9 Numeric representation of regular and special permissions

other has the ability to view and execute the file as the owner and a member of the group, you can use the command chmod 6755 file1, as shown in the following example:

```
[root@server1 ~]# ls -l
total 12
drwx------     3 root     root     4096 Apr  8 07:12 Desktop
drwxr-xr-x     2 root     root     4096 May  3 21:39 dir1
drwx------     2 root     root     4096 May  3 21:41 dir2
-rw-r--r--     1 root     root        0 May  3 21:40 file1
-rw-------     1 root     root        0 May  3 21:41 file2
[root@server1 ~]# chmod 6755 file1
[root@server1 ~]# ls -l
total 12
drwx------     3 root     root     4096 Apr  8 07:12 Desktop
drwxr-xr-x     2 root     root     4096 May  3 21:39 dir1
drwx------     2 root     root     4096 May  3 21:41 dir2
-rwsr-sr-x     1 root     root        0 May  3 21:40 file1
-rw-------     1 root     root        0 May  3 21:41 file2
[root@server1 ~]# _
```

Similarly, to set the sticky bit permission on the directory dir1 used earlier, you can use the command chmod 1777 dir1, which allows all users (including other) to add files to the dir1 directory. This is because you gave the write permission; however, users can only delete the files that they own in dir1 because you set the sticky bit. This is shown in the following example:

```
[root@server1 ~]# ls -l
total 12
drwx------    3 root    root    4096 Apr  8 07:12 Desktop
drwxr-xr-x    2 root    root    4096 May  3 21:39 dir1
drwx------    2 root    root    4096 May  3 21:41 dir2
-rwsr-sr-x    1 root    root       0 May  3 21:40 file1
-rw-------    1 root    root       0 May  3 21:41 file2
[root@server1 ~]# chmod 1777 dir1
[root@server1 ~]# ls -l
total 12
drwx------    3 root    root    4096 Apr  8 07:12 Desktop
drwxrwxrwt    2 root    root    4096 May  3 21:39 dir1
drwx------    2 root    root    4096 May  3 21:41 dir2
-rwsr-sr-x    1 root    root       0 May  3 21:40 file1
-rw-------    1 root    root       0 May  3 21:41 file2
[root@server1 ~]# _
```

Also, remember that assigning special permissions without execute renders those permissions useless. For example, you may forget to give execute permission to either user, group, or other, and the long listing covers the execute permission with a special permission. In that case, the special permission is capitalized, as shown in the following example when dir2 is not given execute underneath the position in the mode that indicates the sticky bit (t):

```
[root@server1 ~]# ls -l
total 12
drwx------    3 root    root    4096 Apr  8 07:12 Desktop
drwxrwxrwt    2 root    root    4096 May  3 21:39 dir1
drwx------    2 root    root    4096 May  3 21:41 dir2
-rwsr-sr-x    1 root    root       0 May  3 21:40 file1
-rw-------    1 root    root       0 May  3 21:41 file2
[root@server1 ~]# chmod 1770 dir2
[root@server1 ~]# ls -l
total 12
drwx------    3 root    root    4096 Apr  8 07:12 Desktop
drwxrwxrwt    2 root    root    4096 May  3 21:39 dir1
drwxrwx--T    2 root    root    4096 May  3 21:41 dir2
-rwsr-sr-x    1 root    root       0 May  3 21:40 file1
-rw-------    1 root    root       0 May  3 21:41 file2
[root@server1 ~]# _
```

Setting Custom Permissions in the Access Control List (ACL)

An access control list (ACL) is a list of users or groups that you can assign permissions to. As discussed earlier, the default ACL used in Linux consists of three entities: user, group, and other. However, there may be situations where you need to assign a specific set of permissions on a file or directory to an individual user or group.

Take, for example, the file doc1:

```
[root@server1 ~]# ls -l doc1
-rw-rw----    1 user1    acctg        0 May  2 22:01 doc1
[root@server1 ~]# _
```

The owner of the file (user1) has read and write permission, the group (acctg) has read and write permission, and everyone else has no access to the file.

Now imagine that you need to give read permission to the bob user without giving permissions to anyone else. The solution to this problem is to modify the ACL on the doc1 file and add a special entry for bob only. This can be accomplished by using the following **setfacl** (set file ACL) command:

```
[root@server1 ~]# setfacl -m u:bob:r-- doc1
[root@server1 ~]# _
```

The –m option in the command above modifies the ACL, and you can use g instead of u to add an additional group to the ACL.

Now, when you perform a long listing of the file doc1, you will see a + symbol next to the mode to indicate that there are additional entries in the ACL for this file. To see these additional members, simply use the **getfacl** (get file ACL) command:

```
[root@server1 ~]# ls -l doc1
-rw-rw----+   1 user1    acctg        0 May  2 22:01 doc1
[root@server1 ~]# getfacl doc1
# file: doc1
# owner: user1
# group: acctg
user::rw-
user:bob:r--
group::rw-
mask::rw-
other::---
[root@server1 ~]# _
```

After running the getfacl command, you will notice an extra node in the output: the mask. The mask is compared to all additional user and group permissions in the ACL. If the mask is more restrictive, it takes precedence when it comes to permissions. For example, if the mask is set to r-- and the user bob has rw-, then the user bob actually gets r-- to the file. When you run the setfacl command, the mask is always made equal to the least restrictive permission assigned so that it does not affect additional ACL entries. The mask was created as a mechanism that could easily revoke permissions on a file that had several additional users and groups added to the ACL.

To remove all extra ACL assignments on the doc1 file, simply use the –b option to the setfacl command:

```
[root@server1 ~]# setfacl -b doc1
[root@server1 ~]# ls -l doc1
-rw-rw----    1 user1    acctg        0 May  2 22:01 doc1
[root@server1 ~]# _
```

Managing Filesystem Attributes

As with the Windows operating system, Linux has file attributes that can be set, if necessary. These attributes work outside Linux permissions and are filesystem-specific. In this section, we'll examine attributes for the ext4 filesystem that you configured earlier during Lab 2.1. Filesystem types will be discussed in more depth in Chapter 5.

To see the filesystem attributes that are currently assigned to a file, you can use the `lsattr` (list attributes) command, as shown here for the doc1 file:

```
[root@server1 ~]# lsattr doc1
-------------e-- doc1
[root@server1 ~]# _
```

By default, all files have the **e** attribute, which writes to the file in "extent" blocks (rather than immediately in a byte-by-byte fashion). If you would like to add or remove attributes, you can use the `chattr` (change attributes) command. The following example assigns the immutable attribute (`i`) to the doc1 file and displays the results:

```
[root@server1 ~]# chattr +i doc1
[root@server1 ~]# lsattr doc1
----i--------e-- doc1
[root@server1 ~]# _
```

The immutable attribute is the most commonly used filesystem attribute and prevents the file from being modified in any way. Since attributes are applied at a filesystem level, not even the root user can modify a file that has the immutable attribute set.

Most filesystem attributes are rarely set, as they provide for low-level filesystem functionality. To view a full listing of filesystem attributes, visit the manual page for the `chattr` command.

Similarly, to remove an attribute, simply use the `chattr` command with the – option, as shown here with the doc1 file:

```
[root@server1 ~]# chattr -i doc1
[root@server1 ~]# lsattr doc1
-------------e-- doc1
[root@server1 ~]# _
```

Chapter Summary

- The Linux directory tree obeys the Filesystem Hierarchy Standard, which allows Linux users and developers to locate system files in standard directories.

- Many file management commands exist to create, change the location of, or remove files and directories. The most common of these include `cp`, `mv`, `rm`, `rmdir`, and `mkdir`.

- You can find files on the filesystem using a preindexed database (the `locate` command) or by the searching directories listed in the PATH variable (the `which` command). However, the most versatile command used to find files is the `find` command, which searches for files based on a wide range of criteria.

- Files can be linked two different ways. In a symbolic link, one file serves as a pointer to another file. In a hard link, one file is a linked duplicate of another file.

- Each file and directory has an owner and a group owner. In the absence of system restrictions, the owner of the file or directory has the ability to change permissions and give ownership to others.

- Permissions can be set on the user or owner of a file, members of the group of the file, as well as everyone on the system (other).

- There are three regular file and directory permissions (read, write, execute) and three special file and directory permissions (SUID, SGID, sticky bit). The definitions of these permissions are different for files and directories.

- Permissions can be changed using the chmod command by specifying symbols or numbers to represent the changed permissions.

- To ensure security, new files and directories receive default permissions from the system, less the value of the umask variable.

- The root user has all permissions to all files and directories on the Linux filesystem. Similarly, the root user can change the ownership of any file or directory on the Linux filesystem.

- The default ACL on a file or directory can be modified to include additional users or groups.

- Filesystem attributes can be set on Linux files to provide low-level functionality such as immutability.

Key Terms

access control list (ACL)   The section within an inode of a file or directory that lists the permissions assigned to users and groups on the file or directory.

chattr (change attributes) command   The command used to change filesystem attributes for a Linux file.

chgrp (change group) command   The command used to change the group owner of a file or directory.

chmod (change mode) command   The command used to change the mode (permissions) of a file or directory.

chown (change owner) command   The command used to change the owner and group owner of a file or directory.

cp (copy) command   The command used to create copies of files and directories.

data blocks   A filesystem allocation unit in which the data that makes up the contents of the file as well as the filename are stored.

Filesystem Hierarchy Standard (FHS)   A standard outlining the location of set files and directories on a Linux system.

find command   The command used to find files on the filesystem using various criteria.

getfacl (get file ACL) command   The command used to list all ACL entries for a particular Linux file or directory.

group   When used in the mode of a certain file or directory, the collection of users who have ownership of that file or directory.

hard link   A file joined to other files on the same filesystem that shares the same inode.

inode   The portion of a file that stores information on the file's attributes, access permissions, location, ownership, and file type.

inode table   The collection of inodes for all files and directories on a filesystem.

interactive mode   The mode that file management commands use when a file can be overwritten; the system interacts with a user asking for the user to confirm the action.

ln (link) command   The command used to create hard and symbolic links.

locate command   The command used to locate files from a file database.

lsattr (list attributes) command   The command used to list filesystem attributes for a Linux file.

mkdir (make directory) command   The command used to create directories.

mode   The part of the inode that stores information on access permissions.

mv (move) command   The command used to move/rename files and directories.

other   When used in the mode of a certain file or directory, all the users on the Linux system.

owner   The user whose name appears in a long listing of a file or directory and who has the ability to change permissions on that file or directory.

PATH variable   A variable that stores a list of directories that will be searched in order when commands are executed without an absolute or relative pathname.

permissions   A list that identifies who can access a file or folder and their level of access.

primary group   The default group to which a user belongs.

recursive   A term referring to itself and its own contents; a recursive search includes all subdirectories in a directory and their contents.

rm (remove) command   The command used to remove files and directories.

rmdir (remove directory) command   The command used to remove empty directories.

setfacl (set file ACL) command   The command used to modify ACL entries for a particular Linux file or directory.

source file/directory   The portion of a command that refers to the file or directory from which information is taken.

superblock   The portion of a filesystem that stores critical information, such as the inode table and block size.

symbolic link   A pointer to another file on the same or another filesystem; commonly referred to as a shortcut.

target file/directory   The portion of a command that refers to the file or directory to which information is directed.

touch command   The command used to create new files. It was originally used to update the time stamp on a file.

umask   A special variable used to alter the permissions on all new files and directories by taking away select default file and directory permissions.

umask command   The command used to view and change the umask variable.

user   When used in the mode of a certain file or directory, the owner of that file or directory.

which command   The command used to locate files that exist within directories listed in the PATH variable.

Review Questions

1. A symbolic link is also known as a soft link and is depicted by an @ symbol appearing at the beginning of the filename when viewed using the `ls -l` command. True or False?

2. What was created to define a standard directory structure and common file location for Linux?

   a. FSH

   b. X.500

   c. FHS

   d. root directory

3. There is no real difference between the "S" and "s" special permissions when displayed using the `ls -l` command. One just means it is on a file, and the other means that it is on a directory. True or False?

4. The default permissions given by the system prior to analyzing the umask are _____ for directories and _____ for files.

   a. rw-rw-rw- and rw-rw-rw-

   b. rw-rw-rw- and r--r--r--

   c. rw-rw-rw- and rwxrwxrwx

   d. rwxrwxrwx and rw-rw-rw-

   e. rwxrw-rw- and rwx-rw-rw-

5. What must a user do to run cp or mv interactively and be asked if she wants to overwrite an existing file?

   a. There is no choice because the new file will overwrite the old one by default.

   b. Type `interactive cp` or `interactive mv`.

   c. Type `cp -i` or `mv -i`.

   d. Type `cp -interactive` or `mv -interactive`.

   e. Just type cp or mv because they run in interactive mode by default.

6. The root user utilizes the chgrp command to give ownership of a file to another user. What must the root user do to regain ownership of the file?

   a. Run chgrp again listing the root user as the new owner.

   b. Nothing, because this is a one-way, one-time action.

   c. Have the new owner run chgrp, and list the root user as the new owner.

   d. Run chown and list the root user as the new owner.

7. After typing the `ls -F` command, you see the following line in the output:

   -rw-r-xr--   1 user1   root   0 Apr 29 15:40 file1

   What does this mean?

   a. User1 has read and write, members of the root group have read and execute, and all others have read permissions to the file.

   b. Members of the root group have read and write, user1 has read and execute, and all others have read permissions to the file.

   c. All users have read and write, members of the root group have read and execute, and user1 has read permissions to the file.

   d. User1 has read and write, all others have read and execute, and members of the root group have read permissions to the file.

8. After typing the command `umask 731`, the permissions on all subsequently created files and directories will be affected. In this case, what will be the permissions on all new files?

   a. rw-rw-rw-

   b. rwxrw-r--

   c. ---r--rw-

   d. ----wx--x

9. You noticed a file in your home directory that has a + symbol appended to the mode. What does this indicate?

   a. Special permissions have been set on the file.

   b. The file has one or more files on the filesystem that are hard linked to it.

   c. The sticky bit directory permission has been set on the file and will remain inactive as a result.

   d. Additional entries exist within the ACL of the file that can be viewed using the `getfacl` command.

10. When you change the data in a file that is hard-linked to three others, _____.

    a. only the data in the file you modified is affected

    b. only the data in the file you modified and any hard-linked files in the same directory are affected

    c. the data in the file you modified and the data in all hard-linked files are modified because they have different inodes

    d. the data in the file you modified as well as the data in all hard-linked files are modified because they share the same data and all have the same inode and file size

11. The command chmod 317 file1 would produce which of the following lines in the
    ls command?

    a. --w-r--rwx 1 user1 root 0 Apr 29 15:40 file1

    b. --wx--xrwx 1 user1 root 0 Apr 29 15:40 file1

    c. -rwxrw-r-x 1 user1 root 0 Apr 29 15:40 file1

    d. --w-rw-r-e 1 user1 root 0 Apr 29 15:40 file1

12. Which of the following commands will change the user ownership and group ownership
    of *file1* to user1 and root, respectively?

    a. chown user1:root file1

    b. chown user1 : root file1

    c. This cannot be done because user and group ownership properties of a file must be
       modified separately.

    d. chown root:user1file1

    e. chown root : user1file1

13. What does the /var directory contain?

    a. various additional programs

    b. spools and log files

    c. temporary files

    d. files that are architecture-independent

    e. local variance devices

14. What does the mv command do? (Choose all that apply.)

    a. It makes a volume.

    b. It makes a directory.

    c. It moves a directory.

    d. It moves a file.

15. A file has the following permissions: *r----x-w-*. The command chmod 143 would have
    the same effect as the command _____. (Choose all that apply.)

    a. chmod u+x-r,g+r-x,o+w file1

    b. chmod u=w,g=rw,o=rx file1

    c. chmod u-r-w,g+r-w,o+r-x file1

    d. chmod u=x,g=r,o=wx file1

    e. chmod u+w,g+r-w,o+r-x file1

    f. chmod u=rw,g=r,o=r file1

16. The which command _____.

    a. can only be used to search for executables

    b. searches for a file in all directories, starting from the root

    c. is not a valid Linux command

    d. searches for a file only in directories that are in the PATH variable

17. Hard links need to reside on the same filesystem as the target, whereas symbolic links need not be on the same filesystem as the target. True or False?

18. When applied to a directory, the SGID special permission _____.

    a. causes all new files created in the directory to have the same group membership as the directory, and not the entity that created them

    b. cannot be used, because it is applied only to files

    c. allows users the ability to use more than two groups for files that they create within the directory

    d. causes users to have their permissions checked before they are allowed to access files in the directory

19. Which command do you use to rename files and directories?

    a. cp

    b. mv

    c. rn

    d. rename

20. What are the three standard Linux permissions?

    a. full control, read-execute, write

    b. read, write, modify

    c. execute, read, write

    d. read, write, examine

21. Given the following output from the ls command, how many files are linked with file1?

    ```
    drwxr-xr-x    3 root    root    4096 Apr  8 07:12 Desktop
    -rw-r--r--    3 root    root     282 Apr 29 22:06 file1
    -rw-r--r--    1 root    root     282 Apr 29 22:06 file2
    -rw-r--r--    4 root    root     282 Apr 29 22:06 file3
    -rw-r--r--    2 root    root     282 Apr 29 22:06 file4
    -rw-r--r--    1 root    root     282 Apr 29 22:06 file5
    -rw-r--r--    1 user1   sys      282 Apr 29 22:06 file6
    ```

    a. one

    b. two

    c. three

    d. four

22. Only the root user can modify a file that has the immutable attribute set. True or False?

Hands-on Projects

These projects should be completed in the order given. The hands-on projects presented in this chapter should take a total of three hours to complete. The requirements for this lab include:

- A computer with Fedora 20 installed according to Hands-on Project 2-1
- Completion of all Hands-on Projects in Chapter 3

Project 4-1

In this hands-on project, you log in to the computer and create new directories.

1. Boot your Fedora Linux virtual machine. After your Linux system has loaded, switch to a command-line terminal (tty2) by pressing **Ctrl+Alt+F2**. Log in to the terminal using the user name of **root** and the password of **LNXrocks!**.

2. At the command prompt, type **ls -F** and press **Enter**. Note the contents of your home folder.

3. At the command prompt, type **mkdir mysamples** and press **Enter**. Next type **ls -F** at the command prompt, and press **Enter**. How many files and subdirectories are there? Why?

4. At the command prompt, type **cd mysamples** and press **Enter**. Next, type **ls -F** at the command prompt and press **Enter**. What are the contents of the subdirectory mysamples?

5. At the command prompt, type **mkdir undermysamples** and press **Enter**. Next, type **ls -F** at the command prompt and press **Enter**. What are the contents of the subdirectory mysamples?

6. At the command prompt, type **mkdir todelete** and press **Enter**. Next, type **ls -F** at the command prompt and press **Enter**. Does the subdirectory todelete you just created appear listed in the display?

7. At the command prompt, type **cd ..** and press **Enter**. Next, type **ls -R** and press **Enter**. Notice that the subdirectory mysamples and its subdirectory undermysamples are both displayed. You have used the recursive option with the **ls** command.

8. At the command prompt, type **cd ..** and press **Enter**. At the command prompt, type **pwd** and press **Enter**. What is your current directory?

9. At the command prompt, type **mkdir foruser1** and press **Enter**. At the command prompt, type **ls -F** and press **Enter**. Does the subdirectory you just created appear listed in the display?

10. Type **exit** and press **Enter** to log out of your shell.

Project 4-2

In this hands-on project, you copy files using the **cp** command.

1. Switch to a command-line terminal (tty2) by pressing **Ctrl+Alt+F2** and log in to the terminal using the user name of **root** and the password of **LNXrocks!**.

2. Next, type **ls -F** at the command prompt and press **Enter**. Note the contents of your home folder.

3. At the command prompt, type **cp sample1** and press **Enter**. What error message was displayed and why?

4. At the command prompt, type **cp sample1 sample1A** and press Enter. Next, type **ls -F** at the command prompt and press Enter. How many files are there, and what are their names? Why?

5. At the command prompt, type **cp sample1 mysamples/sample1B** and press Enter. Next, type **ls -F** at the command prompt and press Enter. How many files are there, and what are their names? Why?

6. At the command prompt, type **cd mysamples** and press Enter. Next, type **ls -F** at the command prompt and press Enter. Was sample1B copied successfully?

7. At the command prompt, type **cp /root/sample2 .** and press Enter. Next, type **ls -F** at the command prompt and press Enter. How many files are there, and what are their names? Why?

8. At the command prompt, type **cp sample1B ..** and press Enter. Next, type **cd ..** at the command prompt and press Enter. At the command prompt, type **ls -F** and press Enter. Was the sample1B file copied successfully?

9. At the command prompt, type **cp sample1 sample2 sample3 mysamples** and press Enter. What message do you get and why? Choose y and press Enter. Next, type **cd mysamples** at the command prompt and press Enter. At the command prompt, type **ls -F** and press Enter. How many files are there, and what are their names? Why?

10. At the command prompt, type **cd ..** and press Enter. Next, type **cp mysamples mysamples2** at the command prompt and press Enter. What error message did you receive? Why?

11. At the command prompt, type **cp –R mysamples mysamples2** and press Enter. Next, type **ls -F** at the command prompt, and press Enter. Was the directory copied successfully? Type **ls –F mysamples2** at the command prompt and press Enter. Were the contents of mysamples successfully copied to mysamples2?

12. Type **exit** and press Enter to log out of your shell.

Project 4-3

In this hands-on project, you use the **mv** command to rename files and directories.

1. Switch to a command-line terminal (tty2) by pressing **Ctrl+Alt+F2** and log in to the terminal using the user name of **root** and the password of **LNXrocks!**.

2. Next, type **ls -F** at the command prompt and press Enter. Note the contents of your home folder.

3. At the command prompt, type **mv sample1** and press Enter. What error message was displayed and why?

4. At the command prompt, type **mv sample1 sample4** and press Enter. Next, type **ls -F** at the command prompt and press Enter. How many files are listed and what are their names? What happened to sample1?

5. At the command prompt, type **mv sample4 mysamples** and press Enter. Next, type **ls -F** at the command prompt and press Enter. How many files are there, and what are their names? Where did sample4 go?

6. At the command prompt, type **cd mysamples** and press **Enter**. Next, type **ls -F** at the command prompt and press **Enter**. Notice that the sample4 file you moved in Step 5 was moved here.

7. At the command prompt, type **mv sample4 ..** and press **Enter**. Next, type **ls -F** at the command prompt and press **Enter**. How many files are there, and what are their names? Where did the sample4 file go?

8. At the command prompt, type **cd ..** and press **Enter**. Next, type **ls -F** at the command prompt and press **Enter** to view the new location of sample4.

9. At the command prompt, type **mv sample4 mysamples/sample2** and press **Enter**. What message appeared on the screen and why?

10. Type **y** and press **Enter** to confirm you want to overwrite the file in the destination folder.

11. At the command prompt, type **mv sample? mysamples** and press **Enter**. Type y and press **Enter** to confirm you want to overwrite the file sample3 in the destination folder.

12. At the command prompt, type **ls -F** and press **Enter**. How many files are there and why?

13. At the command prompt, type **mv sample1* mysamples** and press **Enter**. Type **y** and press **Enter** to confirm you want to overwrite the file sample1B in the destination directory.

14. At the command prompt, type **ls -F** and press **Enter**. Notice that there are no sample files in the /root directory.

15. At the command prompt, type **cd mysamples** and press **Enter**. Next, type **ls -F** at the command prompt and press **Enter**. Notice that all files originally in /root have been moved to this directory.

16. At the command prompt, type **cd ..** and press **Enter**. Next, type **ls -F** at the command prompt and press **Enter**. Type **mv mysamples samples** and press **Enter**. Next, type **ls -F** at the command prompt and press **Enter**. Why did you not need to specify the recursive option to the **mv** command to rename the mysamples directory to samples?

17. Type **exit** and press **Enter** to log out of your shell.

Project 4-4

In this hands-on project, you make and view links to files and directories.

1. Switch to a command-line terminal (tty2) by pressing **Ctrl+Alt+F2** and log in to the terminal using the user name of **root** and the password of **LNXrocks!**.

2. At the command prompt, type **cd samples** and press **Enter**. Next, type **ls -F** at the command prompt and press **Enter**. What files do you see? Next, type **ls -l** at the command prompt and press **Enter**. What is the link count for the sample1 file?

3. At the command prompt, type **ln sample1 hardlinksample** and press **Enter**. Next, type **ls -F** at the command prompt and press **Enter**. Does anything in the terminal output indicate that sample1 and hardlinksample are hard-linked? Next, type **ls -l** at the command prompt and press **Enter**. Does anything in the terminal output indicate that sample1 and hardlinksample are hard-linked? What is the link count for sample1 and hardlinksample? Next, type **ls -li** at the command prompt and press **Enter** to view the inode numbers of each file. Do the two hard-linked files have the same inode number?

4. At the command prompt, type **ln sample1 hardlinksample2** and press **Enter**. Next, type **ls -l** at the command prompt and press **Enter**. What is the link count for the files sample1, hardlinksample, and hardlinksample2? Why?

5. At the command prompt, type **vi sample1** and press **Enter**. Enter a sentence of your choice into the vi editor, and then save your document and quit the vi editor.

6. At the command prompt, type **cat sample1** and press **Enter**. Next, type **cat hardlinksample** at the command prompt and press **Enter**. Next, type **cat hardlinksample2** at the command prompt and press **Enter**. Are the contents of each file the same? Why?

7. At the command prompt, type **ln –s sample2 symlinksample** and press **Enter**. Next, type **ls -F** at the command prompt and press **Enter**. Does anything in the terminal output indicate that sample2 and symlinksample are symbolically linked? Which file is the target file? Next, type **ls -l** at the command prompt and press **Enter**. Does anything in the terminal output indicate that sample2 and symlinksample are symbolically linked? Next, type **ls -li** at the command prompt and press **Enter** to view the inode numbers of each file. Do the two symbolically linked files have the same inode number?

8. At the command prompt, type **vi symlinksample** and press **Enter**. Enter a sentence of your choice into the vi editor, and then save your document and quit the vi editor.

9. At the command prompt, type **ls -l** and press **Enter**. What is the size of the symlinksample file compared to sample2? Why? Next, type **cat sample2** at the command prompt and press **Enter**. What are the contents and why?

10. At the command prompt, type **ln –s /etc/sysconfig/network-scripts netscripts** and press **Enter**. Next, type **ls -F** at the command prompt and press **Enter**. What file type is indicated for netscripts? Next, type **cd netscripts** at the command prompt and press **Enter**. Type **pwd** at the command prompt and press **Enter** to view your current directory. What is your current directory? Next, type **ls -F** at the command prompt and press **Enter**. What files are listed? Next, type **ls -F /etc/sysconfig/network-scripts** at the command prompt and press **Enter**.

    Note that your netscripts directory is merely a pointer to the /etc/sysconfig/network-scripts directory. How can this type of linking be useful?

11. Type **exit** and press **Enter** to log out of your shell.

Project 4-5

In this hands-on project, you find files on the filesystem using the **find**, **locate**, and **which** commands.

1. Switch to a command-line terminal (tty2) by pressing **Ctrl+Alt+F2** and log in to the terminal using the user name of **root** and the password of **LNXrocks!**.

2. At the command prompt, type **touch newfile** and press **Enter**. Next, type **locate newfile** at the command prompt and press **Enter**. Did the **locate** command find the file? Why?

3. At the command prompt, type **updatedb** and press **Enter**. When the command is finished, type **locate newfile** at the command prompt and press **Enter**. Did the **locate** command find the file? If so, how quickly did it find it? Why?

4. At the command prompt, type **find / -name "newfile"** and press **Enter**. Did the **find** command find the file? If so, how quickly did it find it? Why?

5. At the command prompt, type **find /root -name "newfile"** and press **Enter**. Did the **find** command find the file? How quickly did it find it? Why?

6. At the command prompt, type **which newfile** and press **Enter**. Did the **which** command find the file? Why? Type **echo $PATH** at the command prompt and press **Enter**. Is the /root directory listed in the PATH variable? Is the /bin directory listed in the PATH variable?

7. At the command prompt, type **which grep** and press **Enter**. Did the **which** command find the file? Why?

8. At the command prompt, type **find /root –name "sample"** and press **Enter**. What files are listed? Why?

9. At the command prompt, type **find /root –type l** and press **Enter**. What files are listed? Why?

10. At the command prompt, type **find /root –size 0** and press **Enter**. What types of files are listed? Type **find /root –size 0 | more** to see all of the files listed.

11. Type **exit** and press **Enter** to log out of your shell.

Project 4-6

In this hands-on project, you delete files and directories using the **rmdir** and **rm** commands.

1. Switch to a command-line terminal (tty2) by pressing **Ctrl+Alt+F2** and log in to the terminal using the user name of **root** and the password of **LNXrocks!**.

2. At the command prompt, type **cd samples** and press **Enter**. At the command prompt, type **ls -R** and press **Enter**. Note the two empty directories todelete and undermysamples.

3. At the command prompt, type **rmdir undermysamples todelete** and press **Enter**. Did the command work? Why? Next, type **ls -F** at the command prompt and press **Enter**. Were both directories deleted successfully?

4. At the command prompt, type **rm sample1*** and press **Enter**. What message is displayed? Answer **n** to all three questions.

5. At the command prompt, type **rm –f sample1*** and press **Enter**. Why were you not prompted to continue? Next, type **ls -F** at the command prompt and press **Enter**. Were all three files deleted successfully?

6. At the command prompt, type **cd ..** and press **Enter**. Next, type **rmdir samples** at the command prompt and press **Enter**. What error message do you receive and why?

7. At the command prompt, type **rm -Rf samples** and press **Enter**. Next, type **ls –F** at the command prompt and press **Enter**. Was the samples directory and all files within it deleted successfully?

8. Type **exit** and press **Enter** to log out of your shell.

Project 4-7

In this hands-on project, you apply and modify access permissions on files and directories and test their effects.

1. Switch to a command-line terminal (tty2) by pressing **Ctrl+Alt+F2** and log in to the terminal using the user name of **root** and the password of **LNXrocks!**.

2. At the command prompt, type **touch permsample** and press **Enter**. Next, type **chmod 777 permsample** at the command prompt and press **Enter**.

3. At the command prompt, type **ls -l** and press **Enter**. Who has permissions to this file?

4. At the command prompt, type **chmod 000 permsample** and press **Enter**. Next, type **ls -l** at the command prompt and press **Enter**. Who has permissions to this file?

5. At the command prompt, type **rm -f permsample** and press **Enter**. Were you able to delete this file? Why?

6. At the command prompt, type **cd /** and press **Enter**. Next, type **pwd** at the command prompt and press **Enter**. What directory are you in? Type **ls -F** at the command prompt and press **Enter**. What directories do you see?

7. At the command prompt, type **ls -l** and press **Enter** to view the owner, group owner, and permissions on the foruser1 directory created in Hands-on Project 5-1. Who is the owner and group owner? If you were logged in as the user user1, in which category would you be placed (user, group, other)? What permissions do you have as this category (read, write, execute)?

8. At the command prompt, type **cd /foruser1** and press **Enter** to enter the foruser1 directory. Next, type **ls -F** at the command prompt and press **Enter**. Are there any files in this directory? Type **cp /etc/hosts .** at the command prompt and press **Enter**. Next, type **ls -F** at the command prompt and press **Enter** to ensure that a copy of the hosts file was made in your current directory.

9. Switch to a different command-line terminal (tty3) by pressing **Ctrl+Alt+F3** and log in to the terminal using the user name of **user1** and the password of **LNXrocks!**.

10. At the command prompt, type **cd /foruser1** and press **Enter**. Were you successful? Why? Next, type **ls -F** at the command prompt and press **Enter**. Were you able to see the contents of the directory? Why? Next, type **rm -f hosts** at the command prompt and press **Enter**. What error message did you see? Why?

11. Switch back to your previous command-line terminal (tty2) by pressing **Ctrl+Alt+F2**. Note that you are logged in as the root user on this terminal.

12. At the command prompt, type **chmod o+w /foruser1** and press **Enter**. Were you able to change the permissions on the /foruser1 directory successfully? Why?

13. Switch back to your previous command-line terminal (tty3) by pressing **Ctrl+Alt+F3**. Note that you are logged in as the user1 user on this terminal.

14. At the command prompt, type **cd /foruser1** and press **Enter**. Next, type **rm -f hosts** at the command prompt and press **Enter**. Were you successful now? Why?

15. Switch back to your previous command-line terminal (tty2) by pressing **Ctrl+Alt+F2**. Note that you are logged in as the root user on this terminal.

16. At the command prompt, type **cd /foruser1** and press **Enter** to enter the foruser1 directory. Type **cp /etc/hosts .** at the command prompt and press **Enter** to place another copy of the hosts file in your current directory.

17. At the command prompt, type **ls -l** and press **Enter**. Who is the owner and group owner of this file? If you were logged in as the user user1, in which category would you be placed (user, group, other)? What permissions do you have as this category (read, write, execute)?

18. Switch back to your previous command-line terminal (tty3) by pressing **Ctrl+Alt+F3**. Note that you are logged in as the user1 user on this terminal.

19. At the command prompt, type **cd /foruser1** and press **Enter** to enter the foruser1 directory. Type **cat hosts** at the command prompt and press **Enter**. Were you successful? Why? Next, type **vi hosts** at the command prompt to open the hosts file in the vi editor. Delete the first line of this file and save your changes. Were you successful? Why? Exit the vi editor and discard your changes.

20. Switch back to your previous command-line terminal (tty2) by pressing **Ctrl+Alt+F2**. Note that you are logged in as the root user on this terminal.

21. At the command prompt, type **chmod o+w /foruser1/hosts** and press Enter.

22. Switch back to your previous command-line terminal (tty3) by pressing **Ctrl+Alt+F3**. Note that you are logged in as the user1 user on this terminal.

23. At the command prompt, type **cd /foruser1** and press **Enter** to enter the foruser1 directory. Type **vi hosts** at the command prompt to open the hosts file in the vi editor. Delete the first line of this file and save your changes. Why were you successful this time? Exit the vi editor.

24. At the command prompt, type **ls -l** and press **Enter**. Do you have permission to execute the hosts file? Should you make this file executable? Why? Next, type **ls -l /bin** at the command prompt and press **Enter**, Note how many of these files to which you have execute permission. Type **file /bin/*** at the command prompt and press **Enter** to view the file types of the files in the /bin directory. Should these files have the execute permission?

25. Type **exit** and press **Enter** to log out of your shell.

26. Switch back to your previous command-line terminal (tty2) by pressing **Ctrl+Alt+F2**. Note that you are logged in as the root user on this terminal.

27. Type **exit** and press **Enter** to log out of your shell.

Project 4-8

In this hands-on project, you view and manipulate the default file and directory permissions using the umask variable.

1. Switch to a command-line terminal (tty3) by pressing **Ctrl+Alt+F3** and log in to the terminal using the user name of **user1** and the password of **LNXrocks!**.

2. At the command prompt, type **ls -l** and press **Enter**. What files do you see?

3. At the command prompt, type **umask** and press **Enter**. What is the default umask variable?

4. At the command prompt, type **touch utest1** and press **Enter**. Next, type **ls -1** at the command prompt and press **Enter**. What are the permissions on the utest1 file? Do these agree with the calculation in Figure 5-5? Create a new directory by typing the command **mkdir udir1** at the command prompt and pressing **Enter**. Next, type **ls -1** at the command prompt and press **Enter**. What are the permissions on the udir1 directory? Do these agree with the calculation in Figure 5-5?

5. At the command prompt, type **umask 007** and press **Enter**. Next, type **umask** at the command prompt and press **Enter** to verify that your umask variable has been changed to 007.

6. At the command prompt, type **touch utest2** and press **Enter**. Next, type **ls -1** at the command prompt and press **Enter**. What are the permissions on the utest2 file? Do these agree with the calculation in Figure 5-6? Create a new directory by typing the command **mkdir udir2** at the command prompt and pressing **Enter**. Next, type **ls -1** at the command prompt and press **Enter**. What are the permissions on the udir2 directory? Do these agree with the calculation in Figure 5-6?

7. Type **exit** and press **Enter** to log out of your shell.

Project 4-9

In this hands-on project, you view and change file and directory ownership using the **chown** and **chgrp** commands.

1. Switch to a command-line terminal (tty3) by pressing **Ctrl+Alt+F3** and log in to the terminal using the user name of **root** and the password of **LNXrocks!**.

2. At the command prompt, type **touch ownersample** and press **Enter**. Next, type **mkdir ownerdir** at the command prompt and press **Enter**. Next, type **ls -1** at the command prompt and press **Enter** to verify that the file ownersample and directory ownerdir were created and that user1 is the owner and group owner of each.

3. At the command prompt, type **chgrp sys owner*** and press **Enter** to change the group ownership to the sys group for both ownersample and ownerdir. Why were you successful?

4. At the command prompt, type **chown user1 owner*** and press **Enter** to change the ownership to the root user for both ownersample and ownerdir. Why were you successful?

5. At the command prompt, type **chown root.root owner*** and press **Enter** to change the ownership and group ownership back to the root user for both ownersample and ownerdir. Although you are not the current owner of these files, why did you not receive an error message?

6. At the command prompt, type **mv ownersample ownerdir** and press **Enter**. Next, type **ls -1R** at the command prompt and press **Enter** to note that the ownersample file now exists within the ownerdir directory and that both are owned by root.

7. At the command prompt, type **chown -R user1 ownerdir** and press **Enter**. Next, type **ls -1R** at the command prompt and press **Enter**. Who owns the ownerdir directory and ownersample file? Why?

8. At the command prompt, type **rm -Rf ownerdir** and press **Enter**. Why were you able to delete this directory without being the owner of it?

9. Type **exit** and press **Enter** to log out of your shell.

Project 4-10

In this hands-on project, you view and set special permissions on files and directories as well as modify the default ACL on a file.

1. Switch to a command-line terminal (tty3) by pressing **Ctrl+Alt+F3** and log in to the terminal using the user name of **user1** and the password of **LNXrocks!**.

2. At the command prompt, type **touch specialfile** and press Enter. Next, type **ls -l** at the command prompt and press Enter to verify that specialfile was created successfully. Who is the owner and group owner of specialfile?

3. At the command prompt, type **chmod 4777 specialfile** and press Enter. Next, type **ls -l** at the command prompt and press Enter. Which special permission is set on this file? If this file were executed by another user, who would that user be during execution?

4. At the command prompt, type **chmod 6777 specialfile** and press Enter. Next, type **ls -l** at the command prompt and press Enter. Which special permissions are set on this file? If this file were executed by another user, who would that user be during execution, and which group would that user be a member of?

5. At the command prompt, type **chmod 6444 specialfile** and press Enter. Next, type **ls -l** at the command prompt and press Enter. Can you tell if execute is not given underneath the special permission listings? Would the special permissions retain their meaning in this case?

6. Switch to a command-line terminal (tty2) by pressing **Ctrl+Alt+F2** and log in to the terminal using the user name of **root** and the password of **LNXrocks!**.

7. At the command prompt, type **mkdir /public** and press Enter. Next, type **chmod 1777 /public** at the command prompt and press Enter. Which special permission is set on this directory? Who can add or remove files to and from this directory?

8. At the command prompt, type **touch /public/rootfile** and press Enter.

9. Type **exit** and press Enter to log out of your shell.

10. Switch back to your previous command-line terminal (tty3) by pressing **Ctrl+Alt+F3**. Note that you are logged in as the user1 user on this terminal.

11. At the command prompt, type **touch /public/user1file** and press Enter. Next, type **ls -l /public** at the command prompt and press Enter. What files exist in this directory, and who are the owners?

12. At the command prompt, type **rm /public/user1file** and press Enter. Were you prompted to confirm the deletion of the file?

13. At the command prompt, type **rm /public/rootfile** and press Enter. What message did you receive? Why? Press y. Note the error message that you receive.

14. Type **exit** and press Enter to log out of your shell.

15. Switch to a command-line terminal (tty2) by pressing **Ctrl+Alt+F2** and log in to the terminal using the user name of **root** and the password of **LNXrocks!**.

16. At the command prompt, type **touch aclfile** and press Enter. Next, type **getfacl aclfile** at the command prompt and press Enter. Are there any additional entries beyond user, group, and other?

17. At the command prompt, type **setfacl –m u:user1:r-- aclfile** and press Enter. Next, type **ls -l aclfile** at the command prompt and press Enter. Is there a + symbol following the mode? Next, type **getfacl aclfile** at the command prompt and press Enter. Explain the permissions. When would this permission set be useful?

18. At the command prompt, type **setfacl –b aclfile** and press Enter. Next, type **ls -l aclfile** at the command prompt and press Enter. Is there a + symbol following the mode?

19. Type **exit** and press Enter to log out of your shell.

Project 4-11

In this hands-on project, you configure and research filesystem attributes.

1. Switch to a command-line terminal (tty2) by pressing **Ctrl+Alt+F2** and log in to the terminal using the user name of **root** and the password of **LNXrocks!**.

2. At the command prompt, type **touch toughfile** and press Enter. Next, type **lsattr toughfile** at the command prompt and press Enter. What filesystem attributes are set on toughfile by default?

3. At the command prompt, type **chattr +i toughfile** and press Enter. Next, type **lsattr toughfile** at the command prompt and press Enter. Is the immutable attribute set on toughfile?

4. At the command prompt, type **vi toughfile** and press Enter. Does the vi editor warn you that the file is read-only? Add a line of text of your choice in the vi editor and attempt to save your changes using **w!** at the **:** prompt. Were you successful? Quit the vi editor using **q!** at the **:** prompt.

5. At the command prompt, type **rm –f file1** and press Enter. Were you successful? Why?

6. At the command prompt, type **chattr –i file1** and press Enter. Next, type **rm –f file1** and press Enter. Were you successful this time? Why?

7. At the command prompt, type **man chattr** and press Enter. Search the manual page for other filesystem attributes. Which attribute tells the Linux kernel to automatically compress/decompress the file as it is written and read from the filesystem? Which attribute causes the data blocks of a file to be immediately overwritten once the file has been deleted? Type **q** and press Enter to quit out of the manual page when finished.

8. Type **exit** and press Enter to log out of your shell.

Discovery Exercises

1. Use the **ls** command with the **-F** option to explore directories described in the Filesystem Hierarchy Standard starting with /bin. Do you recognize any of the commands in /bin? Explore several other FHS directories and note their contents. Refer to Table 4-1 for a list of directories to explore. Further, visit *http://refspecs. linuxfoundation.org/fhs.shtml* and read about the Filesystem Hierarchy Standard. What benefits does it offer Linux?

2. Write the commands required for the following tasks. Try out each command on your system to ensure that it is correct:

   a. Make a hierarchical directory structure under /root that consists of one directory containing three subdirectories.

   b. Copy two files into each of the subdirectories.

   c. Create one more directory with three subdirectories beneath it and move files from the subdirectories containing them to the counterparts you just created.

   d. Hard-link three of the files. Examine their inodes.

   e. Symbolically link two of the files and examine their link count and inode information.

   f. Make symbolic links from your home directory to two directories in this structure and examine the results.

   g. Delete the symbolic links in your home directory and the directory structure you created under /root.

3. Write the command that can be used to answer the following questions. (*Hint:* Try each out on the system to check your results.)

   a. Find all files on the system that have the word "test" as part of their filename.

   b. Search the PATH variable for the pathname to the awk command.

   c. Find all files in the /usr directory and subdirectories that are larger than 50 kilobytes in size.

   d. Find all files in the /usr directory and subdirectories that are less than 70 kilobytes in size.

   e. Find all files in the / directory and subdirectories that are symbolic links.

   f. Find all files in the /var directory and subdirectories that were accessed less than 60 minutes ago.

   g. Find all files in the /var directory and subdirectories that were accessed less than six days ago.

   h. Find all files in the /home directory and subdirectories that are empty.

   i. Find all files in the /etc directory and subdirectories that are owned by the group bin.

4. For each of the following modes, write the numeric equivalent (e.g., 777):

   a. rw-r--r--

   b. r--r--r--

   c. ---rwxrw-

   d. -wxr-xrw-

   e. rw-rw-rwx

   f. -w-r-----

5. Fill in the permissions in Table 4-7 with checkmarks, assuming that all four files are in the directory /public, which has a mode of rwxr-xr-x.

6. Fill in the permissions in Table 4-8 with checkmarks, assuming that all four files are in the directory /public, which has a mode of rwx--x---.

7. For each of the following umasks, calculate the default permissions given to new files and new directories:
   a. 017
   b. 272
   c. 777
   d. 000
   e. 077
   f. 027

4

Filename	Mode		Read	Edit	Execute	List	Delete
sample1	rw-rw-rw-	User Group Other					
sample2	r--r-----	User Group Other					
sample3	rwxr-x---	User Group Other					
sample4	r-x------	User Group Other					

Table 4-7 Permissions table for Discovery Exercise 5

Filename	Mode		Read	Edit	Execute	List	Delete
sample1	rwxr--r--	User Group Other					
sample2	r-xr--rw-	User Group Other					
sample3	--xr-x---	User Group Other					
sample4	r-xr--r--	User Group Other					

Table 4-8 Permissions table for Discovery Exercise 6

8. For each of the umasks in Question 7, list the umasks that are reasonable to use to increase security on your Linux system and explain why.

9. Starting from the Linux default permissions for file and directories, what umask would you use to ensure that for all new_____?

   a. directories, the owner would have read, write, and execute; members of the group would have read and execute; and others would have read

   b. files, the owner would have read and execute; the group would have read, write, and execute; and others would have execute

   c. files, the owner would have write; the group would have read, write, and execute; and others would have read and write

   d. directories, the owner would have read, write, and execute; the group would have read, write, and execute; and others would have read, write, and execute

   e. directories, the owner would have execute; the group would have read, write, and execute; and others would have no permissions

   f. files, the owner would have read and write; the group would have no permissions; and others would have write

   g. directories, the owner would have read, write, and execute; the group would have read; and others would have read and execute

   h. directories, the owner would have write; the group would have read, write, and execute; and others would have read, write, and execute

   i. files, the owner would have no permissions; the group would have no permissions; and others would have no permissions

10. What chmod command would you use to impose the following permissions?

    a. on a directory such that: the owner would have read, write, and execute; the group would have read and execute; and others would have read

    b. on a file such that: the owner would have read and write; the group would have no permissions; and others would have write

    c. on a file such that: the owner would have write; the group would have read, write, and execute; and others would have read and write

    d. on a file such that: the owner would have read and execute; the group would have read, write, and execute; and others would have execute

    e. on a directory such that: the owner would have execute; the group would have read, write, and execute; and others would have no permissions

    f. on a directory such that: the owner would have write; the group would have read, write, and execute; and others would have read, write, and execute

    g. on a directory such that: the owner would have read, write, and execute; the group would have read; and others would have read and execute

    h. on a directory such that: the owner would have read, write, and execute; the group would have read, write, and execute; and others would have read, write, and execute

    i. on a file such that: the owner would have no permissions; the group would have no permissions; and others would have no permissions

## chapter 5

Linux Filesystem Administration

After completing this chapter, you will be able to:

- Identify the structure and types of device files in the /dev directory
- Understand common filesystem types and their features
- Mount and unmount filesystems to and from the Linux directory tree
- Create and manage filesystems on floppy disks, CDs, DVDs, USB storage devices, Firewire storage devices, and hard disk partitions
- Create and use ISO images
- Use the LVM to create and manage logical volumes
- Monitor free space on mounted filesystems
- Check filesystems for errors
- Use hard disk quotas to limit user space usage

Navigating the Linux directory tree and manipulating files are common tasks that are performed on a daily basis by all users. However, administrators must provide this directory tree for users, as well as manage and fix the disk devices that support it. In this chapter, you learn about the various device files that represent disk devices and the different filesystems that can be placed on those devices. Next, you learn how to create and manage filesystems on a wide variety of different storage devices, as well as learn standard hard disk partitioning, LVM configuration, and filesystem management. The chapter concludes with a discussion of disk usage, filesystem errors, and restricting the ability for users to store files.

The /dev Directory

Fundamental to administering the disks used to store information is an understanding of how these disks are specified by the Linux operating system. Most devices on a Linux system (such as disks, terminals, and serial ports) are represented by a file on the hard disk called a **device file**. There is one file per device, and these files are typically created by the udev system and found in the **/dev directory**. This allows you to specify devices on the system by using the pathname to the file that represents it in the /dev directory.

Perhaps the simplest example of a disk device is a floppy disk, which was primarily used on legacy Linux systems to transfer small amounts of data before the advent of USB flash drives. To specify the first floppy disk in the Linux system, you can type the pathname /dev/fd0 (floppy disk 0) in the appropriate section of a command, and to represent the second floppy disk in the Linux system, you can specify the pathname to the file /dev/fd1 (floppy disk 1).

Furthermore, each device file specifies how data should be transferred to and from the device. You have two methods for transferring data to and from a device. The first method involves transferring information character-by-character to and from the device. Devices that transfer data in this fashion are referred to as **character devices**. The second method transfers chunks or blocks of information at a time by using physical memory to buffer the transfer. Devices that use this method of transfer are called **block devices**; they can transfer information much faster than character devices. Device files that represent disks, such as floppy disks, CDs, DVDs, USB flash drives, and hard disks, are typically block device files because a fast data transfer rate is preferred. Tape drives and most other devices, however, are typically represented by character device files.

To see whether a particular device transfers data character-by-character or block-by-block, recall that the ls –l command displays a c or b character in the type column indicating the type of device file. To view the type of the file /dev/fd0, you can use the following command:

```
[root@server1 ~]# ls -l /dev/fd0
brw-rw----  1 root      floppy    2,   0 Feb 23  16:02   /dev/fd0
[root@server1 ~]#_
```

NOTE

Floppy disk drives are not standard on newer computers today. As a result, Fedora 20 does not load the floppy driver and create the /dev/fd0 device file by default. To load the floppy driver manually (which also creates the /dev/fd0 device file), you can type modprobe floppy at a command prompt as the root user.

Device File	Description	Block or Character
/dev/fd0	First floppy disk on the system	Block
/dev/fd1	Second floppy disk on the system	Block
/dev/hda1	First primary partition on the first PATA hard disk drive (primary master)	Block
/dev/hdb1	First primary partition on the second PATA hard disk drive (primary slave)	Block
/dev/hdc1	First primary partition on the third PATA hard disk drive (secondary master)	Block
/dev/hdd1	First primary partition on the fourth PATA hard disk drive (secondary slave)	Block
/dev/sda1	First primary partition on the first SATA/SCSI hard disk drive	Block
/dev/sdb1	First primary partition on the second SATA/SCSI hard disk drive	Block
/dev/loop0	First loopback interface	Block
/dev/tty1	First local terminal on the system (Ctrl+Alt+F1)	Character
/dev/tty2	Second local terminal on the system (Ctrl+Alt+F2)	Character
/dev/ttyS0	First serial port on the system (COM1)	Character
/dev/ttyS1	Second serial port on the system (COM2)	Character
/dev/psaux	PS/2 mouse port	Character
/dev/lp0	First parallel port on the system (LPT1)	Character
/dev/null	Device file that represents nothing; any data sent to this device is discarded	Character
/dev/st0	First SCSI tape device in the system	Character
/dev/bus/usb/*	USB device files	Character

Table 5-1   Common device files

From the leftmost character in the preceding output, you can see that the /dev/fd0 file is a block device file. Table 5-1 provides a list of some common device files that you may find on your Linux system and their types.

After a typical Fedora Linux installation, you will find several hundred different device files in the /dev directory that represent devices on the system. This large number of device files on a Linux system does not require much disk space because all device files consist of inodes and no data blocks; as a result, the entire contents of the /dev directory is usually less than 100 kilobytes in size. When using the ls –l command to view device files, the portion of the listing describing the file size in kilobytes is replaced by two numbers: the major number and the minor number. The **major number** of a device file points to the device driver for the device in the Linux kernel; several different devices can share the same major number if they are of the same general type (that is, two different floppy disk drives might share the same major number). The **minor number** indicates the particular device itself; the first floppy disk drive in the computer will have a different minor number than the second floppy disk drive in the computer. In the following output, you see that /dev/fd0 and /dev/fd1 share the same major number of 2, yet the minor number for /dev/fd0 is 0 and the minor number for /dev/fd1 is 1, which differentiates them from each other.

```
[root@server1 ~]# ls -l /dev/fd0 /dev/fd1
brw-rw----    1 root      floppy    2,   0 Feb 23 16:02 /dev/fd0
brw-rw----    1 root      floppy    2,   1 Feb 23 16:02 /dev/fd1
[root@server1 ~]#_
```

Together, the device file type (block or character), the major number (device driver), and the minor number (specific device) make up the unique characteristics of each device file. To create a device file, you simply need to know these three pieces of information.

If a device file becomes corrupted, it is usually listed as a regular file instead of a block or character special file. Recall from Chapter 4 that the find /dev -type f command can be used to search for regular files underneath the /dev directory to identify whether corruption has taken place. If you find a corrupted device file or accidentally delete a device file, the **mknod command** can be used to re-create the device file if you know the type, major, and minor numbers. An example of re-creating the /dev/fd0 block device file used earlier with a major number of 2 and a minor number of 0 is shown in the following example:

```
[root@server1 ~]# ls -l /dev/fd0
brw-rw----    1 root      floppy    2,   0 Feb 23 16:02 /dev/fd0
[root@server1 ~]# rm -f /dev/fd0
[root@server1 ~]# ls -l /dev/fd0
[root@server1 ~]# mknod /dev/fd0 b 2 0
[root@server1 ~]# ls -l /dev/fd0
brw-r--r--    1 root      root      2,   0 May  8 13:26 /dev/fd0
[root@server1 ~]#_
```

To see a list of devices that are currently used on the system and their major numbers, you can view the contents of the **/proc/devices** file, as shown here:

```
[root@server1 ~]# cat /proc/devices
Character devices:
  1 mem
  4 /dev/vc/0
  4 tty
  4 ttyS
  5 /dev/tty
  5 /dev/console
  5 /dev/ptmx
  7 vcs
 10 misc
 13 input
 14 sound
 21 sg
 29 fb
116 alsa
128 ptm
136 pts
```

```
   162  raw
   180  usb
   189  usb_device
   202  cpu/msr
   203  cpu/cpuid
   226  drm
   250  hidraw
   251  usbmon
   252  bsg
   253  pcmcia
   254  rtc

Block devices:
     1  ramdisk
     2  fd
     7  loop
     8  sd
     9  md
    11  sr
    65  sd
    69  sd
    70  sd
    71  sd
   128  sd
   134  sd
   135  sd
   253  device-mapper
   254  mdp
[root@server1 ~]#_
```

Filesystems

Recall from Chapter 2 that files must be stored on the hard disk in a defined format called a filesystem so that the operating system can work with them. The type of filesystem used determines how files are managed on the physical hard disk. Each filesystem can have different methods for storing files and features that make the filesystem robust against errors. Although many different types of filesystems are available, all filesystems share three common components, as discussed in Chapter 4: the superblock, the inode table, and the data blocks. On a structural level, these three components work together to organize files and allow rapid access to and retrieval of data. All storage media, such as floppy disks, hard disks, and DVDs, need to contain a filesystem before they can be used.

 Creating a filesystem on a device is commonly referred to as **formatting**.

Filesystem Types

As mentioned, many filesystems are available for use in the Linux operating system. Each has its own strengths and weaknesses, thus some are better suited to some tasks and not as well suited to others. One benefit of Linux is that you need not use only one type of filesystem on the system; you can use several different devices formatted with different filesystems under the same directory tree. In addition, files and directories appear the same throughout the directory tree regardless of whether there is one filesystem or 20 different filesystems in use by the Linux system. Table 5-2 lists some common filesystems available for use in Linux. For a full listing of filesystem types and their features, you can refer to the Filesystem HOWTO at *www.tldp.org/HOWTO/Filesystems-HOWTO.html*.

Filesystem support is typically built into the Linux kernel or added as a package on most distributions. Fedora 20 has native support for btrfs, cramfs, ext2, ext3, ext4, hfs, hfsplus, iso9660, ntfs, reiserfs, vfat, and xfs by default.

Mounting

The term **mounting** originated in the 1960s when information was stored on large tape reels that had to be mounted on computers to make the data available. Today, mounting still refers to making data available. More specifically, it refers to the process whereby a device is made accessible to users via the logical directory tree. This device is attached to a certain directory on the directory tree called a **mount point**. Users can then create files and subdirectories in this mount point directory, which are then stored on the filesystem that was mounted to that particular directory.

Remember that directories are merely files that do not contain data; instead, they contain a list of files and subdirectories organized within them. Thus, it is easy for the Linux system to cover up directories to prevent user access to that data. This is essentially what happens when a device is mounted to a certain directory; the mount point directory is temporarily covered up by that device while the device remains mounted. Any file contents that were present in the mount point directory prior to mounting are not lost; when the device is unmounted, the mount point directory is uncovered, and the previous file contents are revealed. Suppose, for example, that you mount a floppy disk device that contains a filesystem to the /mnt directory. The /mnt directory is an empty directory that is commonly used as a temporary mount point for mounting removable media devices. Before mounting, the directory structure would resemble that depicted in Figure 5-1. After the floppy is mounted to the /mnt directory, the contents of the /mnt directory would be covered up by the floppy filesystem, as illustrated in Figure 5-2.

If a user then stores a file in the /mnt directory, as shown in Figure 5-2, that file will be stored on the floppy disk device. Similarly, if a user creates a subdirectory under the /mnt directory depicted in Figure 5-2, that subdirectory will be made on the floppy disk.

It is important to note that any existing directory can be used as a mount point. If a user mounts a floppy device to the /bin directory, all files in the /bin directory are covered up during the time the floppy disk is mounted, including the command used to unmount the floppy. Thus, it is safe practice to create empty directories used specifically for mounting devices to avoid making existing files inaccessible to users.

Filesystem	Description
bfs	Boot File System—A small, bootable filesystem used to hold the files necessary for system startup; it is commonly used on UNIX systems.
btrfs	B-tree File System—A new filesystem for Linux systems that includes many features that are geared towards large-scale storage. Although still in development, it is envisioned to be a replacement for the ext4 and reiserfs filesystems in the long term. Its name is commonly pronounced as "Butter F S."
cramfs	Compressed ROM filesystem—A read-only filesystem typically used on embedded Linux systems to host system files in a small amount of storage space.
ext2	Second extended filesystem—The traditional filesystem used on Linux, it supports access control lists (individual user permissions). In addition, it retains its name from being the new version of the original extended filesystem, based on the Minix filesystem.
ext3	Third extended filesystem—A variation on ext2 that allows for journaling and, thus, has a faster startup and recovery time.
ext4	Fourth extended filesystem—A variation on ext3 that has larger filesystem support and speed enhancements.
hfs, hfsplus	Hierarchical File System—A filesystem native to Apple Macintosh computers.
hpfs	High Performance File System—An IBM proprietary OS/2 filesystem that provides long filename support and is optimized to manipulate data on large disk volumes.
iso9660	ISO 9660 filesystem—A filesystem that originated from the International Standards Organization recommendation 9660 and is used to access data stored on CDs and DVDs.
minix	MINIX filesystem—The filesystem used by Linus Torvalds in the early days of Linux development.
msdos	DOS FAT filesystem.
ntfs	New Technology File System—A Microsoft proprietary filesystem developed for its Windows operating systems.
reiserfs	Reiser File System—A journalizing filesystem similar to ext3, and more suited for use with databases.
udf	Universal Disk Format filesystem—A filesystem used by software programs that write to a CD-RW or DVD-RW drive.
vfat	DOS FAT filesystem with long filename support.
vxfs	Veritas File System—A journalizing filesystem that offers large file support and supports access control lists (individual user permissions) and is commonly used by major versions of UNIX.
xfs	X File System—A high-performance filesystem created by Silicon Graphics for use on their IRIX UNIX systems. Many Linux administrators prefer to use xfs on systems that need to quickly write large numbers of files to the hard disk.
zfs	Zettabyte File System—A very high-performance filesystem and volume manager originally created by Sun Microsystems that protects against data corruption and has features that support very large distributed storage systems. Many large-scale Linux server systems in industry use the zfs filesystem to store and manage large amounts of data. You will learn how to configure zfs in Chapter 6.

Table 5-2 Common Linux filesystems

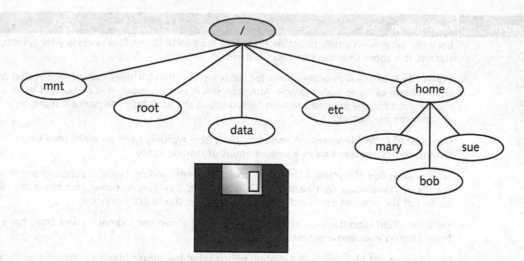

Figure 5-1 The directory structure prior to mounting

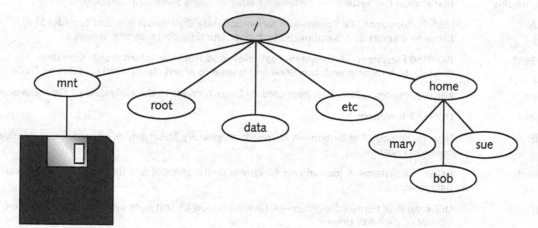

Figure 5-2 The directory structure after mounting a floppy device

Most systems today have several removable media devices—such as CDs, DVDs, USB flash drives, and USB hard drives—that may be connected to your PC for long periods of time. As a result, it is considered good form to create subdirectories under the /media directory on your Linux system to mount these removable media devices and only use the /mnt directory to temporarily mount devices. For example, you could mount your floppy to the /media/floppy directory and your DVD to the /media/DVD directory. You can then access the files on your floppy disk by navigating to the /media/floppy directory, as well as access the files on your DVD by navigating to the /media/DVD directory.

When the Linux system is first turned on, a filesystem present on the hard drive is mounted to the / directory. This is referred to as the **root filesystem** and contains most of the operating system files. Other filesystems present on hard disks inside the computer can also be mounted to various mount point directories underneath the / directory at boot time, as well as via entries in the filesystem table (**/etc/fstab**) discussed in the following sections.

The **mount command** is used to mount devices to mount point directories, and the **umount command** is used to unmount devices from mount point directories; both of these commands are discussed throughout the remainder of this chapter.

Working with Floppy Disks

Traditionally, it was commonplace to use floppy disk removable media to store small files, such as spreadsheets, that needed to be transferred from computer to computer. Today, floppy disks are not available on all systems, but we will examine them here as they are an easy way to practice and learn the commands that are commonly used to work with filesystems and they are emulated in virtualization software.

Recall that each disk device must be formatted with a filesystem prior to being used to store files. To do this, you can use the **mkfs** (**make filesystem**) **command** and specify the filesystem type using the −t switch and the device file representing the floppy disk device. To format the floppy disk inside the first floppy disk drive in the computer with the ext2 filesystem, place a floppy disk in the floppy disk drive and type the following command:

```
[root@server1 ~]# mkfs –t ext2 /dev/fd0
mke2fs 1.42.8 (20-Jun-2013)
Filesystem label=
OS type: Linux
Block size=1024 (log=0)
Fragment size=1024 (log=0)
Stride=0 blocks, Stripe width=0 blocks
184 inodes, 1440 blocks
72 blocks (5.00%) reserved for the super user
First data block=1
Maximum filesystem blocks=1572864
1 block group
8192 blocks per group, 8192 fragments per group
184 inodes per group

Allocating group tables: done
Writing inode tables: done
Writing superblocks and filesystem accounting information: done
[root@server1 ~]#_
```

Alternatively, you can specify a different filesystem after the −t option, such as the DOS FAT filesystem. This results in a different output from the mkfs command, as shown in the following example:

```
[root@server1 ~]# mkfs –t msdos /dev/fd0
mkfs.msdos 3.0.23 (2013-10-15)
[root@server1 ~]#_
```

5

If you do not specify the filesystem using the mkfs command, the default filesystem assumed is the ext2 filesystem, as shown in the following example:

```
[root@server1 ~]# mkfs /dev/fd0
mke2fs 1.42.8 (20-Jun-2013)
Filesystem label=
OS type: Linux
Block size=1024 (log=0)
Fragment size=1024 (log=0)
Stride=0 blocks, Stripe width=0 blocks
184 inodes, 1440 blocks
72 blocks (5.00%) reserved for the super user
First data block=1
Maximum filesystem blocks=1572864
1 block group
8192 blocks per group, 8192 fragments per group
184 inodes per group

Allocating group tables: done
Writing inode tables: done
Writing superblocks and filesystem accounting information: done
[root@server1 ~]#_
```

Although the most common command to create filesystems is the mkfs command, other variants and shortcuts to the mkfs command exist. For example, to create an ext2 filesystem, you could type mke2fs /dev/fd0 on the command line. Other alternatives to the mkfs command are listed in Table 5-3.

After a floppy disk has been formatted with a filesystem, it must be mounted on the directory tree before it can be used. A list of currently mounted filesystems can be obtained by using the mount command with no options or arguments, which reads the information listed in the /etc/mtab (mount table) file, as shown in the following sample output:

```
[root@server1 ~]# mount
/dev/sda1  on  /  type ext4 (rw)
proc  on  /proc type proc (rw)
sysfs  on  /sys type sysfs (rw)
devpts  on  /dev/pts type devpts (rw,gid=5,mode=620)
tmpfs  on  /dev/shm type tmpfs (rw)
none  on  /proc/sys/fs/binfmt_misc type binfmt_misc (rw)
sunrpc  on  /var/lib/nfs/rpc_pipefs type rpc_pipefs (rw)
[root@server1 ~]# cat /etc/mtab
/dev/sda1  /  ext4 rw  0  0
proc  /proc proc rw  0  0
sysfs  /sys sysfs rw  0  0
devpts  /dev/pts devpts rw,gid=5,mode=620  0  0
tmpfs  /dev/shm tmpfs rw  0  0
none  /proc/sys/fs/binfmt_misc binfmt_misc rw  0  0
sunrpc  /var/lib/nfs/rpc_pipefs rpc_pipefs rw  0  0
[root@server1 ~]#_
```

Command	Filesystem It Creates
mkfs	filesystems of most types
mkdosfs mkfs.msdos mkfs.vfat	FAT
mkfs.ext2 mke2fs mke2fs –t ext2	ext2
mkfs.ext3 mke2fs –t ext3	ext3
mkfs.ext4 mke2fs –t ext4	ext4
mkisofs	ISO
mkreiserfs mkfs.reiserfs	REISERFS
mkfs.xfs	XFS
mkntfs mkfs.ntfs	NTFS

Table 5-3   Commands used to create filesystems

From the preceding example output, you can see that the device /dev/sda1 is mounted on the / directory and contains an ext4 filesystem. The other filesystems listed are special filesystems that are used by the system and are discussed later in this book.

To mount a device on the directory tree, you can use the mount command with options and arguments to specify the filesystem type, the device to mount, and the directory on which to mount the device (mount point). It is important to ensure that no user is currently using the mount point directory; otherwise, the system gives you an error message, and the disk is not mounted. To check whether the /media/floppy directory is being used by any users, you can use the **fuser command** with the –u option, as shown in the following output:

```
[root@server1 ~]# fuser -u /media/floppy
[root@server1 ~]#_
```

The preceding output indicates the /media/floppy directory is not being used by any user processes. To mount the first floppy device formatted with the ext2 filesystem to the /media/floppy directory, simply type the following command:

```
[root@server1 ~]# mount –t ext2 /dev/fd0 /media/floppy
[root@server1 ~]# mount
/dev/sda1  on  / type ext4 (rw)
proc  on  /proc type proc (rw)
sysfs  on  /sys type sysfs (rw)
```

```
devpts  on  /dev/pts type devpts  (rw,gid=5,mode=620)
tmpfs  on  /dev/shm type tmpfs  (rw)
none  on  /proc/sys/fs/binfmt_misc type binfmt_misc  (rw)
sunrpc  on  /var/lib/nfs/rpc_pipefs type rpc_pipefs  (rw)
/dev/fd0  on  /media/floppy type ext2  (rw)
[root@server1 ~]#_
```

If you omit the −t option to the mount command, it attempts to automatically detect the filesystem on the device. Thus, the command mount /dev/fd0 /media/floppy will perform the same action as the mount command shown in the preceding output.

Notice that /dev/fd0 appears mounted to the /media/floppy directory in the preceding output of the mount command. To access and store files on the floppy device, you can now treat the /media/floppy directory as the root of the floppy disk. When an ext2 filesystem is created on a disk device, one directory called lost+found is created by default and used by the fsck command discussed later in this chapter. To explore the recently mounted floppy filesystem, you can use the following commands:

```
[root@server1 ~]# cd /media/floppy
[root@server1 floppy]# pwd
/media/floppy
[root@server1 floppy]# ls -F
lost+found/
[root@server1 floppy]#_
```

To copy files to the floppy device, simply specify the /media/floppy directory as the target for the cp command, as shown next:

```
[root@server1 floppy]# cd /etc
[root@server1 etc]# cat issue
Fedora release 20 (Heisenbug)
Kernel \r on an \m (\l)
[root@server1 etc]# cp issue /media/floppy
[root@server1 etc]# cd /media/floppy
[root@server1 floppy]# ls -F
issue lost+found/
[root@server1 floppy]# cat issue
Fedora release 20 (Heisenbug)
Kernel \r on an \m (\l)
[root@server1 floppy]#_
```

Similarly, you can also create subdirectories underneath the floppy device to store files; these subdirectories are referenced underneath the mount point directory. To make a directory called workfiles on the floppy mounted in the previous example and copy the /etc/inittab file to it, you can use the following commands:

```
[root@server1 floppy]# pwd
/media/floppy
[root@server1 floppy]# ls -F
issue lost+found/
```

```
[root@server1  floppy]# mkdir workfiles
[root@server1  floppy]# ls -F
issue lost+found/ workfiles/
[root@server1  floppy]# cd workfiles
[root@server1  workfiles]# pwd
/media/floppy/workfiles
[root@server1  workfiles]# cp /etc/inittab .
[root@server1  workfiles]# ls -F
inittab
[root@server1  workfiles]#_
```

Even though you can eject the floppy disk from the floppy disk drive without permission from the system, doing so is likely to cause error messages to appear on the terminal screen. Before a floppy is ejected, it must be properly unmounted using the umount command. The umount command can take the name of the device to unmount or the mount point directory as an argument. Similar to mounting a floppy disk, unmounting a floppy disk requires that the mount point directory has no users using it. If you try to unmount the floppy disk mounted to the /media/floppy directory while it is being used, you receive an error message similar to the one in the following example:

```
[root@server1  floppy]# pwd
/media/floppy
[root@server1  floppy]# umount /media/floppy
umount: /media/floppy: target is busy.
        (In some cases useful info about processes that use
        the device is found by lsof(8) or fuser(1).)
[root@server1  floppy]# fuser -u /media/floppy
/media/floppy:         17368c(root)
[root@server1  floppy]# cd /root
[root@server1  ~]# umount /media/floppy
[root@server1  ~]# mount
/dev/sda1 on / type ext4 (rw)
proc on /proc type proc (rw)
sysfs on /sys type sysfs (rw)
devpts on /dev/pts type devpts (rw,gid=5,mode=620)
tmpfs on /dev/shm type tmpfs (rw)
none on /proc/sys/fs/binfmt_misc type binfmt_misc (rw)
sunrpc on /var/lib/nfs/rpc_pipefs type rpc_pipefs (rw)
[root@server1  ~]#_
```

Notice from the preceding output that you were still using the /media/floppy directory because it was the current working directory. The fuser command also indicated that the root user had a process using the directory. After the current working directory was changed, the umount command was able to unmount the floppy from the /media/floppy directory, and the output of the mount command indicated that the floppy disk was no longer mounted.

Recall that mounting simply attaches a disk device to the Linux directory tree so that you can treat the device like a directory full of files and subdirectories. A device can be mounted to any existing directory. However, if the directory contains files, those files are inaccessible until the device is unmounted. Suppose, for example, that you create a directory called /flopper for mounting floppy disks and a file inside called samplefile, as shown in the following output:

```
[root@server1 ~]# mkdir /flopper
[root@server1 ~]# touch /flopper/samplefile
[root@server1 ~]# ls -F /flopper
samplefile
[root@server1 ~]#_
```

If the floppy disk used earlier is mounted to the /flopper directory, a user who uses the /flopper directory will be using the floppy disk; however, when nothing is mounted to the /flopper directory, the previous contents are available for use:

```
[root@server1 ~]# mount -t ext2 /dev/fd0 /flopper
[root@server1 ~]# mount
/dev/sda1 on / type ext4 (rw)
proc on /proc type proc (rw)
sysfs on /sys type sysfs (rw)
devpts on /dev/pts type devpts (rw,gid=5,mode=620)
tmpfs on /dev/shm type tmpfs (rw)
none on /proc/sys/fs/binfmt_misc type binfmt_misc (rw)
sunrpc on /var/lib/nfs/rpc_pipefs type rpc_pipefs (rw)
[root@server1 ~]# ls -F /flopper
issue lost+found/ workfiles/
[root@server1 ~]# umount /flopper
[root@server1 ~]# ls -F /flopper
samplefile
[root@server1 ~]#_
```

The mount command used in the preceding output specifies the filesystem type, the device to mount, and the mount point directory. To save time typing on the command line, you can alternatively specify one argument and allow the system to look up the remaining information in the /etc/fstab (filesystem table) file. The /etc/fstab file has a dual purpose; it is used to mount devices at boot time and is consulted when a user does not specify enough arguments on the command line when using the mount command.

There are six fields present in the /etc/fstab file:

```
<device to mount>  <mount point>  <type>  <mount options>  <dump#>  <fsck#>
```

The device to mount can be the path to a device file (i.e., /dev/sda1) or the boot loader label that describes the volume to mount (e.g. UUID=db545f1d-c1ee-4b70-acbe-3dc61b41db20). The mount point specifies where to mount the device. The type can be a specific value (such as ext4) or can be automatically detected. The mount options are additional options that the mount command accepts when mounting the volume (such as read only, or "ro"). Any filesystems with the mount option "noauto" are not automatically mounted at boot time; a complete list of options that the mount command accepts can be found by viewing the manual page for the mount command.

The dump# is used by the dump command (discussed in Chapter 11) when backing up filesystems; a 1 in this field indicates that the filesystem should be backed up, whereas a 0 indicates that no backup is necessary. The fsck# is used by the `fsck` command discussed later in this chapter when checking filesystems at boot time for errors; any filesystems with a 1 in this field are checked before any filesystems with a number 2, and filesystems with a number 0 are not checked.

To mount all filesystems in the /etc/fstab file that are intended to mount at boot time, you can simply type the mount −a command.

The following output displays the contents of a sample /etc/fstab file:

```
[root@server1 ~]# cat /etc/fstab
#
# /etc/fstab
#
# Accessible filesystems, by reference, are maintained under '/dev/disk'
# See man pages fstab(5), findfs(8), mount(8) and/or blkid(8) for info
#
/dev/sda1       /                       ext4        defaults        1 1
/dev/sda2       swap                    swap        defaults        0 0
tmpfs           /dev/shm                tmpfs       defaults        0 0
devpts          /dev/pts                devpts      gid=5,mode=620  0 0
sysfs           /sys                    sysfs       defaults        0 0
proc            /proc                   proc        defaults        0 0
/dev/fd0        /media/floppy           auto        noauto          0 0
[root@server1 ~]# _
```

Thus, to mount the first floppy device (/dev/fd0) to the /mnt/floppy directory and automatically detect the type of filesystem on the device, simply specify enough information for the mount command to find the appropriate line in the /etc/fstab file:

```
[root@server1 ~]# mount /dev/fd0
[root@server1 ~]# mount
/dev/sda1 on / type ext4 (rw)
proc on /proc type proc (rw)
sysfs on /sys type sysfs (rw)
devpts on /dev/pts type devpts (rw,gid=5,mode=620)
tmpfs on /dev/shm type tmpfs (rw)
none on /proc/sys/fs/binfmt_misc type binfmt_misc (rw)
sunrpc on /var/lib/nfs/rpc_pipefs type rpc_pipefs (rw)
/dev/fd0 on /media/floppy type ext2 (rw)
[root@server1 ~]# umount /dev/fd0
[root@server1 ~]#_
```

The mount command in the preceding output succeeded because a line in /etc/fstab described the mounting of the /dev/fd0 device.

Command	Description
mount	Displays mounted filesystems
mount -t <type> <device> <mount point>	Mounts a <device> of a certain <type> to a <mount point> directory
fuser -u <directory>	Displays the users using a particular directory
umount <mount point> or umount <device>	Unmounts a <device> from its <mount point> directory

Table 5-4 Useful commands when mounting and unmounting filesystems

Alternatively, you could specify the mount point as an argument to the mount command to mount the same device via the correct entry in /etc/fstab:

```
[root@server1 ~]# mount /media/floppy
[root@server1 ~]# mount
/dev/sda1 on / type ext4 (rw)
proc on /proc type proc (rw)
sysfs on /sys type sysfs (rw)
devpts on /dev/pts type devpts (rw,gid=5,mode=620)
tmpfs on /dev/shm type tmpfs (rw)
none on /proc/sys/fs/binfmt_misc type binfmt_misc (rw)
sunrpc on /var/lib/nfs/rpc_pipefs type rpc_pipefs (rw)
/dev/fd0 on /media/floppy type ext2 (rw)
[root@server1 ~]# umount /media/floppy
[root@server1 ~]#
```

Table 5-4 lists commands that are useful when mounting and unmounting floppy disks.

Working with CDs, DVDs, and ISO Images

Most software that is not downloaded from the Internet is packaged on CDs and DVDs because they have a much larger storage capacity than floppy disks; one DVD can store more than 3000 times the data a floppy disk can store. Like floppies, CDs and DVDs can be mounted with the mount command and unmounted with the umount command, as shown in Table 5-4; however, the device file used with these commands is different. The device files used by CD and DVD depend on the technology used by the drive itself. If your computer has a PATA CD or DVD drive, you can refer to it using one of the following four standard PATA hard drive configurations (discussed in Chapter 2):

- Primary master (/dev/hda)
- Primary slave (/dev/hdb)
- Secondary master (/dev/hdc)
- Secondary slave (/dev/hdd)

However, if you have a SATA or SCSI CD or DVD drive, Linux may use many different names, depending on your actual CD or DVD drive:

- First SATA/SCSI drive (/dev/sda, /dev/scd0, /dev/sr0, and /dev/sg0)
- Second SATA/SCSI drive (/dev/sdb, /dev/scd1, /dev/sr1, and /dev/sg1)
- Third SATA/SCSI drive (/dev/sdc, /dev/scd2, /dev/sr2, and /dev/sg2)
- And so on

To make the identification of your CD or DVD drive easier, Fedora Linux creates a file called /dev/cdrom, which is merely a symbolic link to the correct device file for your first CD or DVD drive. For example, if your system contains a SATA CD/DVD drive, a long listing of /dev/cdrom may show the following:

```
[root@server1 ~]# ls -l /dev/cdrom
lrwxrwxrwx 1 root root 3 Aug 10 12:39 /dev/cdrom -> sr0
[root@server1 ~]#_
```

In this case, you could use /dev/cdrom or /dev/sr0 to mount CDs or DVDs. To write to a CD or DVD in this same drive, however, you must use disc-burning software that knows how to write data to /dev/cdrom or /dev/sr0.

Nearly all DVD-ROM and DVD-RW drives can also work with CDs.

There are many OSS disc burning software applications available for Linux. One example is the graphical Brasero Disc Burner program that you can install by running the command `yum install brasero` as the root user.

In addition, CDs and DVDs typically use the iso9660 filesystem type and are read-only when accessed using Linux (recall that you must use disc-burning software to record to a CD or DVD). Thus, to mount a CD or DVD to a directory, you should use the filesystem type of iso9660 and add the -r (read-only) option to the mount command. To mount a sample CD to the /media/cd directory and view its contents, you could use the following commands:

```
[root@server1 ~]# mount -r -t iso9660 /dev/cdrom /media/cd
[root@server1 ~]# mount
/dev/sda1 on / type ext4 (rw)
proc on /proc type proc (rw)
sysfs on /sys type sysfs (rw)
devpts on /dev/pts type devpts (rw,gid=5,mode=620)
tmpfs on /dev/shm type tmpfs (rw)
none on /proc/sys/fs/binfmt_misc type binfmt_misc (rw)
sunrpc on /var/lib/nfs/rpc_pipefs type rpc_pipefs (rw)
/dev/cdrom on /media/cd type iso9660 (ro)
[root@server1 ~]# ls -l /media/cdrom
autorun.inf*    install*    graphics/    jungle/    jungle.txt*
joystick/
[root@server1 ~]# umount /media/cdrom
[root@server1 ~]#_
```

The /media/cd directory must exist for the mount command to succeed in the previous example.

As with floppies, you can modify the /etc/fstab file, such that you can specify only a single argument to the mount command to mount a CD or DVD. Also remember that the mount point directory must not be in use to successfully mount or unmount CDs and DVDs; the fuser command can be used to verify this.

Unlike floppy disks, CDs and DVDs cannot be ejected from the drive until they are properly unmounted, because the mount command locks the CD/DVD drive as a precaution.

When you insert a CD or DVD while in a GUI environment, it is automatically mounted by the system to a directory underneath the /run/media/*username* directory (where *username* is the name of the user logged into the GUI environment) that is named for the label on the CD or DVD (specified in the disc-burning software). For example, if you insert a DVD with a label of "Cafe_Scientifique" into your system while logged into a GUI environment as user1, the system will automatically create a /run/media/user1/Cafe_Scientifique directory and mount the device to this directory, as shown here:

```
[root@server1 ~]# mount
/dev/sda1 on / type ext4 (rw)
proc on /proc type proc (rw)
sysfs on /sys type sysfs (rw)
devpts on /dev/pts type devpts (rw,gid=5,mode=620)
tmpfs on /dev/shm type tmpfs (rw)
none on /proc/sys/fs/binfmt_misc type binfmt_misc (rw)
sunrpc on /var/lib/nfs/rpc_pipefs type rpc_pipefs (rw)
gvfs-fuse-daemon on /home/bob/.gvfs type fuse.gvfs-fuse-daemon (rw,
nosuid,nodev,user=bob)
/dev/sr0 on /run/media/user1/Cafe_Scientifique type iso9660
(ro,nosuid,nodev,uhelper=udisks,uid=501,gid=501,iocharset=utf8,
mode=0400,dmode=0500)
[root@server1 ~]#
```

In addition, the system will also place a shortcut to the /run/media/user1/Cafe_Scientifique directory in the Files application within the GUI environment so that you can easily access the contents of your DVD, as shown in Figure 5-3.

When you are finished accessing the files on the DVD, you can click the eject icon next to Cafe_Scientifique, shown in Figure 5-3, to unmount the DVD from the /run/media/user1/Cafe_Scientifique directory and force the DVD drive to eject the DVD.

The iso9660 filesystem type is not limited to CDs and DVDs. You can also create image files, called ISO images, that contain other files. Recall from Chapter 2 that most operating system software available for download from the Internet, such as Linux distributions, are available as an ISO image file. Once downloaded, ISO images can be easily written to a CD or DVD using disc-burning software or mounted and accessed by your Linux system. If you download an ISO image called *sample.iso,* you can mount it to the /mnt directory as a loopback device,

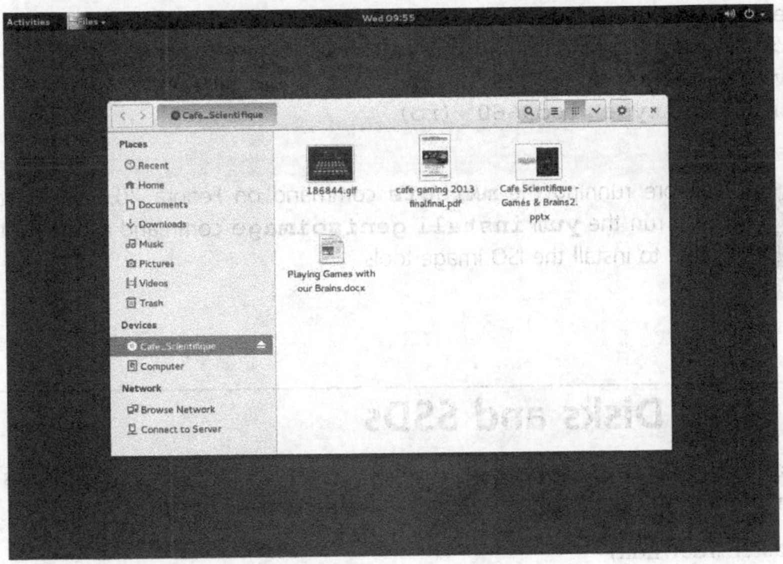

Figure 5-3 Accessing a DVD within the GNOME desktop

which allows your system to access the contents of the *sample.iso* file, using the following command:

```
[root@server1 ~]# mount
[root@server1 ~]# mount -o loop -r -t iso9660 lala.iso /mnt
/dev/sda1 on / type ext4 (rw)
proc on /proc type proc (rw)
sysfs on /sys type sysfs (rw)
devpts on /dev/pts type devpts (rw,gid=5,mode=620)
tmpfs on /dev/shm type tmpfs (rw)
none on /proc/sys/fs/binfmt_misc type binfmt_misc (rw)
sunrpc on /var/lib/nfs/rpc_pipefs type rpc_pipefs (rw)
/dev/loop0 on /mnt type iso9660 (ro)
[root@localhost ~]# ls /mnt
setup.exe tools binaries
[root@server1 ~]#_
```

You can then manipulate, execute, edit files within the /mnt directory, or copy files from the /mnt directory to another directory to extract the contents of the ISO image file.

To create an ISO image from a directory of files, simply use the **mkisofs command**. The following command creates an ISO image called *newimage.iso* from all the information in the /data directory with additional support for the Joliet (-J) and Rock Ridge (-R) standards:

```
[root@localhost ~]# mkisofs -RJ -o newimage.iso /data
[root@localhost ~]# mount -o loop -r -t iso9660 lala.iso /mnt
/dev/sda1 on / type ext4 (rw)
proc on /proc type proc (rw)
sysfs on /sys type sysfs (rw)
devpts on /dev/pts type devpts (rw,gid=5,mode=620)
```

```
tmpfs on /dev/shm type tmpfs (rw)
none on /proc/sys/fs/binfmt_misc type binfmt_misc (rw)
sunrpc on /var/lib/nfs/rpc_pipefs type rpc_pipefs (rw)
/dev/loop0 on /mnt type iso9660 (ro)
[root@server1 ~]#_
```

Before running the **mkisofs** command on Fedora 20, you must first run the **yum install genisoimage** command as the root user to install the ISO image tools.

Working with Hard Disks and SSDs

Hard disks typically come in three flavors: PATA, SATA, and SCSI. PATA hard disks must be set to one of four configurations, each of which has a different device file:

- Primary master (/dev/hda)
- Primary slave (/dev/hdb)
- Secondary master (/dev/hdc)
- Secondary slave (/dev/hdd)

SATA and SCSI hard disks typically have faster data transfer speeds than PATA hard disks, and most systems allow for the connection of more than four SATA or SCSI hard disks. As a result of these benefits, both SATA and SCSI hard disks are well suited to Linux servers that require a great deal of storage space for programs and user files. However, SATA and SCSI hard disks have different device files associated with them:

- First SCSI hard disk drive (/dev/sda)
- Second SCSI hard disk drive (/dev/sdb)
- Third SCSI hard disk drive (/dev/sdc)
- Fourth SCSI hard disk drive (/dev/sdd)
- Fifth SCSI hard disk drive (/dev/sde)
- Sixth SCSI hard disk drive (/dev/sdf)
- And so on

SSDs are a newer technology that use much faster NAND flash storage yet provide a hard disk compatible interface so that they can function as a drop-in replacement for hard disks. Most SSDs on the market are SATA and are treated like a SATA hard disk by the Linux operating system. As a result, /dev/sda could refer to the first SATA hard disk or the first SATA SSD, /dev/sdb could refer to the second SATA hard disk or second SATA SSD, and so on.

For simplicity, we'll refer primarily to hard disk drives when discussing permanent storage throughout the remainder of this book. However, all of the concepts related to hard disk drives apply equally to SSDs.

Standard Hard Disk Partitioning

Recall that hard disks have the largest storage capacity of any device that you use to store information on a regular basis. As helpful as this storage capacity can be, it also poses some problems; as the size of a disk increases, organization becomes more difficult and the chance of error increases. To solve these problems, Linux administrators typically divide a hard disk into smaller, more usable sections called **partitions**. Each partition can contain a separate filesystem and can be mounted to different mount point directories. Recall from Chapter 2 that Linux requires two partitions at minimum: a partition that is mounted to the root directory (the root partition) and a partition used to hold virtual memory (the swap partition). The swap partition does not require a filesystem, because it is written to and maintained by the operating system alone. It is good practice, however, to use more than just two partitions on a Linux system. This division allows you to do the following:

- Segregate different types of data—for example, home directory data is stored on a separate partition mounted to /home.

- Allow for the use of more than one type of filesystem on one hard disk drive—for example, some filesystems are tuned for database use.

- Reduce the chance that filesystem corruption will render a system unusable; if the partition that is mounted to the /home directory becomes corrupted, it does not affect the system because operating system files are stored on a separate partition mounted to the / directory.

- Speed up access to stored data by keeping filesystems as small as possible.

Segregation of data into physically separate areas of the hard disk drive can be exceptionally useful from an organizational standpoint. Keeping different types of data on different partitions gives you the ability to manipulate one type of data without affecting the rest of the system. This also reduces the likelihood that filesystem corruption will affect all files in the directory tree. Access speed is improved because a smaller area needs to be searched in a hard disk drive to locate data. This process is similar to searching for a penny in a 20,000-square-foot warehouse. It takes much less time to find the penny if that warehouse is divided into four separate departments of 5,000 square feet each and you know in which department the penny is located. Searching and maneuvering is much quicker and easier in a smaller, defined space than in a larger one.

On a physical level, hard disks are circular metal platters that spin at a fast speed. Data is read off these disks in concentric circles called **tracks**; each track is divided into **sectors** of information, and sectors are combined into more usable **blocks** of data, as shown in Figure 5-4. Most hard disk drives have several platters inside them, organized on top of each other such that they can be written to simultaneously speed up data transfer. A series consisting of the same concentric track on all of the metal platters inside a hard disk drive is known as a **cylinder**.

 SSDs use circuitry within the drive itself to divide data into logical tracks, sectors, blocks, and cylinders to ensure that the OS can work with SSDs like any hard disk. This allows you to create partitions and filesystems on an SSD in the same way that you would a hard disk. Today, SSDs are much faster at reading and writing data compared to hard disks. As a result, they are typically used on production Linux servers.

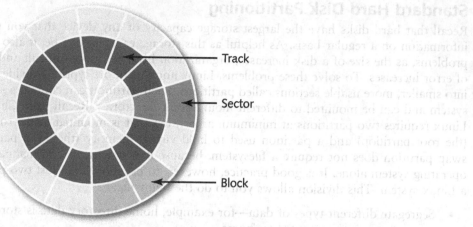

Figure 5-4 The physical areas of a hard disk

Partition definitions are stored in the first readable sector of the hard disk known as the Master Boot Record (MBR) or master boot block (MBB). Large hard disks (> 2TB) and many newer hard disks use a GUID Partition Table (GPT) in place of a MBR to allow for the additional addressing of sectors. If the MBR or GPT area of the hard disk becomes corrupted, the entire contents of the hard disk might be lost.

 It is common for Linux servers to have several hard disks. In these situations, it is also common to configure one partition on each hard disk and mount each partition to different directories on the directory tree. Thus, if one partition fails, an entire hard disk can be replaced with a new one and the data retrieved from a back-up source.

Recall from Chapter 2 that hard disks with a MBR normally contain up to four primary partitions; to overcome this limitation, you can use an extended partition in place of one of these primary partitions. An extended partition can then contain many more subpartitions called logical drives. Because it is on these partitions that you place a filesystem, there exist device files that refer to the various types of partitions that you can have on a hard disk. These device files start with the name of the hard disk (/dev/hda, /dev/hdb, /dev/sda, /dev/sdb, and so on) and append a number indicating the partition on that hard disk. The first primary partition is given the number 1, the second primary partition is given the number 2, the third primary partition is given the number 3, and the fourth primary partition is given the number 4. If any one of these primary partitions is labeled as an extended partition, the logical drives within are named starting with number 5. Table 5-5 lists some common hard disk partition names.

Note from Table 5-5 that any one of the primary partitions can be labeled as an extended partition. Also, for different disk drives than those listed in Table 5-5 (e.g., /dev/hdc), the partition numbers remain the same (e.g., /dev/hdc1, /dev/hdc2, and so on).

Hard disk partitions can be created specific to a certain filesystem. To create a partition that will later be formatted with an ext2, ex3, or ext4 filesystem, you should create a Linux partition (also known as type 83). Similarly, you should create a Linux swap partition (also

Partition	PATA Device Name (Assuming /dev/hda)	SATA/SCSI Device Name (Assuming /dev/sda)
1st primary partition	/dev/hda1	/dev/sda1
2nd primary partition	/dev/hda2	/dev/sda2
3rd primary partition	/dev/hda3	/dev/sda3
4th primary partition	/dev/hda4	/dev/sda4
1st logical drive in the extended partition	/dev/hda5	/dev/sda5
2nd logical drive in the extended partition	/dev/hda6	/dev/sda6
3rd logical drive in the extended partition	/dev/hda7	/dev/sda7
4th logical drive in the extended partition	/dev/hda8	/dev/sda8
5th logical drive in the extended partition	/dev/hda9	/dev/sda9
nth logical drive in the extended partition	/dev/hdan	/dev/sdan

Table 5-5 Common hard disk partition device files for /dev/hda and /dev/sda

known as type 82) if that partition is intended for use as virtual memory. This explicit choice of partition type allows for partitions that better suit the needs of a filesystem.

A typical Linux hard disk structure for the primary master PATA hard disk (/dev/hda) can contain a partition for the / filesystem (/dev/hda1) and an extended partition (/dev/hda2) that further contains a swap partition (/dev/hda5) and some free space, as shown in Figure 5-5.

A more complicated Linux hard disk structure for the first SATA/SCSI hard disk might involve preserving the Windows operating system partition, allowing a user to boot into and use the Linux operating system or boot into and use the Windows operating system. This is known as dual booting and is discussed in Chapter 6.

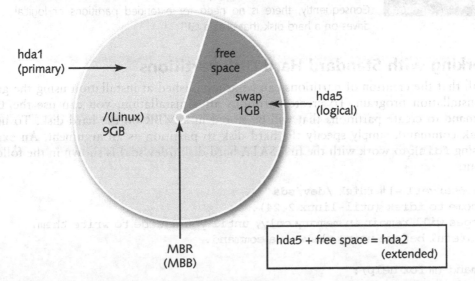

Figure 5-5 A sample Linux partitioning strategy

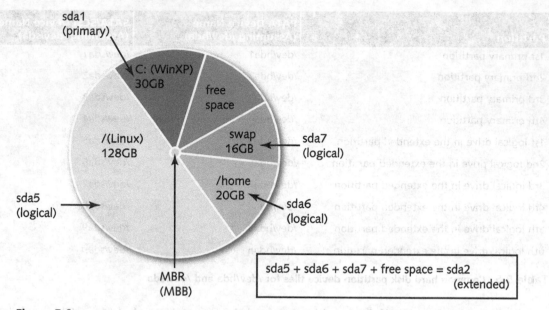

Figure 5-6   A sample dual-boot Linux partitioning strategy

In Figure 5-6, the Windows partition was created as a primary partition (/dev/sda1) and the Linux partitions are contained within the extended partition (/dev/sda2). Figure 5-6 also creates a separate filesystem for users' home directories mounted to /home (/dev/sda6).

Unlike hard disks that use a MBR, GPT hard disks don't need to adhere to the limitation of 4 primary partitions. Instead, you can create as many as 128 primary partitions (/dev/sda1 to /dev/sda128). Consequently, there is no need for extended partitions or logical drives on a hard disk that uses a GPT.

Working with Standard Hard Disk Partitions

Recall that the creation of partitions can be accomplished at installation using the graphical installation program. To create partitions after installation, you can use the **fdisk** command to create partitions that will be stored in a MBR on the hard disk. To use the fdisk command, simply specify the hard disk to partition as an argument. An example of using fdisk to work with the first SATA hard disk (/dev/sda) is shown in the following output:

```
[root@server1 ~]# fdisk /dev/sda
Welcome to fdisk (util-linux 2.24).
Changes will remain in memory only, until you decide to write them.
Be careful before using the write command.

Command (m for help):_
```

Note from the preceding output that the fdisk command displays a prompt for the user to accept fdisk commands; a list of possible fdisk commands can be seen if the user presses the m key at this prompt, as shown in the following example:

```
Command (m for help): m
Help:

    DOS (MBR)
     a   toggle a bootable flag
     b   edit nested BSD disklabel
     c   toggle the dos compatibility flag

    Generic
     d   delete a partition
     l   list known partition types
     n   add a new partition
     p   print the partition table
     t   change a partition type
     v   verify the partition table

    Misc
     m   print this menu
     u   change display/entry units
     x   extra functionality (experts only)

    Save & Exit
     w   write table to disk and exit
     q   quit without saving changes

    Create  a new label
     g   create a new empty GPT partition table
     G   create a new empty SGI (IRIX) partition table
     o   create a new empty DOS partition table
     s   create a new empty Sun partition table

Command (m for help):_
```

To print a list of the partitions currently set on /dev/sda, you could press the p key at the fdisk prompt:

```
Command (m for help): p

Disk /dev/sda: 20 GiB, 21474836480 bytes, 41943040 sectors
Units: sectors of 1 * 512 = 512 bytes
Sector size (logical/physical): 512 bytes / 512 bytes
I/O size (minimum/optimal): 512 bytes / 512 bytes
Disklabel type: dos
Disk identifier: 0x0000996b
```

```
   Device  Boot    Start        End      Blocks   Id  System
/dev/sda1           2048    4196351    2097152   82  Linux swap / Solaris
/dev/sda2     *   4196352   30679039   13241344   83  Linux
/dev/sda3        30679040   41943039    5632000   83  Linux

Command (m for help):_
```

Notice that the device names appear on the left side of the preceding output, including the partition that is booted to (/dev/sda2), the start and end location of partitions on the physical hard disk (start and end cylinders), the number of total blocks for storing information in the partition, as well as the partition type and description (83 is a Linux partition, 82 is a Linux swap partition). A Linux partition can contain a Linux filesystem—for example, ext4.

To remove the /dev/sda3 partition and all the data contained on the filesystem within, you could use the d key noted earlier:

```
Command (m for help): d
Partition number (1-3, default 3): 3

Command (m for help): p

Disk /dev/sda: 20 GiB, 21474836480 bytes, 41943040 sectors
Units: sectors of 1 * 512 = 512 bytes
Sector size (logical/physical): 512 bytes / 512 bytes
I/O size (minimum/optimal): 512 bytes / 512 bytes
Disklabel type: dos
Disk identifier: 0x0000996b

   Device  Boot    Start        End      Blocks   Id  System
/dev/sda1           2048    4196351    2097152   82  Linux swap / Solaris
/dev/sda2     *   4196352   30679039   13241344   83  Linux

Command (m for help):_
```

To create an extended partition using the fourth primary partition (/dev/sda4) with two logical drives (/dev/sda5 and /dev/sda6), you could use the n key noted earlier and specify the partition to create, the starting cylinder on the hard disk, and the size in blocks (+5G makes a 5GB partition):

```
Command (m for help): n
Partition type:
p   primary partition (2 primary, 0 extended, 2 free)
e   extended
Select (default p): e
Partition number (3,4, default 3): 4
First sector (30679040-41943039, default 30679040): 30679040
Last sector, +sectors or +size{K,M,G,T,P} (30679040-41943039, default
41943039): +5G

Created a new partition 3 of type 'Extended' and of size 5 GiB.
```

```
Command (m for help): p

Disk /dev/sda: 20 GiB, 21474836480 bytes, 41943040 sectors
Units: sectors of 1 * 512 = 512 bytes
Sector size (logical/physical): 512 bytes / 512 bytes
I/O size (minimum/optimal): 512 bytes / 512 bytes
Disklabel type: dos
Disk identifier: 0x0000996b


    Device    Boot      Start        End      Blocks    Id   System
/dev/sda1               2048    4196351     2097152    82   Linux swap / Solaris
/dev/sda2      *     4196352   30679039    13241344    83   Linux
/dev/sda4          30679040   41164799     5242880     5   Extended


Command (m for help): n
Partition type:
  p   primary (2 primary, 1 extended, 1 free)
  l   logical (numbered from 5)
Select (default p): l

Adding logical partition 5
First sector (30681088-41164799, default 30681088): 30681088
Last sector, +sectors or +size{K,M,G,T,P} (30681088-41164799, default
41164799): +3GB

Created a new partition 5 of type 'Linux' and of size 2.8 GiB.

Command (m for help): p
Disk /dev/sda: 20 GiB, 21474836480 bytes, 41943040 sectors
Units: sectors of 1 * 512 = 512 bytes
Sector size (logical/physical): 512 bytes / 512 bytes
I/O size (minimum/optimal): 512 bytes / 512 bytes
Disklabel type: dos
Disk identifier: 0x0000996b


Device    Boot      Start        End      Blocks    Id   System
/dev/sda1               2048    4196351     2097152    82   Linux swap / Solaris
/dev/sda2      *     4196352   30679039    13241344    83   Linux
/dev/sda4          30679040   41164799     5242880     5   Extended
/dev/sda5          30681088   36540415     2929664    83   Linux


Command (m for help): n
Partition type:
  p   primary (2 primary, 1 extended, 1 free)
  l   logical (numbered from 5)
Select (default p): l
```

5

```
Adding logical partition 6
First sector (36542464-41164799, default 36542464): 36542464
Last sector, +sectors or +size{K,M,G,T,P} (36542464-41164799, default
41164799): +2G

Created a new partition 6 of type 'Linux' and of size 2 GiB.

Command (m for help): p
Disk /dev/sda: 20 GiB, 21474836480 bytes, 41943040 sectors
Units: sectors of 1 * 512 = 512 bytes
Sector size (logical/physical): 512 bytes / 512 bytes
I/O size (minimum/optimal): 512 bytes / 512 bytes
Disklabel type: dos
Disk identifier: 0x0000996b

    Device   Boot    Start       End   Blocks   Id   System
/dev/sda1            2048   4196351  2097152   82   Linux swap / Solaris
/dev/sda2     *   4196352  30679039 13241344   83   Linux
/dev/sda4         30679040 41164799  5242880    5   Extended
/dev/sda5         30681088 36540415  2929664   83   Linux
/dev/sda6         36542464 40736767  2097152   83   Linux

Command (m for help): _
```

Notice from the preceding output that the default type for new partitions created with fdisk is 83 (Linux); to change this, you can type the t key at the fdisk prompt. To change the /dev/sda6 partition to type 82 (Linux swap), you can do the following at the fdisk prompt:

```
Command (m for help): t
Partition number (1,2,4-6, default 6): 6
Hex code (type L to all list codes): L
```

0	Empty	24	NEC DOS	81	Minix / old Lin	bf	Solaris
1	FAT12	39	Plan 9	82	Linux swap / So	c1	DRDOS/sec (FAT-
2	XENIX root	3c	PartitionMagic	83	Linux	c4	DRDOS/sec (FAT-
3	XENIX usr	40	Venix 80286	84	OS/2 hidden C:	c6	DRDOS/sec (FAT-
4	FAT16 <32M	41	PPC PReP Boot	85	Linux extended	c7	Syrinx
5	Extended	42	SFS	86	NTFS volume set	da	Non-FS data
6	FAT16	4d	QNX4.x	87	NTFS volume set	db	CP/M / CTOS / .
7	HPFS/NTFS	4e	QNX4.x 2nd part	88	Linux plaintext	de	Dell Utility
8	AIX	4f	QNX4.x 3rd part	8e	Linux LVM	df	BootIt
9	AIX bootable	50	OnTrack DM	93	Amoeba	e1	DOS access
a	OS/2 Boot Manag	51	OnTrack DM6 Aux	94	Amoeba BBT	e3	DOS R/O
b	W95 FAT32	52	CP/M	9f	BSD/OS	e4	SpeedStor
c	W95 FAT32 (LBA)	53	OnTrack DM6 Aux	a0	IBM Thinkpad hi	eb	BeOS fs
e	W95 FAT16 (LBA)	54	OnTrackDM6	a5	FreeBSD	ee	GPT
f	W95 Ext'd (LBA)	55	EZ-Drive	a6	OpenBSD	ef	EFI (FAT-12/16/
10	OPUS	56	Golden Bow	a7	NeXTSTEP	f0	Linux/PA-RISC b

11	Hidden FAT12	5c	Priam Edisk	a8	Darwin UFS	f1	SpeedStor
12	Compaq diagnost	61	SpeedStor	a9	NetBSD	f4	SpeedStor
14	Hidden FAT16 <3	63	GNU HURD or Sys	ab	Darwin boot	f2	DOS secondary
16	Hidden FAT16	64	Novell Netware	af	HFS / HFS+	fb	VMware VMFS
17	Hidden HPFS/NTF	65	Novell Netware	b7	BSDI fs	fc	VMware VMKCORE
18	AST SmartSleep	70	DiskSecure Mult	b8	BSDI swap	fd	Linux raid auto
1b	Hidden W95 FAT3	75	PC/IX	bb	Boot Wizard hid	fe	LANstep
1c	Hidden W95 FAT3	80	Old Minix	be	Solaris boot	ff	BBT
1e	Hidden W95 FAT1						

```
Hex code (type L to list all codes): 82
Changed type of partition 'Linux' to 'Linux swap / Solaris'.
Command (m for help): p

Disk /dev/sda: 20 GiB, 21474836480 bytes, 41943040 sectors
Units: sectors of 1 * 512 = 512 bytes
Sector size (logical/physical): 512 bytes / 512 bytes
I/O size (minimum/optimal): 512 bytes / 512 bytes
Disklabel type: dos
Disk identifier: 0x0000996b

    Device Boot    Start      End   Blocks  Id  System
/dev/sda1          2048  4196351  2097152  82  Linux swap / Solaris
/dev/sda2    *  4196352 30679039 13241344  83  Linux
/dev/sda4     30679040 41164799  5242880   5  Extended
/dev/sda5     30681088 36540415  2929664  83  Linux
/dev/sda6     36542464 40736767  2097152  82  Linux swap / Solaris

Command (m for help):_
```

Finally, to save partition changes to the hard disk and attempt to reload the new partition information back into memory, simply use the w key at the fdisk prompt:

```
Command (m for help): w
The partition table has been altered.

Calling ioctl() to re-read partition table.

Re-reading the partition table failed.: Device or resource busy
The kernel still uses the old table. The new table will be used at
the next reboot or after you run partprobe(8) or kpartx(8).
[root@server1 ~]#_
```

If the fdisk command indicates that the new partition information must be reloaded manually (as in the preceding example), simply reboot your machine. This is the most reliable way to ensure that the MBR is reloaded into memory successfully. For this reason, it is good form to always reboot your machine after running fdisk.

An easier alternative to fdisk is the cfdisk utility. When you run the **cfdisk command**, you see the interactive graphical utility shown in Figure 5-7. You can use this utility to

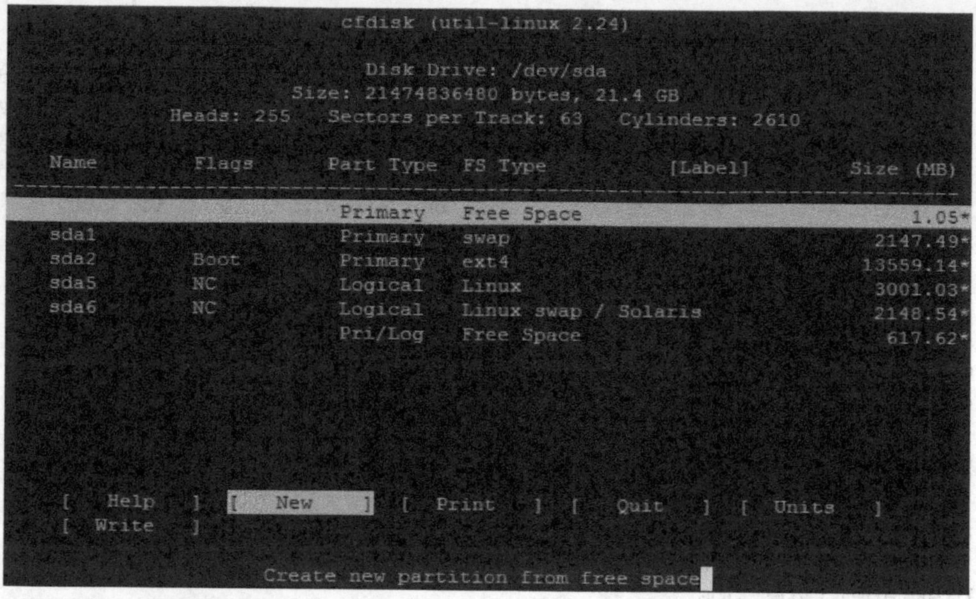

```
                    cfdisk (util-linux 2.24)

                   Disk Drive: /dev/sda
                Size: 21474836480 bytes, 21.4 GB
       Heads: 255   Sectors per Track: 63   Cylinders: 2610

  Name        Flags      Part Type  FS Type           [Label]        Size (MB)
  ----------------------------------------------------------------------------
                        Primary    Free Space                            1.05*
    sda1                Primary    swap                               2147.49*
    sda2      Boot      Primary    ext4                              13559.14*
    sda5      NC        Logical    Linux                              3001.03*
    sda6      NC        Logical    Linux swap / Solaris               2148.54*
                        Pri/Log    Free Space                          617.62*




      [  Help   ]   [   New    ]   [  Print  ]  [  Quit   ]  [  Units   ]
      [  Write  ]

               Create new partition from free space
```

Figure 5-7 The cfdisk utility

quickly create, manipulate, and delete partitions using choices at the bottom of the screen that you can navigate using your cursor keys. As with `fdisk`, after making changes within the cfdisk utility, you should reboot your system to ensure that the MBR is reloaded into memory successfully.

After your computer has rebooted, you can use the `mkfs`, `mount`, and `umount` commands discussed earlier, specifying the partition device file as an argument. To create an ext4 filesystem on the /dev/sda5 partition created earlier, you can use the following command:

```
[root@server1 ~]# mkfs -t ext4 /dev/sda5
mke2fs 1.42.8 (20-Jun-2013)
Filesystem label=
OS type: Linux
Block size=4096 (log=2)
Fragment size=4096 (log=2)
Stride=0 blocks, Stripe width=0 blocks
183264 inodes, 732416 blocks
36620 blocks (5.00%) reserved for the super user
First data block=0
Maximum filesystem blocks=750780416
23 block groups
32768 blocks per group, 32768 fragments per group
7968 inodes per group
Superblock backups stored on blocks:
        32768, 98304, 163840, 229376, 294912

Allocating group tables: done
```

```
Writing inode tables: done
Creating journal (16384 blocks): done
Writing superblocks and filesystem accounting information:done
[root@server1 ~]#_
```

To mount this ext4 filesystem to a new mount point directory called /data and view the contents, you can use the following commands:

```
[root@server1 ~]# mkdir /data
[root@server1 ~]# mount -t ext4 /dev/sda5 /data
[root@server1 ~]# mount
proc on /proc type proc (rw,nosuid,nodev,noexec,relatime)
sysfs on /sys type sysfs (rw,nosuid,nodev,noexec,relatime,seclabel)
/dev/sda2 on / type ext4 (rw,relatime,seclabel,data=ordered)
tmpfs on /tmp type tmpfs (rw,seclabel)
debugfs on /sys/kernel/debug type debugfs (rw,relatime)
mqueue on /dev/mqueue type mqueue (rw,relatime,seclabel)
hugetlbfs on /dev/hugepages type hugetlbfs (rw,relatime,seclabel)
configfs on /sys/kernel/config type configfs (rw,relatime)
/dev/sda5 on /data type ext4 (rw,relatime,seclabel,data=ordered)
[root@server1 ~]# ls -F /data
lost+found/
[root@server1 ~]#_
```

To allow the system to mount this filesystem automatically at every boot, simply edit the /etc/fstab file, such that it has the following entry for /dev/sda5:

```
[root@server1 ~]# cat /etc/fstab
#
# /etc/fstab
# Created by anaconda on Wed Sep 24 15:33:17 2015
#
# Accessible filesystems, by reference, are maintained under '/dev/disk'
# See man pages fstab(5), findfs(8), mount(8) and/or blkid(8) for info
#
/dev/sda2      /            ext4         defaults          1 1
/dev/sda1      swap         swap         defaults          0 0
/dev/sda5      /data        ext4         defaults          0 0
[root@server1 ~]#_
```

Although swap partitions do not contain a filesystem, you must still prepare swap partitions and activate them for use on the Linux system. To do this, you can use the **mkswap** command to prepare the swap partition and the **swapon command** to activate it. To prepare and activate the /dev/sda6 partition that we created earlier as virtual memory, you can use the following commands:

```
[root@server1 ~]# mkswap /dev/sda6
Setting up swapspace version 1, size = 2097148 KiB
no label, UUID=f7999b84-f9e4-48ff-879b-35b3bc941fab
[root@server1 ~]# swapon /dev/sda6
[root@server1 ~]# _
```

 You can also use the **swapoff command** to deactivate a swap partition.

Next, you can edit the /etc/fstab file to ensure that the new /dev/sda6 partition is activated as virtual memory, as shown here:

```
[root@server1 ~]# cat /etc/fstab
#
# /etc/fstab
# Created by anaconda on Wed Sep 24 15:33:17 2015
#
# Accessible filesystems, by reference, are maintained under'/dev/disk'
# See man pages fstab(5), findfs(8), mount(8) and/or blkid(8) for info
#
/dev/sda2       /            ext4      defaults       1 1
/dev/sda1       swap         swap      defaults       0 0
/dev/sda5       /data        ext4      defaults       0 0
/dev/sda6       swap         swap      defaults       0 0
[root@server1 ~]#_
```

If your hard disk uses a GPT instead of a MBR, you can't use the fdisk or cfdisk commands to create and modify partitions before you format them with a filesystem or prepare them for use as Linux swap memory. Instead, you can use the **gdisk** (GPT fdisk) **command** to create and work with up to 128 primary partitions on the GPT hard disk using an interface that is nearly identical to fdisk.

Many Linux distributions also contain the **parted** (GNU Parted) **command**, which can be used to create and modify partitions on both MBR and GPT hard disks. To work with partitions on /dev/sda, you can run the parted command with the device file as an argument. Once in the GNU Parted utility, you can type help to obtain a list of valid commands, or print to print the existing partitions, as shown here:

```
[root@server1 ~]# parted /dev/sda
GNU Parted 3.1
Using /dev/sda
Welcome to GNU Parted! Type 'help' to view a list of commands.
(parted) print
Model: ATA INTEL SSDSA2CW08 (scsi)
Disk /dev/sda: 80.0GB
Sector size (logical/physical): 512B/512B
Partition Table: gpt
Disk Flags:

Number  Start    End     Size    Type     File system    Flags
 1      1049kB   2149MB  2147MB  primary  linux-swap(v1)
 2      2149MB   15.7GB  13.6GB  primary  ext4           boot
(parted)_
```

Note from the previous output that the Intel SSD uses a GPT partition table and contains two partitions: a 2147MB Linux swap partition and a 13.6GB partition that contains the ext4 filesystem (the root filesystem). In the following example, two additional partitions are created using the free space on our hard disk within the GNU parted utility: a 3GB partition with the label "data" (/dev/sda3) and a 2GB partition with the label "logs" (/dev/sda4). During the creation process, you are prompted for the file system type. If you plan on formatting the partition with a Linux filesystem afterwards, choosing the default partition type of ext2 will suffice. However, if you plan on using the partition for swap, you should specify linux-swap when prompted for the file system type.

```
(parted) mkpart
Partition name? []? data
File system type? [ext2]? ext2
Start? 15.7GB
End? 18.7GB
(parted) print
Model: ATA INTEL SSDSA2CW08 (scsi)
Disk /dev/sda: 80.0GB
Sector size (logical/physical): 512B/512B
Partition Table: gpt
```

Number	Start	End	Size	File system	Name	Flags
1	1049kB	2149MB	2147MB	linux-swap(v1)		
2	2149MB	15.7GB	13.6GB	ext4	ext4	boot
3	15.7GB	18.7GB	2989MB		data	

```
(parted) mkpart
Partition name? []? logs
File system type? [ext2]? ext2
Start? 18.7GB
End? 20.7GB
(parted) print
Model: ATA INTEL SSDSA2CW08 (scsi)
Disk /dev/sda: 80.0GB
Sector size (logical/physical): 512B/512B
Partition Table: gpt
```

Number	Start	End	Size	File system	Name	Flags
1	1049kB	2149MB	2147MB	linux-swap(v1)		
2	2149MB	15.7GB	13.6GB	ext4	ext4	boot
3	15.7GB	18.7GB	2989MB		data	
4	18.7GB	20.7GB	1986MB		logs	

```
(parted) quit
Information: You may need to update /etc/fstab.
[root@server1 ~]#_
```

5

After creating GPT partitions that should contain a filesystem, you can proceed to format those partitions with a filesystem using mkfs, mount them to the directory tree with the mount command, and update the /etc/fstab file to mount them automatically, like we did earlier after creating partitions with fdisk. Alternatively, if you've created a Linux swap partition on a GPT hard disk, you can proceed to prepare that partition using mkswap and activate it using the swapon command, as we did earlier after creating partitions with fdisk.

 Recall that parted can also work with disks that contain an MBR. If you create partitions on an MBR hard disk, parted will additionally prompt you for the partition type (primary/extended/logical).

To remove the two GPT partitions that were added in the previous example, you can use the rm command within the parted utility and specify the partition number:

```
[root@server1 ~]# parted /dev/sda
GNU Parted 3.1
Using /dev/sda
Welcome to GNU Parted! Type 'help' to view a list of commands.
(parted) print
Model: ATA INTEL SSDSA2CW08 (scsi)
Disk /dev/sda: 80.0GB
Sector size (logical/physical): 512B/512B
Partition Table: gpt

Number  Start    End      Size    File system     Name    Flags
 1      1049kB   2149MB   2147MB  linux-swap(v1)
 2      2149MB   15.7GB   13.6GB  ext4            ext4    boot
 3      15.7GB   18.7GB   2989MB                  data
 4      18.7GB   20.7GB   1986MB                  logs

(parted) rm 4
(parted) rm 3
(parted) print
Model: ATA INTEL SSDSA2CW08 (scsi)
Disk /dev/sda: 80.0GB
Sector size (logical/physical): 512B/512B
Partition Table: gpt
Disk Flags:

Number  Start    End      Size    Type     File system     Flags
 1      1049kB   2149MB   2147MB  primary  linux-swap(v1)
 2      2149MB   15.7GB   13.6GB  primary  ext4            boot

(parted) quit
Information: You may need to update /etc/fstab.
[root@server1 ~]#_
```

Working with the LVM

In the previous section, you learned how to create standard hard disk partitions on a MBR or GPT hard disk. You also learned how to create filesystems on those partitions and mount the filesystems to a directory within the Linux filesystem hierarchy.

Instead of creating and mounting filesystems that reside on standard partitions, you can use the **Logical Volume Manager** (LVM) to create volumes. These volumes can contain a filesystem and be mounted to directories within the Linux filesystem hierarchy. Using volumes to host filesystems is far more flexible than using standard partitions since it allows you to select free space from unused partitions across multiple hard disks in your computer. This free space is then pooled together into a single group from which volumes can be created. These volumes can then be formatted with a filesystem and mounted to a directory on the Linux filesystem hierarchy. Furthermore, additional hard disks can easily be added to the LVM, where existing volumes can take advantage of the additional storage space.

The LVM consists of several different components:

- **Physical Volumes** (PVs) are unused partitions on hard disks that the LVM can use to store information.

- **Volume Groups** (VGs) contain one or more PVs. They represent the pools of hard disk storage space that are available to the LVM for creating logical volumes. Additional PVs can easily be added to a VG after creation.

- **Logical Volumes** (LVs) are the usable volumes that are created by the LVM from the available storage space within a VG. LVs contain a filesystem and are mounted to a directory in the Linux filesystem hierarchy. In addition, LVs can be resized easily by the LVM to use more or less storage space.

The LVM subsystem in Linux manages the storage of all data that is saved to LVs. The physical location of the data is transparent to the user. Furthermore, the LVM has error correction abilities that minimize the chance that data will become corrupted or lost. Figure 5-8 illustrates the relationships among LVM components in a sample LVM configuration that creates four different PVs from the standard partitions on three different hard disks. These PVs are added to a VG that is divided into three LVs that are each mounted to a directory on the Linux filesystem hierarchy (/directory1, /directory2, and /directory3).

To configure the LVM, you must first create one or more PVs that reference an unused partition on a hard disk in your computer. Say, for example, that you recently created a new partition called /dev/sda4. Rather than placing a filesystem on /dev/sda4, you could instead allow the LVM to use the /dev/sda4 partition using the **pvcreate command,** as shown here:

```
root@server1 ~]# pvcreate /dev/sda4
Physical volume "/dev/sda4" successfully created
[root@server1 ~]#_
```

You should use the pvcreate command to create PVs for each unused partition that you wish to be used by the LVM. For simplicity in code output, we will only create a single PV in this section to demonstrate the configuration of LVM.

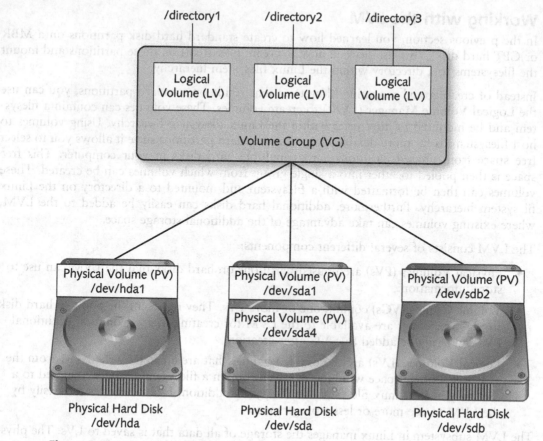

Figure 5-8 A sample LVM configuration

The **pvdisplay** command can be used to display detailed information about each PV. The following pvdisplay command indicates that /dev/sda4 has 32 GB of available space:

```
[root@server1 ~]# pvdisplay
"/dev/sda4" is a new physical volume of "32.00 GiB"
--- NEW Physical volume ---
PV Name               /dev/sda4
VG Name
PV Size               32.00 GiB
Allocatable           NO
PE Size               0
Total PE              0
Free PE               0
Allocated PE          0
PV UUID               YZDmIG-0qFU-54AT-ioB6-bjKa-sHcC-i8IJo0
[root@server1 ~]#_
```

Once you have created PVs, you can create a VG that uses the space in the PVs using the **vgcreate command**. For example, to create a VG called vg00 that uses the /dev/sda4 PV, you could use the following vgcreate command:

```
[root@server1 ~]# vgcreate vg00 /dev/sda4
Volume group "vg00" successfully created
[root@server1 ~]#_
```

To create a VG that uses multiple PVs, simply add multiple device arguments to the vgcreate command. For example, the vgcreate vg00 /dev/sda5 /dev/sdb1 /dev/sdc3 command would create a VG called vg00 that uses three PVs (/dev/sda5, /dev/sdb1, and /dev/sdc3).

When creating a VG, it is important to choose the block size for saving data since it cannot be safely changed later. This is called the **physical extent (PE) size** of the VG. A large PE size results in larger write operations and a larger maximum filesystem size for LVs. For example, a PE size of 32MB will allow for a maximum LV size of 2TB.

By default, the vgcreate command chooses an appropriate PE size according to the current sizes of the PVs that are associated with the VG, but you can use the -s or --physicalextentsize options to the vgcreate command to select a different PE size during VG creation.

The **vgdisplay command** can be used to display detailed information about each VG. The following vgdisplay command indicates that /dev/sda4 has over 31 GB of available space:

```
[root@server1 ~]# vgdisplay
--- Volume group ---
  VG Name                 vg00
  System ID
  Format                  lvm2
  Metadata Areas          1
  Metadata Sequence No    1
  VG Access               read/write
  VG Status               resizable
  MAX LV                  0
  Cur LV                  0
  Open LV                 0
  Max PV                  0
  Cur PV                  1
  Act PV                  1
  VG Size                 32.00 GiB
  PE Size                 4.00 MiB
  Total PE                8192
  Alloc PE / Size         0 / 0
  Free  PE / Size         8192 / 32.00 GiB
  VG UUID                 C2jrUC-LZmR-0tSX-bLqj-43S0-8U7i-0ajUgP
[root@server1 ~]#_
```

Next, you can create LVs from the available space in your VG using the **lvcreate command** and view your results using the **lvdisplay command**. The following commands create an LV called "data" that uses 15GB of space from vg00 as well as an LV called "extras" that uses 16GB of space from vg00, and it displays the results.

```
[root@server1 ~]# lvcreate -L 15GB -n data vg00
  Logical volume "data" created
[root@server1 ~]# lvcreate -L 16GB -n extras vg00
  Logical volume "extras" created
[root@server1 ~]# lvdisplay
--- Logical volume ---
  LV Path                /dev/vg00/data
  LV Name                data
  VG Name                vg00
  LV UUID                hMCr4Z-JNrO-lVcf-5SZk-8UJg-B0ri-Am3siP
  LV Write Access        read/write
  LV Creation host, time localhost.localdomain, 2015-11-25 07:42:30
  LV Status              available
  # open                 0
  LV Size                15.00 GiB
  Current LE             3840
  Segments               1
  Allocation             inherit
  Read ahead sectors     auto
  - currently set to     256
  Block device           253:0

--- Logical volume ---
  LV Path                /dev/vg00/extras
  LV Name                extras
  VG Name                vg00
  LV UUID                yUH5xW-U81b-CD3t-N22K-70gD-xHpm-TTHQca
  LV Write Access        read/write
  LV Creation host, time localhost.localdomain, 2015-11-25 07:42:44
  LV Status              available
  # open                 0
  LV Size                16.00 GiB
  Current LE             4096
  Segments               1
  Allocation             inherit
  Read ahead sectors     auto
  - currently set to     256
  Block device           253:1
[root@server1 ~]#_
```

Notice from the preceding output that the new VGs can be accessed using the device files /dev/vg00/data and /dev/vg00/extras. You can also refer to your new VGs using the device files /dev/mapper/vg00-data and /dev/mapper/vg00-extras, which are typically used by the system when accessing the filesystems on your VGs.

You can work with these files as you would normally work with any other hard disk partition device file. For example, to create an ext4 filesystem on these devices and mount them to the appropriate directories on the filesystem, you could use the following commands:

```
[root@server1 ~]# mke2fs -t ext4 /dev/vg00/data
mke2fs 1.42.8 (20-Jun-2013)
Filesystem label=
OS type: Linux
Block size=4096 (log=2)
Fragment size=4096 (log=2)
Stride=0 blocks, Stripe width=0 blocks
983040 inodes, 3932160 blocks
196608 blocks (5.00%) reserved for the super user
First data block=0
Maximum filesystem blocks=4026531840
120 block groups
32768 blocks per group, 32768 fragments per group
8192 inodes per group
Superblock backups stored on blocks:
     32768, 98304, 163840, 229376, 294912, 819200, 884736, 1605632, 2654208

Writing inode tables: done
Creating journal (32768 blocks): done
Writing superblocks and filesystem accounting information: done

[root@server1 ~]# mke2fs -t ext4 /dev/vg00/extras
mke2fs 1.42.8 (20-Jun-2013)
Filesystem label=
OS type: Linux
Block size=4096 (log=2)
Fragment size=4096 (log=2)
Stride=0 blocks, Stripe width=0 blocks
1048576 inodes, 4194304 blocks
209715 blocks (5.00%) reserved for the super user
First data block=0
Maximum filesystem blocks=0
128 block groups
32768 blocks per group, 32768 fragments per group
8192 inodes per group
Superblock backups stored on blocks:
     32768, 98304, 163840, 229376, 294912, 819200, 884736, 1605632, 2654208,
     4096000

Writing inode tables: done
Creating journal (32768 blocks): done
Writing superblocks and filesystem accounting information: done

[root@server1 ~]# mkdir /data
[root@server1 ~]# mkdir /extras
[root@server1 ~]# mount /dev/vg00/data /data
```

```
[root@server1 ~]# mount /dev/vg00/extras /extras
[root@server1 ~]# mount
/dev/sda1 on / type ext4 (rw)
proc on /proc type proc (rw)
sysfs on /sys type sysfs (rw)
devpts on /dev/pts type devpts (rw,gid=5,mode=620)
tmpfs on /dev/shm type tmpfs (rw)
none on /proc/sys/fs/binfmt_misc type binfmt_misc (rw)
sunrpc on /var/lib/nfs/rpc_pipefs type rpc_pipefs (rw)
/dev/mapper/vg00-data on /data type ext4 (rw)
/dev/mapper/vg00-extras on /extras type ext4 (rw)
[root@server1 ~]#_
```

Next, you can edit the /etc/fstab file to ensure that your new logical volumes are automatically mounted at system startup, as shown here:

```
[root@server1 ~]# cat /etc/fstab
#
# /etc/fstab
# Created by anaconda on Mon Aug  2 09:34:19 2015
#
# Accessible filesystems, by reference, are maintained under'/dev/disk'
# See man pages fstab(5), findfs(8), mount(8) and/or blkid(8) for info
#
/dev/sda1           /            ext4         defaults        1 1
/dev/sda2           swap         swap         defaults        0 0
/dev/vg00/data      /data        ext4         defaults        0 0
/dev/vg00/extras    /extras      ext4         defaults        0 0
[root@server1 ~]#_
```

Three other useful commands that can display information about the PVs, VGs, and LVs that are configured on your system are the **pvscan** command, the **vgscan** command, and **lvscan** command, respectively. Also, you can add additional storage space to your LVs after configuration. More specifically, you can add another PV using the pvcreate command, add this PV to your existing VG using the **vgextend** command, and then increase the size of your LVs to use the additional space using the **lvextend** command. Before using these commands, always consult the manual pages to ensure that you are using the command options and arguments that will perform the desired actions.

Working with USB and Firewire-based Storage Devices

Because of their large capacity and portability, removable storage devices are commonly used today to store backups of data, pictures, music, movies, programs, and documents. These devices, which typically connect to your PC via high speed USB or Firewire cables, include:

- Flash memory drives
- External hard drives
- Digital cameras (that contain flash memory cards)

- Media players (such as Apple iPods)
- Smartphones
- Tablets

Nearly all removable storage device manufacturers emulate the SCSI protocol in the firmware of the device itself. If a GUI environment is loaded, Fedora 20 recognizes removable media devices that connect to your PC via USB or Firewire cables as SCSI devices and automatically mounts them to a new directory under the /run/media/*username* directory named for the label on the device, much like CDs and DVDs. Additionally, you will be able to access or safely eject your device using the associated icon in the Files application within the GUI environment, as shown with the Cafe_Scientifique DVD in Figure 5-3.

Since it is common to work with removable media devices within a GUI environment, understanding the device names and mount point directories used by the devices themselves is often irrelevant. You can work with the files on removable media devices by accessing the appropriate icons in the Files application that represent the devices in the GUI environment. However, if you are working in a command-line terminal (perhaps on a Linux server that does not have a GUI environment), you need to keep track of when a USB or Firewire storage device is plugged into the computer in order to understand which device file the Linux operating system will assign to it.

For example, if your Linux system has two hard disks (/dev/sda and /dev/sdb) and a PATA DVD drive (/dev/hda), the next available device file for a newly inserted USB flash drive would be /dev/sdc and the first partition on that device would be referred to as /dev/sdc1. As a result, you could create a mount point to the directory for the USB flash drive under the /media directory and mount the device to this directory, as shown here (omitting the filesystem type allows the mount command to auto-detect the filesystem type on the device):

```
[root@server1 ~]# mkdir /media/FlashDrive
[root@server1 ~]# mount /dev/sdc1 /media/FlashDrive
[root@server1 ~]#_
```

Monitoring Filesystems

After filesystems are created on devices and those devices are mounted to the directory tree, they should be checked periodically for errors, disk space usage, and inode usage. This minimizes the problems that can occur as a result of a damaged filesystem and reduces the likelihood that a file cannot be saved due to insufficient disk space.

Disk Usage

Several filesystems can be mounted to the directory tree. As mentioned earlier, the more filesystems that are used, the less likely a corrupted filesystem will interfere with normal system operations. Conversely, more filesystems typically results in less hard disk space per filesystem and might result in system errors if certain filesystems fill up with data. Many Linux administrators create filesystems for the /, /usr, and /var directories during installation. The /usr directory contains most utilities and installed programs on a Linux system, and it should have enough space for future software installations. The /var directory grows in size continuously as it stores log files. Old log files should be removed periodically to leave room for new ones. The / filesystem is the most vital of these; it should always contain a great deal of free space used as working space for the operating system. As a result, the / filesystem should be monitored frequently. If free space on the / filesystem falls below 10 percent, the system might suffer from poorer performance or cease to operate.

The easiest method for monitoring free space by mounted filesystems is to use the **df** (disk free space) command, as shown in the following output:

```
[root@server1 ~]# df
Filesystem              1K-blocks      Used   Available   Use%   Mounted on
/dev/sda1               30237648    7227280    21474368    26%   /
devtmpfs                  422820         80      422760     1%   /dev
tmpfs                     480640        272      480368     1%   /dev/shm
/dev/mapper/vg00-data   15481840     169456    14525952     2%   /data
/dev/mapper/vg00-extras 16513960     176108    15498992     2%   /extras
[root@server1 ~]#_
```

From the preceding output, the only filesystems used are the / filesystem, the /data filesystem, and the /extras filesystem; the /usr and /var directories are simply directories on the / filesystem, which increases the importance of monitoring the / filesystem. Because the / filesystem is 26 percent used in the preceding output, there is no immediate concern. However, log files and software installed in the future will increase this number and might warrant the purchase of an additional hard disk for data to reside on.

Alternatively, you can view the output of the df command in a more user-friendly (or human-readable) format by using the –h option, which prints sizes in the most convenient format (G = gigabyte, M = megabyte), as shown here:

```
[root@server1 ~]# df -h
Filesystem              Size    Used    Avail   Use%   Mounted on
/dev/sda1                29G    6.9G      21G    26%   /
devtmpfs                413M     80K     413M     1%   /dev
tmpfs                   470M    272K     470M     1%   /dev/shm
/dev/mapper/vg00-data    15G    166M      14G     2%   /data
/dev/mapper/vg00-extras  16G    172M      15G     2%   /extras
[root@server1 ~]#_
```

It is important to remember that the df command only views mounted filesystems; thus, to get disk free space statistics for a floppy filesystem, you should mount it prior to viewing the output of the df command:

```
[root@server1 ~]# mount /dev/fd0
[root@server1 ~]# df
Filesystem              1K-blocks      Used   Available   Use%   Mounted on
/dev/sda1               30237648    7227280    21474368    26%   /
devtmpfs                  422820         80      422760     1%   /dev
tmpfs                     480640        272      480368     1%   /dev/shm
/dev/mapper/vg00-data   15481840     169456    14525952     2%   /data
/dev/mapper/vg00-extras 16513960     176108    15498992     2%   /extras
/dev/fd0                    1412         17        1323     2%   /mnt/
floppy

[root@server1 ~]# umount /dev/fd0
```

```
[root@server1 ~]# df
Filesystem              1K-blocks     Used   Available  Use%  Mounted on
/dev/sda1               30237648   7227280    21474368   26%  /
devtmpfs                  422820        80      422760    1%  /dev
tmpfs                     480640       272      480368    1%  /dev/shm
/dev/mapper/vg00-data   15481840    169456    14525952    2%  /data
/dev/mapper/vg00-extras 16513960    176108    15498992    2%  /extras
[root@server1 ~]#_
```

If a filesystem is approaching full capacity, it might be useful to examine which directories on that filesystem are taking up the most disk space such that you can remove or move files from that directory to another filesystem that has sufficient space. To view the size of a directory and its contents in kilobytes, you can use the **du** (directory usage) **command**. If the directory is large, you should use either the more or less command to view the output page-by-page, as shown with the following /usr directory:

```
[root@server1 ~]# du /usr |more
56048    /usr/sbin
4        /usr/include/telepathy-1.0
48       /usr/include/python3.3m
40       /usr/include/python2.7
156      /usr/include
8        /usr/libexec/gedit
24       /usr/libexec/spice-gtk-x86_64
20       /usr/libexec/awk
2720     /usr/libexec/ipsec
28       /usr/libexec/plymouth
32       /usr/libexec/shotwell
8        /usr/libexec/totem
12       /usr/libexec/gstreamer-1.0
16       /usr/libexec/utempter
8        /usr/libexec/psacct
12       /usr/libexec/coreutils
1592     /usr/libexec/sssd
20       /usr/libexec/file-roller
36       /usr/libexec/man-db
12       /usr/libexec/gstreamer-0.10
432      /usr/libexec/sudo
1168     /usr/libexec/bluetooth
528      /usr/libexec/openssh
--More--
```

To view only a summary of the total size of a directory, simply use the –s switch to the du command, as shown in the following example with the /usr directory:

```
[root@server1 ~]# du –s /usr
5719324 /usr
[root@server1 ~]# _
```

As with the df command, the du command also accepts the -h option to make the view more human readable; the following indicates that the total size of the /usr directory is 5.5GB:

```
[root@server1 ~]# du -hs /usr
5.5G   /usr
[root@server1 ~]# _
```

Recall that every filesystem has an inode table that contains the inodes for the files and directories on the filesystem; this inode table is made during filesystem creation and is usually proportionate to the size of the filesystem. Each file and directory uses one inode; thus, a filesystem with several small files might use up all of the inodes in the inode table and prevent new files from being created on the filesystem. To view the total number of inodes and free inodes for an ext2, ext3, or ext4 filesystem, you can use the dumpe2fs command with the -h switch, as shown in the following output:

```
[root@server1 ~]# df
Filesystem                 1K-blocks      Used  Available  Use%  Mounted on
/dev/sda1                   30237648   7227280   21474368   26%  /
devtmpfs                      422820        80     422760    1%  /dev
tmpfs                         480640       272     480368    1%  /dev/shm
/dev/mapper/vg00-data       15481840    169456   14525952    2%  /data
/dev/mapper/vg00-extras     16513960    176108   15498992    2%  /extras
[root@server1 ~]# dumpe2fs -h /dev/sda1
dumpe2fs 1.42.8 (20-Jun-2013)
Filesystem volume name:    <none>
Last mounted on:           /
Filesystem UUID:           db545f1d-c1ee-4b70-acbe-3dc61b41db20
Filesystem magic number:   0xEF53
Filesystem revision #:     1 (dynamic)
Filesystem features:       has_journal ext_attr resize_inode dir_index
filetype needs_recovery extent flex_bg sparse_super large_file huge_file
uninit_bg dir_nlink extra_isize
Filesystem flags:          signed_directory_hash
Default mount options:     user_xattr acl
Filesystem state:          clean
Errors behavior:           Continue
Filesystem OS type:        Linux
Inode count:               1921360
Block count:               7680000
Reserved block count:      384000
Free blocks:               5752659
Free inodes:               1663809
First block:               0
Block size:                4096
Fragment size:             4096
Reserved GDT blocks:       1022
Blocks per group:          32768
Fragments per group:       32768
Inodes per group:          8176
```

```
Inode blocks per group:     511
Flex block group size:      16
Filesystem created:         Mon Aug  2 09:27:13 2015
Last mount time:            Thu Aug 12 10:55:03 2015
Last write time:            Mon Aug  2 10:24:23 2015
Mount count:                20
Maximum mount count:        -1
Last checked:               Mon Aug  2 09:27:13 2015
Check interval:             0 (<none>)
Lifetime writes:            13 GB
Reserved blocks uid:        0 (user root)
Reserved blocks gid:        0 (group root)
First inode:                11
Inode size:                 256
Required extra isize:       28
Desired extra isize:        28
Journal inode:              8
First orphan inode:         1705241
Default directory hash:     half_md4
Directory Hash Seed:        cab24941-82b1-43a5-8b3f-18a93adbfd94
Journal backup:             inode blocks
Journal features:           journal_incompat_revoke
Journal size:               128M
Journal length:             32768
Journal sequence:           0x000031fe
Journal start:              1
[root@server1 ~]# _
```

In the preceding output, you can see that there are 1921360 inodes in the inode table and that 1663809 of them are free to use when creating new files and directories.

Checking Filesystems for Errors

Filesystems themselves can accumulate errors over time. These errors are often referred to as **filesystem corruption** and are common on most filesystems. Those filesystems that are accessed frequently are more prone to corruption than those that are not. As a result, such filesystems should be checked regularly for errors.

The most common filesystem corruption occurs because a system was not shut down properly using the shutdown, poweroff, halt, or reboot commands. Data is stored in memory for a short period of time before it is written to a file on the hard disk. This process of saving data to the hard disk is called **syncing**. If the computer's power is turned off, data in memory might not be synced properly to the hard disk and corruption might occur.

Filesystem corruption can also occur if the hard disks are used frequently for time-intensive tasks such as database access. As the usage of any system increases, so does the possibility for operating system errors when writing to the hard disks. Along the same lines, the physical hard disks themselves are mechanical in nature and can wear during time. Some areas of the hard disk platter might become unusable if they cannot hold a magnetic charge; these areas are known as **bad blocks**. When the operating system finds a bad block, it puts a reference to that bad block in the bad blocks table on the filesystem. Any entries in the bad blocks table are not used for any future disk storage.

To check a filesystem for errors, you can use the **fsck** (filesystem check) command, which can check filesystems of many different types. The fsck command takes an option specifying the filesystem type and an argument specifying the device to check; if the filesystem type is not specified, the filesystem is automatically detected. It is also important to note that the filesystem being checked must be unmounted beforehand for the fsck command to work properly, as shown next:

```
[root@server1 ~]# fsck /dev/vg00/data
fsck from util-linux 2.24
e2fsck 1.42.8 (20-Jun-2013)
/dev/mapper/vg00-data is mounted.
e2fsck: Cannot continue, aborting.
[root@server1 ~]# umount /dev/vg00/data
[root@server1 ~]# fsck /dev/vg00/data
fsck from util-linux 2.24
e2fsck 1.42.8 (20-Jun-2013)
/dev/mapper/vg00-data: clean, 11/983040 files, 104064/3932160 blocks
[root@server1 ~]# _
```

 Because the / filesystem cannot be unmounted, you should only run the fsck command on the / filesystem from single-user mode (discussed in Chapter 8) or from live installation media (discussed in Chapter 6).

Notice from the preceding output that the fsck command does not give lengthy output on the terminal screen when checking the filesystem; this is because the fsck command only performs a quick check for errors unless the -f option is used to perform a full check, as shown in the following example:

```
[root@server1 ~]# fsck -f /dev/vg00/data
fsck from util-linux 2.24
e2fsck 1.42.8 (20-Jun-2013)
Pass 1: Checking inodes, blocks, and sizes
Pass 2: Checking directory structure
Pass 3: Checking directory connectivity
Pass 4: Checking reference counts
Pass 5: Checking group summary information
/dev/mapper/vg00-data: 11/983040 files (0.0% non-contiguous),
104064/3932160 blocks
[root@server1 ~]# _
```

Table 5-6 displays a list of common options used with the fsck command.

If the fsck command finds a corrupted file, it displays a message to the user asking whether to fix the error; to avoid these messages, you may use the -a or -y options listed in Table 5-6 to specify that the fsck command should automatically repair any corruption. If there are files that the fsck command cannot repair, it places them in the lost+found directory on that filesystem and renames the file to the inode number.

Option	Description
-f	Performs a full filesystem check
-a or -y	Allows fsck to automatically repair any errors
-A	Checks all filesystems in /etc/fstab that have a 1 or 2 in the sixth field
-Cf	Performs a full filesystem check and displays a progress line
-AR	Checks all filesystems in /etc/fstab that have a 1 or 2 in the sixth field but skips the / filesystem
-V	Displays verbose output

Table 5-6 Common options to the fsck Command

To view the contents of the lost+found directory, simply mount the device and view the contents of the lost+found directory immediately underneath the mount point. Because it is difficult to identify lost files by their inode number, most users delete the contents of this directory periodically. Recall that the lost+found directory is automatically created when an ext2, ext3 or ext4 filesystem is created.

Just as you can use the mke2fs command to make an ext2, ext3, or ext4 filesystem, you can use the e2fsck command to check an ext2, ext3, or ext4 filesystem. The e2fsck command accepts more options and can check a filesytem more thoroughly than fsck. For example, by using the -c option to the e2fsck command, you can check for bad blocks on the hard disk and add them to a bad block table on the filesystem so that they are not used in the future, as shown in the following example:

```
[root@server1 ~]# e2fsck -c /dev/vg00/data
e2fsck 1.42.8 (20-Jun-2013)
Checking for bad blocks (read-only test): done
/dev/vg00/data: Updating bad block inode.
Pass 1: Checking inodes, blocks, and sizes
Pass 2: Checking directory structure
Pass 3: Checking directory connectivity
Pass 4: Checking reference counts
Pass 5: Checking group summary information

/dev/vg00/data: ***** FILE SYSTEM WAS MODIFIED *****
/dev/vg00/data: 11/983040 files (0.0% non-contiguous), 104064/3932160 blocks
[root@server1 ~]# _
```

The badblocks command can be used to perform the same function as the e2fsck command with the -c option.

You cannot use the fsck command to check a btrfs filesystem. Instead, you must use the **btrfs command** to check a btrfs filesystem after unmounting it. For example, the command btrfs check /dev/sda5 will check the unmounted btrfs filesystem on /dev/sda5.

Recall from earlier in this chapter that the fsck command is run at boot time when filesystems are mounted from entries in the /etc/fstab file. Any entries in /etc/fstab that have a 1 in the sixth field are checked first, followed by entries that have a 2 in the sixth field. However, on many Linux systems a full filesystem check is forced periodically each time an ext2, ext3, or ext4 filesystem is mounted. This might delay booting for several minutes or even hours, depending on the size of the filesystems being checked. To change this interval, you can use the -i option to the **tune2fs command**, as shown next:

```
[root@server1 ~]# tune2fs -i 0 /dev/vg00/data
tune2fs 1.42.8 (20-Jun-2013)
Setting interval between check 0 seconds
[root@server1 ~]# _
```

The tune2fs command can be used to change or "tune" filesystem parameters after a filesystem has been created. Changing the interval between checks to 0 seconds, as shown in the preceding example, disables filesystem checks.

Hard Disk Quotas

If there are several users on a Linux system, there must be enough hard disk space to support the files that each user is expected to store on the hard disk. However, if hard disk space is limited or company policy limits disk usage, you should impose limits on filesystem usage. These restrictions, called **hard disk quotas,** can be applied to users or groups of users. Furthermore, **quotas** can restrict how many files and directories a user can create (that is, restrict the number of inodes created) on a particular filesystem or the total size of all files that a user can own on a filesystem. Two types of quota limits are available: soft limits and hard limits. **Soft limits** are hard disk quotas that the user can exceed for a certain period of time (seven days by default), whereas **hard limits** are rigid quotas that the user cannot exceed. Quotas are typically enabled at boot time if there are quota entries in /etc/fstab, but they can also be turned on and off afterward by using the **quotaon** and **quotaoff** commands, respectively.

By default, quota support is not installed on Fedora 20. To obtain quota support, you must run the yum install quota command to download and install the quota package from an Internet software repository. Following this, you can carry out the following steps to set up quotas for the /data filesystem and restrict the user user1:

1. Edit the /etc/fstab file to add the usrquota and grpquota mount options for the /data filesystem. The resulting /etc/fstab file should look like the following:

```
[root@server1 ~]# cat /etc/fstab
#
# /etc/fstab
# Created by anaconda on Mon Aug 2 09:34:19 2015
#
# Accessible filesystems, by reference, are maintained under '/dev/disk'
# See man pages fstab(5), findfs(8), mount(8) and/or blkid(8) for info
#
```

```
/dev/sda1          /       ext4    defaults                   1 1
/dev/sda2          swap    swap    defaults                   0 0
/dev/vg00/data     /data   ext4    defaults,usrquota,grpquota 0 0
[root@server1 ~]# _
```

You can also use journaled quotas on modern Linux kernels, which protects quota data during an unexpected shutdown. To use journaled quotas, simply replace the mount options of `defaults,usrquota,grpquota` in Step 1 with: `defaults,usrjquota=aquota.user,grpjquota=aquota.group,jqfmt=vfsv0`.

2. Remount the /data filesystem as read-write to update the system with the new options from /etc/fstab. The command to do this is:

```
[root@server1 ~]# mount /data -o remount,rw
[root@server1 ~]# _
```

3. Run the `quotacheck –mavugf –F vfsv0` command, which looks on the system for file ownership and creates the quota database (-f) using the default quota format (-F vfsv0) for all filesystems with quota options listed in /etc/fstab (-a), giving verbose output (-v) for all users and groups (-u and -g) even if the filesystem is used by other processes (-m). This creates and places information in the /data/aquota.user and /data/aquota.group files. Sample output from the quotacheck command is shown here:

```
[root@server1 ~]# quotacheck –mavugf –F vfsv0
quotacheck: Your kernel probably supports journaled quota but you are
not using it. Consider switching to journaled quota to avoid running
quotacheck after an unclean shutdown.
quotacheck: Scanning /dev/sda2 [/] done
quotacheck: Checked 8983 directories and 109416 files
[root@server1 ~]# _
```

If you receive any warnings at the beginning of the quotacheck output at this stage, you can safely ignore them since they are the result of newly created *aquota.user* and *aquota.group* files that have not been used yet.

4. Turn user and group quotas on for all filesystems that have quotas configured using the `quotaon -avug` command:

```
[root@server1 ~]# quotaon -avug
/dev/mapper/vg00-data [/data]: group quotas turned on
/dev/mapper/vg00-data [/data]: user quotas turned on
[root@server1 ~]# _
```

You can also enable and disable quotas for individual filesystems. For example, you can use the quotaon /data command to enable quotas for the /data filesystem and the quotaoff /data command to disable them.

5. Edit the quotas for certain users by using the **edquota command** as follows: edquota -u <username>. This brings up the vi editor and allows you to set soft and hard quotas for the number of blocks a user can own on the filesystem (typically, 1 block = 1 kilobyte) and the total number of inodes (files and directories) that a user can own on the filesystem. A soft limit and hard limit of zero (0) indicates that there is no limit. To set a hard limit of 20MB (=20480KB) and 1000 inodes, as well as a soft limit of 18MB (=18432KB) and 900 inodes, you can do the following:

```
[root@server1 ~]# edquota –u user1
Disk quotas for user user1 (uid 500):
Filesystem              blocks   soft   hard   inodes   soft   hard
/dev/mapper/vg00-data    1188      0      0      326      0      0
~
~
~
~
"/tmp//EdP.aclpslv" 3L, 216C
```

Next, place the appropriate values in the columns provided and then save and quit the vi editor:

```
Disk quotas for user user1 (uid 500):
Filesystem              blocks   soft   hard   inodes   soft   hard
/dev/mapper/vg00-data    1188   18432  20480     326    900   1000
~
~
~
:wq
"/tmp/EdP.aclpslv" 3L, 216C written
[root@server1 ~]# _
```

6. Edit the time limit for which users can go beyond soft quotas by using the edquota -u -t command. The default time limit for soft quotas is seven days, but it can be changed as follows:

```
[root@server1 ~]# edquota –u -t
Grace period before enforcing soft limits for users:
Time units may be: days, hours, minutes, or seconds
Filesystem              Block grace period        Inode grace period
/dev/mapper/vg00-data        7days                     7days
~
~
~
"/tmp//EdP.alvzfSy" 4L, 233C
```

7. Ensure that quotas were updated properly by gathering a report for quotas by user on the /data filesystem using the **repquota command**, as shown in the following output:

```
[root@server1 ~]# repquota /data
*** Report for user quotas on device /dev/mapper/vg00-data
Block grace time: 7days; Inode grace time: 7days
```

User	Block limits				File limits			
	used	soft	hard	grace	used	soft	hard	grace
root	--	6420573	0	0		376520	0	0	
daemon	--	8	0	0		3	0	0	
lp	--	4	0	0		1	0	0	
polkitd	--	8	0	0		2	0	0	
abrt	--	24	0	0		4	0	0	
colord	--	20	0	0		4	0	0	
geoclue	--	4	0	0		1	0	0	
chrony	--	12	0	0		3	0	0	
tss	--	12	0	0		2	0	0	
unbound	--	8	0	0		2	0	0	
pulse	--	4	0	0		1	0	0	
gdm	--	128	0	0		32	0	0	
user1	--	1188	18432	20480		326	900	1000	

```
[root@server1 ~]# _
```

Note that most users in the preceding output are system users and do not have quotas applied to them. These users are discussed in Chapter 10.

The aforementioned commands are only available to the root user; however, regular users can view their own quota using the **quota command**. The root user can also use the quota command but can also use it to view quotas of other users:

```
[root@server1 ~]# quota
Disk quotas for user root (uid 0): none
[root@server1 ~]# quota -u user1
Disk quotas for user user1 (uid 500):
Filesystem      blocks   quota   limit   grace   files   quota   limit   grace
/dev/mapper/vg00-data
                  1188   18432   20480            326     900    1000
[root@server1 ~]# _
```

Chapter Summary

- Disk devices are represented by device files that reside in the /dev directory. These device files specify the type of data transfer, the major number of the device driver in the Linux kernel, and the minor number of the specific device.

- Each disk device must contain a filesystem, which is then mounted to the Linux directory tree for usage using the mount command. The filesystem can later be unmounted using the umount command. The directory used to mount the device must not be in use by any logged-in users for mounting and unmounting to take place.

- Hard disks must be partitioned into distinct sections before filesystems are created on those partitions. To partition a hard disk with an MBR, you can use the fdisk, cfdisk, or parted command. To partition a hard disk with a GPT, you can use the gdisk or parted command.

- Many different filesystems are available to Linux; each filesystem is specialized for a certain purpose, and several different filesystems can be mounted to different mount points on the directory tree. You can create a filesystem on a device using the `mkfs` command and its variants.

- The LVM can be used to create logical volumes from the free space within multiple partitions on the various hard disks within your system. Like standard hard disk partitions, logical volumes can contain a filesystem and be mounted to the Linux directory tree. They allow for the easy expansion and reconfiguration of storage.

- USB and Firewire storage devices are recognized as SCSI disks by the Linux system.

- It is important to monitor disk usage using the `df`, `du`, and `dumpe2fs` commands to avoid running out of storage space. Similarly, it is important to check disks for errors using the `fsck` command and its variants.

- If hard disk space is limited, you can use hard disk quotas to limit the space that each user has on filesystems.

Key Terms

/dev directory   The directory off the root where device files are typically stored.

/etc/fstab   A file used to specify which filesystems to mount automatically at boot time and queried by the `mount` command if an insufficient number of arguments are specified.

/etc/mtab   A file that stores a list of currently mounted filesystems.

/proc/devices   A file that contains currently used device information.

bad blocks   The areas of a storage medium unable to store data properly.

block   The unit of data commonly used by filesystem commands; a block can contain several sectors.

block devices   The storage devices that transfer data to and from the system in chunks of many data bits by caching the information in RAM; they are represented by block device files.

btrfs command   A command used to configure btrfs filesystem options and check btrfs filesystems for errors.

cfdisk command   A command used to partition hard disks; displays a graphical interface in which the user can select partitioning options.

character devices   The storage devices that transfer data to and from the system one data bit at a time; they are represented by character device files.

cylinder   A series of tracks on a hard disk that are written to simultaneously by the magnetic heads in a hard disk drive.

device file   A file used by Linux commands that represents a specific device on the system; these files do not have a data section and use major and minor numbers to reference the proper driver and specific device on the system, respectively.

df (disk free space) command   A command that displays disk free space by filesystem.

du (directory usage) command   A command that displays directory usage.

edquota command   A command used to specify quota limits for users and groups.

fdisk command   A command used to create, delete, and manipulate partitions on hard disks.

filesystem   The organization imposed on a physical storage medium that is used to manage the storage and retrieval of data.

filesystem corruption   The errors in a filesystem structure that prevent the retrieval of stored data.

formatting   The process in which a filesystem is placed on a disk device.

fsck (filesystem check) command   A command used to check the integrity of a filesystem and repair damaged files.

fuser command   A command used to identify any users or processes using a particular file or directory.

gdisk (GPT fdisk) command   A command used to create partitions on a GPT hard disk. It uses an interface that is very similar to **fdisk**.

hard disk quotas   The limits on the number of files, or total storage space on a hard disk drive, available to a user.

hard limit   A hard disk quota that the user cannot be exceed.

Logical Volume (LV)   A volume that is managed by the LVM and comprised of free space within a VG.

Logical Volume Manager (LVM)   A set of software components within Linux that can be used to manage the storage of information across several different hard disks on a Linux system.

lvcreate command   A command used to create LVM logical volumes.

lvdisplay command   A command used to view LVM logical volumes.

lvextend command   A command used to add additional space from VGs to existing LVM logical volumes.

lvscan command   A command used to view LVM logical volumes.

major number   The number used by the kernel to identify which device driver to call to interact properly with a given category of hardware; hard disk drives, CDs, and video cards are all categories of hardware; similar devices share a common major number.

minor number   The number used by the kernel to identify which specific hardware device, within a given category, to use a driver to communicate with. See also *major number*.

mkfs (make filesystem) command   A command used to format or create filesystems.

mkisofs command   A command used to create an ISO image from one or more files on the filesystem.

mknod command   A command used to re-create a device file, provided the major number, minor number, and type (character or bock) are known.

mkswap command   A command used to prepare newly created swap partitions for use by the Linux system.

mount command   A command used to mount filesystems on devices to mount point directories.

mount point   The directory in a file structure to which something is mounted.

mounting   A process used to associate a device with a directory in the logical directory tree such that users can store data on that device.

parted (GNU Parted) command   A command used to create partitions on a GPT or MBR hard disk.

partition   A physical division of a hard disk drive.

physical extent (PE) size   The block size used by the LVM when storing data on a volume group.

Physical Volumes (PVs)   A hard disk partition that is used by the LVM.

pvcreate command   A command used to create LVM physical volumes.

pvdisplay command   A command used to view LVM physical volumes.

pvscan command   A command used to view LVM physical volumes.

quota command   A command used to view disk quotas imposed on a user.

quotaoff command   A command used to deactivate disk quotas.

quotaon command   A command used to activate disk quotas.

quotas   The limits that can be imposed on users and groups for filesystem usage.

repquota command   A command used to produce a report on quotas for a particular filesystem.

root filesystem   The filesystem that contains most files that make up the operating system; it should have enough free space to prevent errors and slow performance.

sector   The smallest unit of data storage on a hard disk; sectors are arranged into concentric circles called tracks and can be grouped into blocks for use by the system.

soft limit   A hard disk quota that the user can exceed for a certain period of time.

swapoff command   A command used to disable a partition for use as virtual memory on the Linux system.

swapon command   A command used to enable a partition for use as virtual memory on the Linux system.

syncing   The process of writing data to the hard disk drive that was stored in RAM.

track   The area on a hard disk that forms a concentric circle of sectors.

tune2fs command   A command used to modify ext2 and ext3 filesystem parameters.

umount command   A command used to break the association between a device and a directory in the logical directory tree.

vgcreate command   A command used to create LVM VG.

vgdisplay **command**   A command used to view LVM VG.

vgextend **command**   A command used to add additional physical volumes to an LVM VG.

vgscan **command**   A command used to view LVM VGs.

Volume Group (VG)   A group of PVs that are used by the LVM.

Review Questions

1. Which of the following commands can be used to create partitions on either a MBR or GPT hard disk?

    a. gdisk

    b. cfsck

    c. fdisk

    d. parted

2. After a partition on a hard disk drive is formatted with a filesystem, all partitions on that hard disk drive must use the same filesystem. True or False?

3. You want to see the filesystems that are presently in use on the system. What command could you use?

    a. cat /etc/fstab

    b. ls -l /etc/fstab

    c. cat /etc/mtab

    d. ls -l /etc/fstab

4. Jim has just purchased two new SCSI hard disk drives and a controller card for them. He properly installs the hardware in his machine. Before he can use them for data storage and retrieval, what must he do? (Choose all that apply.)

    a. Mount the two hard drives so they are accessible by the operating system.

    b. Mount a filesystem to each of the hard disk drives.

    c. Create one or more partitions on each of the hard disk drives.

    d. Use the vi editor to edit /etc/mtab and create an entry for the controller card and the hard disk drives.

    e. Mount any partitions created on the two hard drives such that they are accessible by the operating system.

    f. Format any partitions created with a valid filesystem recognized by Linux.

5. Given the following output from /etc/fstab, which filesystems will be automatically checked on boot by the fsck command?

/dev/sda1	/	ext4	defaults	1	1
none	/dev/pts	devpts	gid=5,mode=620	1	0
none	/proc	proc	defaults	0	1
none	/dev/shm	tmpfs	defaults	1	0
/dev/sdc2	swap	swap	defaults	0	1
/dev/dvd	/media/dvd	iso9660	noauto,ro	0	0
/dev/fd0	/media/floppy	auto	noauto	0	0

   a. none, as fsck must be run manually for each filesystem

   b. /, /dev/pts, and /dev/shm

   c. /, /proc, and swap

   d. all of them, as fsck is run automatically at boot for all filesystems

6. A user mounts a device to a mount point directory and realizes afterward there are files previously found within the mount point directory that are needed. What should this user do?

   a. Nothing; the files are lost and cannot ever be accessed.

   b. Nothing; the files could not have been there because you can only mount to empty directories.

   c. Unmount the device from the directory.

   d. Run the fsck command to recover the file.

   e. Look in the lost+found directory for the file.

7. Which command is used to display the amount of free space that exists on a filesystem?

   a. fsck

   b. quota

   c. du

   d. df

8. What must you do to successfully run the fsck command on a filesystem?

   a. Run the fsck command with the -u option to automatically unmount the filesystem first.

   b. Choose yes when warned that running fsck on a mounted filesystem can cause damage.

   c. Unmount the filesystem.

   d. Ensure that the filesystem is mounted.

9. Character devices typically transfer data more quickly than block devices. True or False?

10. What does the du /var command do?

    a. shows the users connected to the /var directory

    b. shows the size of all directories within the /var directory

    c. dumps the /var directory

    d. displays the amount of free space in the /var directory

11. What does the command dumpe2fs -h do?

    a. backs up an ext2 filesystem

    b. displays the number of inodes used and available in an ext2 filesystem

    c. dumps an ext2 filesystem

    d. is not a valid command

12. The first floppy drive on the system is not responding. You enter the file /dev/fd0 command and receive the following output. What is the problem?

    ```
    [root@server1 root]# file /dev/fd0
    /dev/fd0:  ASCII text
    [root@server1 root]#
    ```

    a. The floppy drive cable has come loose.

    b. There is no floppy disk in the drive.

    c. The device file has become corrupt.

    d. The floppy drive is seen as a character device.

13. Which of the following statements are true? (Choose all that apply.)

    a. Quotas can only limit user space.

    b. Quotas can only limit the number of files a user can own.

    c. Quotas can limit both user space and the number of files a user can own.

    d. Hard limits can never be exceeded.

    e. Hard limits allow a user to exceed them for a certain period of time.

    f. Soft limits can never be exceeded.

    g. Soft limits allow a user to exceed them for a certain period of time.

    h. Either a hard limit or a soft limit can be set, but not both concurrently.

14. A device file _____. (Choose all that apply.)

    a. has no inode section

    b. has no data section

    c. has no size

    d. displays a major and minor number in place of a file size

    e. has a fixed size of 300 kilobytes

15. Which of the following statements regarding LVM structure is correct?
    a. PVs are collections of VGs.
    b. LVs are created from the free space available within PVs.
    c. VGs are comprised of one or more PVs.
    d. PVs use the space within LVs to create VGs.

16. The lvextend command can be used to add additional unused space within a volume group to an existing logical volume. True or False?

17. You plug a USB flash memory drive into a system that has two SATA hard disks. How will the partition on this USB flash memory drive be identified by Linux?
    a. /dev/sda1
    b. /dev/sda2
    c. /dev/sdb1
    d. /dev/sdc1

18. Which command mounts all existing filesystems in /etc/fstab?
    a. mount -f
    b. mount -a
    c. mount /etc/fstab
    d. mount /etc/mtab

19. A user runs the fsck command with the -a option on a filesystem that is showing signs of corruption. How would that user locate any files the system was unable to repair?
    a. Look in the root of the filesystem.
    b. The system prompts the user for a target location when it comes across a file it cannot repair.
    c. Mount the filesystem and check the lost+found directory underneath the mount point.
    d. View the contents of the directory /lost+found.

20. Which command is used to format a partition on a hard disk drive with the ext4 filesystem?
    a. format_ext4 *device*
    b. ext4mkfs *device*
    c. e2mkfs –t ext4 *device*
    d. makeext4FS *device*

Hands-on Projects

These projects should be completed in the order given. The hands-on projects presented in this chapter should take a total of three hours to complete. The requirements for this lab include:

- A computer with Fedora 20 installed according to Hands-on Project 2-1

Project 5-1

In this hands-on project, you view and create device files.

1. Boot your Fedora Linux virtual machine. After your Linux system has loaded, switch to a command-line terminal (tty2) by pressing **Ctrl+Alt+F2**. Log in to the terminal using the user name of **root** and the password of **LNXrocks!**.

2. At the command prompt, type **ls –l /dev/tty6** and press **Enter**. What device does /dev/tty6 represent? Is this file a block or character device file? Why? What are the major and minor numbers for this file?

3. At the command prompt, type **rm –f /dev/tty6** and press **Enter**. Next, type **ls –l /dev/tty6** at the command prompt and press **Enter**. Was the file removed successfully?

4. Switch to the command-line terminal (tty6) by pressing **Ctrl+Alt+F6** and attempt to log in to the terminal using the user name of **root** and the password of **LNXrocks!**. Were you successful?

5. Switch back to the command-line terminal (tty2) by pressing **Ctrl+Alt+F2**, type the command **mknod /dev/tty6 c 4 6** at the command prompt, and press **Enter**. What did this command do? Next, type **ls –l /dev/tty6** at the command prompt and press **Enter**. Was the file re-created successfully?

6. At the command prompt, type **reboot** and press **Enter**. After your Linux system has loaded, switch to a command-line terminal (tty6) by pressing **Ctrl+Alt+F6** and log in to the terminal using the user name of **root** and the password of **LNXrocks!**. Why were you successful?

7. At the command prompt, type **ls –l /dev/tty?** and press **Enter**. What is similar about all of these files? Is the major number different for each file? Is the minor number different for each file? Why?

8. At the command prompt, type **find /dev** and press **Enter** to list all of the filenames underneath the /dev directory. Are there many files? Next, type **du –s /dev** at the command prompt and press **Enter**. How large in kilobytes are all files within the /dev directory? Why?

9. At the command prompt, type **cat /proc/devices | more** and press **Enter**. Which devices and major numbers are present on your system? What character devices have a major number of 4? How does this compare with what you observed in Step 2?

10. Type **exit** and press **Enter** to log out of your shell.

Project 5-2

In this hands-on project, you create a filesystem on a floppy disk and practice mounting it to the directory tree.

1. Switch to a command-line terminal (tty2) by pressing **Ctrl+Alt+F2**. Log in to the terminal using the user name of **root** and the password of **LNXrocks!**.

2. At the command prompt, type **poweroff** and press **Enter** to shut down your virtual machine.

3. In your virtualization software, create a new virtual floppy disk and attach it to your virtual machine. Next, boot your virtual machine. After your Linux system has loaded, switch to a command-line terminal (tty2) by pressing **Ctrl+Alt+F2**. Log in to the terminal using the user name of **root** and the password of **LNXrocks!**.

4. At the command prompt, type **modprobe floppy** and press **Enter** to load the floppy driver into the Linux kernel.

5. At the command prompt, type **mkdir /mymount** and press **Enter** to create a new mount point directory. Next, type **ls -F /mymount** at the command prompt and press **Enter**. Are there any files in the /mymount directory? Next, type **cp /etc/hosts /mymount** at the command prompt and press **Enter**. Next, type **ls -F /mymount** at the command prompt and press **Enter** to verify that the hosts file was copied successfully.

6. At the command prompt, type **mkfs -t ext2 /dev/fd0** and press **Enter**.

7. At the command prompt, type **mount -t ext2 /dev/fd0 /mymount** and press **Enter**. Next, type **mount** at the command prompt and press **Enter**. Was your device successfully mounted to the /mymount directory?

8. At the command prompt, type **ls -F /mymount** and press **Enter**. What files do you see? Why? What happened to the hosts file? Next, type **cp /etc/inittab /mymount** at the command prompt and press **Enter**. At the command prompt, type **ls -F /mymount** and press **Enter** to verify that the file was copied to your device.

9. At the command prompt, type **umount /mymount** and press **Enter**. Next, type **mount** at the command prompt and press **Enter**. Was the device successfully unmounted from the /mymount directory?

10. At the command prompt, type **ls -F /mymount** and press **Enter**. What files do you see? Why? What happened to the inittab file and lost+found directory? Is the hosts file present?

11. At the command prompt, type **mount -t ext2 /dev/fd0 /mymount** and press **Enter**.

12. At the command prompt, type **cd /mymount** and press **Enter**. Next, type **ls -F** and press **Enter**. Are the inittab file and lost+found directory available again?

13. At the command prompt, type **umount /mymount** and press **Enter**. What error message did you receive? Next, type **fuser -u /mymount** and press **Enter**. Who is using the /mymount directory?

14. At the command prompt, type **cd** and press **Enter** to return to your home directory. Next, type **umount /mymount** at the command prompt and press **Enter**. Did you receive an error message? Type **mount** at the command prompt and press **Enter** to verify that the device was successfully unmounted from the /mymount directory.

15. Type **exit** and press **Enter** to log out of your shell.

Project 5-3

In this hands-on project, you mount DVDs to the directory tree and view their contents.

1. Switch to a graphical terminal (tty1) by pressing **Ctrl+Alt+F1** and log in to the GNOME desktop using the user name of **user1** and the password of **LNXrocks!**.

2. Click the **Activities** menu and select the **Files** icon to open the Files application.

3. In your virtualization software, attach the DVD ISO image for Fedora Linux (Fedora-Live-Desktop-x86_64-20-1.iso) to the DVD drive for the virtual machine. After you have completed this action, view your Files application. Is there an icon that represents your Fedora Live Desktop DVD in the left pane? Place your mouse over this icon to view the mount point directory. Which directory was your DVD automatically mounted to?

4. Take a few moments to explore the contents of the DVD within the Files application. When finished, click the eject button next to the Fedora Live Desktop DVD icon to eject the DVD.

5. Switch to a command-line terminal (tty2) by pressing **Ctrl+Alt+F2** and log in to the GNOME desktop using the user name of **root** and the password of **LNXrocks!**.

6. In your virtualization software, attach the DVD ISO image for Fedora Linux (Fedora-Live-Desktop-x86_64-20-1.iso) to the DVD drive for the virtual machine. After you have completed this action, type **mount** and press **Enter**. Is the DVD automatically mounted?

7. Next, type **mount /dev/cdrom /mymount** at the command prompt, and press **Enter**. What warning did you receive? Was the DVD successfully mounted to the /mymount directory?

8. At the command prompt, type **ls -F /mymount** and press **Enter**. Do you see the same files as you did in Step 4? Why?

9. At the command prompt, type **ls -l /dev/cdrom** and press **Enter**. What target file does the /dev/cdrom symbolic link point to?

10. At the command prompt, type **mount** and press **Enter**. Note the line at the bottom that lists your mounted DVD. What filesystem was automatically detected earlier when you mounted your DVD? Is the device file identical to the target file shown in Step 9?

11. Next, type **umount /mymount** at the command prompt and press **Enter**. Was the DVD successfully unmounted from the /mymount directory? Type the **mount** command at a command prompt and press **Enter** to verify this.

12. In your virtualization software, deattach the DVD ISO image for Fedora Linux (Fedora-Live-Desktop-x86_64-20-1.iso) to the DVD drive for the virtual machine. This performs the same action as ejecting the DVD from the physical DVD drive.

13. Type **exit** and press **Enter** to log out of your shell.

Project 5-4

In this hands-on project, you work with standard hard disk partitions. You will first create a hard disk partition using the fdisk utility. Next, you create an ext4 filesystem on the partition and mount it to the directory tree. Finally, you use the /etc/fstab file to automatically mount the partition at boot time.

1. Switch to a command-line terminal (tty2) by pressing **Ctrl+Alt+F2** and log in to the terminal using the user name of **root** and the password of **LNXrocks!**.

2. At the command prompt, type **fdisk device_file** and press **Enter**, where **device_file** is the device file for your first hard disk (**/dev/sda** if you have a SCSI or SATA hard disk, or **/dev/hda** if you have a PATA hard disk). At the **fdisk** prompt, type **m** and press **Enter** to view the various **fdisk** commands.

3. At the **fdisk** prompt, type **p** and press **Enter** to view the partition table on your hard disk. Which three partitions are present? When were they created? What are their types?

4. At the **fdisk** prompt, type **n** and press **Enter** to create a new partition. Next, type **e** to select a primary partition and press **Enter**. When prompted for the start sector, observe the valid range within the brackets and press **Enter** to select the default (the first available sector). When prompted for the end cylinder, observe the valid range within the brackets and press **Enter** to select the default (the last available sector).

5. At the **fdisk** prompt, type **p** and press **Enter** to view the partition table on your hard disk. How many partitions are present? What type of partition is /dev/hda4 or /dev/sda4?

6. At the **fdisk** prompt, type **n** and press **Enter** to create a new partition. Note that logical drive is automatically selected as the partition type since all available primary partitions have been used and there is already an extended partition. When prompted for the start sector, observe the valid range within the brackets and press **Enter** to select the default (the first available sector). When prompted for the end cylinder, type **+1GB** and press **Enter**.

7. At the **fdisk** prompt, type **p** and press **Enter** to view the partition table on your hard disk. How many partitions are present? What type of partition is /dev/hda5 or /dev/sda5?

8. At the **fdisk** prompt, type **l** and press **Enter** to view the different partition types. What type is used for Linux swap? Which character would you type at the fdisk prompt to change the type of partition?

9. At the **fdisk** prompt, type **w** and press **Enter** to save the changes to the hard disk and exit the fdisk utility.

10. At the command prompt, type **reboot** and press **Enter** to reboot your machine and ensure that the partition table was read into memory correctly. After your Linux system has been loaded, switch to a command-line terminal (tty2) by pressing **Ctrl+Alt+F2** and log in to the terminal using the user name of **root** and the password of **LNXrocks!**.

11. At the command prompt, type **mkfs –t ext4 device_file** and press **Enter**, where **device_file** is the device file for the first logical drive on your first hard disk (/dev/sda5 if you have a SCSI or SATA hard disk, or /dev/hda5 if you have a PATA hard disk).

12. At the command prompt, type **mkdir /newmount** and press **Enter** to create a mount point directory underneath the / directory for mounting the third partition on your first hard disk.

13. At the command prompt, type **mount –t ext4 device_file /newmount** and press **Enter**, where **device_file** is the device file for the first logical drive on your first hard disk (/dev/sda5 if you have a SCSI or SATA hard disk, or /dev/hda5 if you have a

PATA hard disk). This will mount the filesystem on your first logical drive in the extended partition to the /newmount directory. Next, type the **mount** command and press Enter to verify that the filesystem was mounted correctly.

14. At the command prompt, type **ls -F /newmount** and press Enter. Is the lost+found directory present? Next, type **cp /etc/hosts /newmount** at the command prompt and press Enter to copy the hosts file to the new partition. Verify that the copy was successful by typing the **ls -F /newmount** command at the command prompt again, and press Enter.

15. At the command prompt, type **umount /newmount** and press Enter. Next, type the **mount** command and press Enter to verify that the filesystem was unmounted correctly.

16. At the command prompt, type **vi /etc/fstab** and press Enter. Observe the contents of the file. Add a line to the bottom of the file as shown below, where *device_file* is the device file for the first logical drive on your first hard disk (/dev/sda5 if you have a SCSI or SATA hard disk, or /dev/hda5 if you have a PATA hard disk).

    device_file /newmount ext4 defaults 0 0

17. Save your changes and quit the vi editor.

18. At the command prompt, type **reboot** and press Enter. After your Linux system has been loaded, switch to a command-line terminal (tty2) by pressing **Ctrl+Alt+F2** and log in to the terminal using the user name of **root** and the password of **LNXrocks!**.

19. At the command prompt, type **mount** and press Enter. Is the third partition on your hard disk mounted? Why?

20. At the command prompt, type **umount /newmount** and press Enter. Next, type the **mount** command to verify that the filesystem was unmounted correctly.

21. At the command prompt, type **mount -a** and press Enter. Next, type the **mount** command and press Enter. Is the third partition on your hard disk mounted? Why?

22. Type **exit** and press Enter to log out of your shell.

Project 5-5

In this hands-on project, you create a new partition using the GNU Parted utility, and configure the LVM to host two logical volumes using the space within. Next, you will format these logical volumes and mount them to the directory tree, as well as edit the /etc/fstab file to ensure that they are mounted at boot time.

1. Switch to a command-line terminal (tty2) by pressing **Ctrl+Alt+F2** and log in to the terminal using the user name of **root** and the password of **LNXrocks!**.

2. At the command prompt, type **parted** *device_file* and press Enter, where *device_file* is the device file for your first hard disk (**/dev/sda** if you have a SCSI or SATA hard disk, or **/dev/hda** if you have a PATA hard disk). At the parted prompt, type **help** and press Enter to view the available commands.

3. At the parted prompt, type **print** and press Enter. Write down the End value for your first logical drive (/dev/sda5 or /dev/hda5): _____ (A). Next, write down the End value for your extended partition (/dev/sda4 or /dev/hda4): _____ (B). These two values represent the start and end of the remainder of the free space on your virtual hard disk.

4. At the parted prompt, type **mkpart** and press **Enter** to accept the default of logical drive. Press **Enter** again to accept the default partition type (Linux ext2). When prompted for the Start of the new partition, enter the (A) value you recorded in Step 3 and press **Enter**. When prompted for the End of the new partition, enter the (B) value you recorded in Step 3 and press **Enter**.

5. At the parted prompt, type **p** and press **Enter** to view the partition table on your hard disk. How many partitions are present? What type of partition is /dev/sda6 or /dev/hda6?

6. At the parted prompt, type **quit** and press **Enter** to save the changes to the hard disk and exit the GNU Parted utility.

7. At the command prompt, type **reboot** and press **Enter** to reboot your machine and ensure that the partition table was read into memory correctly. After your Linux system has been loaded, switch to a command-line terminal (tty2) by pressing **Ctrl+Alt+F2** and log in to the terminal using the user name of **root** and the password of **LNXrocks!**.

8. At the command prompt, type **pvcreate *device_file*** and press **Enter**, where ***device_file*** is the device file for your new partition (/dev/sda6 if you have a SCSI or SATA hard disk, or **/dev/hda6** if you have a PATA hard disk). What does this command do?

9. At the command prompt, type **vgcreate vg00 *device_file*** and press **Enter**, where ***device_file*** is the device file for your new partition (/dev/sda6 if you have a SCSI or SATA hard disk, or **/dev/hda6** if you have a PATA hard disk). What does this command do?

10. At the command prompt, type **lvcreate –L 2GB –n volume1 vg00** and press **Enter** to create a 2GB logical volume called volume1 from the vg00 volume group.

11. At the command prompt, type **lvcreate –L 2.5GB –n volume2 vg00** and press **Enter** to create a 2.5GB logical volume called volume2 from the vg00 volume group.

12. At the command prompt, type **mkfs –t ext4 /dev/vg00/volume1** and press **Enter** to format the volume1 logical volume using the ext4 filesystem. Next, type **mkfs –t ext4 /dev/vg00/volume2** and press **Enter** to format the volume2 logical volume using the ext4 filesystem.

13. At the command prompt, type **mkdir /volume1** and press **Enter** to create a mount point for the volume1 logical volume. Next, type **mkdir /volume2** and press **Enter** to create a mount point for the volume2 logical volume.

14. At the command prompt, type **mount –t ext4 /dev/vg00/volume1 /volume1** and press **Enter** to mount the volume1 logical volume to the /volume1 directory. Next, type **mount –t ext4 /dev/vg00/volume2 /volume2** and press **Enter** to mount the volume2 logical volume to the /volume2 directory. When finished, type **mount** and press **Enter** to verify that both filesystems are mounted.

15. At the command prompt, type **ls –F /volume1 /volume2** and press **Enter**. Is there a lost+found directory underneath each directory? Why?

16. At the command prompt, type **vi /etc/fstab** and press **Enter**. Add the following lines to the bottom of the file, as shown below, to ensure that the volume1 and volume2 logical volumes are mounted at boot time:

```
/dev/vg00/volume1      /volume1    ext4     defaults    0 0
/dev/vg00/volume2      /volume2    ext4     defaults    0 0
```

17. Save your changes and quit the vi editor.

18. At the command prompt, type **reboot** and press **Enter**. After your Linux system has been loaded, switch to a command-line terminal (tty2) by pressing **Ctrl+Alt+F2** and log in to the terminal using the user name of **root** and the password of **LNXrocks!**.

19. At the command prompt, type **mount** and press **Enter**. Are volume1 and volume2 mounted? Why? What device file is listed for volume1 and volume2?

20. At the command prompt, type the following commands in turn (pressing **Enter** after each one) and view the information displayed regarding your physical volumes volume group, and logical volumes:

    pvdisplay

    pvscan

    vgdisplay

    vgscan

    lvdisplay

    lvscan

21. Type **exit** and press **Enter** to log out of your shell.

Project 5-6

In this hands-on project, you view disk usage and check filesystems for errors.

1. Switch to a command-line terminal (tty2) by pressing **Ctrl+Alt+F2** and log in to the terminal using the user name of **root** and the password of **LNXrocks!**.

2. At the command prompt, type **df** and press **Enter**. What filesystems are displayed? Can you see the swap partition? Why?

3. At the command prompt, type **dumpe2fs –h /dev/vg00/volume1** and press **Enter**. How many inodes are available to this filesystem? How many inodes are free to be used? Why?

4. At the command prompt, type **fsck /dev/vg00/volume1** and press **Enter**. What error message do you receive and why?

5. At the command prompt, type **umount /volume1** and press **Enter**. Next, type the **mount** command and press **Enter** to verify that the filesystem was unmounted correctly.

6. At the command prompt, type **fsck /dev/vg00/volume1** and press **Enter**. How long did the filesystem check take and why?

7. At the command prompt, type **fsck –f /dev/vg00/volume1** and press **Enter**. How long did the filesystem check take and why?

3. Use the Internet to gather information on four filesystems compatible with Linux. For each filesystem, list the situations for which the filesystem was designed and the key features that the filesystem provides.

4. You have a Linux system that has a 1000GB hard disk drive, which has a 90GB partition containing an ext4 filesystem mounted to the / directory and a 4GB swap partition. Currently, this Linux system is only used by a few users for storing small files; however, the department manager wants to upgrade this system and use it to run a database application that will be used by 100 users. The database application and the associated data will take up over 200GB of hard disk space. In addition, these 100 users will store their personal files on the hard disk of the system. Each user must have a maximum of 5GB of storage space. The department manager has made it very clear that this system must not exhibit any downtime as a result of hard disk errors. How much hard disk space will you require, and what partitions would you need to ensure that the system will perform as needed? Where would these partitions be mounted? What quotas would you implement? What commands would you need to run and what entries to /etc/fstab would you need to create? Justify your answers.

5. You have several filesystems on your hard disk that are mounted to separate directories on the Linux directory tree. The /dev/sdc6 filesystem was unable to be mounted at boot time. What could have caused this? What commands could you use to find more information about the nature of the problem?

chapter 6

Linux Server Deployment

After completing this chapter, you will be able to:

- Identify the types of hardware present in most server systems
- Describe the configuration of SCSI devices
- Explain the different levels of RAID and types of RAID configurations
- Configure the ZFS filesystem
- Install a Linux server distribution
- Troubleshoot the Linux server installation process
- Access an installed system using system rescue

In Chapter 2, you examined a standard Linux installation process using common hardware components and practices. This chapter examines the specialized hardware and software configuration that will affect your choices during the installation of a Linux server distribution. In addition, you install the Ubuntu Server Linux distribution as well as learn how to deal with common installation problems. Finally, this chapter discusses how to access and use system rescue.

Understanding Server Hardware

Recall from Chapter 2 that the minimum hardware requirements for Fedora 20 include a meager 1GHz CPU, 1GB of RAM, and 10GB of disk space, which is far lower than most modern operating systems. However, Linux is incredibly scalable and often configured to work with far more hardware to perform a specialized set of tasks. For example, a Linux computer used as a desktop workstation will usually require enough RAM to run GNOME and desktop applications smoothly, as well as a modern CPU and plenty of disk space to store files, pictures, movies, and so on. An Intel Core i7 system with 8GB of RAM and a 1TB hard disk drive is closer to the type of hardware that you may find on a typical Linux desktop workstation. If that workstation is for personal use or gaming, expect to add a high-end graphics card to the mix that is supported by game platforms, such as Steam. For server computers, the amount of hardware should adequately support its intended use. A Linux Web server that handles e-commerce and a database engine will likely require at least 64 GB of RAM, multiple CPUs, and high-capacity SSDs to host the operating system, Web server software, and database engine.

Nearly all standard server hardware is supported by Linux. If you have recently purchased modern server hardware, there is a high likelihood that your Linux distribution will have all of the drivers that you need. However, if your system has specialized hardware (e.g., a specific Fibrechannel SAN controller), it is important to first verify with the hardware vendor that it has an adequate driver included for your Linux distribution (or available for download).

Moreover, server hardware has a different form factor compared to other computers. Nearly all servers within an organization are housed within a rackmount case that is mounted alongside other servers on a vertical server storage rack. Consequently, we call these servers **rackmount servers.**

 Rackmount servers are sometimes called **blade servers.**

Each rackmount server in the rack may contain a different operating system (or multiple operating systems if virtualization software is used) and will connect to a shared monitor/keyboard/mouse. This shared monitor/keyboard/mouse often folds away into the rack for storage, and it is necessary for initial configuration tasks such as server installation. All other server administration is performed remotely using the remote administration methods discussed in Chapter 12.

Most racks also contain one or more **Storage Area Network (SAN)** devices that provide a large amount of storage for the servers within the rack as well as one or more **uninterruptible** power supply (UPS) devices that provide backup battery power to servers and SANs within the rack in the event of a power loss.

The minimum height of a rackmount server is 1.75 inches; this is called a **1U server**. Most 1U servers have up to two hard drives (or SSDs) and up to two CPUs. Other rackmount servers take up more than one spot on the rack and have a height that is a multiple of a 1U server. For example, a 2U server is twice as high as a 1U server and often contains up to four CPUs and eight hard disks (or SSDs). Rackmount servers rarely exceed 4U.

Figure 6-1 shows a sample server rack configuration that hosts three 1U servers (Web server, file server and firewall server), two 2U servers (database server and email server), a 2U UPS, a 4U SAN, and a management station with a shared monitor/keyboard/mouse.

 Virtualization software is commonly used within server environments today. Consequently, each rackmount server shown in Figure 6-1 could host multiple server operating systems concurrently to better utilize the hardware installed on the rack.

NOTE

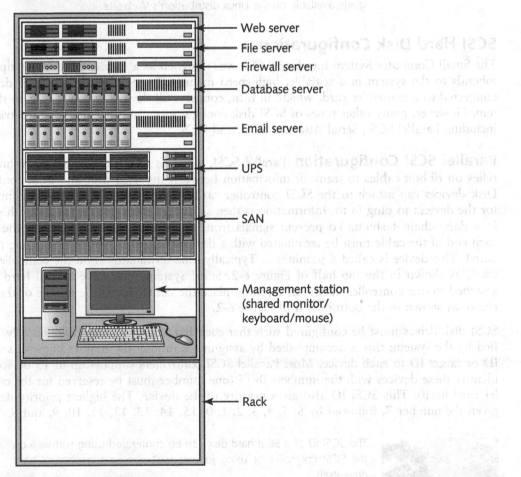

- Web server
- File server
- Firewall server
- Database server
- Email server
- UPS
- SAN
- Management station (shared monitor/ keyboard/mouse)
- Rack

Figure 6-1 A sample server rack

Configuring Server Storage

During the Fedora 20 installation process, described in Chapter 2, one of the most important configuration tasks involves configuring the permanent storage devices that will host the Linux operating system. This involves selecting the storage devices that will be used as well as creating partitions and filesystems. The storage that you configure during installation depends on your specific storage technologies and the space needs of your Linux system. In this section, we examine the configuration of advanced storage technologies that are commonly used on Linux servers, including SCSI, RAID, and ZFS.

You can choose from many different advanced storage technologies. However, because many of these technologies involve proprietary hardware and are used primarily on specialized systems, we will limit our discussion to the general-use technologies discussed in this section. To learn more about configuring other advanced storage technologies during a Linux server installation, consult the installation guide available on the Linux distribution's Web site.

SCSI Hard Disk Configuration

The Small Computer System Interface (SCSI) was designed as a way to connect multiple peripherals to the system in a scalable, high-speed manner. In most systems, a SCSI device is connected to a controller card, which, in turn, connects all devices attached to it to the system. However, many other types of SCSI disk configurations and technologies are available, including Parallel SCSI, Serial Attached SCSI, and iSCSI.

Parallel SCSI Configuration Parallel SCSI, which is the traditional SCSI technology, relies on ribbon cables to transmit information between the hard disk and SCSI controller. Disk devices can attach to the SCSI controller card via one cable, with several connectors for the devices to plug in to. Information is then sent from device to device along this cable in a daisy-chain fashion. To prevent signals from bouncing back and forth on the cable, each end of the cable must be terminated with a device that stops signals from being perpetuated. This device is called a **terminator**. Typically, one terminator is on the controller card itself, as shown in the top half of Figure 6-2. Some systems that have several hard drives attached to one controller, however, typically place the controller in the middle of the daisy chain, as shown in the bottom half of Figure 6-2.

SCSI disk drives must be configured such that each hard disk drive can be uniquely identified by the system; this is accomplished by assigning a unique ID number known as a **SCSI ID** or **target ID** to each device. Most Parallel SCSI controllers support up to 15 devices and identify these devices with the numbers 0–15 (one number must be reserved for the controller card itself). This SCSI ID also gives priority to the device. The highest priority device is given the number 7, followed by 6, 5, 4, 3, 2, 1, 0, 15, 14, 13, 12, 11, 10, 9, and 8.

The SCSI ID of a SCSI hard disk can be configured using software on the SCSI controller or using jumper switches on the physical hard drive itself.

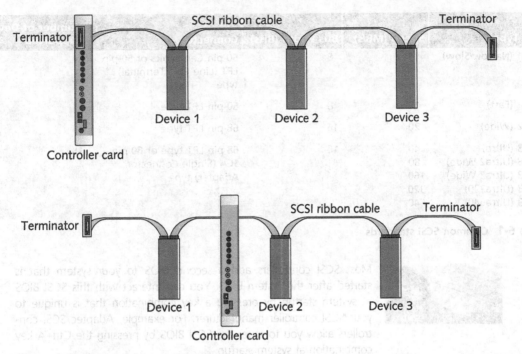

Figure 6-2 Connecting Parallel SCSI devices

 Some SCSI devices act as a gateway to other devices; if this is the case, each device is associated with a unique **Logical Unit Number (LUN)**.

Parallel SCSI technology has evolved over time; it was initially adopted as an industry-defined standard in 1986. At that time, SCSI used an 8-bit-wide data path on a controller card that held up to seven devices and had a data transfer speed of 5MB per second. This was commonly referred to as SCSI-1 (SCSI Standard 1). By 1994, it had evolved to a standard that used a 16-bit-wide data path on a controller card that could hold up to 15 devices and had a transfer speed of 20MB per second. This advance was referred to as SCSI-2 (SCSI Standard 2). SCSI-3 was introduced a short time later and provided speeds of over 160MB per second. Table 6-1 describes various SCSI technologies.

Before you install a Linux system, you must first ensure that you configure your Parallel SCSI devices properly. First, verify that all of your SCSI components (SCSI controller, cables, connectors, hard disks, terminators) support the same technology as listed in Table 6-1. Next, ensure that your SCSI components are connected properly, as shown in Figure 6-1. Finally, make sure your system recognizes the hard drives at system startup. To do this, examine the system BIOS or enter the SCSI BIOS on your SCSI controller card. When you start the Linux installation, your SCSI hard disks will be detected automatically as /dev/sda, /dev/sdb, and so on.

SCSI Type	Speed (MB/s)	Bus Width (Bits)	Connector	Number of Devices Supported
SCSI-1 (Narrow/Slow)	5	8	50-pin Centronics or 50-pin LPT (Line Port Terminal) type	7
SCSI-2 (Fast)	10	8	50-pin LPT type	7
SCSI-2 (Wide)	20	16	68-pin LPT type	15
SCSI-3 (Ultra) SCSI-3 (Ultra2 Wide) SCSI-3 (Ultra3 Wide) SCSI-3 (Ultra320) SCSI-3 (Ultra640)	40 80 160 320 640	16	68-pin LPT type or 80-pin SCA (Single Connector Adapter) type	15

Table 6-1   Common SCSI standards

Most SCSI controllers add a second BIOS to your system that is started after the system BIOS. You can interact with this SCSI BIOS at system startup by pressing a key combination that is unique to your SCSI controller manufacturer. For example, Adaptec SCSI controllers allow you to enter the SCSI BIOS by pressing the Ctrl+A key combination at system startup.

Parallel SCSI hard disks are rarely found on modern Linux servers. However, because Linux performs well with limited hardware, many organizations install Linux on legacy servers to extend their lifetime within the organization and save costs. These legacy servers often use parallel SCSI hard disks.

Serial Attached SCSI Configuration Serial Attached SCSI is a newer SCSI technology that can transfer data at up to 768MB/s. Up to 65,535 Serial Attached SCSI hard disks can be connected to a single SCSI controller via serial cables with small serial connectors (between 7 and 36 pins).

Before you install Linux on a system that includes Serial Attached SCSI hard disks, you must first connect the hard disks to the SCSI controller via the correct serial cable. Then, you must ensure that the hard disks are detected properly by the system or SCSI BIOS. All other Serial Attached SCSI configuration (SCSI ID, LUN, etc.) is performed automatically by the SCSI controller but can be changed manually if you access the SCSI BIOS.

As with Parallel SCSI disks, your Linux installation will detect your Serial Attached SCSI hard disks using /dev/sda, /dev/sdb, and so on.

FireWire (IEEE 1394) is also a serial-based SCSI transfer protocol. It can be used to transfer data to an external hard disk at speeds of over 800MB/s. Unfortunately, FireWire hard disks are not supported for hosting the Linux operating system during installation. Like USB hard disks, they are only intended to be used as removable media and are treated like USB hard disks by the Linux OS.

iSCSI Configuration Internet SCSI (iSCSI) is a recent SCSI technology that uses network cables to transfer data to and from remote hard disks that reside within a SAN or remote system, either on the local network or across the Internet. The computer connected to a remote hard disk via iSCSI is referred to as an **iSCSI initiator**, and the remote hard disk is called the **iSCSI target**. A iSCSI initiator can consist of a software component that is part of the Linux OS, or it can consist of a hardware component that is part of the iSCSI-compliant network card. Typically, iSCSI targets are contained within external network-attached SAN devices that contain multiple hard disks or SSDs (some SAN devices contain over 50 hard disks or SSDs).

A single iSCSI target can be used by multiple computers or iSCSI initiators across a network. The computers that use the same iSCSI target are said to be part of the same SAN. As a result, iSCSI is often referred to as a SAN technology.

The configuration settings for remote iSCSI devices vary by manufacturer. To connect the Linux computer to the remote iSCSI device, you must specify the configuration settings while installing Linux. This means you must understand the configuration settings used by your iSCSI device (name, authentication information, etc.) and ensure that your computer has an iSCSI-compliant network card before starting the installation process. During Linux installation, you need to provide the details regarding your iSCSI target if you want to install Linux on an iSCSI device. For Fedora 20, you will need to select Add a disk, as shown in Figure 2-10. This will allow you to select advanced storage options, as shown in Figure 6-3. You can then click the Add iSCSI Target button shown in Figure 6-3 and supply the TCP/IP configuration of your computer's network card as well as the configuration settings needed to connect to the remote iSCSI device. Following this, the installation will proceed and allow you to create Linux filesystems (e.g., /dev/sda) on your iSCSI device.

Figure 6-3 Configuring advanced storage options during a Fedora 20 installation

RAID Configuration

Recall that you typically create several partitions during installation to decrease the likelihood that the failure of a filesystem on one partition will affect the rest of the system. These partitions should be spread across several different hard disks to minimize the impact of a hard disk failure; if one hard disk fails, the data on the other hard disks is unaffected.

If a hard disk failure occurs, you must power down the computer, replace the failed hard disk drive, power on the computer, and restore the data that was originally on the hard disk drive from a back-up source, such as a tape device. The whole process can take several hours. However, with some systems, such as database servers, no amount of downtime is acceptable. In such situations, hard disk configurations that minimize the time required to recover from a hard disk failure are required. Such **fault tolerant** configurations are typically implemented by a **Redundant Array of Independent Disks (RAID)**. Note that RAID has other uses besides creating a fault tolerant system. It can be used to speed up access to hard disks or combine multiple hard disks into a single volume.

 Most Linux servers and SAN devices use RAID internally to provide for data fault tolerance.

Currently, seven basic RAID configurations, ranging from level 0 to level 6, are available. RAID level 0 configurations are not fault tolerant. One type of RAID level 0, known as **spanning**, consists of two hard disks that the system sees as one large volume. Using this technology, you could, for example, combine two 1TB hard disks into one 2TB partition. Spanning is useful when you need a large amount of storage space in a single volume without fault tolerance.

In another type of RAID level 0, called **disk striping**, an individual file is divided into sections and saved concurrently on multiple disks, one section per disk. For example, suppose you have a disk striping configuration made up of three disks. In that case, when you save a file, it is divided into three sections, with each section written to separate hard disk devices concurrently, in a third of the amount of time it would take to save the entire file on one hard disk device. Note that the system can also read the same file in one-third the amount of time it would take if the file were stored on a single hard drive. Disk striping is useful when you need to speed up disk access, but it is not fault tolerant. If one hard disk fails in a RAID level 0 configuration, all data is lost.

RAID level 1, which is often referred to as **disk mirroring**, provides fault tolerance in the case of a hard disk failure. In this RAID configuration, the same data is written to two separate hard disks at the same time. This results in two hard disks with identical information. If one fails, the copy can replace the failed hard disk in a short period of time. The only drawback to RAID level 1 is the cost, because you need to purchase twice the hard disk space needed for a given computer.

RAID level 2 is no longer used and was a variant of RAID 0 that allowed for error and integrity checking on hard disk drives. Modern hard disk drives do this intrinsically.

RAID level 3 is disk striping with a parity bit, or marker, which indicates what data is where. It requires a minimum of three hard disk drives to function, with one of the hard disks used to store the parity information. Should one of the hard disks that contain data fail, you can replace the hard disk drive and regenerate the data using the parity information stored on the parity disk. If the parity disk fails, the system must be restored from a back-up device.

RAID level 4 is only a slight variant on RAID level 3. RAID level 4 offers greater access speed than RAID level 3, because it can store data in blocks and, thus, does not need to access all disks in the array at once to read data.

RAID level 5 replaces RAID levels 3 and 4; it is the most common RAID configuration as of this writing. It is commonly referred to as **disk striping with parity**. As with RAID levels 3 and 4, it requires a minimum of three hard disk drives for implementation; however, the parity information is not stored on a separate drive, but is intermixed with data on the drives that make up the set. This offers better performance and fault tolerance; if any drive in the RAID configuration fails, the information on the other drives can be used to regenerate the lost information after the failed hard disk has been replaced. If two hard disks fail, the system must be restored from a back-up device. Figure 6-4 shows how a RAID level 5 configuration can be restored using parity information. The parity bits shown in Figure 6-4 are a sum of the information on the other two disks $(22 + 12 = 34)$. If the third hard disk fails, the information can be regenerated because only one element is missing from each equation:

$$22 + 12 = 34$$
$$68 - 65 = 3$$
$$13 - 9 = 4$$

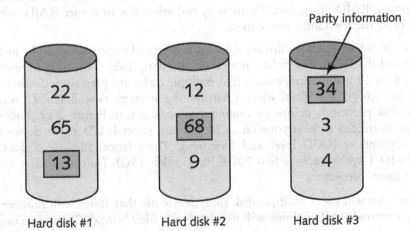

Parity information

Hard disk #1   Hard disk #2   Hard disk #3

Figure 6-4 Organization of data on RAID level 5

RAID level 6 is basically the same as RAID level 5, but it adds a second set of parity bits for added fault tolerance and allows up to two simultaneous hard disk drive failures while remaining fault tolerant.

RAID levels are often combined; RAID level 15 refers to a Stripe Set with Parity (RAID level 5) that is mirrored (RAID level 1) to another Stripe Set with Parity.

RAID configurations can be handled by software running on an operating system (called **software RAID**) but are more commonly handled by the hardware contained within a SCSI or SATA hard disk controller (called **hardware RAID**), or by the system BIOS (called **firmware RAID**).

 Most firmware RAID devices only support RAID level 0 and 1.

To configure hardware RAID, you must use the RAID setup utility for your specific SCSI or SATA hard disk controller. You can access this setup utility by entering the system or SCSI BIOS at system startup, or by using a manufacturer-supplied boot CD or DVD. After you have configured your hardware RAID volumes within the setup utility, they will automatically appear as standard hard disk volumes to the Linux installation program. For example, if you configure three hard disks in a RAID level 5 volume using the RAID setup utility, they will appear as a single volume (/dev/sda1) to the Linux installation program. You can then place a filesystem on /dev/sda1 as you would any other physical hard disk.

To configure firmware RAID, you must first configure a RAID volume using the RAID setup utility within the system BIOS. Next, you can start the Linux installation and select the firmware RAID volume. For a Fedora 20 installation, select Add a disk, as shown in Figure 2-10, highlight the Firmware RAID tab shown Figure 6-3, and select the firmware RAID volumes that you would like to use for Linux installation.

Unlike hardware or firmware RAID, software RAID is configured entirely during the installation process (provided that your system has more than one hard disk). To configure software RAID during a Fedora 20 installation, ensure that multiple disks are present and selected on the screen shown in Figure 2-10. Next, select a partitioning strategy as well as the I want to review/modify my disk partitions before continuing option shown in Figure 2-11. Following this, you can create partitions to host your Linux filesystems, select RAID as the device type, and choose the appropriate RAID level and filesystem. The / (root) filesystem shown in Figure 6-5 uses RAID 1 spread across two 20GB hard disks; 15GB from each disk will be used to store the / (root) filesystem.

Your first RAID volume will use a multiple disk (md) device file that starts with number 127 (/dev/md127). Your second RAID volume will use the device file /dev/md128, and so on. For example, the / (root) filesystem configured in Figure 6-5 will show up as /dev/md127 in the output of the df command, as shown here:

```
[root@server1 ~]# df
Filesystem      1K-blocks      Used    Available   Use%   Mounted on
/dev/md127      14987656    3242408     10960864    23%   /
devtmpfs         1014932          0      1014932     0%   /dev
tmpfs            1022260         80      1022180     1%   /dev/shm
tmpfs            1022260        684      1021576     1%   /run
tmpfs            1022260          0      1022260     0%   /sys/fs/cgroup
tmpfs            1022260         16      1022244     1%   /tmp
/dev/sda1         487652      90207       367749    20%   /boot
[root@server1 ~]# _
```

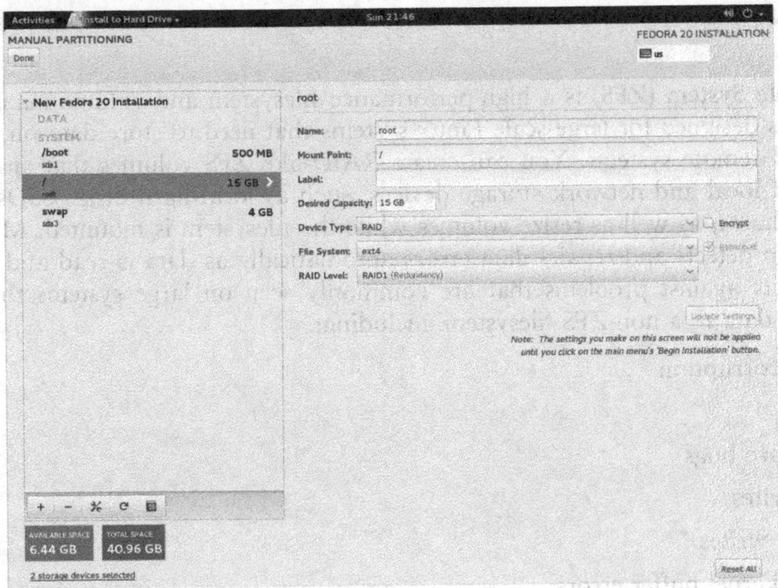

Figure 6-5 Configuring software RAID during a Fedora 20 installation

You can manage your software RAID configuration after installation using the **mdadm** command, as well as obtain details regarding configured software RAID devices by viewing the contents of the /etc/mdadm.conf and /proc/mdstat files, as shown here:

```
[root@server1 ~]# cat /etc/mdadm.conf
# mdadm.conf written out by anaconda
MAILADDR root
AUTO +imsm +1.x -all
ARRAY /dev/md/root level=raid1 num-devices=2 UUID=77d3f6c5:fbc71aa5:426-
b55eb:1e0d9860
[root@server1 ~]#_
[root@server1 ~]# cat /proc/mdstat
Personalities : [raid1]
md127 : active raid1 sda2[0] sdb1[1]
      15360000 blocks super 1.2 [2/2] [UU]
      bitmap: 0/1 pages [0KB], 65536KB chunk

unused devices: <none>
[root@server1 ~]#_
```

ZFS Configuration

Most Linux servers store the Linux operating system and any additional programs within a filesystem on standard partitions, LVM volumes, or RAID volumes. For Linux servers that require a large amount of storage for additional data (e.g., a file server or database server), filesystems are often created on SAN storage devices (e.g., an iSCSI SAN on the same rack as the server) and mounted to a directory on the Linux system that will be used to store the additional data.

The **Zettabyte File System (ZFS)** is a high-performance filesystem and volume management software that was designed for large-scale Linux systems that need to store data on multiple disks, SANs, and remote systems. You can create RAID-like ZFS volumes that span thousands of different local and network storage devices, such as local hard disks, SSDs, SANs, and remote file shares, as well as resize volumes while the filesystem is mounted. Moreover, the ZFS filesystem detects and repairs data errors automatically as data is read and written, as well as protects against problems that are commonly seen on large systems that write large amounts of data to a non-ZFS filesystem, including:

- Silent data corruption
- Bit rot
- Disk firmware bugs
- Phantom writes
- Misdirected writes
- Driver and kernel buffer errors
- Accidental driver overwrites

ZFS also supports new storage technologies such as PCIe SSDs and battery-backed RAM disk devices with ultra-low latency. Additionally, ZFS caches frequently accessed information in RAM and on faster storage devices such as SSDs to provide ultra-fast performance. ZFS also supports nearly all advanced filesystem features, including deduplication (storing one copy of a file that is located in multiple directories until one of the files change), snapshots, cloning, compression, encryption, NFSv4, volume management, and more.

ZFS was initially created by Sun Microsystems in 2001 and is often used by the largest Linux and UNIX systems in the world. It is available for Solaris UNIX, Mac OSX, Linux, FreeBSD, FreeNAS, and more. Since ZFS does not currently have a GPL-compatible license, it cannot be bundled within a Linux distribution, but it can be easily added afterwards. On Linux, ZFS support is maintained by *http://zfsonlinux.org*.

Although ZFS is primarily used on large Linux systems that may have hundreds or thousands of storage devices, it is also used within small and medium-sized organizations that require flexible volume management for data that is easy to configure.

ZFS pools are groups of physical disks that ZFS can manage (local disks, SANs, shared devices, large raw files, remote shares, etc.), and **ZFS volumes** are simply ZFS-managed filesystems that are created from ZFS pools.

Take, for example, a system that hosts several SATA hard disks, with the Linux OS installed on /dev/sda. To create a simple ZFS pool called datastorage1 from the second SATA hard disk, you could use the following **zpool** command:

```
[root@server1 ~]# zpool create datastorage1 /dev/sdb
[root@server1 ~]# _
```

This will also create a new ZFS volume called datastorage1 and mount it to /datastorage1, as shown here in the last line of the mount command output:

```
[root@server1 ~]# mount
/dev/sda1 on / type ext4 (rw,errors=remount-ro)
proc on /proc type proc (rw,noexec,nosuid,nodev)
sysfs on /sys type sysfs (rw,noexec,nosuid,nodev)
tmpfs on /run type tmpfs (rw,noexec,nosuid,size=10%,mode=0755)
systemd on /sys/fs/cgroup/systemd type cgroup
(rw,noexec,nosuid,nodev,none,name=systemd)
datastorage1 on /datastorage1 type zfs (rw,xattr)
[root@server1 ~]# _
```

You can also use the zpool command to view the details for your datastorage1 volume:

```
[root@server1 ~]# zpool list
NAME SIZE ALLOC FREE CAP DEDUP HEALTH ALTROOT
datastorage1 816M 114K 816M 0% 1.00x ONLINE -
[root@server1 ~]# _
```

 You can remove a ZFS volume using the zpool remove command. For example, zpool remove datastorage1 would remove the ZFS volume and pool that we created in the previous output.

If you specify multiple devices when creating a simple ZFS volume, then both devices are automatically added to the ZFS pool and a ZFS volume created from their contents. For example, if you run the following command, the /dev/sdc and /dev/sdd hard disks would be added to the datastorage2 pool, and a ZFS volume called datastorage2 would be created (with a capacity of both hard disks combined) and mounted to the /datastorage2 directory. This would act as the equivalent of a RAID 0 volume, but with the file corruption prevention benefits of ZFS.

```
[root@server1 ~]# zpool create datastorage2 /dev/sdc /dev/sdd
[root@server1 ~]# _
```

To create a ZFS pool and mirrored ZFS volume called datastorage3 from the /dev/sde and /dev/sdf hard disks and mount the volume to /datastorage3, you simply need to specify the mirror keyword during creation, as shown here:

```
[root@server1 ~]# zpool create datastorage3 mirror /dev/sde /dev/sdf
[root@server1 ~]# _
```

The datastorage3 volume is the equivalent of RAID 1 but resize-able under ZFS, and the total size of the volume is identical to the size of one of the hard disks.

 To create a ZFS mirrored volume, you need to specify a minimum of two hard disk devices to protect against a single disk failure.

To view the status of the disks that are part of the datastorage3 pool, you can use the following command:

```
[root@server1 ~]# zpool status datastorage3
  pool: datastorage3
 state: DEGRADED
status: One or more devices could not be used because the label is missing or
        invalid. Sufficient replicas exist for the pool to continue func-
        tioning in a degraded state.
action: Replace the device using 'zpool replace'.
   see: http://zfsonlinux.org/msg/ZFS-8000-4J
  scan: scrub repaired 0 in 0h0m with 0 errors on Tue Sep 30 13:33:11 2014
config:
         NAME          STATE      READ     WRITE     CKSUM
         datastorage3  DEGRADED      0         0         0
           mirror-0    DEGRADED      0         0         0
             /dev/sde  UNAVAIL       0         0         0 corrupted data
             /dev/sdf  ONLINE        0         0         0
errors: No known data errors
[root@server1 ~]# _
```

Notice from the preceding example that one of the disks in the mirror has failed (/dev/sde). In this case, you should detach the device from the pool using the zpool detach datastorage3 /dev/sde command, replace the failed hard disk, and reattach the disk to the mirror using the zpool attach datastorage3 /dev/sdf /dev/sde command. During this process, the filesystem is still available to users for reading and writing data. After reattaching the new hard disk, the output of the zpool status datastorage3 command should resemble the following output:

```
[root@server1 ~]# zpool status datastorage3
  pool: datastorage3
 state: ONLINE
  scan: none requested
config:
         NAME          STATE      READ     WRITE     CKSUM
         datastorage3  ONLINE        0         0         0
           mirror-0    ONLINE        0         0         0
             /dev/sde  ONLINE        0         0         0
             /dev/sdf  ONLINE        0         0         0
errors: No known data errors
[root@server1 ~]# _
```

To create ZFS pool and **RAID-Z** volume (the equivalent of a RAID-5 volume with a variable-sized stripe) called datastorage4 from the /dev/sdg, /dev/sdh, and /dev/sdi hard disks and mount it to /datastorage4, you simply need to specify the **raidz** keyword during creation, as shown here:

```
[root@server1 ~]# zpool create datastorage4 raidz /dev/sdg /dev/sdh /dev/
sdi
[root@server1 ~]# _
```

A RAID-Z volume needs a minimum of three hard disks to protect against a single disk failure and a minimum of seven hard disks to protect against a multi-disk failure.

You can also use `raidz2` (double parity like RAID-6) and `raidz3` (triple parity) in place of `raidz` in the previous command. You need a minimum of four devices for `raidz2` and a minimum of five devices for `raidz3`.

Because ZFS writes parity info with a variable-sized stripe, performance is maximized, and there is virtually no chance of the infamous "RAID 5 Hole" (data loss in the event of a power failure) that plagues traditional RAID systems.

Following this, you can view the state and performance of the RAID-Z volume using the zpool status and zpool iostat -v commands:

```
[root@server1 ~]# zpool status datastorage4
  pool: datastorage4
 state: ONLINE
  scan: none requested
config:
        NAME          STATE      READ    WRITE    CKSUM
        datastorage4  ONLINE        0        0        0
          raidz1-0    ONLINE        0        0        0
            /dev/sdg  ONLINE        0        0        0
            /dev/sdh  ONLINE        0        0        0
            /dev/sdi  ONLINE        0        0        0
errors: No known data errors
root@server1:~# zpool iostat -v datastorage4
                 capacity      operations      bandwidth
pool           alloc   free   read   write   read    write
-----------    -----   -----  ----   -----   -----   -----
datastorage4   220K    970M      0      11    701    10.5K
  raidz1       220K    970M      0      11    701    10.5K
    /dev/sdg      -       -      0      10   25.2K   83.6K
    /dev/sdh      -       -      0      10   25.1K   83.6K
    /dev/sdi      -       -      0      10   1.48K   83.6K
-----------    -----   -----  ----   -----   -----   -----
[root@server1 ~]# _
```

For more granular management of ZFS, you can use the **zfs command** to manage the specific features of the ZFS filesystem stored within ZFS volumes. The zfs command allows you to set a wide variety of ZFS-specific functionality, including directory size quotas and file- and directory-specific features and performance options. Moreover, you can identify specific subdirectories on a ZFS filesystem to tag for ZFS management; these subdirectories are often called **ZFS subfilesystems**. For example, if you create a directory under /datastorage4 called research, you can run the following command to specify that the research subdirectory should be treated as a ZFS subfilesystem:

```
[root@server1 ~]# zfs create datastorage4/research
[root@server1 ~]# _
```

To see a list of ZFS filesystems and subfilesystems that are available for ZFS management, you can run the zfs list command:

```
[root@server1 ~]# zfs list
NAME                    USED    AVAIL    REFER    MOUNTPOINT
datastorage4            286K    970M     42.6K    /datastorage4
datastorage4/research   38.6K   970M     38.6K    /datastorage4/research
[root@server1 ~]# _
```

To list the specific configuration parameters that you can modify for the research subfilesystem, you can use the zfs get all command:

```
[root@server1 ~]# zfs get all datastorage4/research | less
NAME                    PROPERTY       VALUE                      SOURCE
datastorage4/research   type           filesystem                 -
datastorage4/research   creation       Tue Sep 30 13:41 2015      -
datastorage4/research   used           38.6K                      -
datastorage4/research   available      214M                       -
datastorage4/research   referenced     38.6K                      -
datastorage4/research   compressratio  1.00x                      -
datastorage4/research   mounted        yes                        -
datastorage4/research   quota          none                       default
datastorage4/research   reservation    none                       default
datastorage4/research   recordsize     128K                       default
datastorage4/research   mountpoint     /datastorage4/research     default
datastorage4/research   sharenfs       off                        default
datastorage4/research   checksum       on                         default
datastorage4/research   compression    off                        default
datastorage4/research   atime          on                         default
datastorage4/research   atime          on                         default
datastorage4/research   devices        on                         default
datastorage4/research   exec           on                         default
datastorage4/research   setuid         on                         default
datastorage4/research   readonly       off                        default
:
```

You can modify the settings for the research subfilesystem to suit your needs. For example, to limit the total size of files within the research subfilesystem to 10GB, you could use the zfs set quota=10G datastorage4/research command, or to ensure that the contents of the research subfilesystem are read-only, you could run the zfs set readonly=on datastorage4/research command.

On Linux systems, ZFS volumes are mounted by the ZFS system and not via entries within the /etc/fstab file by default. As a result, to ensure that the datastorage1, datastorage2, datastorage3, and datastorage4 volumes created during the examples in this section are mounted at boot time, you simply need to add the line `zfs mount datastorage1 datastorage2 datastorage3 datastorage4` to a system startup script. System startup scripts are discussed in Chapter 8.

Installing a Linux Server Distribution

Any Linux distribution can be used as a server if the necessary packages are installed that provide for server services on the network. However, many Linux distributions also provide a version that is geared for Linux servers. These **Linux server distributions** do not have a GUI environment installed by default, since administration of Linux installed on a rackmount server is often performed using commands within a BASH terminal on a remote computer across the network. Instead, most Linux server distributions ship with a set of packages that are commonly used on Linux servers, including Web server, database server, file server and email server software.

Remote administration methods are discussed in Chapter 12.

The configuration of common server software packages is covered in Chapter 13.

The installation process for a Linux server distribution differs from a standard or live Linux installation process. No GUI environment is loaded during the installation process, and the installation program often prompts you for additional information that is necessary for a server, such that you don't need to configure that same information afterwards, including:

- *The host name and IP configuration of the server*—For a desktop system, the default hostname (localhost) will often suffice. However, for a server system, the host name is often used by the configuration of server services and should match the name that other computers on the network will use when contacting the server. Additionally, many Linux administrators prefer to configure a static IP address on server systems rather than obtain an IP address automatically. This ensures that the IP address of the server cannot change over time.

- *Whether to allow for automatic updating*—Most Linux systems are configured by default to download important OS and application updates periodically. However, for a Linux server, an update could potentially cause problems with software that is currently running on the server. As a result, most Linux administrators prefer to manually update software after testing the update on a non-production computer that contains the same software as the server. Application updates will be discussed in more depth in Chapter 11.

- *Package selection*—While most Linux distributions automatically install a predefined set of software packages during installation without user input, Linux server distributions often prompt you to select the specific software packages that will be needed on the Linux server. This prevents unnecessary packages from being installed and space from being wasted on the server filesystems.

- *Server service configuration*—Some server service packages that are installed require additional configuration in order to provide functionality. The installation program for a Linux server distribution may prompt you for that information during the installation so that you don't need to configure it afterwards.

- *Boot loader configuration*—During the Fedora installation program, you are not prompted to supply information regarding the boot loader that will be used to boot the Linux kernel. However, most Linux server distributions prompt you for the location of the Linux boot loader during the installation. **GRUB (GRand Unified Boot loader)** is the standard boot loader used on Linux systems. By default, most Linux distributions install the first part of GRUB on the MBR/GPT (e.g., /dev/sda). However, you can also choose to install the first part of GRUB on the first sector of the Linux partition that holds the kernel (e.g., /dev/sda1) if you have one or more operating systems already installed on the server system in a multi-boot configuration. Boot loaders will be discussed in more depth in Chapter 8.

In Hands-on Project 6-1, you will install the Ubuntu Server 14.04 Linux distribution. In addition to providing the opportunity to install a Linux server distribution, this project will allow you to apply concepts in later chapters to more than one Linux distribution, as well as configure Linux components that are not found in Fedora Linux, such as the Debian Package Manager, the SysV initialization system, and the system log daemon.

Since servers provide a critical role within the organization, it is important to verify that the installation process has completed successfully and that all hardware components are working properly with the OS after installation.

Dealing with Problems During Installation

Most problems that occur during a Linux installation are related to faulty hardware or an incorrect device driver for a hardware component. In both of these cases, the installation may end abnormally and a "fatal signal 11" error message may appear on the screen. This indicates an error, known as a **segmentation fault**, in which a program accesses a certain area of RAM that was not assigned. If a segmentation fault occurs when you are installing Linux, first check the RAM for errors by running the memtest86 utility shown in Figure 2-6. The memtest86 utility is included on nearly all Linux installation media and can be run from the welcome screen that first appears when you boot the computer from the installation media.

If you experience a segmentation fault during installation and the memtest86 utility finds no RAM errors, first check with the hardware manufacturer of the system (as well as the hardware manufacturer of any additional hardware devices added to the system prior to installation) to determine if an updated driver is available for your distribution of Linux. If one is available that is needed during the installation process (e.g., for a new disk controller card), the manufacturer will often provide instructions that allow you to specify the new driver during the installation process. If you are installing from live media, this is often performed by activating the driver after the live Linux system has loaded. Alternatively, if you are installing from standard installation media, the location of the driver is often specified by modifying the default installation boot options at the welcome screen when you boot the Linux installation media. To access the default installation boot options for Fedora 20, you can press the Tab key at the welcome screen shown in Figure 2-4.

If you experience a segmentation fault during installation and both your RAM and device drivers appear functional, you can assume that some hardware component is faulty. Zeroing in on the right piece of hardware can be tricky. Often, you can fix segmentation faults by turning off the CPU cache memory or by increasing the number of memory wait states in the BIOS. On some computers, the BIOS allows the user to change the voltage for the RAM and CPU; incorrect values could be the source of a segmentation fault. Other causes include power management conflicts and overclocked CPUs.

An **overclocked** CPU is a CPU that is faster than the speed for which the processor was designed. Although this might lead to increased performance, it also makes the processor hotter and can result in intermittent computer crashes.

If the installation fails with an error other than fatal signal 11, consult the support documentation for your distribution of Linux, or check Internet newsgroups and forums.

6

In some cases, the installation process fails to place a boot loader on the hard disk properly; this often occurs with older generation hard disk drives that have over 1024 cylinders. To avoid this problem, ensure that the / partition starts before the 1024th cylinder (the 8GB mark on most hard disks) or create a partition for the /boot directory that starts before the 1024th cylinder.

Dealing with Problems After Installation

Even after a successful Linux installation, problems might arise if the installation program failed to detect the computer's hardware properly or if certain programs were not installed as expected. To ensure no such problems occurred, check the **installation log files** after installation and then verify system settings to ensure that all hardware was detected with the correct values.

The **installation log files** are files that are created by the installation program that record the events that occurred during the installation process, including errors. For Fedora Linux, these log files are stored in the /var/log/anaconda directory; and for Ubuntu Server Linux, these log files are stored in the /var/log/installer directory. To search these files for errors and warnings, you should use the grep command, as their contents are often quite lengthy. For example, the egrep -i "(error|warn)" /var/log/anaconda/* command can be used to search for any errors or warnings within the log files in the /var/log/anaconda directory.

To verify hardware settings, you can examine the content of the /proc directory or boot-up log files. The /proc directory is mounted to a special filesystem contained within RAM that lists system information made available by the Linux kernel; because this is an administrative filesystem, all files within are readable only by the root user. The following sample listing of the /proc directory shows many file and subdirectory contents:

```
[root@server1 ~]# ls -F /proc
1/    1171/ 171/ 3/    415/ 48/  801/         kallsyms     softirqs
10/   12/    172/ 300/ 417/ 484/ 9/           kcore        stat
```

```
1018/ 1224/ 173/ 334/ 418/ 485/  acpi/         keys          swaps
1020/ 1239/ 174/ 361/ 419/ 49/   buddyinfo     key-users     sys/
1024/ 1257/ 175/ 362/ 422/ 5/    bus/          kmsg          sysrq
1028/ 1266/ 176/ 364/ 424/ 548/  cgroups       kpagecount    sysvipc/
1038/ 1282/ 177/ 365/ 425/ 550/  cmdline       kpageflags    timer
1068/ 1284/ 178/ 367/ 426/ 58/   consoles      loadavg       timer_s
1074/ 1288/ 179/ 368/ 428/ 59/   cpuinfo       locks         tty/
1077/ 13/   18/  369/ 434/ 6/    crypto        mdstat        uptime
1084/ 1317/ 180/ 371/ 436/ 60/   devices       meminfo       version
1090/ 14/   187/ 372/ 437/ 62/   diskstats     misc          vmallocin
11/   15/   188/ 373/ 449/ 624/  dma           modules       vmstat
1106/ 16/   19/  383/ 45/  64/   driver/       mounts@       zoneinfo
1109/ 163/  190/ 384/ 455/ 7/    execdomains   mtrr
1112/ 165/  2/   385/ 456/ 72/   fb            net@
1117/ 166/  20/  392/ 459/ 748/  filesystems   pagetypeinfo
1137/ 167/  203/ 393/ 46/  751/  fs/           partitions
1141/ 168/  204/ 394/ 460/ 752/  interrupts    sched_debug
1159/ 169/  205/ 399/ 462/ 755/  iomem         scsi/
1165/ 17/   287/ 410/ 47/  758/  ioports       self@
1168/ 170/  297/ 413/ 478/ 8/    irq/          slabinfo
[root@server1 ~]# _
```

The subdirectories that start with a number in the preceding output are used to display process information; other directories can contain kernel parameters. The files listed in the preceding output are text representations of various parts of the Linux system; they are updated regularly by the Linux kernel and can be viewed using standard text commands, such as cat or less.

To view the information that Linux has detected regarding a computer's CPUs, view the contents of the cpuinfo file in the /proc directory:

```
[root@server1 ~]# cat /proc/cpuinfo
processor       : 0
vendor_id       : GenuineIntel
cpu family      : 6
model           : 58
model name      : Intel(R) Core(TM) i7-3630QM CPU @ 2.40GHz
stepping        : 9
microcode       : 0xffffffff
cpu MHz         : 2394.550
cache size      : 6144 KB
fpu             : yes
fpu_exception   : yes
cpuid level     : 13
wp              : yes
flags           : fpu vme de pse tsc msr pae mce cx8 apic sep mtrr pge mca cmov
pat pse36 clflush mmx fxsr sse sse2 ss syscall nx lm constant_tsc rep_good
nopl eagerfpu pni pclmulqdq ssse3 cx16 sse4_1 sse4_2 popcnt aes xsave avx
f16c rdrand hypervisor lahf_lm xsaveopt fsgsbase smep erms
```

```
bogomips        : 4789.10
clflush size    : 64
cache_alignment : 64
address sizes   : 36 bits physical, 48 bits virtual
power management :
[root@server1 ~]# _
```

The preceding output is from a computer with one processor that runs at 2.4GHz (processor 0), with 6MB of processor cache. If this information is incorrect because Linux failed to detect the processor information properly, you might need to change a setting in BIOS or research a solution to the problem on the mainboard or processor manufacturer's Web site.

After installation, you also need to ensure that Linux has detected the correct amount of RAM. To do this, you can view the contents of the /proc/meminfo file, as shown in the following output:

```
[root@server1 ~]# cat /proc/meminfo
MemTotal:            2044524 kB
MemFree:              821612 kB
Buffers:               88012 kB
Cached:               274340 kB
SwapCached:                0 kB
Active:               335964 kB
Inactive:             246028 kB
Active(anon):         220176 kB
Inactive(anon):          212 kB
Active(file):         115788 kB
Inactive(file):       245816 kB
Unevictable:               0 kB
Mlocked:                   0 kB
SwapTotal:           2097148 kB
SwapFree:            2097148 kB
Dirty:                     0 kB
Writeback:                 0 kB
AnonPages:            219644 kB
Mapped:                71760 kB
Shmem:                   764 kB
Slab:                  95344 kB
SReclaimable:          65104 kB
SUnreclaim:            30240 kB
KernelStack:            2080 kB
PageTables:            10916 kB
NFS_Unstable:              0 kB
Bounce:                    0 kB
WritebackTmp:              0 kB
CommitLimit:         3119408 kB
Committed_AS:         963836 kB
VmallocTotal:      34359738367 kB
VmallocUsed:           30444 kB
```

```
VmallocChunk:        34359698216 kB
HardwareCorrupted:            0 kB
AnonHugePages:           100352 kB
HugePages_Total:              0
HugePages_Free:               0
HugePages_Rsvd:               0
HugePages_Surp:               0
Hugepagesize:              2048 kB
DirectMap4k:              57280 kB
DirectMap2M:            2039808 kB
[root@server1 ~]# _
```

In the preceding output, the total amount of memory (MemTotal) is 2044524KB, or approximately 2GB. If this value is incorrect, you may need to change a setting in BIOS or research a solution to the problem on the mainboard or RAM manufacturer's Web site.

In some cases, it's necessary to insert a device's driver into the Linux kernel as a module. This is typically true of specialized server hardware, such as SAN controller cards. To see a list of modules currently inserted into the Linux kernel, view the /proc/modules file, as shown in the following output:

```
[root@server1 ~]# less /proc/modules
binfmt_misc 17431 1 - Live 0xffffffffa0240000
nf_conntrack_netbios_ns 12665 0 - Live 0xffffffffa023b000
nf_conntrack_broadcast 12527 1 nf_conntrack_netbios_ns, Live
0xffffffffa0236000
ipt_MASQUERADE 12880 1 - Live 0xffffffffa0231000
bnep 19704 2 - Live 0xffffffffa0249000
bluetooth 361772 5 bnep, Live 0xffffffffa01d7000
ip6t_REJECT 12939 2 - Live 0xffffffffa0160000
cfg80211 460310 0 - Live 0xffffffffa0165000
rfkill 21694 4 bluetooth,cfg80211, Live 0xffffffffa0159000
xt_conntrack 12760 42 - Live 0xffffffffa014f000
ebtable_nat 12807 0 - Live 0xffffffffa014a000
ebtable_broute 12731 0 - Live 0xffffffffa0154000
bridge 110624 1 ebtable_broute, Live 0xffffffffa012d000
stp 12868 1 bridge, Live 0xffffffffa0128000
llc 14045 2 bridge,stp, Live 0xffffffffa0123000
ebtable_filter 12827 0 - Live 0xffffffffa011e000
ebtables 30758 3 ebtable_nat,ebtable_broute,ebtable_filter, Live
0xffffffffa0111000
ip6table_nat 13015 1 - Live 0xffffffffa010c000
:
```

If a hardware device is not working with Linux, first consult the hardware vendor's Web site to determine the name of the kernel module. You can then search for this module in the /proc/modules file; if the module isn't present, the driver for that hardware is not loaded into the Linux kernel, and you proceed to add the module manually, as discussed in Chapter 12.

The /proc directory contains many more files than have been presented so far in this chapter. Table 6-2 describes some files that you will find useful when examining a system after installation.

Hardware is detected by the Linux kernel at system startup. However, this information is displayed too quickly to read or hidden by a graphical startup screen. Fortunately, the system logs all information regarding hardware detection and the startup of system processes in log files that can be viewed at a later time.

Filename	Contents
cmdline	Current location of the Linux kernel
cpuinfo	Information regarding the processors in the computer
devices	List of the character and block devices that are currently in use by the Linux kernel
execdomains	List of execution domains for processes on the system; execution domains allow a process to execute in a specific manner
fb	List of framebuffer devices in use on the Linux system; typically, these include video adapter card devices
filesystems	List of filesystems supported by the Linux kernel
interrupts	List of IRQs in use on the system
iomem	List of memory addresses currently used
ioports	List of memory address ranges reserved for device use
kcore	A representation of the physical memory inside the computer; this file should not be viewed
kmsg	Temporary storage location for messages from the kernel
loadavg	Statistics on the performance of the processor
locks	List of files currently locked by the kernel
mdstat	Configuration of multiple-disk RAID hardware
meminfo	Information regarding physical and virtual memory on the Linux system
misc	List of miscellaneous devices (major number=10)
modules	List of currently loaded modules in the Linux kernel
mounts	List of currently mounted filesystems
partitions	Information regarding partition tables loaded in memory on the system
swaps	Information on virtual memory utilization
version	Version information for the Linux kernel and libraries

Table 6-2 **Files commonly found in the /proc directory**

6

To view the hardware detected during boot time, you can use the dmesg command after system startup, as shown in the following output:

```
[root@server1 ~]# dmesg | less
[0.000000] Initializing cgroup subsys cpuset
[0.000000] Initializing cgroup subsys cpu
[0.000000] Initializing cgroup subsys cpuacct
[0.000000] Linux version 3.11.10-301.fc20.x86_64 (mockbuild@bkernel01.
phx2.fedoraproject.org) (gcc version 4.8.2 20131017 (Red Hat 4.8.2-1)
(GCC) ) #1 SMP Thu Dec 5 14:01:17 UTC 2013
[0.000000]   Command   line:   BOOT_IMAGE=/vmlinuz-3.11.10-301.fc20.x86_64
root=/dev/sda3 ro vconsole.font=latarcyrheb-sun16 rhgb quiet LANG=en_US.
UTF-8
[0.000000] e820: BIOS-provided physical RAM map:
[0.000000] BIOS-e820: [mem 0x000000000000-0x000000000009fbff] usable
[0.000000] BIOS-e820: [mem 0x00000009fc00-0x000000009ffff] reserved
[0.000000] BIOS-e820: [mem 0x0000000e0000-0x0000000fffff] reserved
[0.000000] BIOS-e820: [mem 0x000000100000-0x000000007ffeffff] usable
[0.000000] BIOS-e820: [mem 0x00007fff0000-0x000000007fffefff] ACPI data
[0.000000] BIOS-e820: [mem 0x00007ffff000-0x000000007fffffff] ACPI NVS
[0.000000] NX (Execute Disable) protection: active
[0.000000] SMBIOS 2.3 present.
[0.000000]  DMI: Microsoft Corporation Virtual Machine/Virtual Machine,
BIOS
090006 05/23/2012
[0.000000] Hypervisor detected: Microsoft HyperV
[0.000000] HyperV: features 0xe7f, hints 0x2c
[0.000000] e820: update [mem 0x00000000-0x00000fff] usable ==> reserved
[0.000000] e820: remove [mem 0x000a0000-0x000fffff] usable
:
```

You can also view the system processes that started successfully or unsuccessfully during boot time by viewing the contents of the /var/log/boot.log file on most Linux distributions. A sample boot.log file from an Ubuntu Server system is shown in the following output:

```
root@server1:~# tail /var/log/boot.log
* Starting MySQL Server                                              [ OK ]
 * Starting PostgreSQL 9.3 database server                           [ OK ]
 * Starting configure network device security                       [ OK ]
 * Starting configure network device                                [ OK ]
 * Starting Postfix Mail Transport Agent postfix                    [ OK ]
 * Restoring resolver state...                                       [ OK ]
AH00558: apache2: Could not reliably determine the server's fully qualified
domain name, using 127.0.1.1. Set the 'ServerName' directive globally to
suppress this message
 *
 * Starting Tomcat servlet engine tomcat7                            [ OK ]
 * Stopping System V runlevel compatibility                         [ OK ]
root@server1:~# _
```

For more detailed information regarding system processes during the startup process and afterwards, you can view the contents of the /var/log/messages or /var/log/syslog files on most Linux distributions. A sample syslog file from an Ubuntu Server system is shown in the following output:

```
root@server1:~# tail /var/log/syslog
Sep 30 09:56:48 server1 kernel: [ 38.357431] cgroup: systemd-logind (619)
created nested cgroup for controller "memory" which has incomplete
hierarchy support. Nested cgroups may change behavior in the future.
Sep 30 09:56:48 server1 kernel: [ 38.357435] cgroup: "memory" requires
setting use_hierarchy to 1 on the root.
Sep 30 09:57:07 server1 ntpdate[2031]: step time server 91.189.89.199
offset17.350701 sec
Sep 30 09:56:57 server1 kernel: [ 46.667766] audit_printk_skb: 48 callbacks
suppressed
Sep 30 09:56:57 server1 kernel: [ 46.667770] type=1400 audit
(1412085417.259:28): apparmor="STATUS" operation="profile_replace"
profile="unconfined"name="/usr/lib/cups/backend/cups-pdf" pid=2146 com-
m="apparmor_parser"
Sep 30 09:56:57 server1 kernel: [ 46.667776] type=1400 audit
(1412085417.259:29): apparmor="STATUS" operation="profile_replace" pro-
file="unconfined" name="/usr/sbin/cupsd" pid=2146 comm="apparmor_parser"
Sep 30 09:56:57 server1 kernel: [ 46.668185] type=1400 audit
(1412085417.259:30): apparmor="STATUS" operation="profile_replace" pro-
file="unconfined" name="/usr/sbin/cupsd" pid=2146 comm="apparmor_parser"
Sep 30 09:57:13 server1 kernel: [ 63.274963] hv_balloon: Received INFO_
TYPE_MAX_PAGE_CNT
Sep 30 09:57:13 server1 kernel: [ 63.274970] hv_balloon: Data Size is 8
Sep 30 10:09:01 server1 CRON[2290]: (root) CMD ( [ -x /usr/lib/php5/
maxlifetime ] && [ -x /usr/lib/php5/sessionclean ] && [ -d /var/lib/
php5 ] && /usr/lib/php5/sessionclean /var/lib/php5 $(/usr/lib/php5/
maxlifetime))
root@server1:~# _
```

In Fedora 20, the logging system used to record the messages normally stored within /var/log/boot.log, /var/log/messages, or /var/log/syslog has been replaced by a journaling database system called **journald**. You can use the **journalctl command** on a Fedora 20 system with the –b option to view the same information that would normally be stored within /var/log/boot.log, /var/log/messages, or /var/log/syslog files. Since the journalctl command will display entries for each boot process, it is important to narrow down the time frame. The following command only displays boot information from the current day:

```
[root@server1 ~]# journalctl –b --since=today | less
- Logs begin at Tue 2015-09-16 21:56:29 EDT, end at Tue 2015-09-30 10:20:47
EDT. -
Sep 30 11:02:08 localhost.localdomain systemd-journal[71]: Runtime journal
is using 8.0M (max 99.8M, leaving 149.7M of free 990.2M, current limit 99.8M).
Sep 30 11:02:08 localhost.localdomain systemd-journal[71]: Runtime journal
is using 8.0M (max 99.8M, leaving 149.7M of free 990.2M, current limit 99.8M).
```

6

```
Sep 30 11:02:08 localhost.localdomain kernel: Initializing cgroup subsys
cpuset
Sep 30 11:02:08 localhost.localdomain kernel: Initializing cgroup subsys cpu
Sep 30 11:02:08 localhost.localdomain kernel: Initializing cgroup subsys
cpuacct
Sep 30 11:02:08 localhost.localdomain kernel: Linux version 3.11.10-301.
fc20.x86_64  (mockbuild@bkernel01.phx2.fedoraproject.org)  (gcc  version
4.8.2 20131017 (Red Hat 4.8.2-1) (GCC) ) #1 SMP Thu Dec 5 14:01:17 UTC 2013
Sep 30 11:02:08 localhost.localdomain kernel: Command line: BOOT_IMAGE=/
vmlinuz-3.11.10-301.fc20.x86_64 root=/dev/sda3 ro vconsole.font=latarcyrheb-
sun16 rhgb quiet LANG=en_US.UTF-8
Sep 30 11:02:08 localhost.localdomain kernel: e820: BIOS-provided physical
RAM map:
Sep 30 11:02:08 localhost.localdomain kernel: BIOS-e820: [mem
0x0000000000000000-0x000000000009fbff] usable
Sep 30 11:02:08 localhost.localdomain kernel: BIOS-e820: [mem
0x000000000009fc00-0x000000000009ffff] reserved
Sep 30 11:02:08 localhost.localdomain kernel: BIOS-e820: [mem
0x00000000000e0000-0x00000000000fffff] reserved
—More—
```

System Rescue

Booting to a live Linux OS from live installation media offers several benefits to Linux administrators when repairing a damaged Linux system. The live OS contains a small bootable
Linux kernel and virtual filesystem that are loaded into RAM and have access to the filesystems on the underlying hard disk. As a result, you can use the utilities on the live OS to fix
problems within a Linux installation on the hard disk that are preventing the Linux installation from booting, such as:

- Boot loader problems
- Filesystem/partition problems
- Configuration file problems
- Driver problems

All live OS systems contain several utilities that are useful for fixing system problems, including fdisk, parted, e2mkfs, fsck, and several more that will be introduced in later chapters.
Recall from the previous chapter that the `fsck` command can only be run on an unmounted
filesystem. If the / (root) filesystem becomes corrupted, you can boot your system using the live
installation media for your Linux distribution and use the `fsck` command in the live OS to
check the / (root) filesystem on the hard disk since it is not mounted by the live OS by default.

The process of using a live OS to repair problems on another Linux
system installed on the hard disk is commonly called **system rescue**.

You can also configure the Linux kernel loaded by the live OS to use the / (root) filesystem on the hard disk. To do this, simply mount the / (root) filesystem on your local disk under an empty directory in the live OS (e.g., /mnt) and then type chroot /mnt at the command prompt. The **chroot command** will then change the root of the live OS to the /mnt directory, which is actually the / (root) filesystem on the local disk. From this point onwards, you will have root user access to any commands on your / (root) filesystem, as you normally would if you had booted your Linux system on the hard disk. For example, if you run the passwd command (used for changing user passwords), you'll actually be changing the password for the root user on the Linux system installed on the hard drive. This is often used to recover a locally accessible Linux system if the root password has been lost or forgotten.

It is also important to note that this feature is not limited to live installation media. If you install Linux from standard installation media, the welcome screen will often provide a system rescue option that will allow you to boot a small live Linux system that does not contain a GUI environment. This small live Linux system contains the same recovery utilities (fdisk, parted, e2mkfs, fsck, etc.) and will allow you to mount the / (root) filesystem on your hard disk as well as run the chroot command to switch your live Linux system to it.

Chapter Summary

- Linux servers typically use far more hardware that desktop systems. This hardware is installed in a rack using a rackmount form factor.
- Many different SCSI standards have been developed since 1986. Parallel SCSI hard disks are uniquely identified by a SCSI ID and attach to a controller via a terminated cable. SAS is a newer SCSI technology that transfers information to hard disks using a serial cable. iSCSI is a SAN technology used to transfer information from iSCSI initiators to iSCSI targets across a TCP/IP network.
- RAID is often used within Linux servers to combine several hard disks into a single volume for speed or fault tolerance. It can be implemented by software that runs within the OS, hardware on a hard disk controller card, or by the system BIOS.
- The different levels of RAID determine how disks are combined and written to. RAID level 0 is not fault tolerant, whereas RAID levels 1 through 6 provide fault tolerance for data in the event of hard disk failure.
- ZFS is a high-performance, fault tolerant filesystem that is commonly installed on Linux servers. ZFS provides much of the same functionality as RAID, using storage space that spans a wide range of different storage devices, including local disks, SANs, shared devices, large raw files, and remote shares.
- Linux server distributions do not contain a GUI environment and are often administered remotely. They have an installation process that requires additional information compared to other Linux distributions.
- Unsupported hardware, defective RAM, overclocked CPUs, and improper RAM settings can cause a Linux installation to fail.
- The /proc directory contains information regarding detected hardware on the system and is useful when verifying whether an installation was successful.
- You can use the bootable OS found on standard and live Linux installation media to access and repair a damaged Linux installation.

Key Terms

1U server A rackmount server that has a standard height of 1.75 inches.

blade server See *rackmount server*.

chroot command A Linux command that can be used to change the root of one Linux system to another.

disk mirroring A RAID configuration consisting of two identical hard disks to which identical data are written in parallel, thus ensuring fault tolerance. Also known as RAID 1.

disk striping A RAID configuration in which a single file is divided into sections, which are then written to different hard disks concurrently to speed up access time; this type of RAID is not fault tolerant. Also known as RAID 0.

disk striping with parity A RAID configuration that incorporates disk striping for faster file access, as well as parity information to ensure fault tolerance. Also known as RAID 5.

fault tolerant Term used to describe a device that exhibits a minimum of downtime in the event of a failure.

firmware RAID A RAID system controlled by the computer's BIOS.

GRUB (GRand Unified Boot loader) The most common boot loader used on Linux systems. It loads and executes the Linux kernel at boot time.

hardware RAID A RAID system controlled by hardware located on a disk controller card within the computer.

installation log files The files created at installation to record actions that occurred or failed during the installation process.

Internet SCSI (iSCSI) A SCSI technology that transfers data via TCP/IP networks.

iSCSI initiator A term that refers to the computer that connects to the iSCSI target within an iSCSI SAN.

iSCSI target A term that refers to a storage device within an iSCSI SAN.

journalctl command A command used to configure journald, as well as to view log entries in the journald database.

journald A system used to record (or journal) system events on some Linux distributions, such as Fedora 20.

Linux server distribution A Linux distribution that contains packages that are useful for Linux servers.

Logical Unit Number (LUN) A unique identifier for each device attached to any given node in a SCSI chain.

mdadm command A command used to configure software RAID on a Linux system.

overclocked Term used to describe a CPU that runs faster than the clock speed for which it has been rated.

Parallel SCSI The traditional SCSI technology that transfers data across parallel cables.

rackmount server A thin form factor used to house server hardware that is installed in a server rack.

RAID-Z   An implementation of RAID level 5 using ZFS, which uses a variable stripe that provides for better performance and fault tolerance.

Redundant Array of Independent Disks (RAID)   The process of combining the storage space of several hard disk drives into one larger, logical storage unit.

SCSI ID   A number that uniquely identifies and prioritizes devices attached to a SCSI controller.

segmentation fault   An error that software encounters when it cannot locate the information needed to complete its task.

Serial Attached SCSI (SAS)   A SCSI technology that transfers information in serial mode rather than the traditional parallel mode.

software RAID   A RAID system that is controlled by software running within the operating system.

spanning   A type of RAID level 0 that allows two or more devices to be represented as a single large volume.

Storage Area Network (SAN)   A group of computers that access the same storage device across a fast network.

system rescue   The process of using a live Linux OS to access and repair a damaged Linux installation.

target ID   See *SCSI ID*.

terminator   A device used to terminate an electrical conduction medium to absorb the transmitted signal and prevent signal bounce.

uninterruptible power supply (UPS)   A device that contains battery storage and is used to supply power to computers in the event of a power outage.

Zettabyte File System (ZFS)   A high-performance filesystem and volume management software that is often used to create volumes from multiple storage devices on Linux and UNIX systems.

zfs command   A command used to configure ZFS filesystem features.

ZFS pool   A series of storage devices that are managed by ZFS.

ZFS subfilesystem   A subdirectory on a ZFS volume that can be managed as a separate unit by ZFS.

ZFS volume   A volume created from space within a ZFS pool that contains a ZFS filesystem.

zpool command   A command used to configure ZFS pools and volumes.

Review Questions

1. SAS transfers data to SCSI disks via parallel cables. True or False?

2. Which of the following is used to describe a computer that is used to access an iSCSI hard disk across the network?
   a. iSCSI target
   b. iSCSI requestor
   c. iSCSI initiator
   d. iSCSI terminator

3. You want to view log files to get information about a problem that occurred during a Linux installation. In which directory will you likely find the log files?

    a. /root/log

    b. /sys/log

    c. /var/log

    d. /etc/log

4. Which of the following RAID levels is not fault tolerant?

    a. RAID 0

    b. RAID 1

    c. RAID 4

    d. RAID 5

5. Which command can you use during a system rescue to switch from the root of the live OS to the root of the Linux system installed on the hard disk?

    a. `mount`

    b. `sysimage`

    c. `chroot`

    d. `rescue`

6. Which of the following is not a type of RAID?

    a. hardware RAID

    b. software RAID

    c. firmware RAID

    d. serial RAID

7. Where is the /proc filesystem stored?

    a. in RAM

    b. on the hard disk drive in the / directory

    c. on the hard disk drive in the /etc directory

    d. on the hard disk drive in the /var directory

8. Which RAID level uses striping with parity?

    a. 2

    b. 4

    c. 1

    d. 5

9. RAID-Z is functionally equivalent to RAID level 1. True or False?

10. SCSI devices that use an 8-bit-wide data path use _____.

    a. an 8-pin connector

    b. a 15-pin connector

    c. a 50-pin connector

    d. a 68-pin connector

11. Which type of RAID is entirely configured during the Linux installation process?

    a. hardware RAID

    b. software RAID

    c. firmware RAID

    d. serial RAID

12. What command can be used to create a ZFS volume called test from the space on /dev/sdb and /dev/sdc that functions like RAID level 1?

    a. `zpool create test /dev/sdb /dev/sdc`

    b. `zpool create test mirror /dev/sdb /dev/sdc`

    c. `zpool create test raidz /dev/sdb /dev/sdc`

    d. `zpool create test raidz2 /dev/sdb /dev/sdc`

13. To which directory will the test ZFS volume from the previous question be mounted by the ZFS system?

    a. /mnt/test

    b. /media/test

    c. /zfs/test

    d. /test

14. Linux servers are typically installed in a rack using rackmount server hardware. Which of the following is used to describe the minimum height of a rackmount server?

    a. 1U

    b. Series A

    c. Type A

    d. Level 5

15. Which RAID level is also referred to as mirroring?

    a. 0

    b. 1

    c. 4

    d. 5

16. ZFS volumes are mounted at boot time from entries within /etc/fstab by default. True or False?

17. Which of the following could result in a segmentation fault (fatal signal 11) during a Fedora installation?

    a. RAM problems

    b. overclocked CPU

    c. improper device driver

    d. all of the above

18. SCSI-1 is also referred to as _____.

    a. fast and wide

    b. slow and wide

    c. slow and narrow

    d. fast and narrow

19. Which of the following items are you typically required to configure during a Linux server installation? (Choose all that apply.)

    a. package selection

    b. boot loader configuration

    c. system host name

    d. update configuration

20. Which of the following commands can be used on a Fedora 20 system to view hardware and service startup information during the boot process?

    a. `less /var/log/boot.log`

    b. `less /var/log/messages`

    c. `less /var/log/syslog`

    d. `journalctl -b`

Hands-on Projects

These projects should be completed in the order given. The hands-on projects presented in this chapter should take a total of three hours to complete. The requirements for this lab include:

- A computer with Fedora 20 installed according to Hands-on Project 2-1
- The ISO image for Ubuntu Server 14.04 installation media (ubuntu-14.04.1-server-amd64.iso)

Project 6-1

In this hands-on project, you install Ubuntu Server 14.04 Linux within a virtual machine on a Windows computer and examine the LVM partition configuration afterwards.

1. In your virtualization software, create a new virtual machine called **Ubuntu Server Linux** that has the following characteristics:

   a. 2GB of memory

   b. An Internet connection via your PC's network card (preferably using bridged mode)

   c. A 20GB virtual hard disk

   d. The virtual machine DVD drive attached to the ISO file for the Ubuntu Server 14.04 installation media (ubuntu-14.04.1-server-amd64.iso)

2. Start and then connect to your Ubuntu Server Linux virtual machine using your virtualization software.

 The Ubuntu Server Linux installation program does not use a graphical desktop. As a result, you must switch between buttons shown on the screen using the Tab key and press Enter to make your selections.

3. At the Language screen, ensure that **English** is selected and press **Enter**.

4. At the Ubuntu welcome screen, examine the options. Are there options that allow you to check the installation media for defects as well as test RAM for defects (using memtest86)? Ensure that **Install Ubuntu Server** is selected and press **Enter**.

5. At the Select a language page, ensure that **English** is selected and press **Enter**.

6. At the Select your location screen, ensure that **United States** is selected and press **Enter**.

7. At the Configure the keyboard screen, select **Yes** and press **Enter**. Follow the prompts to complete the detection. When the detection process finds a "us" keyboard layout, select **Continue** and press **Enter**.

8. At the Configure the network screen, type a hostname of **UbuntuXX** (where XX is the unique number assigned to you by your instructor during course setup), select **Continue**, and press **Enter**.

9. At the Set up users and passwords page, type **user1** as the full user name, select **Continue**, and press **Enter**. When prompted for the simple user name, ensure that **user1** is displayed, select **Continue**, and press **Enter**. When prompted for a password for user1, type **LNXrocks!**, select **Continue**, and press **Enter**. When prompted to repeat the password, enter **LNXrocks!** again, select **Continue**, and press **Enter**. When prompted to encrypt user1's home directory, ensure that **No** is selected and press **Enter**.

10. At the Configure the clock screen, ensure that the correct time zone is displayed, select **Yes** and press **Enter**. Alternatively, if an incorrect time zone is displayed, select **No**, press **Enter**, select your time zone, and press **Enter**.

11. At the Partition disks screen, note that the default selection is **Guided – use entire disk and set up LVM** and press **Enter**. Press **Enter** again to select your disk (sda or hda), and then select **Yes** and press **Enter** to write your partition changes to the disk. Note that the full size (approx. 20GB) is used for the volume group, select **Continue**, and press **Enter**.

12. At the summary screen, note that Ubuntu will create an LV for the root filesystem with an ext4 filesystem and an LV for swap as well. Select **Yes** and press **Enter** to write the changes to the disk and start the installation of the core system packages.

13. At the Configure the package manager screen, optionally supply the URL address of your classroom proxy (if your classroom uses one), select **Continue**, and press **Enter**.

14. At the Configuring tasksel, ensure that **No automatic updates** is selected and press **Enter**. Why is automatic updating often disabled on production servers?

15. At the Software selection screen, use the spacebar to individually choose all packages (except for Manual package selection), select **Continue**, and press **Enter**.

16. At the Configuring mysql-server-5.5 screen, supply a password of **LNXrocks!**, select **Continue**, and press **Enter**. When prompted to confirm the **password,** type **LNXrocks!**, select **Continue**, and press **Enter**.

17. At the Postfix Configuration screen, ensure that **Internet Site** is selected and press **Enter**. When prompted for a system mail name, ensure that **UbuntuXX** is listed (where XX is the unique number assigned to you by your instructor during course setup), select **Continue**, and press **Enter**.

18. At the configuring dovecot-core screen, ensure that **Yes** is selected and press **Enter** to create an SSL encryption certificate. When prompted for the host name used in the certificate, type **UbuntuXX** in place of localhost (where XX is the unique number assigned to you by your instructor during course setup), select **Continue**, and press **Enter**.

19. At the Install the GRUB boot loader on a hard disk screen, ensure that **Yes** is selected and press **Enter**.

20. At the Finish the installation screen, ensure that **Continue** is selected and press **Enter** to reboot into the new system.

21. After the system has booted, note that a graphical login is not available. Log in as **user1** with the password **LNXrocks!**. At the command prompt, type **who** and press **Enter**. What terminal are you using?

22. The root user password is not set during an Ubuntu Server installation. Instead, the user configured during the installation process (user1) has the ability to configure the root user password following installation. At the command prompt, type **sudo passwd root** and press **Enter**. Supply user1's password of **LNXrocks!** when prompted and press **Enter**. Supply a password of **LNXrocks!** for the root user when prompted and press **Enter**. Confirm the root user password by typing **LNXrocks!** and press **Enter**.

23. At the command prompt, type **su - root** and supply a password of **LNXrocks!** to switch to the root user.

24. At the command prompt, type **df** and press **Enter**. Examine the output of the df command. Why was a /boot partition created on your hard disk? Is the / (root) filesystem a volume managed by the LVM?

25. At the command prompt, type **fdisk -l** and press **Enter**. Note that the remainder of the drive is an extended partition (/dev/sda2 or /dev/hda2) that contains a single logical drive (/dev/sda5 or /dev/hda5) used exclusively by the LVM.

26. At the command prompt, type **lvdisplay** and press **Enter**. Note the logical volumes created for the root filesystem and swap partition within the Ubuntu-XX-vg volume group.

27. Type **exit** and press **Enter** to log out of your shell.

Project 6-2

In this hands-on project, you examine installation log files and system information on Fedora Linux and Ubuntu Server Linux.

1. On your Ubuntu Server Linux virtual machine, log into the command-line terminal (tty1) using the user name of **root** and the password of **LNXrocks!**.

2. At the command prompt, type **ls /var/log/installer** and press **Enter**. What regular log files are present in this directory? From their names, which of these files likely contains system information, and which of these files contains events that occurred during the installation process?

3. At the command prompt, type **egrep -i "(error|warn)" /var/log/installer/syslog** and press **Enter**, View any warnings or errors that occurred during your installation.

4. At the command prompt, type **ls -F /proc** and press **Enter** to view the file and directory contents of the proc filesystem.

5. At the command prompt, type **less /proc/cpuinfo** and press **Enter**. Did the installation detect your CPU correctly? Type **q** to quit the less utility.

6. At the command prompt, type **less /proc/modules** and press **Enter**. What is displayed? What does each entry represent? Type **q** to quit the less utility.

7. At the command prompt, type **less /proc/meminfo** and press **Enter**. Does your Linux system recognize all the memory in your computer? If not, what could you do? Type **q** to quit the less utility.

8. At the command prompt, type **dmesg | less** and press **Enter**. Observe the entries. How do they correspond with the hardware information that you saw in the previous three steps? Type **q** to quit the less utility.

9. At the command prompt, type **less /var/log/boot.log** and press **Enter**. What does each entry represent? Type **q** to quit the less utility.

10. At the command prompt, type **less /var/log/syslog** and press **Enter**. What does each entry represent? How do these lines correspond to the information displayed in the previous two steps? Type **q** to quit the less utility.

11. At the command prompt, type **poweroff** and press **Enter** to shut down your Ubuntu Server Linux virtual machine.

12. Boot your Fedora Linux virtual machine. After your Linux system has loaded, switch to a command-line terminal (tty2) by pressing **Ctrl+Alt+F2**. Log in to the terminal using the user name of **root** and the password of **LNXrocks!**.

13. At the command prompt, type `ls /var/log/anaconda` and press **Enter**. What regular log files are present in this directory? From their names, which of these files likely contains all key events that occurred during the installation process? Which one likely contains information about the programs installed during installation?

14. At the command prompt, type `egrep -i "(error|warn)" /var/log/ana-conda/*` and press **Enter**. View any warnings or errors that occurred during your installation.

15. At the command prompt, type `ls -F /proc` and press **Enter** to view the file and directory contents of the proc filesystem. Do the contents look similar to those from Ubuntu Server Linux? Next, type `less /proc/cpuinfo` and press **Enter**. Do the contents of this file look similar to the contents you saw in Step 5? Why? Type **q** to quit the less utility.

16. At the command prompt, type `dmesg | less` and press **Enter**. Observe the entries. Type **q** to quit the less utility.

17. At the command prompt, type `journalctl -b | less` and press **Enter**. What does each entry represent? Type **q** to quit the less utility.

18. At the command prompt, type `poweroff` and press **Enter** to shut down your Fedora Linux virtual machine.

Project 6-3

In this hands-on project, you install ZFS support on Ubuntu Server and configure the ZFS filesystem.

1. Boot your Ubuntu Server Linux virtual machine. After your Linux system has loaded, log into the command-line terminal (tty1) using the user name of **root** and the password of **LNXrocks!**.

2. At the command prompt, type `apt-get -y install build-essential gawk zlib1g-dev uuid-dev vim-nox python-software-properties` and press **Enter** to download and install ZFS prerequisite packages.

 Ubuntu Server Linux uses a different package manager than Fedora Linux. The `apt-get` command is functionally equivalent to the `yum` command that you used in previous chapters to download and install software from Internet repositories. Both `apt-get` and `yum` are discussed in Chapter 11.

3. At the command prompt, type `add-apt-repository ppa:zfs-native/stable`, press **Enter**, and then press **Enter** again to add the location of the online ZFS software repository on the Internet to the Ubuntu installer. Next, type `apt-get update` and press **Enter** to update the Ubuntu installer with the new repository information.

4. At the command prompt, type **apt-get install ubuntu-zfs** and press Enter to install ZFS on your Ubuntu Server Linux system.

5. Edit the /etc/modules file (**vi /etc/modules**) and add the following lines to the end of the file. When finished, save your changes and quit the vi editor.

```
spl
zavl
znvpair
zunicode
zcommon
zfs
```

6. At the command prompt, type **update-initramfs -u** and press Enter to update the disk and module support for the image used to load kernel modules at boot time.

7. Although ZFS normally works with device files for additional disk devices (/dev/sdb1, /dev/sdc1, /dev/sdd1, and so on), ZFS can work with nearly any device or file that can be used to store data. As a result, we'll create four empty files using the **dd** command that we'll treat as four separate disks to practice ZFS commands. Run the following commands to create four 128MB files called /disk1, /disk2, /disk3, and /disk4:

```
dd if=/dev/zero of=/disk1 bs=1024k count=128
dd if=/dev/zero of=/disk2 bs=1024k count=128
dd if=/dev/zero of=/disk3 bs=1024k count=128
dd if=/dev/zero of=/disk4 bs=1024k count=128
```

8. At the command prompt, type **zpool create webstorage /disk1** and press Enter to create a simple ZFS volume called webstorage from the space on /disk1. Next, type **zpool list** at the command prompt and press Enter to view your configuration.

9. At the command prompt, type **cp /etc/hosts /webstorage** and press Enter to copy the /etc/hosts file to the new ZFS filesystem . Next, type **ls -l /webstorage** at the command prompt and press Enter to view the contents of the filesystem. Was the /etc/hosts file copied successfully?

10. At the command prompt, type **zpool destroy webstorage** and press Enter to remove the webstorage volume.

11. At the command prompt, type **zpool create webstorage mirror /disk1 /disk2** and press Enter to create a mirrored ZFS volume called webstorage from the space on /disk1 and /disk2. Next, type **zpool list** at the command prompt and press Enter to view your configuration. Following this, type **zpool status webstorage** at the command prompt and press Enter. Does you mirror have any problems listed?

12. At the command prompt, type **dd if=/dev/random of=/disk1 bs=512 count=1** and press Enter to overwrite a portion of /disk1 using the dd command, simulating disk corruption. Next, type **zpool scrub webstorage** at the command prompt and press Enter to update the status of the ZFS filesystem, and then type **zpool status webstorage** at the command prompt and press Enter. Does you mirror have any problems listed?

13. At the command prompt, type **zpool detach webstorage /disk1** and press Enter to remove the bad disk (/disk1) from the mirror, and then type **zpool status webstorage** at the command prompt and press **Enter** to verify that it is no longer listed.

14. At the command prompt, type **zpool attach webstorage /disk2 /disk3** and press Enter to mirror the data on /disk2 to a new disk (/disk3), and then type **zpool status webstorage** at the command prompt and press **Enter**. Is the mirror fully functional using /disk2 and /disk3?

15. At the command prompt, type **zpool iostat -v webstorage** and press Enter to view the input and output statistics for your mirror. Next, type **zpool destroy webstorage** and press **Enter** to remove the webstorage mirror.

16. At the command prompt, type **zpool create webstorage raidz /disk2 /disk3 /disk4** and press Enter to create a RAID-Z volume called webstorage using /disk2, /disk3 and /disk4, and then type **zpool status webstorage** at the command prompt and press **Enter** to verify the results. Next, type **zpool iostat -v webstorage** and press **Enter** to view the input and output statistics for your RAID-Z volume.

17. At the command prompt, type each of the following commands in turn and press **Enter** to create three subdirectories under /webstorage:

```
mkdir /webstorage/site1
mkdir /webstorage/site2
mkdir /webstorage/site3
```

18. At the command prompt, type **zfs list** and press **Enter**. Are the site1, site2, and site3 directories listed? Why? Next, type each of the following commands in turn and press **Enter** to create three subfilesystems for site1, site2, and site3:

```
zfs create webstorage/site1
zfs create webstorage/site2
zfs create webstorage/site3
```

19. At the command prompt, type **zfs list** and press **Enter**. Are the site1, site2, and site3 directories listed? Why?

20. At the command prompt, type **zfs get all webstorage/site1** and press Enter to view the available options for the site1 subfilesystem. Next, type **zfs set quota=10G webstorage/site1** at the command prompt and press **Enter** to set a quota of 10GB for the subfilesystem. Next, type **zfs get all webstorage/site1** and press **Enter**. Was your quota listed? Why will this quota never be applied to the webstorage/site1 subfilesystem? (Hint: Think of the total size of the webstorage volume)

21. At the command prompt, type **poweroff** and press **Enter** to shut down your Ubuntu Server Linux virtual machine.

Project 6-4

In this hands-on project, you use system rescue on both Fedora Linux and Ubuntu Server Linux to check your root filesystem for errors and change the root user's password.

1. In your virtualization software, ensure that the DVD for your **Fedora Linux** virtual machine is attached to the ISO image for Fedora 20 Live (Fedora-Live-Desktop-x86_64-20-1.iso). Next, start and then connect to your Fedora Linux virtual machine using your virtualization software.

2. At the Fedora Live welcome screen, press **Enter** to boot Fedora Live.

3. Once the graphical desktop and Welcome to Fedora screen have loaded, select the option **Try Fedora** and click **Close** when prompted.

4. Navigate to **Activities, Show Applications, Utilities, Terminal** within the GNOME desktop to open a BASH terminal.

5. At the command prompt, type **su - root** and press **Enter** to switch to the root user.

6. At the command prompt, type **df** and press **Enter** to view the mounted filesystems. Is the root filesystem on your hard disk mounted?

7. At the command prompt, type **fsck -f /dev/sda3** (or **fsck -f /dev/hda3**) and press **Enter** to check your (/) root filesystem for errors.

8. At the command prompt, type **mount /dev/sda3 /mnt** (or **mount /dev/hda3 /mnt**) and press **Enter** to mount the (/) root filesystem on your hard disk to the /mnt directory on the Fedora live system. Next, type **mount /dev/sda1 /mnt /boot** (or **mount /dev/hda1 /mnt/boot**) and press **Enter** to mount the /boot filesystem on your hard disk to the /mnt/boot directory on the Fedora live system.

9. At the command prompt, type **chroot /mnt** and press **Enter** to switch from the root filesystem on your Live Fedora system to the root filesystem on your hard disk. Next, type **ls /root** and press **Enter**. Do you recognize the files?

10. At the command prompt, type **passwd root** and press **Enter**. Supply a new root user password of **Secret123** and press **Enter** when prompted (twice).

11. Click the power icon in the upper-right corner, select the power icon that appears, and click **Power Off** to shut down your Fedora Live installation image.

12. In the Settings for your virtual machine in your virtualization software, ensure that the DVD drive is no longer attached to the Fedora ISO image.

13. Finally, start your Fedora Linux virtual machine using your virtualization software. After the system has loaded, switch to a command-line terminal (tty2) by pressing **Ctrl+Alt+F2** and log in to the terminal using the user name of **root** and the password of **Secret123**. Were you successful?

14. At the command prompt, type **passwd root** and press **Enter**. Supply a new root user password of **LNXrocks!** and press **Enter** when prompted (twice).

15. At the command prompt, type **poweroff** and press **Enter** to shut down your Fedora Linux virtual machine.

16. In your virtualization software, ensure that the DVD for your **Ubuntu Server Linux** virtual machine is attached to the ISO image for Ubuntu Server 14.04 (ubuntu-14.04.1-server-amd64.iso). Next, start and then connect to your Ubuntu Server Linux virtual machine using your virtualization software.

17. At the language screen, ensure that English is selected and press **Enter**.

18. At the Ubuntu welcome screen, navigate to the **Rescue a broken system** option and press **Enter**.

19. At the Select a language page, ensure that **English** is selected and press **Enter**.

20. At the Select your location screen, ensure that **United States** is selected and press **Enter**.

21. At the Configure the keyboard screen, select **Yes** and press **Enter**. Follow the prompts to complete the detection. When the detection process finds a "us" keyboard layout, select **Continue** and press **Enter**.

22. At the Configure the network screen, view the default hostname supplied, select **Continue**, and press **Enter**.

23. At the Configure the clock screen, ensure that the correct time zone is displayed, select **Yes**, and press **Enter**. Alternatively, if an incorrect time zone is displayed, select **No**, press **Enter**, select your time zone, and press **Enter**.

24. At the Enter rescue mode screen, select **/dev/UbuntuXX-vg/root** (where XX is the unique number assigned to you by your instructor during course setup) and press **Enter**. When prompted to also mount the /boot partition, ensure that **Yes** is selected and press **Enter**.

25. At the Enter rescue mode screen, view the options. Select **Execute a shell in /dev/UbuntuXX-vg/root** (where XX is the unique number assigned to you by your instructor during course setup) and press **Enter**. Ensure that **Continue** is selected and press **Enter** when prompted. This will change the root to the mounted / (root) filesystem on your hard disk with the **chroot** command.

26. At the command prompt, type **df** and press **Enter** to view the mounted filesystems. Is the root filesystem on your hard disk mounted?

27. At the command prompt, type **passwd root** and press **Enter**. Supply a new root user password of **Secret123** and press **Enter** when prompted (twice).

28. At the command prompt, type **exit** and press **Enter**.

29. At the Enter rescue mode screen, select **Reboot the system** and press **Enter**.

30. In the Settings for your virtual machine in your virtualization software, ensure that the DVD drive is no longer attached to the Ubuntu Server ISO image.

31. After the system has loaded, log into the command-line terminal (tty1) using the user name of **root** and the password of Secret123.

32. At the command prompt, type **passwd root** and press **Enter**. Supply a new root user password of **LNXrocks!** and press **Enter** when prompted (twice).

33. At the command prompt, type **poweroff** and press **Enter** to shut down your Ubuntu Server Linux virtual machine.

Discovery Exercises

1. Determine the following about your system by viewing the appropriate files within the /proc directory:

   a. Where is the Linux kernel located?

   b. What version is your Linux kernel

   c. What filesystems are supported by your Linux kernel?

   d. What modules are loaded into the kernel?

   e. Gather information about the physical memory on your system.

2. Use the Internet to gather information on three different commercial iSCSI SAN enclosures that can be used to host Linux, and write a short report that compares and contrasts their features and cost. In what situations would you use each one?

3. Use the Internet to gather information on three different commercial hardware RAID controllers that perform RAID level 5, and write a short report that compares and contrasts their features and cost. In what situations would you use each one?

4. Search the Internet for information about five Linux installation problems that are different than those described in this chapter. How have other people solved these problems? If you had similar difficulties during installation, how could you get help?

5. Linux servers are typically stored in a locked server closet to prevent physical access by unauthorized persons. Given the steps that you performed in Project 6-4, describe why these physical restrictions are warranted.

6

## chapter 7

Working with the BASH Shell

After completing this chapter, you will be able to:

- Redirect the input and output of a command
- Identify and manipulate common shell environment variables
- Create and export new shell variables
- Edit environment files to create variables upon shell startup
- Describe the purpose and nature of shell scripts
- Create and execute basic shell scripts
- Effectively use common decision constructs in shell scripts

A solid understanding of shell features is vital to both administrators and users, who must interact with the shell on a daily basis. The first part of this chapter describes how the shell can manipulate command input and output using redirection and pipe shell metacharacters. Next, you explore the different types of variables present in a BASH shell after login, as well as their purpose and usage. Finally, this chapter ends with an introduction to creating and executing BASH shell scripts.

Command Input and Output

The BASH shell is responsible for providing a user interface and interpreting commands entered on the command line. In addition, the BASH shell can manipulate command input and output, provided the user specifies certain shell metacharacters on the command line alongside the command. Command input and output are represented by labels known as **file descriptors**. For each command that can be manipulated by the BASH shell, there are three file descriptors:

- Standard Input (stdin)
- Standard Output (stdout)
- Standard Error (stderr)

Standard Input (stdin) refers to the information processed by the command during execution; this often takes the form of user input typed on the keyboard. **Standard Output (stdout)** refers to the normal output of a command, whereas **Standard Error (stderr)** refers to any error messages generated by the command. Both Standard Output and Standard Error are displayed on the terminal screen by default. All three components are depicted in Figure 7-1.

As shown in Figure 7-1, each file descriptor is represented by a number, with stdin represented by the number 0, stdout represented by the number 1, and stderr represented by the number 2.

Although all three descriptors are available to any command, not all commands use every descriptor. The `ls /etc/hosts /etc/h` command used in Figure 7-1 gives Standard

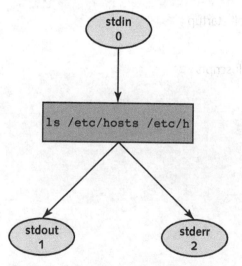

Figure 7-1 The three common file descriptors

Output (the listing of the /etc/hosts file) and Standard Error (an error message indicating that the /etc/h file does not exist) to the terminal screen, as shown in the following output:

```
[root@server1 ~]# ls /etc/hosts /etc/h
ls: cannot access /etc/h: No such file or directory
/etc/hosts
[root@server1 ~]# _
```

Redirection

You can use the BASH shell to redirect Standard Output and Standard Error from the terminal screen to a file on the filesystem. To do this, include the > shell metacharacter followed by the absolute or relative pathname of the file. For example, to redirect only the Standard Output to a file called goodoutput for the command used in Figure 7-1, you append the number of the file descriptor (1) followed by the **redirection** symbol > and the file to redirect the Standard Output to (goodoutput), as shown in the following output:

```
[root@server1 ~]# ls /etc/hosts /etc/h 1>goodoutput
ls: cannot access /etc/h: No such file or directory
[root@server1 ~]# _
```

 You can include a space character after the > metacharacter, but it is not necessary.

In the preceding output, the Standard Error is still displayed to the terminal screen because it was not redirected to a file. The listing of /etc/hosts was not displayed, however; instead, it was redirected to a file called goodoutput in the current directory. If the goodoutput file did not exist prior to running the command in the preceding output, it is created automatically. However, if the goodoutput file did exist prior to the redirection, the BASH shell clears its contents before executing the command. To see that the Standard Output was redirected to the goodoutput file, you can run the following commands:

```
[root@server1 ~]# ls -F
Desktop/  goodoutput
[root@server1 ~]# cat goodoutput
/etc/hosts
[root@server1 ~]# _
```

Similarly, you can redirect the Standard Error of a command to a file; simply specify file descriptor number 2, as shown in the following output:

```
[root@server1 ~]# ls /etc/hosts /etc/h 2>badoutput
/etc/hosts
[root@server1 ~]# cat badoutput
ls: cannot access /etc/h: No such file or directory
[root@server1 ~]# _
```

In the preceding output, only the Standard Error was redirected to a file called badoutput; thus, the Standard Output (a listing of /etc/hosts) was displayed on the terminal screen.

Because redirecting the Standard Output to a file for later use is more common than redirecting the Standard Error to a file, the BASH shell assumes Standard Output in the absence of a numeric file descriptor:

```
[root@server1 ~]# ls /etc/hosts /etc/h >goodoutput
ls: cannot access /etc/h: No such file or directory
[root@server1 ~]# cat goodoutput
/etc/hosts
[root@server1 ~]# _
```

In addition, you can redirect both Standard Output and Standard Error to separate files at the same time, as shown in the following output:

```
[root@server1 ~]# ls /etc/hosts /etc/h >goodoutput 2>badoutput
[root@server1 ~]# cat goodoutput
/etc/hosts
[root@server1 ~]# cat badoutput
ls: cannot access /etc/h: No such file or directory
[root@server1 ~]# _
```

The order of redirection on the command line does not matter; the command ls /etc/hosts /etc/h >goodoutput 2>badoutput is the same as ls /etc/hosts /etc/h 2>badoutput >goodoutput.

It is important to use separate filenames to hold the contents of Standard Output and Standard Error; using the same filename for both results in a loss of data because the system attempts to write both contents to the file at the same time:

```
[root@server1 ~]# ls /etc/hosts /etc/h >goodoutput 2>goodoutput
[root@server1 ~]# cat goodoutput
/etc/hosts
access /etc/h: No such file or directory
[root@server1 ~]# _
```

To redirect both Standard Output and Standard Error to the same file without any loss of data, you must use special notation. To specify that Standard Output be sent to the file goodoutput and Standard Error be sent to the same place as Standard Output, you can do the following:

```
[root@server1 ~]# ls /etc/hosts /etc/h >goodoutput 2>&1
[root@server1 ~]# cat goodoutput
ls: cannot access /etc/h: No such file or directory
/etc/hosts
[root@server1 ~]# _
```

Alternatively, you can specify that the Standard Error be sent to the file badoutput and Standard Output be sent to the same place as Standard Error:

```
[root@server1 ~]# ls /etc/hosts /etc/h 2>badoutput >&2
[root@server1 ~]# cat badoutput
ls: cannot access /etc/h: No such file or directory
/etc/hosts
[root@server1 ~]# _
```

In all of the examples used earlier, the contents of the files used to store the output from commands were cleared prior to use by the BASH shell. Another example of this is shown in the following output when redirecting the Standard Output of the date command to the file dateoutput:

```
[root@server1 ~]# date >dateoutput
[root@server1 ~]# cat dateoutput
Fri Aug 20 07:54:00 EDT 2015
[root@server1 ~]# date >dateoutput
[root@server1 ~]# cat dateoutput
Fri Aug 20 07:54:00 EDT 2015
[root@server1 ~]# _
```

To prevent the file from being cleared by the BASH shell and append output to the existing output, you can specify two > metacharacters alongside the file descriptor, as shown in the following output:

```
[root@server1 ~]# date >dateoutput
[root@server1 ~]# cat dateoutput
Fri Aug 20 07:54:32 EDT 2015
[root@server1 ~]# date >>dateoutput
[root@server1 ~]# cat dateoutput
Fri Aug 20 07:54:32 EDT 2015
Fri Aug 20 07:54:48 EDT 2015
[root@server1 ~]# _
```

You can also redirect a file to the Standard Input of a command using the < metacharacter. Because there is only one file descriptor for input, there is no need to specify the number 0 before the < metacharacter to indicate Standard Input, as shown next:

```
[root@server1 ~]# cat </etc/issue
Fedora release 20 (Heisenbug)
Kernel \r on an \m (\l)

[root@server1 ~]# _
```

In the preceding output, the BASH shell located and sent the /etc/issue file to the cat command as Standard Input. Because the cat command normally takes the filename to be displayed as an argument on the command line (e.g., cat /etc/issue), there is no need to use Standard Input redirection with the cat command as used in the previous example; however, some commands on the Linux system only accept files when they are passed by the shell through Standard Input. The **tr command** is one such command that can be used to replace characters in a file sent via Standard Input. To translate all of the lowercase r characters in the /etc/issue file to uppercase R characters, you can run the following command:

```
[root@server1 ~]# tr r R </etc/issue
FedoRa Release 20 (Heisenbug)
KeRnel \R on an \m (\l)

[root@server1 ~]# _
```

The preceding command does not modify the /etc/issue file; it simply takes a copy of the /etc/issue file, manipulates it, and then sends the Standard Output to the terminal screen. To save a copy of the Standard Output for later use, you can use both Standard Input and Standard Output redirection together:

```
[root@server1 ~]# tr r R </etc/issue >newissue
[root@server1 ~]# cat newissue
FedoRa Release 20 (Heisenbug)
KeRnel \R on an \m (\l)

[root@server1 ~]# _
```

As with redirecting Standard Output and Standard Error in the same command, you should use different filenames when redirecting Standard Input and Standard Output. However, this is because the BASH shell clears a file that already exists before performing the redirection. An example of this is shown in the following output:

```
[root@server1 ~]# sort <newissue >newissue
[root@server1 ~]# cat newissue
[root@server1 ~]# _
```

The newissue file has no contents when displayed in the preceding output. This is because the BASH shell saw that output redirection was indicated on the command line, it cleared the contents of the file newissue, then sorted the blank file and saved the output (nothing in our example) into the file newissue. Because of this feature of shell redirection, Linux administrators commonly use the command >filename at the command prompt to clear the contents of a file.

The contents of log files are typically cleared periodically using the command > /path/to/logfile.

Table 7-1 summarizes the different types of redirection discussed in this section.

Pipes

Note from Table 7-1 that redirection only occurs between a command and a file and vice versa. However, you can send the Standard Output of one command to another command as Standard Input. To do this, you use the pipe | shell metacharacter and specify commands on either side. The shell then sends the Standard Output of the command on the left to the command on the right, which then interprets the information as Standard Input. This process is depicted in Figure 7-2.

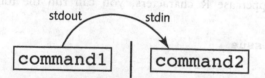

Figure 7-2 Piping information from one command to another

Command	Description
command 1>file command >file	The Standard Output of the command is sent to a file instead of to the terminal screen.
command 2>file	The Standard Error of the command is sent to a file instead of to the terminal screen.
command 1>fileA 2>fileB command >fileA 2>fileB	The Standard Output of the command is sent to fileA instead of to the terminal screen, and the Standard Error of the command is sent to fileB instead of to the terminal screen.
command 1>file 2>&1 command >file 2>&1 command 1>&2 2>file command >&2 2>file	Both the Standard Output and the Standard Error are sent to the same file instead of to the terminal screen.
command 1>>file command >>file	The Standard Output of the command is appended to a file instead of being sent to the terminal screen.
command 2>>file	The Standard Error of the command is appended to a file instead of being sent to the terminal screen.
command 0<file command <file	The Standard Input of a command is taken from a file.

Table 7-1 Common redirection examples

A series of commands that includes the pipe | metacharacter is commonly referred to as a **pipe**.

The pipe symbol can be created on most keyboards by pressing Shift+\.

For example, the Standard Output of the ls -l /etc command is too large to fit on one terminal screen. To send the Standard Output of this command to the less command, which views Standard Input page-by-page, you could use the following command:

```
[root@server1 ~]# ls -l /etc | less
total 1836
drwxr-xr-x  3  root  root  4096  Dec 11  2013   abrt
-rw-r--r--  1  root  root    16  Sep 16  21:54  adjtime
drwxr-xr-x  2  root  root  4096  Sep 17  19:44  akonadi
-rw-r--r--  1  root  root  1518  Jun  7   2013   aliases
drwxr-xr-x  2  root  root  4096  Dec 11  2013   alsa
drwxr-xr-x  2  root  root  4096  Sep 24  10:06  alternatives
-rw-r--r--  1  root  root   541  Sep 25  2013   anacrontab
-rw-r--r--  1  root  root    55  Aug  1   2013   asound.conf
```

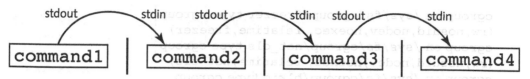

Figure 7-3 Piping several commands

Any command that can take Standard Input and transform it into Standard Output is called a **filter command**. It is important to note that commands such as `ls` and `mount` are not filter commands because they do not accept Standard Input from other commands, but instead find information from the system and display it to the user. As a result, these commands must be at the beginning of a pipe. Other commands, such as `vi`, are interactive and as such cannot exist between two pipe symbols because they cannot take from Standard Input and give to Standard Output.

Several hundred filter commands are available to Linux users. Table 7-2 lists some common ones used throughout this book.

Take, for example, the prologue from Shakespeare's *Romeo and Juliet*:

```
[root@server1 ~]# cat prologue
Two households, both alike in dignity,
In fair Verona, where we lay our scene,
From ancient grudge break to new mutiny,
```

Command	Description
sort	Sorts lines in a file alphanumerically
sort -r	Reverse-sorts lines in a file alphanumerically
wc	Counts the number of lines, words, and characters in a file
wc -l	Counts the number of lines in a file
wc -w	Counts the number of words in a file
wc -c	Counts the number of characters in a file
pr	Formats a file for printing, with several options available; it places a date and page number at the top of each page
pr -d	Formats a file double-spaced
tr	Replaces characters in the text of a file
grep	Displays lines in a file that match a regular expression
nl	Numbers lines in a file
awk	Extracts, manipulates, and formats text using pattern-action statements
sed	Manipulates text using search-and-replace expressions
split	Splits input into several files
unexpand	Converts space characters to tab characters
uniq	Omits repeated lines
xargs	Turns a list of input into arguments that can be used with a command

Table 7-2 Commands that are commonly used within a pipe

```
Where civil blood makes civil hands unclean.
From forth the fatal loins of these two foes
A pair of star-cross'd lovers take their life;
Whole misadventured piteous overthrows
Do with their death bury their parents' strife.
The fearful passage of their death-mark'd love,
And the continuance of their parents' rage,
Which, but their children's end, nought could remove,
Is now the two hours' traffic of our stage;
The which if you with patient ears attend,
What here shall miss, our toil shall strive to mend.
[root@server1 ~]# _
```

Now suppose you want to replace all lowercase "a" characters with uppercase "A" characters in the preceding file, sort the contents by the first character on each line, double-space the output, and view the results page-by-page. To accomplish these tasks, you can use the following pipe:

```
[root@server1 ~]# cat prologue | tr a A | sort | pr -d | less
```

```
2015-08-20 08:06                                             Page 1
A pAir of stAr-cross'd lovers tAke their life;
And the continuAnce of their pArents' rAge,
Do with their deAth bury their pArents' strife.
From Ancient grudge breAk to new mutiny,
From forth the fAtAl loins of these two foes
In fAir VeronA, where we lAy our scene,
Is now the two hours' trAffic of our stAge;
The feArful pAssAge of their deAth-mArk'd love,
The which if you with pAtient eArs Attend,
Two households, both Alike in dignity,
WhAt here shAll miss, our toil shAll strive to mend.
Where civil blood mAkes civil hAnds encleAn.
Which, but their children's end, nought could remove,
Whole misAdventured piteous overthrows
:
```

The command used in the preceding example displays the final Standard Output to the terminal screen via the `less` command. In many cases, you might want to display the results of the pipe while at the same time save copy in a file on the hard disk. The filter command for this job is the **tee command**, which takes information from Standard Input and sends that information to a file, as well as to Standard Output.

To save a copy of the manipulated prologue before displaying it to the terminal screen with the `less` command, you can use the following command:

```
[root@server1 ~]# cat prologue|tr a A|sort|pr -d|tee newfile|less
```

```
2015-08-20 08:06                                             Page 1
A pAir of stAr-cross'd lovers tAke their life;
And the continuAnce of their pArents' rAge,
Do with their deAth bury their pArents' strife.
```

7

```
What here shall miss, our toil shall strive to mend.
[root@server1 ~]# _
```

You can also tell sed the specific lines to search by prefixing the search-and-replace expression. For example, to force sed to replace the string "the" with "THE" globally on lines that contain the string "love," you can use the following command:

```
[root@server1 ~]# cat prologue | sed /love/s/the/THE/g
Two households, both alike in dignity,
In fair Verona, where we lay our scene,
From ancient grudge break to new mutiny,
Where civil blood makes civil hands unclean.
From forth the fatal loins of these two foes
A pair of star-cross'd lovers take THEir life;
Whole misadventured piteous overthrows
Do with their death bury their parents' strife.
The fearful passage of THEir death-mark'd love,
And the continuance of their parents' rage,
Which, but their children's end, nought could remove,
Is now the two hours' traffic of our stage;
The which if you with patient ears attend,
What here shall miss, our toil shall strive to mend.
[root@server1 ~]# _
```

You can also force sed to perform a search-and-replace on certain lines only. To replace the string "the" with "THE" globally on lines 5 to 8 only, you can use the following command:

```
[root@server1 ~]# cat prologue | sed 5,8s/the/THE/g
Two households, both alike in dignity,
In fair Verona, where we lay our scene,
From ancient grudge break to new mutiny,
Where civil blood makes civil hands unclean.
From forth THE fatal loins of THEse two foes
A pair of star-cross'd lovers take THEir life;
Whole misadventured piteous overthrows
Do with THEir death bury THEir parents' strife.
The fearful passage of their death-mark'd love,
And the continuance of their parents' rage,
Which, but their children's end, nought could remove,
Is now the two hours' traffic of our stage;
The which if you with patient ears attend,
What here shall miss, our toil shall strive to mend.
[root@server1 ~]# _
```

You can also use sed to remove unwanted lines of text. To delete all the lines that contain the word "the," you can use the following command:

```
[root@server1 ~]# cat prologue | sed /the/d
Two households, both alike in dignity,
In fair Verona, where we lay our scene,
From ancient grudge break to new mutiny,
Where civil blood makes civil hands unclean.
```

Whole misadventured piteous overthrows
The which if you with patient ears attend,
What here shall miss, our toil shall strive to mend.
[root@server1 ~]# _

Like sed, the awk command searches for patterns of text and performs some action on the text found. However, the awk command treats each line of text as a record in a database, and each word in a line as a database field. For example, the line "Hello, how are you?" has four fields: "Hello," "how," "are," and "you?". These fields can be referenced in the awk command using $1, $2, $3, and $4. For example, to display only the first and fourth words only on lines of the prologue file that contains the word "the," you can use the following command:

```
[root@server1 ~]# cat prologue | awk '/the/ {print $1, $4}'
From fatal
A star-cross'd
Do death
The of
And of
Which, children's
Is two
[root@server1 ~]# _
```

By default, the awk command uses space or tab characters as delimiters for each field in a line. Most configuration files on Linux systems, however, are delimited using colon (:) characters. To change the delimiter that awk uses, you can specify the -F option to the command. For example, the following example lists the last 10 lines of the colon-delimited file /etc/passwd and views only the 6th and 7th fields for lines that contain the word "bob" in the last 10 lines of the file:

```
[root@server1 ~]# tail /etc/passwd
news:x:9:13:News server user:/etc/news:/sbin/nologin
smolt:x:490:474:Smolt:/usr/share/smolt:/sbin/nologin
backuppc:x:489:473::/var/lib/BackupPC:/sbin/nologin
pulse:x:488:472:PulseAudio System Daemon:/var/run/pulse:/sbin/nologin
gdm:x:42:468::/var/lib/gdm:/sbin/nologin
hsqldb:x:96:96::/var/lib/hsqldb:/sbin/nologin
jetty:x:487:467::/usr/share/jetty:/bin/sh
bozo:x:500:500:bozo the clown:/home/bozo:/bin/bash
bob:x:501:501:Bob Smith:/home/bob:/bin/bash
user1:x:502:502:sample user one:/home/user1:/bin/bash
[root@server1 ~]# tail /etc/passwd | awk -F : '/bob/ {print $6, $7}'
/home/bob /bin/bash
[root@server1 ~]# _
```

Both awk and sed allow you to specify regular expressions in the search pattern.

Shell Variables

A BASH shell has several **variables** in memory at any one time. Recall that a variable is simply a reserved portion of memory containing information that might be accessed. Most variables in the shell are referred to as **environment variables** because they are typically set by the system and contain information that the system and programs access regularly. Users can also create their own custom variables. These variables are called **user-defined variables**. In addition to these two types of variables, special variables are available that are useful when executing commands and creating new files and directories.

Environment Variables

Many environment variables are set by default in the BASH shell. To see a list of these variables and their current values, you can use the **set command**, as shown in the following output:

```
[root@server1 ~]# set | less
BASH=/bin/bash
BASHOPTS=checkwinsize:cmdhist:expand_aliases:extglob:extquote:
force_
fignore:histap/bin/bashpend:interactive_comments:login_shell:progcomp:
promptvars:sourcepath
BASH_ALIASES=()
BASH_ARGC=()
BASH_ARGV=()
BASH_CMDS=()
BASH_COMPLETION_COMPAT_DIR=/etc/bash_completion.d
BASH_LINENO=()
BASH_REMATCH=()
BASH_SOURCE=()
BASH_VERSINFO=([0]="4" [1]="2" [2]="45" [3]="1" [4]="release"
[5]="x86_64-redhat-linux-gnu")
BASH_VERSION='4.2.45(1)-release'
COLORS=/etc/DIR_COLORS
COLUMNS=80
COMP_WORDBREAKS=$' \t\n"\'><=;|&(:'
DIRSTACK=()
EUID=0
GROUPS=()
HISTCONTROL=ignoredups
HISTFILE=/root/.bash_history
HISTFILESIZE=1000
HISTSIZE=1000
HOME=/root
HOSTNAME=server1
HOSTTYPE=x86_64
ID=0
IFS=$' \t\n'
INCLUDE=
```

```
KDEDIRS=/usr
LANG=en_US.UTF-8
LESSOPEN='|||/usr/bin/lesspipe.sh %s'
LINES=59
LOGNAME=root
MACHTYPE=x86_64-redhat-linux-gnu
MAIL=/var/spool/mail/root
MAILCHECK=60
OPTERR=1
OPTIND=1
OSTYPE=linux-gnu
PATH=/usr/local/sbin:/usr/local/bin:/usr/sbin:/usr/bin:/root/bin
PIPESTATUS=([0]="0")
PPID=1291
PROMPT_COMMAND='printf "\033]0;%s@%s:%s\007" "${USER}" "${HOSTNAME%%.*}"
"${PWD/#$HOME/~}"'
PS1='[\u@\h \W]\$ '
PS2='> '
PS4='+ '
PWD=/root
QT_GRAPHICSSYSTEM_CHECKED=1
SELINUX_LEVEL_REQUESTED=
SELINUX_ROLE_REQUESTED=
SELINUX_USE_CURRENT_RANGE=
SHELL=/bin/bash
SHELLOPTS=braceexpand:emacs:hashall:histexpand:history:interactive-
comments:monitor
SHLVL=1
SSH_CLIENT='192.168.1.100 43480 22'
SSH_CONNECTION='192.168.1.100 43480 192.168.1.105 22'
SSH_TTY=/dev/pts/0
TERM=xterm
TMP=/tmp/.colorlsn3e
UID=0
USER=root
XDG_RUNTIME_DIR=/run/user/0
XDG_SESSION_ID=2
:
```

Some environment variables shown in the preceding output are used by programs that require information about the system; the OSTYPE (Operating System TYPE) and SHELL (Pathname to shell) variables are examples from the preceding output. Other variables are used to set the user's working environment; the most common of these include the following:

- *PS1*—The default shell prompt
- *HOME*—The absolute pathname to the user's home directory
- *PWD*—The present working directory in the directory tree
- *PATH*—A list of directories to search for executable programs

The PS1 variable represents the BASH shell prompt. To view the contents of this variable only, you can use the **echo command** and specify the variable name prefixed by the $ shell metacharacter, as shown in the following output:

```
[root@server1 ~]# echo $PS1
[\u@\h \W]\$
[root@server1 ~]# _
```

Note that a special notation is used to define the prompt in the preceding output: \u indicates the user name, \h indicates the host name, and \W indicates the name of the current directory. A list of BASH notation can be found by navigating the manual page for the BASH shell.

To change the value of a variable, you specify the variable name followed immediately by an equal sign (=) and the new value. The following output demonstrates how you can change the value of the PS1 variable. The new prompt takes effect immediately and allows the user to type commands.

```
[root@server1 ~]# PS1="This is the new prompt: #"
This is the new prompt: # _
This is the new prompt: # date
Fri Aug 20 08:16:59 EDT 2015
This is the new prompt: # _
This is the new prompt: # who
(unknown) :0          2015-08-20 07:14 (:0)
root      tty2        2015-08-20 07:15
This is the new prompt: # _
This is the new prompt: # PS1="[\u@\h \W]#"
[root@server1 ~]# _
```

The HOME variable is used by programs that require the pathname to the current user's home directory to store or search for files; therefore, it should not be changed. If the root user logs in to the system, the HOME variable is set to /root; alternatively, the HOME variable is set to /home/user1 if the user named user1 logs in to the system. Recall that the tilde ~ metacharacter represents the current user's home directory; this metacharacter is a pointer to the HOME variable, as shown here:

```
[root@server1 ~]# echo $HOME
/root
[root@server1 ~]# echo ~
/root
[root@server1 ~]# HOME=/etc
[root@server1 root]# echo $HOME
/etc
[root@server1 root]# echo ~
/etc
[root@server1 root]# _
```

Like the HOME variable, the PWD (Print Working Directory) variable is vital to the user's environment and should not be changed. PWD stores the current user's location in the directory tree. It is affected by the cd command and used by other commands such as pwd when the current directory needs to be identified. The following output demonstrates how this variable works:

```
[root@server1 ~]# pwd
/root
[root@server1 ~]# echo $PWD
/root
[root@server1 ~]# cd /etc
[root@server1 etc]# pwd
/etc
[root@server1 ~]# echo $PWD
/etc
[root@server1 ~]# _
```

The PATH variable is one of the most important variables in the BASH shell, as it allows users to execute commands by typing the command name alone. Recall that most commands are represented by an executable file on the hard drive. These executables are typically stored in directories named bin or sbin in various locations throughout the Linux directory tree. To execute the ls command, you could either type the absolute or relative pathname to the file (that is, /usr/bin/ls or ../usr/bin/ls) or simply type the letters "ls" and allow the system to search the directories listed in the PATH variable for a command named ls. Sample contents of the PATH variable are shown in the following output:

```
[root@server1 ~]# echo $PATH
/usr/local/sbin:/usr/local/bin:/usr/sbin:/usr/bin:/root/bin
[root@server1 ~]# _
```

In this example, if the user had typed the command ls at the command prompt and pressed Enter, the shell would have noticed the lack of a / character in the pathname and proceeded to search for the file ls in the /usr/local/sbin directory, then the /usr/local/bin directory, the /usr/sbin directory, and then the /usr/bin directory before finding the ls executable file. If no ls file is found in any directory in the PATH variable, the shell returns an error message, as shown here with a misspelled command and any similar command suggestions:

```
[root@server1 ~]# lss
bash: lss: command not found...
Similar command is: 'ls'
[root@server1 ~]# _
```

Thus, if a command is located within a directory that is listed in the PATH variable, you can simply type the name of the command on the command line to execute it. The shell will then find the appropriate executable file on the filesystem. All of the commands used in this book so far have been located in directories listed in the PATH variable. However, if the executable file is not in a directory listed in the PATH variable, the user must specify either the absolute or relative pathname to the executable file. The following example uses the myprogram file in the /root directory (a directory that is not listed in the PATH variable):

```
[root@server1 ~]# pwd
/root
[root@server1 ~]# ls -F
Desktop/ myprogram*
[root@server1 ~]# myprogram
bash: myprogram: command not found...
```

```
[root@server1 ~]# /root/myprogram
This is a sample program.
[root@server1 ~]# ./myprogram
This is a sample program.
[root@server1 ~]# cp myprogram /usr/bin
[root@server1 ~]# myprogram
This is a sample program.
[root@server1 ~]# _
```

After the myprogram executable file was copied to the /usr/bin directory in the preceding output, the user was able to execute it by simply typing its name, because the /usr/bin directory is listed in the PATH variable. Table 7-3 provides a list of environment variables used in most BASH shells.

Variable	Description
BASH	The full path to the BASH shell
BASH_VERSION	The version of the current BASH shell
DISPLAY	The variable used to redirect the output of X Windows to another computer or device that allows remote X connections using the xhost command
ENV	The location of the BASH run-time configuration file (usually ~/.bashrc)
EUID	The effective UID (User ID) of the current user
HISTFILE	The filename used to store previously entered commands in the BASH shell (usually ~/.bash_history)
HISTFILESIZE	The number of previously entered commands that can be stored in the HISTFILE upon logout for use during the next login; it is typically 1000 commands
HISTSIZE	The number of previously entered commands that will be stored in memory during the current login session; it is typically 1000 commands
HOME	The absolute pathname of the current user's home directory
HOSTNAME	The host name of the Linux system
LC_ALL	Defines the locale used by the iconv function within the shell for character encoding (e.g. Unicode UTF-8, ISO-8859), overriding the default locale stored in /usr/bin/locale
LOGNAME	The user name of the current user used when logging in to the shell
MAIL	The location of the mailbox file (where e-mail is stored)
OSTYPE	The current operating system
PATH	The directories to search for executable program files in the absence of an absolute or relative pathname containing a / character
PS1	The current shell prompt
PWD	The current working directory
RANDOM	The variable that creates a random number when accessed
SHELL	The absolute pathname of the current shell
TERM	The variable used to determine the terminal settings; it is typically set to "linux" or "xterm" on newer Linux systems and "console" on older Linux systems
TERMCAP	The variable used to determine the terminal settings on Linux systems that use a TERMCAP database (/etc/termcap)

Table 7-3 Common BASH environment variables

User-Defined Variables

You can set your own variables using the same method discussed earlier to change the contents of existing environment variables. To do so, you simply specify the name of the variable (known as the **variable identifier**) immediately followed by the equal sign (=) and the new contents. When creating new variables, it is important to note the following features of variable identifiers:

- They can contain alphanumeric characters (0–9, A–Z, a–z), the dash (–) character, or the underscore (_) character.
- They must not start with a number.
- They are typically capitalized to follow convention (e.g., HOME, PATH).

To create a variable called MYVAR with the contents "This is a sample variable" and display its contents, you can use the following commands:

```
[root@server1 ~]# MYVAR="This is a sample variable"
[root@server1 ~]# echo $MYVAR
This is a sample variable
[root@server1 ~]# _
```

The preceding command created a variable that is available to the current shell. Most commands that are run by the shell are run in a separate **subshell**, which is created by the current shell. Any variables created in the current shell are not available to those subshells and the commands running within them. Thus, if a user creates a variable to be used within a certain program such as a database editor, that variable should be exported to all subshells using the **export command** to ensure that all programs started by the current shell have the ability to access the variable.

As explained earlier in this chapter, all environment variables in the BASH shell can be listed using the set command; user-defined variables are also indicated in this list. Similarly, to see a list of all exported environment and user-defined variables in the shell, you can use the **env command**. Because the outputs of set and env are typically large, you would commonly redirect the Standard Output of these commands to the grep command to display certain lines only.

To see the difference between the set and env commands as well as export the MYVAR variable created earlier, you can perform the following commands:

```
[root@server1 ~]# set | grep MYVAR
MYVAR='This is a sample variable.'
[root@server1 ~]# env | grep MYVAR
[root@server1 ~]# _
[root@server1 ~]# export MYVAR
[root@server1 ~]# env | grep MYVAR
MYVAR=This is a sample variable.
[root@server1 ~]# _
```

Not all environment variables are exported; the PS1 variable is an example of a variable that does not need to be available to subshells and is not exported as a result. However, it is good form to export user-defined variables because they will likely be used by processes that run in subshells. This means, to create and export a user-defined variable called MYVAR2, you can use the export command alone, as shown in the following output:

```
[root@server1 ~]# export MYVAR2="This is another sample variable"
[root@server1 ~]# set | grep MYVAR2
MYVAR2='This is another sample variable.'
_=MYVAR2
[root@server1 ~]# env | grep MYVAR2
MYVAR2=This is another sample variable.
[root@server1 ~]# _
```

You can also remove a variable from memory using the unset variablename command.

Other Variables

Other variables are not displayed by the set or env commands; these variables perform specialized functions in the shell.

The UMASK variable used earlier in this textbook is an example of a special variable that performs a special function in the BASH shell and must be set by the umask command. Also recall that when you type the cp command, you are actually running an alias to the cp -i command. Aliases are shortcuts to commands stored in special variables that can be created and viewed using the **alias command**. To create an alias to the command mount -t ext2 /dev/fd0 /mnt/floppy called mf and view it, you can use the following commands:

```
[root@server1 ~]# alias mf="mount -t ext2 /dev/fd0 /mnt/floppy"
[root@server1 ~]# alias
alias cp='cp -i'
alias egrep='egrep --color=auto'
alias fgrep='fgrep --color=auto'
alias grep='grep --color=auto'
alias l.='ls -d.* --color=auto'
alias ll='ls -l --color=auto'
alias ls='ls --color=auto'
alias mf='mount -t ext2 /dev/fd0 /mnt/floppy'
alias mv='mv -i'
alias rm='rm -i'
alias which='alias | /usr/bin/which --tty-only --read-alias --show-dot
--show-tilde'
[root@server1 ~]# _
```

Now, you simply need to run the mf command to mount a floppy device that contains an ext2 filesystem to the /mnt/floppy directory, as shown in the following output:

```
[root@server1 ~]# mf
[root@server1 ~]# mount | grep fd0
/dev/fd0 on /mnt/floppy type ext2 (rw)
[root@server1 ~]# _
```

You can also create aliases to multiple commands, provided they are separated by the ; meta-character introduced in Chapter 2. To create and test an alias called dw that runs the date command followed by the who command, you can do the following:

```
[root@server1 ~]# alias dw="date;who"
[root@server1 ~]# alias
alias cp='cp -i'
alias dw='date;who'
alias egrep='egrep --color=auto'
alias fgrep='fgrep --color=auto'
alias grep='grep --color=auto'
alias l.='ls -d .* --color=auto'
alias ll='ls -l --color=auto'
alias ls='ls --color=auto'
alias mf='mount -t ext2 /dev/fd0 /mnt/floppy'
alias mv='mv -i'
alias rm='rm -i'
alias which='alias | /usr/bin/which --tty-only --read-alias --show-dot
--show-tilde'
[root@server1 ~]# dw
Thu Oct 2 08:07:22 EDT 2015
(unknown)  :0              2015-10-02 07:14 (:0)
root       tty2            2015-10-02 07:15
[root@server1 ~]# _
```

It is important to use unique alias names because the shell searches for them before it searches for executable files. If you create an alias called who, that alias would be used instead of the who command on the filesystem.

Environment Files

Recall that variables are stored in memory. When a user exits the BASH shell, all variables stored in memory are destroyed along with the shell itself. To ensure that variables are accessible to a shell at all times, you must place variables in a file that is executed each time a user logs in and starts a BASH shell. These files are called **environment files**. Common BASH shell environment files and the order in which they are typically executed are as follows:

/etc/profile

/etc/bashrc

~/.bashrc

~/.bash_profile

~/.bash_login

~/.profile

The BASH runtime configuration files (/etc/bashrc and ~/.bashrc) are typically used to set aliases and variables that must be present in the BASH shell. They are executed immediately after a new login as well as when a new BASH shell is created after login. The /etc/bashrc file contains aliases and variables for all users on the system, whereas the ~/.bashrc file contains aliases and variables for a specific user.

The other environment files are only executed after a new login. The /etc/profile file is executed after login for all users on the system and sets most environment variables, such as HOME and PATH. After /etc/profile finishes executing, the home directory of the user is searched for the hidden environment files. bash_profile, .bash_login, and .profile. If these files exist, the first one found is executed; as a result, only one of these files is typically used. These hidden environment files allow a user to set customized variables independent of BASH shells used by other users on the system; any values assigned to variables in these files override those set in /etc/profile, /etc/bashrc, and ~/.bashrc due to the order of execution.

To add a variable to any of these files, you simply add a line that has the same format as the command used on the command line. To add the MYVAR2 variable used previously to the .bash_profile file, simply edit the file using a text editor such as vi and add the line `export MYVAR2="This is another sample variable"` to the file.

Variables are not the only type of information that can be entered into an environment file; any command that can be executed on the command line can also be placed inside any environment file. If you want to set the UMASK to 077, display the date after each login, and create an alias, you can add the following lines to one of the hidden environment files in your home directory:

```
umask 077
date
alias dw="date;who"
```

Also, you might want to execute cleanup tasks upon exiting the shell; to do this, simply add those cleanup commands to the .bash_logout file in your home directory.

Shell Scripts

In the previous section, you learned that the BASH shell can execute commands that exist within environment files. The BASH shell also has the ability to execute other text files containing commands and special constructs. These files are referred to as **shell scripts** and are typically used to create custom programs that perform administrative tasks on Linux systems. Any command that can be entered on the command line in Linux can be entered into a shell script because it is a BASH shell that interprets the contents of the shell script itself. The most basic shell script is one that contains a list of commands, one per line, for the shell to execute in order, as shown here in the text file called myscript:

```
[root@server1 ~]# cat myscript
#!/bin/bash
#this is a comment
date
who
ls -F /
[root@server1 ~]# _
```

The first line in the preceding shell script (#!/bin/bash) is called a **hashpling**; it specifies the pathname to the shell that interprets the contents of the shell script. Different shells can use different constructs in their shell scripts. Thus, it is important to identify which shell was used to create a particular shell script. The hashpling allows a user who uses the C shell to use a BASH shell when executing the myscript shell script shown previously. The second line of the shell script is referred to as a comment because it begins with a # character and is ignored by the shell; the only exception to this is the hashpling on the first line of a shell script. The remainder of the shell script shown in the preceding output consists of three commands that will be executed by the shell in order: date, who, and ls.

If you have read permission to a shell script, you can execute the shell script by starting another BASH shell and specifying the shell script as an argument. To execute the myscript shell script shown earlier, you can use the following command:

```
[root@server1 ~]# bash myscript
Fri Aug 20 11:36:18 EDT 2015
user1      tty1        2015-08-20 07:47 (:0)
root       tty2        2015-08-20 11:36
bin/       dev/        home/       media/ proc/   sbin/    sys/  var/
boot/      etc/        lib/        mnt/   public/ selinux/ tmp/
data/      extras/     lost+found/ opt/   root/   srv/     usr/
[root@server1 ~]# _
```

Alternatively, if you have read and execute permission to a shell script, you can execute the shell script like any other executable program on the system, as shown here using the myscript shell script:

```
[root@server1 ~]# chmod a+x myscript
[root@server1 ~]# ./myscript
Fri Aug 20 11:36:58 EDT 2015
user1      tty1        2015-08-20 07:47 (:0)
root       tty2        2015-08-20 11:36
bin/       dev/        home/       media/ proc/   sbin/    sys/  var/
boot/      etc/        lib/        mnt/   public/ selinux/ tmp/
data/      extras/     lost+found/ opt/   root/   srv/     usr/
[root@server1 ~]# _
```

The preceding output is difficult to read because the output from each command is not separated by blank lines or identified by a label. Utilizing the echo command results in a more user-friendly myscript, as shown here:

```
[root@server1 ~]# cat myscript
#!/bin/bash
echo "Today's date is:"
date
echo ""
echo "The people logged into the system include:"
who
echo ""
echo "The contents of the / directory are:"
```

```
ls -F /
[root@server1 ~]#./myscript
Today's date is:
Fri Aug 20 11:37:24 EDT 2015

The people logged into the system include:
user1   tty1        2015-08-20 07:47 (:0)
root    tty2        2015-08-20 11:36
The contents of the / directory are:
bin/    dev/      home/        media/  proc/     sbin/      sys/  var/
boot/   etc/      lib/         mnt/    public/   selinux/   tmp/
data/   extras/   lost+found/  opt/    root/     srv/       usr/
[root@server1 ~]# _
```

Escape Sequences

In the previous example, you used the echo command to manipulate data that appeared on the screen. The echo command also supports several special notations called **escape sequences**. You can use escape sequences to further manipulate the way text is displayed to the terminal screen, provided the –e option is specified to the echo command. Table 7-4 provides a list of these echo escape sequences.

The escape sequences listed in Table 7-4 can be used to further manipulate the output of the myscript shell script used earlier, as shown in the following example:

```
[root@server1 ~]# cat myscript
#!/bin/bash
```

Escape Sequence	Description
\???	Inserts an ASCII character represented by a three-digit octal number (???)
\\	Backslash
\a	ASCII beep
\b	Backspace
\c	Prevents a new line following the command
\f	Form feed
\n	Starts a new line
\r	Carriage return
\t	Horizontal tab
\v	Vertical tab

Table 7-4 Common echo escape sequences

```
echo -e "Today's date is: \c"
date
echo -e "\nThe people logged into the system include:"
who
echo -e "\nThe contents of the / directory are:"
ls -F /
[root@server1 ~]#./myscript
Today's date is: Fri Aug 20 11:44:24 EDT 2015
The people logged into the system include:
user1    tty1         2015-08-20 07:47 (:0)
root     tty2         2015-08-20 11:36

The contents of the / directory are:
bin/      dev/      home/        media/   proc/     sbin/      sys/   var/
boot/     etc/      lib/         mnt/     public/   selinux/   tmp/
data/     extras/   lost+found/  opt/     root/     srv/       usr/
[root@server1 ~]# _
```

Notice from preceding output that the \c escape sequence prevented the newline character at the end of the output "Today's date is:" when myscript was executed. Similarly, newline characters (\n) were inserted prior to displaying "The people logged into the system include:" and "The contents of the / directory are:" to create blank lines between command outputs. This eliminated the need for using the echo " " command shown earlier.

Reading Standard Input

At times, a shell script might need input from the user executing the program; this input can then be stored in a variable for later use. The **read command** takes user input from Standard Input and places it in a variable specified by an argument to the read command. After the input has been read into a variable, the contents of that variable can then be used, as shown in the following shell script:

```
[root@server1 ~]# cat newscript
#!/bin/bash
echo -e "What is your name? --> \c"
read USERNAME
echo "Hello $USERNAME"
[root@server1 ~]# chmod a+x newscript
[root@server1 ~]# ./newscript
What is your name? -->Fred
Hello Fred
[root@server1 ~]# _
```

Note from the preceding output that the echo command used to pose a question to the user ends with --> to simulate an arrow prompt on the screen and the \c escape sequence to place the cursor after the arrow prompt; this is common among Linux administrators when writing shell scripts.

Decision Constructs

Decision constructs are the most common type of construct used in shell scripts. They alter the flow of a program based on whether a command in the program completed successfully or based on a decision that the user makes in response to a question posed by the program. Figures 7-4 and 7-5 illustrate some decision constructs.

The `if` Construct The most common type of decision construct, the `if` construct, has the following syntax:

```
if this is true
then
do these commands
elif this is true
then
do these commands
else
do these commands
fi
```

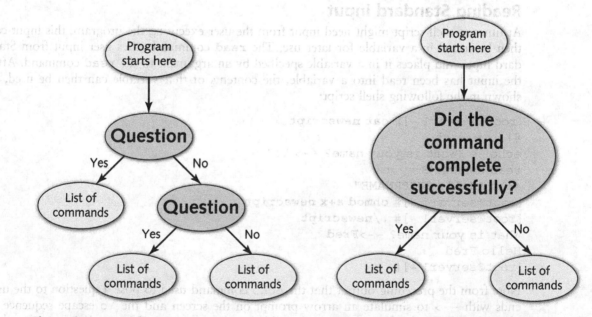

Figure 7-4 A two-question decision construct   **Figure 7-5** A command-based decision construct

Some common rules govern if constructs:

1. elif (else if) and else statements are optional.
2. You can have an unlimited number of elif statements.
3. The *do these* commands section can consist of multiple commands, one per line.
4. The *do these* commands section is typically indented from the left-hand side of the text file for readability but does not need to be.
5. The end of the statement must be a backward "if" (fi).
6. The *this is true* part of the if syntax shown earlier can be a command or a **test statement**:

   * Commands return true if they perform their function properly.
   * Test statements are enclosed within square brackets [ ] or prefixed by the word "test" and used to test certain conditions on the system.

In the following example, a basic if construct is used to ensure that the /etc/hosts file is only copied to the /etc/sample directory if that directory could be created successfully:

```
[root@server1 ~]# cat testmkdir
#!/bin/bash
if mkdir /etc/sample
then
cp /etc/hosts /etc/sample
echo "The hosts file was successfully copied to /etc/sample"
else
echo "The /etc/sample directory could not be created."
fi
[root@server1 ~]# chmod a+x testmkdir
[root@server1 ~]# ./testmkdir
The hosts file was successfully copied to /etc/sample
[root@server1 ~]# _
```

In the preceding output, the mkdir /etc/sample command is always run. If it runs successfully, the shell script proceeds to the cp /etc/hosts /etc/sample and echo "The hosts file was successfully copied to /etc/sample" commands. If the mkdir /etc/sample command is unsuccessful, the shell script skips ahead and executes the echo "The /etc/sample directory could not be created." command. If there were more lines of text following the fi in the preceding shell script, they are executed after the if construct, regardless of its outcome.

Often, it is useful to use the if construct to alter the flow of the program given input from the user. Recall the myscript shell script used earlier:

```
[root@server1 ~]# cat myscript
#!/bin/bash
echo -e "Today's date is: \c"
date
echo -e "\nThe people logged into the system include:"
who
echo -e "\nThe contents of the / directory are:"
```

7

```
ls -F /
[root@server1 ~]# _
```

To ask the user whether to display the contents of the / directory, you could use the following if construct in the myscript file:

```
[root@server1 ~]# cat myscript
#!/bin/bash
echo -e "Today's date is: \c"
date
echo -e "\nThe people logged into the system include:"
who
echo -e "\nWould you like to see the contents of /? (y/n) --> \c"
read ANSWER
if [ $ANSWER = "y" ]
then
echo -e "\nThe contents of the / directory are:"
ls -F /
fi
[root@server1 ~]#./ myscript
Today's date is: Fri Aug 20 11:47:14 EDT 2015

The people logged into the system include:
user1    tty1      2015-08-20 07:47 (:0)
root     tty2      2015-08-20 11:36
Would you like to see the contents of /? (y/n) --> y

The contents of the / directory are:
bin/     dev/      home/       media/ proc/    sbin/    sys/    var/
boot/    etc/      lib/        mnt/   public/  selinux/ tmp/
data/    extras/   lost+found/ opt/   root/    srv/     usr/
[root@server1 ~]# _
```

In the preceding output, the test statement [$ANSWER = "y"] is used to test whether the contents of the ANSWER variable are equal to the letter "y." Any other character in this variable causes this test statement to return false, and the directory listing is then skipped altogether. The type of comparison used previously is called a string comparison because two values are compared for strings of characters; it is indicated by the operator of the test statement, which is the equal sign (=) in this example. Table 7-5 shows a list of common operators used in test statements and their definitions.

The test statement [$ANSWER = "y"] is equivalent to the test statement test $ANSWER = "y".

It is important to include a space character after the beginning square bracket and before the ending square bracket; otherwise, the test statement produces an error.

Test Statement	Returns True if:
[A = B]	String A is equal to String B.
[A != B]	String A is not equal to String B.
[A -eq B]	A is numerically equal to B.
[A -ne B]	A is numerically not equal to B.
[A -lt B]	A is numerically less than B.
[A -gt B]	A is numerically greater than B.
[A -le B]	A is numerically less than or equal to B.
[A -ge B]	A is numerically greater than or equal to B.
[-r A]	A is a file/directory that exists and is readable (r permission).
[-w A]	A is a file/directory that exists and is writable (w permission).
[-x A]	A is a file/directory that exists and is executable (x permission).
[-f A]	A is a file that exists.
[-d A]	A is a directory that exists.

Table 7-5 Common test statements

Test Statement	Returns True if:
[A = B -o C = D]	String A is equal to String B OR String C is equal to String D.
[A = B -a C = D]	String A is equal to String B AND String C is equal to String D.
[! A = B]	String A is NOT equal to String B.

Table 7-6 Special operators in test statements

You can combine any test statement with another test statement using the comparison operators -o (OR) and -a (AND). To reverse the meaning of a test statement, you can use the ! (NOT) operator. Table 7-6 provides some examples of using these operators in test statements.

NOTE

One test statement can contain several -o, -a, and ! operators.

By modifying the myscript shell script in the previous output, you can proceed with the directory listing if the user enters "y" or "Y," as shown in the following example:

```
[root@server1 ~]# cat myscript
#!/bin/bash
echo -e "Today's date is: \c"
date
```

```
    r | R ) echo -e "\nThe contents of the / directory are:"
          ls -F /
          ;;
      *) echo -e "Invalid choice! \a"
          ;;
esac
[root@server1 ~]#./ myscript
What would you like to see?
Todays date (d)
Currently logged in users (u)
The contents of the / directory (r)

Enter your choice(d/u/r)--> d
Today's date is: Fri Aug 20 12:33:08 EDT 2015
[root@server1 ~]# _
```

The preceding example prompts the user with a menu and allows the user to select an item that is then placed into the ANSWER variable. If the ANSWER variable is equal to the letter "d" or "D," the date command is executed; however, if the ANSWER variable is equal to the letter "u" or "U," the who command is executed, and if the ANSWER variable is equal to the letter "r" or "R," the ls command is executed. If the ANSWER variable contains something other than the aforementioned letters, the * wildcard metacharacter matches it and prints an error message to the screen. As with if constructs, any statements present in the shell script following the case construct are executed after the case construct.

The && and || Constructs Although the if and case constructs are versatile, when only one decision needs to be made during the execution of a program, it's faster to use the && and || constructs. The syntax of these constructs is listed as follows:

```
command  &&  command
command  ||  command
```

For the preceding && syntax, the command on the right of the && construct is executed only if the command on the left of the && construct completed successfully. The opposite is true for the || syntax; the command on the right of the || construct is executed only if the command on the left of the || construct did not complete successfully.

Consider the testmkdir example presented earlier in this chapter:

```
[root@server1 ~]# cat testmkdir
#!/bin/bash
if mkdir /etc/sample
then
cp /etc/hosts /etc/sample
echo "The hosts file was successfully copied to /etc/sample"
else
echo "The /etc/sample directory could not be created."
fi
[root@server1 ~]# _
```

You can rewrite the preceding shell script utilizing the && construct as follows:

```
[root@server1 ~]# cat testmkdir
#!/bin/bash
mkdir /etc/sample && cp /etc/hosts /etc/sample
[root@server1 ~]# _
```

The preceding shell script creates the directory /etc/sample and only copies the /etc/hosts file to it if the mkdir /etc/sample command was successful. You can instead use the || construct to generate error messages if one of the commands fails to execute properly:

```
[root@server1 ~]# cat testmkdir
#!/bin/bash
mkdir /etc/sample || echo "Could not create /etc/sample"
cp /etc/hosts /etc/sample || echo "Could not copy /etc/hosts"
[root@server1 ~]#_
```

Loop Constructs

To execute commands repetitively, you can write shell scripts that contain loop constructs. Like decision constructs, **loop constructs** alter the flow of a program based on the result of a particular statement. But unlike decision constructs, which run different parts of a program depending on the results of the test statement, a loop construct simply repeats the entire program. Although several loop constructs are available within the BASH shell, the two most common are for and while.

The for Construct The for construct is the most useful looping construct for Linux administrators because it can be used to process a list of objects, such as files, directories, users, printers, and so on. The syntax of the for construct is as follows:

```
for var_name in string1  string2  string3 … …
do
these commands
done
```

When a for construct is executed, it creates a variable (var_name), sets its value equal to string1, and executes the commands between do and done, which can access the var_name variable. Next, the for construct sets the value of var_name to string2 and executes the commands between do and done again. Following this, the for construct sets the value of var_name to string3 and executes the commands between do and done again. This process repeats as long as there are strings to process. Thus, if there are three strings, the for construct will execute three times. If there are 20 strings, the for construct will execute 20 times.

The following example uses the for construct to e-mail a list of users with a new schedule:

```
[root@server1 ~]# cat emailusers
#!/bin/bash
for NAME in bob sue mary jane frank lisa jason
do
mail -s "Your new project schedule" < newschedule $NAME
```

```
echo "$NAME was emailed successfully"
done
[root@server1 ~]# _
[root@server1 ~]# chmod a+x emailusers
[root@server1 ~]# ./emailusers
bob was emailed successfully
sue was emailed successfully
mary was emailed successfully
jane was emailed successfully
frank was emailed successfully
lisa was emailed successfully
jason was emailed successfully
[root@server1 ~]# _
```

When the for construct in the preceding example is executed, it creates a NAME variable and sets its value to bob. Then it executes the mail command to email bob the contents of the newschedule file with a subject line of Your new project schedule. Next, it sets the NAME variable to sue and executes the mail command to send sue the same email. This process is repeated until the last person receives the email.

A more common use of the for construct within shell scripts is to process several files. The following example renames each file within a specified directory to include a .txt extension.

```
[root@server1 ~]# ls stuff
file1 file2 file3 file4 file5 file6 file7 file8
[root@server1 ~]# _
[root@server1 ~]# cat multiplerename
#!/bin/bash
echo -e "What directory has the files that you would like to rename?
 --> \c"
read DIR
for NAME in $DIR/*
do
mv $NAME $NAME.txt
done
[root@server1 ~]# _
[root@server1 ~]# chmod a+x multiplerename
[root@server1 ~]# ./multiplerename
What directory has the files that you would like to rename? --> stuff
[root@server1 ~]# ls stuff
file1.txt file2.txt file3.txt file4.txt file5.txt file6.txt file7.txt
file8.txt
[root@server1 ~]# _
```

When the for construct in the previous example is executed, it sets the list of strings to stuff/* (which expands to file1 file2 file3 file4 file5 file6 file7 file8). It then creates a NAME variable, sets its value to file1, and executes the mv command to rename file1 to file1.txt. Next, the for construct sets the value of the NAME variable to file2 and executes the mv command to rename file2 to file2.txt. This is repeated until all of the files have been processed. Note that you can also use the seq command to generate a list of numbers for use within a for loop.

The `while` Construct The `while` construct is another common loop construct used within shell scripts. Unlike the `for` construct, the `while` construct begins with a test statement. As long as (or while) the test statement returns true, the commands within the loop construct are executed. When the test statement returns false, the commands within the `while` construct stop executing. A `while` construct typically contains a variable, called a **counter variable**, whose value changes each time through the loop. For the `while` construct to work properly, it must be set up so that, when the counter variable reaches a certain value, the test statement returns false. This prevents the loop from executing indefinitely.

The syntax of the `while` construct is as follows:

```
while this returns true
do
these commands
done
```

The following example illustrates the general use of the `while` construct.

```
[root@server1 ~]# cat echorepeat
#!/bin/bash
COUNTER=0
while [ $COUNTER -lt 7 ]
do
echo "All work and no play makes Jack a dull boy" >> /tmp/redrum
COUNTER=`expr $COUNTER + 1`
done
[root@server1 ~]# _
[root@server1 ~]# chmod a+x echorepeat
[root@server1 ~]# ./echorepeat
[root@server1 ~]# cat /tmp/redrum
All work and no play makes Jack a dull boy
All work and no play makes Jack a dull boy
All work and no play makes Jack a dull boy
All work and no play makes Jack a dull boy
All work and no play makes Jack a dull boy
All work and no play makes Jack a dull boy
All work and no play makes Jack a dull boy
[root@server1 ~]# _
```

The echorepeat shell script shown above creates a counter variable called COUNTER and sets its value to 0. Next, the `while` construct uses a test statement to determine whether the value of the COUNTER variable is less than 7 before executing the commands within the loop. Since the initial value of COUNTER variable is 0, it appends the text `All work and no play makes Jack a dull boy` to the /tmp/redrum file and increments the value of the COUNTER variable to 1. Note the backquotes surrounding the `expr` command, which are required to numerically add 1 to the COUNTER variable (0 + 1 = 1). Because the value of the COUNTER variable at this stage (1) is still less than 7, the `while` construct executes the commands again. This process repeats until the value of the COUNTER variable is equal to 8.

You can use `true` or `:` in place of a test statement to create a `while` construct that executes indefinitely.

Chapter Summary

- Three components are available to commands: Standard Input (stdin), Standard Output (stdout), and Standard Error (stderr). Not all commands use every component.

- Standard Input is typically user input taken from the keyboard, whereas Standard Output and Standard Error are sent to the terminal screen by default.

- You can redirect the Standard Output and Standard Error of a command to a file using redirection symbols. Similarly, you can use redirection symbols to redirect a file to the Standard Input of a command.

- To redirect the Standard Output from one command to the Standard Input of another, you must use the pipe symbol (|).

- Most variables available to the BASH shell are environment variables that are loaded into memory after login from environment files.

- You can create your own variables in the BASH shell and export them to programs started by the shell. These variables can also be placed in environment files, so that they are loaded into memory on every shell login.

- The UMASK variable and command aliases are special variables that must be set using a certain command.

- Shell scripts can be used to execute several Linux commands.

- Decision constructs can be used within shell scripts to execute certain Linux commands based on user input or the results of a certain command.

- Loop constructs can be used within shell scripts to execute a series of commands repetitively.

Key Terms

| A shell metacharacter used to pipe Standard Output from one command to the Standard Input of another command.

< A shell metacharacter used to obtain Standard Input from a file.

> A shell metacharacter used to redirect Standard Output and Standard Error to a file.

alias command A command used to create special variables that are shortcuts to longer command strings.

counter variable A variable that is altered by loop constructs to ensure that commands are not executed indefinitely.

decision construct A special construct used in a shell script to alter the flow of the program based on the outcome of a command or contents of a variable. Common decision constructs include `if`, `case`, `&&`, and `||`.

echo command A command used to display or echo output to the terminal screen. It might utilize escape sequences.

env command   A command used to display a list of exported variables present in the current shell, except special variables.

environment files   The files used immediately after login to execute commands; they are typically used to load variables into memory.

environment variables   The variables that store information commonly accessed by the system or programs executing on the system; together, these variables form the user environment.

escape sequences   The character sequences that have special meaning inside the **echo** command. They are prefixed by the \ character.

export command   A command used to send variables to subshells.

file descriptors   The numeric labels used to define command input and command output.

filter command   A command that can take from Standard Input and send to Standard Output. In other words, a filter is a command that can exist in the middle of a pipe.

hashpling   The first line in a shell script, which defines the shell that will be used to interpret the commands in the script file.

loop construct   A special construct used in a shell script to execute commands repetitively. Common decision constructs include **for** and **while**.

pipe   A string of commands connected by | metacharacters.

read command   A command used to read Standard Input from a user into a variable.

redirection   The process of changing the default locations of Standard Input, Standard Output, and Standard Error.

set command   A command used to view all variables in the shell, except special variables.

shell scripts   The text files that contain a list of commands or constructs for the shell to execute in order.

Standard Error (stderr)   A file descriptor that represents any error messages generated by a command.

Standard Input (stdin)   A file descriptor that represents information input to a command during execution.

Standard Output (stdout)   A file descriptor that represents the desired output from a command.

subshell   A shell started by the current shell.

tee command   A command used to take from Standard Input and send to both Standard Output and a specified file.

test statement   A statement used to test a certain condition and generate a True/False value.

tr command   A command used to transform or change characters received from Standard Input.

user-defined variables   The variables that are created by the user and are not used by the system. These variables are typically exported to subshells.

variable   An area of memory used to store information. Variables are created from entries in environment files when the shell is first created after login, and are destroyed when the shell is destroyed upon logout.

variable identifier   The name of a variable.

14. The `sed` and `awk` commands are filter commands commonly used to format data within a pipe. True or False?

15. What is wrong with the following command string: `ls /etc/hosts >listofhostfile` ?

   a. Nothing is wrong with the command.

   b. The file descriptor was not declared; unless 1 for standard output or 2 for standard error is indicated, the command will fail.

   c. The `ls` command is one of the commands that cannot be used with redirection. You must use | to pipe instead.

   d. The file listofhostfile will always only contain standard error because a file descriptor was not declared.

16. Which of the following is not necessarily generated by every command on the system? (Choose all that apply.)

   a. Standard Input

   b. Standard Deviation

   c. Standard Output

   d. Standard Error

17. Which construct can be used in a shell script to read Standard Input and place it in a variable?

   a. `read`

   b. `sum`

   c. `verify`

   d. `test`

18. A `for` construct is a loop construct that processes a specified list of objects. As a result, it is executed as long as there are remaining objects to process. True or False?

19. What does `>>` accomplish when entered on the command line after a command?

   a. It redirects both Standard Error and Standard Output to the same location.

   b. It does not accomplish anything.

   c. It redirects Standard Error and Standard Input to the same location.

   d. It appends Standard Output to a file.

20. Consider the following shell script:

```
echo -e "What is your favorite color?--> \c"
read REPLY
if ["$REPLY" = "red" -o "$REPLY" = "blue"]
then
echo "The answer is red or blue."
else
echo "The answer is not red nor blue."
fi
```

What would be displayed if a user executes the program in question 20 and answered Blue when prompted?

a. The answer is red or blue.

b. The answer is not red nor blue.

c. The code would cause an error.

d. The answer is red or blue. The answer is not red nor blue.

Hands-on Projects

These projects should be completed in the order given. The hands-on projects presented in this chapter should take a total of three hours to complete. The requirements for this lab include:

- A computer with Fedora Linux installed according to Hands-on Project 2-1.

Project 7-1

In this hands-on project, you use the shell to redirect the Standard Output and Standard Error to a file and take Standard Input from a file.

1. Boot your Fedora Linux virtual machine. After your Linux system has been loaded, switch to a command-line terminal (tty2) by pressing **Ctrl+Alt+F2** and log in to the terminal using the user name of **root** and the password of **LNXrocks!**.

2. At the command prompt, type **touch sample1 sample2** and press **Enter** to create two new files named sample1 and sample2 in your home directory. Verify their creation by typing **ls –F** at the command prompt, and press **Enter**.

3. At the command prompt, type **ls -l sample1 sample2 sample3** and press **Enter**. Is there any Standard Output displayed on the terminal screen? Is there any Standard Error displayed on the terminal screen? Why?

4. At the command prompt, type **ls -l sample1 sample2 sample3 > file** and press **Enter**. Is there any Standard Output displayed on the terminal screen? Is there any Standard Error displayed on the terminal screen? Why?

5. At the command prompt, type **cat file** and press **Enter**. What are the contents of the file and why?

6. At the command prompt, type **ls -l sample1 sample2 sample3 2>file** and press **Enter**. Is there any Standard Output displayed on the terminal screen? Is there any Standard Error displayed on the terminal screen? Why?

7. At the command prompt, type **cat file** and press **Enter**. What are the contents of the file and why? Were the previous contents retained? Why?

8. At the command prompt, type **ls -l sample1 sample2 sample3 > file 2>file2** and press **Enter**. Is there any Standard Output displayed on the terminal screen? Is there any Standard Error displayed on the terminal screen? Why?

9. At the command prompt, type **cat file** and press **Enter**. What are the contents of the file and why?

10. At the command prompt, type **cat file2** and press **Enter**. What are the contents of file2 and why?

11. At the command prompt, type **ls -l sample1 sample2 sample3 > file 2> &1** and press **Enter**. Is there any Standard Output displayed on the terminal screen? Is there any Standard Error displayed on the terminal screen? Why?

12. At the command prompt, type **cat file** and press **Enter**. What are the contents of the file and why?

13. At the command prompt, type **ls -l sample1 sample2 sample3 > &2 2>file2** and press **Enter**. Is there any Standard Output displayed on the terminal screen? Is there any Standard Error displayed on the terminal screen? Why?

14. At the command prompt, type **cat file2** and press **Enter**. What are the contents of file2 and why?

15. At the command prompt, type **date >> file** and press **Enter**.

16. At the command prompt, type **cat file** and press **Enter**. What are the contents of the file and why?

17. At the command prompt, type **date >> file** and press **Enter**.

18. At the command prompt, type **cat file** and press **Enter**. What are the contents of the file and why? Can you tell when each date command was run?

19. At the command prompt, type **tr o O /etc/hosts** and press **Enter**. What error message do you receive and why?

20. At the command prompt, type **tr o O </etc/hosts** and press **Enter**. What happened and why?

21. Type **exit** and press **Enter** to log out of your shell.

Project 7-2

In this hands-on project, you redirect Standard Output and Standard Input using pipe metacharacters.

1. Switch to a command-line terminal (tty2) by pressing **Ctrl+Alt+F2** and log in to the terminal using the user name of **root** and the password of **LNXrocks!**.

2. At the command prompt, type **cat /etc/nsswitch.conf** and press **Enter** to view the */etc/nsswitch.conf* file. Next, type **cat /etc/nsswitch.conf** | less at the command prompt and press **Enter** to perform the same task page-by-page. Explain what the | metacharacter does in the previous command. How is this different from the **less /etc/nsswitch.conf** command?

3. At the command prompt, type **cat /etc/nsswitch.conf | grep nisplus** and press **Enter**. How many lines are displayed? Why did you not need to specify a filename with the grep command?

4. At the command prompt, type **cat /etc/nsswitch.conf | grep nisplus | tr n N** and press **Enter**. Explain the output on the terminal screen.

5. At the command prompt, type **cat /etc/nsswitch.conf | grep nisplus | tr n N | sort –r** and press **Enter**. Explain the output on the terminal screen.

6. At the command prompt, type **cat /etc/nsswitch.conf | grep nisplus | tr n N | sort –r | tee file** and press **Enter**. Explain the output on the terminal screen. Next, type **cat file** at the command prompt and press **Enter**. What are the contents? Why? What does the tee command do in the pipe above?

7. At the command prompt, type **cat /etc/nsswitch.conf | grep nisplus | tr n N | sort –r | tee file | wc –l** and press **Enter**. Explain the output on the terminal screen. Next, type **cat file** at the command prompt and press **Enter**. What are the contents and why?

8. At the command prompt, type **cat /etc/nsswitch.conf/ | grep nisplus | sed /#/d | sed /public/s/nisplus/NISPLUS/** and press **Enter**. Explain the output on the terminal screen. Can this output be obtained with the grep and tr commands instead of sed ?

9. At the command prompt, type **cat /etc/hosts**. Next, type **cat /etc/hosts | awk' /localhost/ {print $1, $3}'** and press **Enter**. Explain the output on the terminal screen.

10. Type **exit** and press **Enter** to log out of your shell.

Project 7-3

In this hands-on project, you create and use an alias, as well as view and change existing shell variables. In addition to this, you export user-defined variables and load variables automatically upon shell startup.

1. Switch to a command-line terminal (tty2) by pressing **Ctrl+Alt+F2** and log in to the terminal using the user name of **root** and the password of **LNXrocks!.**

2. At the command prompt, type **set | less** and press **Enter** to view the BASH shell environment variables currently loaded into memory. Scroll through this list using the cursor keys on the keyboard. When finished, press **q** to quit the less utility.

3. At the command prompt, type **env | less** and press **Enter** to view the exported BASH shell environment variables currently loaded into memory. Scroll through this list using the cursor keys on the keyboard. Is this list larger or smaller than the list generated in Step 2? Why? When finished, press **q** to quit the less utility.

4. At the command prompt, type **PS1="Hello There:"** and press **Enter**. What happened and why? Next, type **echo $PS1** at the command prompt and press **Enter** to verify the new value of the PS1 variable.

5. At the command prompt, type **exit** and press **Enter** to log out of the shell. Next, log in to the terminal using the user name of **root** and the password of **LNXrocks!.** What prompt did you receive and why? How could you ensure that the "Hello There: " prompt occurs at every login?

7

6. At the command prompt, type **vi .bash_profile** and press Enter. At the bottom of the file, add the following lines. When finished, save and quit the vi editor.

```
echo -e "Would you like a hello prompt? (y/n) -->\c"
read ANSWER
if [ $ANSWER = "y" ]
then
PS1="Hello There: "
fi
```

Explain what the preceding lines will perform after each login.

7. At the command prompt, type **exit** and press Enter to log out of the shell. Next, log in to the terminal using the user name of **root** and the password of **LNXrocks!**. When prompted for a hello prompt, type **y** and press Enter. What prompt did you receive and why?

8. At the command prompt, type **exit** and press Enter to log out of the shell. Next, log in to the terminal using the user name of **root** and the password of **LNXrocks!**. When prompted for a hello prompt, type **n** and press Enter to receive the default prompt.

9. At the command prompt, type **MYVAR="My sample variable"** and press Enter to create a variable called MYVAR. Verify its creation by typing **echo $MYVAR** at the command prompt, and press Enter.

10. At the command prompt, type **set | grep MYVAR** and press Enter. Is the MYVAR variable listed? Why?

11. At the command prompt, type **env | grep MYVAR** and press Enter. Is the MYVAR variable listed? Why?

12. At the command prompt, type **export MYVAR** and press Enter. Next, type **env | grep MYVAR** at the command prompt and press Enter. Is the MYVAR variable listed now? Why?

13. At the command prompt, type **exit** and press Enter to log out of the shell. Next, log in to the terminal using the user name of **root** and the password of **LNXrocks!**.

14. At the command prompt, type **echo $MYVAR** and press Enter to view the contents of the MYVAR variable. What is listed and why?

15. At the command prompt, type **vi .bash_profile** and press Enter. At the bottom of the file, add the following line. When finished, save and quit the vi editor.

```
export MYVAR="My sample variable"
```

16. At the command prompt, type **exit** and press Enter to log out of the shell. Next, log in to the terminal using the user name of **root** and the password of **LNXrocks!**.

17. At the command prompt, type **echo $MYVAR** and press Enter to list the contents of the MYVAR variable. What is listed and why?

18. At the command prompt, type **alias** and press Enter. What aliases are present in your shell?

19. At the command prompt, type **alias asample="cd /etc ; cat hosts ; cd ~ ; ls -F"** and press Enter. What does this command do?

20. At the command prompt, type **asample** and press Enter. What happened and why? What environment file could you add this alias to such that it is executed each time a new BASH shell is created?

21. Type **exit** and press Enter to log out of your shell.

Project 7-4

In this hands-on project, you create a basic shell script and execute it on the system.

1. Switch to a command-line terminal (tty2) by pressing **Ctrl+Alt+F2** and log in to the terminal using the user name of **root** and the password of **LNXrocks!.**

2. At the command prompt, type **vi myscript** and press **Enter** to open a new file for editing called myscript in your home directory.

3. Enter the following text into the myscript file. When finished, save and quit the vi editor.

```
#!/bin/bash
echo -e "This is a sample shell script. \t It displays mounted
filesystems \a"
mount
```

4. At the command prompt, type **ls -l myscript** and press **Enter**. What permissions does the myscript file have? Next, type **bash myscript** at the command prompt and press **Enter**. Did the shell script execute? What do the \t and \a escape sequences do?

5. Next, type **./myscript** at the command prompt and press **Enter**. What error message did you receive and why?

6. At the command prompt, type **chmod u+x myscript** and press **Enter**. Next, type **./myscript** at the command prompt and press **Enter**. Did the script execute? Why?

7. Type **exit** and press **Enter** to log out of your shell.

Project 7-5

In this hands-on project, you create a shell script that uses decision and loop constructs to analyze user input.

1. Switch to a command-line terminal (tty2) by pressing **Ctrl+Alt+F2** and log in to the terminal using the user name of **root** and the password of **LNXrocks!.**

2. At the command prompt, type **vi myscript2** and press **Enter** to open a new file for editing called myscript2 in your home directory.

3. Enter the following text into the myscript file. When finished, save and quit the vi editor.

```
#!/bin/bash
echo -e "This program adds entries to a family database file.\n"
echo -e "Please enter the name of the family member -->\c"
read NAME
echo -e "Please enter the family member's relation to you (i.e. mother)
-->\c"
read RELATION
echo -e "Please enter the family member's telephone number -->\c"
read PHONE
echo -e "$NAME\t$RELATION\t$PHONE" >> database
```

4. At the command prompt, type **chmod u+x myscript2** and press **Enter**. Next, type **./myscript2** at the command prompt and press **Enter**. Answer the questions with information regarding one of your family members.

5. At the command prompt, type **cat database** and press **Enter**. Was the entry from Step 4 present? Why?

6. Perform Step 4 several times to populate the database file with entries.

7. At the command prompt, type **vi myscript2** and press Enter. Edit the text inside the myscript2 shell script such that it reads:

```
#!/bin/bash
echo -e "Would you like to add an entry to the family database file?\n"
read ANSWER1
if [ $ANSWER1 = "y" -o $ANSWER1 = "Y" ]
then
echo -e "Please enter the name of the family member -->\c"
read NAME
echo -e "Please enter the family member's relation to you (i.e.
   mother)-->\c"
read RELATION
echo -e "Please enter the family member's telephone number -->\c"
read PHONE
echo -e "$NAME\t$RELATION\t$PHONE" >> database
fi
echo -e "Would you like to search an entry in the family database
   file?\n"
read ANSWER2
if [ $ANSWER2 = "y" -o $ANSWER2 = "Y" ]
then
echo -e "What word would you like to look for? -->\c"
read WORD
grep "$WORD" database
fi
```

8. At the command prompt, type **./myscript2** and press Enter. When prompted to enter an entry into the database, choose **y** and press Enter. Answer the questions with information regarding one of your family members. Next, when prompted to search the database, answer **y** and press Enter. Search for the name that you just entered a few seconds ago. Is it there?

9. At the command prompt, type **./myscript2** and press Enter. When prompted to enter an entry into the database, choose **n** and press Enter. Next, when prompted to search the database, answer **y** and press Enter. Search for a name that you entered earlier in Step 6. Was it there? Why?

10. At the command prompt, type **vi myscript2** and press Enter. Edit the text inside the myscript2 shell script such that it reads:

```
#!/bin/bash
echo -e "What would you like to do?
Add an entry (a)
Search an entry (s)
Enter your choice (a/s)-->\c"
read ANSWER
case $ANSWER in
a|A ) echo -e "Please enter the name of the family member -->\c"
   read NAME
   echo -e "Please enter the family member's relation to you (i.e.
```

```
mother)-->\c"
   read RELATION
   echo -e "Please enter the family member's telephone number -->\c"
   read PHONE
   echo -e "$NAME\t$RELATION\t$PHONE" > > database
   ;;

s|S ) echo -e "What word would you like to look for? -->\c"
   read WORD
   grep "$WORD" database
   ;;
*) echo "You must enter either the letter a or s."
   ;;
esac
```

11. At the command prompt, type **./myscript2** and press **Enter**. Choose **y** and press **Enter**. What error message do you receive and why?

12. At the command prompt, type **./myscript2** and press **Enter**. Choose **a** and press **Enter**. Enter information about another family member. Does it matter whether you entered a or A at the prompt earlier? Why?

13. At the command prompt, type **./myscript2** and press **Enter**. Choose **s** and press **Enter**. Search for the family member entered in Step 12. Does it matter whether you entered s or S at the prompt earlier? Why?

14. At the command prompt, type **vi myscript2** and press **Enter**. Edit the text inside the myscript2 shell script such that it reads:

```
#!/bin/bash
while true
do
clear
echo -e "What would you like to do?
Add an entry (a)
Search an entry (s)
Quit (q)
Enter your choice (a/s/q)-->\c"
read ANSWER
case $ANSWER in
a|A ) echo -e "Please enter the name of the family member -->\c"
   read NAME
   echo -e "Please enter the family member's relation to you (i.e.
mother)-->\c"
   read RELATION
   echo -e "Please enter the family member's telephone number -->\c"
   read PHONE
   echo "$NAME\t$RELATION\t$PHONE" > > database
   ;;
s|S ) echo "What word would you like to look for? -->\c"
   read WORD
   grep "$WORD" database
   sleep 4
```

<aside>7</aside>

```
        ;;
q|Q ) exit
        ;;
*)    echo "You must enter either the letter a or s."
      sleep 4
        ;;
esac
done
```

15. At the command prompt, type **./myscript2** and press **Enter**. Choose **a** and press **Enter**. Enter information about another family member. Does the menu appear again after you were finished? Why? Choose **s** and press **Enter**. Search for the family member that you just entered. Choose **q** to quit the shell script.

16. At the command prompt, type **vi myscript3** and press **Enter** to edit a new file called myscript3 in your home directory.

17. Enter the following text into the myscript3 file. When finished, save and quit the vi editor.

```
#!/bin/bash
echo -e "This program copies a file to the /stuff directory.\n"
echo -e "Which file would you like to copy? -->\c"
read FILENAME
mkdir /stuff || echo "The /stuff directory could not be created."
cp -f $FILENAME /stuff && echo "$FILENAME was successfully copied to /
stuff"
```

18. At the command prompt, type **chmod u+x myscript3** and press **Enter**. Next, type **./myscript3** at the command prompt and press **Enter**. When prompted for a filename, type **/etc/hosts** and press **Enter**. Was the /stuff directory created successfully? Why or why not? Was the /etc/hosts file copied successfully to the /stuff directory? Why or why not?

19. Type **./myscript3** at the command prompt and press **Enter**. When prompted for a filename, type **/etc/inittab** and press **Enter**. Was the /stuff directory created successfully? Why or why not? Was the /etc/inittab file copied successfully to the /stuff directory? Why or why not?

20. At the command prompt, type **vi myscript4** and press **Enter** to edit a new file called myscript4 in your home directory.

21. Enter the following text into the myscript4 file. When finished, save and quit the vi editor.

```
#!/bin/bash
echo "These are the scripts that you have created previously:"
ls -l myscript myscript2 myscript3
sleep 2
echo "This script will now change the permissions on each script such
that the root user has exclusive rights only."
sleep 3
for FILE in myscript myscript2 myscript3
do
chmod 700 $FILE
done

echo "The new permissions are listed below:"
ls -l myscript myscript2 myscript3
```

22. At the command prompt, type **chmod u+x myscript4** and press Enter. Next, type **./myscript4** at the command prompt and press Enter. Were the permissions changed to rwx------ for myscript, myscript2, and myscript3?

23. Type **exit** and press Enter to log out of your shell.

Discovery Exercises

1. Name the command that can be used to do each of the following:

   a. Create an alias called mm that displays only those filesystems that are mounted and contain an ext4 filesystem.

   b. Create and export a variable called NEWHOME that is equivalent to the value contained in the HOME variable.

   c. Find all files that start with the word "host" starting from the /etc directory and save the Standard Output to a file called file1 and the Standard Error to the same file.

   d. Display only the lines from the output of the set command that have the word "bash" in them. This output on the terminal screen should be sorted alphabetically.

   e. Display only the user name (first field) in the colon-delimited /etc/passwd file and save the output to a file called users in the current directory.

2. What would happen if the user executed the following commands?

   ```
   cp /etc/hosts ~
   cd
   tr a A <hosts | sort -r | pr -d >hosts
   ```

   Explain the output.

3. Recall that only Standard Output can be sent across a pipe to another command. Using the information presented in this chapter, how could you send Standard Error across the pipe in the following command?

   ```
   ls /etc/hosts /etc/h | tr h H
   ```

4. Name the test statement that can be used to test the following scenarios:

   a. The user has read permission to the /etc/hosts file.

   b. The user has read and execute permission to the /etc directory.

   c. The contents of the variable $TEST are equal to the string "success."

   d. The contents of the variable $TEST are numerically equal to the contents of the variable $RESULT.

   e. The contents of the variable $TEST are equal to the string "success" and the file /etc/hosts exists.

   f. The contents of the variable $TEST are equal to the string "success," or the number 5, or the contents of the variable $RESULT.

5. Examine the sample */root/.bash_profile* file shown next. Using the information presented in this chapter, describe what each line of this file does.

```
#.bash_profile
# Get the aliases and functions
if [ -f ~/.bashrc ]; then
        . ~/.bashrc
fi
# User specific environment and startup programs

PATH=$PATH:$HOME/bin
BASH_ENV=$HOME/.bashrc
USERNAME="root"
export USERNAME BASH_ENV PATH
```

6. Write a shell script that contains a hashpling and comments. It should perform the following tasks:

   a. Displays a list of currently logged-in users

   b. Displays the system's host name

   c. Displays the time and date

   d. Displays the disk usage

   e. Displays the current working directory

   f. Displays the pathname to the BASH shell

7. Write a shell script that prompts the user for a grade between 0 and 100. The shell script should calculate the corresponding letter for this grade based on the following criteria:

   0–49 = F
   50–59 = D
   60–69 = C
   70–79 = B
   80–100 = A

   Ensure that the shell script continues to prompt the user for grades until the user chooses to exit the shell script.

8. Nearly all of the concepts presented in this chapter apply to all Linux distributions. However, different Linux distributions may use different default environment files. Boot your Ubuntu Server Linux virtual machine and view the hidden environment files in your home directory. Which two files are used to store environment variables and aliases for each Ubuntu user by default? View their contents. Is there a /etc/profile and /etc/bashrc file by default? If not, what are they called? View the contents of both of these files.

System Initialization and X Windows

After completing this chapter, you will be able to:

- Summarize the major steps necessary to boot a Linux system
- Detail the configuration of common Linux boot loaders
- Explain the UNIX SysV and Systemd system initialization processes
- Start, stop, and restart daemons
- Configure the system to start and stop daemons upon entering certain runlevels and targets
- Explain the purpose of the major Linux GUI components: X Windows, window manager, and desktop environment
- List common window managers and desktop environments used in Linux
- Configure X Windows settings

In this chapter, you investigate the boot process in greater detail. You explore how to configure boot loaders and the process used to start daemons after the kernel has loaded. Additionally, you examine the procedures used to start and stop daemons and set them to start automatically at boot time. Finally, you examine the various components the Linux GUI comprises and how to configure these components using common Linux utilities.

The Boot Process

When a computer first initializes, the system BIOS performs a **Power On Self Test (POST)**. Following the POST, the BIOS checks its configuration for boot devices and operating systems to execute. Typically, computers first check for an operating system on floppy disk, CD, DVD, and USB devices since these devices can contain installation media for an operating system. If it fails to find an operating system on any of these options, the BIOS usually checks the MBR/GPT on the first hard disk inside the computer.

Recall that you can alter the order in which boot devices are checked in the computer BIOS.

Also recall that the MBR/GPT stores the list of all partitions on the hard disk.

The MBR/GPT might contain a **boot loader** that can then locate and execute the kernel of the operating system. Alternatively, the MBR/GPT might contain a pointer to a partition on the system that contains a boot loader on the first sector; this partition is referred to as the **active partition**. There can be only one active partition per hard disk.

In addition to storing the list of all partitions on the hard disk, the MBR/GPT stores the location of the active partition.

Regardless of whether the boot loader is loaded from the MBR/GPT or the first sector of the active partition, the remainder of the boot process is the same. The boot loader then executes the Linux kernel from the partition that contains it.

The Linux kernel is stored in the **/boot** directory and is named **vmlinuz-<kernel version>**.

After the Linux kernel is loaded into memory, the boot loader is no longer active; instead, the Linux kernel continues to initialize the system by loading daemons into memory. A **daemon** is a system process that performs useful tasks, such as printing, scheduling, and operating system maintenance. The first daemon process on the system is called the **initialize (init) daemon**; it is responsible for loading all other daemons on the system required to bring the system to a usable state in which users can log in and interact with services. The whole process is depicted in Figure 8-1.

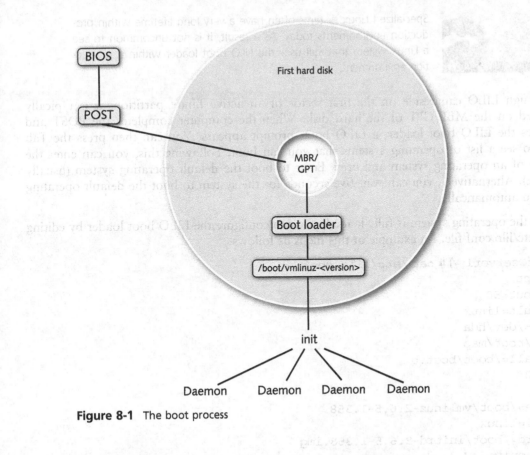

Figure 8-1 The boot process

Boot Loaders

As discussed in the previous section, the primary function of boot loaders during the boot process is to load the Linux kernel into memory. However, boot loaders can perform other functions as well, including passing information to the kernel during system startup and booting other operating systems that are present on the hard disk. Using one boot loader to boot one of several operating systems is known as **multi booting**; the boot loader simply loads a different operating system kernel based on user input.

 Unless virtualization software is used, only one operating system can be active at any one time.

The two most common boot loaders used on Linux systems are LILO, GRUB, and GRUB2.

LILO

Linux Loader (LILO) is the traditional Linux boot loader. Although it is no longer used by most modern Linux distributions, it is often found on other Linux distributions that require a smaller boot loader than GRUB, as well as legacy Linux installations.

Specialized Linux systems often have a very long lifetime within production environments today. As a result, it is not uncommon to see a Linux system that still uses the LILO boot loader within a production environment.

Although LILO can reside on the first sector of an active Linux partition, it is typically located on the MBR/GPT of the hard disk. When the computer completes the POST and locates the LILO boot loader, a LILO boot: prompt appears. You can then press the Tab key to see a list of operating systems that you can boot. Following this, you can enter the name of an operating system and press Enter to boot the default operating system (usually Linux). Alternatively, you can wait five seconds for the system to boot the default operating system automatically.

After the operating system is fully loaded, you can configure the LILO boot loader by editing the **/etc/lilo.conf** file. An example of this file is as follows:

```
[root@server1 ~]# cat /etc/lilo.conf
prompt
timeout=50
default=linux
boot=/dev/hda
map=/boot/map
install=/boot/boot.b
lba32

image=/boot/vmlinuz-2.6.5-1.358
label=linux
initrd=/boot/initrd-2.6.5-1.358.img
read-only
append="rhgb quiet root=/dev/hda1"
[root@server1 ~]# _
```

The preceding /etc/lilo.conf file indicates that LILO boots the linux kernel /boot/vmlinuz-2.6.5-1.358 provided the user chooses the operating system name linux (label=linux). Furthermore, the system continues to boot the default operating system (default=linux) if the user does not enter any input for five seconds (timeout=50). Additionally, the LILO boot loader tells the Linux kernel to use a Red Hat Graphical Boot after it has loaded (rhgb), suppress detailed kernel messages (quiet), and mount the root filesystem on /dev/hda1 (root=/dev/hda1).

Table 8-1 lists some keywords commonly used in /etc/lilo.conf, along with their definitions.

As with shell scripts, you can transform a line in /etc/lilo.conf to a comment by preceding it with a # symbol.

If the kernel does not detect the correct system information, you can use the append= keyword in /etc/lilo.conf to pass information to the Linux kernel manually at boot time. For example, if the Linux kernel did not detect the RAM or hard disk installed in your system

Keyword	Description
image=	Specifies the absolute pathname to the Linux kernel.
root=	Specifies the device and the partition that contains the Linux root filesystem.
prompt	Displays a LILO boot prompt provided there is no message= keyword specified.
message=	Specifies the absolute pathname to the file that contains a graphical LILO screen that can be used instead of a prompt. Y; you can press Ctrl+x at this graphical screen to switch to the LILO boot: prompt.
timeout=	Specifies the number of 1/10th seconds to wait for user input before loading the default operating system kernel.
default=	Specifies the label for the default operating system kernel.
label=	Specifies the friendly name used to identify an operating system kernel within boot loader screens.
boot=	Specifies where LILO should be installed. If the device specified is a partition on a hard disk, LILO is installed at the beginning of the partition. If the device specified is a disk, LILO is installed to the MBR on that device.
linear	Specifies that LILO uses linear sector addressing.
read-only	Initially mounts the Linux root filesystem as read-only to reduce any errors with running fsck during system startup.
initrd=	Specifies the pathname to a ramdisk image used to load modules into memory needed for the Linux kernel at boot time.
password=	Specifies a password required to boot the Linux kernel.
append=	Specifies parameters that are passed to the Linux kernel when loaded.
map=	Specifies the file that contains the exact location of the Linux kernel on the hard disk.
install=	Specifies the file that contains the physical layout of the disk drive.
lba32	Specifies large block addressing (32-bit) for hard drives that have more than 1024 cylinders.

Table 8-1 Common /etc/lilo.conf keywords

properly, you can add the line append="mem=4096M" to /etc/lilo.conf to allow your Linux kernel to recognize that your system has 4096MB of RAM, as well as the line append="hd=2100,16,63" to /etc/lilo.conf to tell your Linux kernel that your hard disk has 2100 cylinders, 16 heads, and 63 sectors.

After changing the /etc/lilo.conf file, LILO must be reinstalled using the new information in /etc/lilo.conf for those changes to take effect. To do this, you can use the **lilo command**:

```
[root@server1 ~]# lilo
Added linux *
[root@server1 ~]# _
```

To uninstall LILO from an active partition or the MBR/GPT, you can use the lilo -U command.

NOTE

Error Message	Description
L	The first part of the LILO boot loader failed to load, usually as a result of incorrect hard disk parameters. Simply rebooting the machine sometimes fixes this problem. However, you might also need to add the word "linear" to /etc/lilo.conf.
LI	The second part of the LILO boot loader failed to load or the /boot/boot.b file is missing. Adding the word "linear" to /etc/lilo.conf might fix the problem.
LIL LIL- LIL?	LILO has loaded properly but cannot find certain files required to operate, such as the /boot/map and /boot/boot.b files. Adding the word "linear" to /etc/lilo.conf might fix the problem.

Table 8-2 LILO error messages

Although LILO is a robust boot loader, it might encounter errors and fail to load properly. In that case, you see an error code indicating the nature of the problem. Table 8-2 lists common LILO error messages and possible solutions.

 **ELILO** is a version of LILO that is available for computers that use Extensible Firmware Interface (EFI). You can download ELILO from the Internet at *www.sourceforge.net/projects/elilo*.

GRUB

GRand Unified Bootloader (GRUB) was created in 1999 and originally intended as a replacement boot loader for LILO. It supports the booting of several different operating systems, including Linux, Mac OSX, UNIX, BSD UNIX, Solaris UNIX, and Windows.

 Although GRUB is no longer in development, due to the release of GRUB2 in 2012, there are a large number of Linux systems installed in production environments that still use it.

The first major part of the GRUB boot loader (called Stage1) typically resides on the MBR/GPT; the remaining parts of the boot loader (called Stage1.5 and Stage2) reside in the /boot/grub directory. GRUB Stage1 simply points to GRUB Stage1.5, which loads filesystem support and proceeds to load GRUB Stage2. GRUB Stage2 performs the actual boot loader functions and displays a graphical boot loader screen similar to that shown in Figure 8-2.

You configure GRUB by editing a configuration file (/boot/grub/grub.conf) that is read directly by the Stage2 boot loader. An example /boot/grub/grub.conf file for a Fedora system is shown next:

```
[root@server1 ~]# cat /boot/grub/grub.conf
# grub.conf generated by anaconda
#
# Note that you do not have to rerun grub after making changes
# NOTICE:   You do not have a /boot partition. This means that
#           all kernel and initrd paths are relative to /, eg.
#           root (hd0,0)
```

Figure 8-2 The GRUB boot screen for a Fedora system

```
#           kernel /boot/vmlinuz-version ro root=/dev/sda1
#           initrd /boot/initrd-[generic-]version.img
boot=/dev/sda
default=0
timeout=5
splashimage=(hd0,0)/boot/grub/splash.xpm.gz
hiddenmenu

title Fedora (2.6.33.3-85.fc13.i686.PAE)
    root (hd0,0)
  kernel /boot/vmlinuz-2.6.33.3-85.fc13.i686.PAE ro root=/dev/sda1
    rhgb quiet
  initrd /boot/initramfs-2.6.33.3-85.fc13.i686.PAE.img
[root@server1 ~]# _
```

Alternatively, you can view and edit the /etc/grub.conf file, which is simply a symbolic link to /boot/grub/grub.conf.

As with LILO, lines can be commented out of /boot/grub/grub.conf by preceding those lines with a # symbol.

Some other Linux distributions, such as Ubuntu Linux, use a /boot/grub/menu.lst file in place of /boot/grub/grub.conf to hold GRUB configuration.

To understand the entries in the /boot/grub/grub.conf file, you must first understand how GRUB refers to partitions on hard disks. Hard disks and partitions on those hard disks are identified by numbers in the following format: (hd<drive#>,<cl:partition#>). Thus, the (hd0,0) notation in the preceding /boot/grub/grub.conf file refers to the first hard disk on the system (regardless of whether it is SCSI, SATA, or PATA) and the first partition on that hard disk, respectively. Similarly, the second partition on the first hard disk is referred to as (hd0,1), and the fourth partition on the third hard disk is referred to as (hd2,3).

In addition, GRUB calls the partition that contains Stage2 of the GRUB boot loader the **GRUB root partition**. Normally, the GRUB root partition is the filesystem that contains the

/boot directory and should not be confused with the Linux root filesystem. If your system has a separate partition mounted to /boot, GRUB refers to the file /boot/grub/grub.conf as /grub/grub.conf. If your system does not have a separate filesystem for the /boot directory, this file is simply referred to as /boot/grub/grub.conf in GRUB.

Thus, the example /boot/grub/grub.conf file shown earlier displays a graphical boot screen (`splashimage=(hd0,0)/boot/grub/splash.xpm.gz`) and boots the default operating system kernel on the first hard drive (`default=0`) in 5 seconds (`timeout=5`) without showing any additional menus (`hiddenmenu`). The default operating system kernel is located on the GRUB root filesystem (`root (hd0,0)`) and is called `/boot/vmlinuz-2.6.33.3-85.fc13.i686.PAE`.

The kernel then mounts the root filesystem on /dev/sda1 (`root=/dev/sda1`) initially as read-only (`ro`) to avoid problems with the `fsck` command and uses a ramdisk image to load modules into RAM that are needed at boot time (`initrd /boot/initramfs-2.6.33.3-85.fc13.i686.PAE.img`).

 Most modern Linux distributions use a GUID label (i.e. `root= UUID= 42c0fce6-bb79-4218-af1a-0b89316bb7d1`) in place of `root=/dev/sda1` to identify the partition that holds the root filesystem.

All other keywords present on the `kernel` line within /boot/grub/grub.conf are used to pass information to the kernel from the GRUB boot loader. For example, the keyword `rhgb` (Red Hat Graphical Boot) tells the Linux kernel to use a graphical boot screen as it is loading daemons, and the keyword `quiet` tells the Linux kernel to avoid printing errors to the screen during system startup. You can add your own keywords to the `kernel` line in /boot/grub/grub.conf to control how your Linux kernel is loaded. For example, appending the text `nosmp` to the `kernel` line disables Symmetric Multi-Processing (SMP) support within the Linux kernel. Alternatively, appending the text `mem=4096M` to the `kernel` line forces your Linux kernel to see 4096MB of physical RAM in the event that your Linux kernel does not detect all of the RAM in your computer properly.

Normally, GRUB allows users to manipulate the boot loader during system startup; to prevent this, you can optionally password protect GRUB modifications during boot time.

Recall from the /boot/grub/grub.conf file shown earlier that you have 5 seconds after the BIOS POST to interact with the GRUB boot screen shown in Figure 8-2. If you press any key within these 5 seconds, you will be presented with a graphical GRUB boot menu screen similar to Figure 8-3 that you can use to manipulate the boot process. If you have several different Linux kernels installed on your system (from updating your system software), you can select the kernel that you would like to boot, or you can highlight your kernel and press a to append keywords to the kernel line, or press e to edit the entire boot configuration for the kernel listed in /boot/grub/grub.conf at boot time. You can also press c to obtain a grub> prompt where you can enter a variety of commands to view system hardware configuration, find and display files, alter the configuration of GRUB, or boot an operating system kernel. Typing `help` at this grub> prompt will display a list of available commands and their usage.

If the GRUB boot loader becomes damaged, you can reinstall it using the **grub-install command** that is available on the system or on a live Linux system used for system rescue.

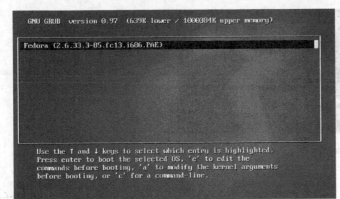

```
GNU GRUB  version 0.97  (639K lower / 1000384K upper memory)

 ┌────────────────────────────────────────────────────────────────────────┐
 │ Fedora (2.6.33.3-85.fc13.i686.PAE)                                      │
 │                                                                          │
 │                                                                          │
 │                                                                          │
 │                                                                          │
 │                                                                          │
 │                                                                          │
 │                                                                          │
 └────────────────────────────────────────────────────────────────────────┘
      Use the ↑ and ↓ keys to select which entry is highlighted.
      Press enter to boot the selected OS, 'e' to edit the
      commands before booting, 'a' to modify the kernel arguments
      before booting, or 'c' for a command-line.
```

Figure 8-3 The GRUB boot menu for a Fedora system

To install GRUB Stage1 on the MBR/GPT of the first SATA hard disk, you can type the following command:

```
[root@server1 ~]# grub-install /dev/sda
Installation finished. No error reported.
This is the contents of the device map /boot/grub/device.map.
Check if this is correct or not. If any of the lines is incorrect,
fix it and re-run the script 'grub-install'.

# this device map was generated by anaconda
(hd0) /dev/sda
[root@server1 ~]# _
```

Alternatively, you can use the `grub-install /dev/sda1` command to install GRUB Stage1 at the beginning of the first primary partition of the same hard disk.

GRUB2

GRand Unified Bootloader version 2 (GRUB2) is the boot loader commonly used on modern Linux systems and the boot loader that you will find on Fedora 20 and Ubuntu Server 14.04 systems.

GRUB2 has additional support for systems that do not use the Intel x86_64 architecture, as well as specialized hardware systems. For example, the Sony Playstation 4 uses the GRUB2 boot loader.

GRUB2 has a similar structure to GRUB. GRUB2 Stage1 typically resides on the MBR/GPT, and Stage1.5 and Stage2 reside in the /boot/grub directory (or /boot/grub2 directory on some Linux distrubutions). However, Stage2 loads a terminal-friendly boot loader screen similar to that shown in Figure 8-4. As with GRUB, you can select the kernel that you would like to boot at the boot loader screen, as well as highlight your kernel and press e to edit the entire boot configuration for the kernel or press c to obtain a prompt where you can enter GRUB configuration commands.

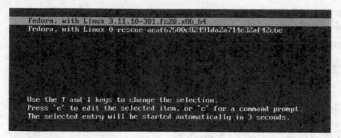

Figure 8-4 The GRUB2 boot screen on a Fedora 20 system

The main configuration file for GRUB2 is /boot/grub/grub.cfg (or /boot/grub2/grub.cfg); this file is automatically built via entries within the /etc/default/grub file, and the output of any shell scripts stored within the /etc/grub.d directory. When you install a device driver that needs to be loaded by the boot loader (e.g., disk controller devices), the device driver package will often add a file to the /etc/grub.d directory that provides the necessary configuration. For any other settings, you should add or modify the existing lines within the /etc/default/grub file. A sample /etc/default/grub file on a Fedora 20 system is shown here:

```
[root@server1 ~]# cat /etc/default/grub
GRUB_TIMEOUT=5
GRUB_DISTRIBUTOR="$(sed 's, release .*$,,g' /etc/system-release)"
GRUB_DEFAULT=saved
GRUB_DISABLE_SUBMENU=true
GRUB_TERMINAL_OUTPUT="console"
GRUB_CMDLINE_LINUX="vconsole.font=latarcyrheb-sun16 $([ -x
/usr/sbin/rhcrashkernel-param ] && /usr/sbin/rhcrashkernel-param || :)
rhgb quiet"
GRUB_DISABLE_RECOVERY="true"
[root@server1 ~]# _
```

From the preceding output, you could change the GRUB_TIMEOUT line to modify the number of seconds that the GRUB2 boot loader screen appears before the default operating system is loaded, or add parameters that are passed to the Linux kernel by modifying the GRUB_CMDLINE_LINUX line. Also note that the /etc/default/grub file does not list any OS paragraphs. This is because GRUB2 uses the /etc/grub.d/30_os-prober script to automatically detect available OSs on the system and configure them for use with GRUB2. If you would like to modify the default OS listed at the GRUB2 boot loader screen, you can set the GRUB_DEFAULT line to the line number, starting from 0. For example, to set the second OS line shown in Figure 8-4 (Fedora, with Linux 0-rescue-aeaf67500c82491da2a714e32af42 c6e) as the default OS to boot, simply set GRUB_DEFAULT=1 in the /etc/default/grub file.

After modifying the /etc/default/grub file, or adding scripts to the /etc/grub.d directory, you can run the **grub2-mkconfig** command to rebuild the /boot/grub/grub.cfg or /boot/grub2/grub. cfg file. For example, to rebuild the /boot/grub2/grub.cfg file, you can use the following:

```
[root@server1 ~]# grub2-mkconfig -o /boot/grub2/grub.cfg
Generating grub.cfg . . .
Found linux image: /boot/vmlinuz-3.11.10-301.fc20.x86_64
Found initrd image: /boot/initramfs-3.11.10-301.fc20.x86_64.img
```

```
Found linux image: /boot/vmlinuz-0-rescue-
034ec8ccdf4642f7a2493195e11d7df6
Found initrd image: /boot/initramfs-0-rescue-
034ec8ccdf4642f7a2493195e11d7df6.img
done
[root@server1 ~]# _
```

As with GRUB, if the GRUB2 boot loader becomes damaged, you can reinstall it. Simply use the **grub2-install command** that is available on the system or on a live Linux system used for system rescue. To reinstall GRUB2 Stage1 on the MBR/GPT of the first SATA hard disk, you can type the following command:

```
[root@server1 ~]# grub2-install /dev/sda
Installation finished. No error reported.
[root@server1 ~]# _
```

Alternatively, you can use the `grub2-install /dev/sda1` command to install GRUB Stage1 at the beginning of the first primary partition of the same hard disk.

The **grubby command** can also be used to configure the LILO, ELILO, GRUB, and GRUB2 boot loaders. For sample usage examples and options, consult the grubby man page.

On some Linux distributions that use GRUB2, such as Ubuntu Server 14.04, GRUB2-related pathnames and commands omit the 2 for simplicity. For example, the Ubuntu Server 14.04 GRUB2 configuration file is /boot/grub/grub.cfg, and the `grub-install` and `grub-mkconfig` commands replace the `grub2-install` and `grub2-mkconfig` commands.

Linux Initialization

Recall that after a boot loader loads the Linux operating system kernel into memory, the kernel resumes control and executes the init daemon, which then performs a **system initialization process** to execute other daemons and bring the system into a usable state.

Up until very recently, Linux systems have used a system initialization process from the **UNIX SysV** standard . However, recent Linux distributions have adopted the **Systemd** system initialization process. Systemd is completely compatible with the UNIX SysV standard yet implements new features for managing all system devices, including Linux kernel modules, daemons, and network sockets. Ubuntu Server 14.04 uses the UNIX SysV system initialization process, whereas Fedora 20 implements the new Systemd system initialization process.

Since Systemd is a recent technology, not all Linux daemons had been rewritten to use it by the time Fedora 20 was released. As a result, Fedora 20 still uses the UNIX SysV system initialization process to initialize some daemons.

Working with the UNIX SysV System Initialization Process

There are two SysV system initialization processes used in most modern Linux systems: the traditional SysV system initialization process and the **upstart** system initialization process. In both systems, the init daemon runs a series of scripts to start other daemons on the system to provide system services and ultimately allow users to log in and use the system. Furthermore, the init daemon is responsible for starting and stopping daemons after system initialization, including stopping daemons before the system is halted or rebooted.

Runlevels Because the init daemon often has to manage several daemons at once, the init daemon categorizes the system into runlevels. A **runlevel** defines the number and type of daemons that are loaded into memory and executed by the kernel on a particular system. At any one time, a Linux system might be in any of the seven standard runlevels defined in Table 8-3.

Because the init daemon is responsible for starting and stopping daemons and, hence, changing runlevels, runlevels are often called **initstates**.

To see the current runlevel of the system and the previous runlevel (if runlevels have been changed since system startup), you can use the **runlevel** command, as shown in the following output:

```
[root@server1 ~]# runlevel
N 5
[root@server1 ~]# _
```

Runlevel	Common Name	Description
0	Halt	A system that has no daemons active in memory and is ready to be powered off.
1 s S single	Single User Mode	A system that has only enough daemons to allow one user (the root user) to log in and perform system maintenance tasks.
2	Multiuser Mode	A system that has most daemons running and allows multiple users the ability to log in and use system services. Most common network services other than specialized network services are available in this runlevel as well.
3	Extended Multiuser Mode	A system that has the same abilities as Multiuser Mode, yet with all extra networking services started (e.g., SNMP, NFS).
4	Not used	Not normally used, but can be customized to suit your needs.
5	Graphical Mode	A system that has the same abilities as Extended Multiuser Mode, yet with a graphical login program. On systems that use the GNOME desktop, this program is called the **GNOME Display Manager (gdm)** and is started on tty1 or tty7 to allow for graphical logins.
6	Reboot	A special runlevel used to reboot the system.

Table 8-3 Linux runlevels

The preceding runlevel command indicates that the system is in runlevel 5 and that the most recent runlevel prior to entering this runlevel is nonexistent (N).

To change the runlevel on a running system, you simply need to specify the **init command** followed by the new runlevel; to change from runlevel 5 to runlevel 1 to perform system maintenance tasks, you can use the following commands:

```
[root@server1 ~]# runlevel
N 5
[root@server1 ~]# init 1
```

*A list of daemons that are being stopped by the init
daemon while the system enters single user mode.*

```
Telling INIT to go to single user mode.
[root@server1 /]# _
[root@server1 /]# runlevel
5 1
[root@server1 /]# _
```

The **telinit command** can be used in place of the init command when changing runlevels. Thus, the command telinit 1 can instead be used to switch to Single User Mode.

You can also pass options from the boot loader to the Linux kernel to force the system to boot to a particular runlevel. If you append the keyword single to the kernel line within the GRUB/GRUB2 configuration screen, you will boot to Single User Mode. Similarly, you can boot to Single User Mode from the LILO boot: prompt by typing the name of the Linux image followed by 1, S, s, or single.

The /etc/inittab file Unless you specify otherwise, the init daemon enters the default runlevel indicated in the /etc/inittab file. In the past, the /etc/inittab file contained the entire configuration for the init daemon. However, on modern systems, the /etc/inittab often contains a single uncommented line that configures the default runlevel, as shown here:

```
[root@server1 ~]# cat /etc/inittab
id:5:initdefault:
[root@server1 ~]# _
```

The line id:5:initdefault: in the /etc/inittab file tells the init daemon that runlevel 5 is the default runlevel to boot to when initializing the Linux system at system startup.

Runlevel 5 is the default runlevel in most Linux distributions that have a GUI environment installed.

Ubuntu Server 14.04 does not contain an /etc/inittab file by default but will use it to set the default runlevel if present. Instead, the default runlevel on Ubuntu Server 14.04 is normally set in the /etc/init/rc-sysinit.conf file.

Runtime Configuration Scripts During the boot process, the init daemon must execute several scripts that prepare the system, start daemons, and eventually bring the system to a usable state. These scripts are called **runtime configuration (rc) scripts**.

On Linux systems that use the traditional UNIX SysV system initialization process, the init daemon identifies the default runlevel in the /etc/inittab file and then proceeds to execute the files within the /etc/rc[runlevel].d directory that start with S or K. If the default runlevel is 5, then the init daemon would execute all files that start with S or K in the /etc/rc5.d directory in alphabetical order. The S or the K indicates whether to Start or Kill (stop) the daemon upon entering this runlevel, respectively. Some sample contents of the /etc/rc.d/rc5.d directory are shown in the following output:

```
[root@server1 ~]# ls /etc/rc5.d
README              S20screen-cleanup      S91apache2
S15bind9            S20zfs-mount           S92tomcat7
S19postgresql       S20zfs-share           S99grub-common
S20postfix          S70dns-clean           S99ondemand
S20rsync            S70pppd-dns            S99rc.local
[root@server1 ~]# _
```

From the preceding output, you can see that the init daemon will start the postfix daemon (S20postfix) upon entering this runlevel. To ensure that the files in the preceding directory are executed in a specific order, a sequence number is added following the S or K at the beginning of the filename. Thus, the file S19postgresql is always executed before the file S20postfix.

Recall that runlevel 1 (Single User Mode) contains only enough daemons for a single user to log in and perform system tasks. If a user tells the init daemon to change to this runlevel using the init 1 command, the init daemon will execute every file that starts with S or K in the /etc/rc1.d directory. Because few daemons are started in Single User Mode, most files in this directory start with a K, as shown in the following output:

```
[root@server1 ~]# ls /etc/rc1.d
K08tomcat7          K20screen-cleanup      K80ebtables      S70dns-clean
K09apache2          K20zfs-mount           K85bind9         S70pppd-dns
K20postfix          K20zfs-share           README           S90single
K20rsync            K21postgresql          S30killprocs
[root@server1 ~]# _
```

Each file in an /etc/rc[runlevel].d directory is merely a symbolic link to an executable rc script in the /etc/init.d directory that can be used to start or stop a certain daemon, depending on whether the symbolic link filename started with an S (start) or K (kill/stop).

Figure 8-5 illustrates the traditional UNIX SysV system initialization process for a system that boots to runlevel 5.

Some Linux distributions use the /etc/rc.d/rc[runlevel].d directory in place of /etc/rc[runlevel].d, and use the /etc/rc.d/init.d directory in place of /etc/init.d.

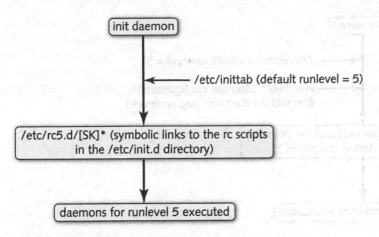

Figure 8-5 A traditional UNIX SysV system initialization process

On Linux systems that use the upstart init system, the /etc/rc[runlevel].d directories are not used. Instead, the init daemon identifies the default runlevel in the /etc/inittab file and then directly executes the rc scripts within the /etc/init.d directory to start or stop the appropriate daemons based on the information specified in the configuration files within the /etc/init directory. Each daemon has a separate configuration file within the /etc/init directory that uses standard wild-card notation to identify the runlevels in which it should be started or stopped. For example, the /etc/init/cron.conf file shown next indicates that the cron daemon should be started in runlevels 2, 3, 4, and 5 ([2345]) and not be stopped in runlevels 2, 3, 4, and 5 ([!2345]):

```
[root@server1 ~]# cat /etc/init/cron.conf
# cron - regular background program processing daemon
#
# cron is a standard UNIX program that runs user-specified programs at
# periodic scheduled times
description    "regular background program processing daemon"

start on runlevel [2345]
stop on runlevel [!2345]

expect fork
respawn

exec cron
[root@server1 ~]# _
```

Figure 8-6 illustrates the upstart system initialization process for a system that boots to runlevel 5.

Some daemons are not compatible with the upstart init system. As a result, Linux distributions that use the upstart init system often host several traditional UNIX SysV daemons that are started via entries in the /etc/rc[runlevel].d directories.

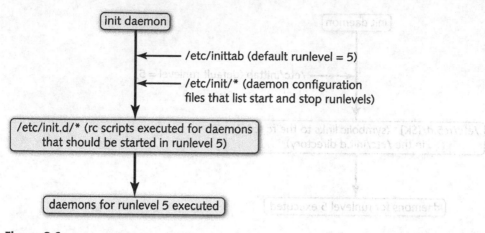

Figure 8-6   An upstart system initialization process

Starting and Stopping Daemons Manually

Recall from the preceding section that the init daemon starts daemons at system initialization as well as starts and stops daemons afterwards when the runlevel is changed by executing the rc scripts within the /etc/init.d directory. To manipulate daemons after system startup, you can execute them directly from the /etc/init.d directory with the appropriate argument (start, stop, or restart). For example, to restart the cron daemon, you could run the following command:

```
[root@server1 ~]# /etc/init.d/cron restart
cron stop/waiting
cron start/running, process 3371
[root@server1 ~]# _
```

You can also use the **service** command to start, stop, or restart any daemons listed within the /etc/init.d directory. For example, you can restart the cron daemon using the following command:

```
[root@server1 ~]# service cron restart
cron stop/waiting
cron start/running, process 3352
[root@server1 ~]# _
```

The upstart init system also provides the **stop** command to stop a daemon, the **start** command to start a daemon, and the **restart** command to restart a daemon. Thus, you could also restart the cron daemon using the following command:

```
[root@server1 ~]# restart cron
cron start/running, process 3389
[root@server1 ~]# _
```

Configuring Daemons to Start in a Runlevel

If your Linux distribution uses the upstart init system, then configuring a daemon to start or stop in a particular runlevel is as easy as modifying the associated daemon configuration file in the /etc/init directory, as shown earlier.

However, for systems that use traditional UNIX SysV system initialization, you must create or modify the symbolic links within the /etc/rc[runlevel].d directories. To make this process easier, there are commands that you can use to do this for you. The **chkconfig command** is available on many Linux systems, and can be used to both list and modify the runlevels that a daemon is started in. For example, the following command indicates that the postfix daemon is not started in any runlevel:

```
[root@server1 ~]# chkconfig --list postfix
postfix          0:off 1:off 2:off 3:off 4:off 5:off 6:off
[root@server1 ~]# _
```

To configure the postfix daemon to start in runlevels 3 and 5 and to verify the results, you could run the following commands:

```
[root@server1 ~]# chkconfig --level 35 postfix on
[root@server1 ~]# chkconfig --list postfix
postfix          0:off 1:off 2:off 3:on 4:off 5:on 6:off
[root@server1 ~]# _
```

Unfortunately, the chkconfig command is not available in Ubuntu Server 14.04 by default. Instead, you can use the **update-rc.d command** on Ubuntu Server 14.04 to configure the files within the /etc/rc[runlevel].d directories. First, you should remove any existing symbolic links within the /etc/rc[runlevel].d directories for the postfix daemon using the following command:

```
[root@server1 ~]# update-rc.d -f postfix remove
Removing any system startup links for /etc/init.d/postfix . . .
    /etc/rc0.d/K20postfix
    /etc/rc1.d/K20postfix
    /etc/rc2.d/S20postfix
    /etc/rc3.d/S20postfix
    /etc/rc4.d/S20postfix
    /etc/rc5.d/S20postfix
    /etc/rc6.d/K20postfix
[root@server1 ~]# _
```

Next, you can use the update-rc.d command to configure the appropriate symbolic links within the /etc/rc[runlevel].d directories for the postfix daemon. Since most daemons are started in runlevels 2 through 5, you can specify the defaults keyword to create symbolic links that start the postfix daemon in runlevels 2 through 5, as shown in the following output:

```
[root@server1 ~]# update-rc.d postfix defaults
Adding system startup for /etc/init.d/postfix . . .
    /etc/rc0.d/K20postfix -> ../init.d/postfix
    /etc/rc1.d/K20postfix -> ../init.d/postfix
    /etc/rc6.d/K20postfix -> ../init.d/postfix
    /etc/rc2.d/S20postfix -> ../init.d/postfix
    /etc/rc3.d/S20postfix -> ../init.d/postfix
    /etc/rc4.d/S20postfix -> ../init.d/postfix
    /etc/rc5.d/S20postfix -> ../init.d/postfix
[root@server1 ~]# _
```

Alternatively, you can specify to start the postfix daemon only in runlevels 2 and 5 using the following command that creates the rc scripts using a sequence number of 20:

```
[root@server1 ~]# update-rc.d postfix start 20 2 5 . stop 20 0 1 3 4 6 .
update-rc.d: warning: start runlevel arguments (5) do not match postfix
Default-Start values (2 3 4 5)
update-rc.d: warning: stop runlevel arguments (1 2 3 4 6) do not match post-
fix Default-Stop values (0 1 6)
    Adding system startup for /etc/init.d/postfix ...
        /etc/rc1.d/K00postfix -> ../init.d/postfix
        /etc/rc3.d/K00postfix -> ../init.d/postfix
        /etc/rc4.d/K00postfix -> ../init.d/postfix
        /etc/rc6.d/K00postfix -> ../init.d/postfix
        /etc/rc2.d/S20postfix -> ../init.d/postfix
        /etc/rc5.d/S20postfix -> ../init.d/postfix
[root@server1 ~]# _
```

Working with the Systemd System Initialization Process

Like the UNIX SysV init daemon, the Systemd init daemon is used to start daemons during system initialization as well as start and stop daemons after system initialization. However, Systemd can also be used to start, stop, and configure many other operating system components. To Systemd, each operating system component is called a unit. Daemons are called **service units** because they provide a system service, and runlevels are called **target units** (or **targets**). By default, each target maps to a UNIX SysV runlevel:

- poweroff.target is the same as Runlevel 0.
- rescue.target is the same as Runlevel 1 (Single User Mode).
- multi-user.target is the same as Runlevel 2, 3 and 4.
- graphical.target is the same as Runlevel 5.
- reboot.target is the same as Runlevel 6.

The graphical.target first loads all daemons from the multi-user.target.

The default target on a system that has a GUI environment installed is the graphical.target. To configure your system to instead boot to the multi-user.target, you can update the /etc/systemd/system/default.target symbolic link to point to the correct runlevel using the following command:

```
[root@server1 ~]# ln -s /lib/systemd/system/runlevel3.target /etc/
systemd/system/default.target
[root@server1 ~]# _
```

Most of the rc scripts that are used by Systemd to start and stop daemons are stored in the /usr/lib/systemd/system directory and called [daemon].service. For example, the script for the cron daemon is /usr/lib/systemd/system/crond.service. To ensure that the cron daemon is

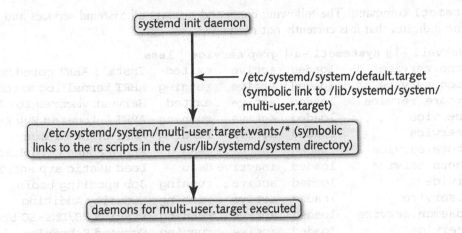

Figure 8-7 A Systemd system initialization process

started when entering the multi-user.target, you can create a symbolic link to /usr/lib/systemd/ system/crond.service called /etc/systemd/system/multi-user.target.wants/crond.service (i.e., the multi-user target wants the crond daemon).

Figure 8-7 illustrates the Systemd system initialization process for a system that boots to multi-user.target.

Both the /lib/systemd/system and /etc/system/system directories contain subdirectories called *.target.wants for loading daemons and other components. By convention, system and OS components are typically loaded from entries in /lib/system/system/*.target.wants directories, whereas other daemons are loaded from entries in /etc/ system/system/*.target.wants directories. For example, components that need to be loaded into the Linux kernel at the beginning of the system initialization process have symbolic links to them in the /lib/ systemd/system/sysinit.target.wants (for core OS components) and /etc/systemd/system/sysinit.target.wants (for optional components) directories.

To start and stop daemons, as well as configure them to automatically start during system initialization, you can use the **systemctl command**. To start, stop, or restart a Systemd daemon, you can specify the appropriate action (start, stop, or restart) and name of the service unit as arguments. For example, to restart the cron daemon, you could use the following command:

```
[root@server1 ~]# systemctl restart crond.service
[root@server1 ~]# _
```

Without arguments, the systemctl command displays a list of all units that are currently executing in memory and their status. You can narrow this list to only services by piping the results to the grep service command. Moreover, to see all possible services regardless of whether they are loaded into memory or not, you can add the –a (or --all) option to the `systemctl` command. The following command displays all Systemd services and their state (dead indicates that it is currently not running):

```
[root@server1 ~]# systemctl -a | grep service | less
abrt-ccpp.service        loaded   active   exited   Install ABRT coredump
abrt-oops.service        loaded   active   running  ABRT kernel log watcher
abrt-vmcore.service      loaded   active   exited   Harvest vmcores for ABRT
abrtd.service            loaded   active   running  ABRT Automated Bug Repo
acpid.service            loaded   active   running  ACPI Event Daemon
alsa-store.service       loaded   inactive dead     Store Sound Card State
arp-ethers.service       loaded   inactive dead     Load static arp entries
atd.service              loaded   active   running  Job spooling tools
auditd.service           loaded   active   running  Security Auditing
avahi-daemon.service     loaded   active   running  Avahi mDNS/DNS-SD Stack
crond.service            loaded   active   running  Command Scheduler
cups.service             loaded   active   running  CUPS Printing Service
dbus-org.bluez.service   error    inactive dead     dbus-org.bluez.service
dbus.service             loaded   active   running  D-Bus System Message Bus
:
```

You can see detailed information about a particular Systemd daemon by using the `status` argument to the `systemctl` command. For example, `systemctl status crond.service` would show detailed information about the cron daemon.

To configure a Systemd daemon to start in the default target (e.g., graphical.target), you can use the `enable` argument to the `systemctl` command. For example, to ensure that the cron daemon is started at system initialization, you can run the `systemctl enable crond.service` command. Alternatively, the `systemctl disable crond.service` would prevent the cron daemon from starting when your system is booted.

The `systemctl` command can also be used to change between targets. You can switch to multi-user.target (which is analogous to runlevel 3) by running either the `systemctl isolate multi-user.target` or `systemctl isolate runlevel3.target` command. Alternatively, you can switch to graphical.target (which is analogous to runlevel 5) by running the `systemctl isolate graphical.target` or `systemctl isolate runlevel5.target` command.

The X Windows System

So far in this chapter, we've focused on performing tasks using a BASH shell command-line interface obtained after logging in to a character terminal. Although most administrators favor the command-line interface, Linux users typically use GUIs for running user programs. Thus, you need to understand the components that make up the Linux GUI. In particular, you need to know how to start, stop, and configure them.

Linux GUI Components

The Linux GUI was designed to function consistently, no matter what video adapter card and monitor are installed on the computer system. It is composed of many components, each of which works separately from the video hardware.

Graphical programs (X clients)

↕

Desktop environment

↕

Window manager

↕

X Windows

↕

Video hardware

Figure 8-8 Components of the Linux GUI

Graphical programs can communicate directly with each other in any X Windows environment via the use of the dbus daemon, or to hardware devices using the hald daemon.

A Linux installation usually includes all of the GUI components listed in Figure 8-8. Together, these GUI components and related programs use over 4GB of storage space on a typical Linux installation.

X Windows The core component of a Linux GUI is **X Windows**, which provides the ability to draw graphical images in windows that are displayed on a terminal screen. The programs that tell X Windows how to draw the graphics and display the results are known as **X clients**. X clients need not run on the same computer as X Windows; you can use X Windows on one computer to send graphical images to an X client on an entirely different computer by changing the DISPLAY environment variable discussed in Chapter 7. Because of this, X Windows is sometimes referred to as the server component of X Windows, or simply the **X server**.

X Windows was jointly developed by Digital Equipment Corporation (DEC) and the Massachusetts Institute of Technology (MIT) in 1984. At that time, it was code-named Project Athena and was released in 1985 as X Windows in hopes that a new name would be found to replace the X. Shortly thereafter, X Windows was sought by many UNIX vendors; and by 1988, MIT released version 11 release 2 of X Windows (X11R2). Since 1988, X Windows has been maintained by The Open Group, which released version 11 release 6 of X Windows (X11R6) in 1995. Since 2004, X Windows has been maintained as Open Source Software by the **X.org** Foundation.

To find out more about X Windows, visit the X.org Foundation's Web site at *www.x.org*.

8

Until recently, X Windows was governed by a separate license than the GPL, which restricted the usage of X Windows and its source code. As a result, open source developers created an open source version of X Windows in the 1990s. This freely available version of X Windows is used in many Linux distributions and is called **XFree86** because it was originally intended for the Intel x86 platform.

To find out more about XFree86, visit The XFree86 Project at *www.xfree86.org*.

Today, Linux distributions offer either X Windows or the XFree86 implementation of X Windows because they are both Open Source Software. Fedora 20 and Ubuntu 14.04 use X Windows instead of XFree86.

Window Managers and Desktop Environments To modify the look and feel of X Windows, you can use a **window manager**. For example, the dimensions and color of windows that are drawn on a graphical screen, as well as the method used to move windows around on a graphical screen, are functions of a window manager.

Many different window managers are available for Linux, including those listed in Table 8-4.

Window Manager	Description
Compiz Fusion	A highly configurable and expandable window manager based on the Compiz and Beryl window managers that utilizes 3D acceleration on modern video cards to produce 3D graphical effects, including 3D window behavior and desktop cube workspaces.
enlightenment	A highly configurable window manager that allows for multiple desktops with different settings. It is commonly used by the GNOME desktop.
fvwm	A window manager based on twm that uses less computer memory and gives the desktop a 3-D look; its full name is "Feeble Virtual Window Manager."
kwin	The window manager used for the KDE desktop.
lxde	A window manager specifically designed for use on underpowered systems such as netbooks, mobile devices, and legacy computers; its full name is "Lightweight X Desktop Environment."
metacity	The default window manager used by the GNOME version 1 and 2 desktop environments.
mutter	The default window manager used by the GNOME version 3 desktop environment.
mwm	A basic window manager that allows the user to configure settings using standard X utilities; its full name is "Motif Window Manager."
sawfish	A window manager commonly used for the GNOME desktop. It allows the user to configure most of its settings via tools or scripts.
twm	One of the oldest and most basic window managers; its full name is "Tab Window Manager."
wmaker	A window manager that provides drag-and-drop mouse movement and imitates the NeXTSTEP operating system interface made by Apple Computer, Inc.; its full name is "Window Maker."

Table 8-4   Common window managers

You can use a window manager alone, or in conjunction with a desktop environment.

A **desktop environment** is a standard set of GUI tools designed to be packaged together, including Web browsers, file managers, and drawing programs. Desktop environments also provide sets of development tools, known as toolkits, that speed up the process of creating new software. As discussed earlier in this book, the two most common desktop environments used on Linux are the **K Desktop Environment (KDE)** and the **GNU Object Model Environment (GNOME)**.

KDE is the traditional desktop environment used on Linux systems. First released by Matthias Ettrich in 1996, KDE uses the **K Window Manager (kwin)** and the **Qt toolkit** for the C++ programming language.

To learn more about KDE, visit *www.kde.org*.

The Qt toolkit included in KDE was created by a company called Trolltech in Norway in the 1990s. However, it took a while to build a following because, at the time, most open source developers preferred to develop in the C programming language instead of C++. Also, the fact that Qt was not released as Open Source Software until 1998 was a drawback, because most developers preferred source code that was freely modifiable.

As a result of the general dissatisfaction with the Qt toolkit, the GNOME Desktop Environment was created in 1997. The latest version of GNOME uses the **mutter window manager** and the **GTK+ toolkit** for the C programming language. The GTK+ toolkit was originally developed for the **GNU Image Manipulation Program (GIMP)**; like the GIMP, it is open source. GNOME is the default desktop environment on most Linux distributions.

8

To learn more about GNOME, visit *www.gnome.org*.

Instead of using the default window manager within the KDE or GNOME desktop environment, you can configure KDE or GNOME to use a different window manager. One popular choice is **Compiz Fusion**, which requires a modern video card with hardware-based 3D acceleration support. After Compiz Fusion is installed, you can use the associated utility to configure its features and advanced graphical effects. The basic functionality of Compiz Fusion allows the user to control window transparency by using the mouse scroll while holding down the Ctrl+Alt keys; it also allows the user to rotate among four desktop displays in a cube effect by using the cursor keys while holding down the Ctrl+Alt keys.

To learn more about Compiz Fusion, including its graphical effects and additional plug-ins, visit *www.compiz.org*.

Starting and Stopping X Windows

As explained earlier in this chapter, when the init daemon boots to runlevel 5 or graphical.target, a program called the gdm is started that displays a graphical login screen. If you click a user account within the gdm and choose the settings icon, you will be able to choose from a list of installed desktop environments or window managers, as shown in Figure 8-9.

 The GNOME Display Manager is a variant of the **X Display Manager (xdm)**, which displays a basic graphical login for users. In addition, some Linux distributions use the **KDE Display Manager (kdm)** to display a KDE style graphical login for users.

The default desktop environment started by the GNOME Display Manager on Fedora 20 is GNOME. However, after you log in as a particular user and select KDE using the Session menu, the GNOME Display Manager will continue to use KDE as the default desktop environment for the user account unless you choose otherwise.

The GNOME Display Manager is the easiest way to log in and access the desktop environments that are available on your system. If, however, you use runlevel 1 (or rescue.target) or runlevel 2 through 4 (multiuser.target), the GNOME Display Manager is not started by

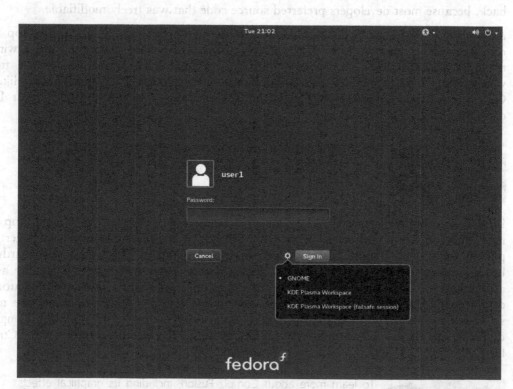

Figure 8-9 Selecting a session within the GNOME Display Manager on Fedora 20

default. In this case, you can type `startx` at a character terminal to start X Windows and the default window manager or desktop environment (e.g., GNOME in Fedora 20).

Configuring X Windows

X Windows is the component of the GUI that interfaces with the video hardware in the computer. For X Windows to perform its function, it needs information regarding the keyboard, mouse, monitor, and video adapter card. By default, X Windows attempts to automatically detect this information. If the automatic detection fails, you may need to specify the correct hardware information manually.

If you use XFree86, X Windows stores its entire configuration in the file /etc/X11/XF86Config. You may edit this file manually or by using a configuration program such as xf86config. If you use X.org, X Windows stores its configuration in the file /etc/X11/xorg.conf. Again, you may edit this file manually or by using a configuration program.

Before modifying the XF86Config or xorg.conf files, first read the contents of the associated man page.

You can also use the xdpyinfo command on certain Linux distributions to display X Windows configuration.

In Fedora 20, Xorg settings are automatically detected rather than being configured manually. Although there is no /etc/X11/xorg.conf file in Fedora 20 by default, it will be used if present. Instead, user-configured settings are stored in files under the /etc/X11/xorg.conf.d directory, and common settings such as the display resolution can be modified using the Displays utility within the GNOME desktop environment. To do this, simply navigate to Activities, Show Applications, Settings within GNOME, click Displays, and select your display to view available settings, as shown in Figure 8-10.

Unknown 0"

| 1 |

| ↶ ↷ |

Size

Aspect Ratio   4:3

Resolution   1152 × 864 (4:3) ∨

Cancel   Apply

Figure 8-10 Selecting a display resolution

8

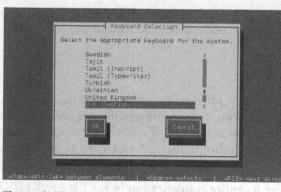

Figure 8-11 Selecting a keyboard layout

Figure 8-12 The xvidtune utility

Keyboard layout is automatically detected during the Fedora 20 installation. However, if you change the keyboard and X Windows cannot detect its layout, you can manually run the **system-config-keyboard** command at a terminal prompt within a desktop environment or at a command-line terminal to start the Keyboard Selection tool. See Figure 8-11.

After configuring X Windows, you can fine-tune the vertical refresh rate (vsync) and horizonal refresh rate (hsync) settings using the **xvidtune** utility within a desktop environment. Simply open a command-line terminal within the desktop environment and type xvidtune to start the utility, as shown in Figure 8-12.

Although most monitors today support a wide range of hsync and vsync values, choosing too high of a value for either might damage the monitor. On the flip side, choosing an hsync or vsync value that is too low is bad for the humans who have to look at the monitors, because they can cause headaches.

The xvidtune utility is not installed on Fedora 20 by default. To install it, run the yum install xvidtune command as the root user.

Chapter Summary

- Boot loaders are typically loaded by the system BIOS from the MBR/GPT or the first sector of the active partition of a hard disk. The most common boot loaders used on Linux systems are LILO, GRUB, and GRUB2.

- After the boot loader loads the Linux kernel, a system initialization process proceeds to load daemons that bring the system to a usable state.

- There are two common system initialization processes: UNIX SysV and Systemd. Modern implementations of UNIX SysV use the upstart system initialization process.

- UNIX SysV uses seven runlevels to categorize a Linux system based on the number and type of daemons loaded in memory. Systemd uses five standard targets that correspond to the seven UNIX SysV runlevels.

- The init daemon is responsible for loading and unloading daemons when switching between runlevels and targets, as well as at system startup and shutdown.

- Daemons are typically executed during system initialization via rc scripts. The /etc/init.d directory contains most UNIX SysV rc scripts, and the /usr/lib/systemd/system directory contains most Systemd rc scripts.

- You can use a variety of different commands to start, stop, and restart daemons following system initialization. The service command is commonly used to start, stop, and restart UNIX SysV daemons, and the systemctl command is commonly used to start, stop, and restart Systemd daemons.

- You can use the chkconfig or update-rc.d commands to configure UNIX SysV daemon startup at boot time, as well as the systemctl command to configure Systemd daemon startup at boot time.

- The Linux GUI has several interchangeable components, including the X server, X clients, window manager, and optional desktop environment.

- X Windows is the core component of the Linux GUI that draws graphics to the terminal screen. It comes in one of two open source implementations: X.org and XFree86. The hardware information required by X Windows is automatically detected but can be modified using several utilities.

- You can start the Linux GUI from runlevel 3 by typing startx at a command prompt, or from runlevel 5 by using the GNOME Display Manager.

Key Terms

active partition   The partition searched for an operating system after the MBR/GPT.

boot loader   A program used to load an operating system.

chkconfig command   A command that can be used to configure UNIX SysV daemon startup by runlevel.

Compiz Fusion   A window manager that is often used alongside the KDE and GNOME desktops to provide advanced graphical effects.

daemon   A Linux system process that provides a system service.

desktop environment   The software that works with a window manager to provide a standard GUI environment that uses standard programs and development tools.

ELILO   A boot loader used with computers that support Intel Extensible Firmware Interface (EFI) technology.

GNOME Display Manager (gdm)   A program that provides a graphical login screen.

GNU Object Model Environment (GNOME)   The default desktop environment in Fedora Linux; it was created in 1997.

GRand Unified Bootloader (GRUB)   A boot loader used to boot a variety of different operating systems (including Linux) on a variety of different hardware platforms.

GRand Unified Bootloader version 2 (GRUB2)   An enhanced version of the GRUB boot loader. It is the most common boot loader used on modern Linux systems.

grub-install command   The command used to install the GRUB boot loader.

grub2-install command   The command used to install the GRUB2 boot loader.

grub2-mkconfig command   The command used to build the GRUB2 configuration file from entries within the /etc/default/grub file and /etc/grub.d directory.

grubby command   A command that can be used to configure the LILO, GRUB and GRUB2 boot loaders.

GRUB root partition   The partition containing the second stage of the GRUB boot loader and the GRUB configuration file.

GTK+ toolkit   A development toolkit for C programming; it is used in the GNOME desktop and the GNU Image Manipulation Program (GIMP).

init command   A UNIX SysV command used to change the operating system from one runlevel to another.

initialize (init) daemon   The first process started by the Linux kernel; it is responsible for starting and stopping other daemons.

initstate   See *runlevel*.

K Desktop Environment (KDE)   A desktop environment created by Matthias Ettrich in 1996.

KDE Display Manager (kdm)   A graphical login screen for users that resembles the KDE desktop.

K Window Manager (kwin)   The window manager that works under the KDE Desktop Environment.

lilo command   The command used to reinstall the LILO boot loader based on the configuration information in /etc/lilo.conf.

Linux Loader (LILO)   A common boot loader used on legacy Linux systems.

multi boot   A configuration in which two or more operating systems exist on the hard disk of a computer; the boot loader allows the user to choose which operating system to load at boot time.

mutter window manager   The default window manager for the GNOME Desktop Environment in Fedora 13.

Power On Self Test (POST)   An initial series of tests run when a computer is powered on to ensure that hardware components are functional.

Qt toolkit   The software toolkit used with the K Desktop Environment.

restart command   A command that can be used to manually restart an upstart daemon.

runlevel   A UNIX SysV term that defines a certain type and number of daemons on a Linux system.

runlevel command   The command used to display the current and most recent (previous) runlevel.

runtime configuration (rc) scripts   Scripts that are used during the system initialization process to start daemons and provide system functionality.

service command   A command that can be used to manually start, stop, and restart UNIX SysV daemons.

service unit   A Systemd term that is used to describe a daemon.

start command   A command that can be used to manually start an upstart daemon.

stop command   A command that can be used to manually stop an upstart daemon.

systemctl command   A command that can be used to manually start, stop and restart Systemd daemons, as well as configure Systemd daemon startup during the system initialization process.

system-config-keyboard command   A command used on Fedora Linux systems to configure a keyboard for use by X Windows.

Systemd   A relatively new software framework used on Linux systems that provides a system initialization process and system management functions.

system initialization process   The process that executes the daemons that provide for system services during boot time and bring the system to a usable state.

target   See *target unit*.

target unit   A Systemd term that is used to describe the number and type of daemons running on a Linux system. It is functionally equivalent to the UNIX SysV term *runlevel*.

telinit command   A UNIX SysV command used to change the operating system from one runlevel to another.

update-rc.d command   A command that can be used to configure UNIX SysV daemon startup by runlevel on Ubuntu Linux systems.

upstart   A recent version of the UNIX SysV system initialization process used on modern Linux distributions.

UNIX SysV   A UNIX standard that is used to provide the structure of the system initialization process on Linux systems.

window manager   The GUI component that is responsible for determining the appearance of the windows drawn on the screen by X Windows.

X client   The component of X Windows that requests graphics to be drawn from the X server and displays them on the terminal screen.

X Display Manager (xdm)   A graphical login screen.

XFree86   A common implementation of X Windows used in Linux distributions.

X.org   A common implementation of X Windows used in Linux distributions.

X server   The component of X Windows that draws graphics to windows on the terminal screen.

xvidtune   A program used to fine-tune the vsync and hsync video card settings for use in X Windows.

X Windows   The component of the Linux GUI that displays graphics to windows on the terminal screen.

Review Questions

1. Which command can be used to fine-tune the vsync and hsync of a video card for use in X Windows?

    a. vidtune

    b. synctune

    c. xvidtune

    d. vhtune

2. Which of the following statements is true?

    a. The GRUB boot loader is stored in the /usr/grub directory.

    b. LILO needs to be reinstalled after it has been modified.

    c. The GRUB2 boot loader is often used on legacy Linux systems.

    d. GRUB needs to be reinstalled after it has been modified.

3. Which directory stores most UNIX SysV rc scripts?

    a. /etc/rc5.d

    b. /etc/rc.d

    c. /etc/init.d

    d. /usr/local/systemd

4. Which runlevel halts the system?

    a. 1

    b. 6

    c. 0

    d. 5

5. Which file does the UNIX SysV init daemon reference on startup to determine the default runlevel?

    a. /etc/initstate

    b. /inittab

    c. /etc/init

    d. /etc/inittab

6. Which command can be used to start X Windows, the window manager, and the default desktop environment?

    a. `startgui`

    b. `startgdm`

    c. `startx`

    d. `gstart`

7. Which of the following statements is true?

    a. The boot loader points to the MBR/GPT.

    b. Either the MBR/GPT or the active partition can contain the boot loader.

    c. Both the MBR/GPT and the active partition point to the boot loader.

    d. The boot loader points to the active partition.

8. Which of the following indicates the second partition on the third hard disk drive to GRUB?

    a. (hd3,2)

    b. (hd4,3)

    c. (hd2,3)

    d. (hd2,1)

9. Which two implementations of X Windows are commonly used in Linux? (Choose two answers.)

    a. X.org

    b. XFce

    c. Xconfigurator

    d. XFree86

10. What is the name of the directory that contains symbolic links to UNIX SysV rc scripts for runlevel 2?

    a. /etc/rc2.d

    b. /etc/init.d/rc2.d

    c. /etc/runlevel/2

    d. /etc/inittab/rc2/d

11. In what directory is Stage2 of the GRUB2 boot loader stored?

    a. /boot

    b. /root

    c. /bin

    d. /

8

12. The first daemon loaded on a Linux system is _____.
    a. initstate
    b. inittab
    c. init
    d. linux

13. Which command causes the system to enter Single User Mode?
    a. `init 0`
    b. `init 1`
    c. `init 6`
    d. `initstate 5`

14. The timeout value in the GRUB configuration file is measured in?
    a. seconds
    b. 1/10 of minutes
    c. 1/10 of seconds
    d. 1/100 of seconds

15. You have recently modified the options within the /etc/default/grub file. What command can you use next to rebuild the GRUB2 configuration file?
    a. `grub2-install`
    b. `grub-install`
    c. `grubby`
    d. `grub2-mkconfig`

16. You wish to configure the runlevels that a particular upstart daemon is started in. What should you do?
    a. Run the appropriate `update-rc.d` command.
    b. Modify the contents of the /etc/rc[runlevel].d directories.
    c. Modify the daemon configuration file within the /etc/init directory.
    d. Run the appropriate `systemctl` command.

17. Which of the following Systemd commands can be used to stop a daemon called lala?
    a. `service stop lala`
    b. `systemctl stop lala.service`
    c. `chkconfig stop lala`
    d. `stop lala`

18. Which of the following commands can be used to start a UNIX SysV daemon called lala in runlevels 1, 2, and 3?

    a. `chkconfig --level 123 lala on`

    b. `update-rc.d lala defaults`

    c. `systemctl enable lala 123`

    d. `service enable lala 123`

19. What Systemd target corresponds to runlevel 5?

    a. multi-user.target

    b. graphical.target

    c. system.target

    d. runlevel5.target

20. What keyword can be specified within a boot loader to force the system to boot to Single User Mode?

    a. `init`

    b. `rescue`

    c. `single`

    d. `telinit`

Hands-on Projects

These projects should be completed in the order given. The hands-on projects presented in this chapter should take a total of three hours to complete. The requirements for this lab include:

- A computer with Fedora Linux installed according to Hands-on Project 2-1 and Ubuntu Server Linux installed according to Hands-on Project 6-1.

Project 8-1

In this hands-on project, you use and configure the GRUB2 boot loader on Fedora 20.

1. Boot your Fedora Linux virtual machine. After your Linux system has been loaded, switch to a command-line terminal (tty2) by pressing **Ctrl+Alt+F2** and log in to the terminal using the user name of **root** and the password of **LNXrocks!**.

2. At the command prompt, type **less /boot/grub2/grub.cfg** and press Enter. Which line sets the default timeout for user interaction at the boot screen? Examine the menuentry paragraphs. Do many of the options match those in the original GRUB bootloader?

3. At the command prompt, type **vi /etc/default/grub** and press Enter to edit the GRUB2 configuration file. Change the value of **GRUB_TIMEOUT** to **30**. Save your changes and quit the vi editor.

4. At the command prompt, type **grub2-mkconfig -o /boot/grub2/grub.cfg** and press **Enter** to rebuild the GRUB2 configuration file with your change.

5. Reboot your system by typing **reboot** and pressing **Enter**. At the GRUB2 boot screen, view the available options. How long do you have to interact with the GRUB2 boot loader after POST before the default operating system is booted? Next, press **c** to obtain a command prompt.

6. At the grub> prompt, type **help** and press **Enter** to see a list of available commands. Next, type **lspci** and press **Enter** to see a list of detected PCI devices. Following this, type **list_env** and press **Enter** to view the variables present. Normally, there should be a single variable called saved_entry that lists the default OS that is booted by GRUB2, although on some systems you may not see this variable. Type **reboot** and press **Enter** to reboot your system.

7. At the GRUB2 boot screen, press **e** to edit your configuration. Where did you see these contents recently?

8. Locate the line that starts with the word "linux" and navigate to the end of this line (the last two keywords on this line should be rhgb and quiet). Add the word **single** after the word quiet and press **F10** to boot your modified configuration. What does this option tell the boot loader to do?

9. Supply your root password of **LNXrocks!** when prompted.

10. Reboot your system by typing **reboot** and pressing **Enter**. Allow your system to boot normally.

Project 8-2

In this hands-on project, you explore and configure the system initialization process on Fedora 20.

1. Switch to a command-line terminal (tty2) by pressing **Ctrl+Alt+F2** and log in to the terminal using the user name of **root** and the password of **LNXrocks!**.

2. At the command prompt, type **runlevel** and press **Enter**. What is your current runlevel? What is the most recent runlevel?

3. At the command prompt, type **cat /etc/inittab** and press **Enter**. View the commented sections. Why is /etc/inittab not used in Fedora 20?

4. At the command prompt, type **ls /usr/lib/systemd/system** and press **Enter**. What do the contents represent?

5. At the command prompt, type **ls /etc/rc.d** and press **Enter**. Do you see init.d and rc[runlevel].d subdirectories? Why?

6. At the command prompt, type **ls /etc/rc.d/init.d** and press **Enter**. Which UNIX SysV daemons are available on Fedora 20?

7. At the command prompt, type **chkconfig --list netconsole** and press **Enter**. In which runlevels is the netconsole daemon started by default?

8. At the command prompt, type **chkconfig --level 23 netconsole on** and press **Enter** to configure the netconsole daemon to start in runlevels 2 and 3. Next, type **ls /etc/rc.d/rc[23].d** and press **Enter**. Does the symbolic link to the netconsole rc script start with S? Why?

9. At the command prompt, type **init 3** and press **Enter** to switch to runlevel 3 (multi-user.target). Note that you are on tty1 and the gdm is not loaded. Log in to the terminal using the user name of **root** and the password of **LNXrocks!.**

10. Next, type **runlevel** and press **Enter**. What is your current and most recent runlevel?

11. At the command prompt, type **init 1** and press **Enter** to switch to single user mode (rescue.target). Supply the root password of **LNXrocks!** when prompted.

12. Next, type **runlevel** and press **Enter**. What is your current and most recent runlevel?

13. At the command prompt, type **systemctl isolate graphical.target** and press **Enter** to switch to runlevel 5 (graphical.target). Note that the gdm is loaded. Press **Ctrl+Alt+F2** and log in to the terminal using the user name of **root** and the password of **LNXrocks!.**

14. At the command prompt, type **systemctl –a | grep crond.service** and press **Enter**. Is the Systemd cron daemon running?

15. At the command prompt, type **systemctl restart crond.service** and press **Enter** to restart the Systemd cron daemon.

16. At the command prompt, type **systemctl disable crond.service** and press **Enter** to prevent the system from starting the cron daemon in your current runlevel/target. Note that the existing symbolic link in the crond.service rc script is removed. Why was this link from the /etc/systemd/system/multi-user.target.wants directory instead of the /etc/systemd/system/graphical.target.wants directory?

17. At the command prompt, type **systemctl enable crond.service** and press **Enter** to start the cron daemon in your current runlevel/target. Was the symbolic link recreated?

18. At the command prompt, type **service netconsole start** and press **Enter**. Note that Systemd started the UNIX SysV netconsole daemon using the systemctl command because Systemd is backwards compatible with UNIX SysV.

19. At the command prompt, type **poweroff** and press **Enter** to power off your Fedora Linux virtual machine.

Project 8-3

In this hands-on project, you explore and configure the system initialization process on Ubuntu Server 14.04.

1. Boot your Ubuntu Server Linux virtual machine. After your Linux system has been loaded, log into tty1 using the user name of **root** and the password of **LNXrocks!.**

2. At the command prompt, type **runlevel** and press **Enter**. What is your current runlevel? What is the most recent runlevel?

3. At the command prompt, type **ls /etc/init.d** and press **Enter**. What do the contents represent?

4. At the command prompt, type **ls /etc/init** and press **Enter**. What do the contents represent?

5. At the command prompt, type **cat /etc/init/ssh.conf** and press **Enter**. In which runlevels is the ssh daemon started?

6. At the command prompt, type **restart ssh** and press **Enter**. Why did the restart command successfully restart the ssh daemon?

7. At the command prompt, type **ls /etc/rc2.d** and press **Enter**. Are there any traditional UNIX SysV daemons started in your current runlevel? Why? Is the postgresql daemon started before or after the apache2 daemon? Why?

8. At the command prompt, type **restart postgresql** and press **Enter**. Why did you receive an error message?

9. At the command prompt, type **/etc/init.d/postgresql restart** and press **Enter**. Did the postgresql daemon restart?

10. At the command prompt, type **update-rc.d –f postgresql remove** and press **Enter** to remove the symbolic links that start the postgresql daemon. Which runlevels was the postgresql daemon originally started in?

11. At the command prompt, type **update-rc.d postgresql defaults** and press **Enter** to configure the symbolic links to start the postgresql daemon in runlevels 2 through 5.

12. At the command prompt, type **telinit 6** and press **Enter** to reboot your system. Could you have used the init command in place of the telinit command?

13. Once your system has rebooted, log into tty1 using the user name of **root** and the password of **LNXrocks!**.

14. At the command prompt, type **poweroff** and press **Enter** to power off your Ubuntu Server Linux virtual machine.

Project 8-4

In this hands-on project, you start X Windows without the gdm and examine X Windows configuration utilities.

1. Boot your Fedora Linux virtual machine. After your Linux system has been loaded, switch to a command-line terminal (tty2) by pressing **Ctrl+Alt+F2** and log in to the terminal using the user name of **root** and the password of **LNXrocks!**.

2. At the command prompt, type **init 3** and press **Enter** to switch to runlevel 3 (multi-user.target). Note that the gdm is no longer loaded in tty1. Log into tty1 using the user name of **root** and the password of **LNXrocks!**.

3. At the command prompt, type **startx** and press **Enter**. What desktop environment was loaded by default and why? Since the root user has not logged into GNOME previously, you will be prompted to choose GNOME preferences.

   a.   At the Welcome screen, ensure that **English (United States)** is selected and click **Next**.

   b.   At the Input Sources screen, ensure that the **English (US)** keyboard layout is selected and click **Next**.

   c.   At the Online Accounts screen, click **Next** to bypass personal account configuration.

   d.   On the Thank You screen, click Start using Fedora.

4. Click the power icon in the upper right of the GNOME desktop, click **root**, **Log Out**, and then click **Log Out** again to log out of the GNOME desktop. Were you returned to your original BASH shell on tty1?

5. At the command prompt, type **init 5** and press **Enter** to switch to runlevel 5 (graphical.target). Note that the gdm is now loaded in tty1. Log into the GNOME desktop using the user name of **user1** and the password of **LNXrocks!**.

6. Click the **Activities** menu and navigate to **Show Applications, Settings**. Click **Displays** and select your display. Note that you can configure the resolution for your current display. Note that the list is limited primarily because you are running a graphical desktop within a virtual machine. Close the Displays window when finished.

7. Click the **Activities** menu and navigate to **Show Applications, Utilities, Terminal** to open a command-line terminal. At the command prompt, type **su - root** and press **Enter** to switch to the root user. Supply the root user password of **LNXrocks!** when prompted.

8. At the command prompt, type **system-config-keyboard** and press **Enter**. Note that you can optionally choose a different keyboard for use with X Windows. Use the Tab key to select the **Cancel** button and press **Enter** to quit the Keyboard Selection utility.

9. At the command prompt, type **yum install xvidtune** and press **Enter**. Press y when prompted to install the xvidtune utility.

10. At the command prompt, type **xvidtune** and press **Enter**. Observe the warning screen and click **OK** to close it. View the available options in the xvidtune utility and close the xvidtune window when finished.

11. At the command prompt, type **poweroff** and press **Enter** to power off your Fedora Linux virtual machine.

Discovery Exercises

1. Describe what would happen if you changed the default runlevel/target on your system to runlevel 6 or reboot.target.

2. Using the Internet, research two boot loaders used for Linux other than LILO and GRUB. What configuration file do they use? What are their benefits and disadvantages compared to LILO and GRUB?

3. On your Fedora Linux virtual machine, examine your X Windows configuration. Does your system have an /etc/X11/xorg.conf file? If it does not, all relevant information needed by X.org has been autodetected. Does your system have any files in the /etc/X11/xorg.conf.d directory? If so, examine their contents. What do these files represent?

4. On your Ubuntu Server Linux virtual machine, perform the same steps that you performed in Project 8-1. In order to accomplish this, you'll need to remember that Ubuntu Server uses slightly different names for GRUB2 configuration files and commands.

5. Use the Internet, books, or other resources to learn more about three Linux window managers or desktop environments that were not discussed in this chapter. For each, describe its common usage and benefits over other window managers and desktop environments. In addition, list how each was developed.

## chapter 9

Managing Linux Processes

After completing this chapter, you will be able to:

- Categorize the different types of processes on a Linux system
- View processes using standard Linux utilities
- Explain the difference between common kill signals
- Describe how binary programs and shell scripts are executed
- Create and manipulate background processes
- Use standard Linux utilities to modify the priority of a process
- Schedule commands to execute in the future using the at daemon
- Schedule commands to execute repetitively using the cron daemon

A typical Linux system can run thousands of processes simultaneously, including those that you have explored in previous chapters. In this chapter, you focus on viewing and managing processes. In the first part of the chapter, you examine the different types of processes on a Linux system and how to view them and terminate them. You then discover how processes are executed on a system, run in the background, and prioritized. Finally, you examine the various methods used to schedule commands to execute in the future.

Linux Processes

Throughout this book, the terms "program" and "process" are used interchangeably. The same is true in the workplace. However, a fine distinction exists between these two terms. Technically, a **program** is an executable file on the hard disk that can be run when you execute it. A **process**, on the other hand, is a program that is running in memory and on the CPU. In other words, a process is a program in action.

If you start a process while logged in to a terminal, that process runs in that terminal and is labeled a **user process**. Examples of user processes include ls, grep, and find, not to mention most of the other commands that you have executed throughout this book. Recall that a system process that is not associated with a terminal is called a **daemon process**; these processes are typically started on system startup, but you can also start them manually. Most daemon processes provide system services, such as printing, scheduling, and system maintenance, as well as network server services, such as Web servers, database servers, file servers, and print servers.

Every process has a unique **process ID (PID)** that allows the kernel to identify it uniquely. In addition, each process can start an unlimited number of other processes called **child processes**. Conversely, each process must have been started by an existing process called a **parent process**. As a result, each process has a **parent process ID (PPID)**, which identifies the process that started it. An example of the relationship between parent and child processes is depicted in Figure 9-1.

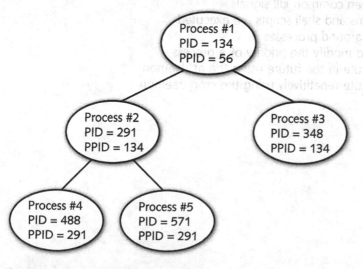

Figure 9-1 Parent and child processes

PIDs are not necessarily given to new processes in sequential order; each PID is generated from free entries in a process table used by the Linux kernel.

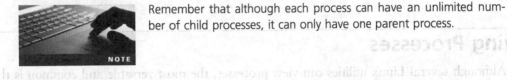

Remember that although each process can have an unlimited number of child processes, it can only have one parent process.

The first process started by the Linux kernel is the initialize (or init) daemon, which has a PID of 1 and a PPID of 0, the latter of which refers to the kernel itself. The init daemon then starts most other daemons during the system initialization process, including those that allow for user logins. After you log in to the system, the login program starts a BASH shell. The BASH shell then interprets user commands and starts all user processes. Thus, each process on the Linux system can be traced back to the init daemon by examining the series of PPIDs, as shown in Figure 9-2.

The init daemon is often referred to as the "grandfather of all user processes."

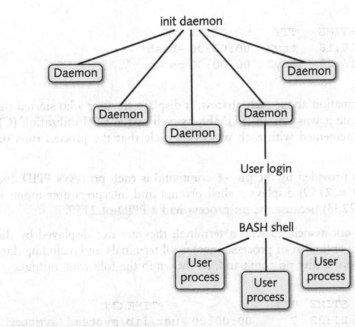

Figure 9-2 Process genealogy

On Linux systems that use the UNIX SysV system initialization process, the init daemon will be listed as `init` within command output. On Linux systems that use the Systemd system initialization process, the init daemon will either be listed as `init` or `systemd` within command output.

Viewing Processes

Although several Linux utilities can view processes, the most versatile and common is the **ps** command. Without arguments, the ps command simply displays a list of processes that are running in the current shell. The following example shows the output of this command while the user is logged in to tty2:

```
[root@server1 ~]# ps
  PID TTY            TIME CMD
 2159 tty2       00:00:00 bash
 2233 tty2       00:00:00 ps
[root@server1 ~]# _
```

The preceding output shows that two processes were running in the terminal tty2 when the ps command executed. The command that started each process (CMD) is listed next to the time it has taken on the CPU (TIME), its PID, and terminal (TTY). In this case, the process took less than one second to run, and so the time elapsed reads nothing. To find out more about these processes, you could instead use the -f, or full, option to the ps command, as shown next:

```
[root@server1 ~]# ps -f
UID         PID  PPID  C STIME    TTY          TIME CMD
root       2159  2156  0 16:18    tty2     00:00:00 -bash
root       2233  2159  3 16:28    tty2     00:00:00 ps -f
[root@server1 ~]# _
```

This listing provides more information about each process. It displays the user who started the process (UID), the PPID, the time it was started (STIME), as well as the CPU utilization (C), which starts at zero and is incremented with each processor cycle that the process runs on the CPU.

The most valuable information provided by the ps -f command is each process's PPID and lineage. The bash process (PID = 2159) displays a shell prompt and interprets user input; it started the ps process (PID = 2233) because the ps process had a PPID of 2159.

Because daemon processes are not associated with a terminal, they are not displayed by the ps -f command. To display an entire list of processes across all terminals and including daemons, you can add the -e option to any ps command, as shown in the following output:

```
[root@server1 ~]# ps -ef
UID         PID  PPID  C  STIME TTY              TIME CMD
root          1     0  0  21:22 ?            00:00:00 /usr/lib/systemd/systemd
root          2     0  0  21:22 ?            00:00:00 [kthreadd]
root          3     2  0  21:22 ?            00:00:00 [ksoftirqd/0]
```

```
root            5      2   0   21:22   ?        00:00:00 [kworker/0:0H]
root            6      2   0   21:22   ?        00:00:00 [kworker/u128:0]
root            7      2   0   21:22   ?        00:00:00 [migration/0]
root            8      2   0   21:22   ?        00:00:00 [rcu_bh]
root            9      2   0   21:22   ?        00:00:00 [rcu_sched]
root           10      2   0   21:22   ?        00:00:00 [watchdog/0]
root           11      2   0   21:22   ?        00:00:00 [khelper]
root           12      2   0   21:22   ?        00:00:00 [kdevtmpfs]
root           13      2   0   21:22   ?        00:00:00 [netns]
root           14      2   0   21:22   ?        00:00:00 [writeback]
root          394      1   0   21:22   ?        00:00:00 /sbin/auditd -n
root          407    394   0   21:22   ?        00:00:00 /sbin/audispd
root          409    407   0   21:22   ?        00:00:00 /usr/sbin/sedispatch
root          411      1   0   21:22   ?        00:00:00 /usr/sbin/alsactl -s -n
root          418      1   0   21:22   ?        00:00:00 /sbin/rngd -f
root          420      1   0   21:22   ?        00:00:00 /usr/sbin/ModemManager
avahi         422      1   0   21:22   ?        00:00:00 avahi-daemon: running
dbus          424      1   0   21:22   ?        00:00:00 /bin/dbus-daemon --system
chrony        430      1   0   21:22   ?        00:00:00 /usr/sbin/chronyd -u
root          431      1   0   21:22   ?        00:00:00 /usr/sbin/crond -n
root          432      1   0   21:22   ?        00:00:00 /usr/sbin/atd -f
root          435      1   0   21:22   ?        00:00:00 /usr/sbin/abrtd -d -s
root          437      1   0   21:22   ?        00:00:00 /usr/bin/abrt-watch-log
root          441      1   0   21:22   ?        00:00:00 /usr/sbin/gdm
root          446      1   0   21:22   ?        00:00:00 /usr/sbin/mcelog
root          481    441   0   21:22   ?        00:00:00 /usr/libexec/gdm-simple
polkitd       482      1   0   21:22   ?        00:00:00 /usr/lib/polkit-1/polkitd
root          488    481   0   21:22   tty1     00:00:00 /usr/bin/Xorg :0
root          551    481   0   21:22   ?        00:00:00 gdm-session-worker
root          552      1   0   21:22   ?        00:00:00 /usr/sbin/NetworkManager
gdm           842    823   0   21:23   ?        00:00:00 (sd-pam)
gdm           852    551   0   21:23   ?        00:00:00 /usr/bin/gnome-session
gdm           856      1   0   21:23   ?        00:00:00 /usr/bin/dbus-launch
gdm          1018      1   0   21:23   ?        00:00:00 /bin/dbus-daemon --fork
root         1020    552   0   21:23   ?        00:00:00 /sbin/dhclient -d -sf
gdm          1025      1   0   21:23   ?        00:00:00 /usr/libexec/at-spi-bus
gdm          1045   1025   0   21:23   ?        00:00:00 /bin/dbus-daemon
root         1072      1   0   21:23   ?        00:00:00 /usr/libexec/upowerd
gdm          1077    852   0   21:23   ?        00:00:03 gnome-shell --mode=gdm
colord       1080      1   0   21:23   ?        00:00:00 /usr/libexec/colord
gdm          1087      1   0   21:23   ?        00:00:00 /usr/bin/pulseaudio
gdm          1114   1111   0   21:23   ?        00:00:00 /usr/libexec/ibus-dconf
gdm          1122   1111   0   21:23   ?        00:00:00 /usr/libexec/ibus-engine
gdm          1148      1   0   21:23   ?        00:00:00 /usr/libexec/goa-daemon
root         1164      1   0   21:23   ?        00:00:00 login -- root
root         1174   1171   0   21:23   ?        00:00:00 (sd-pam)
root         1175   1164   0   21:23   tty2     00:00:00 -bash
root         1208      2   0   21:28   ?        00:00:00 [kworker/0:0]
```

```
root        1213      1   0   21:31   ?       00:00:00 /usr/sbin/sshd -D
root        1216   1213   0   21:32   ?       00:00:00 sshd: root@pts/0
root        1220   1216   0   21:32   pts/0 00:00:00 -bash
root        1253      2   0   21:33   ?       00:00:00 [kworker/0:2]
root        1260      1   0   21:33   ?       00:00:00 /usr/libexec/packagekitd
root        1742   1220   0   21:33   pts/0 00:00:00 ps -ef
[root@server1 ~]# _
```

As shown in the preceding output, the kernel thread daemon (kthreadd) has a PID of 2 and starts most subprocesses within the actual Linux kernel because those subprocesses have a PPID of 2, whereas the init daemon (/usr/lib/systemd/systemd, PID = 1) starts most other daemons because those daemons have a PPID of 1. In addition, there is a ? in the TTY column for daemons and kernel subprocesses because they do not run on a terminal.

Because the output of the ps -ef command can be several hundred lines long on a Linux server, you usually pipe its output to the less command to send the output to the terminal screen page-by-page, or to the grep command, which can be used to display lines containing only certain information. For example, to display only the BASH shells on the system, you could use the following command:

```
[root@server1 ~]# ps -ef | grep bash
user1      2094   2008   0 14:29 pts/1     00:00:00 -bash
root       2159   2156   0 14:30 tty2      00:00:00 -bash
root       2294   2159   0 14:44 tty2      00:00:00 grep –color=auto bash
[root@server1 ~]# _
```

Notice that the grep bash command is also displayed alongside the BASH shells in the preceding output because it was running in memory at the time the ps command was executed. This might not always be the case because the Linux kernel schedules commands to run based on a variety of factors.

The -e and -f options are the most common options used with the ps command; however, many other options are available. The -l option to the ps command lists even more information about each process than the -f option. An example of using this option to view the processes in the terminal tty2 is shown in the following output:

```
[root@server1 ~]# ps -l
F S   UID   PID   PPID  C PRI  NI ADDR SZ WCHAN  TTY       TIME CMD
4 S     0  2159   2156  0  80   0 -  1238 wait    tty2   00:00:00 bash
4 R     0  2295   2159  2  80   0 -   744 -       tty2   00:00:00 ps
[root@server1 ~]# _
```

The process flag (F) indicates particular features of the process; the flag of 4 in the preceding output indicates that the root user ran the process. The **process state** (S) column is the most valuable to systems administrators because it indicates what the process is currently doing. If a process is not being run on the processor at the current time, you see an S (sleeping) in the process state column; processes are in this state most of the time, as seen with bash in the preceding output. You will see an R in this column if the process is currently running on the processor, or a T if it has stopped or is being traced by another process. In addition to these, you might also see a Z in this column, indicating a **zombie process**. When a process finishes executing, the parent process must check to see if it executed successfully and then release the child process's PID so that it can be used again. While a process is waiting for its parent process to release the PID, the process is said to be in a zombie state, because it has finished but still retains a PID. On a busy Linux server, zombie processes can accumulate and prevent new processes from being created; if this occurs, you can simply kill the parent process of the zombies, as discussed in the next section.

 Zombie processes are also known as defunct processes.

 To view a list of zombie processes on your entire system, you could use the `ps -el | grep Z` command.

Process priority (PRI) is the priority used by the kernel for the process; it is measured between 0 (high priority) and 127 (low priority). The **nice value** (NI) can be used to affect the process priority indirectly; it is measured between -20 (a greater chance of a high priority) and 19 (a greater chance of a lower priority). The ADDR in the preceding output indicates the memory address of the process, whereas the WCHAN indicates what the process is waiting for while sleeping. In addition, the size of the process in memory (SZ) is listed and measured in kilobytes; often, it is roughly equivalent to the size of the executable file on the filesystem.

Some options to the `ps` command are not prefixed by a dash character; these are referred to as Berkeley-style options. The two most common of these are the a option, which lists all processes across terminals, and the x option, which lists processes that do not run on a terminal, as shown in the following output for the first 10 processes on the system:

```
[root@server1 ~]# ps ax | head -11
  PID TTY      STAT       TIME COMMAND
    1 ?        S          0:01 /usr/lib/systemd/systemd
    2 ?        S          0:00 [kthreadd]
    3 ?        S          0:00 [migration/0]
    4 ?        S<         0:00 [ksoftirqd/0]
    5 ?        S          0:00 [watchdog/0]
    6 ?        S          0:00 [migration/1]
    7 ?        S          0:00 [ksoftirqd/1]
    8 ?        S          0:00 [watchdog/1]
    9 ?        S          0:00 [events/0]
   10 ?        S          0:00 [events/1]
[root@server1 ~]# _
```

The columns just listed are equivalent to those discussed earlier; however, the process state column is identified with STAT and might contain additional characters to indicate the full nature of the process state. For example, a W indicates that the process has no contents in memory, a < symbol indicates a high-priority process, and an N indicates a low-priority process.

For a full list of symbols that may be shown in the STAT or S columns shown in prior output, consult the manual page for the `ps` command.

Several dozen options to the `ps` command can be used to display processes and their attributes; the options listed in this section are the most common and are summarized in Table 9-1.

The `ps` command is not the only command that can view process information. The kernel exports all process information subdirectories under the /proc directory. Each subdirectory is named for the PID of the process that it contains information for, as shown in the following output:

```
[root@server1 ~]# ls /proc
1       1174  1746  28    407   473   852         irq           slabinfo
10      1175  175   292   409   48    856         kallsyms      softirqs
1018    12    1754  3     411   481   9           kcore         stat
1020    1213  176   307   412   482   acpi        keys          swaps
1025    1216  1760  328   414   488   buddyinfo   key-users     sys
1045    1220  177   350   415   49    bus         kmsg          sysrq
1052    13    178   351   418   5     cgroups     kpagecount    sysvipc
1065    14    179   353   420   551   cmdline     kpageflags    timer_list
1072    15    18    354   421   552   consoles    loadavg       timer_stats
1077    16    180   357   422   58    cpuinfo     locks         tty
1080    164   181   358   424   59    crypto      mdstat        uptime
1087    165   1810  359   430   6     devices     meminfo       version
1097    167   188   370   431   60    diskstats   misc          vmallocinfo
11      168   189   371   432   62    dma         modules       vmstat
1111    169   19    372   435   64    driver      mounts        zoneinfo
1114    17    191   383   437   7     execdomains mtrr
1117    170   2     384   440   72    fb          net
1122    171   20    385   441   748   filesystems pagetypeinfo
1144    172   204   386   446   8     fs          partitions
1148    173   205   387   45    814   interrupts  sched_debug
1164    174   206   388   46    823   iomem       scsi
1171    1745  276   394   47    842   ioports     self
[root@server1 ~]# _
```

Option	Description
-e	Displays all processes running on terminals as well as processes that do not run on a terminal (daemons)
-f	Displays a full list of information about each process, including the UID, PID, PPID, CPU utilization, start time, terminal, processor time, and command name
-l	Displays a long list of information about each process, including the flag, state, UID, PID, PPID, CPU utilization, priority, nice value, address, size, WCHAN, terminal, and command name
a	Displays all processes running on terminals
x	Displays all processes that do not run on terminals

Table 9-1 Common options to the `ps` command

Thus, any program that can read from the /proc directory can display process information. For example, the **pstree command** displays the lineage of a process by tracing its PPIDs until the init daemon. The first 26 lines of this command are shown in the following output:

```
[root@server1 ~]# pstree | head -26
systemd─┬─ModemManager───2*[{ModemManager}]
        ├─NetworkManager─┬─dhclient
        │                └─3*[{NetworkManager}]
        ├─2*[abrt-watch-log]
        ├─abrtd
        ├─accounts-daemon───2*[{accounts-daemon}]
        ├─alsactl
        ├─at-spi-bus-laun─┬─dbus-daemon───{dbus-daemon}
        │                 └─3*[{at-spi-bus-laun}]
        ├─at-spi2-registr───{at-spi2-registr}
        ├─atd
        ├─auditd─┬─audispd─┬─sedispatch
        │        │         └─{audispd}
        │        └─{auditd}
        ├─avahi-daemon───avahi-daemon
        ├─bluetoothd
        ├─chronyd
        ├─colord───2*[{colord}]
        ├─crond
        ├─2*[dbus-daemon───{dbus-daemon}]
        ├─dbus-launch
        ├─dconf-service───2*[{dconf-service}]
        ├─firewalld───{firewalld}
        ├─gdm─┬─gdm-simple-slav─┬─Xorg
        │                       └─gdm-session─┬─gnome-session─┬─gnome-settings
        │                                     │               └─gnome-shell
[root@server1 ~]# _
```

The most common program used to display processes, aside from ps, is the **top command**. The top command displays an interactive screen listing processes organized by processor time. Processes that use the most processor time are listed at the top of the screen. An example of the screen that appears when you type the top command is shown next:

```
top - 21:55:15 up 32 min, 3 users, load average: 1.00, 0.99, 0.89
Tasks: 134 total,  1 running, 133 sleeping,  0 stopped,  0 zombie
%Cpu(s): 0.4 us,  0.4 sy,  0.0 ni, 95.9 id,  2.0 wa,  1.1 hi,  0.1 si,  0.0 st
KiB Mem:  2044524 total, 1066848 used,  977676 free,   19880 buffers
KiB Swap: 2097148 total,       0 used, 2097148 free,  255032 cached

  PID USER  PR NI   VIRT    RES   SHR S %CPU %MEM   TIME+  COMMAND
 1077 gdm   20  0 1518192 150684 36660 R 19.4  7.4 0:33.93 gnome-shell
 2130 root  20  0  123636   1644  1180 R  0.7  0.1 0:00.05 top
    1 root  20  0   51544   7348  2476 S  0.0  0.4 0:00.98 systemd
    2 root  20  0       0      0     0 S  0.0  0.0 0:00.00 kthreadd
    3 root  20  0       0      0     0 S  0.0  0.0 0:00.01 ksoftirqd/0
    5 root   0 -20      0      0     0 S  0.0  0.0 0:00.00 kworker/0:0H
    6 root  20  0       0      0     0 S  0.0  0.0 0:00.02 kworker/u12+
    7 root  rt  0       0      0     0 S  0.0  0.0 0:00.00 migration/0
    8 root  20  0       0      0     0 S  0.0  0.0 0:00.00 rcu_bh
```

9	root	20	0	0	0	0 S	0.0	0.0	0:00.34	rcu_sched
10	root	rt	0	0	0	0 S	0.0	0.0	0:00.00	watchdog/0
11	root	0	-20	0	0	0 S	0.0	0.0	0:00.00	khelper
12	root	20	0	0	0	0 S	0.0	0.0	0:00.00	kdevtmpfs
13	root	0	-20	0	0	0 S	0.0	0.0	0:00.00	netns
14	root	0	-20	0	0	0 S	0.0	0.0	0:00.00	writeback
15	root	0	-20	0	0	0 S	0.0	0.0	0:00.00	kintegrityd
16	root	0	-20	0	0	0 S	0.0	0.0	0:00.00	bioset

Note that the top command displays many of the same columns that the ps command does, yet it contains a summary paragraph at the top of the screen and a cursor between the summary paragraph and the process list. From the preceding output, you can see that the gnome-shell uses the most processor time, followed by the top command itself (top) and the init daemon (systemd).

You might come across a process that has encountered an error during execution and continuously uses up system resources. These processes are referred to as **rogue processes** and appear at the top of the listing produced by the top command. The top command can also be used to change the priority of processes or kill them. Thus, you can stop rogue processes from the top command immediately after they are identified. Process priority and killing processes are discussed later in this chapter.

To get a full listing of the different commands that you can use while in the top utility, simply press h to get a help screen. An example of this help screen is shown next:

```
Help for Interactive Commands - procps-ng version 3.3.8
Window 1:Def: Cumulative mode Off.  System: Delay 3.0 secs; Secure mode Off.

  Z,B,E,e      Global: 'Z' colors; 'B' bold; 'E'/'e' summary/task memory scale
  l,t,m        Toggle Summary: 'l' load avg; 't' task/cpu stats; 'm' memory info
  0,1,2,3,I    Toggle: '0' zeros; '1/2/3' cpus or numa node views; 'I' Irix mode
  f,F,X        Fields: 'f'/'F' add/remove/order/sort; 'X' increase fixed-width

  L,&,<,>      . Locate: 'L'/'&' find/again; Move sort column: '<'/'>' left/right
  R,H,V,J      . Toggle: 'R' Sort; 'H' Threads; 'V' Forest view; 'J' Num justify
  c,i,S,j      . Toggle: 'c' Cmd name/line; 'i' Idle; 'S' Time; 'j' Str justify
  x,y          . Toggle highlights: 'x' sort field; 'y' running tasks
  z,b          . Toggle: 'z' color/mono; 'b' bold/reverse (only if 'x' or 'y')
  u,U,o,O      . Filter by: 'u'/'U' effective/any user; 'o'/'O' other criteria
  n,#,^O       . Set: 'n'/'#' max tasks displayed; Show: Ctrl+'O' other filter(s)
  C,...        . Toggle scroll coordinates msg for: up,down,left,right,home,end

  k,r          Manipulate tasks: 'k' kill; 'r' renice
  d or s       Set update interval
  W,Y          Write configuration file 'W'; Inspect other output 'Y'
  q            Quit
               ( commands shown with '.' require a visible task display window )
Press 'h' or '?' for help with Windows,
Type 'q' or <Esc> to continue
```

Killing Processes

As indicated earlier, a large number of rogue and zombie processes use up system resources. When system performance suffers due to these processes, you should send them a **kill signal**, which terminates a process. The most common command used to send kill signals is the `kill` command. All told, the `kill` command can send 64 different kill signals to a process. Each of these kill signals operates in a different manner. To view the different kill signal names and associated numbers, you can use the `-1` option to the `kill` command, as shown in the following output:

```
[root@server1 ~]# kill -l
 1) SIGHUP        2) SIGINT        3) SIGQUIT       4) SIGILL
 5) SIGTRAP       6) SIGABRT       7) SIGBUS        8) SIGFPE
 9) SIGKILL      10) SIGUSR1      11) SIGSEGV      12) SIGUSR2
13) SIGPIPE      14) SIGALRM      15) SIGTERM      17) SIGCHLD
18) SIGCONT      19) SIGSTOP      20) SIGTSTP      21) SIGTTIN
22) SIGTTOU      23) SIGURG       24) SIGXCPU      25) SIGXFSZ
26) SIGVTALRM    27) SIGPROF      28) SIGWINCH     29) SIGIO
30) SIGPWR       31) SIGSYS       33) SIGRTMIN     34) SIGRTMIN+1
35) SIGRTMIN+2   36) SIGRTMIN+3   37) SIGRTMIN+4   38) SIGRTMIN+5
39) SIGRTMIN+6   40) SIGRTMIN+7   41) SIGRTMIN+8   42) SIGRTMIN+9
43) SIGRTMIN+10  44) SIGRTMIN+11  45) SIGRTMIN+12  46) SIGRTMIN+13
47) SIGRTMIN+14  48) SIGRTMIN+15  49) SIGRTMAX-15  50) SIGRTMAX-14
51) SIGRTMAX-13  52) SIGRTMAX-12  53) SIGRTMAX-11  54) SIGRTMAX-10
55) SIGRTMAX-9   56) SIGRTMAX-8   57) SIGRTMAX-7   58) SIGRTMAX-6
59) SIGRTMAX-5   60) SIGRTMAX-4   61) SIGRTMAX-3   62) SIGRTMAX-2
63) SIGRTMAX-1   64) SIGRTMAX
[root@server1 ~]# _
```

Most of the kill signals listed in the preceding output are not useful for systems administrators. The five most common kill signals used for administration are listed in Table 9-2.

To send a kill signal to a process, you specify the kill signal to send as an option to the `kill` command, followed by the appropriate PID of the process. For example, to send a SIGQUIT to a process called `sample`, you could use the following commands to locate and terminate the process:

```
[root@server1 ~]# ps -ef | grep sample
root      1199    1  0   Jun30 tty3    00:00:00 /sbin/sample
[root@server1 ~]# kill -3 1199
[root@server1 ~]# _
[root@server1 ~]# ps -ef | grep sample
[root@server1 ~]# _
```

The `kill -SIGQUIT 1199` command does the same thing as the `kill -3 1199` command shown in the preceding output.

If you do not specify the kill signal when using the `kill` command, the `kill` command uses the default kill signal, the SIGTERM signal.

9

Name	Number	Description
SIGHUP	1	Also known as the hang-up signal, it stops a process, then restarts it with the same PID. If you edit the configuration file used by a running daemon, that daemon might be sent a SIGHUP to restart the process; when the daemon starts again, it reads the new configuration file.
SIGINT	2	This signal sends an interrupt signal to a process. Although this signal is one of the weakest kill signals, it works most of the time. When you use the Ctrl+c key combination to kill a currently running process, a SIGINT is actually being sent to the process.
SIGQUIT	3	Also known as a core dump, the quit signal terminates a process by taking the process information in memory and saving it to a file called core on the hard disk in the current working directory. You can use the Ctrl+\ key combination to send a SIGQUIT to a process that is currently running.
SIGTERM	15	The software termination signal is the most common kill signal used by programs to kill other processes. It is the default kill signal used by the `kill` command.
SIGKILL	9	Also known as the absolute kill signal, it forces the Linux kernel to stop executing the process by sending the process's resources to a special device file called /dev/null.

Table 9-2 Common administrative kill signals

Some processes have the ability to ignore, or **trap**, certain kill signals that are sent to them. The only kill signal that cannot be trapped by any process is the SIGKILL. Thus, if a SIGINT, SIGQUIT, and SIGTERM do not terminate a stubborn process, you can use a SIGKILL to terminate it. However, you should only use SIGKILL as a last resort because it prevents a process from closing temporary files and other resources properly.

If you send a kill signal to a process that has children, the parent process terminates all of its child processes before terminating itself. Thus, to kill several related processes, you can simply send a kill signal to their parent process. In addition, to kill a zombie process, it is often necessary to send a kill signal to its parent process.

Another command that can be used to send kill signals to processes is the **killall** command. The `killall` command works similarly to the `kill` command in that it takes the kill signal as an option; however, it uses the process name to kill instead of the PID. This allows multiple processes of the same name to be killed in one command. An example of using the `killall` command to send a SIGQUIT to multiple `sample` processes is shown in the following output:

```
[root@server1 ~]# ps -ef | grep sample
root      1729    1    0 Jun30 tty3    00:00:00 /sbin/sample
root     20198    1    0 Jun30 tty4    00:00:00 /sbin/sample
[root@server1 ~]# killall -3 sample
[root@server1 ~]# _
[root@server1 ~]# ps -ef | grep sample
[root@server1 ~]# _
```

Alternatively, you could use the command `killall –SIGQUIT sample` to do the same as the `killall -3 sample` command used in the preceding output.

As with the `kill` command, if you do not specify the kill signal when using the `killall` command, it sends a SIGTERM signal by default.

In addition to the `kill` and `killall` commands, the `top` command can be used to kill processes. While in the `top` utility, simply press the k key and supply the appropriate PID and kill signal when prompted.

Process Execution

You can execute three main types of Linux commands:

- Binary programs
- Shell scripts
- Shell functions

Most commands, such as `ls`, `find`, and `grep`, are binary programs that exist on the filesystem until executed. They were written in a certain programming language and compiled into a binary format that only the computer can understand. Other commands, such as `cd` and `exit`, are built in to the BASH shell running in memory, and they are called shell functions. Shell scripts can also contain a list of binary programs, shell functions, and special constructs for the shell to execute in order.

When executing compiled programs or shell scripts, the BASH shell that interprets the command you typed creates a new BASH shell. This creation of a new subshell is known as **forking** and is carried out by the fork function in the BASH shell. The new subshell then executes the binary program or shell script using its exec function. After the binary program or shell script has completed, the new BASH shell uses its exit function to kill itself and return control to the original BASH shell. The original BASH shell uses its wait function to wait for the new BASH shell to carry out the aforementioned tasks before returning a prompt to the user. Figure 9-3 depicts this process when a user types the `ls` command at the command line.

Running Processes in the Background

As discussed in the previous section, the BASH shell creates, or forks, a subshell to execute most commands on the Linux system. Unfortunately, the original BASH shell must wait for the command in the subshell to finish before displaying a shell prompt to accept new commands. Commands run in this fashion are known as **foreground processes**.

Alternatively, you can omit the wait function shown in Figure 9-3 by appending an ampersand (&) character to the command. Commands run in this fashion are known as **background processes**. When a command is run in the background, the shell immediately returns the shell

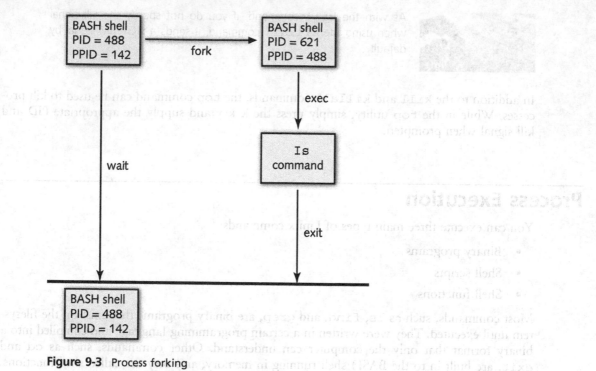

Figure 9-3 Process forking

prompt for the user to enter another command. To run the sample command in the background, you can enter the following command:

```
[root@server1 ~]# sample &
[1] 2583
[root@server1 ~]# _
```

Space characters between the command and the ampersand (&) are optional. In other words, the command sample& is equivalent to the command sample & used in the preceding output.

The shell returns the PID (2583 in the preceding example) and the background job ID (1 in the preceding example) so that you can manipulate the background job after it has been run. After the process has been started, you can use the ps command to view the PID or the **jobs** command to view the background job ID, as shown in the following output:

```
[root@server1 ~]# jobs
[1]+ Running                sample &
[root@server1 ~]# ps | grep sample
2583 tty2    00:00:00 sample
[root@server1 ~]# _
```

To terminate the background process, you can send a kill signal to the PID (as shown earlier in this chapter), or you can send a kill signal to the background job ID. Background job IDs must be prefixed with a % character. To send the sample background process created earlier a SIGINT signal, you could use the following `kill` command:

```
[root@server1 ~]# jobs
[1]+ Running                sample &
[root@server1 ~]# kill -2 %1
[1]+ Interrupt              sample
[root@server1 ~]# jobs
[root@server1 ~]# _
```

 You can also use the `killall -2 sample` command or the `top` utility to terminate the sample background process used in the preceding example.

After a background process has been started, you can move it to the foreground by using the **foreground (fg) command** followed by the background job ID. Similarly, you can pause a foreground process by using the Ctrl+z key combination. You can then send the process to the background with the **background (bg) command**. The Ctrl+z key combination assigns the foreground process a background job ID that is then used as an argument to the bg command. To start a sample process in the background and move it to the foreground, then pause it and move it to the background again, you can use the following commands:

```
[root@server1 ~]# sample &
[1] 7519
[root@server1 ~]# fg %1
sample

Ctrl+z

[1]+ Stopped                sample
[root@server1 ~]# bg %1
[1]+ sample &
[root@server1 ~]# jobs
[1]+ Running                sample &
[root@server1 ~]# _
```

When there are multiple background processes executing in the shell, the `jobs` command indicates the most recent one with a + symbol, and the second most recent one with a − symbol. If you place the % notation in a command without specifying the background job ID, the command operates on the most recent background process. An example of this is shown in the following output, in which four sample processes are started and sent SIGQUIT kill signals using the % notation:

```
[root@server1 ~]# sample &
[1] 7605
[root@server1 ~]# sample2 &
[2] 7613
[root@server1 ~]# sample3 &
[3] 7621
```

9

```
[root@server1 ~]# sample4 &
[4] 7629
[root@server1 ~]# jobs
[1]   Running                 sample &
[2]   Running                 sample2 &
[3]-  Running                 sample3 &
[4]+  Running                 sample4 &
[root@server1 ~]# kill -3 %
[root@server1 ~]# jobs
[1]   Running                 sample &
[2]-  Running                 sample2 &
[3]+  Running                 sample3 &
[root@server1 ~]# kill -3 %
[root@server1 ~]# jobs
[1]-  Running                 sample &
[2]+  Running                 sample2 &
[root@server1 ~]# kill -3 %
[root@server1 ~]# jobs
[1]+  Running                 sample &
[root@server1 ~]# kill -3 %
[root@server1 ~]# jobs
[root@server1 ~]# _
```

Process Priorities

Recall that Linux is a multitasking operating system. That is, it can perform several different tasks at the same time. Because most computers contain only a single CPU, Linux executes small amounts of each process on the processor in series. This makes it seem to the user as if processes are executing simultaneously. The amount of time a process has to use the CPU is called a **time slice**; the more time slices a process has, the more time it has to execute on the CPU and the faster it executes. Time slices are typically measured in milliseconds. Thus, several hundred processes can be executing on the processor in a single second.

The ps -l command lists the Linux kernel priority (PRI) of a process. This value is directly related to the amount of time slices a process has on the CPU. A PRI of 0 is the most likely to get time slices on the CPU, and a PRI of 127 is the least likely to receive time slices on the CPU. An example of this command is shown next:

```
[root@server1 ~]# ps -l
F S   UID  PID PPID  C  PRI NI  ADDR SZ WCHAN  TTY       TIME CMD
4 S     0 3194 3192  0   75  0  - 1238 wait4  pts/1  00:00:00 bash
4 S     0 3896 3194  0   76  0  -  953 -      pts/1  00:00:00 sleep
4 S     0 3939 3194 13   75  0  - 7015 -      pts/1  00:00:01 gedit
4 R     0 3940 3194  0   77  0  -  632 -      pts/1  00:00:00 ps
[root@server1 ~]# _
```

The bash, sleep, gedit, and ps processes all have different PRI values because the kernel automatically assigns time slices based on several factors. You cannot change the PRI directly, but you can influence it indirectly by assigning a certain nice value to a process. A negative nice value increases the likelihood that the process will receive more time slices, whereas a positive nice value does the opposite. The range of nice values is depicted in Figure 9-4.

All users can be "nice" to other users of the same computer by lowering the priority of their own processes by increasing their nice value. However, only the root user has the ability to increase the priority of a process by lowering its nice value.

Processes are started with a nice value of 0 by default, as shown in the NI column of the previous ps –l output. To start a process with a nice value of +19 (low priority), you can use the **nice command** and specify the nice value using the –n option and the command to start. If the –n option is omitted, a nice value of +10 is assumed. To start the ps –l command with a nice value of +19, you can issue the following command:

```
[root@server1 ~]# nice -n 19 ps -l
F S  UID  PID  PPID  C  PRI  NI   ADDR SZ  WCHAN  TTY    TIME CMD
4 S    0 3194  3192  0   75   0    -  1238  wait4  pts/1  00:00:00 bash
4 S    0 3896  3194  0   76   0    -   953  -      pts/1  00:00:00 sleep
4 S    0 3939  3194  0   76   0    -  7015  -      pts/1  00:00:02 gedit
4 R    0 3946  3194  0   99  19    -   703  -      pts/1  00:00:00 ps
[root@server1 ~]#
```

Notice from the preceding output that NI is 19 for the ps command, as compared to 0 for the bash, sleep, and gedit commands. Furthermore, the PRI of 99 for the ps command results in fewer time slices than the PRI of 76 for the sleep and gedit commands and the PRI of 75 for the bash shell.

Conversely, to increase the priority of the ps –l command, you can use the following command:

```
[root@server1 ~]# nice -n -20 ps -l
F S  UID  PID  PPID  C  PRI  NI   ADDR SZ  WCHAN  TTY    TIME CMD
4 S    0 3194  3192  0   75   0    -  1238  wait4  pts/1  00:00:00 bash
4 S    0 3896  3194  0   76   0    -   953  -      pts/1  00:00:00 sleep
4 S    0 3939  3194  0   76   0    -  7015  -      pts/1  00:00:02 gedit
4 R    0 3947  3194  0   60 -20    -   687  -      pts/1  00:00:00 ps
[root@server1 ~]#
```

−20   **0**   **+19**

Most likely to   The default nice value   Least likely to
receive time slices;   for new processes   receive time slices;
the PRI will be   the PRI will be
closer to zero   closer to 127

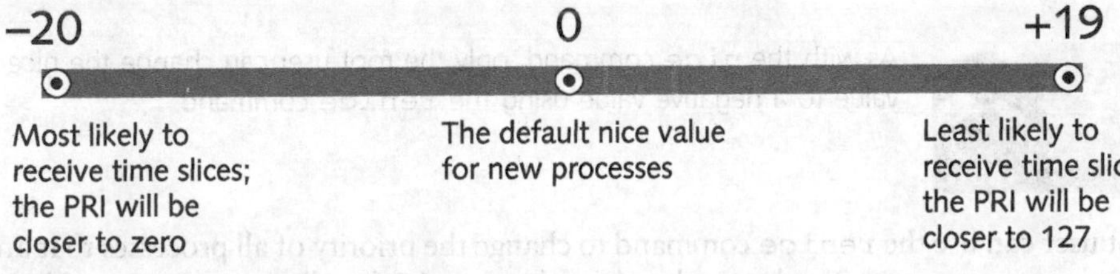

Figure 9-4 The nice value scale

Note from the preceding output that the nice value of -20 for the `ps` command resulted in a PRI of 60, which is more likely to receive time slices than the PRI of 76 for the `sleep` and `gedit` commands and the PRI of 75 for the `bash` shell.

On some Linux systems, background processes are given a nice value of 4 by default to lower the chance they will receive time slices.

After a process has been started, you can change its priority by using the **renice** command and specifying the change to the nice value, as well as the PID of the processes to change. Suppose, for example, three sample processes are currently executing on a terminal:

```
[root@server1 ~]# ps -l
F S  UID   PID  PPID  C PRI  NI ADDR   SZ WCHAN   TTY      TIME CMD
4 S    0  1229  1228  0  71   0  -     617 wait4   pts/0 00:00:00 bash
4 S    0  1990  1229  0  69   0  -     483 nanosl  pts/0 00:00:00 sample
4 S    0  2180  1229  0  70   0  -     483 nanosl  pts/0 00:00:00 sample
4 S    0  2181  1229  0  71   0  -     483 nanosl  pts/0 00:00:00 sample
4 R    0  2196  1229  0  75   0  -     768 -       pts/0 00:00:00 ps
[root@server1 ~]# _
```

To lower priority of the first two sample processes by changing the nice value from 0 to +15 and view the new values, you can execute the following commands:

```
[root@server1 ~]# renice +15 1990 2180
1990 (process ID) old priority 0, new priority 15
2180 (process ID) old priority 0, new priority 15
[root@server1 ~]# ps -l
F S  UID   PID  PPID  C PRI  NI ADDR   SZ WCHAN   TTY      TIME CMD
4 S    0  1229  1228  0  71   0  -     617 wait4   pts/0 00:00:00 bash
4 S    0  1990  1229  0  93  15  -     483 nanosl  pts/0 00:00:00 sample
4 S    0  2180  1229  0  96  15  -     483 nanosl  pts/0 00:00:00 sample
4 S    0  2181  1229  0  71   0  -     483 nanosl  pts/0 00:00:00 sample
4 R    0  2196  1229  0  75   0  -     768 -       pts/0 00:00:00 ps
[root@server1 ~]# _
```

You can also use the `top` utility to change the nice value of a running process. Simply press the `r` key, then supply the PID and the nice value when prompted.

As with the `nice` command, only the root user can change the nice value to a negative value using the `renice` command.

The root user can use the `renice` command to change the priority of all processes that are owned by a certain user or group. To change the nice value to +15 for all processes owned by the users mary and bob, you could execute the command `renice +15 -u mary bob` at the command prompt. Similarly, to change the nice value to +15 for all processes started by members of the group sys, you could execute the command renice +15 -g sys at the command prompt.

Scheduling Commands

Although most processes are begun by users executing commands while logged in to a terminal, at times you might want to schedule a command to execute at some point in the future. For example, scheduling system maintenance commands to run during nonworking hours is good practice, as it does not disrupt normal business activities.

You can use two different daemons to schedule commands: the **at daemon (atd)** and the **cron daemon (crond)**. The at daemon can be used to schedule a command to execute once in the future, whereas the cron daemon is used to schedule a command to execute repeatedly in the future.

Scheduling Commands with atd

To schedule a command or set of commands for execution at a later time by the at daemon, you can specify the time as an argument to the **at command**; some common time formats used with the **at** command are listed in Table 9-3.

Command	Description
at 10:15pm	Schedules commands to run at 10:15 PM on the current date
at 10:15pm July 15	Schedules commands to run at 10:15 PM on July 15
at midnight	Schedules commands to run at midnight on the current date
at noon July 15	Schedules commands to run at noon on July 15
at teatime	Schedules commands to run at 4:00 PM on the current date
at tomorrow	Schedules commands to run the next day
at now + 5 minutes	Schedules commands to run in five minutes
at now + 10 hours	Schedules commands to run in 10 hours
at now + 4 days	Schedules commands to run in four days
at now + 2 weeks	Schedules commands to run in two weeks
at now at batch	Schedules commands to run immediately
at 9:00am 01/03/2016 at 9:00am 01032016 at 9:00am 03.01.2016	Schedules commands to run at 9:00 AM on January 3, 2016

Table 9-3 Common at commands

After being invoked, the at command displays an at> prompt allowing you to type commands to be executed, one per line. After the commands have been entered, use the Crtl+d key combination to schedule the commands using atd.

The at daemon uses the current shell's environment when executing scheduled commands. The shell environment and scheduled commands are stored in the **/var/spool/at** directory on Fedora systems and the **/var/spool/cron/atjobs** directory on Ubuntu systems.

If the standard output of any command scheduled using atd has not been redirected to a file, it is normally mailed to the user. You can check your local mail by typing mail at a command prompt. More information about the mail utility can be found in its manual page or info page.

Fedora 20 does not install a mail daemon by default. As a result, it is important to ensure that the output of any Fedora 20 commands scheduled using atd are redirected to a file.

To schedule the commands date and who to run at 10:15 PM on July 15th, you can use the following commands:

```
[root@server1 ~]# at 10:15pm July 15
at> date > /root/atfile
at> who >> /root/atfile
at> Ctrl+d
job 1 at Wed Jul 15 22:15:00 2015
[root@server1 ~]# _
```

As shown in the preceding output, the at command returns an at job ID. You can use this ID to query or remove the scheduled command. To display a list of at job IDs, you can specify the -1 option to the at command:

```
[root@server1 ~]# at -1
1        Wed Jul 15 22:15:00 2015 a root
[root@server1 ~]# _
```

Alternatively, you can use the atq command to see scheduled at jobs. The atq command is simply a shortcut to the at -1 command.

When running the at -1 command, a regular user only sees his own scheduled at jobs; however, the root user sees all scheduled at jobs.

To see the contents of the at job listed in the previous output alongside the shell environment at the time the at job was scheduled, you can use the -c option to the at command and specify the appropriate at job ID:

```
[root@server1 ~]# at -c 1
#!/bin/sh
# atrun uid=0 gid=0
# mail    root 0
umask 22
XDG_VTNR=2; export XDG_VTNR
XDG_SESSION_ID=1; export XDG_SESSION_ID
HOSTNAME=server1; export HOSTNAME
SHELL=/bin/bash; export SHELL
HISTSIZE=1000; export HISTSIZE
QT_GRAPHICSSYSTEM_CHECKED=1; export QT_GRAPHICSSYSTEM_CHECKED
USER=root; export USER
MAIL=/var/spool/mail/root; export MAIL
PATH=/usr/local/sbin:/usr/local/bin:/sbin:/bin:/usr/sbin:/usr/bin:/
root/bin; export PATH
PWD=/root; export PWD
LANG=en_US.UTF-8; export LANG
KDEDIRS=/usr; export KDEDIRS
HISTCONTROL=ignoredups; export HISTCONTROL
SHLVL=1; export SHLVL
XDG_SEAT=seat0; export XDG_SEAT
HOME=/root; export HOME
LOGNAME=root; export LOGNAME
LESSOPEN=\|\|/usr/bin/lesspipe.sh\ %s; export LESSOPEN
XDG_RUNTIME_DIR=/run/user/0; export XDG_RUNTIME_DIR
cd /root || {
        echo 'Execution directory inaccessible' >&2
        exit 1
}
${SHELL:-/bin/sh} << 'marcinDELIMITER2b2a920e'
date >/root/atfile
who >>/root/atfile

marcinDELIMITER2b2a920e
[root@server1 ~]# _
```

To remove the at job used in the preceding example, simply specify the -d option to the at command, followed by the appropriate at job ID, as shown in the following output:

```
[root@server1 ~]# at -d 1
[root@server1 ~]# at -l
[root@server1 ~]# _
```

Alternatively, you can use the atrm 1 command to remove the first at job. The atrm command is simply a shortcut to the at -d command.

If there are many commands to be scheduled using the at daemon, you can place these commands in a shell script and then schedule the shell script to execute at a later time using the −f option to the at command. An example of scheduling a shell script called myscript using the at command is shown next:

```
[root@server1 ~]# cat myscript
#this is a sample shell script
date > /root/atfile
who >> /root/atfile
[root@server1 ~]# at 10:15pm July 16 -f myscript
job 2 at Thu Jul 16 22:15:00 2015
[root@server1 ~]# _
```

If the **/etc/at.allow** and **/etc/at.deny** files do not exist, only the root user is allowed to schedule tasks using the at daemon. To give this ability to other users, simply create an /etc/at.allow file and add the names of users allowed to use the at daemon, one per line. Conversely, you can use the /etc/at.deny file to deny certain users access to the at daemon; any user not listed in this file is then allowed to use the at daemon. If both files exist, the system checks the /etc/at.allow file and does not process the entries in the /etc/at.deny file.

On Fedora systems, only an /etc/at.deny file exists by default. Because this file is initially left blank, all users are allowed to use the at daemon. On Ubuntu systems, only an /etc/at.deny file exists by default. Because only daemon user accounts are listed in this file by default, the root user and other regular user accounts are allowed to use the at daemon.

Scheduling Commands with cron

The at daemon is useful for scheduling tasks that occur on a certain date in the future but is ill suited for scheduling repetitive tasks, because each task requires its own at job ID. The cron daemon is better suited for repetitive tasks because it uses configuration files called **cron tables** to specify when a command should be executed.

A cron table includes six fields separated by space or tab characters. The first five fields specify the times to run the command, and the sixth field is the absolute pathname to the command to be executed. As with the at command, you can place commands in a shell script and schedule the shell script to run repetitively; in this case, the sixth field is the absolute pathname to the shell script. Each of the fields in a cron table is depicted in Figure 9-5.

Thus, to execute the /root/myscript shell script at 5:20 PM and 5:40 PM Monday to Friday regardless of the day of the month or month of the year, you could use the cron table depicted in Figure 9-6.

The first field in Figure 9-6 specifies the minute past the hour. Because the command must be run at 20 minutes and 40 minutes past the hour, this field has two values, separated by a comma. The second field specifies the time in 24-hour format, with 5 PM being the 17th hour. The third and fourth fields specify the day of month and month of year, respectively, to run the command. Because the command might run during any month regardless of the day of month, both fields use the * wildcard shell metacharacter to match all values. The final field indicates the day of the week to run the command; as

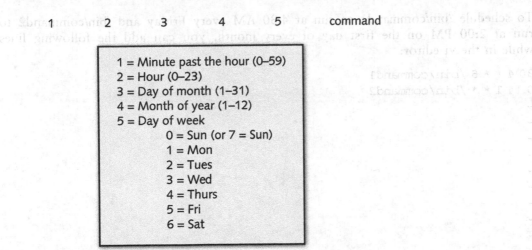

Figure 9-5 User cron table format

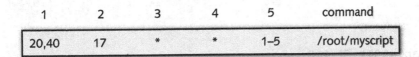

Figure 9-6 Sample user cron table entry

with the first field, the command must be run on multiple days, but a range of days was specified (day 1 to day 5).

Two different types of cron tables are used by the cron daemon: user cron tables and system cron tables. User cron tables represent tasks that individual users schedule and exist in the **/var/spool/cron** directory on Fedora systems and the **/var/spool/cron/crontabs** directory on Ubuntu systems. System cron tables contain system tasks and exist in the **/etc/crontab** file as well as the **/etc/cron.d** directory.

User Cron Tables On a newly installed Fedora system, all users have the ability to schedule tasks using the cron daemon because the **/etc/cron.deny** file has no contents. However, if you create an **/etc/cron.allow** file and add a list of users to it, only those users will be able to schedule tasks using the cron daemon. All other users are denied. Conversely, you can modify the /etc/cron.deny file to list those users who are denied the ability to schedule tasks. Thus, any users not listed in this file are allowed to schedule tasks only. If both files exist, only the /etc/cron.allow file is processed. If neither file exists, all users are allowed to schedule tasks, which is the case on a newly installed Ubuntu system.

To create or edit a user cron table, you can use the -e option to the **crontab** command, which opens the vi editor. You can then enter the appropriate cron table entries. Suppose, for example, that the root user executed the crontab -e command.

To schedule /bin/command1 to run at 4:30 AM every Friday and /bin/command2 to run at 2:00 PM on the first day of every month, you can add the following lines while in the vi editor:

```
30 4 * * 5 /bin/command1
0 14 1 * * /bin/command2
~
~
~
~
~
~
~
~
~
~
~
~
~
~
"/tmp/crontab.4101" 2L 41C
```

When the user saves the changes and quits the vi editor, the information is stored in the file /var/spool/cron/*username*, where *username* is the name of the user who executed the cron-tab -e command. In the preceding example, the file would be named /var/spool/cron/root.

To list your user cron table, you can use the -l option to the crontab command. The following output lists the cron table created earlier:

```
[root@server1 ~]# crontab -l
30 4 * * 5 /bin/command1
0 14 1 * * /bin/command2
[root@server1 ~]# _
```

Furthermore, to remove a cron table and all scheduled jobs, you can use the -r option to the crontab command, as illustrated next:

```
[root@server1 ~]# crontab -r
[root@server1 ~]# crontab -l
no crontab for root
[root@server1 ~]# _
```

The root user can edit, list, or remove any other user's cron table by using the -u option to the crontab command followed by the user name. For example, to edit the cron table for the user mary, the root user could use the command crontab -e -u mary at the command prompt. Similarly, to list and remove mary's cron table, the root user could execute the commands crontab -l -u mary and crontab -r -u mary, respectively.

System Cron Tables Linux systems are typically scheduled to run many commands during nonbusiness hours. These commands might perform system maintenance, back up data, or run CPU-intensive programs. Most of these commands are scheduled by the cron daemon from entries in the system cron table /etc/crontab, which can only be edited by the root user. The default /etc/crontab file on a Fedora system is shown in the following output:

```
[root@server1 ~]# cat /etc/crontab
SHELL=/bin/bash
PATH=/sbin:/bin:/usr/sbin:/usr/bin
MAILTO=root

# For details see man 4 crontabs

# Example of job definition:
# .---------------- minute (0 - 59)
# |  .------------- hour (0 - 23)
# |  |  .---------- day of month (1 - 31)
# |  |  |  .------- month (1 - 12) OR jan,feb,mar,apr ...
# |  |  |  |  .---- day of week (0 - 6) (Sunday=0 or 7) OR
# |  |  |  |  |           sun,mon,tue,wed,thu,fri,sat
# |  |  |  |  |
# *  *  *  *  * command to be executed
[root@server1 ~]#
```

The initial section of the cron table specifies the environment used while executing commands. The remainder of the file contains comments that identify the format of a cron table entry. If you add your own cron table entries to the bottom of this file, they will be executed as the root user. Alternatively, you may prefix the command within a system cron table entry with the user account that it should be executed as. For example, the /bin/cleanup command shown in the following output will be executed as the apache user:

```
[root@server1 ~]# cat /etc/crontab
SHELL=/bin/bash
PATH=/sbin:/bin:/usr/sbin:/usr/bin
MAILTO=root

# For details see man 4 crontabs

# Example of job definition:
# .---------------- minute (0 - 59)
# |  .------------- hour (0 - 23)
# |  |  .---------- day of month (1 - 31)
# |  |  |  .------- month (1 - 12) OR jan,feb,mar,apr ...
# |  |  |  |  .---- day of week (0 - 6) (Sunday=0 or 7) OR
# |  |  |  |  |           sun,mon,tue,wed,thu,fri,sat
# |  |  |  |  |
# *  *  *  *  * command to be executed

 30 23  *  * 5 apache  /bin/cleanup

[root@server1 ~]# _
```

You can also place a cron table with the same information in the /etc/cron.d directory. Any cron tables found in this directory can have the same format as /etc/crontab and are run by the system. For example, if the sysstat package is installed on your system, the sa1 command is run every 10 minutes as the root user by the cron daemon from the file /etc/cron.d/sysstat, as shown next:

```
[root@server1 ~]# cat /etc/cron.d/sysstat
# Run system activity accounting tool every 10 minutes
*/10 * * * * root /usr/lib/sa/sa1 -S DISK 1 1
# 0 * * * * root /usr/lib/sa/sa1 -S DISK 600 6 &
# Generate a daily summary of process accounting at 23:53
53 23 * * * root /usr/lib/sa/sa2 -A
[root@server1 ~]# _
```

Notice in the preceding output that the second uncommented line (the sa2 command) runs at 11:53 PM as the root user.

Many administrative tasks are performed on an hourly, daily, weekly, or monthy basis. If you have a task of this type, you don't need to create a system cron table. Instead, you can place a shell script that runs the appropriate commands in one of the following directories:

- Scripts that should be executed hourly in the /etc/cron.hourly/ directory
- Scripts that should be executed daily in the /etc/cron.daily/ directory
- Scripts that should be executed weekly in the /etc/cron.weekly/ directory
- Scripts that should be executed monthly in the /etc/cron.monthly/ directory

On Fedora systems, the cron daemon runs the /etc/cron.d/0hourly script, which executes the contents of the /etc/cron.hourly directory 1 minute past the hour, every hour on the hour. The /etc/cron.hourly/0anacron file starts the anacron daemon, which then executes the contents of the /etc/cron.daily/, /etc/cron.weekly/, and /etc/cron.monthy/ directories at the times specified in /etc/anacrontab.

On Ubuntu systems, cron table entries within the /etc/crontab file are used to execute the contents of the /etc/cron.hourly, /etc/cron.daily/, /etc/cron.weekly/, and /etc/cron.monthy/ directories.

Chapter Summary

- Processes are programs that are executing on the system.
- User processes are run in the same terminal as the user who executed them, whereas daemon processes are system processes that do not run on a terminal.
- Every process has a parent process associated with it and, optionally, several child processes.
- Process information is stored in the /proc filesystem. You can use the ps, pstree, and top commands to view this information.
- Zombie and rogue processes that exist for long periods of time use up system resources and should be killed to improve system performance.

- You can send kill signals to a process using the `kill`, `killall`, and `top` commands.
- The BASH shell creates, or forks, a subshell to execute most commands.
- Processes can be run in the background by appending an & to the command name. The BASH shell assigns each background process a background job ID, such that it can be manipulated afterward.
- The priority of a process can be affected indirectly by altering its nice value; nice values range from -20 (high priority) to +19 (low priority). Only the root user can increase the priority of a process.
- You can use the at and cron daemons to schedule commands to run at a later time. The at daemon schedules tasks to occur once at a later time, whereas the cron daemon uses cron tables to schedule tasks to occur repetitively in the future.

Key Terms

/etc/at.allow   A file listing all users who can use the `at` command.

/etc/at.deny   A file listing all users who cannot access the `at` command.

/etc/cron.allow   A file listing all users who can use the `cron` command.

/etc/cron.d   A directory that contains additional system cron tables.

/etc/cron.deny   A file listing all users who cannot access the `cron` command.

/etc/crontab   The default system cron table.

/var/spool/at   A directory that stores the information used to schedule commands using the at daemon on Fedora systems.

/var/spool/cron   A directory that stores user cron tables on a Fedora system.

/var/spool/cron/atjobs   A directory that stores the information used to schedule commands using the at daemon on Ubuntu systems.

/var/spool/cron/crontabs   A directory that stores user cron tables on an Ubuntu system.

at command   The command used to schedule commands and tasks to run at a preset time in the future.

at daemon (atd)   The system daemon that executes tasks at a future time; it is configured with the at command.

background (bg) command   The command used to run a foreground process in the background.

background process   A process that does not require the BASH shell to wait for its termination. Upon execution, the user receives the BASH shell prompt immediately.

child process   A process that was started by another process (parent process).

cron daemon (crond)   The system daemon that executes tasks repetitively in the future and that is configured using cron tables.

cron table   A file specifying tasks to be run by the cron daemon; there are user cron tables and system cron tables.

crontab command   The command used to view and edit user cron tables.

daemon process   A system process that is not associated with a terminal.

foreground (fg) command   The command used to run a background process in the foreground.

foreground process   A process for which the BASH shell that executed it must wait for its termination.

forking   The act of creating a new BASH shell child process from a parent BASH shell process.

jobs command   The command used to see the list of background processes running in the current shell.

kill command   The command used to kill or terminate a process.

kill signal   The type of signal sent to a process by the kill command; different kill signals affect processes in different ways.

killall command   The command that kills all instances of a process by command name.

nice command   The command used to change the priority of a process as it is started.

nice value   The value that indirectly represents the priority of a process; the higher the value, the lower the priority.

parent process   A process that has started other processes (child processes).

parent process ID (PPID)   The PID of the parent process that created the current process.

process   A program currently loaded into physical memory and running on the system.

process ID (PID)   A unique identifier assigned to every process as it begins.

process priority   A number assigned to a process, used to determine how many time slices on the processor that process will receive; the higher the number, the lower the priority.

process state   The current state of the process on the processor; most processes are in the sleeping or running state.

program   A structured set of commands stored in an executable file on a filesystem. A program can be executed to create a process.

ps command   The command used to obtain information about processes currently running on the system.

pstree command   A command that displays processes according to their lineage, starting from the init daemon.

renice command   The command used to alter the nice value of a process currently running on the system.

rogue process   A process that has become faulty in some way and continues to consume far more system resources than it should.

time slice   The amount of time a process is given on a CPU in a multiprocessing operating system.

top command   The command used to give real-time information about the most active processes on the system; it can also be used to renice or kill processes.

trapping   The process of ignoring a kill signal.

user process   A process begun by a user and which runs on a terminal.

zombie process   A process that has finished executing but whose parent has not yet released its PID; the zombie still retains a spot in the kernel's process table.

Review Questions

1. Which command entered without arguments is used to display a list of processes running in the current shell?

   a. ppid

   b. list

   c. pid

   d. ps

2. Which of the following statements is true? (Choose all that apply.)

   a. If /etc/at.allow exists, only users listed in it can use the at command.

   b. If /etc/cron.allow exists, only users listed in it can use the cron command.

   c. If /etc/cron.deny exists and /etc/cron.allow does not exist, any user not listed in /etc/cron.deny can use the cron command.

   d. If /etc/cron.allow and /etc/cron.deny exist, only users listed in the former can use the cron command, and any users listed in the latter are denied access to the cron command.

   e. If a user is listed in both /etc/cron.allow and /etc/cron.deny, then /etc/cron.deny takes precedence and the user cannot access the crontab command.

3. Where are individual user tasks scheduled to run with the cron daemon stored on a Fedora system?

   a. /etc/crontab

   b. /etc/cron/(the user's login name)

   c. /var/spool/cron

   d. /var/spool/cron/(the user's login name)

4. Which process will always have a PID of 1 and a PPID of 0?

   a. the kernel itself

   b. ps

   c. init

   d. top

5. A process spawning or initiating another process is referred to as _____.

   a. a child process

   b. forking

   c. branching

   d. parenting

6. As daemon processes are not associated with terminals, you must use the -e switch with the ps command to view them. True or False?

7. Which of the following commands will most likely increase the chance of a process receiving more time slices?

   a. `renice 0`

   b. `renice 15`

   c. `renice -12`

   d. `renice 19`

8. How can you bypass the wait function and send a user process to the background?

   a. This cannot happen once a process is executing; it can be done only when the command is started by placing an ampersand (&) after it.

   b. This cannot happen; only daemon processes can run in the background.

   c. You can use the `ps` command.

   d. You can use the Ctrl+z key combination and the `bg` command.

9. The `at` command is used to _____.

   a. schedule processes to run periodically in the background

   b. schedule processes to run periodically on a recurring basis in the future

   c. schedule processes to run at a single instance in the future

   d. schedule processes to run in the foreground

10. What command is used to view and modify user jobs scheduled to run with cron?

   a. `crontab`

   b. `cron`

   c. `ps`

   d. `sched`

11. Every process has a process ID and a _____.

   a. fork process

   b. daemon

   c. child process

   d. parent process ID

12. The `killall` command terminates _____.

   a. all instances of a process with the same PPID

   b. all instances of a process with the same PID

   c. all instances of a process with the same priority

   d. all instances of a process with the same name

13. Nice values are used to affect process priorities using a range between _____.

    a. 0 and 20

    b. 0 and –19

    c. –19 and 20

    d. –20 and 19

14. What is the name given to a process not associated with a terminal?

    a. child process

    b. parent process

    c. user process

    d. daemon process

15. To kill a process running in the background, you must place a % character before its process ID. True or False?

16. What kill level signal cannot be trapped?

    a. 1

    b. 9

    c. 3

    d. 15

17. A runaway process that is faulty and consuming mass amounts of system resources _____.

    a. is a zombie process

    b. is an orphaned process

    c. has a PPID of Z

    d. is a rogue process

18. When you run the ps command, how are daemon processes recognized?

    a. The terminal is listed as tty0.

    b. There is a question mark in the TTY column.

    c. There is an asterisk in the STIME column.

    d. There is a "d" for daemon in the terminal identification column.

19. Which command is used to gain real-time information about processes running on the system, with the most processor-intensive processes appearing at the beginning of the list?

    a. ps

    b. ps -elf

    c. top

    d. top -1

20. Which command can be used to see processes running in the background?

    a. bg

    b. jobs

    c. ps -%

    d. fg

Hands-on Projects

These projects should be completed in the order given. The hands-on projects presented in this chapter should take a total of three hours to complete. The requirements for this lab include:

- A computer with Fedora Linux installed according to Hands-on Project 2-1

Project 9-1

In this hands-on project, you view characteristics of processes using the ps command.

1. Boot your Fedora Linux virtual machine. After your Linux system has been loaded, switch to a command-line terminal (tty2) by pressing **Ctrl+Alt+F2** and log in to the terminal using the user name of **root** and the password of **LNXrocks!**.

2. At the command prompt, type **ps –ef | less** and press **Enter** to view the first processes started on the entire Linux system.

3. Fill in the following information from the data displayed on the terminal screen after typing the command:

    a. Which process has a Process ID of 1? (PID = 1) _____

    b. What character do most processes have in the terminal column (tty)? _____

    c. What does this character in the terminal column indicate? _____

    d. Which user started most of these processes? _____

    e. Most processes that are displayed on the screen are started by a certain parent process indicated in the Parent Process ID column (PPID). Which process is the parent to most processes? _____

    Type **q** at the MORE prompt to quit.

4. At the command prompt, type **ps –el | less** and press **Enter** to view the process states for the first processes started on the entire Linux system.

5. Fill in the following information from the data displayed on the terminal screen after typing the command:

    a. What character exists in the State (S) column for most processes, and what does this character indicate? _____

    b. What range of numbers is it possible to have in the Nice (NI) column? _____

   c. Which processes have the number 4 in the Flag (F) column, and what does this number indicate? _____

   Type **q** at the MORE prompt to quit.

6. At the command prompt, type **ps -el | grep Z** and press **Enter** to display zombie processes on your Linux system. Are there any zombie processes indicated in the State (S) column?

7. Type **exit** and press **Enter** to log out of your shell.

Project 9-2

In this hands-on project, you use kill signals to terminate processes on your system.

1. On your Fedora Linux virtual machine, switch to a command-line terminal (tty2) by pressing **Ctrl+Alt+F2** and log in to the terminal using the user name of **root** and the password of **LNXrocks!**.

2. At the command prompt, type **ps -ef | grep bash** and press **Enter** to view the bash shells that are running in memory on your computer. Record the PID of the bash shell running in your terminal (tty2): _____.

3. At the command prompt, type **kill -1** and press **Enter** to list the available kill signals that you can send to a process.

4. At the command prompt, type **kill -2 PID** (where PID is the PID that you recorded in Question 2) and press **Enter**. Did your shell terminate?

5. At the command prompt, type **kill -3 PID** (where PID is the PID that you recorded in Question 2) and press **Enter**. Did your shell terminate?

6. At the command prompt, type **kill -15 PID** (where PID is the PID that you recorded in Question 2) and press **Enter**. Did your shell terminate?

7. At the command prompt, type **kill -9 PID** (where PID is the PID that you recorded in Question 2) and press **Enter**. Did your shell terminate? Why did this command work when the others did not?

Project 9-3

In this hands-on project, you run processes in the background, kill them using the kill and killall commands, and change their priorities using the nice and renice commands.

1. On your Fedora Linux virtual machine, switch to a command-line terminal (tty2) by pressing **Ctrl+Alt+F2** and log in to the terminal using the user name of **root** and the password of **LNXrocks!**.

2. At the command prompt, type **sleep 6000** and press **Enter** to start the sleep command, which waits 6000 seconds in the foreground. Do you get your prompt back after you enter this command? Why? Send the process an INT signal by typing the **Ctrl+c** key combination.

3. At the command prompt, type **sleep 6000&** and press **Enter** to start the sleep command, which waits 6000 seconds in the background. Observe the background Job ID and PID that is returned.

9. When you finish typing, save and quit the vi editor and observe the output on the terminal screen.

10. At the command prompt, type **crontab -l** and press **Enter** to list your cron table. When will the /bin/false command run?

11. At the command prompt, type **cat /var/spool/cron/root** and press **Enter** to list your cron table from the cron directory. Is it the same as the output from the previous command?

12. At the command prompt, type **crontab -r** and press **Enter** to remove your cron table.

13. Type **exit** and press Enter to log out of your shell.

Project 9-6

In this hands-on project, you view information that is exported by the Linux kernel to the /proc directory.

1. On your Fedora Linux virtual machine, switch to a command-line terminal (tty2) by pressing **Ctrl+Alt+F2** and log in to the terminal using the user name of **root** and the password of **LNXrocks!**.

2. At the command prompt, type **cd /proc** and press Enter to change your current directory to /proc. Then type **ls** to list the directory contents and examine the output on the terminal screen. Why are the subdirectories named using numbers?

3. At the command prompt, type **cat meminfo | less** and press Enter to list information about total and available memory. How does the value for total memory (MemTotal) compare to the information from Step 3 in Project 9-4?

4. At the command prompt, type **cat swaps** and press Enter to list information about total and available swap memory. How does the value for total swap memory (Size) compare to the information from Step 3 in Project 9-4?

5. At the command prompt, type **cd 1** and press Enter to enter the subdirectory that contains information about the init daemon (PID = 1).

6. At the command prompt, type **ls** and press Enter to list the files in the /proc/1 directory. Next, type **cat status | less** and press Enter. What is the state of the init daemon? Does it list the correct PID and PPID?

7. Type **exit** and press Enter to log out of your shell.

Discovery Exercises

1. Type the command **sleep 5** at a command prompt and press Enter. When did you receive your shell prompt? Explain the events that occurred by referencing Figure 9-3. Next, type **exec sleep 5** at a command prompt and press Enter. What happened? Can you explain the results using Figure 9-3? Redraw Figure 9-3 to indicate what happens when a command is directly executed.

2. Using the man or info pages, research four more options to the ps command. What processes does each option display? What information is given about each process?

3. Log in to the GNOME desktop on your Fedora 20 system as user1 and open a command-line terminal. At a shell prompt, type **xeyes** to execute the xeyes program. Does the terminal window stay open? Click the terminal window to bring it to the foreground. Do you see your shell prompt? Why? Close your terminal window by clicking the **X** symbol in the upper-right corner. What happened to the xeyes program? Why?

   Next, open another command-line terminal and type **xeyes&** at the command prompt to execute the xeyes program in the background. Click the terminal window to bring it to the foreground. Do you see your shell prompt? Why? Close your terminal window by clicking the **X** symbol in the upper-right corner. What happened to the xeyes program? Why?

   Finally, open another command-line terminal and type **nohup xeyes&** at the command prompt to execute the xeyes program in the background from the nohup command. Click the terminal window to bring it to the foreground and press **Enter**. Do you see your shell prompt? Why? Close your terminal window by clicking the **X** symbol in the upper-right corner. Notice that the xeyes program is still available. Research the nohup manual page and explain why.

4. You are the systems administrator for a large trust company. Most of the Linux servers in the company host databases that are accessed frequently by company employees. One particular Linux server has been reported as being very slow today. Upon further investigation using the top utility, you have found a rogue process that is wasting a great deal of system resources. Unfortunately, the rogue process is a database maintenance program and should be killed with caution. Which kill signal would you send this process and why? If the rogue process traps this signal, which other kill signals would you try? Which command could you use as a last resort to kill the rogue process?

5. Write the lines that you could use in your user cron table to schedule the **/bin/ myscript** command to run:

   a. every Wednesday afternoon at 2:15 PM

   b. every hour on the hour every day of the week

   c. every 15 minutes on the first of every month

   d. only on February 25th at 6:00 PM

   e. on the first Monday of every month at 12:10 PM

6. Time-permitting, perform Project 9-1 through 9-6 on your Ubuntu Server virtual machine. Note any differences between the Fedora and Ubuntu distributions.

9

## chapter 10

Common Administrative Tasks

After completing this chapter, you will be able to:

- Set up, manage, and print to printers on a Linux system
- Understand the purpose of log files and how they are administered
- Create, modify, manage, and delete user and group accounts

In previous chapters, you learned how to administer filesystems, X Windows, system startup, and processes. In this chapter, you examine other essential areas of Linux administration. First, you learn about the print process and how to administer and set up printers, followed by a discussion on managing log files and the logrotate utility. Finally, you examine system databases that store user and group information, and the utilities that can be used to create, modify, and delete user and group accounts on a Linux system.

Printer Administration

Printing work files is commonly required by most users on a Linux system, and printing log files and system configuration information is good procedure in case of a system failure. Thus, a firm understanding of how to set up, manage, and print to printers is vital for those who set up and administer Linux servers.

The Common UNIX Printing System

Today, the most common printing system used on Linux computers is the **Common Unix Printing System (CUPS)**. Fundamental to using CUPS on a Linux system is an understanding of the process by which information is sent to a printer. A set of information that is sent to a printer at the same time is called a **print job**. Print jobs can consist of a file, several files, or the output of a command. To send a print job to a printer, you must first use the **lp command** and specify what to print.

Next, the **CUPS daemon (cupsd)** assigns the print job a unique **print job ID** and places a copy of the print job into a temporary directory on the filesystem called the **print queue**, provided the printer is accepting requests. If the printer is rejecting requests, the CUPS daemon prints an error message stating that the printer is not accepting print jobs.

Accepting print jobs into a print queue is commonly called **spooling** or **queuing**.

The print queue for a printer is typically /var/spool/cups. Regardless of how many printers you have on your Linux system, all print jobs are sent to the same directory.

After a print job is in the print queue, it is ready to be printed. If the printer is enabled and ready to accept the print job, the CUPS daemon then sends the print job from the print queue to the printer and removes the copy of the print job in the print queue. Conversely, if the printer is disabled, the print job remains in the print queue.

Sending print jobs from a print queue to a printer is commonly called printing.

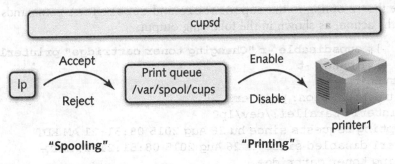

Figure 10-1 The print process

An example of this process for a printer called printer1 is illustrated in Figure 10-1.

To see a list of all printers on the system and their status, you can use the -t (total) option to the **lpstat command,** as shown in the following output:

```
[root@server1 ~]# lpstat -t
scheduler is running
system default destination: printer1
device for printer1: parallel:/dev/lp0
printer1 accepting requests since Thu 26 Aug 2015 08:34:30 AM EDT
printer printer1 is idle. enabled since Thu 26 Aug 2015 08:42:23 AM EDT
[root@server1 ~]# _
```

The preceding output indicates that there is only one printer on the system, called *printer1*, that it prints to a printer connected to the first parallel port on the computer (parallel:/dev/lp0) and that there are no print jobs in its print queue. In addition, the CUPS daemon (scheduler) is running and accepting jobs into the print queue for this printer. Also, the CUPS daemon sends print jobs from the print queue to the printer because the printer is enabled.

You can manipulate the status of a printer using either the **cupsaccept, cupsreject, cupsenable,** or **cupsdisable** command followed by the printer name. Thus, to enable spooling and disable printing for the printer *printer1*, you can use the following commands:

```
[root@server1 ~]# cupsaccept printer1
[root@server1 ~]# cupsdisable printer1
[root@server1 ~]# lpstat -t
scheduler is running
system default destination: printer1
device for printer1: parallel:/dev/lp0
printer1 accepting requests since Thu 26 Aug 2015 08:51:21 AM EDT
printer printer1 disabled since Thu 26 Aug 2015 08:51:21 AM EDT -
        Paused
[root@server1 ~]# _
```

Any print jobs now sent to the printer *printer1* are sent to the print queue but remain in the print queue until the printer is started again.

You can also use the -r option to the cupsdisable and cupsreject commands to specify a reason for the action, as shown in the following output:

```
[root@server1 ~]# cupsdisable -r "Changing toner cartridge" printer1
[root@server1 ~]# lpstat -t
scheduler is running
system default destination: printer1
device for printer1: parallel:/dev/lp0
printer1 accepting requests since hu 26 Aug 2015 08:51:21 AM EDT
printer printer1 disabled since hu 26 Aug 2015 08:51:21 AM EDT -
        Changing toner cartridge
[root@server1 ~]# _
```

Managing Print Jobs

Recall that you create a print job by using the lp command. To print a copy of the /etc/inittab file to the printer *printer1* shown in earlier examples, you can use the following command, which returns a print job ID that you can use to manipulate the print job afterward:

```
[root@server1 ~]# lp -d printer1 /etc/inittab
request id is printer1-1 (1 file(s))
[root@server1 ~]# _
```

The lp command uses the -d option to specify the destination printer name. If this option is omitted, the lp command assumes the default printer on the system. Because *printer1* is the only printer on the system and, hence, is the default printer, the command lp /etc/inittab is equivalent to the one used in the preceding output.

You can set the default printer for all users on your system by using the lpoptions -d printername command, where printername is the name of the default printer. This information is stored in the /etc/cups/lpoptions file.

Alternatively, each user on a Linux system can specify his own default printer by adding the line default printername to the .lpoptions file in her home directory, where printername is the name of the default printer. Alternatively, you can use the PRINTER or LPDEST variables to set the default printer. For example, to specify printer2 as the default printer, you can add either the line export PRINTER=printer2 or the line export LPDEST=printer2 to an environment file in your home directory, such as .bash_profile.

Table 10-1 lists some common options to the lp command.

You can also specify several files to be printed using a single lp command by specifying the files as arguments. In this case, only one print job is created to print all of the files. To print the files /etc/hosts and /etc/issue to the printer *printer1*, you can execute the following command:

```
[root@server1 ~]# lp -d printer1 /etc/hosts /etc/issue
request id is printer1-2 (2 file(s))
[root@server1 ~]# _
```

Option	Description
-d printername	Specifies the name of printer to send the print job.
-i print job ID	Specifies a certain print job ID to modify.
-n number	Prints a certain *number* of copies.
-m	Mails you confirmation of print job completion.
-o option	Specifies certain printing options. Common printing options include the following: cpi=number—Sets the characters per inch to *number*. landscape—Prints in landscape orientation. number-up=number—Prints *number* pages on a single page, where *number* is 1, 2, or 4. sides=string—Sets double-sided printing, where *string* is either 'two-sided-short-edge' or 'two-sided-long-edge'.
-q priority	Specifies a print job priority from 1 (low priority) to 100 (high priority). By default, all print jobs have a priority of 50.

Table 10-1 Common options to the lp command

The lp command accepts information from Standard Input; thus, you can place the lp command at the end of a pipe to print information. To print a list of logged-in users, you can use the following pipe:

```
[root@server1 ~]# who | lp -d printer1
request id is printer1-3 (1 file(s))
[root@server1 ~]# _
```

To see a list of print jobs in the queue for *printer1*, you can use the lpstat command. Without arguments, this command displays all jobs in the print queue that you have printed:

```
[root@server1 ~]# lpstat
printer1-1     root     2048   Thu 26 Aug 2015 08:54:18 AM EDT
printer1-2     root     3072   Thu 26 Aug 2015 08:54:33 AM EDT
printer1-3     root     1024   Thu 26 Aug 2015 08:54:49 AM EDT
[root@server1 ~]# _
```

Table 10-2 lists other options that you can use with the lpstat command.

Option	Description
-a	Displays a list of printers that are accepting print jobs
-d	Displays the default destination printer
-o printername	Displays the print jobs in the print queue for printername only
-p	Displays a list of printers that are enabled
-r	Shows whether the CUPS daemon (scheduler) is running
-t	Shows all information about printers and their print jobs

Table 10-2 Common options to the lpstat command

To remove a print job that is in the print queue, you can use the **cancel command** followed by the print job IDs of the jobs to remove. To remove the print job IDs printer1-1 and printer1-2 created earlier, you can use the following command:

```
[root@server1 ~]# cancel printer1-1 printer1-2
[root@server1 ~]# lpstat
printer1-3     root    3072  Thu 26 Aug 2015 08:54:49 AM EDT
[root@server1 ~]# _
```

You can instead remove all jobs started by a certain user; simply specify the –u option to the cancel command followed by the user name. To remove all jobs in a print queue, you can use the –a option to the cancel command, as shown in the following example, which removes all jobs destined for printer1:

```
[root@server1 ~]# cancel –a printer1
[root@server1 ~]# lpstat
[root@server1 ~]# _
```

Not all users might be allowed access to a certain printer. As a result, you can restrict access to certain printers by using the **lpadmin** command. For example, to deny all users other than root and user1 from printing to the *printer1* printer created earlier, you can use the following command:

```
[root@server1 ~]# lpadmin –u allow:root,user1 –u deny:all –d printer1
[root@server1 ~]# _
```

The LPD Printing System

Although CUPS is the preferred printing system for Linux computers today, many older Linux computers use the traditional **Line Printer Daemon (LPD)** printing system. In this printing system, the **lpr command** is used to print documents to the print queue much like the lp command; the **lpc command** can be used to view the status of printers; the **lpq command** can be used to view print jobs in the print queue, much like the lpstat command; and the **lprm command** can be used to remove print jobs, much like the cancel command.

For those who are used to using the LPD printing system, CUPS contains versions of the lpr, lpc, lpq, and lprm commands. The following output displays the status of all printers on the system, prints two copies of /etc/inittab to *printer1*, views the print job in the queue, and removes the print job:

```
[root@server1 ~]# lpc status
printer1:
        printing is enabled
        queuing is enabled
        no entries
        daemon present
[root@server1 ~]# lpr -#2 -P printer1 /etc/inittab
[root@server1 ~]# lpq
printer1 is ready and printing
Rank    Owner    Job    File(s)    Total Size
1st     root     1      inittab    2048 bytes
[root@server1 ~]# lprm 1
```

```
[root@server1 ~]# lpq
printer1 is ready
no entries
[root@server1 ~]# _
```

Configuring Printers

Recall that the core component of printing is the CUPS daemon, which accepts print jobs into a queue and sends them to the printer. The file that contains settings for the CUPS daemon is **/etc/cups/cupsd.conf**, and the file that contains the configuration information for each printer installed on the system is **/etc/cups/printers.conf**. By default, the CUPS daemon detects locally connected and network-shared printers and automatically adds an entry for them in the /etc/cups/printers.conf file using a name based on the printer model number (e.g., HP Laserjet 6M). For any printers that the CUPS daemon does not detect and configure, you must provide the necessary information.

Since the format of the /etc/cups/printers.conf file is rigid, it is safer to use a program to create or modify entries within them. You can provide a series of options to the `lpadmin` command discussed earlier to configure a printer on the system, or you can use one of several graphical utilities within a desktop environment that can do the same. On Fedora 20 systems, the **Printers tool** within the GNOME desktop (shown in Figure 10-2) can be used to create new printers, print a test page, view print jobs, control spooling, and specify basic printing options. You can access the Printers tool within the GNOME desktop environment on Fedora 20 by navigating to the Activities menu, Show Applications, Settings, Printers.

To manually add a printer within the Printers tool, you can click the + symbol in the lower-left corner. The Printers tool then prompts you to select your device from a list of detected printers, or specify the name or IP address of a printer on the network.

The Printers tool provides for a quick and easy method of configuring printers on a system. It does not allow you to specify detailed printer configuration when adding a printer.

The most comprehensive way to create and manage CUPS printers is by using the **CUPS Web administration tool**, which gives Linux administrators the ability to create and manage all

10

![The Printers tool showing printer1 Ready, Location —, Model Local Raw Printer, IP Address localhost, Supply Level, Jobs 1 active, Default, with Print Test Page and Options buttons]

Figure 10-2 The Printers tool

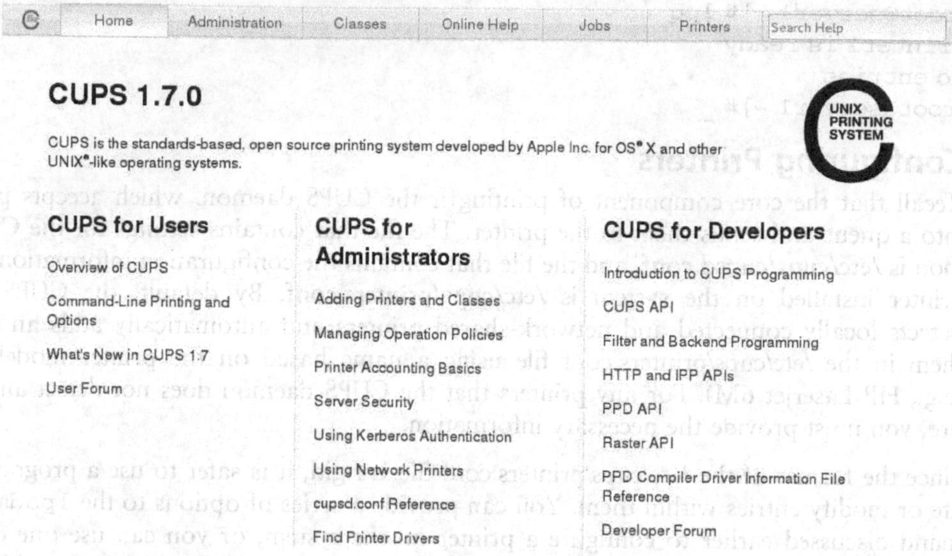

Figure 10-3 The CUPS Web administration tool

printer settings. You can access the CUPS Web administration tool using a Web browser on TCP port 631 by navigating to http://servername:631, as shown in Figure 10-3.

To create a new printer using this tool, select the Administration tab, click Add Printer, and log in using the root username and password. You will then be prompted to choose the type of printer, as shown in Figure 10-4. You can choose to print to a printer that is connected to a local serial, parallel, or USB port, to a printer connected to the network using Hewlett-Packard JetDirect technology, or to a printer that is shared on a remote computer across a network with the **Internet Printing Protocol (IPP)**, the Line Printer Daemon (LPD), or the Windows (SAMBA) printing service.

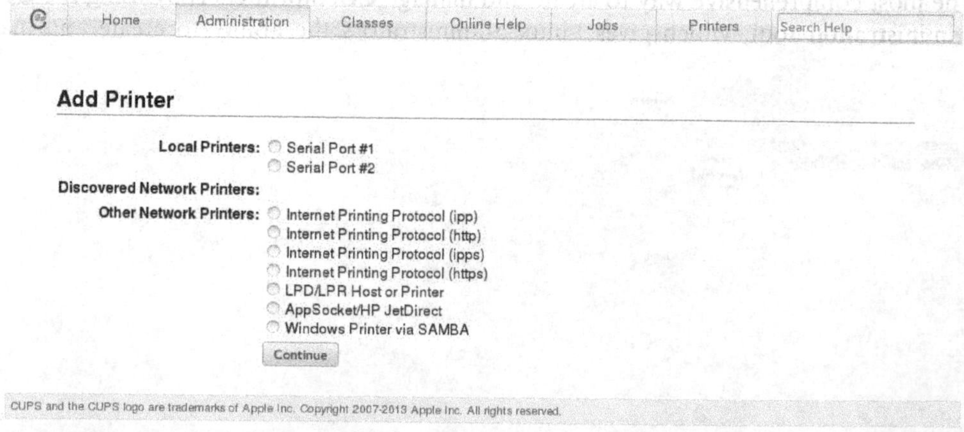

Figure 10-4 Selecting the printer type for a new printer

The ports available in the Local Printers section of Figure 10-4 reflect the local ports that are available on your system. The system shown in Figure 10-4 only contains two local serial ports.

After selecting a printer type, you will be presented with several screens that prompt you to specify information that relates to the printer type (e.g., the network address for an network printer), as well as a printer name, description, manufacturer and model, default printer options, and whether to share the printer using IPP to other systems on the network.

After creating a printer, you can use the other options available on the Administration tab of the CUPS Web administration tool to configure and manage the CUPS printing service, as shown in Figure 10-5.

The Find New Printers button shown in Figure 10-5 performs a detailed local and network search for new printer devices, and the Manage Printers button (which switches to the Printers tab) allows you to configure individual printer settings.

CUPS also allows you to configure collections of printers that can be used as a single unit. These collections are called **printer classes**. When you print to a printer class, the print job is sent to the first available printer in the printer class. Printer classes are often used in larger organizations, where multiple printers are stored in a print room for users to print to. To create a printer class, select the Add Class button shown in Figure 10-5 and supply a name and description for the new class as well as choose the printers that should be included in the class. Following this, you can click the Manage Classes button (which switches to the Classes tab) to configure settings for your new printer class.

Clicking Manage Jobs in Figure 10-5 (which switches to the Jobs tab) allows you to view, modify, and delete print jobs that have submitted to the queue. Regular users can also access the CUPS Web administration tool and select the Jobs tab to manage their own jobs after logging in with their username and password.

Figure 10-5 CUPS administration options

The Server section shown in Figure 10-5 allows you to edit the CUPS configuration file and access log files as well as perform advanced functions. Selecting the Allow remote administration option allows the CUPS Web administration tool to be accessed from other computers on the network. By selecting the Share printers connected to this system and Allow printing from the Internet options, IPP printer sharing will be enabled for all printers that allow IPP printer sharing in their settings. To configure a shared printer on a remote system using IPP, you can specify the URL *http://servername:631/printers/printername* when adding the printer.

To allow for IPP printer sharing, any firewalls must allow TCP port 80, 443, and 631. Firewall configuration is discussed in Chapter 14.

Log File Administration

To identify and troubleshoot problems on a Linux system, you must view the events that occur over time. Because administrators cannot observe all events that take place on a Linux system, most daemons record information and error messages to files stored on the filesystem. These files are referred to as **log files** and are typically stored in the **/var/log** directory. Many programs store their log files in subdirectories of the /var/log directory. For example, the /var/log/samba directory contains the log files created by the samba file-sharing daemons. Table 10-3 lists some common log files that you may find in the /var/log directory, depending on your Linux distribution.

Log File	Contents
boot.log	Basic information regarding daemon startup obtained during system initialization
cron	Information and error messages generated by the cron and at daemons
dmesg	Detected hardware information obtained during system startup
mail.log	Information and error messages generated by the sendmail or postfix daemon
secure	Information and error messages regarding network access generated by daemons such as sshd and xinetd
wtmp	A history of all login sessions
rpmpkgs	A list of packages installed by the Red Hat Package Manager and related error messages
dpkg.log	A list of packages installed by the Debian Package Manager and related error messages
xferlog	Information and error messages generated by the FTP daemon
Xorg.0.log XFree86	Information and error messages generated by X Windows
lastlog	A list of users and their last login time; must be viewed using the `lastlog` command
messages syslog	Detailed information regarding daemon startup obtained at system initialization as well as important system messages produced after system initialization

Table 10-3 Common Linux log files found in /var/log

Daemons that provide a service to other computers on the network typically manage their own log files within the /var/log directory. The logging for other daemons and operating system components is performed by a logging daemon. The two most common logging daemons used on Linux systems today are the **System Log Daemon (rsyslogd)** and the **Systemd Journal Daemon (journald)**.

Working with the System Log Daemon

The System Log Daemon (rsyslogd) is the traditional and most common logging daemon used on Linux systems. When this daemon is loaded upon system startup, it creates a socket (/dev/log) for other system processes to write to. It then reads any information written to this socket and saves the information in the appropriate log file according to entries in the /etc/rsyslog.conf file and any files within the /etc/rsyslog.d directory. A sample /etc/rsyslog.conf file is shown in the following output:

```
[root@server1 ~]# cat /etc/rsyslog.conf
#### MODULES ####

$ModLoad imuxsock.so    # provides support for local system logging
(e.g. via logger command)
$ModLoad imklog.so      # provides kernel logging support (previously done
by rklogd)
#$ModLoad immark.so     # provides --MARK-- message capability

# Provides UDP syslog reception
#$ModLoad imudp
#$UDPServerRun 514

# Provides TCP syslog reception
#$ModLoad imtcp
#$InputTCPServerRun 514

#### RULES ####
# Log all kernel messages to the console.
# Logging much else clutters up the screen.
#kern.*                                                 /dev/console

# Log anything (except mail) of level info or higher.
# Don't log private authentication messages!
*.info;mail.none;news.none;authpriv.none;cron.none    /var/log/messages

# The authpriv file has restricted access.
authpriv.*                                             /var/log/secure

# Log all the mail messages in one place.
mail.*                                                 -/var/log/maillog

# Log cron stuff
cron.*                                                 /var/log/cron
```

```
# Everybody gets emergency messages
*.emerg                                              *

# Save news errors of level crit and higher in a special file.
uucp,news.crit                              /var/log/spooler

# Save boot messages also to boot.log
local7.*                                    /var/log/boot.log
# INN
news.=crit                                  /var/log/news/news.crit
news.=err                                   /var/log/news/news.err
news.notice                                 /var/log/news/news.notice
news.=debug                                 /var/log/news/news.debug
[root@server1 ~]# _
```

 On legacy Linux systems, the System Log Daemon is represented by syslogd and configured using the /etc/syslog.conf file.

Lines in the /etc/rsyslog.conf file or in files within the /etc/rsyslog.d directory that start with a # character are comments. All other entries have the following format:

```
facility.priority     /var/log/logfile
```

The **facility** is the area of the system to listen to, whereas the **priority** refers to the importance of the information. For example, a facility of kern and priority of warning indicates that the System Log Daemon should listen for kernel messages of priority warning and more serious. When found, the System Log Daemon places these messages in the /var/log/logfile file. The aforementioned entry would read:

```
kern.warning     /var/log/logfile
```

To only log warning messages from the kernel to /var/log/logfile, you can use the following entry instead:

```
kern.=warning     /var/log/logfile
```

Alternatively, you can log all error messages from the kernel to /var/log/logfile by using the * wildcard, as shown in the following entry:

```
kern.*     /var/log/logfile
```

In addition, you can specify multiple facilities and priorities; to log all error messages except warnings from the kernel to /var/log/logfile, you can use the following entry:

```
kern.*;kern.!=warn     /var/log/logfile
```

To log all error messages from the kernel and news daemons, you can use the following entry:

```
kern,news.*     /var/log/logfile
```

To log all warnings from all facilities except for the kernel, you can use the "none" keyword, as shown in following entry:

```
*.=warn;kern.none    /var/log/logfile
```

You can also prefix the pathname to the log file in any entry to ensure that the system synchronizes changes to the disk immediately after a new event occurs, as shown in the following entry:

```
*.=warn;kern.none    -/var/log/logfile
```

Table 10-4 describes the different facilities available and their descriptions.

Table 10-5 displays the different priorities available listed in ascending order.

The /etc/rsyslog.conf file may also send logging information to another computer using the format `facility.priority@hostname:portnumber`; however the remote computer must have the modules that listen on either the TCP or UDP protocol uncommented in the /etc/rsyslog.conf file. For example, by uncommenting the same lines shown next in the /etc/rsyslog.conf file, you allow your system to accept incoming requests from another System Log Daemon on TCP and UDP port 514 (the default System Log Daemon port):

```
# Provides UDP syslog reception
$ModLoad imudp
$UDPServerRun 514
```

Facility	Description
auth or security	Specifies messages from the login system, such as the login program, the getty program, and the su command
authpriv	Specifies messages from the login system when authenticating users across the network or to system databases
cron	Specifies messages from the cron and at daemons
daemon	Specifies messages from system daemons such as the FTP daemon
kern	Specifies messages from the Linux kernel
lpr	Specifies messages from the printing system (lpd)
mail	Specifies messages from the e-mail system (sendmail)
mark	Specifies time stamps used by syslogd; used internally only
news	Specifies messages from the Inter Network News daemon and other USENET daemons
syslog	Specifies messages from the syslog daemon
user	Specifies messages from user processes
uucp	Specifies messages from the uucp (UNIX to UNIX copy) daemon
local0-7	Specifies local messages; these are not used by default but can be defined for custom use

Table 10-4   **Facilities used by the System Log Daemon**

10

Priority	Description
debug	Indicates all information from a certain facility
info	Indicates normal information messages as a result of system operations
notice	Indicates information that should be noted for future reference, yet does not indicate a problem
warning or warn	Indicates messages that might be the result of an error but are not critical to system operations
error or err	Indicates all other error messages not described by other priorities
crit	Indicates system critical errors such as hard disk failure
alert	Indicates an error that should be rectified immediately, such as a corrupt system database
emerg or panic	Indicates very serious system conditions that would normally be broadcast to all users

Table 10-5 Priorities used by the System Log Daemon

```
# Provides TCP syslog reception
$ModLoad imtcp
$InputTCPServerRun 514
```

Working with the Systemd Journal Daemon

The Systemd Journal Daemon (journald) replaces the System Log Daemon on Linux distributions that use Systemd, such as Fedora 20. As with the System Log Daemon, journald creates a socket (/dev/log) for other system processes to write to and reads any information that is written to this socket. However, the events logged are not controlled by specific rules. Instead, journald logs all information to a database under the /var/log/journal directory structure, and events are tagged with labels that identify the same facility and priority information that we examined earlier with the rsyslogd daemon.

You can configure daemon settings for journald, including the ability to forward events to the System Log Daemon, by editing its configuration file, **/etc/systemd/journald.conf**.

To view events within the journald database, you can use the same `journalctl` command that we introduced in Chapter 6 to view boot-related messages. If you type `journalctl` at a command prompt and press the Tab key, you will see a list of areas and criteria that can be queried, as shown here:

```
[root@server1 ~]# journalctl
_AUDIT_LOGINUID=        __MONOTONIC_TIMESTAMP=
_AUDIT_SESSION=         _PID=
_BOOT_ID=               PRIORITY=
```

```
_CMDLINE=                    __REALTIME_TIMESTAMP=
CODE_FILE=                   _SELINUX_CONTEXT=
CODE_FUNC=                   _SOURCE_REALTIME_TIMESTAMP=
CODE_LINE=                   SYSLOG_FACILITY=
_COMM=                       SYSLOG_IDENTIFIER=
COREDUMP_EXE=                SYSLOG_PID=
__CURSOR=                    _SYSTEMD_CGROUP=
ERRNO=                       _SYSTEMD_OWNER_UID=
_EXE=                        _SYSTEMD_SESSION=
_GID=                        _SYSTEMD_UNIT=
_HOSTNAME=                   _TRANSPORT=
_KERNEL_DEVICE=              _UDEV_DEVLINK=
_KERNEL_SUBSYSTEM=           _UDEV_DEVNODE=
_MACHINE_ID=                 _UDEV_SYSNAME=
MESSAGE=                     _UID=
MESSAGE_ID=
```

Say, for example, that you wish to search for information in the logs from a particular command on the system. You can type journalctl _COMM= and press the Tab key to see the available commands that perform logging via journald on the system, as shown here:

```
[root@server1 ~]# journalctl _COMM=
abrtd             dnsmasq            mtp-probe         sh         tgtd
anacron           gnome-keyring-d    network           smartd     udisksd
avahi-daemon      hddtemp            polkit-agent-he   smbd       umount
bash              journal2gelf       polkitd           sshd       userhelper
blueman-mechani   kdumpctl           pulseaudio        sssd_be    yum
chronyd           krb5_child         qemu-system-x86   su
colord            libvirtd           sealert           sudo
crond             logger             sendmail          systemd
dbus-daemon       mcelog             setroubleshootd   systemd-journal
```

To see the logs from the cron daemon (crond), you can run the command journalctl _COMM=crond | less since there will likely be many lines of output. However, when troubleshooting an issue regarding the cron daemon, it is more useful to narrow down the time period. The following command displays crond log entries from 1:00 p.m. (13:00) until 2:00 p.m. (14:00) from the current day:

```
[root@server1 ~]# journalctl _COMM=crond --since "13:00" --until "14:00"
-- Logs begin at Tue 2015-09-16 21:56:29 EDT, end at Tue 2015-10-14 20:43:32
EDT
Oct 14 13:50:58 server1 crond[457]: (CRON) INFO (RANDOM_DELAY will be
scaled with factor 30% if used.)
Oct 14 13:50:59 server1 crond[457]: (CRON) INFO (running with inotify sup-
port)
[root@server1 ~]# _
```

The time format used within the journalctl command follows the standard YYYY-MM-DD HH-MM-SS. Thus, to obtain crond events since 5:30 pm (17:30) on August 22,

2015, you could instead run the `journalctl _COMM=crond --since "2015-08-22 17:30:00"` command.

You can also query events related to a specific process or daemon if you specify the path name to the executable file or PID. For example, since the Systemd init daemon has a path of /usr/lib/systemd/systemd and a PID of 1, you could run the `journalctl /usr/lib/systemd/systemd` command or the `journalctl _PID=1` command to view events related to the Systemd init daemon.

Managing Log Files and the journald Database

Although log files and the journald database contain important system information, they might take up unnecessary space on the filesystem over time. On systems that use Systemd, you can limit the size of the journald database by uncommenting and configuring the System-MaxUse line in /etc/systemd/journald.conf. For example, SystemMaxUse=75M would limit the database to 75MB, and the oldest events would be deleted as new events are logged. To prevent key older events from being overwritten, you can create a shell script that executes the appropriate `journalctl` commands and either prints the results or saves them to a text file. You can then configure the cron daemon to execute this shell script periodically, as discussed in Chapter 9.

For log files within the /var/log directory, you can periodically clear their contents to reclaim space on the filesystem.

Do not remove log files, because the permissions and ownership will be removed as well.

Before clearing important log files, it is good form to save them to a different location or print their contents for future reference.

To clear a log file, recall that you can use a > redirection symbol. The following commands display the size of the /var/log/wtmp log file before and after it has been printed and cleared:

```
[root@server1 ~]# ls -l /var/log/wtmp
-rw-------  1 root    utmp   21705 Aug 27 10:52 /var/log/wtmp
[root@server1 ~]# lp -d printer1 /var/log/wtmp
[root@server1 ~]# >/var/log/wtmp
[root@server1 ~]# ls -l /var/log/wtmp
-rw-------  1 root    utmp       0 Aug 27 10:52 /var/log/wtmp
[root@server1 ~]# _
```

Alternatively, you can schedule the **logrotate command** to back up and clear log files from entries stored in the **/etc/logrotate.conf** file and files stored in the /etc/logrotate.d directory. The `logrotate` command typically renames (or rotates) log files on a cyclic basis; the log file will be renamed to contain a numeric or date extension, and a new log file will be created to accept system information. You can specify the type of extension as well as the number of log files that logrotate keeps. If logrotate is configured to keep only two copies of old log files, then after two log rotations, the oldest log file will automatically be removed.

An example of the /etc/logrotate.conf file is shown in the following output:

```
[root@server1 ~]# cat /etc/logrotate.conf
# see "man logrotate" for details
# rotate log files weekly
weekly

# keep 4 weeks worth of backlogs
rotate 4

# create new (empty) log files after rotating old ones
create

# use date as a suffix of the rotated file
dateext

# uncomment this if you want your log files compressed
#compress

# RPM packages drop log rotation information into this directory
include /etc/logrotate.d

# no packages own wtmp and btmp -- we'll rotate them here
/var/log/wtmp {
    monthly
    create 0664 root utmp
    minsize 1M
    rotate 1
}

/var/log/btmp {
    missingok
    monthly
    create 0600 root utmp
    rotate 1
}

[root@server1 ~]# _
```

In the preceding output, any # characters indicate a comment and are ignored. The other lines indicate that log files contained in this file and all other files in the /etc/logrotate.d directory (include /etc/logrotate.d) are rotated on a weekly basis unless otherwise specified (weekly) using a date extension (dateext), and up to 4 weeks of log files will be kept (rotate 4).

The bottom of the /etc/logrotate.conf file has two entries that override these values. For the file /var/log/wtmp, this rotation occurs monthly instead of weekly, only if the size of the log file is greater than 1MB. Only one old log file is kept, and the new log file created has the permissions 0664 (rw-rw-r--), the owner root, and the group utmp. For the file /var/log/btmp, this rotation occurs monthly instead of weekly, and no errors are reported if the log file is missing. Only one old log file is kept, and the new log file created has the permissions 0600 (rw-------), the owner root, and the group utmp.

Most rotation information within /etc/logrotate.conf is overridden from files stored in the /etc/logrotate.d directory. Take the file /etc/logrotate.d/psacct as an example:

```
[root@server1 ~]# cat /etc/logrotate.d/psacct
# Logrotate file for psacct RPM

/var/account/pacct {
    compress
    delaycompress
    notifempty
    daily
    rotate 31
    create 0600 root root
    postrotate
      if /etc/init.d/psacct status >/dev/null 2>&1; then
        /usr/sbin/accton /var/account/pacct
      fi
    endscript
}
[root@server1 ~]# _
```

This file indicates that the /var/account/pacct file should be rotated daily if it is not empty, and that new log files will be owned by the root user/group and have the permissions 0600 (rw-------). Up to 31 old log files will be kept and compressed, but only on the next rotation (delaycompress). In addition, the /usr/sbin/accton /var/account/pacct command is run after each rotation if the /etc/init.d/psacct status command returns true.

On most Linux systems, the logrotate utility is automatically scheduled to run daily via the file /etc/cron.daily/logrotate; however, you might choose to run it manually by typing the command logrotate /etc/logrotate.conf at a command prompt.

Over time, the logrotate command generates several copies of each log file, as shown in the following listing of the /var/log directory:

```
[root@server1 ~]# ls /var/log
anaconda.log              dmesg              ppp
anaconda.program.log      dmesg.old          prelink
anaconda.storage.log      gdm                sa
anaconda.syslog           httpd              samba
anaconda.xlog             jetty              sa-update.log
anaconda.yum.log          lastlog            secure
audit                     mail               secure-20150808
BackupPC                  maillog            secure-20150818
bittorrent                maillog-20150808   secure-20150823
boot.log                  maillog-20150818   setroubleshoot
```

```
boot.log-20150808      maillog-20150823      speech-dispatcher
boot.log-20150818      messages              spooler
boot.log-20150823      messages-20150808     spooler-20150808
btmp                   messages-20150818     spooler-20150818
ConsoleKit             messages-20150823     spooler-20150823
cron                   mysqld.log            squid
cron-20150808          news                  sssd
cron-20150818          ntpstats              tallylog
cron-20150823          pm-powersave.log      wtmp
cups                   pm-suspend.log        Xorg.0.log
[root@server1 ~]# _
```

Given the preceding output, the most recent events for the cron daemon are recorded in the cron.log file, followed by the cron-20150823 file, followed by the cron-20150818 file and the cron-20150808 file.

Administering Users and Groups

You must log in to a Linux system with a valid user name and password before a BASH shell is granted. This process is called **authentication** because the user name and password are authenticated against a system database that contains all **user account** information. Authenticated users are then granted access to files, directories, and other resources on the system based on their user account.

The system database that contains user account information typically consists of two files: **/etc/passwd** and **/etc/shadow**. Every user typically has a line that describes the user account in /etc/passwd and a line that contains the encrypted password and expiration information in /etc/shadow.

Older Linux systems stored the encrypted password in the /etc/passwd file and did not use an /etc/shadow file at all. This is considered poor security today because processes often require access to the user information in /etc/passwd. Storing the encrypted password in a separate file that cannot be accessed by processes prevents a process from obtaining all user account information. By default, Fedora 13 configures passwords using an /etc/shadow file. However, you can use the **pwunconv command** to revert to using an /etc/passwd file only. Also, you can use the **pwconv command** to configure the system again using an /etc/shadow file for password storage.

Each line of the /etc/passwd file has the following colon-delimited format:

```
name:password:UID:GID:GECOS:homedirectory:shell
```

The name in the preceding output refers to the name of the user. If an /etc/shadow is not used, the password field contains the encrypted password for the user; otherwise, it just contains an x character as a placeholder for the password stored in /etc/shadow.

The **User Identifier (UID)** specifies the unique User ID that is assigned to each user. Typically, UIDs that are less than 500 refer to user accounts that are used by daemons when logging in to the system. The root user always has a UID of zero.

The **Group Identifier (GID)** is the primary Group ID for the user. Each user can be a member of several groups, but only one of those groups can be the primary group. The **primary group** of a

10

user is the group that is made the group owner of any file or directory that the user creates. Similarly, when a user creates a file or directory, that user becomes the owner of that file or directory.

GECOS represents a text description of the user and is typically left blank; this information was originally used in the **General Electric Comprehensive Operating System (GECOS)**. The last two fields represent the absolute pathname to the user's home directory and the shell, respectively.

An example of an **/etc/passwd** file is shown next:

```
[root@server1 ~]# cat /etc/passwd
root:x:0:0:root:/root:/bin/bash
bin:x:1:1:bin:/bin:/sbin/nologin
daemon:x:2:2:daemon:/sbin:/sbin/nologin
adm:x:3:4:adm:/var/adm:/sbin/nologin
lp:x:4:7:lp:/var/spool/lpd:/sbin/nologin
sync:x:5:0:sync:/sbin:/bin/sync
shutdown:x:6:0:shutdown:/sbin:/sbin/shutdown
halt:x:7:0:halt:/sbin:/sbin/halt
mail:x:8:12:mail:/var/spool/mail:/sbin/nologin
uucp:x:10:14:uucp:/var/spool/uucp:/sbin/nologin
operator:x:11:0:operator:/root:/sbin/nologin
games:x:12:100:games:/usr/games:/sbin/nologin
gopher:x:13:30:gopher:/var/gopher:/sbin/nologin
ftp:x:14:50:FTP User:/var/ftp:/sbin/nologin
nobody:x:99:99:Nobody:/:/sbin/nologin
dbus:x:81:81:System message bus:/:/sbin/nologin
usbmuxd:x:113:113:usbmuxd user:/:/sbin/nologin
avahi-autoipd:x:499:499:avahi-autoipd:/var/lib/avahi-autoipd:/sbin/nologin
rpc:x:32:32:Rpcbind Daemon:/var/lib/rpcbind:/sbin/nologin
rpcuser:x:29:496:RPC Service User:/var/lib/nfs:/sbin/nologin
nfsnobody:x:65534:65534:Anonymous NFS User:/var/lib/nfs:/sbin/nologin
named:x:25:25:Named:/var/named:/sbin/nologin
apache:x:48:486:Apache:/var/www:/sbin/nologin
gdm:x:42:468::/var/lib/gdm:/sbin/nologin
hsqldb:x:96:96::/var/lib/hsqldb:/sbin/nologin
jetty:x:487:467::/usr/share/jetty:/bin/sh
user1:x:1000:1000:sample user one:/home/user1:/bin/bash
[root@server1 ~]# _
```

The root user is usually listed at the top of the /etc/passwd file, as just shown, followed by user accounts used by daemons when logging in to the system, followed by regular user accounts. The final line of the preceding output indicates that the user user1 has a UID of 1000, a primary GID of 1000, a GECOS of "sample user one," the home directory /home/user1, and uses the BASH shell.

Like /etc/passwd, the /etc/shadow file is colon-delimited yet has the following format:

```
name:password:lastchange:min:max:warn:disable1:disable2:
```

Although the first two fields in the /etc/shadow file are the same as those in /etc/passwd, the contents of the password field are different; the password field in the /etc/shadow file contains the encrypted password, whereas the password field in /etc/passwd contains an x character because it is not used.

The lastchange field represents the date of the most recent password change; it is measured in the number of days since January 1, 1970. For example, the number 10957 represents January 1, 2000, because January 1, 2000, is 10957 days after January 1, 1970.

Traditionally, a calendar date was represented by a number indicating the number of days since January 1, 1970. Many calendar dates found in configuration files follow the same convention.

To prevent unauthorized access to a Linux system, it is good form to change passwords for user accounts regularly. To ensure that passwords are changed, you can can set them to expire at certain intervals. The next three fields of the /etc/shadow file indicate information about password expiration: min represents the number of days a user must wait before he changes his password after receiving a new one, max represents the number of days a user can use the same password without changing it, and warn represents the number of days before a password would expire that a user is warned to change his password.

By default on Red Hat Fedora Linux systems, min is equal to zero days, max is equal to 99999 days, and warn is equal to seven days. This means you can change your password immediately after receiving a new one, your password expires in 99999 days, and you are warned seven days before your password needs to be changed.

When a password has expired, the user is still allowed to log in to the system for a certain period of time, after which point the user is disabled from logging in. The number of days after a password expires that a user account is disabled is represented by the disable1 field in /etc/shadow. In addition, you can choose to disable a user from logging in at a certain date, such as the end of an employment contract. The disable2 field in /etc/shadow represents the number of days since January 1, 1970 that a user account will be disabled.

An example /etc/shadow file is shown next:

```
[root@server1 ~]# cat /etc/shadow
root:$6$vIoletCT$E5zaz6q.5UTH/SriWiFlh9.OgHMFvSH3R515uyxyj9p-
jezZb8mWG8pKpIwvfUatNzCw3tiaXU1bqDYQeeBTK2.:14841:0:99999:7:::
bin:*:14715:0:99999:7:::
daemon:*:14715:0:99999:7:::
adm:*:14715:0:99999:7:::
lp:*:14715:0:99999:7:::
sync:*:14715:0:99999:7:::
shutdown:*:14715:0:99999:7:::
halt:*:14715:0:99999:7:::
mail:*:14715:0:99999:7:::
uucp:*:14715:0:99999:7:::
operator:*:14715:0:99999:7:::
games:*:14715:0:99999:7:::
gopher:*:14715:0:99999:7:::
ftp:*:14715:0:99999:7:::
nobody:*:14715:0:99999:7:::
```

```
dbus:!!:14823:::::
usbmuxd:!!:14823:::::
avahi-autoipd:!!:14823::::::
rpc:!!:14823:0:99999:7:::
rpcuser:!!:14823:::::
nfsnobody:!!:14823:::::
named:!!:14823:::::
apache:!!:14823:::::
gdm:!!:14823:::::
hsqldb:!!:14823:::::
jetty:!!:14823:::::
user1:$6$PVyl5FBX$nK5DvuCfTaFX0U3.h38n.doqSc824YzuINXdBjQ/
nEUREPQlpqrZ3qxPg3eWlS84fYtJoDPvDUdumcT.dNIWF1:16342:0:99999:7:::
[root@server1 ~]# _
```

Note from the preceding output that most user accounts used by daemons do not receive an encrypted password.

Although every user must have a primary group listed in the /etc/passwd file, each user can be a member of multiple groups. All groups and their members are listed in the **/etc/group** file. The /etc/group file has the following colon-delimited fields:

```
name:password:GID:members
```

The first field is the name of the group, followed by a group password.

The password field usually contains an x, because group passwords are rarely used. If group passwords are used on your system, you need to specify a password to change your primary group membership using the newgrp command discussed later in this chapter. These passwords are set using the gpasswd command and can be stored in the /etc/gshadow file for added security. Refer to the gpasswd manual or info page for more information.

The GID represents the unique Group ID for the group, and the members field indicates the list of group members. An example /etc/group file is shown next:

```
[root@server1 ~]# cat /etc/group
root:x:0:root
bin:x:1:root,bin,daemon
daemon:x:2:root,bin,daemon
sys:x:3:root,bin,adm
adm:x:4:root,adm,daemon
tty:x:5:
disk:x:6:root
lp:x:7:daemon,lp
mem:x:8:
kmem:x:9:
wheel:x:10:root
mail:x:12:mail
uucp:x:14:uucp
```

```
man:x:15:
games:x:20:
gopher:x:30:
video:x:39:
dip:x:40:
ftp:x:50:
named:x:25:
rtkit:x:495:
nscd:x:494:
abrt:x:493:
apache:x:486:
haldaemon:x:482:
sshd:x:476:
gdm:x:468:
hsqldb:x:96:
jetty:x:467:
user1:x:500:
[root@server1 ~]# _
```

From the preceding output, the "bin" group has a GID of 1 and three users as members: root, bin, and daemon.

Creating User Accounts

You can create user accounts on the Linux system by using the **useradd command**, specifying the user name as an argument, as shown next:

```
[root@server1 ~]# useradd bobg
[root@server1 ~]# _
```

In this case, all other information, such as the UID, shell, and home directory location, is taken from two files that contain user account creation default values.

The first file, **/etc/login.defs**, contains parameters that set the default location for e-mail, password expiration information, minimum password length, and the range of UIDs and GIDs available for use. In addition, it determines whether home directories will be automatically made during user creation, as well as the password hash algorithm used to store passwords within /etc/shadow.

A sample /etc/login.defs file is depicted in the following example:

```
[root@server1 ~]# cat /etc/login.defs
# *REQUIRED*
# Directory where mailboxes reside, _or_ name of file, relative to the
# home directory. If you _do_ define both, MAIL_DIR takes precedence.
# QMAIL_DIR is for Qmail
#
#QMAIL_DIR     Maildir
MAIL_DIR       /var/spool/mail
#MAIL_FILE     .mail
```

10

```
# Password aging controls:
#
# PASS_MAX_DAYS     Maximum number of days a password may be used.
# PASS_MIN_DAYS     Minimum number of days allowed between password changes
# PASS_MIN_LEN      Minimum acceptable password length.
# PASS_WARN_AGE     Number of days warning given before a password expires
#
PASS_MAX_DAYS     99999
PASS_MIN_DAYS     0
PASS_MIN_LEN      5
PASS_WARN_AGE     7


#
# Min/max values for automatic uid selection in useradd
#
UID_MIN                    1000
UID_MAX                    60000
# System accounts
SYS_UID_MIN                201
SYS_UID_MAX                999


#
# Min/max values for automatic gid selection in groupadd
#
GID_MIN                    1000
GID_MAX                    60000
# System accounts
SYS_GID_MIN                201
SYS_GID_MAX                999


#
# If defined, this command is run when removing a user.
# It should remove any at/cron/print jobs etc. owned by
# the user to be removed (passed as the first argument).
#
#USERDEL_CMD    /usr/sbin/userdel_local
#


# If useradd should create home directories for users by default
# On RH systems, we do. This option is overridden with the -m flag on
# useradd command line.
#
CREATE_HOME     yes


# The permission mask is initialized to this value. If not specified,
# the permission mask will be initialized to 022.
UMASK           077
```

```
# This enables userdel to remove user groups if no members exist.
#
USERGROUPS_ENAB yes

# Use SHA512 to encrypt password.
ENCRYPT_METHOD SHA512
[root@server1 ~]# _
```

The second file, **/etc/default/useradd**, contains information regarding the default primary group, the location of home directories, the default number of days to disable accounts with expired passwords, the date to disable user accounts, the shell used, and the skeleton directory used. The **skeleton directory**, which is **/etc/skel** on most Linux systems, contains files that are copied to all new users' home directories when the home directory is created. Most of these files are environment files, such as .bash_profile and .bashrc.

A sample /etc/default/useradd file is shown in the following output:

```
[root@server1 ~]# cat /etc/default/useradd
# useradd defaults file
GROUP=100
HOME=/home
INACTIVE=-1
EXPIRE=
SHELL=/bin/bash
SKEL=/etc/skel
CREATE_MAIL_SPOOL=yes
[root@server1 ~]# _
```

To override any of the default parameters for a user in the /etc/login.defs and /etc/default/useradd files, you can specify options to the useradd command when creating user accounts. For example, to create a user named maryj with a UID of 762, you can use the –u option to the useradd command, as shown in the following example:

```
[root@server1 ~]# useradd –u 762 maryj
[root@server1 ~]# _
```

Table 10-6 lists some common options available to the useradd command and their descriptions.

After a user account has been added, the password field in the /etc/shadow file contains either two ! characters or a single * character, indicating that no password has been set for the user account. To set the password, simply type the **passwd command**, type the name of the new user account at a command prompt, and then supply the appropriate password when prompted. An example of setting the password for the bobg user is shown in the following:

```
[root@server1 ~]# passwd bobg
Changing password for user bobg.
New UNIX password:
Retype new UNIX password:
passwd: all authentication tokens updated successfully.
[root@server1 ~]# _
```

10

Option	Description
-c "description"	Adds a description for the user to the GECOS field of /etc/passwd.
-d homedirectory	Specifies the absolute pathname to the user's home directory.
-e expirydate	Specifies a date to disable the account from logging in.
-f days	Specifies the number of days until a user account with an expired password is disabled.
-g group	Specifies the primary group for the user account. By default in Fedora Linux, a group is created with the same name as the user and made the primary group for that user.
-G group1, group2, etc.	Specifies all other group memberships for the user account.
-m	Specifies that a home directory should be created for the user account. By default in Fedora Linux, home directories are created for all users via an entry in the /etc/login.defs file. However, in many other Linux distributions, a home directory is not created unless this option is specified.
-k directory	Specifies the skeleton directory used when copying files to a new home directory.
-s shell	Specifies the absolute pathname to the shell used for the user account.
-u UID	Specifies the UID of the user account.

Table 10-6 Common options to the useradd command

Without arguments, the passwd command changes the password for the current user.

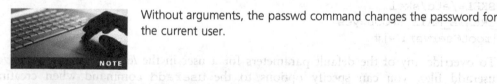

All user accounts must have a password set before they are used to log in to the system.

The root user can set the password on any user account using the passwd command; however, regular users can change their password only using this command.

Passwords should be difficult to guess and contain a combination of uppercase, lowercase, and special characters to increase system security. An example of a good password is C2Jr1;Pwr.

Modifying User Accounts

To modify the information regarding a user account after creation, you can edit the /etc/passwd or /etc/shadow file. This is not recommended, however, because typographical errors in these files might prevent the system from functioning. Instead, it's better to use the **usermod command**, which you can use to modify most information regarding user accounts. For example, to change the login name of the user bobg to barbg, you can use the -1 option to the usermod command:

```
[root@server1 ~]# usermod -l barbg bobg
[root@server1 ~]# _
```

Table 10-7 displays a complete list of options used with the usermod command to modify user accounts.

 If installed, the finger command can be used to view information about users. This information is stored in the GECOS field of /etc/passwd. As a result, instead of using the −c option to the usermod command, users can change their own GECOS, or finger information, using the **chfn command**.

The only user account information that the usermod command cannot modify is the password expiration information stored in /etc/shadow (min, max, warn), discussed earlier. To change this information, you can use the **chage command** with the appropriate option. For example, to specify that the user bobg must wait 2 days before changing his password after receiving a new password, as well as to specify that his password expires every 50 days with 7 days of warning prior to expiration, you can use the following options to the chage command:

```
[root@server1 ~]# chage -m 2 -M 50 -W 7 bobg
[root@server1 ~]# _
```

Sometimes it's necessary to **lock an account**—that is, to temporarily prevent a user from logging in. To lock an account, you can use the command usermod −L *username* at the command prompt. This places a ! character at the beginning of the encrypted password field in the /etc/shadow file. To unlock the account, simply type usermod −U *username* at the command prompt, which removes the ! character from the password field in the /etc/shadow file.

Alternatively, you can use the passwd −l *username* command to lock a user account, and the passwd −u *username* command to unlock a user account. These commands place and

Option	Description
-c "description"	Specifies a new description for the user in the GECOS field of /etc/passwd
-d homedirectory	Specifies the absolute pathname to a new home directory
-e expirydate	Specifies a date to disable the account from logging in
-f days	Specifies the number of days until a user account with an expired password is disabled
-g group	Specifies a new primary group for the user account
-G group1, group2, etc.	Specifies all other group memberships for the user account
-l name	Specifies a new login name
-s shell	Specifies the absolute pathname to a new shell used for the user account
-u UID	Specifies a new UID for the user account

Table 10-7 Common options to the usermod command

10

remove two ! characters at the beginning of the encrypted password field in the /etc/shadow file, respectively.

Yet another method commonly used to lock a user account is to change the shell specified in /etc/passwd for a user account from /bin/bash to an invalid shell such as /bin/false or /sbin/nologin. Without a valid shell, a user cannot use the system. To lock a user account this way, you can edit the /etc/passwd file and make the appropriate change, use the -s option to the usermod command, or use the **chsh command**. The following example uses the chsh command to change the shell to /bin/false for the user bobg:

```
[root@server1 ~]# chsh -s /bin/false bobg
Changing shell for bobg.
chsh: Warning: "/bin/false" is not listed in /etc/shells
Shell changed.
[root@server1 ~]# _
```

Deleting User Accounts

To delete a user account, you can use the **userdel command** and specify the user name as an argument. This removes entries from the /etc/passwd and /etc/shadow files corresponding to the user account. Furthermore, you can specify the -r option to the userdel command to remove the home directory for the user and all of its contents.

When a user account is deleted, any files that were previously owned by the user become owned by a number that represents the UID of the deleted user. Any future user account that is given the same UID then becomes the owner of those files.

Suppose, for example, that the user bobg leaves the company. To delete bobg's user account and display the ownership of his old files, you can use the following commands:

```
[root@server1 ~]# userdel bobg
[root@server1 ~]# ls -la /home/bobg
total 52
drwx------    4 1002    1002    4096 Jul 17 15:37 .
drwxr-xr-x    5 root    root    4096 Jul 17 15:37 ..
-rw-r--r--    1 1002    1002      24 Jul 17 15:37 .bash_logout
-rw-r--r--    1 1002    1002     191 Jul 17 15:37 .bash_profile
-rw-r--r--    1 1002    1002     124 Jul 17 15:37 .bashrc
-rw-r--r--    1 1002    1002    5542 Jul 17 15:37 .canna
-rw-r--r--    1 1002    1002     820 Jul 17 15:37 .emacs
-rw-r--r--    1 1002    1002     118 Jul 17 15:37 .gtkrc
-rw-r--r--    3 1002    1002    4096 Jul 17 15:37 .kde
drwxr-xr-x    2 1002    1002    4096 Jul 17 15:37 .xemacs
-rw-r--r--    1 1002    1002    3511 Jul 17 15:37 .zshrc
[root@server1 ~]# _
```

From the preceding output, you can see that the UID of the bobg user was 1002. Now suppose the company hires Sue—that is, the user sueb—to replace bobg. You can then assign the UID of 1002 to Sue's user account. Although she will have her own home directory (/home/sueb), she will also own all of bobg's old files within /home/bobg and otherwise. She can then copy the files that she needs to her own home directory and remove any files that she doesn't need as part of her job function.

To create the user sueb with a UID of 1002 and list the ownership of the files in bobg's home directory, you can use the following commands:

```
[root@server1 ~]# useradd -u 1002 sueb
[root@server1 ~]# ls -la /home/bobg
total 52
drwx------      4 sueb     sueb         4096 Jul 17 15:37 .
drwxr-xr-x      5 root     root         4096 Jul 17 18:56 ..
-rw-r--r--      1 sueb     sueb           24 Jul 17 15:37 .bash_logout
-rw-r--r--      1 sueb     sueb          191 Jul 17 15:37 .bash_profile
-rw-r--r--      1 sueb     sueb          124 Jul 17 15:37 .bashrc
-rw-r--r--      1 sueb     sueb         5542 Jul 17 15:37 .canna
-rw-r--r--      1 sueb     sueb          820 Jul 17 15:37 .emacs
-rw-r--r--      1 sueb     sueb          118 Jul 17 15:37 .gtkrc
-rw-r--r--      3 sueb     sueb         4096 Jul 17 15:37 .kde
drwxr-xr-x      2 sueb     sueb         4096 Jul 17 15:37 .xemacs
-rw-r--r--      1 sueb     sueb         3511 Jul 17 15:37 .zshrc
[root@server1 ~]# _
```

Managing Groups

By far, the easiest way to add groups to a system is to edit the /etc/group file using a text editor. Another method is to use the **groupadd command**. To add a group called group1 to the system and assign it a GID of 492, you can use the following command:

```
[root@server1 ~]# groupadd –g 492 group1
[root@server1 ~]# _
```

Then, you can use the -G option to the usermod command to add members to the group. To add the user maryj to this group and view the addition, you can use the following usermod command:

```
[root@server1 ~]# usermod –G group1 maryj
[root@server1 ~]# tail -1 /etc/group
group1:x:492:maryj
[root@server1 ~]# _
```

There also exists a **groupmod command**, which can be used to modify the group name and GID, and a **groupdel command**, which can be used to remove groups from the system.

To see a list of groups of which you are a member, simply run the **groups command**; to see the GIDs for each group, simply run the **id command**. The primary group is always listed first by each command. The following output shows sample output of these commands when executed by the root user:

```
[root@server1 ~]# groups
root bin daemon sys adm disk wheel
[root@server1 ~]# id
uid=0(root)     gid=0(root)         groups=0(root),1(bin),2(daemon),3(sys),
4(adm),6(disk),10(wheel)
[root@server1 ~]# _
```

10

In the preceding output the primary group for the root user is the root group. This group is attached as the group owner for all files that are created by the root user, as shown in the following output:

```
[root@server1 ~]# touch samplefile1
[root@server1 ~]# ls -l samplefile1
-rw-r--r--   1 root    root          0 Aug 27 19:22 samplefile1
[root@server1 ~]# _
```

To change the primary group temporarily to another group that is listed in the output of the groups and id commands, you can use the **newgrp command**. Any new files created afterward will then have the new group owner. The following output demonstrates how changing the primary group for the root user affects file ownership:

```
[root@server1 ~]# newgrp sys
[root@server1 root]# id
uid=0(root)      gid=3(sys)       groups=0(root),1(bin),2(daemon),3(sys),
4(adm),6(disk),10(wheel)
[root@server1 ~]# touch samplefile2
[root@server1 ~]# ls -l samplefile2
-rw-r--r--   1 root    sys          0 Aug 27 19:28 samplefile2
[root@server1 ~]# _
```

If you use group passwords as described earlier in this section, you can use the newgrp command to change your primary group to a group of which you are not a member, provided you supply the appropriate group password when prompted.

The root user can use the newgrp command to change her primary group to any other group.

Although command-line utilities are commonly used to administer users and groups, you can instead use a graphical utility to create, modify, and delete user and group accounts on the system. These utilities run the appropriate command-line utility in the background. To create and manage users and groups in Fedora 20 from within a desktop environment, you can open a terminal application in the desktop environment, switch to the root user, and run the system-config-users command to open the User Manager utility shown in Figure 10-6.

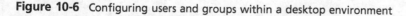

Figure 10-6 Configuring users and groups within a desktop environment

Chapter Summary

- Print jobs are spooled to a print queue before being printed to a printer.
- You can configure spooling or printing for a printer by using the `cupsaccept`, `cupsreject`, `cupsenable`, and `cupsdisable` commands.
- Print jobs are created using the `lp` command, can be viewed in the print queue using the `lpstat` command, and are removed from the print queue using the `cancel` command.
- You can configure printers using the `lpadmin` command, the CUPS Web administration tool, or by modifying the /etc/cups/printers.conf file.
- Most log files on a Linux system are stored in the `/var/log` directory.
- System events are typically logged to files by the System Log Daemon (rsyslogd) or to a database by the Systemd Journal Daemon (journald).
- You can use the `jounalctl` command to view the contents of the journald database.
- Log files should be cleared or rotated over time to save disk space; the logrotate utility can be used to rotate log files.
- User and group account information is typically stored in the `/etc/passwd`, `/etc/shadow`, and `/etc/group` files.
- You can use the `useradd` command to create users and the `groupadd` command to create groups.
- All users must have a valid password before logging in to a Linux system.
- Users can be modified with the `usermod`, `chage`, `chfn`, `chsh`, and `passwd` commands, and groups can be modified using the `groupmod` command.
- The `userdel` and `groupdel` commands can be used to remove users and groups from the system, respectively.

Key Terms

/etc/cups/cupsd.conf   A file that holds daemon configuration for the cups daemon.

/etc/cups/printers.conf   A file that holds printer configuration for the cups daemon.

/etc/default/useradd   A file that contains default values for user creation.

/etc/group   The file that contains group definitions and memberships.

/etc/login.defs   A file that contains default values for user creation.

/etc/logrotate.conf   The file used by the logrotate utility to specify rotation parameters for log files.

/etc/passwd   The file that contains user account information.

/etc/rsyslog.conf   The main configuration file for the System Log Daemon.

/etc/shadow   The file that contains the encrypted password as well as password and account expiry parameters for each user account.

/etc/skel   A directory that contains files that are copied to all new users' home directories upon creation.

/etc/systemd/journald.conf   The configuration file for the Systemd Journal Daemon.

/var/log   A directory that contains most log files on a Linux system.

authentication   The act of verifying a user's identity by comparing a user name and password to a system database (/etc/passwd and /etc/shadow).

`cancel` **command**   The command used to remove print jobs from the print queue in the CUPS print system.

`chage` **command**   The command used to modify password expiry information for user accounts.

`chfn` **command**   The command used to change the GECOS for a user.

`chsh` **command**   The command used to change a valid shell to an invalid shell.

Common Unix Printing System (CUPS)   The printing system commonly used on Linux computers.

CUPS daemon (cupsd)   The daemon responsible for printing in the CUPS printing system.

CUPS Web administration tool   A Web-based management tool for the CUPS printing system.

`cupsaccept` **command**   The command used to allow a printer to accept jobs into the print queue.

`cupsdisable` **command**   The command used to prevent print jobs from leaving the print queue.

`cupsenable` **command**   The command used to allow print jobs to leave the print queue.

`cupsreject` **command**   The command used to force a printer to reject jobs from entering the print queue.

facility   The area of the system from which information is gathered when logging system events.

General Electric Comprehensive Operating System (GECOS)   The field in the /etc/passwd file that contains a description of the user account.

Group Identifier (GID)   A unique number given to each group.

`groupadd` **command**   The command used to add a group to the system.

`groupdel` **command**   The command used to delete a group from the system.

`groupmod` **command**   The command used to modify the name or GID of a group on the system.

`groups` **command**   The command that lists group membership for a user.

`id` **command**   The command that lists UIDs for a user and the GIDs for the groups that the same user belongs to.

Internet Printing Protocol (IPP)   A printing protocol that can be used to send print jobs across a TCP/IP network, such as the Internet, using HTTP or HTTPS.

`journalctl` **command**   The command used to query the database created by the Systemd Journal Daemon.

Line Printer Daemon (LPD)   A printing system typically used on legacy Linux computers.

lock an account To make an account temporarily unusable by altering the password information for it stored on the system.

log file A file containing information about the Linux system.

logrotate command The command used to rotate log files; typically uses the configuration information stored in /etc/logrotate.conf.

lp command The command used to create print jobs in the print queue in the CUPS printing system.

lpadmin command The command used to perform printer administration in the CUPS printing system.

lpc command The command used to view the status of and control printers in the LPD printing system.

lpq command The command used to view the contents of print queues in the LPD printing system.

lpr command The command used to create print jobs in the print queue in the LPD printing system.

lprm command The command used to remove print jobs from the print queue in the LPD printing system.

lpstat command The command used to view the contents of print queues and printer information in the CUPS printing system.

newgrp command The command used to temporarily change the primary group of a user.

passwd command The command used to modify the password associated with a user account.

primary group The group that is specified for a user in the /etc/passwd file and that is specified as group owner for all files created by a user.

print job The information sent to a printer for printing.

print job ID A unique numeric identifier used to mark and distinguish each print job.

print queue A directory on the filesystem that holds print jobs that are waiting to be printed.

printer class A group of CUPS printers that are treated as a single unit for the purposes of printing and management.

Printers tool A graphical utility used to configure printers on a Fedora 20 system.

priority The importance of system information when logging system events.

pwconv command The command used to enable the use of the /etc/shadow file.

pwunconv command The command used to disable the use of the /etc/shadow file.

queuing See *spooling*.

skeleton directory A directory that contains files that are copied to all new users' home directories upon creation; the default skeleton directory on Linux systems is /etc/skel.

spooling The process of accepting a print job into a print queue.

System Log Daemon (rsyslogd) The daemon that logs system events to various log files via information stored in /etc/rsyslog.conf and files within the /etc/rsyslog.d directory.

Systemd Journal Daemon (journald)   A Systemd component that logs system events to a journal database.

user account   The information regarding a user that is stored in a system database (/etc/passwd and /etc/shadow), which can be used to log in to the system and gain access to system resources.

User Identifier (UID)   A unique number assigned to each user account.

`useradd` **command**   The command used to add a user account to the system.

`userdel` **command**   The command used to remove a user account from the system.

`usermod` **command**   The command used to modify the properties of a user account on the system.

Review Questions

1. The process of sending print jobs from the print queue to the printer is called _____.
   a. spooling
   b. queuing
   c. redirecting
   d. printing

2. You can clear a log file simply by redirecting nothing into it. True or False?

3. When a printer is disabled, _____.
   a. the print queue does not accept jobs and sends a message to the user noting that the printer is unavailable
   b. the print queue accepts jobs into the print queue and holds them there until the printer is enabled again
   c. the printer appears as off-line when an `lp` request is sent
   d. the print queue redirects all print jobs sent to it to /dev/null

4. What is the name used to describe a user providing a user name and password to log in to a system?
   a. validation
   b. authorization
   c. login
   d. authentication

5. Which command can you use to lock a user account?
   a. `lock username`
   b. `secure username`
   c. `usermod -L username`
   d. `useradd -L username`

6. Which command can be used to alter the primary group associated with a given user temporarily?

   a. usermod

   b. chggrp

   c. gpasswd

   d. newgrp

7. Which command can be used to send a print job to the default printer named Printer1? (Choose all that apply.)

   a. lp -d Printer1 file

   b. lp Printer1 file

   c. lp file

   d. lp -m Printer1 file

8. What is the name of the file that contains a listing of all users on the system and their home directories?

   a. /etc/passwd

   b. /etc/users

   c. /etc/shadow

   d. /etc/password

9. UIDs and GIDs are unique to the system and, once used, can never be reused. True or False?

10. What is the name of the utility used to rotate log files?

    a. syslog

    b. jetpack

    c. logrotate

    d. logbackup

11. You can lock a user account by changing the default login shell to an invalid shell in /etc/passwd. True or False?

12. When a printer is rejecting requests, _____.

    a. the print queue does not accept jobs and sends a message to the user noting that the printer is unavailable

    b. the print queue accepts jobs into the print queue and holds them there until the printer is accepting requests again

    c. the printer appears as off-line when a lp request is sent

    d. the print queue redirects all print jobs sent to it to /dev/null

13. When referring to the /etc/rsyslog.conf file, _____ specifies information from a certain area of the system, whereas _____ is the level of importance of that information.

   a. section, priority

   b. service, precedents

   c. process, degree

   d. facility, priority

14. Most log files on the system are found in which directory?

   a. /etc/logfiles

   b. /etc/log

   c. /var/log

   d. /dev/log

15. Which file contains default information such as UID and GID ranges and minimum password length to be used at user creation?

   a. /etc/skel

   b. /etc/passwd

   c. /etc/login.defs

   d. /etc/default/useradd

16. What command can you use to view journald log entries on a system that uses Systemd?

   a. `less`

   b. `journalctl`

   c. `syslog`

   d. `catlog`

17. Which command would you use to unlock a user account?

   a. `unlock username`

   b. `open username`

   c. `usermod -U username`

   d. `useradd -U username`

18. Along with a listing of user accounts, the /etc/passwd file contains information on account expiry. True or False?

19. You use `lpstat` and determine that a user named User1 has placed two large print jobs in the queue for Printer1 that have yet to start printing. They have print job IDs of Printer1-17 and Printer1-21, respectively. Which command would you use to remove these two jobs from the print queue?

   a. `cancel Printer1-17 Printer1-21`

   b. `cancel -u Printer1-17 Printer1-21`

   c. `cancel -a Printer1-17 Printer1-21`

   d. `cancel 17 21`

20. Which command is used to delete a user account?

    a. `usermod –d username`

    b. `del username`

    c. `userdel username`

    d. `rm username`

Hands-on Projects

These projects should be completed in the order given. The hands-on projects presented in this chapter should take a total of three hours to complete. The requirements for this lab include:

- A computer with Fedora Linux installed according to Hands-On Project 2-1 and Ubuntu Server Linux installed according to Hands-On Project 6-1.

Project 10-1

In this hands-on project, you use commands to create and configure a printer as well as submit and manage print jobs.

1. Boot your Fedora Linux virtual machine. After your Linux system has been loaded, switch to a command-line terminal (tty2) by pressing **Ctrl+Alt+F2** and log in to the terminal using the user name of **root** and the password of **LNXrocks!**.

2. At the command prompt, type **lpadmin -p printer1 -E -v /dev/null -m raw** and press **Enter** to create a sample printer called printer1 that prints to the /dev/null device using a raw print driver.

3. At the command prompt, type **lpoptions –d printer1** and press **Enter** to ensure that printer1 is the default printer on the system.

4. At the terminal screen prompt, type **cat /etc/cups/printers.conf** and press **Enter**. Do you see an entry for printer1 that prints to /dev/null?

5. At the command prompt, type **lpstat -t** and press **Enter**. Is the CUPS daemon running? Is printer1 enabled and accepting requests? Is printer1 the default printer on the system?

6. At the command prompt, type **cupsdisable –r "To keep print jobs in the queue" printer1** and press **Enter** to disable printer1 with an appropriate reason. Next, type **lpstat -t** at the command prompt and press Enter. Is printer1 disabled with a reason?

7. At the command prompt, type **lp –n 2 /etc/inittab** and press **Enter** to print two copies of /etc/inittab to printer1. What is the print job ID? Why did you not need to specify the printer name when running the lp command?

8. At the command prompt, type **lp /etc/hosts /etc/nsswitch.conf** and press **Enter** to print the /etc/hosts and /etc/nsswitch.conf files. What is the print job ID?

9. At the command prompt, type **mount | lp** and press **Enter** to print the output of the mount command to printer1. What is the print job ID?

10

10. At the command prompt, type **lpstat** and press Enter. Are your print jobs shown in the queue? How long will they remain in the queue and why?

11. At the command prompt, type **ls /var/spool/cups** and press Enter. You should notice contents within this directory for your three print jobs. The data for your print jobs should have file names that start with d, and the settings for your print jobs should have file names that start with c. Type **cat /var/spool/cups/d00001-001** at the command prompt and press Enter to view the data for the first print job on the system. What is shown and why?

12. At the command prompt, type **cancel printer1-1** and press Enter to remove the first print job from the queue. Next, type **lpstat printer1** at the command prompt and press Enter. Has the printer1-1 job been removed?

13. At the command prompt, type **lpc status** and press Enter to view the status of CUPS using the traditional BSD lpc command. Is the CUPS daemon running? Is the status of printing and spooling correct? Next, type **lpq** at the command prompt and press Enter. Do you see the two remaining jobs in the print queue for printer1? Do the job numbers displayed correspond with the job numbers in the lpstat output from the previous step?

14. At the command prompt, type **lpr -#2 /etc/inittab** and press Enter to print two copies of /etc/inittab to the default printer using the traditional BSD lpr command. Next, type **lpq** at the command prompt and press Enter. Do you see an additional job in the print queue? What is the job ID?

15. At the command prompt, type **lprm 4** and press Enter to remove the most recent print job that you submitted. Next, type **lpq** at the command prompt and press Enter. Was print job 4 removed successfully?

16. Type **exit** and press Enter to log out of your shell.

Project 10-2

In this hands-on project, you submit a print job from a graphical program as well as explore the Printers tool and the CUPS Web administration tool.

1. On your Fedora Linux virtual machine, switch to a graphical terminal (tty1) by pressing **Ctrl+Alt+F1** and log in to the GNOME desktop using the user name of **user1** and the password of **LNXrocks!**.

2. In the GNOME desktop, click the **Activities** menu and select the **LibreOffice Writer** icon. Type a line of your choice within the document, select the **File** menu, and choose **Print**. Is printer1 listed as the default printer? Click **OK** to print one copy of your document. Close the LibreOffice Writer window and click **Close without saving** when prompted.

3. In the GNOME desktop, click the **Activities** menu, select the **Show Applications** icon, and click **Settings** to open the Settings window. Next, click **Printers** to open the graphical Printers tool and note that printer1 is displayed.

4. In the Printers tool, click **Show Jobs** and note that your recently submitted print job is shown. Why aren't the two other print jobs in the printer1 queue shown? Click **Close** when finished.

5. In the Printers tool, click **Print Test Page** to submit a test page print job. Next, click **Show Jobs** and note that two jobs are now displayed. Highlight your Test page job,

click the Stop icon to remove the job from the queue and click **Close** when finished. Close the Printers tool when finished.

6. In the GNOME desktop, click the **Activities** menu and select the **Firefox** icon. Enter the address **localhost:631** in the address bar and press Enter to access the CUPS Web administration tool.

7. In the CUPS Web administration tool, select the **Administration** tab and select the **Allow remote administration, Share printers connected to this system,** and **Allow printing from the Internet** options. Click the **Change Settings** button to activate your changes. Supply the user name **root** and password **LNXrocks!** when prompted and click **OK**.

8. On the Administration tab of the CUPS Web administration tool, click **Add Class,** supply a name of **SampleClass,** select **printer1,** and click **Add Class.**

9. Select the **Printers** tab of the CUPS Web administration tool and click printer1. Select the **Maintenance** drop-down menu and note the maintenance tasks that you perform for printer1. Next, select the **Administration** drop-down menu and note the administrative tasks that you can perform for printer1. View the print jobs at the bottom of the page and note the management functions that you can perform for each one.

10. Highlight the **Jobs** tab of the CUPS Web administration tool. Are the jobs shown the same as those shown on the Printers tab for printer1? Can you perform the same management functions for each job?

11. Highlight the **Classes** tab of the CUPS Web administration tool and click **SampleClass.** Select the **Maintenance** drop-down menu and note the maintenance tasks that you perform for printer1. Next, select the **Administration** drop-down menu and note the administrative tasks that you can perform for printer1. Do these options match those shown in on the Printers tab for printer1?

12. Close the Firefox Web browser window and switch to a command-line terminal (tty2) by pressing **Ctrl+Alt+F2** and log in to the terminal using the user name of **root** and the password of **LNXrocks!.**

13. At the command prompt, type **lpstat -t** and press **Enter.** Is your SampleClass shown in the output? Why is user1 listed as the user for the most recent print job?

14. At the command prompt, type **lp –d SampleClass /etc/hosts** and press **Enter** to print a copy of /etc/hosts to the SampleClass printer class. Why does the print job ID reflect the printer class name and not printer1?

15. At the command prompt, type **lpstat -t** and press **Enter.** Is the print job submitted to your printer class shown?

16. At the command prompt, type **cancel –a printer1 SampleClass** and press **Enter** to remove all print jobs in the queue for printer1 and SampleClass. Next, type **lpstat -t** and press **Enter** to verify that no print jobs exist within the print queue.

17. Type **exit** and press **Enter** to log out of your shell.

Project 10-3

In this hands-on project, you view the configuration of the System Log Daemon and the logrotate utility on Ubuntu Server Linux.

1. Boot your Ubuntu Server Linux virtual machine. After your Linux system has been loaded, log into tty1 using the user name of **root** and the password of **LNXrocks!.**

10

2. At the command prompt, type `ls -l /dev/log` and press Enter. What is the file type? Which daemon on Ubuntu Server Linux uses this file and what is its purpose?

3. At the command prompt, type `less /etc/rsyslog.conf` and press Enter to view the configuration file for the System Log Daemon. Are there any entries that specify facilities, priorities, or log file locations? What does the last line of the file specify? Press q when finished to quit the less utility.

4. At the command prompt, type `less /etc/rsyslog.d/50-default.conf` and press Enter. Where do kernel messages of any priority get logged to by default? What does the – character next to the filename indicate? Press q when finished to quit the less utility.

5. At the command prompt, type `tail /var/log/kern.log` and press Enter. Observe the entries.

6. At the command prompt, type `ls /var/log/cups` and press Enter. What daemon creates the log files within the /var/log/cups directory?

7. At the command prompt, type `cat /etc/cron.daily/logrotate` and press Enter to observe the `logrotate` command that is run each day.

8. At the command prompt, type `less /etc/logrotate.conf` and press Enter to view the configuration file for the `logrotate` command. How many copies of old log files are kept by default? When finished, press q to quit the less utility.

9. At the command prompt, type `ls /etc/logrotate.d` and press Enter. How many files are in this directory? Will entries in these files override the same entries in */etc/log-rotate.conf*?

10. At the command prompt, type `cat /etc/logrotate.d/cups-daemon` and press Enter. How many copies of old log files are kept for the log files in the /var/log/cups directory? Will the log files be rotated if they contain no contents?

11. Type `exit` and press Enter to log out of your shell.

Project 10-4

In this hands-on project, you view the configuration and log entries created by the Systemd Journal Daemon as well as the configuration of the logrotate utility on Fedora Linux.

1. On your Fedora Linux virtual machine, switch to a command-line terminal (tty2) by pressing **Ctrl+Alt+F2** and log in to the terminal using the user name of **root** and the password of **LNXrocks!**.

2. At the command prompt, type `ls -l /dev/log` and press Enter. What is the file type? Which daemon on Fedora Linux uses this file and what is its purpose?

3. At the command prompt, type `cat /etc/systemd/journald.conf` and press Enter to view the configuration file for the Systemd Journal Daemon. What line could you uncomment and configure to set a maximum size for the journald database?

4. At the command prompt, type `journalctl _COMM=` and press the **Tab** key twice. Which keyword could you use to view log entries from the GNOME display manager? Press Ctrl+c to return to your command prompt. Next, type `journalctl _COMM=gdm` and press Enter to view log entries from the GNOME display manager. Are entries shown for multiple days?

5. At the command prompt, type **journalctl --COMM=gdm --since "5:00"** and press **Enter** to view log entries from the GNOME display manager since 5:00am.

6. At the command prompt, type **which crond** and press **Enter**. What is the path to the cron daemon executable file? Next, type **journalctl /sbin/crond --since "5:00"** and press **Enter**. What entries are shown?

7. At the command prompt, type **ls /var/log** and press **Enter**. Observe the entries. Are there log files within /var/log created by daemons that do not log entries via journald?

8. At the command prompt, type **ls /var/log/cups** and press **Enter**. Are the contents similar to those from Step 6 in Project 10-3?

9. At the command prompt, type **cat /etc/cron.daily/logrotate** and press **Enter** to observe the **logrotate** command that is run each day.

10. At the command prompt, type **less /etc/logrotate.conf** and press **Enter** to view the configuration file for the **logrotate** command. How many copies of old log files are kept by default? When finished, press q to quit the less utility.

11. At the command prompt, type **ls /etc/logrotate.d** and press **Enter**. How many files are in this directory? Will entries in these files override the same entries in /etc/logrotate.conf?

12. At the command prompt, type **cat /etc/logrotate.d/cups** and press **Enter**. How many copies of old log files are kept for the log files in the /var/log/cups directory? Will the log files be rotated if they contain no contents?

13. Type **exit** and press **Enter** to log out of your shell.

Project 10-5

In this hands-on project, you observe user account databases on Fedora Linux and create a user account using command-line utilities.

1. On your Fedora Linux virtual machine, switch to a command-line terminal (tty2) by pressing **Ctrl+Alt+F2** and log in to the terminal using the user name of **root** and the password of **LNXrocks!**.

2. At the command prompt, type **less /etc/passwd** and press **Enter**. Where is the line that describes the root user located in this file? Where is the line that describes the user1 user in this file? How many daemon accounts are present? What is in the password field for all accounts? When finished, press the q key to quit the less utility.

3. At the command prompt, type **ls -l /etc/passwd** and press **Enter**. Who is the owner and group owner of this file? Who has permission to read this file?

4. At the command prompt, type **less /etc/shadow** and press **Enter**. What is in the password field for the root user and user1 user accounts? What is in the password field for most daemon accounts? Press the q key to quit the less utility.

5. At the command prompt, type **ls -l /etc/shadow** and press **Enter**. Who is the owner and group owner of this file? Who has permission to read this file? Compare the permissions for /etc/shadow to those of /etc/passwd obtained in Step 3 and explain the difference.

10

6. At the command prompt, type **pwunconv** and press **Enter**. Next, type **less /etc/ shadow** at the command prompt and press **Enter**. What error message do you receive? Why?

7. At the command prompt, type **less /etc/passwd** and press **Enter**. What is in the password field for all accounts? Why? When finished, press the **q** key to quit the less utility.

8. At the command prompt, type **pwconv** and press **Enter**. What does the pwconv command do?

9. Next, type **less /etc/shadow** at the command prompt and press **Enter**. Verify that the file has contents and press **q** when finished. Next, type **less /etc/passwd** at the command prompt and press **Enter**. Verify that the file has contents and press **q** when finished.

10. At the command prompt, type **cat /etc/default/useradd** and press **Enter**. What is the default shell used when creating users? What is the default location of the skel directory used when creating users? Where are user home directories created by default?

11. At the command prompt, type **ls -a /etc/skel** and press **Enter**. What files are stored in this directory? What is the purpose of this directory when creating users?

12. At the command prompt, type **cp /etc/inittab /etc/skel** and press **Enter** to create a copy of the inittab file in the /etc/skel directory.

13. At the command prompt, type **useradd -m bozo** and press **Enter**. What does the -m option specify? From where is the default shell, home directory information taken?

14. At the command prompt, type **less /etc/login.defs** and press **Enter**. Observe the entries and descriptive comments. Did you need to specify the -m option to the user-add command in Step 13? Explain. Press the **q** key to quit the less utility.

15. At the command prompt, type **cat /etc/passwd** and press **Enter**. What shell and home directory does bozo have? What is bozo's UID?

16. At the command prompt, type **cat /etc/shadow** and press **Enter**. Does bozo have a password? Can bozo log in to the system?

17. At the command prompt, type **passwd bozo** and press **Enter**. Enter the password of LNXrocks! and press **Enter**. Enter the password of LNXrocks! again to confirm and press **Enter**.

18. At the command prompt, type **ls -a /home/bozo** and press **Enter**. How many files are in this directory? Compare this list to the one obtained in Step 11. Is the **inittab** file present?

19. Type **exit** and press **Enter** to log out of your shell.

Project 10-6

In this hands-on project, you modify user accounts on Fedora Linux using command-line utilities.

1. On your Fedora Linux virtual machine, switch to a command-line terminal (tty2) by pressing **Ctrl+Alt+F2** and log in to the terminal using the user name of **root** and the password of **LNXrocks!**.

2. At the command prompt, type **cat /etc/passwd** and press **Enter**. Record the line used to describe the user bozo.

3. At the command prompt, type **cat /etc/shadow** and press **Enter**. Record the line used to describe the user bozo.

4. At the command prompt, type **usermod –l bozo2 bozo** and press **Enter** to change the login name for the user bozo to bozo2. Next, type **cat /etc/passwd** at the command prompt and press **Enter**. Was the login name changed from bozo to bozo2? Was the UID changed? Was the home directory changed?

5. At the command prompt, type **usermod –l bozo bozo2** and press **Enter** to change the login name for the user bozo2 back to bozo.

6. At the command prompt, type **usermod –u 666 bozo** and press **Enter** to change the UID of the user bozo to 666. Next, type **cat /etc/passwd** at the command prompt and press **Enter**. Was the UID changed?

7. At the command prompt, type **usermod –f 14 bozo** and press **Enter** to disable bozo's user account 14 days after the password expires. Next, type **cat /etc/shadow** at the command prompt and press **Enter**. Which field was changed?

8. At the command prompt, type **usermod –e "01/01/2025" bozo** and press **Enter** to expire bozo's user account on January 1, 2025. Next, type **cat /etc/shadow** at the command prompt and press **Enter**. Which field was changed? What does the number represent in this field?

9. At the command prompt, type **chage –m 2 bozo** and press **Enter** to require that the user bozo wait at least two days before making password changes. Next, type **cat /etc/shadow** at the command prompt and press **Enter**. Which field was changed?

10. At the command prompt, type **chage –M 40 bozo** and press **Enter** to require that the user bozo change passwords every 40 days. Next, type **cat /etc/shadow** at the command prompt and press **Enter**. Which field was changed?

11. At the command prompt, type **chage –W 5 bozo** and press **Enter** to warn the user bozo five days before a password change is required. Next, type **cat /etc/shadow** at the command prompt and press **Enter**. Which field was changed?

12. Type **exit** and press **Enter** to log out of your shell.

Project 10-7

In this hands-on project, you lock and unlock user accounts on Fedora Linux using command-line utilities.

1. On your Fedora Linux virtual machine, switch to a command-line terminal (tty2) by pressing **Ctrl+Alt+F2** and log in to the terminal using the user name of **root** and the password of **LNXrocks!**.

2. At the command prompt, type **cat /etc/shadow** and press **Enter**. Record the encrypted password for bozo's user account.

3. At the command prompt, type **passwd –l bozo** and press **Enter** to lock bozo's user account.

4. At the command prompt, type **cat /etc/shadow** and press **Enter**. What has been changed regarding the original encrypted password recorded in Step 2?

5. Switch to a command-line terminal (tty5) by pressing **Ctrl+Alt+F5** and attempt to log in to the terminal using the user name of **bozo** and the password of **LNXrocks!**. Were you successful?

6. Switch back to the command-line terminal (tty2) by pressing **Ctrl+Alt+F2**.

7. At the command prompt, type **passwd –u bozo** and press **Enter** to unlock bozo's user account.

8. At the command prompt, type **cat /etc/shadow** and press **Enter**. Compare the encrypted password for bozo's user account to the one recorded in Step 2.

9. Switch to a command-line terminal (tty5) by pressing **Ctrl+Alt+F5** and attempt to log in to the terminal using the user name of **bozo** and the password of **LNXrocks!**. Were you successful?

10. Type **exit** and press **Enter** to log out of your shell.

11. Switch back to the command-line terminal (tty2) by pressing **Ctrl+Alt+F2**.

12. At the command prompt, type **chsh –s /bin/false bozo** and press **Enter** to change bozo's shell to /bin/false. What message did you receive? Was the shell changed? Type **cat /etc/passwd** at a command prompt to verify that the shell was changed to /bin/false for bozo's user account.

13. Switch to a command-line terminal (tty5) by pressing **Ctrl+Alt+F5** and attempt to log in to the terminal using the user name of **bozo** and the password of **LNXrocks!**. Were you successful?

14. Switch back to the command-line terminal (tty2) by pressing **Ctrl+Alt+F2**.

15. At the command prompt, type **chsh –s /bin/bash bozo** and press **Enter** to change bozo's shell to /bin/bash.

16. Switch to a command-line terminal (tty5) by pressing **Ctrl+Alt+F5** and attempt to log in to the terminal using the user name of **bozo** and the password of **LNXrocks!**. Were you successful?

17. Type **exit** and press **Enter** to log out of your shell.

18. Switch back to the command-line terminal (tty2) by pressing **Ctrl+Alt+F2**.

19. Type **exit** and press **Enter** to log out of your shell.

Project 10-8

In this hands-on project, you remove a user account on Fedora Linux and create a new user account in its place using command-line utilities.

1. On your Fedora Linux virtual machine, switch to a command-line terminal (tty2) by pressing **Ctrl+Alt+F2** and log in to the terminal using the user name of **root** and the password of **LNXrocks!**.

2. At the command prompt, type **ls –la /home/bozo** and press **Enter**. Who owns most files in this directory? Why?

3. At the command prompt, type **userdel bozo** and press **Enter**. Was the home directory removed for bozo as well?

4. At the command prompt, type **ls -la /home/bozo** and press **Enter**. Who owns most files in this directory? Why?

5. At the command prompt, type **useradd -m -u 666 bozoette** and press **Enter**. What do the -m and the -u options do in this command?

6. At the command prompt, type **passwd bozoette** and press **Enter**. Enter the password of **LNXrocks!** and press **Enter**. Enter the password of **LNXrocks!** again to confirm and press **Enter**.

7. At the command prompt, type **cat /etc/passwd** and press **Enter**. What is bozoette's home directory? What is bozoette's UID?

8. At the command prompt, type **ls -la /home/bozo** and press **Enter**. Who owns most files in this directory? Why? Can bozoette manage these files?

9. Type **exit** and press **Enter** to log out of your shell.

Project 10-9

In this hands-on project, you create, use, and delete groups on Fedora Linux using command-line utilities.

1. On your Fedora Linux virtual machine, switch to a command-line terminal (tty2) by pressing **Ctrl+Alt+F2**, and log in to the terminal using the user name of **root** and the password of **LNXrocks!**.

2. At the command prompt, type **vi /etc/group** and press **Enter** to open the /etc/group file in the vi editor. Add a line to the bottom of this file that reads:

   groupies:x:1234:root,bozoette

   This adds a group to the system with a GID of 1234, the members root, and bozoette. When finished, save and quit the vi editor.

3. Switch to a command-line terminal (tty5) by pressing **Ctrl+Alt+F5** and log in to the terminal using the user name of **bozoette** and the password of **LNXrocks!**.

4. At the command prompt, type **groups** and press **Enter**. Of which groups is bozoette a member?

5. At the command prompt, type **id** and press **Enter**. Which group is the primary group for the user bozoette?

6. At the command prompt, type **touch file1** and press **Enter** to create a new file called file1 in the current directory.

7. At the command prompt, type **ls -l** and press **Enter**. Who is the owner and group owner of the file file1? Why?

8. At the command prompt, type **newgrp groupies** and press **Enter** to temporarily change bozoette's primary group to groupies.

9. At the command prompt, type **touch file2** and press **Enter** to create a new file called file2 in the current directory.

10. At the command prompt, type **ls -l** and press **Enter**. Who is the owner and group owner of the file file2? Why?

10

11. Type **exit** and press **Enter** to log out of the new shell created when you used the **newgrp** command. Next, type **exit** and press **Enter** to log out of your shell.

12. Switch back to the command-line terminal (tty2) by pressing **Ctrl+Alt+F2**.

13. At the command prompt, type **groupdel groupies** and press **Enter** to remove the group groupies from the system. Which file is edited by the **groupdel** command?

14. Type **exit** and press **Enter** to log out of your shell.

Discovery Exercises

1. Indicate which entry you could add to /etc/rsyslog.conf to:

   a. Log all critical messages from the kernel to /var/log/alert

   b. Log all messages from the user processes to /var/log/userlog

   c. Log all debug messages, as well as more serious messages, from the printing daemon to /var/log/printer

   d. Log all messages except notices from the mail daemon to /var/log/mailman

   e. Log all alerts and critical error messages to /var/log/serious

   f. Log all warnings and errors from the kernel and the printing daemon to /var/log/shared

2. Use the man or info pages to find a description of the –D option to the useradd command. What does this option do? What file does it edit? Use this option with the useradd command to set the date that all new user accounts will be disabled to March 5, 2055. What command did you use?

3. In Project 10-2, you enabled the remote administration and IPP print sharing options within the CUPS remote administration tool on your Fedora Linux virtual machine. However, in order to access CUPS remotely or print to your shared IPP printers, you must allow the ports for the HTTP (TCP port 80), HTTPS (TCP port 443), and IPP (TCP port 631) protocols in the firewall that is enabled by default in Fedora 20. Run the following commands to enable those ports:

   ```
   firewall-cmd --add-service http
   firewall-cmd --add-service https
   firewall-cmd --add-service ipp
   ```

   Next, use the ifconfig command to determine the IP address of your Fedora Linux virtual machine. Following this, access the CUPS administration Web site using the Web browser on your Windows host computer (URL: http://IP address:631). Finally, add a new printer within Control Panel on your Windows host computer that prints to the URL http://IP address:631/printers/printer1. Print to this new printer from a Windows program of your choice and verify that the job was submitted to the printer1 print queue using the lpstat -t command on your Fedora Linux virtual machine.

4. The CUPS commands introduced in this chapter work identically on both Fedora 20 and Ubuntu Server 14.04 systems. Since remote administration of the CUPS Web administration tool is disabled by default and Ubuntu Server 14.04 does not contain a GUI environment that allows you to access a Web browser and the CUPS Web administration tool, you must manually enable remote administration within the /etc/cups/cupsd.conf file.

On your Ubuntu Server Linux virtual machine, edit the *etc/cups/cupsd.conf* file and change the line that reads Listen localhost:631 to Port 631 as well as add three Allow from all lines within the access sections, as shown here:

```
# Restrict access to the server...
<Location />
  Order allow,deny
  Allow from all
</Location>

# Restrict access to the admin pages...
<Location /admin>
  Order allow,deny
  Allow from all
</Location>

# Restrict access to configuration files...
<Location /admin/conf>
  AuthType Default
  Require user @SYSTEM
  Order allow,deny
  Allow from all
</Location>
```

Next, save your changes, run the service cups restart command to restart the CUPS daemon, and run the ifconfig command to determine the IP address of your Ubuntu Server Linux virtual machine. Finally, access the CUPS administration Web site using the Web browser on your Windows host computer (URL: http://IP address:631).

5. When adding several user accounts, you might want to use the newusers utility, which can process a text file full of entries to add user accounts. Use the man or info page to find out how to use this utility, and use it to add three users. When finished, view the /etc/passwd, /etc/shadow, and /etc/group files to verify that the users were added successfully.

10

6. Write commands to accomplish the following (use the manual or info pages if necessary):

a. Create a user with a login name of bsmith, a UID of 733, a GECOS field entry of "accounting manager," and a password of Gxj234

b. Delete the user jdoe, but leave the home directory intact

c. Change the properties of the existing user wjones such that the user has a new comment field of "shipping" and an account expiry of March 23, 2022

d. Lock the account of wjenkins

e. Change the password of bsmith to We34Rt

f. Change the properties of the existing user tbanks such that the user is a member of the managers group and has a login name of artbanks

g. Create a user with the same UID and primary group as root and a login name of wjones

h. Create a new user with a login name of jdoe who has a password of he789R and no home directory

i. Change the primary group of the user wsmith to root

j. Add the users tbanks and jdoe to the group acctg

Compression, System Backup, and Software Installation

After completing this chapter, you will be able to:

- Outline the features of common compression utilities
- Compress and decompress files using common compression utilities
- Perform system backups using the `tar`, `cpio`, and `dump` commands
- View and extract archives using the `tar`, `cpio`, and `restore` commands
- Use burning software to back up files to CD and DVD
- Describe common types of Linux software
- Compile and install software packages from source code
- Install, manage, and remove software packages using the Red Hat Package Manager (RPM)
- Install, manage, and remove software packages using the Debian Package Manager (DPM)

In the preceding chapter, you examined common administrative tasks that are performed on a regular basis. In this chapter, you also learn about tasks that are performed frequently, but you focus on file- and software-related administration. You begin this chapter by learning about utilities commonly used to compress files on filesystems, followed by a discussion of system backup and archiving utilities. Finally, you learn about the different forms of software available for Linux systems, how to compile source code into functional programs, and about the features and usage of the Red Hat Package Manager (RPM) and Debian Package Manager (DPM).

Compression

At times, you might want to reduce the size of a file or set of files due to limited disk space. You might also want to compress files that are sent across the Internet or other computer network to decrease transfer time. In either case, you can choose from several utilities that reduce a file's size by stripping out characters via a process known as **compression**. The standard set of instructions used to compress a file is known as a **compression algorithm**. To decompress a file, you run the compression algorithm in reverse.

Because compression utilities use different compression algorithms, they achieve different rates of compression, or **compression ratios**, for similar files types. To calculate the compression ratio for a utility, you subtract the compressed percentage from 100. For example, if a compression utility compresses a file to 52 percent of its original size, it has a compression ratio of 48 percent.

Many compression utilities are available to Linux users; this section examines the three most common:

- compress
- GNU zip
- bzip2

Using compress

The `compress` command is one of the oldest compression utilities common to most UNIX and Linux systems. Its compression algorithm, which is called Adaptive Lempel-Ziv coding (LZW), has an average compression ratio of 40–50 percent.

To compress a file using `compress`, you specify the files to compress as arguments. Each file is renamed with a `.Z` filename extension to indicate that it is compressed. In addition, you can use the `-v` (verbose) option to the `compress` command to display the compression ratio during compression. The following output displays the filenames and size of the samplefile and samplefile2 files before and after compression:

```
[root@server1 ~]# ls -l
total 28
drwx------   3 root    root     4096 Jul 21 08:15 Desktop
-rw-r--r--   1 root    root    20239 Jul 21 08:15 samplefile
-rw-rw-r--   1 root    root      574 Jul 21 08:18 samplefile2
[root@server1 ~]# compress -v samplefile samplefile2
samplefile: -- replaced with samplefile.Z Compression: 48.06%
samplefile2: -- replaced with samplefile2.Z Compression: 26.13%
```

```
[root@server1 root]# ls -l
total 20
drwx------   3 root    root        4096 Jul 21 08:15 Desktop
-rw-rw-r--   1 root    root         424 Jul 21 08:18 samplefile2.Z
-rw-r--r--   1 root    root       10512 Jul 21 08:15 samplefile.Z
[root@server1 ~]# _
```

The `compress` command is not installed on Fedora 20 or Ubuntu Server 14.04 by default. To install it from a software repository on the Internet, you can run the `yum install ncompress` command as the root user on Fedora 20, or the `apt-get install ncompress` command as the root user on Ubuntu Server 14.04.

The `compress` command preserves the original ownership, modification, and access time for each file that it compresses.

By default, `compress` does not compress symbolic links or very small files unless you use the `-f` option.

You can compress all of the files in a certain directory by using the `-r` option and specifying the directory name as an argument to the `compress` command.

After compression, the **zcat command** can be used to display the contents of a compressed file, as shown in the following output:

```
[root@server1 ~]# zcat samplefile2.Z
Hi there, I hope this day finds you well.

Unfortunately we were not able to make it to your dining
room this year while vacationing in Algonquin Park - I
especially wished to see the model of the Highland Inn
and the train station in the dining room.

I have been reading on the history of Algonquin Park but
no where could I find a description of where the Highland
Inn was originally located on Cache lake.

If it is no trouble, could you kindly let me know such that
I need not wait until next year when I visit your lodge?

Regards,
Mackenzie Elizabeth

[root@server1 ~]# _
```

11

You can use the **zmore command** and the **zless command** to view the contents of a compressed file page-by-page.

To decompress files that have been compressed with the compress command, simply use the **uncompress command** followed by the names of the files to be decompressed. This restores the original filename. The following output decompresses and displays the filenames for the samplefile.Z and samplefile2.Z files created earlier:

```
[root@server1 ~]# uncompress -v samplefile.Z samplefile2.Z
samplefile.Z: -- replaced with samplefile
samplefile2.Z: -- replaced with samplefile2
[root@server1 ~]# ls -l
total 28
drwx------  3 root    root        4096 Jul 21 08:15 Desktop
-rw-r--r--  1 root    root       20239 Jul 21 08:15 samplefile
-rw-rw-r--  1 root    root         574 Jul 21 08:18 samplefile2
[root@server1 ~]# _
```

The uncompress command prompts you for confirmation if any existing files will be overwritten during decompression. To prevent this confirmation, you can use the −f option to the uncompress command.

You can omit the .Z extension when using the uncompress command. The command uncompress −v samplefile samplefile2 would achieve the same results as the command shown in the preceding output.

Furthermore, the compress utility is a filter command that can take information from Standard Input and send it to Standard Output. For example, to send the output of the who command to the compress utility and save the compressed information to a file called file.Z, you can execute the following command:

```
[root@server1 ~]# who | compress -v > file.Z
Compression: 21.35%
[root@server1 ~]# _
```

Following this, you can display the contents of file.Z using the zcat command, or decompress it using the uncompress command, as shown in the following output:

```
[root@server1 ~]# zcat file.Z
root    pts/1    Jul 20 19:22 (3.0.0.2)
root    tty5     Jul 15 19:03
root    pts/1    Jul 17 19:58
[root@server1 root]# uncompress -v file.Z
file.Z:  -- replaced with file
[root@server1 ~]# _
```

Option	Description
-c	When used with the uncompress command, it displays the contents of the compressed file to Standard Output (same function as the zcat command).
-f	When used with the compress command, it can be used to compress symbolic links. When used with the uncompress command, it overwrites any existing files without prompting the user.
-r	Specifies to compress or decompress all files recursively within a specified directory.
-v	Displays verbose output (compression ratio and filenames) during compression and decompression.

Table 11-1 Common options used with the compress utility

Table 11-1 provides a summary of options commonly used with the compress utility.

Using GNU Zip

GNU zip uses a Lempel-Ziv compression algorithm (LZ77) that varies slightly from the one used by the compress command. Typically, this algorithm yields better compression than the one used by compress. The average compression ratio for GNU zip is 60–70 percent. To compress files using GNU zip, you can use the **gzip command**.

Like compress, symbolic links are not compressed by the gzip command unless the –f option is given, and the –r option can be used to compress all files in a certain directory. In addition, the ownership, modification, and access times of compressed files are preserved by default, and the –v option to the gzip command can be used to display the compression ratio and filename. However, gzip uses the .gz filename extension by default.

To compress the samplefile and samplefile2 files shown earlier and view the compression ratio, you can use the following command:

```
[root@server1 ~]# gzip –v samplefile samplefile2
samplefile:          56.8% -- replaced with samplefile.gz
samplefile2:         40.7% -- replaced with samplefile2.gz
[root@server1 ~]# _
```

You can also use the zcat and zmore commands to send the contents of a compressed file to Standard Output. Along the same lines, the gzip command can accept information via Standard Input. Thus, to compress the output of the date command to a file called file.gz and view its contents afterward, you can use the following commands:

```
[root@server1 ~]# date | gzip -v > file.gz
6.8%
[root@server1 ~]# zcat file.gz
Sun Jul 25 19:24:56 EDT 2015
[root@server1 ~]# _
```

To decompress the file.gz file in the preceding output, you can use the –d option to the gzip command, or the **gunzip command**, as shown in the following output:

```
[root@server1 ~]# gunzip -v file.gz
file.gz:             6.8% -- replaced with file
[root@server1 ~]# _
```

11

Like the uncompress command, the gunzip command prompts you to overwrite existing files unless the -f option is specified. Furthermore, you can omit the .gz extension when decompressing files, as shown in the following example:

```
[root@server1 ~]# ls -l
total 20
drwx------  3 root     root      4096 Jul 21 08:15 Desktop
-rw-rw-r--  1 root     root       370 Jul 21 08:18 samplefile2.gz
-rw-r--r--  1 root     root      8763 Jul 21 08:15 samplefile.gz
[root@server1 ~]# gunzip -v samplefile samplefile2
samplefile.gz:  56.8% -- replaced with samplefile
samplefile2.gz: 40.7% -- replaced with samplefile2
[root@server1 ~]# ls -l
total 28
drwx------  3 root     root      4096 Jul 21 08:15 Desktop
-rw-r--r--  1 root     root     20239 Jul 21 08:15 samplefile
-rw-rw-r--  1 root     root       574 Jul 21 08:18 samplefile2
[root@server1 ~]# _
```

One of the largest advantages that gzip has over compress is its ability to control the level of compression via a numeric option. The -1 option is also known as fast compression and results in a lower compression ratio. Alternatively, the -9 option is known as best compression and results in the highest compression ratio at the expense of time. If no level of compression is specified, the gzip command assumes the number 6.

The following command compresses the samplefile file shown earlier using fast compression and displays the compression ratio:

```
[root@server1 ~]# gzip -v -1 samplefile
samplefile:            51.3% -- replaced with samplefile.gz
[root@server1 ~]# _
```

Notice from the preceding output that samplefile was compressed with a compression ratio of 51.3 percent, which is much lower than the compression ratio of 56.8 percent obtained earlier when samplefile was compressed with the default level of 6.

 You need not specify the level of compression when decompressing files, as it is built in to the compressed file itself.

Many more options are available to gzip than to compress, and many of these options have a POSIX option equivalent. Table 11-2 shows a list of these options.

Using bzip2

The **bzip2 command** differs from the compress and gzip commands previously discussed in that it uses the Burrows-Wheeler Block Sorting Huffman Coding algorithm when compressing files. In addition, bzip2 cannot be used to compress a directory full of files, the zcat and zmore commands cannot be used to view files compressed with bzip2, and the compression ratio is 50–75 percent on average.

Option	Description
-#	Specifies how thorough the compression will be, where # can be the number 1–9. The option -1 represents fast compression, which takes less time to compress but results in a lower compression ratio. The option -9 represents thorough compression, which takes more time but results in a higher compression ratio.
--best	Results in a higher compression ratio; same as the -9 option.
-c --stdout --to-stdout	Displays the contents of the compress file to Standard Output (same function as the zcat command) when used with the gunzip command.
-d --decompress --uncompress	Decompresses the files specified (same as the gunzip command) when used with the gzip command.
-f --force	Compresses symbolic links when used with the gzip command. When used with the gunzip command, it overwrites any existing files without prompting the user.
--fast	Results in a lower compression ratio; same as the -1 option.
-h --help	Displays the syntax and available options for the gzip and gunzip commands.
-l --list	Lists the compression ratio for files that have been compressed with gzip.
-n --no-name	Does not allow gzip and gunzip to preserve the original modification and access time for files.
-q --quiet	Suppresses all warning messages.
-r --recursive	Specifies to compress or decompress all files recursively within a specified directory.
-S .suffix --suffix .suffix	Specifies a file suffix other than .gz when compressing or decompressing files.
-t --test	Performs a test decompression such that a user can view any error messages before decompression, when used with the gunzip command; it does not decompress files.
-v --verbose	Displays verbose output (compression ratio and filenames) during compression and decompression.

Table 11-2 Common options used with the gzip command

As with compress and gzip, symbolic links are only compressed if the –f option is used, and the –v option can be used to display compression ratios. Also, file ownership, modification, and access time are preserved during compression.

The filename extension given to files compressed with bzip2 is .bz2. To compress the samplefile and samplefile2 files and view their compression ratios and filenames, you can use the following commands:

```
[root@server1 ~]# bzip2 -v samplefile samplefile2
samplefile: 2.637:1, 3.034 bits/byte, 62.08% saved, 20239 in, 7675 out.
```

```
s? samplefile2: 1.483:1, 5.394 bits/byte, 32.58% saved, 574 in, 387 out.
[root@server1 ~]# ls -l
total 16
drwx------  3 root    root     4096 Jul 21 08:15 Desktop
-rw-rw-r--  1 root    root      387 Jul 21 08:18 samplefile2.bz2
-rw-r--r--  1 root    root     7675 Jul 21 08:15 samplefile.bz2
[root@server1 ~]# _
```

Because the compression algorithm is different than the one used by compress and gzip, you must use the **bzcat command** to display the contents of compressed files to Standard Output, as shown in the following example:

```
[root@server1 ~]# bzcat samplefile2.bz2
Hi there, I hope this day finds you well.

Unfortunately we were not able to make it to your dining
room this year while vacationing in Algonquin Park - I
especially wished to see the model of the Highland Inn
and the train station in the dining room.

I have been reading on the history of Algonquin Park but
no where could I find a description of where the Highland
Inn was originally located on Cache lake.

If it is no trouble, could you kindly let me know such that
I need not wait until next year when I visit your lodge?

Regards,
Mackenzie Elizabeth

[root@server1 ~]# _
```

 You can also use the **bzmore** and a **bzless commands** also exist to view the contents of a bzip2-compressed file page by page.

To decompress files, you can use the **bunzip2 command** followed by the filename(s) to decompress; unlike with compress and gzip, you must include the filename extension when decompressing files. To decompress the samplefile and samplefile2 files created earlier and view the results, you can use the following command:

```
[root@server1 ~]# bunzip2 -v samplefile.bz2 samplefile2.bz2
  samplefile.bz2: done
  samplefile2.bz2: done
[root@server1 ~]# _
```

If any files are about to be overwritten, the bunzip2 command prompts the user for confirmation. To skip this confirmation, you can include the –f option. Table 11-3 lists other common options used with the bzip2 utility.

Option	Description
-#	Specifies the block size used during compression; -1 indicates a block size of 100KB, whereas -9 indicates a block size of 900KB.
-c --stdout	Displays the contents of the compressed file to Standard Output when used with the bunzip2 command.
-d --decompress	Decompresses the files specified (same as the bunzip2 command) when used with the bzip2 command.
-f --force	Compresses symbolic links when used with the bzip2 command. When used with the bunzip2 command, it overwrites any existing files without prompting the user.
-k --keep	Keeps the original file during compression; a new file is created with the extension .bz2.
-q --quiet	Suppresses all warning messages.
-s --small	Minimizes memory usage during compression.
-t --test	Performs a test decompression such that a user can view any error messages before decompression, when used with the bunzip2 command; it does not decompress files.
-v --verbose	Displays verbose output (compression ratio) during compression and decompression.

Table 11-3   Common options used with the bzip2 utility

System Backup

It's a good idea to create backup copies of files and directories regularly and store them at an alternate location. You can then distribute these back-up copies to other computers or use them to restore files lost as a result of a system failure. This entire process is known as **system backup**, and the back-up copies of files and directories are called **archives**.

You can create archives on many different types of media, such as tapes, CDs, DVDs, or hard disks. Traditionally, tapes were used to back up data. Today, large backups are typically performed using separate hard disks. Smaller backups are performed using CDs or DVDs, which require special burning software described later in this chapter.

Table 11-4 shows a list of some common device files for use with different tape devices.

A typical Linux system can include hundreds of thousands of files, but you don't have to include all of them in an archive. For example, you don't have to include temporary files in the /tmp and /var/tmp directories, nor do you need to include any cached Internet content found in the .mozilla directory (if you use the Mozilla Firefox Web browser) under each user's home directory.

As a rule of thumb, you should back up user files from home directories and any important system configuration files such as /etc/passwd. In addition to this, you might want to back up files used by system services. For example, you need to back up Web site files if the Linux computer is used as a Web server. Programs such as grep and vi need not be backed up because they can be restored from the original installation media in the event of a system failure.

Device File	Description
/dev/st0	First SCSI tape device (rewinding)
/dev/st1	Second SCSI tape device (rewinding)
/dev/st2	Third SCSI tape device (rewinding)
/dev/nst0	First SCSI tape device (nonrewinding)
/dev/ht0	First ATAPI IDE tape device (rewinding)
/dev/nht0	First ATAPI IDE tape device (nonrewinding)
/dev/ftape	First floppy tape device

Table 11-4 Common tape device files

After files have been selected for system backup, you can use a back-up utility to copy the files to the appropriate media. Several back-up utilities are available to Linux administrators. The most common are the following:

- Tape archive (tar)
- Copy in/out (cpio)
- dump/restore
- Disc burning software

Using Tape Archive (tar)

The **tape archive (tar)** utility is one of the oldest, most widely used back-up utilities and is executed via the **tar command**. It can create an archive in a file on a filesystem or directly on a device.

Like the compression utilities discussed earlier, the tar command accepts options to determine the location of the archive and the action to perform on the archive. Any arguments specified to the tar command list the file(s) to place in the archive. Table 11-5 depicts a list of common options used with the tar command.

Because tar is a widely used utility, the options shown in Table 11-5 are often used in other similar commands. One example is the jar command, which archives reusable class files used by the Java programming language.

To create an archive called /backup.tar that contains the contents of the current directory and view the results, you can use the following commands:

```
[root@server1 ~]# tar -cvf /backup.tar *
Desktop/
Desktop/Home.desktop
Desktop/trash.desktop
samplefile
samplefile2
[root@server1 ~]# ls -l /backup.tar
-rw-r--r--   1 root     root      40960 Jul 27 10:49 /backup.tar
[root@server1 ~]# _
```

Option	Description

`-A`
`--catenate`
`--concatenate`
	Appends whole archives to another archive

`-c` `--create`	Creates a new archive
`--exclude PATTERN`	Excludes files that have a matching *PATTERN* in their filename when creating an archive
`-f FILENAME` `--file FILENAME`	Specifies the location of the archive (*FILENAME*); it can be a file on a filesystem or a device file
`-h` `--dereference`	Prevents tar from backing up symbolic links; instead, `tar` backs up the target files of symbolic links
`-j` `--bzip`	Compresses/decompresses the archive using the `bzip2` utility
`-P` `--absolute-paths`	Stores filenames in an archive using absolute pathnames
`-r` `--append`	Appends files to an existing archive
`--remove-files`	Removes files after adding them to an archive
`-t` `--list`	Lists the filename contents (table of contents) of an existing archive
`-u` `--update`	Appends files to an existing archive only if they are newer than the same filename inside the archive
`-v` `--verbose`	Displays verbose output (file and directory information) when manipulating archives

`-w`
`--interactive`
`--confirmation`
	Prompts the user for confirmation of each action

`-W` `--verify`	Verifies the contents of each archive after creation

`-x`
`--extract`
`--get`
	Extracts the contents of an archive

`-z`
`--gzip`
`--ungzip`
	Compresses/decompresses the archive using the `gzip` utility

`-Z`
`--compress`
`--uncompress`
	Compresses/decompresses the archive using the `compress` utility

Table 11-5   Common options used with the tar utility

11

Note from the preceding command that the –f option is followed by the pathname of the archive and that the * metacharacter indicates that all files in the current directory will be added to this archive. Also note that files are backed up recursively by default and stored using relative pathnames; to force the use of absolute pathnames when creating archives, simply use the –P option to the tar command.

 The filename used for an archive need not have an extension. However, it is good practice to name archive files with an extension to identify their contents, as with /backup.tar in the preceding example.

 The tar utility cannot back up device files or files with filenames longer than 255 characters.

After creating an archive, you can view its detailed contents by specifying the –t (table of contents) option to the tar command and the archive to view. For example, to view the detailed contents of the /backup.tar archive created earlier, you can issue the following command:

```
[root@server1 ~]# tar -tvf /backup.tar
drwx------ root/root       0 2015-07-21 08:15 Desktop/
-rw-r--r-- root/root    3595 2015-06-21 20:32 Desktop/Home.desktop
-rw-r--r-- root/root    3595 2015-06-21 20:32 Desktop/trash.desktop
-rw-r--r-- root/root   20239 2015-07-21 08:15 samplefile
-rw-rw-r-- root/root     574 2015-07-21 08:18 samplefile2
[root@server1 ~]# _
```

You can use the –x option with the tar command to extract a specified archive. To extract the contents of the /backup.tar file to a new directory called /tartest and view the results, you can issue the following commands:

```
[root@server1 ~]# mkdir /tartest
[root@server1 ~]# cd /tartest
[root@server1 tartest]# tar -xvf /backup.tar
Desktop/
Desktop/Home.desktop
Desktop/trash.desktop
samplefile
samplefile2
[root@server1 tartest]# ls -F
Desktop/ samplefile samplefile2
[root@server1 tartest]# _
```

After an archive has been created in a file on a filesystem, that file can be sent to other computers across a network or the Internet. This is the most common form of backup today and a common method used to distribute software across the Internet. Unfortunately, the tar utility does not compress files inside the archive. Thus, the amount of time needed to transfer the archive across a network is high. To reduce transfer times, you can compress the archive using a compression utility before transmission. Because this is a common task, the tar command accepts options that allow you to compress an archive immediately after creation using the compress, gzip, or bzip2 command.

To create a gzip-compressed archive called /backup.tar.gz that contains the contents of the current directory and view the results, you can use the following commands:

```
[root@server1 ~]# tar -zcvf /backup.tar.gz *
Desktop/
Desktop/Home.desktop
Desktop/trash.desktop
samplefile
samplefile2
[root@server1 ~]# ls -l /backup.tar*
-rw-r--r--   1 root    root        40960 Jul 27 10:49 /backup.tar
-rw-r--r--   1 root    root        12207 Jul 27 11:18 /backup.tar.gz
[root@server1 ~]# _
```

Note in the preceding output that the –z option indicated compression using the gzip utility, and that we chose to end the filename with the .tar.gz extension. In addition, the size of the /backup.tar.gz file is much less than the /backup.tar file created earlier.

 Filenames that end with the .tar.gz or .tgz extension are commonly called **tarballs** since they represent compressed tar archives.

To view the contents of a gzip-compressed archive, you must use the –z option in addition to the –t option followed by the archive to view. The detailed contents of the /backup.tar.gz file can be viewed using the following command:

```
[root@server1 ~]# tar -ztvf /backup.tar.gz
drwx------   root/root          0 2015-07-21 08:15 Desktop/
-rw-r--r--   root/root       3595 2015-06-21 20:32 Desktop/Home.desktop
-rw-r--r--   root/root       3595 2015-06-21 20:32 Desktop/trash.desktop
-rw-r--r--   root/root      20239 2015-07-21 08:15 samplefile
-rw-rw-r--   root/root        574 2015-07-21 08:18 samplefile2
[root@server1 ~]# _
```

Similarly, when extracting a gzip-compressed archive, you must supply the –z option to the tar command. To extract the contents of the /backup.tar.gz file to a new directory called /tartest2 and view the results, you can issue the following commands:

```
[root@server1 ~]# mkdir /tartest2
[root@server1 ~]# cd /tartest2
[root@server1 tartest2]# tar -zxvf /backup.tar.gz
Desktop/
Desktop/Home.desktop
Desktop/trash.desktop
samplefile
samplefile2
[root@server1 tartest2]# ls -F
Desktop/ samplefile samplefile2
[root@server1 tartest2]# _
```

11

Backing up files to a compressed archive on a filesystem is useful when you plan to transferr the archived data across a network. However, you can use tar to back up data directly to a device such as a tape. To back up files to a device, you can use the −f option to the tar command to specify the pathname to the appropriate device file. Files are then transferred directly to the device, overwriting any other data or filesystems that might be present.

For example, to create an archive on the first rewinding SCSI tape device containing the contents of the current directory, you can use the following command:

```
[root@server1 ~]# tar -cvf /dev/st0 *
Desktop/
Desktop/Home.desktop
Desktop/trash.desktop
samplefile
samplefile2
[root@server1 ~]#
```

You can then view the contents of the archive on the tape device used in the preceding example using the command tar −tvf /dev/st0 or extract the contents of the archive on the tape device using the command tar −xvf /dev/st0 in a similar fashion to the examples shown earlier.

Because tape devices can hold large amounts of information, you might want to add to a tar archive that already exists on the tape device. To do this, simply replace the −c option with the −r option when using the tar utility. For example, to append a file called samplefile3 to the archive created in the previous output and view the results, you can use the following commands:

```
[root@server1 ~]# tar -rvf /dev/st0 samplefile3
samplefile3
[root@server1 ~]# tar -tvf /dev/st0
drwx------   root/root        0 2010-07-21 08:15 Desktop/
-rw-r--r--   root/root     3595 2010-06-21 20:32 Desktop/Home.desktop
-rw-r--r--   root/root     3595 2010-06-21 20:32 Desktop/trash.desktop
-rw-r--r--   root/root    20239 2010-07-21 08:15 samplefile
-rw-rw-r--   root/root      574 2010-07-21 08:18 samplefile2
-rw-r--r--   root/root      147 2010-07-27 16:15 samplefile3
[root@server1 ~]# _
```

Using Copy In/Out (cpio)

Another common back-up utility is **copy in/out (cpio)**, which can be executed via the **cpio** command. Although cpio uses options similar to tar, it has some added features, including long filenames and the ability to back up device files.

Because its primary use is to back up files in case of system failure, cpio uses absolute pathnames by default when archiving. In addition, cpio normally takes a list of files to archive from Standard Input and sends the files "out" to the archive specified by the −O option. Conversely, when extracting an archive, you must include the −I option to indicate the archive from which to read "in" files.

Table 11-6 provides a list of commonly used options to the cpio command and their descriptions.

Option	Description
-A --append	Appends files to an existing archive
-B	Changes the default block size from 512 bytes to 5KB, thus speeding up the transfer of information
-c	Uses a storage format (SVR4) that is widely recognized by different versions of cpio for UNIX and Linux
-d --make-directories	Creates directories as needed during extraction
-i --extract	Reads files from an archive
-I FILENAME	Represents the input archive; it is the file or device file of the archive used when viewing or extracting files
-L --dereference	Prevents cpio from backing up symbolic links; instead, cpio backs up the target files of symbolic links
--no-absolute-filenames	Stores filenames in an archive using relative pathnames
-o --create	Creates a new archive
-O FILENAME	Represents the output archive; it is the file or device file of the target archive when backing up files
-t --list	Lists the filename contents (table of contents) of an existing archive
-u --unconditional	Overwrites existing files during extraction without prompting for user confirmation
-v --verbose	Displays verbose output (file and directory information) when manipulating archives

Table 11-6 Common options used with the cpio utility

To create an archive using cpio, you must first generate a list of filenames. You can do this using the find command. To list all filenames underneath the /root/sample directory, you can use the following command:

```
[root@server1 ~]# find /root/sample
/root/sample
/root/sample/samplefile
/root/sample/samplefile2
[root@server1 ~]# _
```

Next, you can send this list via Standard Input to the cpio command. For example, to verbosely back up all files in /root/sample to the first SCSI tape device using a block size of 5KB and a common format, you can use the following command:

```
[root@server1 ~]# find /root/sample | cpio -vocB -O /dev/st0
/root/sample
/root/sample/samplefile
/root/sample/samplefile2
```

```
5 blocks
[root@server1 ~]# _
```

To view the verbose table of contents of this archive, you can use the following command:

```
[root@server1 ~]# cpio -vitB -I /dev/st0
drwxr-xr-x   2 root    root        0 Jul 27 13:40 /root/sample
-rw-r-r--    1 root    root    20239 Jul 21 08:15 /root/sample/samplefile
-rw-rw-r--   1 root    root      574 Jul 21 08:18 /root/sample/samplefile2
5 blocks
[root@server1 ~]# _
```

Following this, you can extract the archive on /dev/st0, creating directories and overwriting files as needed by using the following command:

```
[root@server1 ~]# cpio -vicduB -I /dev/st0
/root/sample
/root/sample/samplefile
/root/sample/samplefile2
5 blocks
[root@server1 ~]# _
```

Like tar, the cpio command can be used to create an archive on a file on the filesystem; to do this, simply specify the filename after the –O option. To create an archive called /root/sample.cpio that contains the files from the directory /root/sample, using a block size of 5KB as well as a common header, and to view the results, you can issue the following commands:

```
[root@server1 ~]# find /root/sample | cpio -vocB –O /root/sample.cpio
/root/sample
/root/sample/samplefile
/root/sample/samplefile2
5 blocks
[root@server1 ~]# ls -l sample.cpio
-rw-rw-rw-   1 root  root   25600 Jul 27 13:45 sample.cpio
[root@server1 ~]# _
```

As with the tar utility, cpio archive filenames need not have an extension to identify their contents. However, it is good practice to use extensions, as shown with /root/sample.cpio in the preceding example.

Using dump/restore

Like tar and cpio, the **dump command** can be used to back up files and directories to a device or to a file on the filesystem, and the **restore command** can be used to restore those files and directories. However, dump and restore can only work with files on ext2, ext3, and ext4 filesystems.

The dump and restore commands are not installed on Fedora 20 or Ubuntu Server 14.04 by default. To install them from a software repository on the Internet, you can run the yum install dump command as the root user on Fedora 20, or the apt-get install dump command as the root user on Ubuntu Server 14.04.

Although dump can be used to back up only certain files and directories, it was designed to back up entire filesystems to an archive and keep track of these filesystems in a file called **/etc/dump-dates**. Because archiving all data on a filesystem (known as a **full backup**) might take a long time, you can choose to perform a full backup only on weekends and incremental backups each evening during the week. An **incremental backup** backs up only the data that has been changed since the last backup. In the case of a system failure, you can restore the information from the full backup and then restore the information from all subsequent incremental backups in sequential order. You can perform up to nine different incremental backups using dump; number 0 represents a full backup, whereas numbers 1 through 9 represent incremental backups.

Suppose, for example, that you perform a full backup of the /dev/sda3 filesystem on Sunday, perform incremental backups from Monday to Wednesday, and on Thursday the /dev/sda3 filesystem becomes corrupted, as depicted in Figure 11-1.

After the filesystem has been re-created, you should restore the full backup (0) followed by the first incremental backup (1), the second incremental backup (2), and the third incremental backup (3) to ensure that data has been properly recovered.

The dump and restore commands have many options available; Table 11-7 provides a list of these options.

Take, for example, the output from the following df command:

```
[root@server1 ~]# df
Filesystem     1K-blocks      Used   Available   Use%   Mounted on
/dev/sda1      30237648    6885728    21815920    24%   /
tmpfs            480640        272      480368     1%   /dev/shm
/dev/sda3      15481840     169484    14525924     2%   /data
[root@server1 ~]# _
```

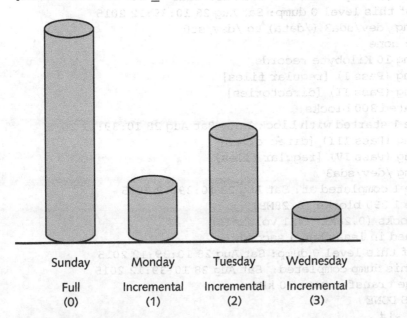

Sunday   Monday   Tuesday   Wednesday

Full   Incremental   Incremental Incremental
(0)   (1)   (2)   (3)

Figure 11-1 A sample back-up strategy

11

Option	Description
-#	Specifies the type of backup when used with the dump command; if # is 0, a full backup is performed. If # is 1 through 9, the appropriate incremental backup is performed.
-b NUM	Specifies a certain block size (NUM) to use in kilobytes; the default block size is 10KB.
-f FILENAME	Specifies the pathname to the archive; the FILENAME can be a file on a filesystem or a device file.
-u	Specifies to update the /etc/dumpdates file after a successful backup.
-n	Notifies the user if any errors occur and when the backup has completed.
-r	Extracts an entire archive when used with the restore command.
-x FILENAME	Extracts a certain file or files represented by FILENAME when used with the restore command.
-i	Restores files interactively, prompting the user for confirmation for all actions, when used with the restore command.
-t	Lists the filename contents (table of contents) of an existing archive when used with the restore command.
-v	Displays verbose output (file and directory information) when manipulating archives.

Table 11-7 Common options used with dump/restore

To perform a full backup of the /data partition (/dev/sda3) to the first rewinding SCSI tape device and update the /etc/dumpdates file when completed, you can issue the following command:

```
[root@server1 ~]# dump -0uf /dev/st0 /dev/sda3
  DUMP: Date of this level 0 dump: Sat Aug 28 10:39:12 2015
  DUMP: Dumping /dev/sda3 (/data) to /dev/st0
  DUMP: Label: none
  DUMP: Writing 10 Kilobyte records
  DUMP: mapping (Pass I) [regular files]
  DUMP: mapping (Pass II) [directories]
  DUMP: estimated 300 blocks.
  DUMP: Volume 1 started with block 1 at: Sat Aug 28 10:39:12 2015
  DUMP: dumping (Pass III) [directories]
  DUMP: dumping (Pass IV) [regular files]
  DUMP: Closing /dev/sda3
  DUMP: Volume 1 completed at: Sat Aug 28 10:39:12 2015
  DUMP: Volume 1 290 blocks (0.28MB)
  DUMP: 290 blocks (0.28MB) on 1 volume(s)
  DUMP: finished in less than a second
  DUMP: Date of this level 0 dump: Sat Aug 28 10:39:12 2015
  DUMP: Date this dump completed:  Sat Aug 28 10:39:12 2015
  DUMP: Average transfer rate: 0 kB/s
  DUMP: DUMP IS DONE
[root@server1 ~]# _
```

Alternatively, you can specify the filesystem mount point when using the dump command. The command `dump -0uf /dev/st0 /data` is equivalent to the one used in the preceding example.

The contents of the /etc/dumpdates file now indicate that a full backup has taken place:

```
[root@server1 ~]# cat /etc/dumpdates
/dev/sda3 0 Sat Aug 28 10:39:12 2015 -0400
[root@server1 ~]# _
```

To perform the first incremental backup and view the contents of the /etc/dumpdates file, you can place a new tape into the SCSI tape drive and issue the following commands:

```
[root@server1 ~]# dump -1uf /dev/st0 /dev/sda3
  DUMP: Date of this level 1 dump: Sat Aug 28 10:41:09 2015
  DUMP: Date of last level 0 dump: Sat Aug 28 10:39:12 2015
  DUMP: Dumping /dev/sda3 (/data) to /dev/st0
  DUMP: Label: none
  DUMP: Writing 10 Kilobyte records
  DUMP: mapping (Pass I) [regular files]
  DUMP: mapping (Pass II) [directories]
  DUMP: estimated 255 blocks.
  DUMP: Volume 1 started with block 1 at: Sat Aug 28 10:41:10 2015
  DUMP: dumping (Pass III) [directories]
  DUMP: dumping (Pass IV) [regular files]
  DUMP: Closing /dev/sda3
  DUMP: Volume 1 completed at: Sat Aug 28 10:41:10 2015
  DUMP: Volume 1 250 blocks (0.24MB)
  DUMP: 250 blocks (0.24MB) on 1 volume(s)
  DUMP: finished in less than a second
  DUMP: Date of this level 1 dump: Sat Aug 28 10:41:09 2015
  DUMP: Date this dump completed: Sat Aug 28 10:41:10 2015
  DUMP: Average transfer rate: 0 kB/s
  DUMP: DUMP IS DONE
[root@server1 ~]# cat /etc/dumpdates
/dev/sda3 0 Sat Aug 28 10:39:12 2015 -0400
/dev/sda3 1 Sat Aug 28 10:41:09 2015 -0400
[root@server1 ~]# _
```

To view the contents of an archive, you can specify the -t option to the restore command followed by the archive information. To view the contents of the full backup performed earlier, you can place the appropriate tape into the tape drive and execute the following command:

```
[root@server1 ~]# restore -tf /dev/st0
Dump date: Sat Aug 28 10:39:12 2015
Dumped from: the epoch
Level 0 dump of /data on server1.class.com:/dev/sda3
```

```
Label: none
    2    .
   11    ./lost+found
   12    ./inittab
   13    ./hosts
   14    ./issue
   17    ./aquota.user
   15    ./aquota.group
[root@server1 ~]# _
```

To extract the full backup shown in the preceding output, you can specify the −r option to the restore command, followed by the archive information. In addition, you can specify the −v option to list the filenames restored, as shown in the following example:

```
[root@server1 ~]# restore -vrf /dev/st0
Verify tape and initialize maps
Input is from a local file/pipe
Input block size is 32
Dump   date: Sat Aug 28 10:39:12 2015
Dumped from: the epoch
Level 0 dump of /data on server1.class.com:/dev/sda3
Label: none
Begin level 0 restore
Initialize symbol table.
Extract directories from tape
Calculate extraction list.
Make node ./lost+found
Extract new leaves.
Check pointing the restore
extract file ./inittab
extract file ./hosts
extract file ./issue
extract file ./aquota.group
extract file ./aquota.user
Add links
Set directory mode, owner, and times.
Check the symbol table.
Check pointing the restore
[root@server1 ~]# _
```

Using Burning Software

The tar, cpio, and dump commands copy data to a back-up medium in a character-by-character or block-by-block format. As a result, they are typically used to create back-up copies of files on tape and hard disk media because those media accept data in that format. To write files to CD and DVD media, you must use a program that allows you to select the data to copy, organize that data, build a CD or DVD filesystem, and write the entire filesystem (including the data) to the CD or DVD. Recall from Chapter 2 that the programs that can be used to do this are called disc-burning software. Figure 11-2 shows the **GnomeBaker CD/DVD Writer** disc-burning software. You can install GnomeBaker CD/DVD Writer on a Fedora 20 system using the yum install gnomebaker command as the root user, and launch it from the GNOME desktop by navigating to Activies, Show Applications, Gnome-Baker CD/DVD Writer.

Figure 11-2 The GnomeBaker CD/DVD Writer

Software Installation

Primary responsibilities of most Linux administrators typically include installing and maintaining software packages. Software for Linux can consist of binary files that have been precompiled to run on certain hardware architectures such as 64-bit Intel (x86_64), or as source code, which must be compiled on the local architecture before use. The largest advantage to obtaining and compiling source code is that the source code is not created for a particular hardware architecture. After being compiled, the program executes natively on the architecture from which it was compiled.

NOTE The most common method for obtaining software for Linux is via the Internet. Appendix C lists some common Web sites that host Linux Open Source Software for download.

NOTE When downloading software files from the Internet, you may notice that the Internet sites list a **checksum** value for the file, which was calculated from the exact file contents. To ensure that the file was received in its entirety after you download it, you should verify that the checksum value is still the same. You can use one of several ***sum commands**, depending on the algorithm used to create the checksum. For example, you can use the md5sum `programfile` command to check an MD5 checksum, the sha1sum `programfile` command to check an SHA-1 checksum, the sha256sum `programfile` command to check an SHA-256 checksum, or the sha512sum `programfile` command to check an SHA-512 checksum.

11

Program source code is typically distributed as a format, which you can uncompress. After you have uncompressed it, you can extract the source code and compile it. Precompiled binary programs can also be distributed in tarball format, but they are typically distributed in a format for use with a package manager.

Recall from Chapter 1 that a **package manager** provides a standard format for distributing programs as well as a central database to store information about software packages installed on the system; this allows software packages to be queried and easily uninstalled. Most Linux distributions today, including Fedora, use the **Red Hat Package Manager (RPM)**. However, Debian and Debian-based Linux distributions, such as Ubuntu Linux, use the **Debian Package Manager (DPM)**.

RPM or DPM are used by nearly all mainstream Linux distributions. However, they are not the only package managers available on Linux systems. For example, Arch Linux uses the Pacman package manager.

Compiling Source Code into Programs

The procedure for compiling source code into binary programs is standardized today among most Open Source Software developers. Because most source code comes in tarball format, you must uncompress and extract the files. This creates a subdirectory under the current directory containing the source code. In addition, this directory typically contains a README file with information about the program and an INSTALL file with instructions for installation.

While inside the source code directory, the first step to installation is to run the `configure` program. This performs a preliminary check for system requirements and creates a list of what to compile inside a file called Makefile in the current directory.

Next, you can type the `make` command, which looks for the Makefile file and uses the information in it to compile the source code into binary programs using the appropriate compiler program for the local hardware architecture. For example, software written in the C programming language is compiled using the **GNU C Compiler (gcc)**. After compilation, the binary files the program comprises remain in the source code directory. To copy the files to the appropriate location on the filesystem, such as a directory listed in the PATH variable, you must type `make install`.

Most Linux programs are installed to a subdirectory of the /usr/local directory after compilation.

After the program has been compiled and copied to the correct location on the filesystem, you can remove the source code directory and its contents from the system.

Suppose, for example, that you download the source code for rdesktop (Remote Desktop Protocol client) version 1.8.2 from the Internet at *www.sourceforge.net*:

```
[root@server1 ~]# ls -F
Desktop/ rdesktop-1.8.2.tar.gz
[root@server1 ~]# _
```

The first step to installing this program is to uncompress and extract the tarball, as shown in the following output. This creates a directory called rdesktop-1.8.2 containing the source code and supporting files.

```
[root@server1 ~]# tar -zxvf rdesktop-1.8.2.tar.gz
rdesktop-1.8.2/COPYING
rdesktop-1.8.2/README
rdesktop-1.8.2/configure
rdesktop-1.8.2/configure.ac
rdesktop-1.8.2/config.sub
rdesktop-1.8.2/config.guess
rdesktop-1.8.2/bootstrap
rdesktop-1.8.2/install-sh
rdesktop-1.8.2/Makefile.in
rdesktop-1.8.2/rdesktop.spec
rdesktop-1.8.2/asn.c
rdesktop-1.8.2/bitmap.c
rdesktop-1.8.2/cache.c
rdesktop-1.8.2/channels.c
rdesktop-1.8.2/cliprdr.c
rdesktop-1.8.2/cssp.c
rdesktop-1.8.2/ctrl.c
rdesktop-1.8.2/disk.c
rdesktop-1.8.2/ewmhints.c
rdesktop-1.8.2/iso.c
rdesktop-1.8.2/licence.c
rdesktop-1.8.2/lspci.c
rdesktop-1.8.2/mcs.c
rdesktop-1.8.2/mppc.c
rdesktop-1.8.2/orders.c
rdesktop-1.8.2/parallel.c
rdesktop-1.8.2/printer.c
rdesktop-1.8.2/printercache.c
rdesktop-1.8.2/pstcache.c
rdesktop-1.8.2/rdesktop.c
rdesktop-1.8.2/rdp5.c
rdesktop-1.8.2/rdp.c
rdesktop-1.8.2/rdpdr.c
rdesktop-1.8.2/rdpsnd_alsa.c
rdesktop-1.8.2/rdpsnd.c
rdesktop-1.8.2/rdpsnd_dsp.c
rdesktop-1.8.2/rdpsnd_libao.c
```

```
checking for stdint.h... yes
checking for unistd.h... yes
checking whether byte ordering is bigendian... no
checking for X... libraries , headers
checking for gethostbyname... yes
checking for connect... yes
checking for remove... yes
checking for shmat... yes
checking for IceConnectionNumber in -lICE... no
checking for pkg-config... /usr/bin/pkg-config
checking for library containing socket... none required
checking for library containing inet_aton... none required
checking sys/select.h usability... yes
checking sys/select.h presence... yes

<Additional checks omitted here>

checking for struct statvfs.f_namemax... yes
checking for struct statfs.f_namelen... yes
checking for struct statvfs.f_namelen... no
checking for special C compiler options needed for large files... no
checking for _FILE_OFFSET_BITS value needed for large files... no
checking mntent.h usability... yes
checking mntent.h presence... yes
checking for mntent.h... yes
checking for setmntent... yes
configure: creating ./config.status
config.status: creating Makefile
[root@server1 rdesktop-1.8.2]# _
```

After the configure script has run, a Makefile exists in the current directory, as shown in the following output:

```
[root@server1 rdesktop-1.8.2]# head Makefile
#
# rdesktop: A Remote Desktop Protocol client
# Makefile.in
# Copyright (C) Matthew Chapman 1999-2007
#
prefix = /usr/local
exec_prefix = ${prefix}
bindir = ${exec_prefix}/bin
mandir = ${datarootdir}/man
[root@server1 rdesktop-1.8.2]# _
```

This Makefile contains most of the information and commands necessary to compile the program. Some program source code that you download might contain commented lines that you need to uncomment to enable certain features of the program or to allow the program to compile on your computer architecture. Instructions for these commented areas are documented in the Makefile itself; thus, it is good form to read the Makefile after you run the configure script. You can also edit the Makefile if you want to change the location to which the program is installed. For rdesktop, simply change the line `prefix=/usr/local` shown in the preceding output to reflect the new directory.

Next, you must compile the program according to the settings stored in the Makefile by typing the `make` command while in the source code directory. This uses the `gcc` program to compile the source code files, as shown in the following output:

```
[root@server1 rdesktop-1.8.2]# make
gcc -g -O2 -Wall -I/usr/include -I/usr/include/alsa -
DPACKAGE_NAME=\"rdesktop\" -DPACKAGE_TARNAME=\"rdesktop\" -
DPACKAGE_VERSION=\"1.8.2\" -DPACKAGE_STRING=\"rdesktop\ 1.8.2\" -
DPACKAGE_BUGREPORT=\"\" -DSTDC_HEADERS=1 -DHAVE_SYS_TYPES_H=1 -
DHAVE_SYS_STAT_H=1 -DHAVE_STDLIB_H=1 -DHAVE_STRING_H=1 -
DHAVE_MEMORY_H=1 -DHAVE_STRINGS_H=1 -DHAVE_INTTYPES_H=1 -
DHAVE_STDINT_H=1 -DHAVE_UNISTD_H=1 -DL_ENDIAN=1 -DHAVE_SYS_SELECT_H=1 -
DHAVE_LOCALE_H=1 -DHAVE_LANGINFO_H=1 -Dssldir=\"/usr\" -
DEGD_SOCKET=\"/var/run/egd-pool\" -DWITH_RDPSND=1 -DRDPSND_OSS=1 -
DRDPSND_ALSA=1 -DHAVE_DIRENT_H=1 -DHAVE_DIRFD=1 -DHAVE_DECL_DIRFD=1 -
DHAVE_ICONV_H=1 -DHAVE_ICONV=1 -DICONV_CONST= -DHAVE_SYS_VFS_H=1 -
DHAVE_SYS_STATVFS_H=1 -DHAVE_SYS_STATFS_H=1 -DHAVE_SYS_PARAM_H=1 -
DHAVE_SYS_MOUNT_H=1 -DSTAT_STATVFS=1 -DHAVE_STRUCT_STATVFS_F_NAMEMAX=1
-DHAVE_STRUCT_STATFS_F_NAMELEN=1 -D_FILE_OFFSET_BITS=64 -
DHAVE_MNTENT_H=1 -DHAVE_SETMNTENT=1 -
DKEYMAP_PATH=\"/usr/local/share/rdesktop/keymaps/\" -o rdesktop.
o -c rdesktop.c
gcc -g -O2 -Wall -I/usr/include -I/usr/include/alsa   -
DPACKAGE_NAME=\"rdesktop\" -DPACKAGE_TARNAME=\"rdesktop\" -
DPACKAGE_VERSION=\"1.8.2\" -DPACKAGE_STRING=\"rdesktop\ 1.8.2\" -
DPACKAGE_BUGREPORT=\"\" -DSTDC_HEADERS=1 -DHAVE_SYS_TYPES_H=1 -
DHAVE_SYS_STAT_H=1 -DHAVE_STDLIB_H=1 -DHAVE_STRING_H=1 -
DHAVE_MEMORY_H=1 -DHAVE_STRINGS_H=1 -DHAVE_INTTYPES_H=1 -
DHAVE_STDINT_H=1 -DHAVE_UNISTD_H=1 -DL_ENDIAN=1 -DHAVE_SYS_SELECT_H=1 -
DHAVE_LOCALE_H=1 -DHAVE_LANGINFO_H=1 -Dssldir=\"/usr\" -
DEGD_SOCKET=\"/var/run/egd-pool\" -DWITH_RDPSND=1 -DRDPSND_OSS=1 -
DRDPSND_ALSA=1 -DHAVE_DIRENT_H=1 -DHAVE_DIRFD=1 -DHAVE_DECL_DIRFD=1 -
DHAVE_ICONV_H=1 -DHAVE_ICONV=1 -DICONV_CONST= -DHAVE_SYS_VFS_H=1 -
DHAVE_SYS_STATVFS_H=1 -DHAVE_SYS_STATFS_H=1 -DHAVE_SYS_PARAM_H=1 -
DHAVE_SYS_MOUNT_H=1 -DSTAT_STATVFS=1 -DHAVE_STRUCT_STATVFS_F_NAMEMAX=1
-DHAVE_STRUCT_STATFS_F_NAMELEN=1 -D_FILE_OFFSET_BITS=64 -
DHAVE_MNTENT_H=1 -DHAVE_SETMNTENT=1 -
DKEYMAP_PATH=\"/usr/local/share/rdesktop/keymaps/\" -o xwin.o -c xwin.c

<Additional gcc commands omitted here>

DKEYMAP_PATH=\"/usr/local/share/rdesktop/keymaps/\" -o rdesktop
rdesktop.o xwin.o xkeymap.o ewmhints.o xclip.o cliprdr.o rdpsnd.o
rdpsnd_dsp.o rdpsnd_oss.o rdpsnd_alsa.o tcp.o iso.o mcs.o secure.o
licence.o rdp.o orders.o bitmap.o cache.o rdp5.o channels.o rdpdr.o
```

11

```
serial.o printer.o disk.o parallel.o printercache.o mppc.o pstcache.o
lspci.o seamless.o ssl.o -L/usr/lib -lcrypto -lasound      -lX11
[root@server1 rdesktop-1.8.2]# _
```

After you compile the source code files, you can copy the compiled executable programs to the correct location on the filesystem by typing the following command:

```
[root@server1 rdesktop-1.8.2]# make install
mkdir -p /usr/local/bin
/usr/bin/install -c rdesktop /usr/local/bin
strip /usr/local/bin/rdesktop
chmod 755 /usr/local/bin/rdesktop
mkdir -p /usr/local/share/rdesktop/keymaps/
cp keymaps/?? keymaps/??-?? /usr/local/share/rdesktop/keymaps/
cp keymaps/common /usr/local/share/rdesktop/keymaps/
cp keymaps/modifiers /usr/local/share/rdesktop/keymaps/
chmod 644 /usr/local/share/rdesktop/keymaps//*
mkdir -p /usr/local/share/man/man1
cp doc/rdesktop.1 /usr/local/share/man/man1
chmod 644 /usr/local/share/man/man1/rdesktop.1
[root@server1 rdesktop-1.8.2]# _
```

After you copy the executable programs files to the appropriate directory, you can remove the source code and tarball and locate the main binary file for the program, as shown in the following example:

```
[root@server1 rdesktop-1.8.2]# cd ..
[root@server1 ~]# rm -Rf rdesktop-1.8.2
[root@server1 ~]# rm -f rdesktop-1.8.2.tar.gz
[root@server1 ~]# which rdesktop
/usr/local/bin/rdesktop
[root@server1 ~]# _
```

Finally, you can view the rdesktop manual page, then switch to a desktop environment and run the command rdesktop remote_server_name to connect to a remote Windows server that runs the Remote Desktop Protocol (RDP), as shown in Figure 11-3.

Working with the Red Hat Package Manager (RPM)

RPM is the most widely used format for Linux software distributed via the Internet. RPM packages have filenames that indicate the hardware architecture for which the software was compiled and end with the .rpm extension. The following output indicates that the bluefish RPM package (a Web page editor) version 2.2.6-3 was compiled for Fedora 20 (fc20) on the Intel x86_64 platform:

```
[root@server1 ~]# ls -F
Desktop/    bluefish-2.2.6-3.fc20.x86_64.rpm
[root@server1 ~]# _
```

To install an RPM package, you can use the –i option to the **rpm command**. In addition, you can use the –v and –h options to print the verbose information and hash marks, respectively, during installation.

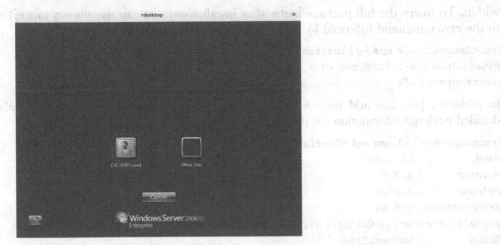

Figure 11-3 The rdesktop program

 You can convert an RPM package to a cpio archive using the `rpm2cpio` command.

Some RPM packages require that other RPM packages be installed on your system first. This type of relationship is known as a **package dependency**. If you attempt to install an RPM package that has package dependencies, you receive an error message that indicates the RPM packages that need to be installed first. After installing these prerequisite packages, you can successfully install your desired RPM package. Say, for example, that you download the RPM package for the bluefish Web page editor and run the following command to install it:

```
[root@server1 ~]# rpm -ivh bluefish-2.2.6-3.fc20.x86_64.rpm
error: Failed dependencies:
        bluefish-shared-data = 2.2.6-3.fc20 is needed by bluefish-2.2.6-3.
fc20.x86_64
[root@server1 ~]# _
```

The error shown in the preceding output indicates that there is a package dependency for the bluefish RPM package called bluefish-shared-data. Consequently, you must download the bluefish-shared-data package for your architecture. Following this, you can run the following command to install both packages:

```
[root@server1 ~]# rpm -ivh bluefish-shared-data-2.2.6-3.fc20.noarch.rpm
bluefish-2.2.6-3.fc20.x86_64.rpm
Preparing...                          ######################### [100%]
Updating / installing...
 1:bluefish-2.2.6-3.fc20               ######################### [ 50%]
 2:bluefish-shared-data-2.2.6-3.fc20  ######################### [100%]
[root@server1 ~]# _
```

After you install an RPM package, the RPM database (stored within files in the /var/lib/rpm directory) is updated to contain information about the package and the files contained within. To query the full package name after installation, you can use the -q (query) option to the rpm command followed by the common name of the package:

```
[root@server1 ~]# rpm -q bluefish
bluefish-2.2.6-3.fc20.x86_64
[root@server1 ~]# _
```

In addition, you can add the -i (info) option to the preceding command to display the detailed package information for the bluefish package:

```
[root@server1 ~]# rpm -qi bluefish
Name         : bluefish
Version      : 2.2.6
Release      : 3.fc20
Architecture : x86_64
Install Date : Mon 20 Oct 2014 05:40:55 PM EDT
Group        : Unspecified
Size         : 1495592
License      : GPLv3+
Signature    : RSA/SHA256, Fri 18 Jul 2014 02:17:53 PM EDT, Key ID 2eb161fa246110c1
Source RPM   : bluefish-2.2.6-3.fc20.src.rpm
Build Date   : Thu 17 Jul 2014 03:17:58 PM EDT
Build Host   : buildhw-08.phx2.fedoraproject.org
Relocations  : (not relocatable)
Packager     : Fedora Project
Vendor       : Fedora Project
URL          : http://bluefish.openoffice.nl/
Summary      : GTK2 web development application for experienced users
Description  :
Bluefish is a powerful editor for experienced web designers and programmers. Bluefish
supports many programming and markup languages, but it focuses on editing dynamic and
interactive websites.
[root@server1 ~]# _
```

Because the Red Hat Package Manager keeps track of all installed files, you can find the executable file for the bluefish program by using the -q and -l (list) options followed by the RPM package name to list all files contained within the package. The following command lists the first 10 files in the bluefish package:

```
[root@server1 ~]# rpm -ql bluefish
/usr/bin/bluefish
/usr/lib64/bluefish
/usr/lib64/bluefish/about.so
/usr/lib64/bluefish/charmap.so
/usr/lib64/bluefish/entities.so
/usr/lib64/bluefish/htmlbar.so
/usr/lib64/bluefish/infbrowser.so
/usr/lib64/bluefish/snippets.so
/usr/lib64/bluefish/zencoding.so
[root@server1 ~]# _
```

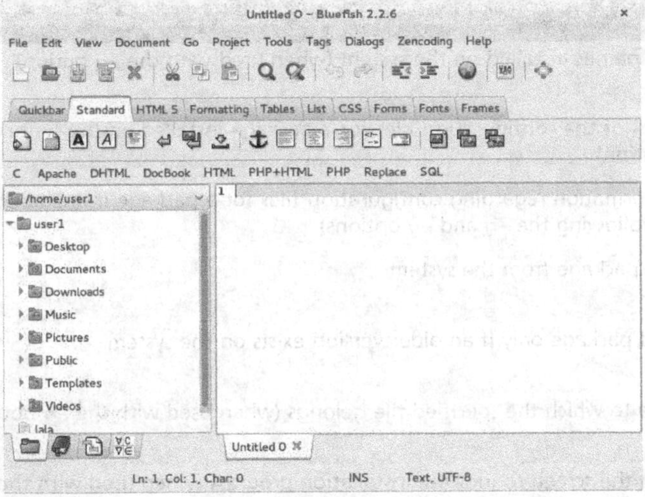

Figure 11-4 The bluefish program

From the preceding output, you can see that the pathname to the executable file is /usr/bin/bluefish, which resides in a directory that is in our PATH variable. Upon execution in a desktop environment, you see the screen depicted in Figure 11-4.

Conversely, you can find out to which RPM package a certain file belongs by using the -q and -f (file) options with the rpm command, followed by the filename:

```
[root@server1 ~]# rpm -qf /usr/bin/bluefish
bluefish-2.2.6-3.fc20.x86_64
[root@server1 ~]# _
```

To remove an RPM package from the system, you can use the -e option to the rpm command; all files that belong to the package will be removed as well. To remove the bluefish and bluefish-shared-data RPM packages and verify the deletion, you can use the following commands:

```
[root@server1 ~]# rpm -e bluefish bluefish-shared-data
[root@server1 ~]# rpm -q bluefish bluefish-shared-data
package bluefish is not installed
package bluefish-shared-data is not installed
[root@server1 ~]# _
```

Table 11-8 displays a list of common options used with the rpm command.

There are thousands of different RPM packages available for free download on Internet servers called **software repositories**. Moreover, each RPM on a software repository may have several package dependencies. Luckily, you can use the **yum** (**Yellowdog Updater Modified**) **command** to search Internet software repositories for RPM packages that map to your architecture, and automatically install or upgrade those packages on your system. Prior to installing the desired RPM package, the yum command also downloads and installs any package dependencies.

The **yum command**, which is installed by default on Fedora 20, uses the /etc/yum.conf and /etc/yum.repos.d/* files to specify the locations of Internet software repositories. During the

Option	Description
-a --all	Displays all package names installed on the system (when used with the –q option)
-c --configfiles	Displays the locations of the configuration files for a package installed on the system (when used with the –q option)
--dump	Displays detailed information regarding configuration files for a package installed on the system (when used following the –q and –c options)
-e --erase	Removes a specified package from the system
-F --freshen	Upgrades a specified package only if an older version exists on the system
-f --file	Displays the package to which the specified file belongs (when used with the –q option)
-h --hash	Prints hash marks on the screen to indicate installation progress (when used with the –i option)
-i --install	Installs a specified package (provided the –q option is not used)
-i --info	Displays full information about the specified package (when used with the –q option)
-K	When used before a filename argument, validates the checksum listed within the RPM file
-l --list	Lists the filenames the specified package comprises (when used with the –q option)
--nodeps	Forces the RPM to avoid checking for dependencies before installing packages (when used following the –i option)
-q --query	Queries information about packages on the system
--test	Performs a test installation only (when used with the –i option)
-U --upgrade	Upgrades a specified package; the package is installed even if no older version exists on the system
-V --verify	Verifies the location of all files that belong to the specified package
-v	Prints verbose information when installing or manipulating packages

Table 11-8   Common options used with the rpm command

Fedora 20 installation, files are added to the /etc/yum.repos.d directory that list standard software repositories on the Internet that contain RPM packages. Thus, if you forgot to choose a particular RPM package during the Fedora installation, you can easily install it afterwards using the yum install packagename command.

You used the yum command discussed in previous chapters to install several different programs on your Fedora 20 virtual machine from software repositories on the Internet.

Multiple software packages can be installed using a single yum command. For example, the yum install package1name package2name package3name command will install three packages, including any package dependencies.

Since newer versions of RPM packages are frequently added to software repositories, you can also upgrade an installed package to the latest version using the yum update packagename command. For example, to upgrade your BASH shell to the latest version, you could use the following command and press y when prompted to download and install the latest packages:

```
[root@server1 ~]# yum update bash
Loaded plugins: langpacks, refresh-packagekit
Resolving Dependencies
---> Running transaction check
---> Package bash.x86_64 0:4.2.45-4.fc20 will be updated
---> Package bash.x86_64 0:4.2.53-1.fc20 will be an update
---> Finished Dependency Resolution

Dependencies Resolved

================================================================
Package      Arch      Version          Repository    Size
================================================================
Updating:
bash         x86_64    4.2.53-1.fc20    updates       998 k

Transaction Summary

================================================================
Upgrade  1 Package

Total download size: 998 k
Is this ok [y/d/N]: y

Downloading packages:
Delta RPMs reduced 998 k of updates to 453 k (54% saved)
bash-4.2.45-4.fc20_4.2.53-1.fc20.x86_64.drpm   | 453 kB   00:00
Finishing delta rebuilds of 1 package(s) (998 k)
Running transaction check100% [========] 0.0 B/s | 998 kB  --:-- ETA
Running transaction test
Transaction test succeeded
Running transaction
  Updating  : bash-4.2.53-1.fc20.x86_64                    1/2
  Cleanup   : bash-4.2.45-4.fc20.x86_64                    2/2
  Verifying : bash-4.2.53-1.fc20.x86_64                    1/2
  Verifying : bash-4.2.45-4.fc20.x86_64                    2/2

Updated:
  bash.x86_64 0:4.2.53-1.fc20

Complete!
[root@server1 ~]# _
```

Without a package name argument, the `yum update` command will attempt to update all installed packages. You can also use the `yum check-update` command to check for installed software updates.

Note from the previous output that the `yum` command did not find any other package dependencies for BASH that needed updating. You may also find that the `yum` command tries several different software repositories that contain the necessary software (called **software mirrors**) before finding one that accepts a connection. This is common, because software repositories limit their concurrent download connections to allow for fast download. When a software repository reaches its concurrent connection limit, it returns a negative response to the `yum` command, and the `yum` command searches for the RPM package on the next software mirror listed in the `yum` configuration files.

In some cases, you may not know the exact RPM package name to use alongside the `yum` command. Luckily, you can use the `yum search keyword` command to search a software repository by keyword, or the `yum list available` command to list available RPM packages. The `yum grouplist` command will display a list of package group names. A **package group** is a group of related RPM packages that are often installed together to provide a key function. For example, to install the Development Tools package group on Fedora 20 (which contains the `make` and `gcc` commands), you can use the `yum groupinstall "Development Tools"` command.

RPM packages that are not hosted on the default software repositories can still be downloaded and installed using the `yum` command. Many software authors host their RPM packages on private software repositories and include instructions on their Web site that guide you through the process of adding the private software repository to your `yum` configuration files (usually by installing a special RPM package) and installing the RPM packages using the `yum` command. For example, if you want to install the VideoLAN VLC media player on Fedora 20, you can access the instructions for Fedora 20 from the VideoLAN Web site (*www.videolan.org*). Since the VideoLAN VLC media player is hosted on the private RPM Fusion software repository, the VideoLAN Web site instructs you to run the following command to update your `yum` configuration files with the location of the RPM Fusion software repository:

```
[root@server1 ~]# rpm -ivh http://download1.rpmfusion.org/free/fedora/
rpmfusion-free-release-stable.noarch.rpm
Retrieving   http://download1.rpmfusion.org/free/fedora/rpmfusion-free-
release-stable.noarch.rpm
warning: /var/tmp/rpm-tmp.cV8N0a: Header V3 RSA/SHA256 Signature, key ID
172ff33d: NOKEY
Preparing...                          ######################### [100%]
Updating / installing...
  1:rpmfusion-free-release-19-1        ######################### [100%]
[root@server1 ~]# _
```

Next, you can run the `yum install vlc` command to install the VLC media player.

The `yum` command can also be used to view and manage installed RPM packages. The `yum list installed` command will list installed RPM packages, and the `yum info packagename` command will display detailed information for an installed RPM package. You can also use the `yum remove packagename` command to remove an installed RPM package, or the yum groupremove packagegroupname command to remove all of the RPM packages within a particular package group.

The GNOME and KDE desktop environments on Fedora 20 contain a utility that periodically checks for updated RPM packages for the software installed on your system. If you select the Install Updates option in the notification window, this utility notifies you of any newer packages and automatically downloads and installs them using the yum command. You can also run the graphical **Software utility** shown in Figure 11-5 to check for software updates manually, search for and install new RPM software packages, or manage installed RPM software packages. To start the Software utility within the GNOME desktop environment, navigate to Activities, Show Applications, Software.

Working with the Debian Package Manager (DPM)

The Debian Package Manager (DPM) is used by default on Linux distributions that are based on the Debian Linux distribution, such as Ubuntu Linux. Like RPM packages, DPM packages contain software that has been precompiled for a specific platform, and they may have package dependencies. However, DPM packages use the .deb extension and are installed and maintained by the **dpkg command**. For example, to install the bluefish Web page editor on an Ubuntu Linux system from the downloaded DPM file bluefish_2.2.6-1_amd64.deb, you can use the dpkg -i bluefish_2.2.6-1_amd64.deb command. Table 11-9 displays a list of common options used with the dpkg command.

Figure 11-5 The Software utility

Option	Description
`-i` `--install`	Installs a specified package
`--ignore-depends`	Ignores any dependency checking for a specified package
`-l` `--list`	Displays information for a specified package by name or wildcard pattern (or all packages if no argument is given); it may also be used with the `dpkg-query` command
`-L` `--listfiles`	Displays the files that comprise a specified package; it may also be used with the `dpkg-query` command
`-p` `--print-avail`	Displays detailed package information for a specified package; it may also be used with the `dpkg-query` command
`-P` `--purge`	Removes a specified package from the system, including any configuration files used by the package
`-r` `--remove`	Removes a specified package from the system, excluding any configuration files used by the package
`-S` `--search`	Displays the package to which the specified file belongs; it may also be used with the `dpkg-query` command
`-s` `--status`	Displays the status for a specified package; it may also be used with the `dpkg-query` command
`--test`	Performs a test installation only (when used with the `-i` option)
`-V` `--verify`	Verifies the location of all files that belong to the specified package

Table 11-9   Common options used with the `dpkg` command

The amd64 architecture is identical to the x86_64 architecture; you will often find amd64 used in place of x86_64 within DPM package names. Additionally, some DPM packages prompt you for configuration information when installed using the `dpkg` command. You can reconfigure this information afterwards using the `dpkg-reconfigure` command.

After you install a DPM package, the DPM database (stored within files in the /var/lib/dpkg directory) is updated to contain information about the package and the files contained within. As with the RPM, you can query package information for installed packages. For example, to list information about the BASH shell package, you can use the following command:

```
[root@server1 ~]# dpkg –l bash
Desired=Unknown/Install/Remove/Purge/Hold
| Status=Not/Inst/Conf-files/Unpacked/halF-conf/Half-inst/trig-aWait/
Trig-pend
|/ Err?=(none)/Reinst-required (Status,Err: uppercase=bad)
||/ Name          Version     Architecture Description
+++-=============-===========-============-=================================
ii bash          4.3-7ubuntu1 amd64       GNU Bourne Again SHell
[root@server1 ~]# _
```

You can instead use the **dpkg-query command** when searching for DPM package information. The dpkg-query command takes the same search arguments as the dpkg command.

Alternatively, you could use the following command to list detailed information about the BASH shell package:

```
[root@server1 ~]# dpkg –p bash

Package: bash
Essential: yes
Priority: required
Section: shells
Installed-Size: 1480
Maintainer: Ubuntu Developers <ubuntu-devel-discuss@lists.ubuntu.com>
Architecture: amd64
Multi-Arch: foreign
Version: 4.3-7ubuntu1
Replaces: bash-completion (<< 20060301-0), bash-doc (<= 2.05-1)
Depends: base-files (>= 2.1.12), debianutils (>= 2.15)
Pre-Depends: dash (>= 0.5.5.1-2.2), libc6 (>= 2.15), libtinfo5
Recommends: bash-completion (>= 20060301-0)
Suggests: bash-doc
Conflicts: bash-completion (<< 20060301-0)
Filename: pool/main/b/bash/bash_4.3-6ubuntu1_amd64.deb
Size: 574520
MD5sum: 4829101773fd90ae0574fa83e474603a
Description: GNU Bourne Again SHell
 Bash is an sh-compatible command language interpreter that executes
 commands read from the standard input or from a file. Bash also
 incorporates useful features from the Korn and C shells (ksh and csh).
 .
 Bash is ultimately intended to be a conformant implementation of the
 IEEE POSIX Shell and Tools specification (IEEE Working Group 1003.2).
 .
 The Programmable Completion Code, by Ian Macdonald, is now found in
 the bash-completion package.
Homepage: http://tiswww.case.edu/php/chet/bash/bashtop.html
Original-Maintainer: Matthias Klose <doko@debian.org>
[root@server1 ~]# _
```

Since the Debian Package Manager keeps track of all installed files, you can also list the files that belong to a DPM package, verify DPM package contents, or search for the DPM package name for a specified file using the appropriate options from Table 11-9. For example, the following command lists the first 10 files in the BASH shell DPM package:

```
[root@server1 ~]# dpkg –L bash | head
/.
/etc
```

11

```
/etc/bash.bashrc
/etc/skel
/etc/skel/.profile
/etc/skel/.bashrc
/etc/skel/.bash_logout
/usr
/usr/share
/usr/share/menu
[root@server1 ~]# _
```

As with RPM, most DPM packages are hosted on Internet software repositories for free download. To download and install DPM packages, including any dependency packages, you can use the **apt-get** (**Advanced Package Tool**) **command.**

 You used the apt-get command in Chapter 6 to install the DPM packages required for ZFS on your Ubuntu Server Linux virtual machine.

The apt-get command is as easy to use as the yum command with the RPM. For example, to install the conky DPM package (a system monitoring tool) from an Internet software repository, you could run the following command:

```
[root@server1 ~]# apt-get install conky
Reading package lists... Done
Building dependency tree
Reading state information... Done
The following NEW packages will be installed:
  conky
0 upgraded, 1 newly installed, 0 to remove and 119 not upgraded.
Need to get 3,284 B of archives.
After this operation, 43.0 kB of additional disk space will be used.
Get:1 http://us.archive.ubuntu.com/ubuntu/ trusty/universe conky all
1.9.0-4 [3,284 B]
Fetched 3,284 B in 0s (51.0 kB/s)
Selecting previously unselected package conky.
(Reading database ... 75913 files and directories currently installed.)
Preparing to unpack .../archives/conky_1.9.0-4_all.deb ...
Unpacking conky (1.9.0-4) ...
Setting up conky (1.9.0-4) ...
[root@server1 ~]# _
```

To remove the conky DPM package, excluding any conky configuration files, you could use the apt-get remove conky command. Alternatively, you could use the apt-get purge conky command to remove the conky DPM package, including all conky configuration files. You can also use the apt-get update command to update the list of available DPM packages from Internet software repositories, as well as the apt-get upgrade command to upgrade the DPM packages on your system to the latest versions, based on the updated package list.

Figure 11-6 The Aptitude utility

DPM repository information is stored in the /etc/apt/sources.list file and in the /etc/apt/sources.list.d directory. You can add new repositories using the **add-apt-repository command**, or search available repository information using the **apt-cache command**. For example, to search software repositories for DPM packages that contain the word conky, you could use the `apt-cache search conky` command. To list all DPM packages available on available software repositories, you could use the `apt-cache search .` command.

 You used the `add-apt-repository` command in Chapter 6 to add the ZFS software repository to your Ubuntu Server Linux virtual machine.

You can also use the **Aptitude** utility (shown in Figure 11-6) to install, query, and remove DPM packages. You can start this utility by executing the **aptitude command** in a command-line or graphical terminal. In a command-line terminal, you can access the different Aptitude menus by pressing the Ctrl+t key combination. The `aptitude` command also accepts many of the same arguments as apt-get. For example, `aptitude install conky` will install the conky DPM package from an Internet repository, `aptitude remove conky` will remove the installed conky DPM package (excluding conky configuration files), and `aptitude purge conky` will remove the installed conky DPM package (including conky configuration files).

Chapter Summary

- Many compression utilities are available for Linux systems; each of them uses a different compression algorithm and produces a different compression ratio.
- Files can be backed up to an archive using a back-up utility. To back up files to CD-RW or DVD-RW, you must use burning software instead of a back-up utility.

tar (tape archive) command   The most common command used to create archives.

tarball   A gzip-compressed tar archive.

uncompress command   A command used to decompress files compressed by the compress command.

yum (Yellowdog Updater Modified) command   A command used to install and upgrade RPM packages from software repositories, as well as manage and remove installed RPM packages.

zcat command   A command used to view the contents of an archive created with compress or gzip to Standard Output.

zless command   A command used to view the contents of an archive created with compress or gzip to Standard Output in a page-by-page fashion.

zmore command   A command used to view the contents of an archive created with compress or gzip to Standard Output in a page-by-page fashion.

Review Questions

1. Most source code is available on the Internet in tarball format. True or False?

2. Which dump level indicates a full backup?

    a.   0

    b.   9

    c.   1

    d.   f

3. Which filename extension indicates a tarball?

    a.   .tar.gz

    b.   .cpio

    c.   .dump

    d.   .tar

4. Files that have been compressed using the compress utility typically have the _____ extension.

    a.   .tar.gz

    b.   .gz

    c.   .Z

    d.   .bz2

5. The bzip2 and gzip utilities use similar compression algorithms. True or False?

6. When compiling source code into a binary program, which command does the compiling using the GNU C Compiler?

    a. `tar`

    b. `./configure`

    c. `make`

    d. `make install`

7. The -9 option to the gzip command results in a higher compression ratio. True or False?

8. You have created a full backup and four incremental backups. In which order must you restore these backups?

    a. 0, 1, 2, 3, 4

    b. 0, 4, 3, 2, 1

    c. 4, 3, 2, 1, 0

    d. 1, 2, 3, 4, 0

9. Which of the following commands extracts an archive?

    a. `cpio -vocBL /dev/fd0`

    b. `cpio -vicdu -I /dev/fd0`

    c. `cpio -vicdu -O /dev/fd0`

    d. `cpio -vti -I /dev/fd0`

10. The Debian Package Manager (DPM) is the default package manager used by Fedora 20. True or False?

11. Which of the following commands can be used to list the files contained within an installed RPM package?

    a. `rpm -qa packagename`

    b. `rpm -qi packagename`

    c. `rpm -ql packagename`

    d. `rpm -q packagename`

12. Which of the following command can be used to remove the test DPM package, including any test configuration files?

    a. `dpkg remove test`

    b. `apt-get remove test`

    c. `dpkg purge test`

    d. `apt-get purge test`

13. To install a new program from RPM software repositories on the Internet, you can use the yum update programname command. True or False?

11

14. Which file contains full and incremental back-up information for use with the dump/restore utility?

    a. /etc/dumps

    b. /etc/dumpdates

    c. /etc/dumpfile

    d. /etc/dump.conf

15. Which of the following represents the first nonrewinding SCSI tape device on a system?

    a. /dev/st0

    b. /dev/ht0

    c. /dev/nht0

    d. /dev/nst0

16. Which option to the dpkg command can be used to list the files that comprise a package?

    a. -l

    b. -L

    c. -s

    d. -i

17. Which option to the rpm command can be used to remove a package from the system?

    a. -r

    b. -e

    c. -u

    d. -U

18. Which of the following commands creates an archive?

    a. tar -cvf /dev/st0

    b. tar -xvf /dev/st0

    c. tar -tvf /dev/st0

    d. tar -zcvf /dev/st0 *

19. When compiling source code into a binary program, which command performs a system check and creates the Makefile?

    a. tar

    b. ./configure

    c. make

    d. make install

20. Which of the following commands can be used to search for packages that contain the word "oobla" on RPM software repositories?

    a. `yum search oobla`

    b. `rpm -qS oobla`

    c. `yum list oobla`

    d. `rpm -ql oobla`

Hands-on Projects

These projects should be completed in the order given. The hands-on projects presented in this chapter should take a total of three hours to complete. The requirements for this lab include:

- A computer with Fedora Linux installed according to Hands-on Project 2-1 and Ubuntu Server Linux installed according to Hands-on Project 6-1.

Project 11-1

In this hands-on project, you use common compression utilities to compress and uncompress information on Fedora 20.

1. Boot your Fedora Linux virtual machine. After your Linux system has been loaded, switch to a command-line terminal (tty2) by pressing **Ctrl+Alt+F2** and log in to the terminal using the user name of **root** and the password of **LNXrocks!**.

2. At the command prompt, type **yum install ncompress** and press **Enter**. Press y when prompted to complete the installation of the ncompress RPM package (and any package dependencies).

3. At the command prompt, type **cp /etc/services ~** and press **Enter** to make a copy of the /etc/services file in your home directory. Next, type **ls -l** at the command prompt and press **Enter**. How large is the services file?

4. At the command prompt, type **compress -v services** and press **Enter** to compress the services file. What was the compression ratio? Next, type **ls -l** at the command prompt and press **Enter**. What extension does the services file have and how large is it?

5. At the command prompt, type **uncompress -v services.Z** and press **Enter** to decompress the services file.

6. At the command prompt, type **cp /etc/hosts /etc/inittab Desktop** and press **Enter** to copy the hosts and inittab file to your Desktop subdirectory.

7. At the command prompt, type **compress -vr Desktop** and press **Enter** to compress the contents of the Desktop subdirectory. Next, type **ls -lR Desktop** at the command prompt and press **Enter** to view the contents of the Desktop directory. Which files were compressed? If there were symbolic links in this directory, how could you force the compress utility to compress these files as well?

8. At the command prompt, type **uncompress -vr Desktop** and press **Enter** to decompress the contents of the Desktop subdirectory. Next, type **ls –lR Desktop** at the command prompt and press **Enter** to verify that these files were uncompressed.

9. At the command prompt, type **ps –ef | compress –v >psfile.Z** and press **Enter** to compress the output of the **ps –ef** command to a file called psfile.Z. What was the compression ratio?

10. At the command prompt, type **zmore psfile.Z** and press **Enter** to view the compressed contents of the psfile.Z file. When finished, press **q** to quit the more utility.

11. At the command prompt, type **gzip -v services** and press **Enter** to compress the services file. What was the compression ratio? How does this ratio compare to the one obtained in Step 4? Why? Next, type ls –l at the command prompt and press **Enter**. What extension does the services file have and how large is it?

12. At the command prompt, type **gunzip -v services.gz** and press **Enter** to decompress the services file.

13. At the command prompt, type **gzip -v -9 services** and press **Enter** to compress the services file. What was the compression ratio? Why?

14. At the command prompt, type **gunzip -v services.gz** and press **Enter** to decompress the services file.

15. At the command prompt, type **gzip -v -1 services** and press **Enter** to compress the services file. What was the compression ratio? Why?

16. At the command prompt, type **gunzip -v services.gz** and press **Enter** to decompress the services file.

17. At the command prompt, type **bzip2 -v services** and press **Enter** to compress the services file. What was the compression ratio? How does this compare to the ratios from Step 4 and Step 11? Why? Next, type **ls –l** at the command prompt and press **Enter**. What extension does the services file have and how large is it?

18. At the command prompt, type **bunzip2 -v services.bz2** and press **Enter** to decompress the services file.

19. Type **exit** and press **Enter** to log out of your shell.

Project 11-2

In this hands-on project, you create, view, and extract archives using the tar utility.

1. On your Fedora Linux virtual machine, switch to a command-line terminal (tty2) by pressing **Ctrl+Alt+F2** and log in to the terminal using the user name of **root** and the password of **LNXrocks!**.

2. At the command prompt, type **tar –cvf test1.tar /etc/samba** and press **Enter** to create an archive called test1.tar in the current directory that contains the /etc/samba directory and its contents. Next, type **ls –l** at the command prompt and press **Enter**. How large is the test1.tar file?

3. At the command prompt, type **tar –tvf test1.tar** and press **Enter**. What is displayed?

4. At the command prompt, type **mkdir /new1** and press **Enter**. Next, type **cd /new1** at the command prompt and press **Enter** to change the current directory to the /new1 directory.

5. At the command prompt, type **tar -xvf /root/test1.tar** and press **Enter** to extract the contents of the test1.tar archive. Next, type **ls -RF** at the command prompt and press **Enter** to view the contents of the /new1 directory. Was the extraction successful?

6. At the command prompt, type **cd** and press **Enter** to return to your home directory.

7. At the command prompt, type **tar -zcvf test2.tar.gz /etc/samba** and press **Enter** to create a **gzip**-compressed archive called test2.tar.gz in the current directory that contains the /etc/samba directory and its contents. Next, type ls -l at the command prompt and press **Enter**. How large is the test2.tar.gz file? How does this compare to the size obtained for test1.tar in Step 2? Why?

8. At the command prompt, type **tar -ztvf test2.tar.gz** and press **Enter**. What is displayed?

9. At the command prompt, type **mkdir /new2** and press **Enter**. Next, type **cd /new2** at the command prompt and press **Enter** to change the current directory to the /new2 directory.

10. At the command prompt, type **tar -zxvf /root/test2.tar.gz** and press **Enter** to uncompress and extract the contents of the test2.tar.gz archive. Next, type **ls -RF** at the command prompt and press **Enter** to view the contents of the /new2 directory. Was the extraction successful?

11. At the command prompt, type **cd** and press **Enter** to return to your home directory.

12. At the command prompt, type **modprobe floppy** and press **Enter**. This will load the floppy disk driver. The process of creating and managing an archive on a floppy disk is identical to that of creating and managing an archive on a tape device.

13. At the command prompt, type **tar -cvf /dev/fd0 /etc/samba** and press **Enter** to create an archive on the device /dev/fd0 that contains the /etc/samba directory and its contents.

14. At the command prompt, type **tar -tvf /dev/fd0** and press **Enter**. What is displayed?

15. At the command prompt, type **mkdir /new3** and press **Enter**. Next, type **cd /new3** at the command prompt and press **Enter** to change the current directory to the /new3 directory.

16. At the command prompt, type **tar -xvf /dev/fd0** and press **Enter** to extract the contents of the archive stored on the first floppy disk. Next, type **ls -F** at the command prompt and press **Enter** to view the contents of the /new3 directory. Was the extraction successful?

17. At the command prompt, type **mount /dev/fd0 /mnt** and press **Enter** to mount the floppy to the /mnt directory. What error message do you receive and why? Why was the filesystem type not automatically detected? Can this floppy be mounted?

18. At the command prompt, type **rm -Rf /new[123]** and press **Enter** to remove the directories created in this hands-on project.

19. At the command prompt, type **rm –f /root/test*** and press **Enter** to remove the tar archives created in this hands-on project.

20. Type **exit** and press **Enter** to log out of your shell.

Project 11-3

In this hands-on project, you create, view, and extract archives using the cpio and dump utilities.

1. On your Fedora Linux virtual machine, switch to a command-line terminal (tty2) by pressing **Ctrl+Alt+F2** and log in to the terminal using the user name of **root** and the password of **LNXrocks!**.

2. At the command prompt, type **find /etc/samba | cpio -ovcBL –O test.cpio** and press **Enter** to create an archive in the file test.cpio that contains the /etc/samba directory and its contents. What does each option indicate in the aforementioned command?

3. At the command prompt, type **cpio -ivtB –I test.cpio** and press **Enter**. What is displayed? What does each option indicate in the aforementioned command?

4. At the command prompt, type **cpio -ivcdumB –I test.cpio** and press **Enter** to extract the contents of the archive in the test.cpio file. To what location were the files extracted? Were any files overwritten? What does each option indicate in the aforementioned command?

5. At the command prompt, type **yum install dump** and press **Enter**. Press **y** when prompted to complete the installation of the dump RPM package (and any package dependencies).

6. At the command prompt, type **dump -0uf test.dump /dev/sda1** and press **Enter** to create an archive of the /boot filesystem in the archive file test.dump. What type of backup was performed? Will the /etc/dumpdates file be updated?

7. At the command prompt, type **cat /etc/dumpdates** and press **Enter**. Does the file indicate your full backup and time?

8. At the command prompt, type **mkdir /new** and press **Enter**. Next, type **cd /new** at the command prompt and press **Enter** to change the current directory to the /new directory.

9. At the command prompt, type **restore -rf /root/test.dump** and press **Enter**. What was displayed? Are absolute or relative pathnames used?

10. Type **ls –F** at the command prompt and press **Enter** to view the contents of the /new directory. What is displayed?

11. At the command prompt, type **cd** and press **Enter** to return to your home directory.

12. At the command prompt, type **rm –Rf /new** and press **Enter** to remove the directory created in this hands-on project.

13. At the command prompt, type **rm –f /root/test*** and press **Enter** to remove the archives created in this hands-on project.

14. Type **exit** and press **Enter** to log out of your shell.

Project 11-4

In this hands-on project, you compile and install a program from source code.

1. On your Fedora Linux virtual machine, switch to a graphical terminal (tty1) by pressing **Ctrl+Alt+F1** and log in to the GNOME desktop using the user name of **user1** and the password of **LNXrocks!**.

2. Open the Firefox Web browser and download the source code tarball for rdesktop 1.8.2 (rdesktop-1.8.2.tar.gz) from *www.rdesktop.org*. Save the source code tarball to the default location (/home/user1/Downloads) and log out of the GNOME desktop when finished.

3. Next, switch to a command-line terminal (tty2) by pressing **Ctrl+Alt+F2** and log in to the terminal using the user name of **root** and the password of **LNXrocks!**.

4. At the command prompt, type **yum groupinstall "Development Tools"** and press **Enter** to install the compiler tools from a software repository.

5. At the command prompt, type **yum install libX11-devel openssl-devel** and press **Enter** to install the X11 and OpenSSL development libraries from a software repository.

6. At the command prompt, type **cp ~user1/Downloads/rdesktop-1.8.2.tar.gz ~** and press **Enter** to copy the rdesktop source code tarball to your home directory.

7. At the command prompt, type **tar –zxvf rdesktop-1.8.2.tar.gz** and press **Enter** to uncompress and extract the contents of the tarball. Next, type **ls -F** at the command prompt and press **Enter**. What directory was created?

8. At the command prompt, type **cd rdesktop-1.8.2** and press **Enter**. Next, type **ls -F** at the command prompt and press **Enter**. Is there an executable configure program? Are there README and INSTALL files present?

9. At the command prompt, type **./configure --disablecredssp --disable-smartcard** and press **Enter** to run the configure script without configuring for credssp and smartcard support. What does this program do? Near the bottom of the output, can you see whether the Makefile was created successfully?

10. At the command prompt, type **make** and press **Enter**. What does the make program do? Which program compiles the different parts of the program?

11. At the command prompt, type **make install** and press **Enter**. What does the make install command do?

12. At the command prompt, type **cd** and press **Enter** to return to your home directory. Next, type **rm –Rf rdesktop-1.8.2** to remove the source code directory for rdesktop.

13. At the command prompt, type **which rdesktop** and press **Enter**. Which directory contains the rdesktop executable program? Is a central database updated with this information?

14. At the command prompt, type **man rdesktop** and press **Enter**. View the available options for the **rdesktop** command and press **q** to quit when finished.

15. Type **exit** and press **Enter** to log out of your shell.

11

Project 11-5

In this hands-on project, you use the **rpm** and **yum** commands to query, remove, and install the ncompress RPM package.

1. On your Fedora Linux virtual machine, switch to a command-line terminal (tty2) by pressing **Ctrl+Alt+F2** and log in to the terminal using the user name of **root** and the password of **LNXrocks!**.

2. At the command prompt, type **rpm -qa | less** and press **Enter** to view the RPM packages installed on your computer. Are there many of them? Briefly scroll through the list and press **q** when finished to exit the less utility.

3. At the command prompt, type **rpm -q ncompress** and press **Enter**. Is the ncompress RPM package installed on your computer? When did you install it?

4. At the command prompt, type **rpm -qi ncompress** and press **Enter** to view the information about the ncompress RPM package. What license does this package use?

5. At the command prompt, type **rpm -ql ncompress** and press **Enter** to view the locations of all files that belong to the ncompress package. What directory holds the compress and uncompress executables?

6. At the command prompt, type **rpm -e ncompress** and press **Enter**. What does this option to the rpm command do?

7. At the command prompt, type **rpm -q ncompress** and press **Enter**. Is the ncompress RPM package installed?

8. At the command prompt, type **yum search compress | less** and press **Enter**. Is the ncompress RPM package listed? Press **q** to quit the less utility.

9. At the command prompt, type **yum list available | grep compress** and press **Enter**. Is the ncompress RPM package available for installation from a software repository?

10. At the command prompt, type **yum install ncompress** and press **Enter**. Press **y** when prompted to complete the installation.

11. At the command prompt, type **rpm -q ncompress** and press **Enter**. Is the ncompress RPM package installed?

12. Type **exit** and press **Enter** to log out of your shell.

Project 11-6

In this hands-on project, you use the **dpkg** and **apt-get** commands to install, query, and remove the ncompress DPM package.

1. Boot your Ubuntu Server Linux virtual machine, and log into tty1 using the user name of **root** and the password of **LNXrocks!**.

2. At the command prompt, type **dpkg -l | less** and press **Enter** to view the DPM packages installed on your computer. Are there many of them? Briefly scroll through the list and press **q** when finished to exit the less utility.

3. At the command prompt, type **dpkg -L ncompress** and press **Enter** to list the files that comprise the ncompress package, Is the ncompress DPM package installed on your computer?

4. At the command prompt, type **apt-cache search compress | less** and press **Enter**. Is ncompress listed? Press **q** to quit the less utility when finished.

5. At the command prompt, type **apt-get install ncompress** and press **Enter** to install the ncompress DPM package from a software repository.

6. At the command prompt, type **dpkg -L ncompress** and press **Enter** to list the files that comprise the ncompress package. Next, type **dpkg -p ncompress** at the command prompt and press **Enter** to view the detailed information about the ncompress package.

7. At the command prompt, type **apt-get purge ncompress** and press **Enter**. Press **y** when prompted. What does the purge option do?

8. At the command prompt, type **aptitude install ncompress** and press **Enter**. What does this command do?

9. Type **exit** and press **Enter** to log out of your shell.

Discovery Exercises

1. On your Fedora Linux virtual machine, open the Firefox Web browser and navigate to *www.sourceforge.net*. Browse the available software and download a source tarball for a program of your choice and compile it on your system. Next, download an RPM package for a program of your choice and install it on your system.

2. Write the command that can be used to perform the following:

   a. Compress the symbolic link /root/sfile using the compress utility and display the compression ratio.

   b. Compress the contents of the directory /root/dir1 using the gzip utility and display the compression ratio.

   c. Decompress the file /root/letter.bz2.

   d. Compress the file /root/letter using gzip fast compression.

   e. Find the compression ratio of the file /root/letter.gz.

   f. Perform a test compression of the file /root/sample using the bzip2 utility.

   g. Compress the file /root/sample using the bzip2 utility while minimizing memory usage during the compression.

3. Write the command that can be used to perform the following:

   a. Back up the contents of the /var directory (which contains symbolically linked files) to the second nonrewinding SCSI tape device on the system using the tar utility.

   b. Append the file /etc/inittab to the archive created in Exercise 3a.

   c. Create a tarball called /stuff.tar.gz that contains all files in the /root/stuff directory.

11

    d. Use the cpio utility to back up all files in the /var directory (which contains symbolically linked files) to the first rewinding IDE tape device that has a block size of 5KB.

    e. Perform a full filesystem backup of the /var filesystem using the dump utility and record the event in the /etc/dumpdates file.

    f. View the contents of the archives created in Exercises 3a, c, d, and e.

    g. Extract the contents of the archives created in Exercises 3a and c to the /root directory.

    h. Extract the contents of the archives created in Exercises 3d and e to their original locations.

4. Use the Internet, the library, or other resources to research two other package managers available for Linux systems other than RPM and DPM. For each package manager, list the command and options required to install, query, and remove packages. Also list the benefits that the package manager offers to Linux users and from where it can be downloaded on the Internet.

## chapter 12

Network Configuration

After completing this chapter, you will be able to:

- Describe the purpose and types of networks, protocols, and media access methods
- Explain the basic configuration of TCP/IP
- Configure a network interface to use TCP/IP
- Configure a modem, ISDN, and DSL interface
- Describe the purpose of host names and how they are resolved to IP addresses
- Configure TCP/IP routing
- Identify common network services
- Use command-line and graphical utilities to perform remote administration

Throughout this book, you have examined the installation and administration of local Linux services. This chapter focuses on configuring Linux to participate on a network. First, you become acquainted with some common network terminology, then you learn about TCP/IP and the procedure for configuring a network interface. Next, you learn about the Domain Name Space and the processes by which host names are resolved to IP addresses. Finally, you learn how to configure TCP/IP routing as well as how to set up and use various utilities to perform remote administration of a Linux system.

Networks

Most functions that computers perform today involve the sharing of information between computers. Information is usually transmitted from computer to computer via media such as fiber optic, telephone, coaxial, or unshielded twisted pair (UTP) cable, but it can also be transmitted via wireless media such as radio, micro, or infrared waves. These media typically interact directly with a peripheral card on the computer, such as a network interface card (NIC) or modem device.

Two or more computers connected via media that can exchange information are called a **network**. Networks that connect computers within close proximity are called **local area networks (LANs)**, whereas networks that connect computers separated by large distances are called **wide area networks (WANs)**.

Many companies use LANs to allow employees to connect to databases and other shared resources such as printers. Home users can also use LANs to connect several home computers together. Alternatively, home users can use a WAN to connect home computers to an **Internet service provider (ISP)** to gain access to resources such as Web sites on the worldwide public network called the Internet.

 The Internet (the name is short for "inter-network") is merely several interconnected public networks. Both home and company networks can be part of the Internet. Special computers called *routers* transfer information from one network to another.

Network media serve as the conduit for information as it travels across a network. But simply sending information through this conduit is not enough. In order for the devices on the network to make sense of this information, it must be organized according to a set of rules, or protocols. A network **protocol** breaks information down into **packets** that can be recognized by workstations, routers, and other devices on a network.

You can configure many different network protocols in Linux, including but not limited to the following:

- TCP/IP (Transmission Control Protocol/Internet Protocol)
- UDP/IP (User Datagram Protocol/Internet Protocol)
- IPX/SPX (Internetwork Packet Exchange/Sequenced Packet Exchange)
- AppleTalk
- DLC (Data Link Control)
- DECnet (Digital Equipment Corporation network)

The most common LAN protocol used today is TCP/IP. It is the standard protocol used to transmit information across the Internet and the one discussed in this chapter.

When transmitting information across a WAN, you might use a WAN protocol in addition to a specific LAN protocol to format packets for safer transmission. The two most common WAN protocols are Serial Line Internet Protocol (SLIP) and Point-to-Point Protocol (PPP).

Another important part of the puzzle, the **media access method,** is a set of rules that govern how the various devices on the network share the network media. The media access method is usually contained within the hardware on the NIC or modem. Although many media access methods are available, the one most commonly used to send TCP/IP packets onto network media is called **Ethernet.** It ensures that any TCP/IP packets are retransmitted onto the network if a network error occurs. Another media access method, **Token Ring,** controls which computer has the ability to transmit information by passing a special packet of information, called a token, around the network. Only the computer that currently has the token can transmit information.

Wireless-Fidelity (Wi-Fi) LANs also use Ethernet to place packets onto the network medium (in this case, the air).

The TCP/IP Protocol

The TCP/IP protocol is actually a set, or suite, of protocols with two core components: TCP and IP. Together, these two protocols ensure that information packets travel across a network as quickly as possible, without getting lost or mislabeled.

When you transfer information across a network such as the Internet, that information is often divided into many thousands of small packets. Each of these packets may take a different physical route when reaching its destination since routers can transfer information to multiple interconnected networks. TCP ensures that packets can be assembled in the correct order at their destination regardless of the order in which they arrive. Additionally, TCP ensures that any lost packets are retransmitted.

IP is responsible for labeling each packet with the destination address. As a result, each computer that participates on a TCP/IP network must have a valid **Internet Protocol (IP) address** that identifies itself to the IP protocol. Nearly all computers on the Internet use a version of the IP protocol called **IP version 4 (IPv4).** However, a small number of computers use a next-generation IP protocol called **IP version 6 (IPv6).** We will examine the structure and configuration of IPv4 and IPv6 in this chapter.

The IPv4 Protocol

To participate on an IPv4 network, your computer must have a valid IP address as well as a **subnet mask.** Optionally, you can configure a **default gateway** to participate on larger networks such as the Internet.

12

IPv4 Addresses An IP address is a unique number assigned to the computer that identifies itself on the network, similar to a unique postal address that identifies your location in the world. If any two computers on the same network have the same IP address, it is impossible for information to be correctly delivered to them. Directed communication from one computer to another single computer using TCP/IP is referred to as a **unicast**.

The most common format for IPv4 addresses is four numbers called **octets** that are separated by periods. Each octet represents an 8-bit binary number (0–255). An example of an IP address in this notation is 192.168.5.69.

You can convert between decimal and binary by recognizing that an 8-bit binary number represents the decimal binary powers of two in the following order:

128 64 32 16 8 4 2 1

Thus, the number 255 is 11111111 (128+64+32+16+8+4+2+1) in binary, and the number 69 is 01000101 (64+4+1) in binary. When the computer looks at an IP address, the numbers are converted to binary. To learn more about binary/decimal number conversion, visit *www.wikihow.com/Convert-from-Decimal-to-Binary*.

All IPv4 addresses are composed of two parts: the network ID and the host ID. The **network ID** represents the network on which the computer is located, whereas the **host ID** represents a single computer on that network. No two computers on the same network can have the same host ID; however, two computers on different networks can have the same host ID.

The network ID and the host ID are similar to postal mailing addresses, which are made up of a street name and a house number. The street name is similar to a network ID. No two streets can have the same name, just as no two networks can have the same network ID. The host ID is like the house number. Two houses can have the same house number as long as they are on different streets, just as two computers can have the same host ID as long as they are on different networks.

Only computers with the same network ID can communicate with each other without the use of a router. This allows administrators to logically separate computers on a network; computers in the Accounting Department could use one network ID, whereas computers in the Sales Department could use a different network number. If the two departments are connected by a router, computers in the Accounting Department can communicate with computers in the Sales Department and vice versa.

If your TCP/IP network is not connected to the Internet, the choice of IP address is entirely up to you. However, if your network is connected to the Internet, you might need to use preselected IP addresses for the computers on your network. IP addresses that can be used on the Internet are assigned by your Internet service provider.

The IP address 127.0.0.1 is called the loopback IP address. It always refers to the local computer. In other words, on your computer, 127.0.0.1 refers to your computer. On your coworker's computer, 127.0.0.1 refers to your coworker's computer.

Subnet Masks Each computer with an IPv4 address must also be configured with a subnet mask to define which part of its IP address is the network ID and which part is the host ID. Subnet masks are composed of four octets, just like an IP address. The simplest subnet masks use only the values 0 and 255. An octet in a subnet mask containing 255 is part of the network ID. An octet in a subnet mask containing 0 is part of the host ID. Your computer uses the binary process called **ANDing** to find the network ID. ANDing is a mathematical operation that compares two binary digits and gives a result of 1 or 0. If both binary digits being compared have a value of 1, the result is 1. If one digit is 0 and the other is 1, or if both digits are 0, the result is 0.

When an IP address is ANDed with a subnet mask, the result is the network ID. Figure 12-1 shows an example of how the network ID and host ID of an IP address can be calculated using the subnet mask.

Thus, the IP address shown in Figure 12-1 identifies the first computer (host portion 0.1) on the 192.168 network (network portion 192.168).

IP addresses and their subnet masks are often written using the **classless interdomain routing (CIDR) notation**. For example, the notation 172.11.4.66/16 refers to the IP address 172.11.4.66 with a 16-bit subnet mask (255.255.0.0).

The IP addresses 0.0.0.0 and 255.255.255.255 cannot be assigned to a host computer because they refer to all networks and all computers on all networks, respectively. Similarly, using the number 255 (all 1s in binary format) in an IP address can specify many hosts. For example, the IP address 192.168.255.255 refers to all hosts on the 192.168.0.0 network; this IP address is also called the **broadcast** address for the 192.168 network.

A computer uses its IP address and subnet mask to determine what network it is on. If two computers are on the same network, they can deliver packets directly to each other. If two computers are on different networks, they must use a router to communicate.

12

IP Address 192 . 168 . 0 . 1
11000000.10101000.00000000.00000001

Subnet mask
    255   255   0   0
11111111.11111111.00000000.00000000

Network Portion	Host Portion

Figure 12-1 A sample IP address and subnet mask

Default Gateway Typically, all computers on a LAN are configured with the same network ID and different host IDs. A LAN can connect to another LAN by means of a router, which has IP addresses for both LANs and can forward packets to and from each network. Each computer on a LAN can contain the IP address of a router in its TCP/IP configuration; any packets that are not destined for the local LAN are then sent to the router, which can then forward the packet to the appropriate network or to another router. The IP address of the network interface on the router to which you send packets is called the default gateway.

A router is often a dedicated hardware device from a vendor such as Cisco, D-Link, or Linksys. Other times, a router is actually a computer with multiple network cards. The one consistent feature of routers, regardless of the manufacturer, is that they can distinguish between different networks and move (or route) packets between them. A router has an IP address on every network to which it is attached. When a computer sends a packet to the default gateway for further delivery, the address of the router must be on the same network as the computer, as computers can send packets directly to devices only on their own network.

IPv4 Classes and Subnetting IPv4 addresses are divided into classes to make them easier to manage. The class of an IP address defines the default subnet mask of the device using that address. All of the IP address classes can be identified by the first octet of the address, as shown in Table 12-1.

Class A addresses use 8 bits for the network ID and 24 bits for the host ID. You can see this is true by looking at the subnet mask, 255.0.0.0. The value of the first octet will always be somewhere in the range 1 to 127. This means there are only 127 potential Class A networks available for the entire Internet. Class A networks are only assigned to very large companies and Internet providers.

Class B addresses, which are identified by the subnet mask 255.255.0.0, use 16 bits for the network ID and 16 bits for the host ID. The value of the first octet ranges from 128 to 191. There are 16,384 Class B networks, with 65,534 hosts on each network. Class B networks are assigned to many larger organizations, such as governments, universities, and companies with several thousand users.

Class C addresses, which are identified by the subnet mask 255.255.255.0, use 24 bits for the network ID and 8 bits for the host ID. The value of the first octet ranges from 192 to 223. There are 2,097,152 Class C networks, with 254 hosts on each network. Although there are very many Class C networks, they have a relatively small number of hosts; thus, they are suited only to smaller organizations.

Class	Subnet Mask	First Octet	Maximum Number of Networks	Maximum Number of Hosts	Example IP Address
A	255.0.0.0	1–127	127	16,777,214	3.4.1.99
B	255.255.0.0	128–191	16,384	65,534	144.129.188.1
C	255.255.255.0	192–223	2,097,152	254	192.168.1.1
D	N/A	224–239	N/A	N/A	224.0.2.1
E	N/A	240–254	N/A	N/A	N/A

Table 12-1 IP address classes

Class D addresses are not divided into networks, and they cannot be assigned to computers as IP addresses; instead, Class D addresses are used for multicasting. **Multicast** addresses are used by groups of computers. A packet addressed to a multicast address is delivered to each computer in the multicast group. This is better than a broadcast message because routers can be configured to allow multicast traffic to move from one network to another. In addition, all computers on the network process broadcasts, while only computers that are part of that multicast group process multicasts. Streaming media and network conferencing software often use multicasting to communicate to several computers at once.

Like Class D addresses, Class E addresses are not typically assigned to a computer. Class E addresses are considered experimental and are reserved for future use.

Notice from Table 12-1 that Class A and B networks can have many thousands or millions of hosts on a single network. Because this is not practically manageable, Class A and B networks are typically subnetted. **Subnetting** is the process in which a single large network is subdivided into several smaller networks to control traffic flow and improve manageability. After a network has been subnetted, a router is required to move packets from one subnet to another.

 You can subnet any Class A, B, or C network.

To subnet a network, you take some bits from the host ID and give them to the network ID. Suppose, for example, that you want to divide the 3.0.0.0/8 network into 17 subnets. The binary representation of this network is:

```
3.0.0.0   = 00000011.00000000.00000000.00000000
255.0.0.0 = 11111111.00000000.00000000.00000000
```

You then borrow some bits from the host portion of the subnet mask. Because the number of combinations of binary numbers can be represented in binary powers of two, and because valid subnet masks do not contain all 0s or 1s, you can use the equation $2^n - 2$ to represent the minimum number of subnets required, where n is the number of binary bits that are borrowed from the host portion of the subnet mask. For our example, this is represented as:

$$2^n - 2 \geq 15$$
$$2^n \geq 17$$

Thus, n = 5 (because $2^4 = 16$ is less than 17, but $2^5 = 32$ is greater than 17). Following this, our subnet mask borrows five bits from the default Class A subnet mask:

```
255.248.0.0 = 11111111.11111000.00000000.00000000
```

Similarly, because there are 19 zeros in the preceding subnet mask, you can use the $2^n - 2$ equation referred to previously to identify the number of hosts per subnet:

```
2^19 - 2 = number of hosts per subnet
         = 524,286 hosts per subnet
```

You can then work out the IP address ranges for each of the network ranges. Because three bits in the second octet were not borrowed during subnetting, the ranges of IP addresses that can be given to each subnet must be in ranges of 23 = 8. Thus, the first five ranges that can be given to different subnets on the 3.0.0.0/8 network that use the subnet mask 255.248.0.0 are as follows:

```
3.0.0.1-3.7.255.254
3.8.0.1-3.15.255.254
3.16.0.1-3.23.255.254
3.24.0.1-3.31.255.254
3.32.0.1-3.39.255.254
```

From the preceding ranges, a computer with the IP address 3.34.0.6/13 cannot communicate with the computer 3.31.0.99/13 because they are on different subnets. To communicate, there must be a router between them.

When subnetting a Class C network, ensure that you discard the first and last IP address in each range to account for the broadcast and network address for the subnet.

The IPv6 Protocol

As the Internet grew in the 1990s, ISPs realized that the number of IP addresses available using IPv4 was inadequate to accommodate future growth. As a result, the IPv6 protocol was designed in 1998 to accommodate far more IP addresses. IPv6 uses 128 bits to identify computers, whereas IPv4 only uses 32 bits (4 octets). This allows IPv6 to address up to 340,282,366,920,938,463,463,374,607,431,768,211,456 (or 340 trillion trillion trillion) unique computers.

Due to the large address space, subnetting is not necessary using IPv6.

IPv6 IP addresses are written using 8 colon-delimited 16-bit hexadecimal numbers—for example, 2001:0db8:3c4d:0015:0000:0000:adb6:ef12. If an IPv6 IP address contains 0000 segments, they are often omitted in most notation, thus 2001:0db8:3c4d:0015:::adb6:ef12 is equivalent to 2001:0db8:3c4d:0015:0000:0000:adb6:ef12. The IPv6 loopback address is 0000:0000:0000:0000:0000:0000:0000:0001, but it is often referred to as ::1 for simplicity.

Unlike our traditional decimal numbering scheme, hexadecimal uses an expanded numbering system that includes the letters A through F in addition to the numbers 0–9. Thus, the number 10 is called A in hexadecimal, the number 11 is called B in hexadecimal, the number 12 is called C in hexadecimal, the number 13 is called D in hexadecimal, the number 14 is called E in hexadecimal, and the number 15 is called F in hexadecimal.

Although IPv6 addresses can be expressed several different ways, the first half of an IPv6 address is assigned by your ISP and typically identifies your network. The last half of an IPv6 address is called the **link local** portion and is used to uniquely identify the computers in your LAN.

Although most operating systems today support IPv6, very few networks and computers on the Internet have adopted it. In 2014, Google reported that less than 3 percent of all computers in any country have adopted IPv6. This slow adoption of IPv6 is primarily the result of two technologies that allow IPv4 to address many more computers than was previously possible: **proxy servers** and **Network Address Translation (NAT)** routers.

Proxy servers and NAT routers are computers or hardware devices that have an IP address and access to a network such as the Internet. Other computers on the network can use a proxy server or NAT router to obtain network or Internet resources on their behalf. Moreover, there are three reserved ranges of IPv4 addresses that are not distributed to computers on the Internet and intended only for use behind a proxy server or NAT router:

- The entire 10.0.0.0 Class A network (10.0.0.0/8)
- The 172.16 through 172.31 Class B networks (172.16–31.0.0/16)
- The 192.168 Class C networks (192.168.0–255.0/24)

Thus, a computer behind a proxy server in Iceland and a computer behind a NAT router in Seattle could use the same IPv4 address—say, 10.0.5.4—without problems since each of these computers only requests Internet resources using its own proxy server or NAT router. A company may use a Cisco NAT router, for example, to allow other networks and computers in the company to gain access to the Internet. Similarly, a high-speed home Internet modem typically functions as a NAT router to allow multiple computers in your home to access the Internet.

Most computers in the world today obtain Internet access via a proxy server or NAT router. Since these computers share IPv4 addresses on a reserved network range, rather than using a unique IP address, the number of available IPv4 addresses has remained high and slowed the adoption of IPv6.

Configuring a Network Interface

Linux computers in a business environment typically connect to the company network via a wired or wireless NIC. At home, more and more people are connecting to the Internet by means of a NIC, using technologies such as Fiber optic, WiMAX, Digital Subscriber Line (DSL), and Broadband Cable Networks (BCNs).

If the NIC was detected during installation, Fedora Linux automatically configures the appropriate driver to allow the Linux kernel to work with the NIC driver. However, some NICs are not detected upon installation because an appropriate Linux driver for the NIC is not included in the installation media.

NIC drivers are usually contained within modules that can be inserted into the Linux kernel. Modules end with the .ko (kernel object) extension and are typically stored in the /lib/modules directory. They can be manually loaded into the Linux kernel using the **insmod** or **modprobe command**. To see a list of modules that are currently loaded into the Linux kernel, you can use the **lsmod command**. You can remove a module from the Linux kernel using the **rmmod command**.

Older Linux kernels loaded modules automatically at boot time from entries within the /etc/modprobe.conf or /etc/modules.conf file. Modern Linux kernels use a hardware detection process that automatically loads modules at boot time. However, you can add the name of a specific module to a file to ensure that a modern Linux kernel loads the module automatically at boot time. This is useful for devices that aren't automatically detected during the boot process or for modules that provide additional kernel features.

To load a specific module at boot time on Ubuntu Server 14.04, you can simply add the name of the module to the /etc/modules file. For Fedora 20 systems, additional modules are loaded at boot time from files within the /etc/modprobe.d directory. For example, to load the module for the DEC tulip wired NIC into the kernel at boot time and give it the alias eth0, simply add the line `alias eth0 tulip` to a new file within the /etc/modprobe.d directory. The tulip module will then be located from subdirectories of /lib/modules and loaded into the Linux kernel and called eth0.

In Project 6-3, you modified the /etc/modules file to ensure that the ZFS modules were loaded at boot time.

The first wired Ethernet NIC in your system is typically called eth0, the second wired Ethernet NIC in your system is typically called eth1, and so on. Similarly, the first wireless NIC in your system is called wlan0, the second wireless NIC in your system is called wlan1, and so on.

Some Linux distributions provide hardware-specific aliases for wired NICs. For example, em1 may refer to the first wired NIC embedded on the motherboard, and p2p1 may refer to the first wired NIC (p1) located in the second PCI expansion slot (p2) on your motherboard.

You can use the **lshw command** to view specific hardware devices. For example, the `lshw -C network` command will display details regarding NIC hardware in your system, including the kernel module used.

After a driver module for the NIC has been loaded into the Linux kernel, you can configure it to use TCP/IP. The **ifconfig (interface configuration) command** can be used to assign a TCP/IP configuration to a NIC as well as view the configuration of all network interfaces in the computer. To assign eth0 the IP address of 3.4.5.6 with a subnet mask of 255.0.0.0 and broadcast address of 3.255.255.255, you can use the following command at the command prompt:

```
ifconfig eth0 3.4.5.6 netmask 255.0.0.0 broadcast 3.255.255.255
```

Alternatively, you can receive TCP/IP configuration from a Dynamic Host Configuration Protocol (DHCP) or Boot Protocol (BOOTP) server on the network. To obtain and configure TCP/IP information from a server on the network for the first Ethernet adapter, you can use the command `dhclient eth0` at the command prompt.

The process of obtaining an IP address for your NIC varies, depending on whether your computer is on an IPv4 or IPv6 network. If you attempt to obtain IPv4 configuration for your NIC from a DHCP or BOOTP server and no DHCP or BOOTP server exists on your network, your system will assign an IPv4 address of 169.254.*x.x* where *x.x* is a randomly generated host ID. This automatic assignment feature is called **Automatic Private IP Addressing (APIPA)**. If your network has IPv6-configured routers, an IPv6 address is automatically assigned to each NIC. This is because NICs use **Internet Control Message Protocol version 6**

(**ICMPv6**) router discovery messages to probe their network for IPv6 configuration information. Alternatively, you can obtain your IPv6 configuration from a DHCP server on the network. If there are no IPv6-configured routers or DHCP servers on your network from which you can obtain an IPv6 configuration for your NIC, your system will assign an IPv6 link local address that begins with the hexadecimal equivalent of your IPv4 address and ends with the last half of your NIC's hardware address.

A single NIC can have both an IPv4 and an IPv6 address. Each address can be used to access the Internet using the IPv4 and IPv6 protocols, respectively.

To view the configuration of all interfaces, you can use the `ifconfig` command without any arguments, as shown in the following output:

```
[root@server1 ~]# ifconfig
eth0: flags=4163<UP,BROADCAST,RUNNING,MULTICAST> mtu 1500
        inet 3.4.5.6 netmask 255.0.0.0 broadcast 0.0.0.0
        inet6 fe80::280:c6ff:fef9:1b8c prefixlen 64  scopeid 0x20<link>
        ether 00:80:C6:F9:1B:8C txqueuelen 1000  (Ethernet)
        RX packets 1550  bytes 611332 (597.0 KiB)
        RX errors 0  dropped 0  overruns 0  frame 0
        TX packets 722  bytes 62170 (60.7 KiB)
        TX errors 0  dropped 0 overruns 0  carrier 0  collisions 0

lo:     flags=73<UP,LOOPBACK,RUNNING> mtu 65536
        inet 127.0.0.1 netmask 255.0.0.0
        inet6 ::1 prefixlen 128  scopeid 0x10<host>
        loop txqueuelen 0  (Local Loopback)
        RX packets 4  bytes 340 (340.0 B)
        RX errors 0  dropped 0  overruns 0 frame 0
        TX packets 4  bytes 340 (340.0 B)
        TX errors 0  dropped 0 overruns 0  carrier 0  collisions 0
[root@server1 ~]# _
```

The output of the `ifconfig` command shows that the eth0 NIC has an IPv4 address of `3.4.5.6` and an IPv6 address of `fe80::280:c6ff:fef9:1b8c` that was automatically configured by the system, since the end of the IPv6 is identical to the last half of the hardware address (ether `00:80:C6:F9:1B:8C`). It also shows interface statistics and the special loopback adapter (lo) with the IP address 127.0.0.1; this IP address represents the local computer and is required on all computers that use TCP/IP.

The `netstat -i` command can also be used to show interface statistics.

If you restart the computer, the TCP/IP information configured for eth0 will be lost. To allow the system to activate and configure the TCP/IP information for an interface at each boot time, simply place entries in a configuration file that is read at boot time by your Linux distribution when

12

activating the network. For Fedora 20 systems, you can add entries to the /etc/sysconfig/network-scripts/ifcfg-*interface* file, where *interface* is the name of the network interface. An example of the configuration file for the first Ethernet interface (eth0) is shown in the following output:

```
[root@server1 ~]# cat /etc/sysconfig/network-scripts/ifcfg-eth0
DEVICE=eth0
BOOTPROTO=none
HWADDR=00:80:C6:F9:1B:8C
IPADDR=3.4.5.6
NETMASK=255.0.0.0
GATEWAY=3.0.0.1
ONBOOT=yes
TYPE=Ethernet
IPV6INIT=yes
USERCTL=no
DEFROUTE=yes
IPV4_FAILURE_FATAL=yes
NAME="System eth0"
UUID=5fb06bd0-0bb0-7ffb-45f1-d6edd65f3e03
PEERDNS=yes
PEERROUTES=yes
IPV6_AUTOCONF=yes
IPV6_DEFROUTE=yes
IPV6_PEERDNS=yes
IPV6_PEERROUTES=yes
IPV6_FAILURE_FATAL=no
[root@server1 ~]# _
```

The entries in the preceding output indicate that the TCP/IP configuration for the first Ethernet adapter (eth0) will be activated at boot time (ONBOOT=yes), and IPv6 will be automatically configured using ICMPv6 if an IPv6-configured router is available (IPV6_AUTOCONF=yes). The NIC does not obtain information from a DHCP server (BOOTPROTO=none). IPv4 is instead configured using the IP address 3.4.5.6, a subnet mask of 255.0.0.0, and a default gateway of 3.0.0.1. Also, you can change the BOOTPROTO=none line to BOOTPROTO=dhcp to obtain all TCP/IP configuration information from a DHCP server on the network.

After editing the /etc/sysconfig/network-scripts/ifcfg-eth0 file, you do not need to reboot your system to have the new TCP/IP configuration take effect. Instead, simply run the command ifdown eth0 to unconfigure the eth0 network interface, followed by ifup eth0 to configure the eth0 network interface, using the settings in the /etc/sysconfig/network-scripts/ifcfg-eth0 file. Alternatively, you can use the ifconfig eth0 down and ifconfig eth0 up commands to deactivate and activate the eth0 network interface.

Ubuntu Linux systems don't store network configuration within files under the /etc/sysconfig/network-scripts directory. Instead, all network interfaces are configured from information stored within the /etc/network/interfaces file. A sample /etc/network/interfaces file that has a static IP assigned to eth0 (3.4.5.6) is shown in the following output:

```
[root@server1 ~]# cat /etc/network/interfaces
# This file describes the network interfaces available on your system
```

```
# and how to activate them.  For more information, see interfaces(5).

# The loopback network interface
auto lo
iface lo inet loopback

# The primary network interface
auto eth0
iface eth0 inet static
address 3.4.5.6
netmask 255.0.0.0
gateway 3.0.0.254
[root@server1 ~]# _
```

To instead use DHCP configuration for eth0, you can simply change the line `iface eth0 inet static` to `iface eth0 inet dhcp` and remove the `address`, `netmask` and gateway lines in the preceding example and then reload your configuration by using the `ifdown eth0` command followed by the `ifup eth0` command, as you would in Fedora Linux, to deactivate and activate the network interface.

To make the configuration of a network interface easier, you may access your configuration from within a GUI environment. Most Linux distributions contain a graphical network configuration tool that can be run if a GUI environment is installed. On Fedora 20, you can configure IP on your NICs using the **Network utility**. Simply navigate to Activities, Show Applications, Settings, Network, and click the cog wheel icon shown in Figure 12-2.

Figure 12-2 The Network utility

After a NIC has been configured to use TCP/IP, you should test the configuration by using the **ping (Packet Internet Groper) command**. The `ping` command sends a small TCP/IP packet to another IP address and awaits a response. By default, the `ping` command sends packets continuously every second until the Ctrl+c key combination is pressed; to send only five ping requests to the loopback interface, simply use the `-c` option to the `ping` command, as shown in the following example:

```
[root@server1 ~]# ping -c 5 127.0.0.1
PING 127.0.0.1 (127.0.0.1) 56(84) bytes of data.
64 bytes from 127.0.0.1: icmp_seq=0 ttl=64 time=0.154 ms
64 bytes from 127.0.0.1: icmp_seq=1 ttl=64 time=0.109 ms
```

```
64 bytes from 127.0.0.1: icmp_seq=2 ttl=64 time=0.110 ms
64 bytes from 127.0.0.1: icmp_seq=3 ttl=64 time=0.119 ms
64 bytes from 127.0.0.1: icmp_seq=4 ttl=64 time=0.111 ms

--- 127.0.0.1 ping statistics ---
5 packets transmitted, 5 received, 0% packet loss, time 3999ms
rtt min/avg/max/mdev = 0.109/0.120/0.154/0.020 ms
[root@server1 ~]# _
```

If the `ping` command fails to receive any responses from the loopback interface, there is a problem with TCP/IP itself.

Next, you need to test whether the Linux computer can ping other computers on the same network; the following command can be used to send five ping requests to the computer that has the IP address 3.0.0.2 configured:

```
[root@server1 ~]# ping -c 5 3.0.0.2
PING 3.0.0.2 (3.0.0.2) 56(84) bytes of data.
64 bytes from 3.0.0.2: icmp_seq=0 ttl=128 time=0.448 ms
64 bytes from 3.0.0.2: icmp_seq=1 ttl=128 time=0.401 ms
64 bytes from 3.0.0.2: icmp_seq=2 ttl=128 time=0.403 ms
64 bytes from 3.0.0.2: icmp_seq=3 ttl=128 time=0.419 ms
64 bytes from 3.0.0.2: icmp_seq=4 ttl=128 time=0.439 ms

--- 3.0.0.2 ping statistics ---
5 packets transmitted, 5 received, 0% packet loss, time 4001ms
rtt min/avg/max/mdev = 0.401/0.422/0.448/0.018 ms
[root@server1 ~]# _
```

If the `ping` command fails to receive any responses from other computers on the network, there is a problem with the network media.

Configuring a PPP Interface

Instead of configuring TCP/IP to run on a NIC to gain network access, you can instead run TCP/IP over serial lines (such as telephone lines) using a WAN protocol, such as SLIP or PPP. PPP is a newer technology than SLIP and incorporates all of SLIP's features; thus, PPP is the standard protocol for connecting to remote networks over serial lines.

Three common technologies use PPP to connect computers to the Internet or other networks:

- Modems
- ISDN
- DSL

Modem (modulator-demodulator) devices use PPP to send TCP/IP information across normal telephone lines; they were the most common method for home users to gain Internet access in the 1990s. Modem connections are considered slow today compared to most other technologies; most modems can only transmit data at 56KB/s. Because modems transmit information on a serial port, the system typically makes a symbolic link called /dev/modem that points to the correct serial port device, such as /dev/ttyS0 for COM1.

Integrated Services Digital Network (ISDN) is a set of standards designed for transmitting voice, video, and data over normal copper telephone lines. It allows data to be transferred at 128KB/s. ISDN uses an ISDN modem device to connect to a different type of media than regular phone lines. Although ISDN is popular in Europe, it does not have a large presence in North America.

One of the most popular connection technologies in North America is DSL. DSL has many variants, such as asynchronous DSL (ADSL), which is the most common DSL used in homes across North America, and high-bit-rate DSL (HDSL), which is common in business environments; for simplification, all variants of DSL are referred to as xDSL. You use an Ethernet NIC to connect to a DSL modem using TCP/IP and PPP; as a result, DSL connections are said to use **PPP over Ethernet (PPPoE)**. The DSL modem then transmits information across normal telephone lines at speeds that can exceed 100MB/s.

Since modem, ISDN, and DSL connections require additional configuration information that is specific to the ISP, they are not normally configured during the Linux installation and must be configured manually.

Configuring a PPP connection requires support for PPP compiled into the kernel or available as a module, the PPP daemon (pppd), and a series of supporting utilities such as the chat program, which is used to communicate with a modem. PPP configuration in the past was tedious at best; you needed to create a chat script that contained the necessary information to establish a PPP connection (user name, password, and so on), a connection script that contained device parameters used by the PPP daemon, as well as use a program such as minicom to initiate network communication. Because the TCP/IP configuration is typically assigned by the ISP to which you connect, it rarely needs to be configured during the process.

Since modems and ISDN modems are relatively rare today, modern Linux distributions typically don't ship with a graphical configuration tool by default. However, you can download and install the **Modem Manager utility** to configure modems and ISDN modems. On a Fedora 20 system, you can run the yum install modem-manager-gui command as the root user to install this package, and then execute the modem-manager-gui command within a graphical terminal to start the Modem Manager shown in Figure 12-3. The Modem

Figure 12-3 The Modem Manager utility

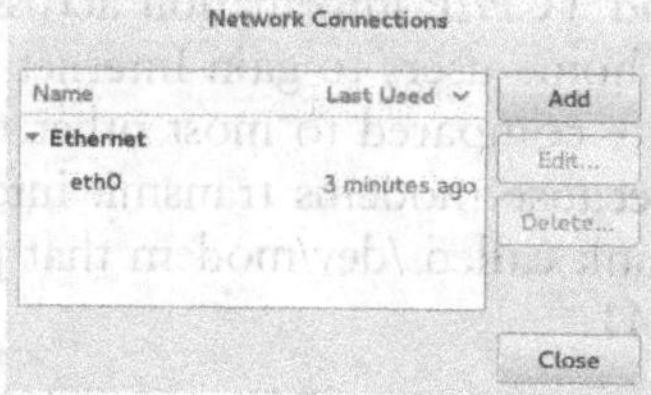

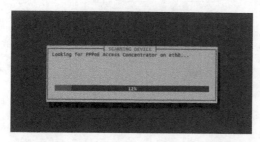

Figure 12-4 The Network Connections utility

Manager automatically detects any modem or ISDN hardware in your computer and allows you configure the associated ISP configuration, and an ISP account username and password.

DSL connections are very common today. As a result, nearly all modern Linux distributions contain a utility that can configure your network interface to work with a DSL modem. On Fedora 20, you can either execute the **pppoe-setup command** at a command-line terminal or the nm-connection-editor command within a terminal in a GUI environment. The **nm-connection-editor command** starts the graphical **Network Connections tool** shown in Figure 12-4. If you click the Add button shown in Figure 12-4 and choose your device type (DSL), The Network Connections tool will attempt to detect your DSL modem and prompt you to supply the ISP account username and password.

To configure a DSL connection on Ubuntu Server 14.04, you can execute the **pppoeconf command**, which will open a basic graphical screen within your terminal and scan for DSL devices, as shown in Figure 12-5. If a DSL device is found, you will be prompted to supply the ISP account username and password to complete the configuration.

Once a PPP modem, ISDN, or DSL connection has been configured, it will normally be activated automatically at boot time like other NICs on the system. On a Fedora 20 system, you will notice a new file for the connection within the /etc/sysconfig/network-scripts directory; and on an Ubuntu Server 14.04 system, there will an additional paragraph added to the /etc/network/interfaces file. Other configuration used by the PPP daemon is stored within the /etc/ppp and /etc/isdn directories. It is good form to double-check the passwords used to connect to the ISP because incorrect passwords represent the most common problem with PPP connections. These passwords are stored in two files: /etc/ppp/pap-secrets (Password Authentication

Figure 12-5 The pppoeconf utility

Protocol secrets) and /etc/ppp/chap-secrets (Challenge Handshake Authentication Protocol secrets). If the ISP accepts passwords sent across the network in text form, the /etc/ppp/pap-secrets file is consulted for the correct password; however, if the ISP requires a more secure method for validating the identity of a user, the passwords in the /etc/ppp/chap-secrets file are used. When you configure a PPP connection, this information is automatically added to both files, as shown in the following output:

```
[root@server1 ~]# cat /etc/ppp/pap-secrets
# Secrets for authentication using PAP
# client      server    secret           IP addresses
####### system-config-network will overwrite this part!!! (begin) ####
"user1"       "isp"     "secret"
####### system-config-network will overwrite this part!!! (end) ######
[root@server1 ~]# cat /etc/ppp/chap-secrets
# Secrets for authentication using CHAP
# client      server    secret           IP addresses
####### system-config-network will overwrite this part!!! (begin) ####
"user1"       "isp"     "secret"
####### system-config-network will overwrite this part!!! (end) ######
[root@server1 ~]# _
```

After a PPP device has been configured, the ifconfig command indicates the PPP interface using the appropriate name; ppp0 is typically used for the first modem or xDSL device, and ippp0 is typically used for the first ISDN device. The following output shows the IP configuration (obtained from the ISP) when the first xDSL interface (ppp0) is activated:

```
[root@server1 ~]# ifconfig
eth0      Link encap:EthernetHWaddr 00:80:C6:F9:1B:8C
          inet addr:3.4.5.6 Bcast:3.255.255.255 Mask:255.0.0.0
          inet6addr: fe80::280:c6ff:fef9:1b8c/64 Scope:Link
          UP BROADCAST RUNNING MULTICAST MTU:1500 Metric:1
          RX packets:47 errors:0 dropped:0 overruns:0 frame:0
          TX packets:13 errors:5 dropped:0 overruns:0 carrier:5
          collisions:0 txqueuelen:1000
          RX bytes:5560 (5.4 Kb)  TX bytes:770 (770.0 b)
          Interrupt:10 Base address:0x8000

lo        Link encap:LocalLoopback
          inet6addr: ::1/128 Scope:Host
          UP LOOPBACK RUNNING MTU:16436 Metric:1
          RX packets:3142 errors:0 dropped:0 overruns:0 frame:0
          TX packets:3142 errors:0 dropped:0 overruns:0 carrier:0
          collisions:0 txqueuelen:0
          RX bytes:3443414 (3.2 Mb)  TX bytes:3443414 (3.2 Mb)

ppp0      Link encap:Point-to-Point Protocol
          inet addr:65.95.13.217 P-t-P:65.95.13.1 Mask:255.255.255.255
          UP POINTOPOINT RUNNING NOARP MULTICAST MTU:1492 Metric:1
```

12

```
        RX packets:15 errors:0 dropped:0 overruns:0 frame:0
        TX packets:31 errors:0 dropped:0 overruns:0 carrier:0
        collisions:0 txqueuelen:3
        RX bytes:1448 (1.4 Kb)  TX bytes:3088 (3.0 Kb)

[root@server1 ~]# _
```

Like other network interfaces, a PPP interface can be activated using the `ifup interface-name` command and deactivated using the `ifdown interfacename` command.

Name Resolution

Computers that communicate on a TCP/IP network identify themselves using unique IP addresses; however, this identification scheme is impractical for human use because it is difficult to remember IP addresses. As a result, every computer on a network is identified by a name that makes sense to humans, such as "Accounting1" or "Reception." Because each computer on a network is called a host, the name assigned to an individual computer is its **host name**.

For computers that require a presence on the Internet, simple host names are rarely used. Instead, they are given a host name called a **fully qualified domain name (FQDN)** according to a hierarchical naming scheme called **Domain Name Space (DNS)**. At the top of the Domain Name Space is the root domain, which is really just a theoretical starting point for the branching, tree-like structure. Below the root domain are the top-level domain names, which identify the type of organization in which a network is located. For example, the com domain is primarily used for business, or commercial, networks. Several second-level domains exist underneath each top-level domain name to identify the name of the organization, and simple host names are listed underneath the second-level domains. Figure 12-6 shows a portion of the Domain Name Space.

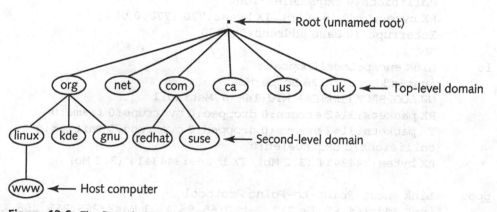

Figure 12-6 The Domain Name Space

For simplicity, FQDNs are often referred to as host names.

Thus, the host computer shown in Figure 12-6 has an FQDN of *www.linux.org*.

The host name www (World Wide Web) is often used by servers that host Web pages.

Second-level domains must be purchased and registered with an ISP in order to be recognized by other computers on the Internet. You can use the **whois command** to obtain registration information about any domain within the Domain Name Space. For example, to obtain information about the organization responsible for maintaining the linux.org domain, you can use the following command:

```
[root@server1 ~]# whois linux.org | head -30
Domain Name:LINUX.ORG
Domain ID: D2338975-LROR
Creation Date: 1994-05-10T04:00:00Z
Updated Date: 2012-11-23T22:47:33Z
Registry Expiry Date: 2018-05-11T04:00:00Z
Sponsoring Registrar:Network Solutions, LLC (R63-LROR)
Sponsoring Registrar IANA ID: 2
WHOIS Server:
Referral URL:
Domain Status: clientTransferProhibited
Registrant ID:22275688-NSI
Registrant Name:Linux Online, Inc
Registrant Organization:Linux Online, Inc
Registrant Street: 314 Franklin Street #2
Registrant City:Ogdensburg
Registrant State/Province:NY
Registrant Postal Code:13669
Registrant Country:US
Registrant Phone:+1.3153931978
Registrant Phone Ext:
Registrant Fax: +1.3153931978
Registrant Fax Ext:
Registrant Email:mmclagan@INVLOGIC.COM
Admin ID:15412138-NSI
Admin Name:Michelle McLagan
Admin Organization:Linux Online, Inc.
Admin Street: P.O. Box 822
Admin City:OGDENSBURG
Admin State/Province:NY
```

12

```
Admin Postal Code:13669
[root@server1 ~]# _
```

You can view or set the host name for a Linux computer using the **hostname** command, as shown in the following output:

```
[root@server1 ~]# hostname
server1.class.com
[root@server1 ~]# hostname computer1.sampledomain.com
[root@server1 ~]# hostname
computer1.sampledomain.com
[root@server1 ~]# _
```

To configure the host name shown in the preceding output at every boot time, simply modify the HOSTNAME line in the /etc/hostname file, or run the **hostnamectl** command. For example, the commands in the following output set the host name to computer1.sampledomain.com and verifies the configuration within /etc/hostname:

```
[root@server1 ~]# hostnamectl set-hostname computer1.sampledomain.com
[root@server1 ~]# cat /etc/hostname
computer1.sampledomain.com
[root@server1 ~]# _
```

 Many network server daemons record the system host name in their configuration files during installation. As a result, most Linux server distributions prompt you for the host name during the Linux installation to ensure that you don't need to modify network server daemon configuration files afterwards.

Although host names are easier to use when specifying computers on the network, TCP/IP cannot use them to identify computers. Thus, you must map host names to their associated IP addresses so that applications that contact other computers across the network can find the appropriate IP address for a host name.

The simplest method for mapping host names to IP addresses is by placing entries into the /etc/hosts file, as shown in the following example:

```
[root@server1 ~]# cat /etc/hosts
127.0.0.1    server1  server1.class.com  localhost  localhost.localdomain
::1          server1 server1.class.com localhost6 localhost6.localdomain6
3.0.0.2      ftp.sampledomain.com fileserver
10.3.0.1     alpha
[root@server1 ~]# _
```

The entries in the preceding output identify the local computer, 127.0.0.1, by the host names server1, server1.class.com, localhost, and localhost.localdomain. Similarly, you can use the host name ftp.sampledomain.com or fileserver to refer to the computer with the IP address of 3.0.0.2. Also, the computer with the IP address of 10.3.0.1 can be referred to using the name alpha.

You can use the Network Information Service (NIS) to share the /etc/hosts configuration file among several Linux computers on the network. NIS is discussed in Chapter 13.

Because it would be cumbersome to list names for all hosts on the Internet in the /etc/hosts file, ISPs can list FQDNs in DNS servers on the Internet. Applications can then ask DNS servers for the IP address associated with a certain FQDN. To configure your system to resolve names to IP addresses by contacting a DNS server, simply specify the IP address of the DNS server in the /etc/resolv.conf file. This file can contain up to three DNS servers; if the first DNS server is unavailable, the system attempts to contact the second DNS server, followed by the third DNS server listed in the file. An example /etc/resolv.conf file is shown in the following output:

```
[root@server1 ~]# cat /etc/resolv.conf
nameserver 209.121.197.2
nameserver 192.139.188.144
nameserver 6.0.4.211
[root@server1 ~]# _
```

Each network interface can have a different set of DNS servers that it uses for name resolution. To do this, simply specify the DNS servers within the IP configuration for the network interface. For example, to set the same DNS servers listed in the previous output in the configuration file for eth0 on a Fedora 20 system, simply add the following lines to the /etc/sysconfig/network-scripts/ifcfg-eth0 file:

```
DNS1=209.121.197.2
DNS2=192.139.188.144
DNS3=6.0.4.211
```

On an Ubuntu Server 14.04 system, you could instead add the following line in the paragraph for the eth0 interface:

```
dns-nameservers 209.121.197.2 192.139.188.144 6.0.4.211
```

The /etc/resolv.conf file is only used if no DNS servers are listed within the IP configuration for a network interface.

On Ubuntu Server 14.04, the /etc/resolv.conf file is built dynamically at each boot. To manually add a DNS server, simply add lines to /etc/resolvconf/resolv.conf.d/base, and they will be incorporated into /etc/resolv.conf on each subsequent boot.

To test the DNS configuration by resolving a name to an IP address, you can type `nslookup name`, `dig name`, or `host name` at a command prompt, where name is the host name or FQDN of a remote host.

When you specify a host name while using a certain application, that application must then resolve that host name to the appropriate IP address by searching either the local /etc/hosts file, a DNS server, or an NIS server. The method that applications use to resolve host names is determined by the "hosts" line in the /etc/nsswitch.conf file; an example of this file is shown in the following output:

```
[root@server1 ~]# grep hosts /etc/nsswitch.conf
#hosts:    db files nisplus nis dns
hosts:     files dns nis
[root@server1 ~]# _
```

The preceding output indicates that applications first try to resolve host names using the /etc/hosts file (files). If unsuccessful, applications contact the DNS servers listed in the IP configuration or /etc/resolv.conf file (dns), followed by a NIS server (nis) if one is configured.

On older Linux computers, the /etc/host.conf file was used instead of /etc/nsswitch.conf; the /etc/host.conf file still exists today to support older application programs and should contain the same name resolution order as /etc/nsswitch.conf. An example /etc/host.conf file that tells applications to search the /etc/hosts file (hosts) followed by DNS servers (bind) and NIS servers (nis) is shown in the following output:

```
[root@server1 ~]# cat /etc/host.conf
multi on
order hosts,bind,nis
[root@server1 ~]# _
```

Routing

Every computer on a network maintains a list of TCP/IP networks so that packets are sent to the appropriate location; this list is called a **route table** and is stored in system memory. To see the route table, you can simply use the **route command**, as shown in the following output:

```
[root@server1 ~]# route
Kernel IP routing table
Destination   Gateway       Genmask      Flags Metric Ref Use Iface
10.0.0.0      *             255.255.0.0  U     2      0   0   wlan0
192.168.0.0   *             255.255.0.0  U     0      0   0   eth0
127.0.0.0     *             255.0.0.0    U     0      0   0   lo
default       192.168.0.1   0.0.0.0      UG    0      0   0   eth0
[root@server1 ~]# _
```

 The netstat -r command is equivalent to the route command.

The route table shown in the preceding output indicates that all packets destined for the 10.0.0.0 network will be sent to the device wlan0. Similarly, all packets destined for the 192.168.0.0 network will be sent to the device eth0, and packets destined for the 127.0.0.0 network will be sent to the loopback adapter (lo). Packets that must be sent to any other network will be sent to the default gateway; the final line in the preceding output indicates that the default gateway is a computer with the IP address 192.168.0.1, via the eth0 device.

 Recall that the default gateway route is loaded when a network interface is activated. The default gateway for eth0 would be loaded from the GATEWAY= line in the /etc/sysconfig/network-scripts/ifcfg-eth0 file on a Fedora 20 system, or from the gateway line within the eth0 paragraph in the /etc/network/interfaces file on an Ubuntu Server 14.04 system.

If your computer has more than one network interface configured, the route table will have more entries that define the available TCP/IP networks; computers that have more than one network interface are called **multihomed hosts**. Multihomed hosts can be configured to forward packets from one interface to another to aid a packet in reaching its destination; this process is commonly called **routing** or **IP forwarding**. To enable routing on your Linux computer, simply place the number 1 in the file /proc/sys/net/ipv4/ip_forward for IPv4 or /proc/sys/net/ipv6/conf/all/forwarding for IPv6, as shown in the following output:

```
[root@server1 ~]# cat /proc/sys/net/ipv4/ip_forward
0
[root@server1 ~]# cat /proc/sys/net/ipv6/conf/all/forwarding
0
[root@server1 ~]# echo 1 > /proc/sys/net/ipv4/ip_forward
[root@server1 ~]# echo 1 > /proc/sys/net/ipv6/conf/all/forwarding
[root@server1 ~]# cat /proc/sys/net/ipv4/ip_forward
1
[root@server1 ~]# cat /proc/sys/net/ipv6/conf/all/forwarding
[root@server1 ~]# _
```

To enable IPv4 routing at every boot, ensure that the line `net.ipv4.ip_forward = 1` exists in the /etc/sysctl.conf file. To enable IPv6 routing at every boot, ensure that the line `net.ipv6.conf.default.forwarding = 1` exists in the /etc/sysctl.conf file.

If your computer has more than one network interface and routing is enabled, your computer will route packets only to networks for which it has a network interface. On larger networks, however, you might have several routers, in which case packets might have to travel through several routers to reach their destination. Because routers only know the networks to which they are directly connected, you might need to add entries to the route table on a router so that it knows where to send packets that are destined for a remote network. Suppose, for example, your organization has three TCP/IP networks (1.0.0.0/8, 2.0.0.0/8, and 3.0.0.0/8) divided by two routers, as shown in Figure 12-7.

12

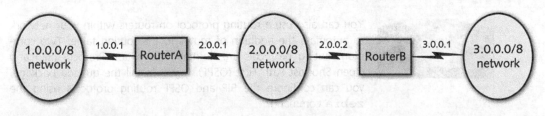

Figure 12-7 A sample routed network

RouterA has an entry in its route table that says it is connected to: 1) the 1.0.0.0/8 network via the network interface that has the IP address 1.0.0.1; and 2) the 2.0.0.0/8 network via the network interface that has the IP address 2.0.0.1. These two routes are automatically established when TCP/IP is configured. If RouterA receives a packet that is destined for the 3.0.0.0/8 network, it does not know where to forward it because it does not have a route for the 3.0.0.0/8 network in its routing table. To add the appropriate route to the 3.0.0.0/8 network on RouterA, you can run the following command on RouterA:

```
[root@server1 ~]# route add -net 3.0.0.0 netmask 255.0.0.0 gw 2.0.0.2
[root@server1 ~]# _
```

Now RouterA sends any packets destined for the 3.0.0.0/8 network to the computer 2.0.0.2 (RouterB). RouterB then forwards the packets to the 3.0.0.0/8 network because it has a route in its route table that says it is connected to the 3.0.0.0/8 network via the network interface that has the IP address 3.0.0.1.

Similarly, for RouterB to forward packets it receives destined for the 1.0.0.0/8 network, it must have a route that sends those packets to RouterA via the interface 2.0.0.1:

```
[root@server1 ~]# route add -net 1.0.0.0 netmask 255.0.0.0 gw 2.0.0.1
[root@server1 ~]# _
```

You can use the `route del <route>` command to remove entries from the route table.

The **ip command** can also be used to manipulate the route table. For example, the command `ip route add 1.0.0.0/8 via 2.0.0.1` can be used to add the route shown in the previous output to the route table.

The contents of the route table are lost when the computer is powered off; to load the additional route shown in the previous output to the route table at every boot time, simply add the line `1.0.0.0/8 via 2.0.0.1 dev eth0` to the /etc/sysconfig/network-scripts/route-eth0 file on a Fedora 20 system, or add the line `up route add -net 1.0.0.0 netmask 255.0.0.0 gw 2.0.0.1` to the eth0 section of the /etc/network/interfaces file on an Ubuntu Server 14.04 system.

You can also use a routing protocol on routers within your network to automate the addition of routes to the routing table. Two common routing protocols are Routing Information Protocol (RIP) and Open Shortest Path First (OSPF). If you install the quagga package, you can configure the RIP and OSPF routing protocols using the `zebra` command.

Because the list of all routes on large networks such as the Internet is too large to be stored in a route table on a router, most routers are configured with a default gateway. Any packets that are addressed to a destination that is not listed in the route table are sent to the default gateway, which is a router that can forward the packet to the appropriate network or to the router's own default gateway and so on until the packets reach their destination.

If computers on your network are unable to connect to other computers on a remote network, the problem is likely routing-related. A common utility used to troubleshoot routing is the **traceroute command**; it displays all routers between the current computer and a remote computer. To trace the path from the local computer to the computer with the IP address 3.4.5.6, you can use the following command:

```
[root@server1 ~]# traceroute 3.4.5.6
traceroute to 3.4.5.6 (3.4.5.6), 30 hops max, 38 byte packets
1  linksys (192.168.0.1)  2.048 ms  0.560 ms  0.489 ms
2  apban.pso.com (7.43.111.2)  2.560 ms  0.660 ms  0.429 ms
3  tfs.ihtfcid.net (3.0.0.1)  3.521 ms  0.513 ms  0.499 ms
4  sr1.lala.com (3.4.5.6)  5.028 ms  0.710 ms  0.554 ms
[root@server1 ~]# _
```

A common alternative to the traceroute command is the **tracepath command**.

To trace an IPv6 route, you can use the **traceroute6** or **tracepath6 commands**.

Network Services

Recall from Chapter 1 that Linux provides a wide variety of services that are available to users across a network. Before you are able to configure the appropriate network services to meet your organization's needs, you must first identify the types and features of network services.

Network services are processes that run on your computer and provide some type of valuable service for client computers on the network. They are often represented by a series of daemon processes that listen for certain requests on the network. Daemons identify the packets to which they should respond using a **port** number that uniquely identifies each network service. Different daemons listen for different port numbers. A port number is like an apartment number for the delivery of mail. The network ID of the IP address ensures that the packet is delivered to the correct street (network); the host ID ensures that the packet is delivered to the correct building (host); and the transport layer protocol and port number ensure that the packet is delivered to the proper apartment (service).

Ports and their associated protocols are defined in the /etc/services file. To see to which port the telnet daemon listens, you can use the following command:

```
[root@server1 ~]# grep telnet /etc/services
telnet            23/tcp
telnet            23/udp
rtelnet           107/tcp              # Remote Telnet
rtelnet           107/udp
telnets           992/tcp
telnets           992/udp
skytelnet         1618/tcp             # skytelnet
skytelnet         1618/udp             # skytelnet
hp-3000-telnet    2564/tcp             # HP 3000 NS/VT block mode telnet
hp-3000-telnet    2564/udp             # HP 3000 NS/VT block mode telnet
tl1-telnet        3083/tcp             # TL1-TELNET
tl1-telnet        3083/udp             # TL1-TELNET
telnetcpcd        3696/tcp             # Telnet Com Port Control
telnetcpcd        3696/udp             # Telnet Com Port Control
scpi-telnet       5024/tcp             # SCPI-TELNET
scpi-telnet       5024/udp             # SCPI-TELNET
ktelnet           6623/tcp             # Kerberos V5 Telnet
ktelnet           6623/udp             # Kerberos V5 Telnet
[root@server1 ~]# _
```

The preceding output indicates that the telnet daemon listens on port 23 using both TCP/IP and UDP/IP.

The **User Datagram Protocol/Internet Protocol (UDP/IP)** is a faster and consequently less-reliable version of TCP/IP.

Ports range in number from 0 to 65534. The ports 0–1023 are called **well-known ports** because they represent commonly used services. Table 12-2 provides a list of common well-known ports.

Many protocols have a secure version that uses encrypted communication. For example, secure HTTP is called HTTPS and uses a different port number as a result.

Network utilities can connect to daemons that provide network services directly; these daemons are called **stand-alone daemons**. Alternatively, network utilities can connect to network services via the **Internet Super Daemon (inetd)** or **Extended Internet Super Daemon (xinetd)**, which starts the appropriate daemon in order to provide the network service as needed. This structure is shown in Figure 12-8.

The inetd or xinetd daemons are typically used to start and manage connections for smaller network daemons such as telnet and rlogin. Ubuntu Server 14.04 installed the inetd daemon by default, but you can optionally install the xinetd daemon via a software repository. Fedora

Service	Port
FTP	TCP 20, 21
Secure Shell (SSH)	TCP 22
Telnet	TCP 23
SMTP	TCP 25
HTTP / HTTPS	TCP 80 / TCP 443
rlogin	TCP 513
DNS	TCP 53, UDP 53
Trivial FTP (TFTP)	UDP 69
POP3 / POP3S	TCP 110 / TCP 995
NNTP / NNTPS	TCP 119 / TCP 563
IMAP4 / IMAP4S	TCP 143 / TCP 993

Table 12-2 Common well-known ports

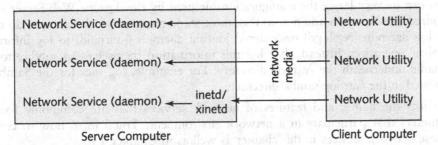

Figure 12-8 Interacting with network services

20 systems do not contain the inetd or xinetd daemons by default, but you can install xinetd from a software repository.

The inetd daemon is configured by editing the /etc/inetd.conf file. For example, if you install the telnet daemon, you can configure the following line within /etc/inetd.conf to ensure that it can be started by inetd:

```
[root@server1 ~]# grep telnet /etc/inetd.conf
telnet  stream tcp nowait root /usr/sbin/tcpd /usr/sbin/in.telnetd
[root@server1 ~]# _
```

The preceding output displays the full path to the telnet daemon (/usr/sbin/in.telnetd).

The xinetd daemon is configured via entries within the /etc/xinetd.conf file. Normally, this file incorporates all of the files in the /etc/xinetd.d directory as well. Most daemons that are managed by xinetd are configured by files in the /etc/xinetd.d directory named after the daemons. For example, if you install the telnet daemon, you can configure it to be started by xinetd via the /etc/xinetd.d/telnet file, as shown in the following output:

```
[root@server1 ~]# cat /etc/xinetd.d/telnet
service telnet
{
  flags              = REUSE
  socket_type        = stream
  wait               = no
  user               = root
  server             = /usr/sbin/in.telnetd
  log_on_failure    += USERID
  disable            = no
}
[root@server1 ~]# _
```

Large network daemons are rarely started by inetd or xinetd. Instead, they are stand-alone daemons that are started at boot time from rc scripts as part of the UNIX SysV or Systemd system initialization process.

Many stand-alone and inetd/xinetd-managed daemons also have configuration files that control how they operate and indicate the pathname to other important files used by the daemon. For simplicity, many of these daemons store all information in only one configuration file that contains comments that indicate the syntax and purpose of each line. As a result, these configuration files can be very large; the configuration file used by the Apache Web Server is often several hundred lines long. In addition to this, most stand-alone network daemons do not use the system log daemon (rsyslogd) or Systemd journal daemon (journald) to log information related to their operation. Instead, they log this information themselves to subdirectories of the same name underneath the /var/log directory. For example, log files for the Samba daemon are located in the /var/log/samba directory.

Table 12-3 lists the names and features of network services that are commonly found on Linux computers that participate in a network environment. You'll learn how to configure many of these network services in this chapter as well as in Chapter 13.

Network Service	Type	Port	Description
Apache Web Server (httpd)	Stand-alone	TCP 80 TCP 443	Serves Web pages using HTTP/HTTPS to other computers on the network that have a Web browser Configuration file: /etc/httpd/conf/httpd.conf or /etc/apache2/apache2.conf
BIND / DNS Server (named)	Stand-alone	TCP 53 UDP 53	Resolves fully qualified domain names to IP addresses for a certain namespace on the Internet Configuration file: /etc/named.conf
DHCP Server (dhcpd)	Stand-alone	UDP 67 UDP 68	Provides IP configuration for computers on a network Configuration file: /etc/dhcp/dhcpd.conf
Washington University FTP Server (in.ftpd)	inetd/xinetd	TCP 20 TCP 21 UDP 69	Transfers files to and accepts files from other computers on the network with an FTP utility Configuration file: /etc/ftpaccess Hosts denied FTP access: /etc/ftphosts Users denied FTP access: /etc/ftpusers FTP data compression: /etc/ftpconversions

Table 12-3 Common network services

Network Service	Type	Port	Description
Very Secure FTP Server (vsftpd)	Stand-alone	TCP 20 TCP 21 UDP 69	Transfers files to and accepts files from other computers on the network with an FTP utility Configuration file: /etc/vsftpd/vsftpd.conf Users denied FTP access: /etc/vsftpd.ftpusers and /etc/vsftpd.user_list
Internetwork News Server (innd)	Stand-alone	TCP 119 TCP 563	Accepts and manages newsgroup postings and transfers them to other news servers Configuration file: /etc/news/inn.conf
NFS Server (rpc.nfsd)	Stand-alone	TCP 2049	Shares files to other computers on the network that have an NFS client utility Configuration file: /etc/exports
NIS Server (ypserv & ypbind)	Stand-alone	TCP 111	Shares configuration information to NIS clients that are members of an NIS domain Configuration file: /etc/ypserv.conf
POP3 Server (ipop3d)	Stand-alone	TCP 110 TCP 995	Allows users with an e-mail reader to obtain e-mail from the server using the Post Office Protocol version 3
IMAP4 Server (imapd)	Stand-alone	TCP 143 TCP 993	Allows users with an e-mail reader to obtain e-mail from the server using the Intenet Message Access Protocol
Sendmail Email Server (sendmail)	Stand-alone	TCP 25	Accepts and sends e-mail to users or other e-mail servers on the Internet using the Simple Mail Transfer Protocol (SMTP) Configuration file: /etc/sendmail.cf
Postfix Email Server (postfix)	Stand-alone	TCP 25	Accepts and sends e-mail to users or other e-mail servers on the Internet using the Simple Mail Transfer Protocol (SMTP). Configuration file: /etc/postfix/main.cf
rlogin Daemon (in.rlogind)	inetd/xinetd	TCP 513	Allows users who use the rlogin and rcp utilities the ability to copy files and obtain shells on other computers on the network
rsh Daemon (in.rshd)	inetd/xinetd	TCP 514	Allows users who use the rsh utility the ability to run commands on other computers on the network
Samba Server (smbd & nmbd)	Stand-alone	TCP 137 TCP 138 TCP 139 TCP 445	Allows Windows users to view shared files and printers on a Linux server Configuration file: /etc/samba/smb.conf
Secure Shell Daemon (sshd)	Stand-alone	TCP 22	Provides a secure alternative to the telnet, rlogin, and rsh utilities by using encrypted communication Configuration file: /etc/ssh/sshd_config
Squid Proxy Server (squid)	Stand-alone	TCP 3128	Allows computers on a network to share one connection to the Internet. It is also known as a proxy server Configuration file: /etc/squid/squid.conf
telnet Daemon (in.telnetd)	inetd/xinetd	TCP 23	Allows users who have a telnet utility the ability to log in to the system from across the network and obtain a shell

Table 12-3 Common network services (continued)

Remote Administration

As we discussed in Chapter 6, Linux servers are typically installed on a rackmount server system that is located on a rack in a server room and administered remotely. There are several ways to perform command-line and graphical administration of remote Linux servers, including telnet, remote commands, Secure Shell (SSH), and Virtual Network Computing (VNC).

Telnet

The easiest way to perform administration on a remote Linux computer is via a command-line interface. The **telnet command** has traditionally been used to obtain a command-line shell on remote UNIX and Linux servers across the network that run a telnet server daemon. Nearly all Macintosh, Linux, and UNIX systems come with a telnet command. For Windows systems, you can download the free **Putty** program at *www.chiark.greenend.org.uk/~sgtatham/putty/* to start a telnet session to another computer.

The telnet server daemon is not installed by default on most modern Linux distributions, but it can easily be installed from a software repository. On systems that use the Systemd system initialization process, such as Fedora 20, the telnet server daemon is managed directly by Systemd as a stand-alone daemon. On other systems, such as Ubuntu Server 14.04, the telnet server daemon is managed by inetd or xinetd.

 By default, you are prevented from logging in and obtaining a shell as the root user to certain network services such as telnet due to entries in the /etc/securetty file. Removing or renaming this file allows the root user to log in and receive a shell across the network using the telnet command.

Once the telnet daemon has been configured, you can connect to it from a remote computer. Simply specify the host name or IP address of the target computer to the telnet command and log in with the appropriate user name and password. A shell obtained during a telnet session runs on a pseudoterminal (a terminal that does not obtain input directly from the computer keyboard) rather than a local terminal, and it works much the same way a normal shell does; you can execute commands and use the exit command to kill the BASH shell and end the session. A sample telnet session is shown in the following output using a computer with a host name of server1:

```
[root@server1 ~]# telnet server1
Trying 192.168.1.105…
Connected to server1.
Escape character is '^]'.
Fedora release 20 (Heisenbug)
Kernel 3.11.10-301.fc20.x86_64 on an x86_64 (1)
server1 login: root
Password: LNXrocks!
Last login: Fri Oct 24 16:55:33 from 192.168.1.100
[root@server1 ~]# who
(unknown)  :0         2015-10-24 16:15 (:0)
root       tty2       2015-10-24 16:16
root       pts/0      2015-10-24 16:55 (server1)
[root@server1 ~]# exit
```

```
Connection closed by foreign host.
[root@server1 ~]# _
```

Secure Shell (SSH)

Although the `telnet` command can be quickly used to perform remote administration, it doesn't encrypt the information that passes between computers. **Secure Shell (SSH)** was designed as a secure replacement for telnet (and other legacy commands, such as `rsh`, `rlogin`, and `rcp`) that encrypts information that passes across the network. As a result, the SSH daemon (sshd) is installed by default on nearly all Linux distributions.

On Fedora 20, sshd is installed by default but not set to start automatically at boot time.

To connect to a remote Linux computer running sshd, you can use the **ssh command** followed by the host name or IP address of the target computer. For example, you can connect to a computer with the host name of appserver using the `ssh appserver` command. Your local user name will be passed to the server automatically during the SSH request, and you will be prompted to supply the password for the same user on the target computer. If you need to log in using a different user name on the remote appserver computer, you can instead use the `ssh -l username appserver` command or the `ssh username@appserver` command. A sample `ssh` session is shown in the following output:

```
[root@server1 ~]# ssh root@appserver
root@appserver's password:
Last login: Thu Sep  2 14:29:06 2015 from 10.0.1.3
[root@server1 ~]# who
root     :0           Aug 10 14:13
root     pts/8        Aug 10 14:14 (:0.0)
root     pts/9        Aug 10 14:14 (10.0.1.3)
[root@server1 ~]# exit
Connection to appserver closed.
[root@server1 ~]# _
```

You can also use the Putty program on a Windows computer to connect to sshd running on a Linux, UNIX, or Macintosh computer.

When you connect to a new computer for the first time using SSH, you will be prompted to accept the RSA encryption fingerprint for the target computer, which is stored in ~/.ssh/known_hosts for subsequent connections. If the target computer's encryption keys are regenerated, you will need to remove the old key from the ~/.ssh/known_hosts file before you connect again.

You can regenerate the keys used by sshd using the `ssh-keygen` command.

12

SSH can also be used to transfer files between computers. For example, to transfer the /root/ sample file on a remote computer called appserver to the /var directory on the local computer, you could run the following command:

```
[root@server1 ~]# ssh root@appserver cat /root/sample > /var/sample
root@appserver's password:
[root@server1 ~]# _
```

Alternatively, to transfer the /root/sample file on the local computer to the /var directory on a remote computer called appserver, you could run the following command:

```
[root@server1 ~]# ssh root@appserver cat </root/sample ">" /var/sample
root@appserver's password:
[root@server1 ~]# _
```

Although SSH is used to perform command-line administration of remote systems, the –X option to the ssh command can be used to tunnel X Windows information through the SSH connection if you are using the ssh command within a GUI environment. For example, if you start a command-line terminal within a GNOME desktop and run the command ssh –X root@appserver, you will receive a command prompt where you can type commands as you would in any command-line SSH session. However, if you type a graphical command (e.g., gnome-control-center), you will execute the graphical utility on appserver across the SSH tunnel. All graphics, keystrokes, and mouse movement will be passed between X Windows on appserver and X Windows on the local system.

Since SSH is typically used to perform remote administration, sshd is usually configured to allow root logins and a wide range of encryption algorithms by default. However, you can configure the functionality of sshd by editing the /etc/ssh/sshd_config file. Most of this file is commented and should only be edited to change the default settings that sshd uses when servicing SSH clients. The most commonly changed options in this file are those that deal with authentication and encryption. By default, sshd uses a secure challenge-response authentication method that ensures that the password is not transmitted on the network, but this can be changed to Kerberos authentication.

On Ubuntu Server 14.04, root access via SSH is denied by default. To enable it, you can modify the value of PermitRootLogin to yes within the /etc/ssh/sshd.config file.

Organizations use many types of encryption to secure communication on the network. Each type of encryption differs in its method of encryption and the cryptography key length used to encrypt data; the longer the key length, the more difficult it is for malicious users to decode the data. The main types of encryption supported by sshd are as follows:

- Triple Data Encryption Standard (3DES), which encrypts blocks of data in three stages using a 168-bit key length
- Advanced Encryption Standard (AES), an improvement on 3DES encryption and is available in 128-, 192-, and 256-bit key lengths
- Blowfish, an encryption algorithm that is much faster than 3DES and can use keys up to 448 bits in length

- Carlisle Adams Stafford Tavares (CAST), a general-purpose encryption similar to 3DES that is commonly available using a 128-bit key length
- ARCfour, a fast encryption algorithm that operates on streams of data instead of blocks of data and uses variable-length keys up to 2048 bits in length

In addition, all of the aforementioned types of encryption except ARCfour typically use Cipher Block Chaining (CBC), which can be used to encrypt larger amounts of data.

Client computers can use a /etc/ssh/ssh_config or ~/ssh/ssh_config file to set SSH options for use with the ssh command, including the encryption types that can be used. However, the encryption types on the client computer must match those supported by the SSH server for a connection to be successful.

Virtual Network Computing (VNC)

Like the −X option of ssh, **Virtual Network Computer (VNC)** is another graphical option for administrating a Linux system remotely. After you install a VNC server daemon on a computer, other computers that run a VNC client can connect to the VNC server daemon across a network to obtain a desktop environment. VNC uses a special platform-independent protocol called Remote FrameBuffer (RFB) to transfer graphics, mouse movements, and keystrokes across the network.

 VNC server software and client software exist for Linux, UNIX, Mac, and Windows systems. You can use a single system to obtain the desktop of all of the Linux, UNIX, Mac, and Windows systems on your network.

 Since X Windows is not installed on Ubuntu Server 14.04 by default, we'll focus on the configuration of VNC on Fedora 20 in this section. However, the steps are similar on other Linux distributions.

On Fedora 20, you can install a VNC server by running the yum install tigervnc-server command. Next, you must configure the VNC server by creating a VNC server configuration file that listens on a certain display number. To create a VNC server configuration file that listens on the third X Windows display, you can use the following command to copy it from the /lib/systemd/system/vncserver@.service template:

```
[root@localhost ~]# cp /lib/systemd/system/vncserver@.service
/lib/systemd/system/vncserver@:3.service
[root@localhost ~]# _
```

 On systems that do not use the Systemd system initialization system, the /etc/sysconfig/vncservers configuration file is used in place of /lib/systemd/system/vncserver@:3.service.

 The port number to which the VNC server listens is 5900 plus the display number. The VNC server listed in the preceding output would be listed on port 5903.

12

Next, you must edit the VNC server configuration file and, at minimum, modify the line(s) that indicate(s) the user that can connect (replace <USER> with a valid username). It's also good form to set the window geometry that is used when the session is started. For example, to grant user1 the ability to obtain a VNC window with dimensions 1024x768, you could edit the following line within /lib/systemd/system/vncserver@:3.service to indicate the login name of user1 and geometry of 1024x768:

```
ExecStart=/sbin/runuser -l user1 -c "/usr/bin/vncserver %i -geometry
1024x768"
```

Following this, you can execute the `systemctl daemon-reload` command to force all running daemons to re-read their configuration files, log in as user1, and run the **vncpasswd command** to set the VNC password that will be used for the VNC connection. The VNC password is stored in the ~/.vnc/passwd file; for user1, the VNC password will be stored in the /home/user1/.vnc/passwd file.

Finally, you can log back in as the root user, start the VNC server instance for the display number, and configure it to start automatically at system initialization using the following commands:

```
[root@localhost ~]# systemctl enable vncserver@:3.service
[root@localhost ~]# systemctl start vncserver@:3.service
[root@localhost ~]# _
```

Next, other computers can connect to the VNC server using a **VNC viewer** program, such as RealVNC. When using a VNC viewer program to connect to a remote VNC server, you can specify the server name or IP address, port, and display number using the syntax *server:port:display*. For example, to connect to the VNC server that uses display number 2 on the computer server1.class.com, you could use the syntax `server1.class.com:5903:3`. You will then obtain a desktop session on the remote computer, as shown in Figure 12-9.

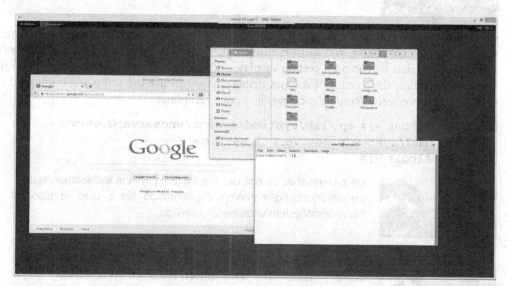

Figure 12-9 A remote VNC session

Many VNC viewers allow you to specify the server name or IP address and either the port or display number. For example, you could specify `server1.class.com:5903` or `server1.class.com:3` within a VNC viewer to connect to the server shown in Figure 12-9.

Chapter Summary

■ A network is a collection of connected computers that share information.

■ A protocol is a set of rules that define the format of information that is transmitted across a network. The protocol suite used by the Internet and most networks is TCP/IP.

■ Each computer on a TCP/IP network must have a valid IPv4 or IPv6 address.

■ The IPv4 configuration of a network interface can be specified manually, obtained automatically from a DHCP or BOOTP server, or autoconfigured by the system.

■ The IPv6 configuration of a network interface can be obtained from a router using ICMPv6, from a DHCP server, or autoconfigured by the system.

■ On a Fedora 20 system, the /etc/sysconfig/network-scripts directory contains the configuration for NIC and PPP interfaces. On an Ubuntu Server 14.04 system, most NIC and PPP interface configuration is stored within the /etc/network/interfaces file.

■ Host names are computer names that, unlike IP names, are easy for humans to remember. Host names that are generated by the hierarchical Domain Name Space are called FQDNs.

■ Host names must be resolved to an IP address before network communication can take place.

■ Routers are devices that forward TCP/IP packets from one network to another. Each computer and router has a route table that it uses to determine how TCP/IP packets are forwarded.

■ Network services are started by a stand-alone daemon or an Internet Super Daemon (inetd or xinetd). In either case, they listen for requests on a certain port.

■ There are many ways to remotely administer a Linux system. You can perform command-line administration remotely via the `telnet` and `ssh` commands. For graphical remote administration, you can use the `ssh -X` command or VNC.

Key Terms

ANDing The process by which binary bits are compared to calculate the network and host IDs from an IP address and subnet mask.

Automatic Private IP Addressing (APIPA) A feature that automatically configures a network interface using an IPv4 address on the 169.254.0.0 network.

broadcast The TCP/IP communication destined for all computers on a network.

classless interdomain routing (CIDR) notation A notation that is often used to represent an IP address and its subnet mask.

default gateway The IP address of the router on the network used to send packets to remote networks.

Domain Name Space (DNS) A hierarchical namespace used for host names.

Ethernet The most common media access method used in networks today.

Extended Internet Super Daemon (xinetd) A network daemon that is used to start other network daemons on demand.

fully qualified domain name (FQDN) A host name that follows DNS convention.

host ID The portion of an IP address that denotes the host.

host name A user-friendly name assigned to a computer.

hostname command A command used to display and change the host name of a computer.

hostnamectl command A command used to change the host name of a computer as well as ensure that the new host name is loaded at boot time.

ifconfig (interface configuration) command A command used to display and modify the TCP/IP configuration information for a network interface.

insmod command A command used to insert a module into the Linux kernel.

Internet Control Message Protocol version 6 (ICMPv6) A protocol used by computers to obtain an IPv6 configuration from a router on the network.

Internet Protocol (IP) address A series of four 8-bit numbers that represent a computer on a network.

Internet service provider (ISP) A company that provides Internet access.

Internet Super Daemon (inetd) A network daemon that is used to start other network daemons on demand.

ip command A command used to manipulate the route table.

IP forwarding The act of forwarding TCP/IP packets from one network to another. See also *routing*.

IP version 4 (IPv4) The most common version of IP used on the Internet. It uses a 32-bit addressing scheme organized into different classes.

IP version 6 (IPv6) A recent version of IP that is used by some hosts on the Internet. It uses a 128-bit addressing scheme.

link local The portion of an IPv6 address that refers to a unique computer. It is analogous to the host portion of an IPv4 address.

local area networks (LANs) Networks in which the computers are all in close physical proximity.

lshw command A command used to list details regarding hardware devices in a Linux system.

lsmod command A command used to list the modules that are currently used by the Linux kernel.

media access method   A system that defines how computers on a network share access to the physical medium.

Modem Manager utility   A graphical utility that can be used to configure modem settings on Linux systems.

`modprobe` **command**   A command used to insert a module into the Linux kernel.

multicast   The TCP/IP communication destined for a certain group of computers.

multihomed hosts   The computers that have more than one network interface.

network   Two or more computers joined together via network media and able to exchange information.

Network Address Translation (NAT)   A technology used on routers that allows computers on a network to obtain Internet resources via a single network interface on the router itself.

Network Connections tool   A graphical utility in Fedora 20 that can be used to configure DSL settings.

network ID   The portion of an IP address that denotes the network.

network service   A process that responds to network requests.

Network utility   A graphical utility in Fedora 20 that can be used to configure network settings for the NICs on the system.

`nm-connection-editor` **command**   A command used to start the Network Connections tool on Fedora 20 systems.

octet   A portion of an IP address that represents eight binary bits.

`ping` **(Packet Internet Groper) command**   A command used to check TCP/IP connectivity on a network.

packets   The packages of data formatted by a network protocol.

port   A number that uniquely identifies a network service.

PPP over Ethernet (PPPoE)   The protocol used by DSL to send PPP information over an Ethernet connection.

`pppoe-setup` **command**   A command used to configure a DSL connection on Fedora 20 systems.

`pppoeconf` **command**   A command used to configure a DSL connection on Ubuntu Server 14.04 systems.

protocol   A set of rules of communication used between computers on a network.

proxy server   A network server that accepts Internet requests from other computers on the same LAN and obtains the desired resource on their behalf.

Putty   A cross-platform SSH client.

`rmmod` **command**   A command used to remove a module from the Linux kernel.

`route` **command**   A command used to manipulate the route table.

route table   A table of information used to indicate which networks are connected to network interfaces.

12

routers The devices capable of transferring packets from one network to another.

routing The act of forwarding data packets from one network to another.

Secure Shell (SSH) A technology that can be used to run remote applications on a Linux computer; it encrypts all client-server traffic.

ssh command A command that connects to a remote SSH daemon to perform remote administration.

stand-alone daemons The daemons that configure themselves at boot time without assistance from inetd or xinetd.

subnet mask A series of four 8-bit numbers that determine the network and host portions of an IP address.

subnetting The process in which a single large network is subdivided into several smaller networks to control traffic flow.

telnet command A command used to run remote applications on a Linux computer.

Token Ring A media access method commonly used by industrial networks.

tracepath command A command used to trace the path an IPv4 packet takes through routers to a destination host.

tracepath6 command A command used to trace the path an IPv6 packet takes through routers to a destination host.

traceroute command A command used to trace the path an IPv4 packet takes through routers to a destination host.

traceroute6 command A command used to trace the path an IPv6 packet takes through routers to a destination host.

unicast The TCP/IP communication destined for a single computer.

User Datagram Protocol/Internet Protocol (UDP/IP) A faster but unreliable version of TCP/IP.

Virtual Network Computer (VNC) A cross-platform technology that allows users to connect to a graphical desktop across a network.

vncpasswd command A command used to set a VNC password for a user.

VNC viewer A program used to connect to a VNC server and obtain a graphical desktop.

well-known ports Of the 65,535 possible ports, the ports from 0 to 1024, which are used by common networking services.

whois command A command used to obtain information about the organization that maintains a DNS domain.

Wireless-Fidelity (Wi-Fi) A LAN technology that uses Ethernet to transmit data over the air.

wide area networks (WANs) Networks in which computers are separated geographically by large distances.

Review Questions

1. A subnet mask is used to differentiate the host portion from the network portion in a TCP/IP address. True or False?

2. Which Windows program is often used to connect to a Linux server via SSH?

    a. SSHD

    b. Putty

    c. Rdesktop

    d. mstsc

3. Stand-alone daemons are started on demand using inetd or xinetd. True or False?

4. Which file stores the TCP/IP addresses of the DNS servers used to resolve host names if no DNS servers are specified within the network configuration file for the NIC?

    a. /etc/hosts

    b. /etc/host.conf

    c. /etc/resolve

    d. /etc/resolv.conf

5. To test DNS configuration by resolving a host name to an IP address, which command or commands can you use? (Choose all that apply.)

    a. `nslookup hostname`

    b. `dig hostname`

    c. `host hostname`

    d. `resolve hostname`

6. Which two commands can be used to modify the route table on a Linux computer? (Choose two answers.)

    a. `route`

    b. `ipconfig`

    c. `ip`

    d. `traceroute`

7. Which file holds the methods to be used and the order in which they will be applied for host name resolution?

    a. /etc/nsswitch.conf

    b. /etc/resolve.conf

    c. /etc/hosts

    d. /etc/dns.conf

12

8. What are two means available to resolve a host name to the appropriate TCP/IP address? (Choose two answers.)

    a. DHCP

    b. DNS

    c. /etc/hosts

    d. /etc/resolve.conf

9. SSH encrypts all traffic that passes across the network, whereas telnet does not. True or False?

10. What devices are used to transfer information from one network to another?

    a. routers

    b. LANs

    c. DNS servers

    d. DHCP servers

11. Which of the following are graphical remote administration technologies? (Choose all that apply.)

    a. telnet

    b. ssh -X

    c. ssh

    d. VNC

12. The daemons associated with network services listen for network traffic associated with a particular _____.

    a. station

    b. port

    c. TCP/IP address

    d. allocation number

13. The TCP/IP address of 127.0.0.1 is also referred to as the _____.

    a. local address

    b. lookup address

    c. local host

    d. loopback address

14. The line that configures the host name for the computer at boot time can be found in /etc/hostname. True or False?

15. Which command would be used to activate the NIC aliased as eth0?

    a. ifup

    b. ifup eth0

    c. ipup eth0

    d. ifdown eth0

16. Which of the following port numbers is associated with telnet?

    a. 20

    b. 137

    c. 49

    d. 23

17. Which file would you modify to permanently change the TCP/IP address of the first wired NIC on a Fedora 20 system?

    a. /etc/sysconfig/network-scripts/ifcfg-eth1

    b. /etc/sysconfig/network-scripts/ifcfg-eth0

    c. /etc/sysconfig/network-scripts/ipcfg-eth0

    d. /etc/sysconfig/network-scripts/ipcfg-eth1

18. Before a computer can use a router, with what configuration information must it be provided?

    a. routing table

    b. subnet mask

    c. default gateway

    d. default router

19. Which of the following are stand-alone daemons? (Choose all that apply.)

    a. Apache (httpd)

    b. Washington University FTP (in.ftpd)

    c. telnet (in.telnetd)

    d. DNS (named)

20. Which of the following utilities can be used to check TCP/IP configuration and test network connectivity? (Choose all that apply.)

    a. ifconfig

    b. ipconfig

    c. ping

    d. netstat −i

Hands-on Projects

These projects should be completed in the order given. The hands-on projects presented in this chapter should take a total of three hours to complete. The requirements for this lab include:

- A computer with Fedora Linux installed according to Hands-on Project 2-1 and Ubuntu Server Linux installed according to Hands-on Project 6-1.

Project 12-1

In this hands-on project, you view and modify the TCP/IP configuration of the network interface on your Fedora Linux and Ubuntu Server Linux virtual machines.

1. Boot your Fedora Linux virtual machine. After your Linux system has been loaded, log into the GNOME desktop using the user name of **user1** and the password of **LNXrocks!**.

2. Navigate to the **Activities** menu, **Show Applications, Settings** and click **Network**. Note the IPv4 and IPv6 configuration for your Wired network interface.

3. Next, click the cog wheel icon in the lower-right corner and highlight **IPv4** in the left pane. Click the drop-down box next to Addresses and select **Manual**. Supply the IP address, netmask, default gateway, and DNS server information shown in the previous step and click **Apply**.

4. Switch to a command-line terminal (tty2) by pressing **Ctrl+Alt+F2** and log in to the terminal using the user name of **root** and the password of **LNXrocks!**.

5. At the command prompt, type **ifconfig** and press **Enter**. What IPv4 and IPv6 configuration do you see?

> The steps within the hands-on projects in this chapter assume that your first network interface is called eth0. If your network interface has a different name, use it in place of eth0 in any steps.

6. At the command prompt, type **cat /etc/sysconfig/network-scripts/ifcfg-eth0** and press **Enter**. Is your configuration listed?

7. Switch back to your graphical terminal (tty1) pressing **Ctrl+Alt+F1**. In the Network utility, click the cog wheel icon in the lower-right corner and highlight IPv4 in the left pane. Click the drop-down box next to Addresses, select **Automatic (DHCP)**, and click **Apply**.

8. Close the Network utility and log out of the GNOME desktop.

9. Switch back to tty2 by pressing **Ctrl+Alt+F2**.

10. At the command prompt, type **cat /etc/sysconfig/network-scripts/ifcfg-eth0** and press **Enter**. What is the BOOTPROTO line equal to? Will the static IP configuration listed in this file be used?

11. At the command prompt, type **ifdown eth0** and press **Enter**. Next, type **ifconfig** at the command prompt and press **Enter**. Is eth0 listed?

12. At the command prompt, type **ifup eth0** and press **Enter**. Did the command probe for a DHCP server? Next, type **ifconfig** at the command prompt and press **Enter**. Is eth0 listed?

13. At the command prompt, type **ping *interfaceIP*** and press **Enter**, where ***interfaceIP*** is the IPv4 address of eth0. Do you receive ping responses from your network interface? Press **Ctrl+c** when finished to quit the ping command.

14. At the command prompt, type **netstat -i** and press **Enter**. View the statistics for your network interfaces. If necessary, consult the netstat manual page to determine the meaning of each column displayed.

15. Type **exit** and press **Enter** to log out of your shell.

16. Boot your Ubuntu Server Linux virtual machine. After your Linux system has been loaded, log into tty1 using the user name of **root** and the password of **LNXrocks!**.

17. At the command prompt, type **ifconfig** and press **Enter**. What IPv4 and IPv6 configuration do you see for eth0?

18. At the command prompt, type **cat /etc/network/interfaces** and press **Enter**. Is IP information obtained automatically for eth0? What lines could you modify and add to this file to set a static IP configuration?

19. At the command prompt, type **ifdown eth0 ; ifup eth0** and press **Enter**. Did the command probe for a DHCP server?

20. Type **exit** and press **Enter** to log out of your shell.

Project 12-2

In this hands-on project, you view your host name as well as resolve host names and configure host name resolution.

1. On your Fedora Linux virtual machine, switch to a command-line terminal (tty2) by pressing **Ctrl+Alt+F2** and log in to the terminal using the user name of **root** and the password of **LNXrocks!**.

2. At the command prompt, type **hostname** and press **Enter**. What is your host name? Next, type **cat /etc/hostname** at the command prompt and press **Enter**. What host name is listed here? Why?

3. At the command prompt, type **cat /etc/resolv.conf** and press **Enter**. Do you have a DNS server configured?

4. At the command prompt, type **less /etc/nsswitch.conf** and press **Enter**. Will files such as /etc/hosts be used for name resolution before DNS? Press **q** to quit the less utility.

5. Edit the **/etc/hosts** file with a text editor such as vi. Add a line to the bottom of the file that reads:

```
1.2.3.4   fakehost.fakedomain.com sample
```

When finished, save your changes and quit the editor.

6. At the command prompt, type **ping –c 5 localhost** and press **Enter**. Was the name resolved correctly?

7. At the command prompt, type **ping –c 5 fakehost.fakedomain.com** and press **Enter**. Was the name resolved correctly? Was the ping command able to contact the host?

8. At the command prompt, type **ping –c 5 sample** and press **Enter**. Was the name resolved correctly? Was the ping command able to contact the host?

9. Type **exit** and press **Enter** to log out of your shell.

10. On your Ubuntu Server Linux virtual machine, log into tty1 using the user name of **root** and the password of **LNXrocks!**. Perform Steps 2 through 9 and note any differences.

12

Project 12-3

In this hands-on project, you test name resolution using your ISP's DNS server on your Ubuntu Server Linux virtual machine.

1. On your Ubuntu Server Linux virtual machine, log into tty1 using the user name of **root** and the password of **LNXrocks!**.

2. At the command prompt, type **host ftp.kernel.org** and press **Enter**. What IP address was returned for ftp.kernel.org? Is there another name for ftp.kernel.org?

3. At the command prompt, type **nslookup ftp.kernel.org** and press **Enter**. How do you know that this information came from your ISP's DNS server?

4. At the command prompt, type the command **dig ftp.kernel.org** and press **Enter**. What additional information does dig provide compared to the nslookup and host utilities?

5. Type **exit** and press Enter to log out of your shell.

Project 12-4

In this hands-on project, you view and configure the route table on your Fedora Linux virtual machine as well as view and test your routing configuration.

1. On your Fedora Linux virtual machine, switch to a command-line terminal (tty2) by pressing **Ctrl+Alt+F2** and log in to the terminal using the user name of **root** and the password of **LNXrocks!**.

2. At the command prompt, type **route** and press **Enter**. What entries are listed? What does each entry represent? What IPv4 address is listed as your default gateway?

3. At the command prompt, type **ip route add 1.0.0.0/8 via _gwIP_** and press **Enter**, where **_gwIP_** is the IPv4 address of your default gateway.

4. At the command prompt, type **route** and press **Enter**. Is the route added in Step 3 visible? Will this route interfere with traffic that is sent to the 1.0.0.0 network? Explain.

5. At the command prompt, type **traceroute ftp.kernel.org** and press **Enter**. How many routers are used to pass your packet to the ftp.kernel.org computer?

6. At the command prompt, type **tracepath** ftp.kernel.org and press **Enter**. Is the same path taken? If not, explain why.

7. At the command prompt, type the command **cat /proc/sys/net/ipv4/ip_forward** and press **Enter**. Is your system configured as an IPv4 router? Next, type the command **cat /proc/sys/net/ipv6/conf/all/forwarding** and press **Enter**. Is your system configured as an IPv6 router?

8. Type **exit** and press Enter to log out of your shell.

Project 12-5

In this hands-on project, you install and configure the Extended Internet Super Daemon and telnet server daemon on your Ubuntu Server Linux virtual machine. Next, you test remote administration of your Ubuntu Server Linux virtual machine using the telnet command on your Ubuntu host as well as the Putty program on your Windows host. Finally, you install the telnet server daemon on your Fedora Linux virtual machine and perform remote administration using a telnet session.

1. On your Ubuntu Server Linux virtual machine, log into tty1 using the user name of **root** and the password of **LNXrocks!**.

2. At the command prompt, type **yum install xinetd telnetd** and press **Enter**.

3. Edit the /etc/xinetd.d/telnet file (it will be a new file) with a text editor such as vi and add the following contents:

```
service telnet
{
disable = no
flags = REUSE
socket_type = stream
wait = no
user = root
server = /usr/sbin/in.telnetd
log_on_failure += USERID
}
```

When finished, save your changes and quit the editor.

4. At the command prompt, type **service xinetd restart** and press **Enter** to restart the Extended Internet Super Daemon.

5. At the command prompt, type **telnet localhost** and press **Enter**. Supply the user name of **user1** and password of **LNXrocks!** when prompted.

6. Next, type **who** at the command prompt and press **Enter**. Are you using a pseudoterminal through a local connection?

7. Type **exit** and press **Enter** to log out of your remote shell.

8. At the command prompt, type **telnet localhost** and press **Enter**. Supply the user name of **root** when prompted. What error did you receive?

9. At the command prompt, type **mv /etc/securetty /etc/securetty.backup** and press **Enter**.

10. At the command prompt, type **telnet localhost** and press **Enter**. Supply the user name of **root** and password of **LNXrocks!** when prompted.

11. Type **exit** and press **Enter** to log out of your remote shell.

12. On your Windows host, use a Web browser to download the putty.exe program from **www.chiark.greenend.org.uk/~sgtatham/putty/download.html** and save the executable file on your Windows desktop.

13. Double-click the putty.exe file on your Windows desktop. What is the default connection type? Select **Telnet** as the connection type, enter the IP address of your Ubuntu Server Linux virtual machine in the Host Name (or IP address) box and click **Open**. Log into your Ubuntu Server Linux virtual machine using the user name of **root** and password of **LNXrocks!**. Next, type **who** at the command prompt and press **Enter**. What is listed in brackets next to your pseudoterminal session and why?

12

14. Type **exit** and press **Enter** to log out of your remote shell (this closes the Putty program). Finally, type **exit** and press **Enter** to log out of your local shell.

15. On your Fedora Linux virtual machine, switch to a command-line terminal (tty2) by pressing **Ctrl+Alt+F2** and log in to the terminal using the user name of **root** and the password of **LNXrocks!**.

16. At the command prompt, type **telnet *IP***, where ***IP*** is the IP address of your Ubuntu Server Linux virtual machine, and press **Enter**. Supply the user name of **root** and password of **LNXrocks!** when prompted.

17. At the command prompt, type **who** and press **Enter**. What is listed in brackets next to your pseudoterminal session and why? Type **exit** and press **Enter** to log out of your remote shell.

18. At the command prompt, type **yum install telnet-server telnet** and press **Enter** to install the telnet daemon and **telnet** command on your Fedora Linux virtual machine. Press **y** when prompted to complete the installation.

19. At the command prompt, type **systemctl start telnet.socket** and press **Enter** to start the telnet daemon.

20. At the command prompt, type **mv /etc/securetty /etc/securetty.backup** and press **Enter**.

21. At the command prompt, type **telnet localhost** and press **Enter**. Supply the user name of **root** and password of **LNXrocks!** when prompted. Why was the root login successful? Type **exit** and press **Enter** to log out of your remote shell.

22. At the command prompt, type **firewall-cmd --add-service telnet** and press **Enter** to add an exception to the firewall on your Fedora Linux virtual machine for telnet. We discuss firewalls in Chapter 14.

23. Next, type **exit** and press **Enter** to log out of your shell.

24. On your Windows host, double-click the putty.exe file on your desktop. Select **Telnet** as the connection type, enter the IP address of your Fedora Linux virtual machine in the Host Name (or IP address) box, and click **Open**. Log into your Fedora Linux virtual machine using the user name of **root** and password of **LNXrocks!**.

25. Next, type **who** at the command prompt and press **Enter**. What is listed in brackets next to your pseudoterminal session and why? Type **exit** and press **Enter** to log out of your remote shell (this closes the Putty program).

Project 12-6

In this hands-on project, you configure SSH on your Ubuntu Server Linux and Fedora Linux virtual machines. Additionally, you perform remote administration of your Ubuntu Server Linux and Fedora Linux virtual machines using SSH.

1. On your Fedora Linux virtual machine, switch to a command-line terminal (tty2) by pressing **Ctrl+Alt+F2** and log in to the terminal using the user name of **root** and the password of **LNXrocks!**.

2. At the command prompt, type **ps -ef | grep sshd** and press **Enter**. Is the SSH daemon started by default?

3. At the command prompt, type **systemctl enable sshd.service; systemctl start sshd.service** and press **Enter** to start the SSH daemon and ensure that it is started at boot time.

4. At the command prompt, type **ssh root@localhost** and press **Enter**. When prompted to connect to the remote system, type **yes** and press **Enter**. Next, supply the root user's password of **LNXrocks!** and press **Enter**.

5. At the command prompt, type **who** and press **Enter**. Are you on a pseudoterminal? Type **exit** and press **Enter** to log out of your remote shell.

6. Switch to a graphical terminal by pressing **Ctrl+Alt+F1** and log in to the GNOME desktop using the user name of **user1** and the password of **LNXrocks!**. Next, open a command-line terminal (Activities, Show Applications, Utilities, Terminal).

7. At the command prompt, type **ssh -X root@localhost** and press **Enter**. When prompted to connect to the remote system, type **yes** and press **Enter**. Supply the root user's password of **LNXrocks!** and press **Enter** when prompted.

8. At the command prompt, type **system-config-abrt** and press **Enter**. Note that this command starts the remote Problem Reporting Utility in a graphical window. Close the Problem Reporting Utility, type **exit**, and press **Enter** to close your remote shell. Log out of the GNOME desktop when finished.

9. Switch back to tty2 by pressing **Ctrl+Alt+F2** and type **ssh user1@** *IP*, where *IP* is the IP address of your Ubuntu Server Linux virtual machine. When prompted to connect to the remote system, type **yes** and press **Enter**. Supply the root user password of **LNXrocks!** when prompted. Why is the SSH daemon started by default in Ubuntu Server?

10. At the command prompt, type **su - root** and press **Enter**. Supply the root user password of **LNXrocks!** when prompted to obtain a root shell.

11. At the command prompt, type **vi /etc/ssh/sshd_config** and press **Enter**. Modify the **PermitRootLogin without-password** line such that it reads **PermitRootLogin yes**, save your changes, and quit the vi editor.

12. At the command prompt, type **service ssh reload** and press **Enter** to force the SSH daemon to reload its configuration file.

13. Type **exit** and press **Enter** to log out of your remote shell.

14. At the command prompt, type **ssh user1@** *IP*, where *IP* is the IP address of your Ubuntu Server Linux virtual machine, and supply the root user password of **LNXrocks!** when prompted. Next, type **exit** and press **Enter** to log out of your remote shell.

15. Supply the root user password of **LNXrocks!** when prompted At the command prompt, type **ssh root@** *IP* **cat /etc/issue > /root/partner_issue** and press **Enter**, where *IP* is the IP address of your partner's computer. Next, supply the root user's password of **LNXrocks!** and press **Enter**.

16. At the command prompt, type **cat partner_issue** and press **Enter**. Was your partner's issue file transferred successfully?

17. At the command prompt, type **less /etc/ssh/ssh_config** and press **Enter**. Examine the SSH client options available. Note the encryption algorithms supported in the commented Ciphers line. Press **q** when finished.

12

18. At the command prompt, type **less /etc/ssh/sshd_config** and press **Enter**. Examine the SSH daemon options available. What line would allow root connections to the SSH daemon if they were not allowed by default? Press **q** when finished.

19. At the command prompt, type **cat /root/.ssh/known_hosts** and press **Enter**. What two hosts are listed in this file and why?

20. Type **exit** and press **Enter** to log out of your shell.

21. On your Windows host, double-click the putty.exe file on your desktop. Note that the default connection type is SSH, enter the IP address of your Fedora Linux virtual machine in the Host Name (or IP address) box, and click **Open**. Log into your Fedora Linux virtual machine using the user name of **root** and password of **LNXrocks!**. When finished, type **exit** and press **Enter** to log out of your remote shell.

22. On your Windows host, double-click the putty.exe file on your desktop. Note that the default connection type is SSH, enter the IP address of your Ubuntu Server Linux virtual machine in the Host Name (or IP address) box, and click **Open**. Log into your Ubuntu Server Linux virtual machine using the user name of **root** and password of **LNXrocks!**. When finished, type **exit** and press **Enter** to log out of your remote shell.

Project 12-7

In this hands-on project, you configure a VNC server on your Fedora Linux virtual machine and connect to it remotely from your Windows host.

1. On your Fedora Linux virtual machine, switch to a command-line terminal (tty2) by pressing **Ctrl+Alt+F2** and log in to the terminal using the user name of **root** and the password of **LNXrocks!**.

2. At the command prompt, type **yum install tigervnc-server** and press **Enter**. Press **y** when prompted to complete the installation of the tiger VNC server.

3. At the command prompt, type **cp /lib/systemd/system/vncserver@.service /lib/systemd/system/vncserver@:3.service** and press **Enter** to create a VNC configuration for display number 3.

4. At the command prompt, type **vi /lib/systemd/system/vncserver@:3.service** and press **Enter**. Change all instances of <USER> to **user1**. Save your changes and quit the vi editor when finished.

5. At the command prompt, type **systemctl daemon-reload** and press **Enter** to force all daemons to re-read their configuration files.

6. At the command prompt, type **su - user1** and press **Enter** to switch your shell to user1. Next, type **vncpasswd** and press **Enter** to set a VNC password. Supply a password of **LNXrocks!** when prompted (twice).

7. At the command prompt, type **exit** and press **Enter** to return to your root shell.

8. At the command prompt, type **systemctl enable vncserver@:3.service; systemctl start vncserver@:3.service** and press **Enter** to start the VNC daemon and ensure that it starts at boot time.

9. At the command prompt, type **firewall-cmd --permanent --zone=public --add-service vnc-server** and press **Enter** to add a permanent firewall exception for the VNC server.

10. At the command prompt, type **reboot** and press **Enter** to reboot your Fedora Linux virtual machine.

11. On your Windows host, open a Web browser and download the RealVNC Viewer for Windows EXE program from **https://www.realvnc.com/download/viewer/**. Install the program when finished and open the program following installation.

12. In the VNC Viewer program, enter **IP:5903** in the VNC Server dialog box, where **IP** is the IP address of your Fedora Linux virtual machine, and click **Connect**. Supply the VNC password of **LNXrocks!** when prompted. Explore your user1 desktop and close the VNC Viewer window when finished.

Discovery Exercises

1. Assuming that your company uses the Class A network 100.0.0.0/8, with what subnet mask would you need to configure all computers on the network to divide this network 11 times to match the company's 11 departments? How many hosts can you have per network? What are the first five ranges of addresses that you can assign to different departments?

2. In Project 12-6, you used the following method to transfer a file from a remote system to your local computer:

   ```
   ssh remotecomputer cat remotefile > localfile
   ```

   Using your knowledge of redirection, briefly describe how this command achieves this transfer. Can this command be used to transfer a binary file? Explain.

3. Use the Internet, books, or other resources to find out how to register a FQDN on a DNS server for use on the Internet. Describe the procedure and cost involved. Also, find three domain names that would be free for you to register if you wanted to.

4. Use the Internet, books, or other resources to research the history of DNS. How and where did it start? Are there different versions of DNS? If so, what are their differences?

5. On legacy UNIX and Linux systems, the remote commands (rlogin, rsh, and rcp) were used to execute commands on remote systems, obtain remote shells, and copy files between systems. These commands were often called the r commands, and they allowed access to remote computers without a password, provided the remote computer has trusted access—in other words, permission to do so via an entry within the /etc/hosts.equiv file or the ~/.rhosts file. While the security subsystem on modern Linux distributions does not allow for trusted access using the r commands, you can still install the r commands and use them (provided that you supply a password). Use the Internet to research the use of the r commands and the packages that you need to host them. Next, install those packages on your Ubuntu Server Linux virtual machine, examine the /etc/inetd.conf file (used to start the associated services), and use the r commands to perform remote administration on your local Ubuntu Server Linux virtual machine.

12

Configuring Network Services

After completing this chapter, you will be able to:

- Configure infrastructure network services, including DHCP, DNS, NTP, and NIS
- Configure Web services using the Apache Web server
- Configure file-sharing services, including Samba, NFS, and FTP
- Configure e-mail services using Postfix
- Configure database services using PostgreSQL

In the previous chapter, you examined the concepts and procedures that allow Linux to participate on a network. You also learned about the network services that are commonly used on Linux systems. In this chapter, you examine the configuration of network services that provide infrastructure, Web, file sharing, e-mail, and database services to users across a network.

Infrastructure Services

Some networking services provide network configuration and support for other computers on a network in the form of TCP/IP configuration, name resolution, time management, and centralized authentication. These services, which are collectively called **infrastructure services**, include DHCP, DNS, NTP, and NIS.

DHCP

Recall from the previous chapter that your network interface can be configured manually or automatically using Dynamic Host Configuration Protocol (DHCP). If your network interface is configured using DHCP, it sends a DHCP broadcast on the network requesting IP configuration information. If a DHCP server on the network has a range of IP addresses, it leases an IP address to the client computer for a certain period of time; after this lease has expired, the client computer must send another DHCP request. Because DHCP servers keep track of the IP addresses they lease to client computers, they can ensure that no two computers receive the same IP address. If two computers are accidentally configured manually with the same IP address, neither would be able to communicate using the IP protocol.

DHCP servers can also send client computers other IP configuration information, such as the default gateway and the DNS server they should use.

The DHCP Lease Process The process by which a DHCP client requests IP configuration from a DHCP server involves several stages. First, the client sends a request (DHCPDISCOVER packet) to all hosts on the network. In reply, a DHCP server sends an offer (DHCPOFFER packet) that contains a potential IP configuration. The DHCP client then selects (accepts) the offer by sending a DHCPREQUEST packet to the associated DHCP server. Next, the DHCP server sends to the client an acknowledgement indicating the amount of time the client can use the IP configuration (DHCPACK packet). Finally, the client configures itself with the IP configuration. This process is illustrated in Figure 13-1.

 If there are multiple DHCP servers on your network, DHCP clients will accept the first offer that they receive and decline all other offers by sending a DHCPDECLINE packet to the other DHCP servers.

Halfway through the time period specified by its lease (i.e., at 50 percent of its lease), the DHCP client will send another DHCPREQUEST packet to its DHCP server to renew its IP configuration. If its DHCP server is unreachable, it will try to renew its IP configuration again at 87.5 percent of its lease by sending a DHCPDISCOVER packet to all hosts on the network to allow any DHCP server on the network to respond with an offer. Once the lease is up, the DHCP client discards its IP configuration obtained from the DHCP server and automatically configures the network interface using APIPA (the IPv4 169.254.0.0 network).

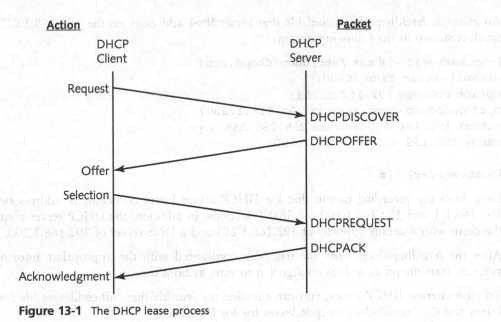

Figure 13-1 The DHCP lease process

To configure your Linux system as a DHCP server, you must first install the DHCP daemon, which is available from online software repositories. The two most common DHCP daemons available for Linux are the **DHCP daemon (dhcpd)** and **BusyBox DHCP daemon (udhcpd)**.

Configuring a Linux DHCP Server Using dhcpd Most Linux systems, including Fedora 20, use the dhcpd daemon to provide for DHCP functionality on the network. To configure a Fedora 20 system using dhcpd, you must first add a dhcpd user account (no password required) that will be used by dhcpd. Next, you must add lines to the appropriate configuration files to list the appropriate IP address range for your network, as well as lease information and other IP configuration options. The dhcpd configuration files for IPv4 and IPv6 are as follows:

- /etc/dhcp/dhcpd.conf stores IPv4 configuration
- /etc/dhcp/dhcpd6.conf stores IPv6 configuration

You don't need to configure the /etc/dhcp/dhcpd.conf file unless you wish to configure IPv4 clients. Similarly, you don't need to configure the /etc/dhcp/dhcpd6.conf file unless you wish to configure IPv6 clients.

You can refer to the manual page for the dhcpd.conf file to obtain a complete list of parameters that can be configured within the /etc/dhcp/dhcpd.conf and /etc/dhcp/dhcpd6.conf files.

An example /etc/dhcp/dhcpd.conf file that leases IPv4 addresses on the 192.168.1.0/24 network is shown in the following output:

```
[root@server1 ~]# cat /etc/dhcp/dhcpd.conf
default-lease-time 36000;
option routers 192.168.1.254;
option domain-name-servers 192.168.1.200;
subnet 192.168.1.0 netmask 255.255.255.0 {
range 192.168.1.1 192.168.1.100;
}
[root@server1 ~]# _
```

Note from the preceding output that the DHCP server leases clients an IP address between 192.168.1.1 and 192.168.1.100 for 36,000 seconds. In addition, the DHCP server configures the client with a default gateway of 192.168.1.254 and a DNS server of 192.168.1.200.

After the /etc/dhcp/dhcpd.conf file has been configured with the appropriate information, you can start dhcpd as well as configure it to start at boot time.

To view current DHCP leases, you can examine the /var/lib/dhcpd/dhcpd.leases file for IPv4 leases and the /var/lib/dhcp/dhcpd6.leases file for IPv6 leases.

After changing the /etc/dhcp/dhcpd.conf or /etc/dhcp/dhcpd6.conf configuration files, you must restart the dhcpd daemon for the changes to take effect.

Configuring a Linux DHCP Server Using udhcpd

Some Linux systems, including Ubuntu Server 14.04, use the udhcpd daemon to provide for IPv4 DHCP functionality on the network. To configure an Ubuntu Server14.04 system using udhcpd, you must first change the DHCPD_ENABLED="no" line within the /etc/default/udhcpd file to read DHCPD_ENABLED="yes" and save your changes. Next, you must specify the appropriate IP address range for your network as well as lease information and other IP configuration options within the /etc/udhcpd.conf. The following udhcpd.conf file leases clients an IP address between 192.168.1.1 and 192.168.1.100 on eth0 for 36,000 seconds as well as configures the client with a default gateway of 192.168.1.254 and a DNS server of 192.168.1.200:

```
[root@server1 ~]# cat /etc/udhcpd.conf
start           192.168.1.1
end             192.168.1.100
interface       eth0
option subnet   255.255.255.0
option router   192.168.1.254
option dns      192.168.1.200
option lease    36000
lease_file      /var/lib/misc/udhcpd.leases
[root@server1 ~]# _
```

Also note from the preceding output that the location of the file that stores IPv4 lease information (/var/lib/misc/udhcpd.leases) is also set within the /etc/udhcpd.conf file. If you do not specify the location of a lease file within /etc/udhcpd.conf, you can still view DHCP lease information by executing the **dumpleases** command.

Finally, you can start udhcpd and configure it to start at boot time.

After changing the /etc/udhcpd.conf configuration file, you must restart the udhcpd daemon for the changes to take effect.

DNS

Recall that DNS is a hierarchical namespace used to identify computers on large TCP/IP networks such as the Internet. Each part of this namespace is called a **zone**, and DNS servers contain all host name information for a zone. DNS servers typically resolve FQDNs to IP addresses (called a **forward lookup**), but they can also resolve IP addresses to FQDNs (called a **reverse lookup**).

The DNS Lookup Process When you contact a Web server on the Internet using a Web browser, the Web browser performs a forward lookup of the FQDN such that it can contact the IP address of the Web server. This forward lookup can be performed by a DNS server or a series of DNS servers. The whole process used to resolve the FQDN *www.linux. org* is illustrated in Figure 13-2.

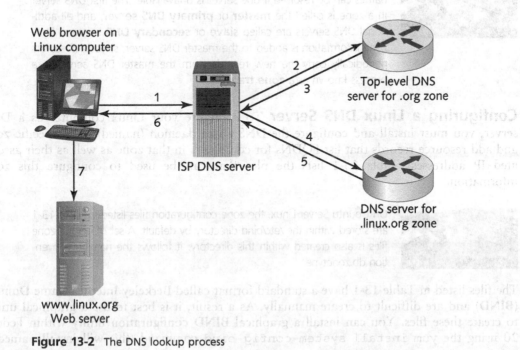

Figure 13-2 The DNS lookup process

In the first step from Figure 13-2, the Linux computer sends a forward lookup request for *www.linux.org* to the DNS server that is configured in NIC properties or /etc/resolv.conf; this is typically the DNS server at your ISP. If the ISP DNS server has recently resolved the FQDN and placed the result in its local DNS cache, you receive the response immediately (a DNS lookup query that generates a reply from a DNS cache is called an **iterative query**). If it has not, the ISP DNS server normally contacts the DNS server for the .org top-level zone (Step 2) and repeats the forward lookup request for *www.linux.org* (called a **recursive query**). The .org DNS server will not contain the IP address for the *www.linux.org* computer in its zone but will reply with the IP address of the DNS server for the linux.org zone (Step 3).

All DNS servers contain a **DNS cache file** that contains the IP addresses of DNS servers that hold top-level DNS zones.

Your ISP DNS server then contacts the DNS server for the linux.org zone (Step 4) and repeats the forward lookup request for *www.linux.org* (another recursive query). The DNS server for the linux.org domain contains a record that lists the IP address for the *www.linux.org* computer and returns this IP address to the ISP DNS server (Step 5). The ISP DNS server then returns the result to the client Web browser (Step 6), which then uses the IP address to connect to the Web server (Step 7).

Each zone typically has more than one DNS server to ensure that names can be resolved if one server is unavailable. The first DNS server in a zone is called the **master** or **primary DNS server**, and all additional DNS servers are called **slave** or **secondary DNS servers**. New zone information is added to the master DNS server; slave DNS servers periodically copy the new records from the master DNS server in a process known as a **zone transfer**.

Configuring a Linux DNS Server To configure your Linux computer as a DNS server, you must install and configure the DNS name daemon (named) for a specific zone and add resource records that list FQDNs for computers in that zone as well as their associated IP addresses. Table 13-1 lists the files that can be used to configure this zone information.

On Ubuntu Server Linux, the zone configuration files listed in Table 13-1 are stored within the /etc/bind directory by default. A set of default zone files is also created within this directory; it follows the naming convention db.zonetype.

The files listed in Table 13-1 have a standard format called **Berkeley Internet Name Domain (BIND)** and are difficult to create manually. As a result, it is best to use a graphical utility to create these files. You can install a graphical **BIND configuration utility** within Fedora 20 using the yum install system-config-bind command (this will install named if

File	Description
/etc/named.conf	Contains the list of DNS zones and their type (master/slave) that the name daemon will manage.
/var/named/*zone_name*.db or /var/named/*zone_name*.zone	Contains **resource records** used to perform forward lookups for a particular *zone_name*. Lines in this file have a type that determines the kind of resource record: • A (add host) records map FQDNs to IPv4 addresses. • AAAA (add host) records map FQDNs to IPv6 addresses. • CNAME (canonical name) records provide additional aliases for A records. • NS (name server) records provide the names of DNS servers for the zone. • MX (mail exchange) records provide the IP address for the e-mail server for a zone. • SOA (start of authority) determines the parameters used for zone transfers as well as how long information can be cached by the computer performing the forward or reverse lookup (called the **Time-To-Live**, or **TTL**).
/var/named/*reverse_network_ID*.in-addr.arpa or /var/named/*network_ID*.db or /var/named/*network_ID*.zone	Contains resource records of type PTR (pointer), which list names used for reverse lookups for a particular network. The network is incorporated into the filename itself; for example, the filename that contains PTR records for the 192.168.1.0 IPv4 network would be called 1.168.192.in-addr.arpa or 192.168.1.db or 192.168.1.zone.
/var/named/named.local & /var/named/named.ip6.local or /var/named/named.localhost or /var/named/named.loopback	Contains PTR records used to identify the loopback adapter (127.0.0.1 for IPv4, ::1 for IPv6).
/var/named/named.ca or /var/named/named.root	Contains the IP addresses of top-level DNS servers; it is commonly called the DNS cache file.

Table 13-1 Common zone configuration files

not already installed). Next, you can run the system-config-bind command at a BASH terminal prompt within a desktop environment and configure the appropriate zones, as shown in Figure 13-3.

After you configure the appropriate zones within the graphical BIND utility shown in Figure 13-3, you must click the Save button to save your configuration to the /etc/named.conf file and the appropriate files within the /var/named directory.

After the files that contain the zone information have been created, you can start the DNS name daemon to provide DNS services on the network, as well as configure the DNS name daemon to start at boot time.

BIND configuration GUI

File   Help

New   Properties   Delete   Import   Preview   Save

Search:

⊞ 🌐 DNS Server

⊞ 📇 ::1   Internet Reverse IPv6 ARPA Zone

⊞ 📇 192.168.1   Internet Reverse IPv4 Zone

⊞ 📇   Internet Forward Zone

⊞ 📇 localhost.localdomain   Internet Forward Zone

⊞ 📇 0   Internet Reverse IPv4 Zone

⊞ 📇 127.0.0.1   Internet Reverse IPv4 Zone

⊟ 📇 class.com   Internet Forward Zone

⊞ 🗐   Zone Authority Information   SOA

⊞ ✉   Mail Exchange   MX

⊞ 🗐   Name Server   localhost   NS

⊞ 🖥   gateway   ->   192.168.1.1   A

⊞ 🖥   server1   ->   192.168.1.105   A

⊞ ⇒   alias ->   server1.class.com   CNAME

⊞ 📇 localhost   Internet Forward Zone

Select an object; press and release the right-hand mouse button.

Figure 13-3 The BIND configuration utility

The name of the DNS service differs in each Linux distribution. For example, to restart named on Fedora 20, you can use the `systemctl restart named.service` command. However, to restart named on Ubuntu Server 14.04, you use the `service bind9 restart` command.

If you modify any files associated with the name daemon (for example, to add additional resource records), you must restart the name daemon for those changes to take effect.

Recall from Chapter 12 that you can use the `dig` command to test name resolution. The `dig` command can also query the records that exist on a specific DNS server using the format `dig @server record type`, where `server` is the name or IP address of the DNS server, `record` is the name of the resource record or domain, and `type` is the type of record (A, CNAME, PTR, MX, NS, SOA, ANY, etc.). This is especially useful if you want to see whether a zone from a primary (master) DNS server to a secondary (slave) DNS server was successful. Simply query the secondary DNS server to find out whether the new records have been added.

NTP

Most system components and network services require the correct date and time in order to function properly. The BIOS on each computer contains a system clock that stores the current date and time. Operating systems can choose to use the time from this system clock or obtain time information from other servers on the network using the **Network Time Protocol** (**NTP**).

You can view and modify the date and time within the BIOS using the BIOS configuration utility on your computer or by using the `hwclock command`.

NTP is one of the oldest Internet protocols still commonly used on the Internet. It is designed to simplify the setting of time and date information on computers across the Internet using UDP port 123. The two NTP daemons that are commonly used on Linux systems are the **NTP daemon (ntpd)** and **Chrony NTP daemon (chronyd)**.

Understanding NTP Strata NTP uses a hierarchical series of time sources called **strata**. Stratum 0 is at the top of this hierarchy and consists of atomic devices or GPS clocks. Stratum 1 devices obtain their time directly from Stratum 0 devices. Stratum 2 devices obtain their time from Stratum 1 servers, and so on. This organization is shown in Figure 13-4.

The stratum is not an indication of quality or reliability since NTP servers typically obtain time information from multiple time sources (NTP servers) and use an algorithm to determine the most reliable time information. As a result, it is common to find a Stratum 3 device that is more accurate than a Stratum 2 device.

NTP supports up to 256 strata.

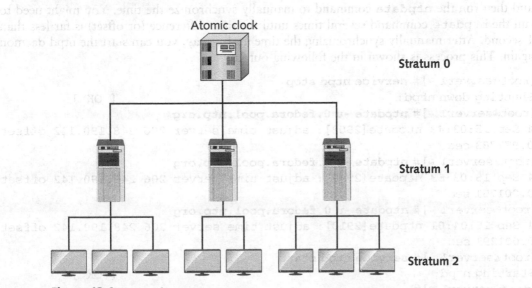

Figure 13-4 A sample strata structure

Most Internet time servers, such as time.apple.com, are Stratum 1 devices.

Working with ntpd   Most Linux systems use ntpd to provide for NTP functionality. It can act as both an NTP client to obtain time from an Internet time server or an NTP server that other computers can query for time information. Although most Linux distributions install ntpd during the Linux installation process, it can be installed from a software repository if it is not available.

To configure a Linux system as an NTP client using ntpd, you can modify the /etc/ntp.conf file and add lines for different NTP servers the client can query. These servers could be any strata or combinations of different strata.

For example, the following lines in /etc/ntp.conf query three time servers: ntp.research.gov, ntp.redhat.com, and 0.fedora.pool.ntp.org.

```
server ntp.research.gov
server ntp.redhat.com
server 0.fedora.pool.ntp.org
```

Each of the FQDNs listed in the preceding output may point to multiple servers since NTP servers typically have several A (host) records in DNS that list the name FQDN for different IP addresses. This allows NTP requests to be spread across all servers to reduce server load.

If your time differs significantly from the time on these time servers, you must first stop ntpd and then run the **ntpdate command** to manually synchronize the time. You might need to run the ntpdate command several times until the time difference (or **offset**) is far less than 1 second. After manually synchronizing the time in this way, you can start the ntpd daemon again. This process is shown in the following output:

```
[root@server1 ~]# service ntpd stop
Shutting down ntpd:                                          [ OK ]
[root@server1 ~]# ntpdate -u 0.fedora.pool.ntp.org
4 Sep 15:03:43 ntpdate[2908]: adjust time server 206.248.190.142 offset
0.977783 sec
[root@server1 ~]# ntpdate -u 0.fedora.pool.ntp.org
4 Sep 15:03:53 ntpdate[2909]: adjust time server 206.248.190.142 offset
0.001751 sec
[root@server1 ~]# ntpdate -u 0.fedora.pool.ntp.org
4 Sep 15:04:01 ntpdate[2910]: adjust time server 206.248.190.142 offset
0.001291 sec
[root@server1 ~]# service ntpd start
Starting ntpd:                                              [ OK ]
[root@server1 ~]# _
```

After restarting the ntpd daemon, you can use the **ntpq command** to see what actual time servers you are synchronizing with. Since time varies greatly by location, NTP uses a **jitter** buffer to store the difference between the same time measurements from different NTP servers. The jitter information is used by NTP when determining the most reliable time when several NTP servers are queried for time information. The `ntpq -p` command shows the offset and jitter in milliseconds, as shown here:

```
[root@server1 ~]# ntpq -p
remote          refid           st t when  poll reach delay  offset jitter
==============================================================================
ox.eicat.ca     139.78.135.14   2  u  6    64    3    28.662 11.138 0.046
adelaide.ph     142.3.100.15    3  u  2    64    3    62.211 30.870 0.574
one.trx.com     209.51.161.238  2  u  3    64    3    43.329 22.867 0.190
[root@server1 ~]#
```

By default, the NTP daemon is not configured as an NTP server, since there is only a single NTP `restrict` line within the /etc/ntp.conf file:

```
restrict 127.0.0.1
```

This line allows your local client to query the NTP daemon for time information with no restrictions. If you want to allow other computers to query your NTP daemon (ntpd) for time information, simply edit the /etc/ntp.conf file again and add a line that identifies the specific computers or networks that are allowed to query your NTP daemon. For example, the following line within /etc/ntp.conf allows all computers on the 192.168.1.0 network to query your NTP daemon for time information but prevents other computers from modifying your NTP server configuration (`nomodify notrap`).

```
restrict 192.168.1.0 mask 255.255.255.0 nomodify notrap
```

If you modify the /etc/ntp.conf file, you must restart ntpd for those changes to take effect.

Working with chronyd Some modern Linux distributions, such as Fedora 20, use chronyd in place of ntpd, since it offers a faster response time and is backwards-compatible with ntpd. It uses the /etc/chrony.conf configuration file, which has a format nearly identical to that of /etc/ntp.conf. You can add different NTP servers to query using the same syntax used within /etc/ntp.conf, as well as add lines that allow other NTP servers to query you on a particular subnet. Rather than using a `restrict` line to allow other NTP clients to query your time as seen earlier in /etc/ntp.conf, you can simply add the line `allow` *subnet* to /etc/chrony.conf. For example, the line `allow 192.168.1/24` would allow NTP clients to connect from the 192.168.1.0 network (with a 24-bit subnet mask of 255.255.255.0).

For management, chronyd uses the **chronyc command** to provide the functionality that the ntpdate and ntpq commands do with ntpd. For example, to view the servers that you are currently polling for time, simply run the chronyc sources command, as shown here:

```
[root@server1 ~]# chronyc sources
210 Number of sources=4
```

```
MS Name/IP address      Stratum  Poll   LastRx    Last sample
===============================================================================
^+ 209.167.68.100           2      6      22      +11ms [  +11ms]  +/-   87ms
^+ 66.102.79.92             2      6      32      +3556us[+3669us]  +/-   62ms
^+ ox.eicat.ca              2      6      42      -4311us[-4198us]  +/-   75ms
^* 216.234.161.11           2      6      50       -41us [  +72us]  +/-   81ms
[root@server1 ~]# _
```

When run without arguments, the chronyc command provides an interactive chronyc> prompt that you can use to type additional commands. Typing help at the chronyc> prompt will display a list of common commands, including polltarget (which can be used to poll a specified NTP server) and settime (which can be used to manually set the date and time to a specified value).

Nearly all desktop environments installed today obtain time from an Internet time server using NTP and allow for NTP client configuration using a graphical application. For example, to obtain time from an Internet time server using chronyd on a Fedora 20 system, you can navigate to the Activities menu, Show Applications, Settings, Date & Time within the GNOME desktop to open the **Date & Time utility** shown in Figure 13-5.

 All system date information is calculated relative to the time zone that you selected during Linux installation. The configuration of each time zone is stored in the /usr/share/zoneinfo directory. If you need to manually change the time zone following installation, you can use the **tzselect command** or set OFF next to Automatic Time Zone in Figure 13-5 and select your desired time zone.

NIS

You can use the **Network Information Service (NIS)** to coordinate common configuration files, such as /etc/passwd and /etc/hosts, across several Linux computers within an organization. Each computer that participates in NIS belongs to an **NIS domain** and uses an **NIS map** for accessing certain information rather than use the local configuration file. Furthermore, you can configure a **NIS master server** to send all NIS map configuration to **NIS slave servers**, which then distribute these NIS maps to all other Linux computers, known as **NIS clients**. Alternatively, a master NIS server can send NIS map configuration directly to NIS clients.

 Some Linux systems store their timezone information within the /etc/timezone or /etc/localtime file. You can use the tzconfig command to modify these files.

Date & Time

Automatic Date & Time Requires internet access	ON
Automatic Time Zone Requires internet access	ON
Date & Time	11 August 2014, 11:32
Time Zone	EDT (Toronto, Canada)
Time Format	24-hour

Figure 13-5   The Date & Time utility

NOTE The steps used to configure NIS servers and clients vary considerably between Linux distributions. As a result, we'll limit our discussion to the configuration of NIS servers and NIS clients on Fedora 20 within this section. For other Linux distributions, consult the configuration steps provided for NIS on the distribution Web site.

Configuring an NIS Server on a Fedora 20 System The most common configuration files that companies use NIS to coordinate across multiple systems are password databases (/etc/passwd and /etc/shadow). This allows users to log in to several different Linux servers using the same user name and password. The steps required to set up an NIS server for this purpose are as follows:

1. Install the ypserv and rpcbind packages from a software repository.

2. Define the NIS domain name by typing the command ypdomainname NIS_domain_name at a command prompt.

3. Edit the file /var/yp/Makefile, navigate to the line that starts with `all:`, and edit the list of files to be made into maps. If you have no slave servers, also ensure that NOPUSH=-true is in this file. If you have slave servers, they must be listed in the /var/yp/ypservers file.

4. Add the names or IP addresses of allowed clients to the /var/yp/securenets file.

5. Allow the clients from Step 3 access to the appropriate maps in the /etc/ypserv.conf file.

6. Start the ypserv and rpcbind daemons and set them to start at boot time.

7. Generate the configuration file maps by typing /usr/lib/yp/ypinit -m at a command prompt (or cd /var/yp ; make).

Configuring an NIS Client on a Fedora 20 System After configuring an NIS server, you must configure NIS clients to obtain their configuration information from the NIS server. To set up an NIS client to obtain user and password information from an NIS server, you can perform the following steps:

1. Install the ypbind and rpcbind packages from a software repository.

2. Define the NIS domain name by typing the command ypdomainname NIS_domain_name at a command prompt.

3. Change the line USENIS=no to USENIS=yes within the /etc/sysconfig/authconfig file.

4. Edit the /etc/yp.conf file and add the following line to query a specific NIS server:

   domain NIS_domain server NIS_server

   Alternatively, you can add the following line to listen for NIS broadcasts on the network:

   domain NIS_domain broadcast

5. Start the ypbind and rpcbind daemons and set them to start automatically at boot time.

6. Locate the NIS server by typing the command ypwhich at a command prompt.

13

7. Edit the /etc/nsswitch.conf file and add the keyword nis (or nisplus) before other methods for user, group, and host name lookup, as shown in the following example:

```
passwd:   nis files
shadow:   nis files
```

After the NIS server and client have been set up, ensure that all users on NIS clients use the yppasswd command to change their NIS password; using the passwd command only modifies the local password database.

NIS was originally called Yellow Pages; as a result, many configuration commands and files are prefixed with the letters yp.

Web Services

Apache is the world's most common Web server. It started as the HTTP Daemon (httpd) developed by Rob McCool for the NCSA (National Center for Supercomputing Applications) at the University of Illinois. In the early-1990s, Rob McCool became too busy to continue the project single-handedly, so he released the source code for httpd under the GPL. Open Source Software developers then made patches to this code, with each patch improving one component of the system. These patches gave rise to the name Apache server (a patchy server). After these early days, the Apache Group of Open Source Developers took over development of Apache. (To learn more about this group, go to *www.apache.org*.)

Recall that Web servers hand out HTML files and other Web content using the Hyper Text Transfer Protocol (HTTP) from a specific directory in the directory tree. This directory is called the **document root** directory and contains the default Web site that is used on the server. The default document root directory is /var/www/html, and the default document that is handed out from this directory is index.html. The main configuration file for Apache differs based on your Linux distribution. On Fedora 20, the main Apache configuration file is /etc/httpd/conf/httpd.conf, and for Ubuntu 14.04, the main Apache configuration file is /etc/apache2/apache2.conf. Each line in the httpd.conf file is called a **directive**. Table 13-2 lists some common directives.

The main Apache configuration file often references several other configuration files that contain directives used by Apache.

The name of the Apache service differs in each Linux distribution. For example, to install Apache on Fedora 20, you can install the httpd package and use the command systemctl start httpd. service to start Apache. However, to install Apache on Ubuntu Server 14.04, you can install the apache2 package and use the command service apache2 start to start Apache.

Directive	What It Specifies
Listen 80	Apache daemon will listen for HTTP requests on port 80.
ServerName server1.class.com	Name of the local server is server1.class.com.
DocumentRoot "/var/www/html"	Document root directory is /var/www/html on the local computer.
DirectoryIndex index.html	Index.html file in the document root directory will be sent to clients who request an HTML document.
ServerRoot /etc/httpd	All paths listed within the /etc/httpd/conf/httpd.conf file are relative to the /etc/httpd directory.
ErrorLog logs/error_log	All Apache daemon messages will be written to the /etc/httpd/logs/error_log file.
CustomLog logs/access_log combined	All Web requests will be written to the /etc/httpd/logs/access_log file using a combined log format.
MaxClients 150	Maximum number of simultaneous requests cannot exceed 150.
User apache	Apache daemon will run as the "apache" local user account.
Group apache	Apache daemon will run as the "apache" local group account.
<Directory /var/www/html> Order allow,deny Allow from all Deny from 192.168.1.51 </Directory>	All hosts are allowed to access HTML files and other Web content from the /var/www/html directory except for the computer with the IP address 192.168.1.51.

Table 13-2   Common httpd.conf directives

The default settings in the httpd.conf file are sufficient for most simple Web servers; thus, you simply need to copy the appropriate HTML files to the /var/www/html directory, including the index.html file, start Apache to host Web content on your network, and ensure that Apache is started automatically at boot time. Client computers can then enter the location *http://servername_or_IPaddress* in their Web browser to obtain the default Web page. Each time a client request is received by the Apache Web server (called a **Web page hit**), a separate httpd daemon is started to service the request.

You can also use the **curl command** at a BASH command prompt to obtain a Web page. For example, the curl http://127.0.0.1/ command can be used to test your local Apache Web server to ensure that your Apache Web server is sending the correct Web page to clients.

On a busy Web server, there may be several hundred httpd daemons running on the system responding to client requests. The first httpd daemon is started as the root user and is used to start all other httpd daemons. These non-root httpd daemons are started as a regular user account to prevent privileged access to the system. For example, the User apache directive

13

shown in Table 13-2 will ensure that non-root httpd daemons are started as the apache user. In this case, any Web content must have Linux permissions that allow it to be readable by the apache user. When you restart Apache, the root httpd daemon is restarted, which in turn restarts all other httpd daemons. If you change the HTML content inside the document root directory, you do not need to restart Apache. However, if you change the contents of an Apache configuration file, you need to restart Apache to activate those changes.

The **apachectl command** is useful when managing Apache. The `apachectl graceful` command can be used to restart Apache without dropping any client connections, whereas the `apachectl configtest` command checks the syntax of lines within Apache configuration files and notes any errors.

The **ab (Apache benchmark) command** can be used to monitor the performance of the Apache Web server by sending null requests to it. To send 1000 requests to the local Apache Web server (100 at a time), you could use the `ab -n1000 -c100 http://127.0.0.1/` command.

File Sharing Services

There are many different file sharing services available on Linux systems. Each is tailored for a specific purpose and has a different configuration method. The most common include Samba, NFS, and FTP.

Samba

Microsoft Windows is the most commonly used client computer operating system, so you need to know how to configure your Linux system to communicate with Windows computers. Windows computers format TCP/IP data using the **Server Message Blocks (SMB)** protocol. To share information with Windows client computers, you can use the Samba daemon (smbd), which emulates the SMB protocol. In addition, Windows computers advertise their computer names using the **NetBIOS** protocol. To create and advertise a NetBIOS name that Windows computers can use to connect to your Linux server, you can use the NetBIOS name daemon (nmbd).

NetBIOS names can be up to 15 characters long and are normally resolved on the network using a WINS (Windows Internet Name Service) server or NetBIOS broadcasts. All NetBIOS names that are successfully resolved are placed in a NetBIOS name cache to speed future access to the same servers. The **nmblookup command** can be used to test NetBIOS name resolution in Linux.

Because of the widespread popularity of SMB, nearly all operating systems, including UNIX, Linux, Macintosh OS X, and Microsoft Windows, can connect to directories that are shared using the SMB protocol.

Configuring a Samba Server When a Windows client computer accesses a shared directory using SMB, the Windows user name and password are transmitted alongside the request in case the shared directory allows access to certain users only. As a result, you should first create local Linux user accounts for each Windows user and create a Samba password for them using the **smbpasswd command** that matches the password that they use on their Windows computer, as shown in the following output:

```
[root@server1 ~]# useradd mary
[root@server1 ~]# passwd mary
Changing password for user mary.
New UNIX password:
Retype new UNIX password:
passwd: all authentication tokens updated successfully.
[root@server1 ~]# smbpasswd -a mary
New SMB password:
Retype new SMB password:
Added user mary.
[root@server1 ~]# _
```

Following this, you can edit the main configuration file for Samba, /etc/samba/smb.conf. Like the Apache configuration file, the smb.conf contains directives that can be used to set your NetBIOS name, server settings, shared directories, and shared printers. On most Linux systems, the default settings within smb.conf file shares all printers and home directories (for recognized Windows users). However, you need to add a line under the [global] section of this file to set your NetBIOS name. For example, to set your NetBIOS name to server1, you could add the directive netbios name = server1 to the smb.conf file. As with Apache, if you change the smb.conf file, you must restart the Samba and NetBIOS name daemons.

You can use the **testparm command** to ensure that there are no syntax errors in the /etc/samba/smb.conf file. As a result, it is good practice to run this command after you edit the /etc/samba/smb.conf file.

13

Connecting to a Samba Server After configuring Samba, you should test its functionality to ensure that it is functioning normally. To do this, you could log into a Windows client and enter *Samba_server* in the Run dialog box, where *Samba_server* is the NetBIOS name or IP address of your Samba server. If successful, the Windows operating system will open a new window that displays your home directory, shared printers, and other shared directories that you have permission to, as shown in Figure 13-6.

Alternatively, you could connect to your Samba server using the **smbclient command** on your Linux computer. Simply log into a BASH terminal using the login information for an established Windows user account. Then run the smbclient -L *Samba_server* command, where *Samba_server* is the NetBIOS name or IP address of your Samba server. This connects your computer to the Samba server using your current user account credentials

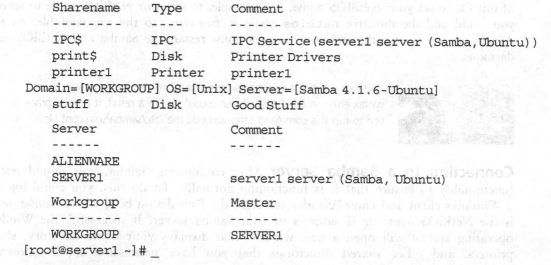

Figure 13-6 Accessing a Samba server from a Windows client

and lists the shared directories and available printers, as shown in the following sample output:

```
[root@server1 ~]# smbclient -L server1
Enter root's password:
Domain=[WORKGROUP] OS=[Unix] Server=[Samba 4.1.6-Ubuntu]

    Sharename      Type        Comment
    ---------      ----        -------
    IPC$           IPC         IPC Service(server1 server (Samba,Ubuntu))
    print$         Disk        Printer Drivers
    printer1       Printer     printer1
Domain=[WORKGROUP] OS=[Unix] Server=[Samba 4.1.6-Ubuntu]
    stuff          Disk        Good Stuff

    Server                     Comment
    ------                     -------
    ALIENWARE
    SERVER1                    server1 server (Samba, Ubuntu)

    Workgroup                  Master
    ---------                  ------
    WORKGROUP                  SERVER1
[root@server1 ~]# _
```

You can use the smbclient command to connect to both Samba and Windows servers.

Additionally, you can use the smbclient command to display an FTP-like interface for transferring files to and from shared directories on Samba or Windows servers. The following output demonstrates how to connect to the stuff shared directory on server1 using an FTP-like interface:

```
[root@server1 root]# smbclient //server1/stuff
Enter root's password:
Domain=[MYGROUP] OS=[Unix] Server=[ Samba 4.1.6-Ubuntu]
smb: \> dir
  .                              D        0    Mon Sep  6 22:28:12 2015
  ..                             D        0    Mon Sep  6 22:28:12 2015
  Final Exam.doc                 A    26624    Mon Sep  6 23:17:30 2015
  homework questions.doc         A    46080    Mon Sep  6 23:33:03 2015
  Part 0.DOC                     A    13312    Mon Sep  6 23:27:51 2015
  Part 1.DOC                     A    35328    Mon Sep  6 23:24:44 2015
  Part 2.doc                     A    70656    Mon Sep  6 23:25:28 2015
  Part 3.DOC                     A    38912    Mon Sep  6 23:26:07 2015
  Part 4.doc                     A    75776    Mon Sep  6 23:26:57 2015
  Part 5.DOC                     A    26624    Mon Sep  6 23:27:23 2015
  Part 6.doc                     A    59904    Mon Sep  6 23:05:32 2015
  TOC.doc                        A    58880    Mon Sep  6 23:09:16 2015
  39032 blocks of size 262144. 14180 blocks available

smb: \> help
?               allinfo         altname         archive         backup
blocksize       cancel          case_sensitive  cd              chmod
chown           close           del             dir             du
echo            exit            get             getfacl         geteas
hardlink        help            history         iosize          lcd
link            lock            lowercase       ls              l
mask            md              mget            mkdir           more
mput            newer           notify          open            posix
posix_encrypt   posix_open      posix_mkdir     posix_rmdir     posix_unlink
print           prompt          put             pwd             q
queue           quit            readlink        rd              recurse
reget           rename          reput           rm              rmdir
showacls        setea           setmode         stat            symlink
tar             tarmode         timeout         translate       unlock
volume          vuid            wdel            logon           listconnect
showconnect     tcon            tdis            tid             logoff
..              !
smb: \> get TOC.doc
getting file \TOC.doc of size 58880 as TOC.doc (16.0 KiloBytes/sec) (aver-
age 16.0 KiloBytes/sec)
smb: \> exit
[root@server1 root]#
```

NFS

Network File System (NFS) allows UNIX, Linux, and Macintosh OS X computers to share files transparently. In NFS, one computer shares (or **exports**) a directory in the directory tree by placing the name of that directory in the /etc/exports file. The other computer can then access that directory across the network by using the mount command to mount the remote directory on the local computer.

Configuring a Linux NFS Server To configure an NFS server in Linux, perform the following steps:

1. Install the NFS server package from a software repository.

2. Create a directory that contains the information that is to be shared to client computers. Although you can use an existing directory, try to avoid doing so because you might accidentally give client computers the ability to view or modify existing system files.

3. Edit the /etc/exports file and add a line that lists the directory to be shared and the appropriate options. For example, the following lines in the /etc/exports file share the /source directory to the computer server1, allowing users to read and write data and ensuring that the root user is treated as an anonymous user on the NFS server, as well as share the /admin directory to all users, allowing users to read and write data:

```
/source server1(rw,root_squash)

/admin  *(rw)
```

4. Save your changes to the /etc/exports file and return to the command prompt.

5. Run the command exportfs -a to update the list of exported filesystems in memory from the /etc/exports file.

6. Restart the NFS daemon.

The name of the NFS server package differs based on Linux distribution. On Fedora 20, you can install the nfs-utils package, and on Ubuntu Server 14.04, you can install the nfs-kernel-server package.

The name of the NFS daemon is nfsd. To restart this daemon, you can use the systemctl restart nfs.service command on Fedora 20 or the service nfs-kernel-server restart command on Ubuntu Server 14.04.

Connecting to a Linux NFS Server You can see a list of available NFS shared directories on a remote server using the **showmount command**. For example, to see a list of the shared directories on the server nfs.sampledomain.com, you could use the following command:

```
[root@server1 ~]# showmount -e nfs.sampledomain.com
Export list for 192.168.1.104:
/var *
[root@server1 ~]# mount
```

From the preceding output, the /var directory on the nfs.sampledomain.com server is shared to all hosts (*).

To access files using NFS, you mount a directory from a remote NFS server on the network to a directory on your local computer. That is, you specify the nfs filesystem type, server name or IP address, remote directory, and local directory as arguments to the mount command. For example, to mount the /var directory on the remote computer named nfs.sampledomain.com (IP address 192.168.0.1) to the /mnt directory on the local computer using NFS and view the results, you can use the following commands:

```
[root@server1 ~]# mount -t nfs nfs.sampledomain.com:/var /mnt
[root@server1 ~]# mount
/dev/sda1 on / type ext4 (rw)
proc on /proc type proc (rw)
sysfs on /sys type sysfs (rw)
devpts on /dev/pts type devpts (rw,gid=5,mode=620)
tmpfs on /dev/shm type tmpfs (rw)
/dev/mapper/vg00-data on /data type ext4 (rw,usrquota,grpquota)
none on /proc/sys/fs/binfmt_misc type binfmt_misc (rw)
sunrpc on /var/lib/nfs/rpc_pipefs type rpc_pipefs (rw)
192.168.0.1:/var on /mnt type nfs (rw,vers=4,clientaddr=192.168.0.1)
[root@server1 ~]# ls /mnt
arpwatch      ftpkerberos    lock      mailman     nis         run        tux
cachegdm      lib            log       mars_nwe    opt         spool      www
dbiptraf      local          mail      named       preserve    tmpyp
[root@server1 ~]# _
```

After running these commands, you can use the /mnt directory as any other local directory, with all file operations performed in the /var directory on the remote computer. You can then dismount the NFS filesystem using the umount command.

FTP

The protocol most commonly used to transfer files on public networks is the **File Transfer Protocol (FTP)**. FTP hosts files differently than NFS. In anonymous access, a special directory is available to any user who wants to connect to the FTP server. Alternatively, users can log in, via an FTP client program, to a home directory on the FTP server.

Configuring a Linux FTP Server The traditional FTP server program is the Washington University FTP daemon (wu-ftpd). However, most Linux systems today use the **Very Secure FTP daemon (vsftpd)**. This stand-alone daemon is much easier to configure than wu-ftpd. The following steps show how to configure vsftpd to host files that can be downloaded from a client computer by user1 after user1 logs in with a valid password:

1. Create a directory underneath user1's home directory and ensure that user1 owns this directory. This directory will be used to host the files.

2. Edit the /etc/vsftpd.conf file and modify the appropriate commented options to control what actions the vsftpd daemon will allow from FTP clients. This includes:

   a. Whether to allow anonymous connections

   b. Whether to allow local user connections

   c. Whether to allow users to upload files

   d. Whether to prevent users from accessing files outside their home directory (called a "chroot jail")

3. Start the vsftpd daemon and ensure that it is started at boot time.

13

When you connect to the vsftpd daemon using an FTP client utility, you are prompted to log in. If you log in as the user "anonymous," you will be placed in the /var/ftp or /srv/ftp directory, depending on your Linux distribution. Alternatively, if you log in as a valid user account on the system, you will be place in that user's home directory.

The root user is not allowed to connect to vsftpd by default. To log in as the root user to vsftpd, you must remove the line **root** from the /etc/ftpusers file.

On Fedora 20, the configuration files for vsftpd are stored within the /etc/vsftpd directory. For example, the configuration file for vsftpd on Fedora 20 would be /etc/vsftpd/vsftpd.conf.

Connecting to a Linux FTP Server Most Web browsers have a built-in FTP utility that allows you to access files and directories on a remote computer. To connect to an FTP server using a Web browser, simply specify the location *ftp://servername_or_IPaddress* in your Web browser for anonymous access or the location *ftp://user:password@servername_or_IPaddress* to log in as a particular user account and password. A sample FTP session within a Web browser is shown in Figure 13-7.

Clicking a file displayed in Figure 13-7 displays a dialog box that allows you to save the file to the appropriate location on a local filesystem.

Figure 13-7 Using a Web browser FTP client

Most operating systems also come with a command-line FTP utility that can connect to an FTP server. To use such a utility, you specify the host name or IP address of an FTP server as an argument to the **ftp command**. This opens a connection that allows the transfer of files to and from that computer. You can then log in as a valid user on that computer, in which case you are automatically placed in your home directory. Alternatively, you can log in as the user "anonymous" and be placed in the /var/ftp directory. After you logged in, you receive an ftp> prompt that accepts FTP commands. A list of common FTP commands is depicted in Table 13-3.

 Most FTP servers require the user to enter a password when logging in as the anonymous user via a command-line FTP utility; this password is typically the user's e-mail address.

Command	Description
Help	Displays a list of commands
Pwd	Displays the current directory on the remote computer
dir ls	Displays a directory listing from the remote computer
cd *directory*	Changes the current directory to *directory* on the remote computer
lcd *directory*	Changes the current directory to *directory* on the local computer
get *filename*	Downloads the *filename* to the current directory on the local computer
ascii	Specifies text file downloads (default)
binary	Specifies binary file downloads
mget *filename*	Downloads the file named *filename* to the current directory on the local computer; it also allows the use of wildcard metacharacters to specify the *filename*
put *filename*	Uploads the *filename* from the current directory on the local computer to the current directory on the remote computer
mput *filename*	Uploads the *filename* from the current directory on the local computer to the current directory on the remote computer; it also allows the use of wildcard metacharacters to specify the *filename*
!	Runs a shell on the local computer
close	Closes the FTP connection to the remote computer
open *hostname or IP*	Opens an FTP connection to the *hostname or IP* address specified
bye quit	Quits the FTP utility

Table 13-3 Common FTP commands

13

The exact output displayed during an FTP session varies slightly depending on the version of the FTP software used on the FTP server. The following output is an example of using the ftp command to connect to an FTP server named ftp.sampledomain.com as the root user:

```
[root@server1 ~]# ftp ftp.sampledomain.com
Connected to ftp.sampledomain.com.
220 (vsFTPd 2.2.2)
Name (ftp.sampledomain.com:root): root
331 Please specify the password.
Password:
230 Login successful.
Remote system type is UNIX.
Using binary mode to transfer files.
ftp>
```

The current directory on the remote computer is the home directory for the root user in the preceding output. To verify this and see a list of files to download, you can use the following commands at the ftp> prompt:

```
ftp> pwd
257 "/root"
ftp> ls
227 Entering Passive Mode (192,168,0,1,56,88).
150 Here comes the directory listing.
total 2064
-rw-r--r--    1 root      root         1756    Aug 14 08:48   file1
-rw-r--r--    1 root      root          160    Aug 14 08:48   file2
-rw-r--r--    1 root      root      1039996    Aug 14 08:39   file3
drwxr-xr-x    2 root      root         4096    Aug 14 08:50   stuff
226 Directory send OK.
ftp>
```

The preceding output shows three files and one subdirectory. To download file3 to the current directory on the local computer, you can use the following command:

```
ftp> get file3
local: file3 remote: file3
227 Entering Passive Mode (192,168,0,1,137,37)
150 Opening BINARY mode data connection for file3 (1039996 bytes).
226 Transfer complete.
ftp>
```

Similarly, to change the current directory on the remote computer to /root/stuff and upload a copy of file4 from the current directory on the local computer to it, as well as view the results and then exit the ftp utility, you can use the following commands at the ftp> prompt:

```
ftp> cd stuff
250 Directory successfully changed.
ftp> pwd
257 "/root/stuff"
```

```
ftp> mput file4
mput file4? y
227 Entering Passive Mode (192,168,0,1,70,109)
150 Opening BINARY mode data connection for file4.
226 Transfer complete.
929 bytes sent in 0.00019 seconds (4.8e+03 Kbytes/s)
ftp> ls
227 Entering Passive Mode (192,168,0,1,235,35)
150 Opening ASCII mode data connection for directory listing.
total 8
-rw-r--r--      1 root    root      929 Aug 14 09:26 file4
226 Transfer complete.
ftp> bye
221 Goodbye.
[root@server1 ~]# _
```

In addition to using a Web browser or command-line ftp client included with your computer's operating system, you can choose from many third-party graphical FTP client programs, such as Filezilla.

E-mail Services

E-mail servers typically accept e-mail and route it over the Internet using Simple Mail Transfer Protocol (SMTP) or Enhanced Simple Mail Transfer Protocol (ESMTP) on TCP port 25. Additionally, client computers can retrieve e-mail from e-mail servers using a variety of different protocols such as Post Office Protocol (POP) or Internet Message Access Protocol (IMAP). Client computers can also send e-mail to e-mail servers using SMTP/ESMTP for later relay on the Internet.

Most e-mail servers provide the functions of the Mail Transfer Agent (MTA) and Mail Delivery Agent (MDA) described earlier in Chapter 1.

To relay e-mail to other servers on the Internet, an e-mail server must look up the name of the target e-mail server in the domain's MX (Mail Exchanger) records, which are stored on a public DNS server. For example, if your local e-mail server needs to send e-mail to jason.eckert@trios.com, the e-mail server locates the name of the target e-mail server by looking up the MX record for the trios.com domain. It then resolves the target e-mail server name to the appropriate IP address using the A (host) record for the server on the public DNS server.

Daemons and other system components on Linux systems rely on e-mail to send important information to the root user. The most common e-mail daemon used on modern Linux systems is **Postfix**.

Fedora 20 is one of the few Linux distributions that does not install an e-mail daemon by default.

The Postfix daemon is configured by default to accept e-mail on TCP port 25 and route it to the appropriate user on the Linux system. To test this, you can use the telnet command with port 25 as an argument. This displays a Welcome banner that identifies the e-mail server, as shown in the following output. Additionally, you can use the EHLO command to test ESMTP support and the HELO command to test SMTP support, as shown in the following output:

```
[root@server1 ~]# telnet localhost 25
Connected to localhost.
Escape character is '^]'.
220 server1.class.com ESMTP Postfix
EHLO sample.com
250-server1.class.com
250-PIPELINING
250-SIZE 10240000
250-VRFY
250-ETRN
250-ENHANCEDSTATUSCODES
250-8BITMIME
250 DSN
HELO sample.com
250 server1.class.com
quit
221 2.0.0 Bye
Connection closed by foreign host.
[root@server1 ~]#
```

To check your e-mail on your local Linux system, you can use the **mail command**, as shown here:

```
[root@server1 ~]# mail
Mail version 8.1.2 01/15/2001. Type ? for help.
"/var/spool/mail/root": 13 messages 6 new 10 unread
 U  1 Cron Daemon           Sat Jul 11 07:01   26/981    "Cron"
 U  2 logwatch@localhost.1  Mon Jul 20 11:43   42/1528   "Logwatch"
 U  3 logwatch@localhost.1  Tue Jul 21 12:32  151/4669   "Logwatch"
 N  4 jason.eckert@trios.c  Wed Sep 29 15:53   11/430
 &  4
Message 4:
From jason.eckert@trios.com Wed Sep 29 15:53:25 2009
Return-Path: <jason.eckert@trios.com>
Date: Wed, 29 Sep 2010 15:52:36 -0400
From: jason.eckert@trios.com
Status: R
```

Hey dude

```
& q
[root@server1 ~]# _
```

The mail command is an example of a Mail User Agent (MUA), as described in Chapter 1. E-mail for each user is stored within a file named for the user in the /var/spool/mail directory. For example, the e-mail for the bob user will be stored within the /var/spool/mail/bob file.

The /etc/aliases file contains other e-mail names that are used to identify the different users on the system. From the entries in the /etc/aliases file shown next, you can use the names post-master, bin, daemon, or adm to refer to the root user:

```
[root@server1 ~]# head -17 /etc/aliases
# See man 5 aliases for format
postmaster: root
bin:        root
daemon:     root
adm:        root
[root@server1 ~]# _
```

If you modify the /etc/aliases file, you need to run the **newaliases command** in order to rebuild the aliases database (/etc/aliases.db) based on the entries in the /etc/aliases file. Only the aliases database is used by the Postfix daemon.

 Users can also create a .forward file in their home directory that lists the user name or email address that mail items should be forwarded to.

While Postfix is normally configured to accept and route local e-mail only, you can also configure it to relay e-mail to other servers on the Internet as well as accept connections from e-mail clients on your network using POP and IMAP. To do this, you must edit its configuration file: /etc/postfix/main.cf. A common set of lines that you should modify or add at minimum is listed in Table 13-4.

Line	Change
mydomain = sample.com	Sets the e-mail domain name; changes to desired name
myorigin = $mydomain	Sets local access to the domain name
inet_interfaces = all	Configures Postfix to listen for e-mail on all interfaces
mydestination = $myhostname, localhost.$mydomain, localhost, $mydomain	Configures destination domain for e-mail
mynetworks_style=class	Trusts e-mail from computers on the local network

Table 13-4 Sample lines in /etc/postfix/main.cf to modify or add when configuring Postfix

Database Services

Databases are large files that store important information in the form of **tables.** A table organizes information into a list. Within the list, the set of information about a particular item is called a **record.** For example, in a list of customer mailing addresses, a single record would contain a customer's first name, last name, street address, city, state, and Zip code. The various categories of information within a record are called **fields.** For example, in our customer mailing address example, one field contains the city information, one contains the state information, and so on.

Most databases consist of dozens or hundreds of tables that store information used by applications. For example, accounting software typically stores financial data within a database. In large databases, information within certain tables can be related to information within other tables in the same database. These databases are called **relational databases,** and the tables within are usually linked by a common field. Figure 13-8 shows a simple relational database that consists of two tables with a related EmployeeID field.

Structured Query Language (SQL) is a special programming language used to store and access the data in databases. The database server programs that allow users to access and update the data stored within a database are called **SQL servers.** Table 13-5 lists common SQL statements that are used to manipulate data on SQL servers.

EmployeeID	FirstName	LastName	Address	ZIP	Home Phone	Mobile Phone
A518	Bob	Smith	14 Wallington St.	49288	555-123-1399	555-144-2039
A827	Jill	Sagan	51 York Ave. N.	49282	555-132-1039	
A988	Frank	Kertz	623 Queen St.	44922	555-209-1039	555-199-2938
A472	Bethany	Weber	82 Shepherd Ave.	49100	555-299-0199	555-203-1000
A381	John	Lauer	55 Rooshill Ave.	49288	555-123-2883	555-203-2811

Common field

EmployeeID	Week	Hours	MgrOK
A518	08/20/10	37	Yes
A827	08/20/10	40	Yes
A988	08/20/10	40	Yes
A472	08/20/10	40	Yes
A381	08/20/10	22	Yes
A518	08/27/10	40	Yes
A827	08/27/10	35	Yes
A988	08/27/10	0	Yes
A472	08/27/10	40	Yes
A381	08/27/10	22	Yes

Field names

Record

Figure 13-8 A simple relational database structure

Command	Description
CREATE DATABASE *database_name*	Creates a database
DROP DATABASE *database_name*	Deletes a database
CREATE TABLE *table_name* *field_definitions*	Creates a table within a database
DROP TABLE *table_name*	Deletes a table within a database
INSERT INTO *table_name* VALUES *record*	Inserts a new record within a table
UPDATE *table_name* SET *record_modifications*	Modifies records within a table
DELETE FROM *table_name* *record*	Deletes a record within a table
SELECT * FROM *table_nam*	Displays all records within a table
SELECT *fields* FROM *table_name* WHERE *criteria*	Displays one or more fields for records within a table that meet a specific criteria
SELECT *fields* FROM *table_name* GROUP BY *field*	Displays one or more fields for records within a table and groups the results according to the values within a common field
SELECT *fields* FROM *table_name* ORDER BY *field* [ASC/DESC]	Displays one or more fields for records within a table and sorts the results in ascending or descending order according to the values within a common field
SELECT *fields* FROM *table1* INNER JOIN *table2* ON *table1.common_field* = *table2.common_field*	Displays one or more fields for records within two related tables (*table1* and *table2*) that have a common field; only records that have matching information within the common field in both tables are displayed
SELECT *fields* FROM *table1* LEFT OUTER JOIN *table2_name* ON *table1_name.common_field* = *table2_name.common_field*	Displays one or more fields for all records within *table1* and any records within *table2* that have matching information within a common field
SELECT *fields* FROM *table1* RIGHT OUTER JOIN *table2_name* ON *table1_name.common_field* = *table2_name.common_field*	Displays one or more fields for all records within *table2* and any records within *table1* that have matching information within a common field
CREATE USER *user_name* WITH PASSWORD *password*	Creates a user that can access the SQL server
GRANT *permissions* ON *table1* TO *user_name*	Assigns permissions to a user that give the user the ability to work with the table, where *permissions* can include INSERT, UPDATE, SELECT, or DELETE

Table 13-5   Common SQL statements

SQL servers usually offer advanced backup, repair, replication, and recovery utilities for the data within the database. In addition, SQL servers can store multiple databases, and they allow programs to access these databases from across the network. Thus, a single SQL server can store the data needed by all programs that exist on servers and client computers within the network. Although there are several SQL servers available for Linux, PostgreSQL is one of the most widely used.

13

Configuring PostgreSQL

PostgreSQL is a powerful SQL server that provides a large number of features. Although many Linux server distributions allow you to install PostgreSQL SQL during the Linux installation process, you can easily install it from a software repository afterwards. During installation, the PostgreSQL installation creates a postgres user within the /etc/passwd and /etc/shadow files that has a home directory of /var/lib/postgresql and a shell of /bin/bash.

Next, you can prepare PostgreSQL for use by following these steps:

1. Assign the postgres user a password using the `passwd postgres` command.

2. Optionally modify the PostgreSQL configuration file, postgresql.conf. The location of this file differs depending on your Linux distribution, but it is often stored under the /var/lib/postgresql directory or the /etc/postgresql directory.

3. Start the PostgreSQL daemon and configure it to start at boot time.

Configuring PostgreSQL Databases

To configure PostgreSQL databases, you must first log in as the postgres user. Next, you can execute one of several PostgreSQL command-line utilities to create and manage databases. These commands are summarized in Table 13-6.

For example, to create a database called sampled after logging in as the postgres user, you could use the following command:

```
[root@server1 ~]$ createdb sampledb
[root@server1 ~]$ _
```

Command	Description
clusterdb	Associates a PostgreSQL database to another database on a different server
createdb	Creates a PostgreSQL database
createlang	Allows a new programming language to be used with PostgreSQL
createuser	Creates a PostgreSQL user
dropdb	Deletes a PostgreSQL database
droplang	Removes support for a programming language within PostgreSQL
dropuser	Deletes a PostgreSQL user
pg_dump	Backs up PostgreSQL database settings
pg_dumpall	Backs up a PostgreSQL database cluster settings
pg_restore	Restores PostgreSQL database settings
psql	The PostgreSQL utility
reindexdb	Reindexes a PostgreSQL database
vacuumdb	Analyzes and regenerates internal PostgreSQL database statistics

Table 13-6 PostgreSQL command-line utilities

Next, you can run the **psql command** to connect to the employee database using the interactive **PostgreSQL utility**, where you can obtain information about the SQL and psql commands that can perform most database administration.

```
[root@server1 ~]$ psql sampledb
psql (9.3.4)
Type "help" for help.

sampledb=# help
You are using psql, the command-line interface to PostgreSQL.
Type:  \copyright for distribution terms
       \h for help with SQL commands
       \? for help with psql commands
       \g or terminate with semicolon to execute query
       \q to quit
sampledb=# _
```

You can create tables and add records within the PostgreSQL utility using the appropriate SQL statements. The following output shows how to: 1) create a table called "employee" with three fields (Name, Dept, Title) that each allow 20 characters of information; 2) add three employee records; and 3) display the results.

```
sampledb=# CREATE TABLE employee (Name char(20), Dept char(20), Title
char(20));
CREATE TABLE
sampledb=# INSERT INTO employee VALUES ('Jeff
Smith','Research','Analyst');
INSERT 0 1
sampledb=# INSERT INTO employee VALUES ('Mary
Wong','Accouting','Manager');INSERT 0 1
sampledb=# INSERT INTO employee VALUES ('Pat
Clarke','Marketing','Coordinator');
INSERT 0 1
sampledb=# SELECT * from employee;
          name        |        dept        |        title
----------------------+--------------------+--------------------
 Jeff Smith           | Research           | Analyst
 Mary Wong            | Accounting         | Manager
 Pat Clarke           | Marketing          | Coordinator
(3 rows)

sampledb=# _
```

Each SQL statement that is entered within the PostgreSQL utility must end with a ; metacharacter.

Command	Description
\l	Lists available databases
\c database_name	Connects to a different database
\d	Lists the tables within the current database
\d table_name	Lists the fields within a table
\q	Exits the PostgreSQL utility

Table 13-7 Common built-in PostgreSQL utility commands

In addition to SQL statements, the PostgreSQL utility has many built-in commands. These commands, which are prefixed with a \ character, can be used to obtain database information or perform functions within the PostgreSQL utility. The most common of these built-in commands are listed in Table 13-7.

Chapter Summary

- DHCP, DNS, NTP, and NIS are called infrastructure services as they provide network-related services to other computers on the network.

- DHCP servers lease other computers an IPv4 or IPv6 configuration. The two most common DHCP servers are dhcpd and udhcpd.

- DNS servers provide name resolution services for other computers on the network. Each DNS server can contain several zones that store resource records for names that can be resolved.

- Linux computers can use the system time stored within the computer BIOS or obtain their time from an NTP server across the network. NTP servers obtain their time from other NTP servers in a hierarchical organization that consists of several strata. The two most common NTP servers are ntpd and chronyd.

- NIS servers provide key configuration files such as /etc/passwd and /etc/shadow to other Linux computers that are configured as NIS clients.

- The Apache server shares Web pages from its document root directory to computers on the network using the HTTP protocol.

- Samba can be used to share files to Linux, UNIX, Macintosh, and Windows computers using the SMB protocol.

- NFS can be used to natively share files amongst Linux, UNIX, and Macintosh systems. NFS clients access these files by mounting shared directories on an NFS server.

- FTP can be used to share files to any computer that has an FTP client utility and is the most common method for file sharing on the Internet. The most common FTP daemon on modern Linux systems is vsftpd.

- E-mail servers deliver e-mails from one user to another on your system. They also accept new e-mails from users and relay it to other e-mail servers on the Internet for delivery. The most common e-mail server used on Linux systems is Postfix.

■ Many large applications store their data within databases on a database server. These applications use SQL statements to add, manipulate, and retrieve information within a database across the network. PostgreSQL is a common database server that provides advanced configuration and utilities.

Key Terms

ab (Apache benchmark) command   A command that can be used to obtain performance benchmarks for a Web server such as Apache.

apachectl command   A command that can be used to start, stop, and restart the Apache Web server as well as check for syntax errors within the Apache configuration file.

Berkeley Internet Name Domain (BIND)   The standard that all DNS servers and DNS configuration files adhere to.

BIND configuration utility   A graphical utility that can be used to generate and modify the files that are used by the DNS name daemon.

BusyBox DHCP daemon (udhcpd)   A lightweight Linux daemon used to provide IPv4 addresses to other computers on the network.

Chrony NTP daemon (chronyd)   A daemon that provides fast time synchronization services on Linux computers.

chronyc command   A command that can query the state of an NTP server or client as well as synchronize the system time with an NTP server.

curl command   A command that can be used to obtain a Web page from a Web server.

database   A file that contains data that is organized into tables.

Date & Time utility   A graphical utility within Fedora 20 that can be used to set the date, time, and timezone information for a system.

DHCP daemon (dhcpd)   The most common Linux daemon used to provide IPv4 and IPv6 addresses to other computers on the network.

directive   A line within a configuration file.

document root   The directory on a Web server that stores Web content for distribution to Web browsers.

DNS cache file   A file that contains the IP addresses of top-level DNS servers.

dumpleases command   A command that can be used to obtain current DHCP leases from the BusyBox DHCP daemon (udhcpd).

export   To share a directory using NFS to other computers.

field   An attribute within a record in a database table.

File Transfer Protocol (FTP)   The most common protocol used to transfer files across networks such as the Internet.

forward lookup   A DNS name resolution request whereby a FQDN is resolved to an IP address.

13

ftp command   A command-line FTP client program that is found in most operating systems.

hwclock command   A command that can be used to view and modify the system clock within the computer BIOS.

infrastructure services   Services that provide TCP configuration, name resolution, time synchronization, or system configuration to other computers on a network.

iterative query   A DNS resolution request that was resolved without the use of top-level DNS servers.

jitter   The difference between time measurements from several different NTP servers.

mail command   A common e-mail client on UNIX, Linux, and Macintosh systems.

master DNS server   See *primary DNS server*.

NetBIOS   A protocol used by Windows computers that adds a unique 15-character name to file- and printer-sharing traffic.

Network File System (NFS)   A set of software components that can be used to share files natively between UNIX, Linux, and Macintosh computers on a network.

Network Information Service (NIS)   A set of software components that can be used to standardize the configuration files across several different Linux and UNIX computers.

Network Time Protocol (NTP)   A protocol that can be used to obtain time information from other computers on the Internet.

newaliases command   A command that can be used to rebuild the e-mail alias database based on the entries within the /etc/aliases file.

NIS client   A computer in an NIS domain that receives its configuration from an NIS master server or NIS slave server.

NIS domain   A group of computers that share the same NIS configuration.

NIS map   A system configuration that is shared by the computers within an NIS domain.

NIS master server   The computer in an NIS domain that contains the master copy of all NIS maps.

NIS slave server   A computer in an NIS domain that receives a read-only copy of all NIS maps from an NIS master server.

nmblookup command   A command that can test NetBIOS name resolution on a Linux system.

NTP daemon (ntpd)   The most common daemon used to provide time synchronization services on Linux computers.

ntpdate command   A command that can view the current system time as well as synchronize the system time with an NTP server.

ntpq command   A command that can query the state of an NTP server or client.

offset   The difference in time between two computers that use the NTP protocol.

Postfix   A common e-mail server daemon used on Linux systems.

PostgreSQL   A common SQL server used on Linux computers.

PostgreSQL utility   The program used to perform most database management on a PostgreSQL server.

primary DNS server   The DNS server that contains a read/write copy of the zone.

`psql` **command**   The command used to start the PostgreSQL utility.

record   A line within a database table that represents a particular object.

recursive query   A DNS resolution request that was resolved with the use of top-level DNS servers.

relational database   A database that contains multiple tables that are linked by common fields.

resource records   The records within a zone on a DNS server that provide name resolution for individual computers.

reverse lookup   A DNS name resolution request whereby an IP address is resolved to a FQDN.

secondary DNS server   A DNS server that contains a read-only copy of the zone.

Server Message Blocks (SMB)   The protocol that Windows computers use to format file- and printer-sharing traffic on TCP/IP networks.

`showmount` **command**   A command used to view NFS shared directories on a remote computer.

slave DNS server   See *secondary DNS server*.

`smbclient` **command**   A command that can be used to connect to a remote Windows or Samba server and transfer files.

`smbpasswd` **command**   A command used to generate a Samba password for a user.

strata   The levels used within an NTP hierarchy that describe the relative position of a server to an original time source such as an atomic clock.

Structured Query Language (SQL)   A language used by database servers to query, add, and modify the data within a database.

SQL server   A server service that gives other programs and computers the ability to access a database.

table   A database structure that organizes data using records and fields.

Time-To-Live (TTL)   The amount of time that a computer is allowed to cache name resolution information obtained from a DNS server.

`testparm` **command**   A command that can be used to check for syntax errors within the Samba configuration file as well as display the current Samba configuration.

`tzselect` **command**   A command that can be used to change the time zone of a Linux computer.

Very Secure FTP daemon (vsftpd)   The default FTP server program used in modern Linux distributions.

Web page hit   A single HTTP request that is sent from a Web browser to a Web server.

zone   A portion of the Domain Name Space that is administered by one or more DNS servers.

zone transfer   The process of copying resource records for a zone from a master to a slave DNS server.

13

Review Questions

1. NFS can be used to share files natively with computers running the Microsoft Windows operating system. True or False?

2. Which file stores the Apache configuration in Fedora 20?
   a. /etc/apache2/httpd.conf
   b. /etc/apache2.conf
   c. /etc/httpd.conf
   d. /etc/httpd/conf/httpd.conf

3. Which DNS resource record is an alias to other records?
   a. A
   b. AAAA
   c. CNAME
   d. NS

4. NIS clients use NIS records to access their configuration information. True or False?

5. Which command can be used to connect to check the /etc/samba/smb.conf file for syntax errors?
   a. `apachectl`
   b. `sambactl`
   c. `testparm`
   d. `psql`

6. You have modified the /etc/aliases file to include a new e-mail alias. However, when you send e-mail to the alias, it can not be delivered. What should you do?
   a. Add the line to the /etc/aliases.db file instead.
   b. Run the `newaliases` command.
   c. Restart the Postfix daemon.
   d. Log out of the system and then log back into the system and resend the e-mail.

7. Which command within the command-line FTP utility can be used to change the current directory on the local computer?
   a. `cd`
   b. `dir`
   c. `lcd`
   d. `get`

8. You have opened a telnet session on port 25 with your e-mail server. What command can you type within your telnet session to start an e-mail session? (Choose all that apply.)

   a. START

   b. HELO

   c. EHLO

   d. WAZUP

9. Which of the following must you perform to share a directory using NFS? (Choose all that apply.)

   a. Edit the /etc/exports file.

   b. Mount the directory to the /etc/exports directory using the mount command.

   c. Run the exportfs -a command.

   d. Start or restart the NFS daemons.

10. DHCP clients send a DHCPREQUEST packet when they require a new IP configuration. True or False?

11. Which command can be used to connect to a remote Windows share called data on the server called fileserver?

    a. smbclient -L fileserver:data

    b. smbclient -L //fileserver/data

    c. smbclient //fileserver/data

    d. smbclient \\fileserver\data

12. The lines within the Apache configuration file that modify the functionality of the Apache are called directives. True or False?

13. Which of the following can be used to create a database within PostgreSQL? (Choose all that apply.)

    a. the CREATE DATABASE statement within the PostgreSQL utility.

    b. the ADD DATABASE statement within the PostgreSQL utility.

    c. the adddb command.

    d. the createdb command.

14. Stratum 1 NTP servers do not obtain time information from other NTP servers. True or False?

15. What must you do to transform your computer into a DNS server? (Choose all that apply.)

    a. Create zone files.

    b. Create resource records for DNS lookups.

    c. Create NIS maps.

    d. Run the name daemon (named).

13

16. What directory are you placed in when you log in as the anonymous user to an Ubuntu Server 14.04 FTP server?

    a. /srv/ftp

    b. /var/www/ftp

    c. /home/anonymous

    d. /var/ftp/pub

17. Chronyd is an NTP daemon that offers a faster response time compared to the ntpd daemon. True or False?

18. Which SQL statement key word can be used to delete a record within a table?

    a. DELETE

    b. DROP

    c. REMOVE

    d. CLEAR

19. Which command can you use to synchronize ntpd with an NTP time source?

    a. ntp

    b. ntpquery

    c. ntpq

    d. hwclock

20. Mary is a system administrator in your organization. She has recently made changes to the DHCP configuration file, but the DHCP daemon does not seem to recognize the new changes. What should she do?

    a. Log in as the root user and reedit the configuration file.

    b. Run the dhcpconf command to edit the configuration file.

    c. Restart the DHCP daemon.

    d. Restart the xinetd daemon.

Hands-on Projects

These projects should be completed in the order given. The hands-on projects presented in this chapter should take a total of three hours to complete. The requirements for this lab include:

- A computer with Fedora Linux installed according to Hands-on Project 2-1 and Ubuntu Server Linux installed according to Hands-on Project 6-1.

Project 13-1

In this hands-on project, you configure the DHCP daemon on your Fedora Linux virtual machine and test your configuration by obtaining an IPv4 address from your Ubuntu Server Linux virtual machine.

1. Boot your Fedora Linux virtual machine. After your Linux system has been loaded, switch to a command-line terminal (tty2) by pressing **Ctrl+Alt+F2** and log in to the terminal using the user name of **root** and the password of **LNXrocks!**.

2. At the command prompt, type **yum install dhcp** and press **Enter** to install the DHCP server daemon. Type **y** and press **Enter** when prompted to continue the installation.

3. Edit the **/etc/dhcp/dhcpd.conf** file with a text editor by adding the following lines:

   ```
   default-lease-time 72000;
   option routers IP_address_of_your_class_default_gateway;
   option domain-name-servers IP_address_of_your_class_DNS_server;
   subnet class_network netmask subnet_mask {
     range class_network.50 class_network.100;
   }
   ```

   For example, if your class uses the 192.168.1 network (subnet mask 255.255.255.0) and a default gateway and DNS server of 192.168.1.254, you would add the following lines:

   ```
   default-lease-time 72000;
   option routers 192.168.1.254;
   option domain-name-servers 192.168.1.254;
   subnet 192.168.1.0 netmask 255.255.255.0 {
     range 192.168.1.50 192.168.1.100;
   }
   ```

   When finished, save your changes and quit the editor.

4. At the command prompt, type **useradd -m dhcpd** and press **Enter** to create a dhcpd user account for the DHCP daemon.

5. At the command prompt, type **systemctl start dhcpd.service** and press **Enter** to start the DHCP daemon.

6. At the command prompt, type **ps -ef | grep dhcpd** and press **Enter** to ensure that the DHCP daemon has loaded successfully. If the DHCP daemon is not listed, check for errors in your /etc/dhcp/dhcpd.conf file and repeat the previous step.

7. At the command prompt, type **firewall-cmd --add-service dhcp** and press **Enter** to allow DHCP traffic through the firewall on your Fedora Linux virtual machine.

8. In your virtualization software, disable the virtual DHCP server used for your Ubuntu Server Linux virtual machine. Next, boot your Ubuntu Server Linux virtual machine and log into tty1 using the user name of **root** and the password of **LNXrocks!**.

9. At the command prompt on your Ubuntu Server Linux virtual machine, type **dhclient eth0** and press **Enter** to request a DHCP address.

10. At the command prompt on your Fedora Linux virtual machine, type **cat /var/lib/dhcpd/dhcpd.leases** and press **Enter**. Note the line that details the lease information.

11. At the command prompt on your Fedora Linux virtual machine, type **systemctl stop dhcpd.service** and press **Enter** to stop the DHCP daemon.

13

12. At the command prompt on your Fedora Linux virtual machine, type **exit** and press **Enter** to log out of your shell.

13. At the command prompt on your Ubuntu Server Linux virtual machine, type **poweroff** and press **Enter** to shut down the system. Next, enable the virtual DHCP server used for your Ubuntu Server Linux virtual machine within your virtualization software.

Project 13-2

In this hands-on project, you configure and test the DNS daemon on your Fedora Linux virtual machine.

1. On your Fedora Linux virtual machine, switch to a command-line terminal (tty2) by pressing **Ctrl+Alt+F2** and log in to the terminal using the user name of root and the password of **LNXrocks!**.

2. At the command prompt, type **yum install system-config-bind** and press **Enter** to install the graphical BIND configuration utility, which also installs the dependency package BIND (the named daemon). Type **y** and press **Enter** when prompted to continue the installation.

3. Switch to a graphical terminal by pressing **Ctrl+Alt+F1** and log in to the GNOME desktop with the user name user1 and the password of LNXrocks!. Next, open a command-line terminal (**Activities menu, Show Applications, Utilities, Terminal**).

4. At the command prompt, type **su - root** and press **Enter**. Supply the password of **LNXrocks!** and press **Enter** when prompted to switch to the root user.

5. At the command prompt, type **system-config-bind&** and press **Enter** to start the BIND configuration GUI program.

6. Highlight **DNS Server** and click **Properties**. Add the **forwarders** option to the Current Options box. In the New List Element section, highlight **IPV4 Address** and supply the IPv4 address of your classroom DNS server for this option and click **OK** when finished. Click **OK** to close the DNS server property window. This configures your DNS server to forward requests to the classroom DNS server if it cannot resolve the destination address using the information within its own zone files.

7. Click **New, Zone** and accept the default zone scope of **Internet** by clicking **OK** underneath the Class drop-down box. Next, accept the default zone type of **Forward** by clicking **OK** below the Origin Type drop-down box and type the zone name **class.com.** (taking care to include the trailing . in the zone name). Accept the default DNS server zone role of **master** by clicking **OK**.

8. Examine the default SOA record parameters. What is the default minimum TTL? Briefly explain what this setting does. Click **OK** to return to the BIND configuration utility window.

9. Expand your **class.com** zone. What default records are created in this new zone?

10. Highlight the **class.com** zone and click **New, A IPv4 Address**. Type **gateway.class.com.** in the Domain Name dialog box (taking care to include the trailing . in the FQDN) and supply the IPv4 address of your classroom's default gateway. Click **OK** to create the A record.

11. Highlight the **class.com** zone and click **New, A IPv4 Address**. Type **server1.class.com.** in the Domain Name dialog box (taking care to include the trailing . in the FQDN) and supply your computer's IPv4 address. Click **OK** to create the A record.

12. Highlight the **class.com** zone and click **New, CNAME Alias**. Type **alias.class.com.** in the Domain Name dialog box, and type **server1.class.com.** in the Canonical Name dialog box (taking care to include the trailing . in both FQDNs). Click **OK** to create the CNAME record.

13. Highlight the **class.com** zone and click **New, MX Mail Exchange**. Note the default domain of class.com. in the Domain Name dialog box and type **server1.class.com.** in the Mail Server Name dialog box (taking care to include the trailing . in the FQDN). Click **OK** to create the MX record.

14. Expand your **class.com** zone. Are the new records visible?

15. Expand the zone that represents your classroom network. Are PTR records available for reverse lookups?

16. Click **Save**. Click **OK** when prompted to save your changes to the configuration files on the hard drive.

17. Close the BIND configuration utility, log out of the GNOME desktop environment, and switch back to tty2 by pressing **Ctrl+Alt+F2**.

18. At the command prompt, type **systemctl start named.service** and press **Enter** to start the DNS name daemon.

19. Edit the /etc/resolv.conf file with a text editor and remove any existing nameserver lines. Add the line **nameserver 127.0.0.1** to ensure that your Linux computer uses the local DNS server daemon for name resolution. Save your changes and quit the editor when finished.

20. At the command prompt, type **ping −c 4 gateway.class.com** and press **Enter**. Was the name resolved successfully? Explain.

21. At the command prompt, type **ping −c 4 server1.class.com** and press **Enter**. Was the name resolved successfully? Explain.

22. At the command prompt, type **ping −c 4 alias.class.com** and press **Enter**. Was the name resolved successfully? Explain.

23. At the command prompt, type **ping −c 4 www.yahoo.com** and press **Enter**. Was the name resolved successfully? Explain.

24. At the command prompt, type **dig @localhost class.com ANY** and press **Enter**. Are your resources records returned successfully?

25. At the command prompt, type **less /etc/named.conf** and press **Enter**. View the entries. Is class.com a Master zone? Do you see a line that forwards unknown requests to your classroom DNS server? Press q when finished.

26. At the command prompt, type **cat /var/named/class.com.db** and press **Enter**. View the entries. Are your resource records present?

27. At the command prompt, type **cat /var/named/network_ID.db** and press **Enter** where *network_ID* is your classroom network ID. View the entries. Are PTR resource records present?

28. At the command prompt, type **less /var/named/named.ca** and press **Enter**. View the entries. What do these entries represent?

29. Type **exit** and press **Enter** to log out of your shell.

13

Project 13-3

In this hands-on project, you install and explore the NTP daemon on your Ubuntu Server Linux virtual machine as well as explore the Chrony NTP daemon on your Fedora Linux virtual machine.

1. Boot your Ubuntu Server Linux virtual machine and log into tty1 using the user name of **root** and the password of **LNXrocks!**.

2. At the command prompt, type **apt-get install ntp** and press **Enter**. Press **y** when prompted to install the NTP daemon. Next, type **ps -ef | grep ntpd** and press **Enter** to verify that the NTP daemon is running.

3. At the command prompt, type the **less /etc/ntp.conf** command. What lines indicate that your system is configured as an NTP client? Is your system configured as an NTP server? If not, what line could you modify to allow computers on your network to query your NTP server?

4. At the command prompt, type **service ntp stop** and press **Enter** to stop the NTP daemon.

5. At the command prompt, type **ntpdate -u 0.ubuntu.pool.ntp.org** and press **Enter** to synchronize your clock with the first time server listed in /etc/ntp.conf. Repeat this command several times until the offset is very low.

6. At the command prompt, type **service ntp start** and press **Enter** to start the NTP daemon.

7. At the command prompt, type **ntpq -p** and press **Enter** to view information about the time servers that you are synchronizing with (peers).

8. Type **exit** and press **Enter** to log out of your shell.

9. On your Fedora Linux virtual machine, switch to a command-line terminal (tty2) by pressing **Ctrl+Alt+F2** and log in to the terminal using the user name of **root** and the password of **LNXrocks!**.

10. At the command prompt, type **less /etc/chrony.conf** and press **Enter**. What lines indicate that your system is configured as an NTP client? Is your system configured as an NTP server? If not, what line could you modify to allow computers on your network to query your NTP server?

11. At the command prompt, type **chronyc sources -v** and press **Enter** to view information about the time servers that you are synchronizing with (peers).

12. Type **exit** and press **Enter** to log out of your shell.

Project 13-4

In this hands-on project, you configure the Apache Web server on your Fedora Linux virtual machine and test daemon permissions to files on the system.

1. On your Fedora Linux virtual machine, switch to a command-line terminal (tty2) by pressing **Ctrl+Alt+F2** and log in to the terminal using the user name of **root** and the password of **LNXrocks!**.

2. At the command prompt, type **yum install httpd** and press Enter. Press y when prompted to complete the installation of the Apache Web server.

3. At the command prompt, type **grep DocumentRoot /etc/httpd/conf/httpd. conf** and press Enter. What is the document root directory?

4. At the command prompt, type **grep DirectoryIndex /etc/httpd/conf/httpd. conf** and press Enter. What file(s) will automatically be handed out by the Apache daemon from the document root directory?

5. At the command prompt, type **grep "User " /etc/httpd/conf/httpd.conf** and press Enter. What user does the Apache daemon run as locally?

6. At the command prompt, type **grep "Group " /etc/httpd/conf/httpd.conf** and press Enter. What user does the Apache daemon run as locally?

7. At the command prompt, type **apachectl configtest** and press Enter. Are there any syntax errors within your /etc/httpd/conf/httpd.conf file?

8. Edit the **/var/www/html/index.html** file with a text editor such as vi. Are there any entries? Add the following lines:

```
<html>
<body>
<h1>My sample website</h1>
</body>
</html>
```

When finished, save your changes and quit the editor.

9. At the command prompt, type **systemctl start httpd.service** and press Enter to start the Apache Web server.

10. At the command prompt, type **curl http://127.0.0.1/** and press Enter. Was your Web page successfully returned by Apache?

11. At the command prompt, type **ab -n 1000 http://127.0.0.1/** and press Enter. How long did Apache take to respond to 1000 requests?

12. At the command prompt, type **less /etc/httpd/logs/access_log** and press Enter. How many Web page hits are shown? Explain.

13. At the command prompt, type **firewall-cmd --add-service http** and press Enter to allow inbound HTTP connections in your firewall.

14. On your Windows host, open a Web browser and navigate to the location **http://IPaddress** (where *IPaddress* is the IP address of your Fedora Linux virtual machine). Is your Web page displayed?

15. Return to tty2 on your Fedora Linux virtual machine. At the command prompt, type **ls -l /var/www/html/index.html** and press Enter. Who owns the file? What is the group owner? What category do the Apache daemons use when they run as the user apache and group apache?

16. At the command prompt, type **chmod 640 /var/www/html/index.html** and press Enter.

13

17. In the Web browser on your Windows host, refresh the Web page for **http://IPaddress** (where *IPaddress* is the IP address of your Fedora Linux virtual machine). What error do you receive and why?

18. Return to tty2 on your Fedora Linux virtual machine. At the command prompt, type **chmod 644 /var/www/html/index.html** and press **Enter**.

19. In the Web browser on your Windows host, refresh the Web page for **http://IPaddress** (where *IPaddress* is the IP address of your Fedora Linux virtual machine). Does your page display properly now? Close the Web browser on your Windows host.

20. Return to tty2 on your Fedora Linux virtual machine, type **poweroff**, and press **Enter** to shut down your virtual machine.

Project 13-5

In this hands-on project, you configure and test Samba file sharing on your Ubuntu Server Linux virtual machine.

1. On your Ubuntu Server Linux virtual machine, log into tty1 using the user name of **root** and the password of **LNXrocks!**.

2. At the command prompt, type **ps −ef | grep mbd** and press **Enter**. Are the Samba daemons installed and started by default.

3. Edit the **/etc/samba/smb.conf** file with the vi text editor. Spend a few minutes examining the comments within this file to understand the available Samba configuration options. Under the Share Definitions section, notice that the only two shares configured by default are the [printers] share (which shares all printers to Windows hosts) and the hidden [print$] share (which shares print drivers to Windows hosts).

4. Add the following line underneath the [global] line in this file, where *hostname* is the host name configured on your Ubuntu Server Linux virtual machine:
   netbios name = *hostname*

5. Uncomment/modify the following section that shares out all home directories to users who authenticate successfully:
   [homes]
       comment = Home Directories
       browseable = no
       read only = no

6. Next, add the following share definition to the bottom of the file to share out the /etc directory to all users as read-only:
   [etc]
       comment = The etc directory
       path = /etc
       guest ok = yes
       read only = yes

7. When finished, save your changes and quit the editor.

8. At the command prompt, type **testparm** and press **Enter**. Were any syntax errors reported within /etc/samba/smb.conf? Press **Enter** to view your Samba configuration.

9. At the command prompt, type **service samba restart** and press **Enter** to restart the Samba daemons.

10. At the command prompt, type **smbpasswd -a root** and press **Enter**. When prompted, supply the password **LNXrocks!**. Repeat the same password when prompted a second time.

11. At the command prompt, type **smbclient -L 127.0.0.1** and press **Enter**. Supply your Samba password of **LNXrocks!** when prompted. Do you see your shared home directory? Do you see any printer shares?

12. At the command prompt, type **smbclient //127.0.0.1/root** and press **Enter**. Supply your Samba password of **LNXrocks!** when prompted.

13. At the smb:\> prompt, type **dir** and press **Enter**. Are you in your home directory?

14. At the smb:\> prompt, type **exit** and press **Enter**.

15. At the command prompt type **poweroff** and press **Enter** to shut down your virtual machine.

16. On your Windows host, add a local user account called **root** with a password of **LNXrocks!** that has administrative ability on your PC. Next, log in to your Windows host as the root user and start your Ubuntu Server Linux virtual machine.

17. Once your Ubuntu Server Linux virtual machine has started, open the Run dialog box on your Windows host, type **\\IPaddress**, and press **Enter**. What shared directories and printers do you see and why? Are you able to copy files from your Windows host to your home directory share? Are you able to copy files from your Windows host to your /etc directory share? Explain.

18. Close the Windows Explorer window when finished.

Project 13-6

In this hands-on project, you export the /etc directory using NFS on your Ubuntu Server Linux virtual machine and access it from your Fedora Linux virtual machine.

1. On your Ubuntu Server Linux virtual machine, log into tty1 using the user name of **root** and the password of **LNXrocks!**.

2. At the command prompt, type **apt-get install nfs-kernel-server** and press **Enter** to install NFS.

3. Edit the /etc/exports file with the vi text editor and add a line that reads:

   /etc * (rw)

   When finished, save your changes and quit the editor.

4. At the command prompt, type **exportfs -a** and press **Enter**.

5. At the command prompt, type **service nfs-kernel server restart** and press **Enter** to restart NFS.

6. Boot your Fedora Linux virtual machine. After your Linux system has been loaded, switch to a command-line terminal (tty2) by pressing **Ctrl+Alt+F2** and log in to the terminal using the user name of **root** and the password of **LNXrocks!**.

7. At the command prompt, type **yum install nfs-utils** and press **Enter**. Press **y** when prompted to complete the installation of NFS.

13

8. At the command prompt, type `mount -t nfs IPaddress:/etc /mnt` (where *IPaddress* is the IP address of your Ubuntu Server Linux virtual machine) and press **Enter**.

9. At the command prompt, type `df` and press **Enter**. What is mounted to the /mnt directory?

10. At the command prompt, type `ls -F /mnt` and press **Enter**. What directory are you observing? Type `cat /mnt/issue` at the command prompt and press **Enter**. Can you tell that the issue file is on your Ubuntu Server Linux virtual machine?

11. At the command prompt, type `umount /mnt` and press **Enter** to unmount the NFS filesystem.

12. Type `exit` and press **Enter** to log out of your shell.

Project 13-7

In this hands-on project, you install and configure the Very Secure FTP daemon on your Ubuntu Server Linux virtual machine.

1. On your Ubuntu Server Linux virtual machine, log into tty1 using the user name of **root** and the password of **LNXrocks!**.

2. At the command prompt, type `apt-get install vsftpd` and press **Enter** to install vsftpd.

3. At the command prompt, type `cp /etc/hosts ~user1/file1 ; cp /etc/hosts ~user1/file2 ; cp /etc/hosts /srv/ftp/file3` and press **Enter** to create two copies of the file /etc/hosts within user1's home directory called file1 and file2 as well as a copy of the file /etc/hosts within the /srv/ftp directory called file3.

4. Edit the /etc/vsftpd.conf file using the vi editor. Take a few moments to read the options in this file and the comments that describe each option. Next, uncomment the `write_enable=YES` line, modify the anonymous_enable line to read `anonymous_enable=YES`, save your changes, and quit the vi editor.

5. At the command prompt, type `service vsftpd restart` and press **Enter** to restart vsftpd.

6. At the command prompt, type `ftp localhost` and press **Enter**. Log in as **user1** using the password **LNXrocks!** when prompted.

7. At the ftp> prompt, type `dir` and press **Enter** to list the contents of the /home/user1 directory.

8. At the ftp> prompt, type `lcd /etc` and press **Enter** to change the current working directory on the FTP client to /etc.

9. At the ftp> prompt, type `put issue` and press **Enter** to upload the issue file to the remote FTP server.

10. At the ftp> prompt, type `dir` and press **Enter** to list the contents of the /home/user1 directory. Was the issue file uploaded successfully?

11. At the ftp> prompt, type `lcd /` and press **Enter** to change the current working directory on the FTP client to /.

12. At the ftp> prompt, type **get issue** and press **Enter** to download the issue file to the / directory on the local computer.

13. At the ftp> prompt, type **mget file*** and press **Enter** to download file1 and file2 to the / directory on the local computer.

14. At the ftp> prompt, type **help** and press **Enter** to list the commands available within the FTP client program.

15. At the ftp> prompt, type **bye** and press **Enter** to exit the FTP client program.

16. At the command prompt, type **ls /** and press **Enter**. Were the issue, file1, and file2 files downloaded to the / directory successfully?

17. At the command prompt, type **ftp localhost** and press **Enter**. Log in as **anonymous** using the password **nothing** when prompted (the actual password is not relevant for the anonymous user; you could use any password).

18. At the ftp> prompt, type **dir** and press **Enter** to list the contents of the /var/ftp directory.

19. At the ftp> prompt, type **lcd /** and press **Enter** to change the current working directory on the FTP client to /.

20. At the ftp> prompt, type **get file3** and press **Enter** to download the hosts file to the / directory on the local computer.

21. At the ftp> prompt, type **bye** and press **Enter** to exit the FTP client program.

22. At the command prompt, type **ls /** and press **Enter**. Was file3 downloaded to the / directory successfully?

23. At the command prompt, type **ftp localhost** and press **Enter**. Log in as the **root** user and the password **LNXrocks!** when prompted. Were you able to log in? At the ftp> prompt, type **bye** and press **Enter** to exit the FTP client program.

24. Edit the /etc/ftpusers file using the vi editor and remove the following line:

    root

    When finished, save your changes and quit the editor.

25. At the command prompt, type **ftp localhost** and press **Enter**. Log in as the **root** user with the password **LNXrocks!** when prompted.

26. At the ftp> prompt, type **dir** and press **Enter** to list the contents of the /root directory.

27. At the ftp> prompt, type **bye** and press **Enter** to exit the FTP client program.

28. Type **exit** and press **Enter** to log out of your shell.

29. On your Windows host, open a Web browser and enter the location **ftp://IPaddress**, where *IPaddress* is the IP address of your Ubuntu Server Linux virtual machine. What directory are you placed in and why? Next, enter the location **ftp://user1:LNXrocks! @IPaddress**, where *IPaddress* is the IP address of your Ubuntu Server Linux virtual machine. What directory are you placed in and why? Close your Web browser when finished.

13

30. On your Windows host, download and install the free Filezilla FTP client program from *https://filezilla-project.org/*. Next, open the Filezilla program and enter *IPaddress* in the Host dialog box (where *IPaddress* is the IP address of your Ubuntu Server Linux virtual machine). Next, enter **user1** in the Username dialog box and **LNXrocks!** in the Password dialog box and click **Quickconnect**. Explore copying files between your Windows host and Ubuntu Server Linux virtual machine, and close Filezilla when finished.

Project 13-8

In this hands-on project, you explore the Postfix e-mail daemon on your Ubuntu Server Linux virtual machine.

1. On your Ubuntu Server Linux virtual machine, log in to tty1 using the user name of **root** and the password of **LNXrocks!**.

2. At the command prompt, type **ps -ef | grep postfix** and press **Enter**. Is the Postfix daemon running?

3. Edit the /etc/aliases file with a text editor and add the following line:

   webmaster: user1

   When finished, save your changes and quit the editor.

4. At the command prompt, type **newaliases** and press **Enter** to update the aliases database using the information within the /etc/aliases file.

5. At the command prompt, type **mail webmaster** and press **Enter** to compose a new e-mail to the users admin and user1. When prompted for a subject, type **Test email** and press **Enter**. Next, type **This is a test email that will be delivered using the Postfix daemon** and press **Enter**. Next, type **.** (a period) and press **Enter**. Press **Enter** again to complete and send the e-mail.

6. At the command prompt, type **su - user1** to switch to a new shell as user1.

7. At the command prompt, type **mail** to check your mailbox for e-mail messages. The last e-mail should have a subject line of Test e-mail. If you don't see this message, type **z** to advance to the next screen of messages. Note the number of the e-mail message that has the subject line of Test e-mail and type this number at the & prompt to read your e-mail message. Type **q** when finished to exit the mail program.

8. At the command prompt, type **exit** and press **Enter** to return to your root shell.

9. At the command prompt, type **telnet localhost 25** and press **Enter**. Can you tell that you are interacting with the Postfix daemon?

10. Type **EHLO localhost** and press **Enter**. Does your Postfix daemon support 8-bit MIME? Type **quit** and press **Enter** to quit the telnet session.

11. Type **exit** and press **Enter** to log out of your shell.

Project 13-9

In this hands-on project, you create, query, and manage a database using PostgreSQL on your Ubuntu Server Linux virtual machine.

1. On your Ubuntu Server Linux virtual machine, log into tty1 using the user name of **root** and the password of **LNXrocks!**.

2. At the command prompt, type **passwd postgres** and press **Enter**. Type a password of **LNXrocks!** and press **Enter** at both prompts to set a password of LNXrocks! for the postgres user account.

3. At the command prompt, type **su - postgres** and press **Enter** to start a new shell as the postgres user.

4. At the command prompt, type **createdb sales** and press **Enter**.

5. At the command prompt, type **psql sales** and press **Enter** to start the PostgreSQL utility.

6. At the sales=# prompt, type **\l** and press **Enter** to view the databases on your PostgreSQL server. The postgres database stores all information used internally by the PostgreSQL server, and the template databases are used when creating new databases. Note that your sales database is listed and uses the UTF-8 character set for information.

7. At the sales=# prompt, type **CREATE TABLE customer (Name char(20),Address char(40),Balance char(10));** and press **Enter** to create a customer table that has three fields (Name, Address, Balance).

8. At the sales=# prompt, type **\d** and press **Enter** to view the tables within your database. Is the customer database listed?

9. At the sales=# prompt, type **\d customer** and press **Enter** to view the fields within the customer table. How many characters are allowed in each of the three fields?

10. At the sales=# prompt, type **INSERT INTO customer VALUES ('Lily Bopeep','123 Rutherford Lane','526.80');** and press **Enter** to add a record to your table.

11. At the sales=# prompt, type **INSERT INTO customer VALUES ('Lily Bopeep','123 Rutherford Lane','526.80');** and press **Enter** to add a record to your table.

12. At the sales=# prompt, type **INSERT INTO customer VALUES ('Harvey Lipshitz','51 King Street','122.19');** and press **Enter** to add a record to your table.

13. At the sales=# prompt, type **INSERT INTO customer VALUES ('John Escobar','14-6919 Franklin Drive','709.66');** and press **Enter** to add a record to your table.

14. At the sales=# prompt, type **SELECT * from customer;** and press **Enter** to view all records within your table.

15. At the sales=# prompt, type **SELECT * from cusomter ORDER BY Balance DESC;** and press **Enter** to view all records within your table in descending order by balance.

16. At the sales=# prompt, type **SELECT * from customer WHERE Name= 'Harvey Lipshitz';** and press **Enter** to view the record for Harvey Lipshitz.

17. At the sales=# prompt, type **CREATE USER bob WITH PASSWORD 'supersecret';** and press **Enter** to create a user account within PostgreSQL that can access the customer database.

18. At the sales=# prompt, type **GRANT ALL PRIVILEGES ON customer TO bob** and press **Enter** to grant SELECT, UPDATE, DELETE, and INSERT permission on the customer table to the bob user.

13

19. At the sales=# prompt, type **\q** and press **Enter** to quit the PostgreSQL utility.

20. Type **exit** and press **Enter** to log out of your shell.

Discovery Exercises

1. In Project 13-1, you configured the DHCP daemon (dhcpd) on your Fedora Linux virtual machine. On your Ubuntu Server Linux virtual machine, install and configure udhcpd to provide the same functionality described in Project 13-1, and test your settings by configuring your Fedora Linux virtual machine as a DHCP client that obtains IPv4 configuration from udhcpd. Finally, restore your original configuration.

2. In Project 13-2, you installed and configured the DNS daemon (named) on your Fedora Linux virtual machine. The DNS daemon is already installed and running on your Ubuntu Server Linux virtual machine. Spend a few moments to view the /etc/bind/named.conf file as well as any files referenced by the /etc/bind/named.conf file (/etc/bind/named.conf.local, /etc/bind/named.conf.options, and /etc/bind/named.conf.default-zones). Next, view the contents of the sample zone files referenced by /etc/bind/named.conf.default-zones. Do the contents follow the same convention that you saw in Project 13-2? How could you configure the DNS daemon on your Ubuntu Server Linux virtual machine to host the same zone files that you configured on your Fedora Linux virtual machine?

3. In Project 13-3, you configured your NTP daemon to share time information to other computers on your classroom network. Edit the /etc/ntp.conf on your partner's computer to obtain time information from your computer and test the results using the ntpq command. Next, restore your original configuration.

4. In Project 13-4, you configured the Apache Web server on your Fedora Linux virtual machine. Perform the same configuration on the Apache Web server running on your Ubuntu Server Linux virtual machine. Note any pathname and configuration file differences.

5. The file sharing servers discussed in this chapter (vsftpd, NFS, and Samba) were configured on your Ubuntu Server Linux virtual machine during the hands-on projects. Perform the same configuration on your Fedora Linux virtual machine, installing packages as necessary from software repositories.

6. Fedora 20 does not contain an e-mail daemon by default but will use one if available. Install and configure Postfix and the `mail` command on your Fedora Linux virtual machine and test your results using the `mail` and `telnet` commands.

7. Use the steps outlined in this chapter to configure your system as an NIS master server, and then configure NIS maps for the /etc/passwd and /etc/shadow files on your Fedora Linux virtual machine. Next, use the Internet to research the steps needed to configure Ubuntu Server 14.04 as an NIS client, and then configure your Ubuntu Server Linux virtual machine to obtain its /etc/passwd and /etc/shadow configuration from your NIS master server. Test your configuration using the yppasswd command. When finished, restore your original configuration.

## chapter 14

Troubleshooting, Performance, and Security

After completing this chapter, you will be able to:

- Describe and outline good troubleshooting practices
- Effectively troubleshoot common hardware- and software-related problems
- Monitor system performance using command-line and graphical utilities
- Identify and fix common performance problems
- Describe the different facets of Linux security
- Increase the security of a Linux computer
- Outline measures and utilities that can be used to detect a Linux security breach

Throughout this textbook, you have examined various elements of a Linux system. In this chapter, you focus on fixing common problems that affect these elements. First, you explore system maintenance, troubleshooting procedures, common system problems, and performance utilities. Next, you learn security concepts, good security practices, as well as the utilities that you can use to prevent and detect both local and network-related security breaches.

Troubleshooting Methodology

After you have successfully installed Linux, configured services on the system, and documented settings, you must maintain the system's integrity over time. This includes monitoring, proactive maintenance, and reactive maintenance, as illustrated in Figure 14-1.

Monitoring, the activity on which Linux administrators spend the most time, involves examining log files and running performance utilities periodically to identify problems and their causes. **Proactive maintenance** involves taking the required steps to minimize the chance of future problems as well as their impact. Performing regular system backups and identifying potential problem areas are examples of proactive maintenance. All proactive maintenance tasks should be documented for future reference. This information, along with any data backups, is vital to the reconstruction of your system, should it suffer catastrophic failure.

Reactive maintenance is used to correct problems when they arise during monitoring. When a problem is solved, it needs to be documented and the system adjusted proactively to reduce the likelihood that the same problem will occur in the future. Furthermore, documenting the solution to problems creates a template for action, allowing subsequent or similar problems to be remedied faster.

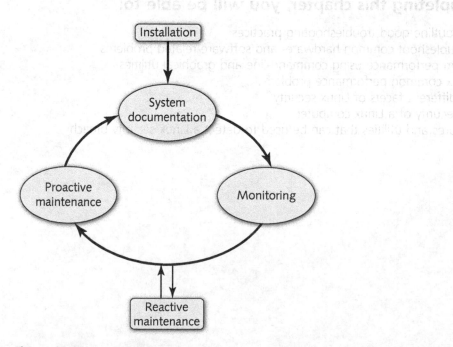

Figure 14-1 The maintenance cycle

Any system **documentation** should be printed and kept in a log book because this information might be lost during a system failure if kept on the Linux system itself.

Reactive maintenance is further composed of many procedures known as **troubleshooting procedures**, which can be used to efficiently solve a problem in a systematic manner.

When a problem occurs, you need to gather as much information about the problem as possible. This might include examining system log files and viewing the contents of the /proc filesystem, as well as running information utilities, such as ps or mount. In addition, you might research the symptoms of the problem on the Internet; Web sites and newsgroups often list log files and commands that can be used to check for certain problems.

The `tail -f /path/to/logfile` command opens a specific log file for continuous viewing; this allows you to see entries as they are added, which is useful when gathering information about system problems. If your system uses Systemd, you can use the `--follow` option to the `journalctl` command to do the same. For example, to view chronyd events as they are added, you can use the `journalctl _COMM=chronyd --follow` command.

Following this, you need to try to isolate the problem by examining the information gathered. Determine whether the problem is persistent or intermittent and whether it affects all users or just one.

Given this information, you might then generate a list of possible causes and solutions organized by placing the most probable solution at the top of the list and the least probable solution at the bottom of the list. Using the Internet at this stage is beneficial because solutions for many Linux problems are posted on Web sites or newsgroups. In addition, posing the problem at a local Linux Users Group will likely generate many possible solutions.

Next, you need to implement and test each possible solution for results until the problem is resolved. When implementing possible solutions, it is very important that you only apply one change at a time. If you make multiple modifications, it will be unclear as to what worked and why.

After the problem has been solved, document the solution for future reference and proceed to take proactive maintenance measures to reduce the chance of the same problem recurring in the future. These troubleshooting procedures are outlined in Figure 14-2.

The troubleshooting procedures listed in Figure 14-2 serve as a guideline only. You might need to alter your approach for certain problems. Remember, troubleshooting is an art that you will begin to master only with practice. There are, however, two golden rules that should guide you during any troubleshooting process:

- *Prioritize problems*—If you need to solve multiple problems, prioritize the problems according to severity and spend the most time on the most severe problems. Becoming fixated on a small problem and ignoring larger issues results in much lower productivity. If a problem is too difficult to solve in a given period of time, it is good practice to ask for help.

14

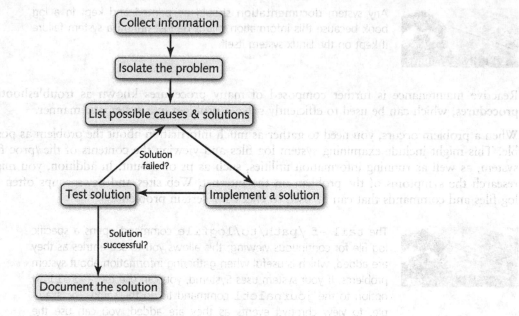

Figure 14-2 Common troubleshooting procedures

- *Try to solve the root of the problem*—Some solutions might appear successful in the short term yet fail over the long term because of an underlying problem. Effective troubleshooting requires good instincts, which in turn comes from a solid knowledge of the system hardware and configuration. To avoid missing the underlying cause of any problem, try to justify why a certain solution was successful. If it is unclear why a certain solution was successful, it is likely that you have missed an underlying cause to the problem that might need to be remedied in the future to prevent the same problem from recurring.

Resolving Common System Problems

The possible problems that can arise on Linux systems are too numerous to list here. However, as a troubleshooter, you'll most often face a set of the common problems described in this section. All Linux problems can be divided into three categories: hardware-related, software-related, and user interface-related.

Hardware-Related Problems

Although hardware problems might be the result of damaged hardware, many hardware-related problems involve improper hardware or software configuration. This is most likely the case if the hardware problem presents itself immediately after Linux installation.

As discussed in earlier chapters, ensuring that all Parallel SCSI drives are properly terminated, that the video card and monitor settings have been configured properly, and that all hardware is on the Hardware Compatibility List minimizes problems later. In addition, if the POST does not complete or alerts the user with two or more beeps at system startup, there is likely a peripheral card, cable, or memory stick that is loose or connected improperly inside the computer.

Some hardware-related problems prevent the use of hardware with the Linux operating system. These problems are typically specific to the type of hardware. Viewing the output of the dmesg command, journalctl -b command (if Systemd is used), or the contents of the /var/log/syslog, /var/log/boot.log, and /var/log/messages log files can isolate most hardware problems.

The absence of a device driver also prevents the operating system from using the associated hardware device. Normally, the Linux kernel detects new hardware devices at boot time and configures the device driver module for them automatically. However, if the Linux kernel doesn't have access to the appropriate driver module for a certain hardware device, the device cannot be used. You can view the hardware that is detected by the Linux kernel by viewing the output of the dmesg command or lshw command. To only view the USB devices detected by the Linux kernel, you could instead use the **lsusb command**, as shown here:

```
[root@server1 ~]# lsusb
Bus 002 Device 002: ID 05ac:0302 Apple, Inc. Optical Mouse [Fujitsu]
Bus 002 Device 001: ID 1d6b:0001 Linux Foundation 1.1 root hub
Bus 001 Device 001: ID 1d6b:0002 Linux Foundation 2.0 root hub
[root@server1 ~]# _
```

Alternatively, you could use the **lscpu command** to view the features of your CPU, or the **lspci command** to view the PCI devices detected by the Linux kernel, as shown in the following output:

```
[root@server1 ~]# lspci
00:00.0 RAM memory: nVidia Corporation C51 Host Bridge (rev a2)
00:00.1 RAM memory: nVidia Corporation C51 Memory Controller 0 (rev a2)
00:00.2 RAM memory: nVidia Corporation C51 Memory Controller 1 (rev a2)
00:00.3 RAM memory: nVidia Corporation C51 Memory Controller 5 (rev a2)
00:00.4 RAM memory: nVidia Corporation C51 Memory Controller 4 (rev a2)
00:00.5 RAM memory: nVidia Corporation C51 Host Bridge (rev a2)
00:00.6 RAM memory: nVidia Corporation C51 Memory Controller 3 (rev a2)
00:00.7 RAM memory: nVidia Corporation C51 Memory Controller 2 (rev a2)
00:03.0 PCI bridge: nVidia Corporation C51 PCI Express Bridge (rev a1)
00:05.0 VGA compatible controller: nVidia Corporation C51 [GeForce Go
6100] (rev a2)
00:09.0 RAM memory: nVidia Corporation MCP51 Host Bridge (rev a2)
00:0a.0 ISA bridge: nVidia Corporation MCP51 LPC Bridge (rev a3)
00:0a.1 SMBus: nVidia Corporation MCP51 SMBus (rev a3)
00:0a.3 Co-processor: nVidia Corporation MCP51 PMU (rev a3)
00:0b.0 USB Controller: nVidia Corporation MCP51 USB Controller (rev a3)
00:0b.1 USB Controller: nVidia Corporation MCP51 USB Controller (rev a3)
00:0d.0 IDE interface: nVidia Corporation MCP51 IDE (rev f1)
00:10.0 PCI bridge: nVidia Corporation MCP51 PCI Bridge (rev a2)
00:10.1 Audio device: nVidia Corporation MCP51 High Definition Audio
 (rev a2)
00:14.0 Bridge: nVidia Corporation MCP51 Ethernet Controller (rev a3)
```

14

```
00:18.0 Host bridge: Advanced Micro Devices [AMD] K8 [Athlon64/Opteron]
HyperTransport Technology Configuration
00:18.1 Host bridge: Advanced Micro Devices [AMD] K8 [Athlon64/Opteron]
Address Map
00:18.2 Host bridge: Advanced Micro Devices [AMD] K8 [Athlon64/Opteron]
DRAM Controller
00:18.3 Host bridge: Advanced Micro Devices [AMD] K8 [Athlon64/Opteron]
Miscellaneous Control
06:09.0 Ethernet controller: Realtek Semiconductor Co., Ltd. RTL-8185
IEEE 802.11a/b/g Wireless LAN Controller (rev 20)
[root@server1 ~]# _
```

Recall from Chapter 13 that the lsmod command lists the driver modules loaded into the Linux kernel. By comparing the output of the dmesg, lshw, lsusb, and lspci commands to the output of the lsmod command, you can determine whether a driver module is missing for a hardware device in your system. By searching Linux forums on the Internet or the hardware vendor's Web site, you will likely find a package that you can add to your system that provides a driver module for this hardware device. After installing this package, simply reboot to allow the Linux kernel to detect your hardware and load the appropriate driver module.

Although less common than other hardware problems, hardware failure can also render a device unusable. In this case, you must replace the hardware and allow the Linux kernel to detect it and load the appropriate driver module or obtain the appropriate driver module from the Internet, as described earlier. Because hard disks are used frequently and consist of moving parts, they are the most common hardware component to fail on Linux systems. If the Linux system uses hardware RAID level 1 or 5, the data on the hard disk can be regenerated using the RAID configuration utility after you replace the failed hard disk.

If, however, the Linux system does not use hardware RAID and the hard disk that failed contained partitions that were mounted on noncritical directories, such as /home or /var, then you can perform the following steps:

1. Power down the computer and replace the failed hard disk.
2. Boot the Linux system.
3. Create partitions on the replaced hard disk.
4. Optionally configure LVM logical volumes from the partitions created in Step 3.
5. Use mkfs to create filesystems on the partitions or LVM logical volumes.
6. Restore the original data using a backup utility.
7. Ensure that /etc/fstab has the appropriate entries to mount the filesystems at system startup.

Alternatively, if the hard disk that contains the / filesystem fails, you can perform the following steps:

1. Power down the computer and replace the failed hard disk.
2. Reinstall Linux on the new hard disk (remembering to recreate the original partition and volume structure during installation).
3. Restore the original configuration and data files using a backup utility.

Software-Related Problems

Software-related problems are typically more difficult to identify and resolve than hardware-related problems. As a result, you should identify whether the software-related problem is related to application software or operating system software.

Application-Related Problems Applications can fail during execution for a number of reasons, including missing program libraries and files, process restrictions, or conflicting applications.

As discussed in Chapter 11, when a package is installed, the package manager does a preliminary check to ensure that all shared program libraries and prerequisite packages (package dependencies) required for the application to work properly have been installed. If these are missing, an error message is printed to the screen or the necessary libraries and dependencies are downloaded and installed from a software repository (if yum or apt-get is used, for example). Similarly, uninstalling a package may fail if the package being uninstalled is a dependency for another package. Also, when compiling source code, the configure script checks for the presence of any required shared program libraries and programs and fails to create the Makefile if they are absent. Thus, you must download and install the necessary shared libraries and/or packages before installing software packages using these methods.

Some programs, however, might fail to check for dependencies during installation, or files that belong to a package dependency might be accidentally removed from the system over time. If this is the case, certain programs fail to execute properly.

To identify any missing files in a package or package dependency, recall that you can use the –V option to the rpm command (for RPM) or dpkg command (for DPM), followed by the name of the package. The following output indicates that there are two missing files in the bash RPM package:

```
[root@server1 ~]# rpm -V bash
missing  d /usr/share/doc/bash-4.2.53/COPYING
missing  d /usr/share/doc/bash-4.2.53/README
[root@server1 ~]# _
```

To identify which shared libraries are required by a certain program, you can use the **ldd** command. For example, the following output displays the shared libraries required by the /bin/bash program:

```
[root@server1 ~]# ldd /bin/bash
    linux-vdso.so.1 => (0x00007fff2fe36000)
    libtinfo.so.5 => /lib64/libtinfo.so.5 (0x00007f5e0ebf7000)
    libdl.so.2 => /lib64/libdl.so.2 (0x00007f5e0e9f3000)
    libc.so.6 => /lib64/libc.so.6 (0x00007f5e0e634000)
    /lib64/ld-linux-x86-64.so.2 (0x00007f5e0ee3f000)
[root@server1 ~]# _
```

If any shared libraries listed by the ldd command are missing, you can download the appropriate library from the Internet and install it to the correct location, which is typically underneath the /lib, /lib64, /usr/lib, or /usr/lib64 directories. After downloading and installing any shared libraries, it is good practice to run the **ldconfig command** to ensure that

14

the list of shared library directories (/etc/ld.so.conf) and the list of shared libraries (/etc/ld.so.cache) are updated. Alternatively, you can create a variable in your BASH shell called LD_LIBRARY_PATH that lists the directories that contain the shared libraries.

Processes are restricted by a number of constraints that can also prevent them from executing properly. Recall that all processes require a PID from the system process table. Too many processes running on the system can use all available PIDs in the process table; this is typically the result of a large number of zombie processes. Killing the parent process of the zombie processes then frees several entries in the process table.

In addition, processes can initiate numerous connections to files on the filesystem in addition to Standard Input, Standard Output, and Standard Error. These connections are called **file handles**. The shell restricts the number of file handles that programs can open to 1024 by default; to increase the maximum number of file handles to 5000, you can run the command ulimit -n 5000. The **ulimit command** can also be used to increase the number of processes that users can start in a shell; this might be required for programs that start a great deal of child processes. For example, to increase the maximum number of user processes to 30000, you can use the command ulimit -u 30000.

To isolate application problems that are not related to missing dependencies or restrictions, you should first check the log file produced by the application. Most application log files are stored in the /var/log directory or subdirectories of the /var/log directory named for the application. Even if an application stores its log files elsewhere, it usually hard links its log files to files within the /var/log directory. For example, to view the errors for the Apache daemon, you can view the appropriate log files created by the Apache daemon under the /var/log/httpd directory (Fedora 20) or /var/log/apache2 directory (Ubuntu Server 14.04).

Applications might run into difficulties gaining resources during execution and stop functioning. Often, restarting the process using a SIGHUP solves this problem. This condition might also be caused by another process on the system that attempts to use the same resources. To determine if this is the case, attempt to start the application when fewer processes are loaded, such as in single user-mode (runlevel 1). If resource conflict seems to be the cause of the problem, check the Internet for a newer version of the application or an application fix.

Operating System-Related Problems

Many software-related problems are related to the operating system itself. These typically include problems with X Windows, boot loaders, and filesystems.

There are many different video card and monitor models today. As a result, some video cards and monitors may not be detected properly by the kernel, or an updated device driver may be required to properly use them with the Linux kernel. If you configure custom display settings and your X Windows or gdm fails to start, you can usually isolate the problems by viewing the Xorg or XFree86 configuration file, or by executing the **xwininfo** command.

As discussed in Chapter 8, boot loaders can encounter problems while attempting to load the operating system kernel. For the LILO boot loader, placing the word "linear" and removing the word "compact" from the /etc/lilo.conf file usually remedies the problem. For the GRUB and GRUB2 boot loaders, errors are typically the result of a missing file in the /boot directory. Also, ensuring that the Linux kernel resides before the 1024th cylinder of the hard disk and that 32-bit large block addressing (lba32) keyword is specified in the boot loader configuration file typically eliminates BIOS problems with large hard disks.

GRUB2 automatically sets lba32.

Because the operating system transfers data to and from the hard disk frequently, the filesystem can become corrupted over time; a corrupted filesystem can be identified by very slow write requests, errors printed to the console, or failure to mount. If the filesystem on a partition mounted to a noncritical directory, such as /home or /var, becomes corrupted, you should perform the following troubleshooting steps:

1. Unmount the filesystem if mounted.
2. Run the `fsck` command with the `-f` (full) option on the filesystem device.
3. If the `fsck` command cannot repair the filesystem, use the `mkfs` command to re-create the filesystem.
4. Restore the original data for the filesystem using a backup utility.

Do not restore data onto a damaged filesystem; ensure that the filesystem has been recreated first.

If the / filesystem becomes corrupted, the system is unstable and must be turned off. Following this, you can perform the following troubleshooting steps:

1. Boot your system from your installation or live media to perform system rescue, as described in Chapter 6.
2. At the BASH shell prompt during system rescue, use the `mkfs` command to recreate the filesystem on the appropriate partition or volume that originally hosted the / filesystem.
3. At the BASH shell prompt during system rescue, use the appropriate utility (e.g., `tar`, `restore`, or `cpio`) to restore the original data to the recreated / filesystem.
4. Boot your system normally following the system rescue.

Some Linux administrators prefer to download a bootable CD, DVD, or USB flash drive-based Linux distribution that contains more filesystem repair utilities than the Fedora installation media. Many small Linux distributions are available on the Internet that are designed for this purpose; one example is **Knoppix Linux** (www.knoppix.net). Simply download the ISO image for the Linux distribution and write the image to a CD, DVD, or USB flash drive. Following this, you can boot your computer using this CD, DVD, or USB flash drive, and use the utilities on it to repair your / filesystem and restore the files from backup.

User Interface-Related Problems

Because of the large number of open source productivity software applications available, Linux desktop environments are fast becoming popular within organizations as an alternative to the Windows operating system.

14

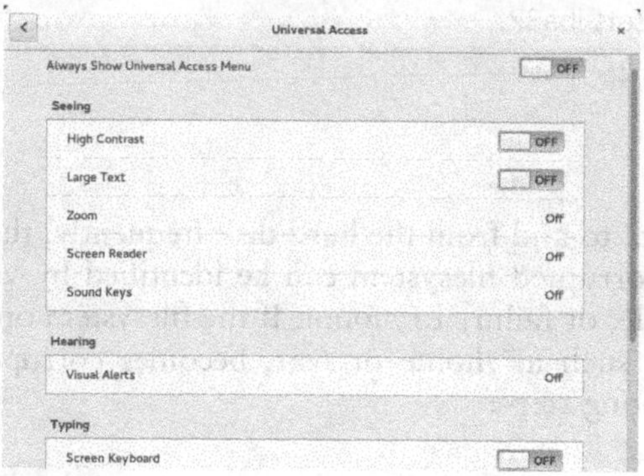

Figure 14-3 The Universal Access utility

In order to use productivity software properly, Linux users need to understand how to use their desktop environment as well as modify it to suit their needs. As a Linux administrator, you may need to assist users with desktop problems. The tools that users can use to modify their desktop experience are collectively called **assistive technologies**. You can configure assistive technologies within Fedora 20 using the **Universal Access utility**, as shown in Figure 14-3. To start this utility within the GNOME desktop environment, open the Activities menu and navigate to Show Applications, Settings, Universal Access.

If you turn on the Always Show Universal Access Menu option shown within Figure 14-3, you can enable and disable each assistive technology using the Universal Access icon in the upper right of the GNOME desktop. Following is a list of the assistive technologies that you can configure within the Universal Access utility or desktop icon:

- High Contrast, which modifies the color scheme to suit those with low vision
- Large Text, which increases the font size of text to suit those with low vision
- Zoom, which allows you to enable magnification for parts of the screen that your mouse follows, as well as modify the color and crosshair effects during magnification
- Screen Reader, which narrates the text on the active window on the screen
- Sound Keys, which beeps when the Num Lock or Caps Lock keys are pressed
- Visual Alerts, which displays a visual alert in place of beep sounds
- Screen Keyboard, which displays an on-screen keyboard that can be used with a mouse
- Typing Assist, which provides three keyboard assistive features:
  - Sticky keys, which simulate simultaneous key presses when two keys are pressed in sequence
  - Slow keys, which add a delay following each key press
  - Bounce keys, which ignore fast duplicate key presses
- Mouse keys, which allow the user to control the mouse using the cursor keys on the keyboard
- Click Assist, which can be used to simulate a right-click by holding down a left-click for a period of time, or trigger a left-click by hovering the mouse pointer over an area of the desktop

Performance Monitoring

Some problems that you will encounter on a Linux system are not as noticeable as those discussed in the previous section. Such problems affect the overall performance of the Linux system. Like the problems discussed earlier, performance problems can be caused by software or hardware or a combination of the two.

Hardware that is improperly configured might still work, but at a slower speed. In addition, when hardware ages, it might start to malfunction by sending large amounts of information to the CPU when not in use. This process, known as **jabbering**, can slow down a CPU and, hence, the rest of the Linux system. To avoid this hardware malfunction, most companies retire computer equipment after two to three years of use.

Software can also affect the overall performance of a system. Software that requires too many system resources monopolizes the CPU, memory, and peripheral devices. Poor performance can also be the result of too many processes running on a computer, processes that make a great deal of read/write requests to the hard disk (such as databases), or rogue processes. To remedy most software performance issues, you can remove software from the system to free up system resources. If the software is needed for business activity, you can instead choose to move the software to another Linux system that has more free system resources.

Software performance problems can also sometimes be remedied by altering the hardware. Upgrading or adding another CPU allows the Linux system to execute processes faster and reduce the number of processes running concurrently on the CPU. Alternatively, some peripheral devices can perform a great deal of processing that is normally performed by the CPU; this is known as **bus mastering**. Using bus mastering peripheral components reduces the amount of processing the CPU must perform and, hence, increases system speed.

Adding RAM to the computer also increases system speed because it gives processes more working space in memory and the system will swap much less information to and from the hard disk. Because the operating system, peripheral components, and all processes use RAM constantly, adding RAM to any system often has a profound impact on system performance.

In addition, replacing slower hard disk drives with faster ones or using disk striping RAID improves the performance of programs that require frequent access to filesystems. SCSI hard disks typically have faster rotational speeds and hence faster access speeds than other hard disks; many Linux servers use SCSI hard disks for this reason. In addition, CD and DVD drives have a slower access speed than hard disks. Thus, keeping CD and DVD drives on a separate hard disk controller also improves hard disk performance.

To make it easier to identify performance problems, you should run performance utilities on a healthy Linux system on a regular basis during normal business hours and record the results in a system log book. The average results of these performance utilities are known as **baseline** values because they represent normal system activity. When performance issues arise, you can compare the output of performance utilities to the baseline values recorded in the system log book. Values that have changed dramatically from the baseline can help you pinpoint the source of the performance problem.

Although many performance utilities are available to Linux administrators, the most common of these belong to the sysstat package, described next.

14

Monitoring Performance with sysstat Utilities

The **System Statistics (sysstat)** package contains a wide range of utilities that monitor the system using information from the /proc directory and system devices. The sysstat package isn't added during the installation process on most Linux distributions but can be installed from a software repository afterwards.

To monitor CPU performance, you can use the **mpstat (multiple processor statistics) command**. Without arguments, the mpstat command gives average CPU statistics for all processors on the system since the most previous system boot, as shown in the following output:

```
[root@server1 ~]# mpstat
Linux 3.11.10-301.fc20.x86_64 (server1) 11/01/2015 _x86_64_ (2 CPU)

06:38:42 PM CPU %usr %nice %sys %iowait %irq %soft %steal %guest %gnice %idle
06:38:42 PM all 17.53 1.48  6.21 11.73  0.19 0.00  0.00   0.00   0.00  62.85
[root@server1 ~]# _
```

 If your system has multiple CPUs, you can measure the performance of a single CPU by specifying the −P # option to the mpstat command, where # represents the number of the processor, starting from zero. Thus, the command mpstat −P 0 displays statistics for the first processor on the system.

The **%usr** value shown in the preceding output indicates the percentage of time the processor spent executing user programs and daemons, whereas the **%nice** value indicates the percentage of time the processor spent executing user programs and daemons that had nondefault nice values. These numbers combined should be greater than the value of **%sys**, which indicates the amount of time the system spent maintaining itself such that it can execute user programs and daemons.

 A system that has a high **%sys** compared to **%usr** and **%nice** is likely executing too many resource-intensive programs.

The **%iowait** value indicates the percentage of time the CPU was idle when an outstanding disk I/O request existed. The **%irq** and **%soft** values indicate the percentage of time the CPU is using to respond to normal interrupts and interrupts that span multiple CPUs, respectively. If these three values rapidly increase over time, the CPU cannot keep up with the number of requests it receives from software. If you have virtualization software installed, the **%guest** value indicates the percentage of time the CPU is executing another virtual CPU, **%gnice** value indicates the percentage of time the processor spent executing user programs and daemons in the virtual CPU that had nondefault nice values, and the **%steal** indicates the percentage of time the CPU is waiting to respond to virtual CPU requests.

The **%idle** value indicates the percentage of time the CPU did not spend executing tasks. Although it might be zero for short periods of time, **%idle** should be greater than 25 percent over a long period of time.

 A system that has a `%idle` less than 25 percent over a long period of time might require faster or additional CPUs.

Although the average values given by the `mpstat` command are very useful in determining the CPU health of a Linux system, you might choose to take current measurements using `mpstat`. To do this, simply specify the interval in seconds and number of measurements as arguments to the `mpstat` command. For example, the following command takes five current measurements, one per second:

```
[root@server1 ~]# mpstat 1 5
Linux 3.11.10-301.fc20.x86_64 (server1)  11/01/2015 _x86_64_  (2 CPU)

07:05:10 AM  CPU  %usr  %nice  %sys  %iowait  %irq  %soft  %steal  %guest  %gnice  %idle
07:05:11 AM  all  8.91  1.98   0.00  0.00     0.99  0.00   0.00    0.00    0.00    88.12
07:05:12 AM  all  7.07  2.02   0.00  0.00     0.00  0.00   0.00    0.00    0.00    90.91
07:05:13 AM  all  7.92  1.98   0.99  0.00     0.00  0.00   0.00    0.00    0.00    89.11
07:05:14 AM  all  7.07  2.02   0.00  0.00     0.00  0.00   0.00    0.00    0.00    90.91
07:05:15 AM  all  6.93  2.97   0.99  0.00     0.00  0.00   0.00    0.00    0.00    89.11
Average:     all  7.58  2.20   0.40  0.00     0.20  0.00   0.00    0.00    0.00    89.62
[root@server1 ~]# _
```

The preceding output must be used with caution because it was taken over a short period of time. If, for example, the `%idle` values are under 25 percent on average, they are not necessarily abnormal because the system might be performing a CPU-intensive task during the short time the statistics were taken.

Another utility in the sysstat package, **`iostat`** (**input/output statistics**), measures the flow of information to and from disk devices. Without any arguments, the `iostat` command displays CPU statistics similar to `mpstat`, followed by statistics for each disk device on the system. If your Linux system has one SATA hard disk drive (/dev/sda), the `iostat` command produces output similar to the following:

```
[root@server1 ~]# iostat
Linux 3.11.10-301.fc20.x86_64 (server1)  11/01/2015 _x86_64_  (2 CPU)

avg-cpu:  %user   %nice  %system  %iowait  %steal  %idle
          0.10    0.01   0.15     0.39     0.00    99.35

Device:   tps    kB_read/s  kB_wrtn/s  kB_read  kB_wrtn
sda       0.76   20.94      5.51       1619316  426256
dm-0      0.00   0.01       0.00       890      8
dm-1      0.00   0.01       0.00       472      0

[root@server1 ~]# _
```

The output from `iostat` displays the number of transfers per second (`tps`) as well as the number of kilobytes read per second (`kB_read/s`) and written per second (`kB_wrtn/s`), followed by the total number of kilobytes read (`kB_read`) and written (`kB_wrtn`) for the device since the last boot. An increase over time in these values indicates an increase in disk

14

usage by processes. If this increase results in slow performance, the hard disks should be replaced with faster ones or a RAID striping configuration. Like mpstat, the iostat command can take current measurements of the system. Simply specify the interval in seconds, followed by the number of measurements as arguments to the iostat command.

Although iostat and mpstat can be used to get quick information about system status, they are limited in their abilities. The **sar** (system activity reporter) **command** that is contained in the sysstat package can be used to display far more information than iostat and mpstat. As such, it is the most widely used performance monitoring tool on UNIX and Linux systems.

By default, sar commands are scheduled using the cron daemon to run every 10 minutes on Fedora 20 and Ubuntu Server 14.04. All performance information obtained is logged to a file in the /var/log/sa directory (Fedora 20) or /var/log/sysstat directory (Ubuntu Server 14.04) called sa#, where # represents the day of the month. If today were the 14th day of the month, the output from the sar command that is run every 10 minutes would be logged to the file sa14. Next month, this file will be overwritten on the 14th day. In other words, only one month of records is kept at any one time.

You can change the sar logging interval by editing the cron table /etc/cron.d/sysstat.

Without arguments, the sar command displays the CPU statistics taken every 10 minutes for the current day, as shown in the following output:

```
[root@server1 ~]# sar
Linux 3.11.10-301.fc20.x86_64 (server1) 11/01/2015 _x86_64_ (2 CPU)

03:40:01 AM     CPU    %user    %nice    %system    %iowait    %steal    %idle
03:50:01 AM     all     0.06     0.00      0.13       0.27       0.00     99.54
04:00:01 AM     all     0.06     0.00      0.12       0.23       0.00     99.58
04:10:01 AM     all     0.08     0.00      0.14       0.19       0.00     99.60
04:20:01 AM     all     0.06     0.00      0.13       0.38       0.00     99.43
04:30:01 AM     all     0.06     0.00      0.12       0.20       0.00     99.61
04:40:01 AM     all     0.05     0.00      0.12       0.24       0.00     99.59
04:50:01 AM     all     0.06     0.00      0.12       0.21       0.00     99.61
05:00:01 AM     all     0.07     0.00      0.12       0.22       0.00     99.59
05:10:01 AM     all     0.08     0.00      0.13       0.19       0.00     99.59
05:20:01 AM     all     0.06     0.00      0.12       0.37       0.00     99.45
05:30:01 AM     all     0.07     0.00      0.12       0.20       0.00     99.61
05:40:01 AM     all     0.06     0.00      0.13       0.28       0.00     99.53
05:50:01 AM     all     0.06     0.00      0.12       0.22       0.00     99.60
06:00:01 AM     all     0.07     0.00      0.12       0.22       0.00     99.59
06:10:01 AM     all     0.08     0.00      0.14       0.18       0.00     99.60
06:20:01 AM     all     0.06     0.00      0.12       0.36       0.00     99.46
06:30:01 AM     all     0.07     0.00      0.13       0.20       0.00     99.60
06:40:01 AM     all     0.07     0.00      0.13       0.24       0.00     99.57
06:50:01 AM     all     0.06     0.00      0.13       0.26       0.00     99.56
```

```
07:00:01 AM    all     0.10    0.00     0.15      0.27    0.00     99.49
07:10:01 AM    all     0.09    0.00     0.15      0.31    0.00     99.45
07:20:01 AM    all     1.79    0.00     0.99      4.19    0.00     93.04
Average:       all     0.11    0.05     0.15      0.35    0.00     99.34
[root@server1 ~]# _
```

To view the CPU statistics for the 6th of the month, you can specify the pathname to the appropriate file using the −f option to the sar command:

```
[root@server1 ~]# sar -f /var/log/sa/sa06 | head
Linux 3.11.10-301.fc20.x86_64 (server1)  10/06/2015 _x86_64_  (2 CPU)

12:00:01 AM    CPU     %user   %nice   %system    %iowait  %steal   %idle
12:10:01 AM    all     0.07    0.00     0.14      0.56    0.00     99.22
12:20:01 AM    all     0.07    0.00     0.14      0.51    0.00     99.28
12:30:01 AM    all     0.07    0.00     0.13      0.53    0.00     99.28
12:40:01 AM    all     0.06    0.00     0.13      0.58    0.00     99.22
12:50:01 AM    all     0.07    0.00     0.13      0.54    0.00     99.26
01:00:01 AM    all     0.07    0.00     0.13      0.58    0.00     99.22
01:10:01 AM    all     0.07    0.00     0.14      0.60    0.00     99.19
[root@server1 ~]# _
```

You must use the −f option to the sar command to view files in the /var/log/sa (or /var/log/sysstat) directory with the aforementioned filenames because they contain binary information. A sar text report is also written to the /var/log/sa/sar# file (or /var/log/sysstat/sar# file) at the end of each day, where # represents the day of the month. To view a sar report file, you can use any text command, such as less.

As with the iostat and mpstat commands, the sar command can be used to take current system measurements. To take four CPU statistics every two seconds, you can use the following command:

```
[root@server1 ~]# sar 2 4
Linux 3.11.10-301.fc20.x86_64 (server1)  11/01/2015 _x86_64_  (2 CPU)

08:24:41 AM    CPU     %user   %nice   %system    %iowait  %steal   %idle
08:24:43 AM    all     0.00    0.00     0.50      0.00    0.00     99.50
08:24:45 AM    all     0.00    0.00     0.25      0.00    0.00     99.75
08:24:47 AM    all     0.25    0.00     0.76      0.00    0.00     98.99
08:24:49 AM    all     0.00    0.00     0.27      0.00    0.00     99.73
Average:       all     0.06    0.00     0.45      0.00    0.00     99.49
[root@server1 ~]# _
```

Although the sar command displays CPU statistics by default, you can display different statistics by specifying options to the sar command. Table 14-1 lists common options used with the sar command.

From Table 14-1, you can see that the −b and −d options to the sar command display information similar to the output of the iostat command. In addition, the −u option displays CPU statistics equivalent to the output of the mpstat command.

14

Option	Description
-A	Displays the most information; this option is equivalent to all options
-b	Displays I/O statistics
-B	Displays swap statistics
-d	Displays Input/Output statistics for each block device on the system
-f file_name	Displays information from the specified file; these files typically reside in the /var/log/sa directory
-n ALL	Reports all network statistics
-o file_name	Saves the output to a file in binary format
-P CPU#	Specifies statistics for a single CPU (the first CPU is 0, the second CPU is 1, and so on)
-q	Displays statistics for the processor queue
-r	Displays memory and swap statistics
-R	Displays memory statistics
-u	Displays CPU statistics; this is the default action when no options are specified
-v	Displays kernel-related filesystem statistics
-W	Displays swapping statistics

Table 14-1 Common options to the sar command

Another important option to the sar command is –q, which shows processor queue statistics. A processor queue is an area of RAM that stores information temporarily for quick retrieval by the CPU. To view processor queue statistics every five seconds, you can execute the following command:

```
[root@server1 ~]# sar -q 1 5
Linux 3.11.10-301.fc20.x86_64 (server1)  11/01/2015 _x86_64_  (2 CPU)

08:34:36 AM   runq-sz   plist-sz  ldavg-1   ldavg-5   ldavg-15  blocked
08:34:37 AM   0         252       0.00      0.00      0.00      0
08:34:38 AM   0         252       0.00      0.00      0.00      0
08:34:39 AM   0         252       0.00      0.00      0.00      0
08:34:40 AM   0         252       0.00      0.00      0.00      0
08:34:41 AM   0         252       0.00      0.00      0.00      0
Average:      0         252       0.00      0.00      0.00      0
[root@server1 ~]# _
```

The runq-sz (run queue size) indicates the number of processes that are waiting for execution on the processor run queue. For most Intel architectures, this number is typically 2 or less on average.

A runq-sz much greater than 2 for long periods of time indicates that the CPU is too slow to respond to system requests.

The plist-sz (process list size) value indicates the number of processes currently running in memory, and the ldavg-1 (load average −1 minute), ldavg-5 (load average −5 minutes), and ldavg-15 (load average −15 minutes) values represent an average CPU load for the last 1 minute, 5 minutes, and 15 minutes, respectively. These four statistics display an overall picture of processor activity. A rapid increase in these values is typically caused by CPU-intensive software that is running on the system.

The blocked value represents the number of tasks currently blocked from completion because they are waiting for I/O requests to complete. If this value is high, there are likely one or more disk devices that cannot keep up with system requests.

Recall that all Linux systems use a swap partition to store information that cannot fit into physical memory; this information is sent to and from the swap partition in units called pages. The number of pages that are sent to the swap partition (pswpin/s) and the pages that are taken from the swap partition (pswpout/s) can be viewed using the −W option to the sar command, as shown in the following output:

```
[root@server1 ~]# sar -W 1 5
Linux 3.11.10-301.fc20.x86_64 (server1) 11/01/2015 _x86_64_ (2 CPU)

08:37:01 AM       pswpin/s       pswpout/s
08:37:02 AM         0.00            0.00
08:37:03 AM         0.00            0.00
08:37:04 AM         0.00            0.00
08:37:05 AM         0.00            0.00
08:37:06 AM         0.00            0.00
Average:            0.00            0.00
[root@server1 ~]# _
```

If a large number of pages are being sent to and taken from the swap partition, the system will suffer from slower performance. To remedy this, you can add more physical memory (RAM) to the system.

Other Performance Monitoring Utilities

The sysstat package utilities are not the only performance-monitoring utilities available on Linux systems. The top utility discussed in Chapter 9 also displays CPU statistics, memory usage, swap usage, and average CPU load at the top of the screen, as shown here:

```
top - 08:40:07 up 22:43,  3 users,  load average: 0.00, 0.00, 0.00
Tasks: 166 total, 1 running, 165 sleeping, 0 stopped, 0 zombie
Cpu(s): 0.5%us, 0.3%sy, 0.0%ni, 99.2%id, 0.0%wa, 0.0%hi, 0.0%si, 0.0%st
KiB Mem:  961284 total, 814576 used, 146708 free, 126036 buffers
KiB Swap: 4095992 total,    212 used, 4095780 free,  480740 cached

  PID USER   PR NI  VIRT   RES   SHR  S %CPU %MEM   TIME+ COMMAND
 5693 root   20  0  2696  1120   852  R  1.0  0.1 0:00.08 top
    1 root   20  0  2828  1312  1144  S  0.0  0.1 0:01.43 init
    2 root   20  0     0     0     0  S  0.0  0.0 0:00.00 kthreadd
    3 root   RT  0     0     0     0  S  0.0  0.0 0:00.01 migration/0
    4 root   20  0     0     0     0  S  0.0  0.0 0:00.11 ksoftirqd/0
```

14

```
    5  root RT  0        0        0        0 S   0.0  0.0  0:00.00 watchdog/0
    6  root RT  0        0        0        0 S   0.0  0.0  0:00.01 migration/1
    7  root 20  0        0        0        0 S   0.0  0.0  0:00.45 ksoftirqd/1
    8  root RT  0        0        0        0 S   0.0  0.0  0:00.00 watchdog/1
    9  root 20  0        0        0        0 S   0.0  0.0  0:00.66 events/0
   10  root 20  0        0        0        0 S   0.0  0.0  0:00.57 events/1
   11  root 20  0        0        0        0 S   0.0  0.0  0:00.00 cpuset
   12  root 20  0        0        0        0 S   0.0  0.0  0:00.00 khelper
```

Furthermore, the **free command** can be used to display the total amounts of physical and swap memory in kilobytes and their utilizations, as shown in the following output:

```
[root@server1 ~]# free
                total       used       free     shared    buffers     cached
Mem:           961284     814820     146464          0     126120     480740
-/+ buffers/cache:        207960     753324
Swap:         4095992        212    4095780
[root@server1 ~]# _
```

The Linux kernel reserves some memory for its own use (`cached`) to hold requests from hardware devices (`buffers`); the `total` memory in the preceding output is calculated with and without these values to indicate how much memory the system has reserved. The output from the preceding `free` command indicates that there is sufficient memory in the system because little swap is used and a great deal of free physical memory is available.

Like the free utility, the vmstat utility can be used to indicate whether more physical memory is required by measuring swap performance:

```
[root@server1 ~]# vmstat
procs --------- memory---------- -swap- --io-- system ----- cpu-----
 r b swpd    free    buff   cache si so bi bo  in cs us sy id wa st
 1 0  212 146496 126144  480752  0  0  5  2  49 51  0  0 99  0  0
[root@server1 ~]# _
```

The **vmstat command** shown in the previous output indicates more information than the free command used earlier, including the following:

- The number of processes waiting to be run (`r`)
- The number of sleeping processes (`b`)
- The amount of swap memory used, in Kilobytes (`swpd`)
- The amount of free physical memory (`free`)
- The amount of memory used by buffers, in Kilobytes (`buff`)
- The amount of memory used as cache (`cache`)
- The amount of memory in Kilobytes per second swapped in to the disk (`si`)
- The amount of memory in Kilobytes per second swapped out to the disk (`so`)
- The number of blocks per second sent to block devices (`bi`)
- The number of blocks per second received from block devices (`bo`)
- The number of interrupts sent to the CPU per second (`in`)

- The number of context changes sent to the CPU per second (cs)
- The CPU user time (us)
- The CPU system time (sy)
- The CPU idle time (id)
- The time spent waiting for I/O (wa)
- The time stolen from a virtual machine (st)

Thus, the output from vmstat shown previously indicates that little swap memory is being used because swpd is 212 KB and si and so are both zero; however, it also indicates that the reason for this is that the system is not running many processes at the current time (r=1, id=99).

Security

In the past decade, hundreds of new services have been made available to Linux systems, and the number of Linux users has risen to tens of millions. In addition, Linux systems today are typically made available across networks such as the Internet. As a result, Linux is more prone today to security loopholes and attacks, both locally and from across networks. To protect your Linux computer, you should take steps to improve local and network security as well as understand how to detect intruders who manage to breach your Linux system.

Securing the Local Computer

One of the most important security-related practices is to limit access to the physical Linux computer itself. If a malicious user has access to the Linux computer, that user could boot the computer using a USB flash drive, CD, or DVD that contains a small operating system and use it to access files on the partitions on the hard disk of the Linux computer without having to log in to the operating system installed on the hard disk. To prevent this, you should lock important computers, such as Linux servers, in a specific room to which only Linux administrators or trusted users have key access. This room is commonly called a **server closet**. Unfortunately, some Linux computers, such as Linux workstations, must be located in public areas. For these computers, you should remove the CD and DVD drives from the computer. In addition, you should ensure that the boot order listed in the computer BIOS prevents booting from the USB ports, as well as ensure that a system BIOS password is set to prevent other users from changing the boot order.

Another important security consideration for Linux computers is to limit access to graphical desktops and shells. If you walk away from your workstation for a few minutes and leave yourself logged in to the system, another person can use your computer while you are away. To avoid such security breaches, it is good security practice to lock your desktop environment or exit your command-line shell before leaving the computer.

Both the GNOME and KDE desktop environments allow you to lock your screen. For the GNOME desktop, you can click the power symbol icon in the upper-right corner menu and choose the lock icon. To use your desktop again, you need to enter your password.

While it is good practice to exit a command-line shell before leaving your workstation, doing so necessarily ends any background processes because the parent of those processes is your shell. If you run background processes that take a long time to complete, you can avoid problems associated with exiting the command-line shell by running the processes using the **nohup command**. This allows you to exit your command-line shell without ending any background processes. For example, to run the updatedb command and then exit your system (so that you can leave your workstation), perform the following commands:

```
[root@server1 ~]# nohup updatedb &
[1] 3773
nohup: ignoring input and appending output to 'nhup.out'
[root@server1 ~]# exit

Fedora release 20 (Heisenbug)
Kernel 3.11.10-301.fc20.x86_64 on an x86_64 (tty2)

server1 login:
```

If you have root access to a Linux system, it is important to minimize the time that you are logged in as the root user to reduce the chance that another user can access your terminal if you accidentally leave your system without locking your desktop or exiting your shell. It is best practice to create a regular user account that you can use to check e-mails and perform other day-to-day tasks. Recall from Chapter 2 that you can then use the su command to obtain root access only when you need to perform an administrative task. When you are finished, you can use the exit command to return to your previous shell, where you are logged in as a regular user account.

 The root user can use the su command to switch to any other user account without specifying the user account password.

Still, some users, such as software developers, need to run certain commands as the root user in certain situations. Instead of giving them the root password, it is best to give them the ability to run certain commands as the root user via the **sudo command**. The sudo command checks the /etc/sudoers file to see if you have rights to run a certain command as a different user. The following /etc/sudoers file gives software developers mary and bob the ability to run the kill and killall commands as the root user on the computers server1 and server2:

```
[root@server1 ~]# cat /etc/sudoers
User_Alias SD = mary, bob
Cmnd_Alias KILL = /bin/kill, /usr/bin/killall
Host_Alias SERVERS = server1, server2

SD    SERVERS = (root)   KILL
[root@server1 ~]# _
```

Now, if mary needs to kill the cron daemon on server1 (which was started as the root user) to test a program that she wrote, she needs to use the sudo command, as shown in the following output, and supply her own password:

```
[mary@server1 ~]$ ps -ef |grep crond
root    2281    1  0 21:20 ?    00:00:00 crond
[mary@server1 ~]$ kill -9 2281
```

```
-bash: kill: (2281) - Operation not permitted
[mary@server1 ~]$ sudo kill -9 2281
[sudo] password for mary: ******
[mary@server1 ~]$ _
```

Protecting Against Network Attacks

Recall from earlier in this chapter that network services listen for network traffic on a certain port number and interact with that traffic. As long as network services exist on a computer, there is always the possibility that hackers can manipulate the network service by interacting with it in unusual ways. One example of this type of network attack is a **buffer overrun**, which can replace program information used by the network service in memory with new program information, consequently altering how the network service operates.

Network Security Essentials The first step to securing your computer against network attacks such as buffer overruns is to minimize the number of network services running. If you run only the minimum number of network services necessary for your organization, you greatly reduce the chance of network attacks. To see what network services are running on your network, you can run the **nmap** (network mapper) command. The following output demonstrates how nmap can be used to determine the number of services running on the server1 computer:

```
[root@server1 ~]# nmap -sT server1.class.com
Starting Nmap 6.45 (http://nmap.org) at 2015-11-01 15:14 EDT
Nmap scan report for server1.class.com (192.168.1.105)
Host is up (0.0019s latency).
rDNS record for 192.168.1.105: server1.class.com
Not shown: 995 closed ports
PORT       STATE     SERVICE
22/tcp     open      ssh
111/tcp    open      rpcbind
631/tcp    open      ipp
5903/tcp   open      vnc-3
6003/tcp   open      X11:3

Nmap done: 1 IP address (1 host up) scanned in 0.13 seconds
[root@server1 ~]# _
```

 The nmap command is not normally installed on a Linux distribution by default, but it can be added from a software repository.

From the preceding output, you can determine which services are running on your computer by viewing the service name or by searching the descriptions for the port numbers in the /etc/services file or on the Internet. For services that are not needed, ensure that they are not started automatically when entering your runlevel.

For services that must be used because they are essential to your organization, you can take certain steps to ensure that they are as secure as possible. You should ensure that network

14

service daemons are not run as the root user on the system when possible. If a hacker gains access to your system via a network service daemon run as the root user, the hacker has root access as well. Many network daemons, such as Apache, set the user account by which they execute in their configuration files.

Similarly, for daemons such as Apache that run as a non-root user, you should ensure that the shell listed in /etc/passwd for the daemon is set to an invalid shell, such as /sbin/nologin. If a hacker attempted to remotely log into the system using a well-known daemon account, she would not be able to get a BASH shell. Instead, the /sbin/nologin simply prints the warning listed in the /etc/nologin.txt file to the screen and exits. If the /etc/nologin.txt file doesn't exist, the /sbin/nologin program prints a standard warning.

In addition, because network attacks are reported in the open source community, new versions of network services usually include fixes for known network attacks. As such, these new versions are more resilient to network attacks. Because of this, it is good form to periodically check for new versions of network services, install them, and check the associated documentation for new security-related parameters that can be set in the configuration file.

If you use network services that are started by inetd or xinetd, you can use TCP wrappers to provide extra security. A **TCP wrapper** is a program (/usr/sbin/tcpd) that can start a network daemon. To enable TCP wrappers, you must modify the /etc/inetd.conf file (for inetd) or the appropriate file in the /etc/xinetd.d directory (for xinetd) and start the network daemon as an argument to the TCP wrapper. For the telnet daemon started by xinetd, you modify the /etc/xinetd.d/telnet file, as shown in the following example:

```
[root@server1 ~]# cat /etc/xinetd.d/telnet
# default: on
# description: The telnet server serves telnet sessions; it uses \
#      unencrypted username/password pairs for authentication.
service telnet
{
            flags             = REUSE
            socket_type       = stream
            wait              = no
            user              = root
            server            = /usr/sbin/tcpd
            server_args       = /usr/sbin/in.telnetd
            log_on_failure    += USERID
            disable           = no
}
[root@server1 ~]# _
```

Now, the telnet daemon (/usr/sbin/in.telnetd) will be started by the TCP wrapper (/usr/sbin/tcpd). Before a TCP wrapper starts a network daemon, it first checks the /etc/hosts.allow and /etc/hosts.deny files. This allows you to restrict the network service such that it can only be accessed by certain hosts within your organization. The following /etc/hosts.allow and /etc/hosts.deny files only give the computers client1 and client2 the ability to use the telnet utility to connect to your telnet server.

```
[root@server1 ~]# cat /etc/hosts.deny
in.telnetd: ALL
```

```
[root@server1 ~]# _
[root@server1 ~]# cat /etc/hosts.allow
in.telnetd: client1, client2
[root@server1 ~]# _
```

Another important component of network security involves local file permissions. If everyone had read permission on the /etc/shadow file, any user could read the encrypted passwords for all user accounts, including the root user, and possibly decrypt the password using a decryption program. Fortunately, the default permissions on the /etc/shadow file allow read permission for the root user only to minimize this possibility. However, similar permission problems exist with many other important files, and hackers typically exploit these files as a result. Thus, you need to carefully examine the permissions on files and directories associated with system and network services.

Take, for example, the Apache Web server discussed in Chapter 13. Apache daemons are run as the user apache and the group apache by default. These daemons read HTML files from the document root directory such that they can give the information to client Web browsers. The following directory listing from a sample document root directory shows that the Apache daemons also have write permission because they own the index.html file:

```
[root@server1 ~]# ls -l /var/www/html
total 64
-rw-r--r-- 1 apache apache 61156 Sep 5 08:36 index.html
[root@server1 ~]# _
```

Thus, if a hacker were able to manipulate an Apache daemon, the hacker would have write access to the index.html file and would be able to modify it. It is secure practice to ensure that the index.html is owned by the Web developer (who needs to modify the file) and that the Apache daemons are given read access only through membership in the other category. If your Web developer logs into the system as the user account webma, you could perform the following commands to change the permissions on the Web content and verify the results:

```
[root@server1 ~]# chown webma /var/www/html/index.html
[root@server1 ~]# ls -l /var/www/html
total 64
-rw-r--r-- 1 webma apache  61156 Sep 5 08:36 index.html
[root@server1 ~]# _
```

Configuring a Firewall Another method that you can use to ensure that network services are as secure as possible is to configure a firewall on your Linux computer using a component of the Linux kernel called **netfilter**. Recall from Chapter 1 that firewalls can be used in your organization to block unwanted network traffic; as a result, firewalls are typically enabled on router interfaces.

Netfilter discards certain network packets according to **chains** of **rules** that are stored in your computer's memory. By default, you can specify firewall rules for three types of chains:

- INPUT chain, for network packets destined for your computer
- FORWARD chain, for network packets that must pass through your computer (if you are a router)
- OUTPUT chain, for network packets that originate from your computer

14

 Netfilter can also be used to configure a Linux computer with two or more NICs as a NAT router. To do this, you would use the PREROUTING, OUTPUT, and POSTROUTING chains. Consult the `iptables` manual page for more information.

In most cases, no rules exist for the INPUT, FORWARD, or OUTPUT chains after a Linux installation. To create rules that are used for each chain, you must use the **iptables** command. Rules can be based on the source IP address, destination IP address, protocol used (TCP, UDP, ICMP), or packet status. For example, to flush all previous rules from memory, specify that forwarded packets are dropped by default and that packets are only to be forwarded if they originate from the 192.168.1.0 network, you can use the following commands:

```
[root@server1 ~]# iptables -F
[root@server1 ~]# iptables -P FORWARD DROP
[root@server1 ~]# iptables -A FORWARD -s 192.168.1.0/24 -j ACCEPT
[root@server1 ~]#
```

You can then verify the list of rules for each chain in memory by using the following command:

```
[root@server1 ~]# iptables -L
Chain INPUT (policy ACCEPT)
target       prot opt source              destination

Chain INPUT (policy DROP)
target       prot opt source              destination
ACCEPT       all -- 192.168.1.0/24        anywhere

Chain INPUT (policy ACCEPT)
target       prot opt source              destination
[root@server1 ~]#
```

The previous firewall example uses static packet filtering rules. Most technologies today start by using a specific port and then switch to a random port above 30000. A good example of this is SSH. The first SSH packet is addressed to port 22, but the port number is changed in the return packet to a random port above 30000 for subsequent traffic. In a static filter, you would need to allow traffic for all ports above 30000 in order to use SSH.

Instead of doing this, you can use a dynamic (or stateful) packet filter rule by specifying the −m state option to the `iptables` command. **Stateful packet filters** remember traffic that was originally allowed in an existing session and adjust their rules appropriately. For example, to forward all packets from your internal interface eth1 to your external interface eth0 on your Linux router that are addressed to port 22, you could use the following command:

```
[root@server1 ~]# iptables -A FORWARD -i eth1 -o eth0 -m state
--state NEW -dport 22 -j ACCEPT
[root@server1 ~]#
```

Next, you can allow all subsequent packets that are part of an allowed existing session, as shown in the following output (remember that only SSH is allowed):

```
[root@server1 ~]# iptables -A FORWARD -i eth1 -o eth0 -m state
--state ESTABLISHED,RELATED -j ACCEPT
[root@server1 ~]#
```

Option	Description
-s address	Specifies the source address of packets for a rule.
-d address	Specifies the destination address of packets for a rule.
-sport port#	Specifies the source port number for a rule.
-dport port#	Specifies the destination port number for a rule.
-p protocol	Specifies the protocol type for a rule.
-i interface	Specifies the input network interface.
-o interface	Specifies the output network interface.
-j action	Specifies the action that is taken for a rule.
-m match	Specifies a match parameter that should be used within the rule. The most common match used is state, which creates a stateful packet filtering firewall.
-A chain	Specifies the chain used.
-L chain	Lists rules for a certain chain. If no chain is given, all chains are listed.
-P policy	Specifies the default policy for a certain chain type.
-D number	Deletes a rule for a chain specified by additional arguments. Rules start at number 1.
-R number	Replaces a rule for a chain specified by additional arguments. Rules start at number 1.
-F chain	Removes all rules for a certain chain. If no chain is specified, it removes all rules for all chains.

Table 14-2 Common iptables options

Table 14-2 provides a list of common options to the iptables command.

The order in which firewall rules are defined is the order in which they are applied. Normally, firewall rules are defined to first DROP all traffic destined for the computer (the INPUT chain) and allow only specific traffic by port number.

You can use the ip6tables command to configure firewall rules for IPV6.

Because chains and rules are stored in memory, they are lost when your computer is shut down. To ensure that they are loaded on each boot on a Fedora 20 system, run the service iptables save command to save all current chains and rules to the /etc/sysconfig/iptables file. To ensure that they are loaded on each boot on an Ubuntu Server 14.04 system, simply run the apt-get install iptables-persistent command; during the installation of the iptables-persistent package, you will be asked if you wish to save your iptables configuration to a file loaded by a line within /etc/network/interfaces.

14

Older Linux kernels (version 2.2.36 and earlier) used the `ipchains` command to provide firewall services; support for this utility is not supported by newer Linux kernels.

Since firewall rules can quickly become complex, some Linux distributions, such as Fedora 20, implement a **firewall daemon (firewalld)** that can configure iptables with more flexibility through the use of network zones and service names. A **network zone** defines the level of trust for network connections and can be mutable (modification to its definition is allowed) or immutable (its definition cannot be changed). Table 14-3 lists common network zones used by firewalld.

The default zone used on your system is defined in /etc/firewalld/firewalld.conf, and custom zone configuration is stored in /etc/firewalld/zones. You can manage zones and firewall rules that allow or deny traffic by service or port through the use of the **firewall-cmd command**. Some common options to the `firewall-cmd` command are listed in Table 14-4.

To define a firewall exception for postgresql in your default (current) zone and also ensure that this exception is loaded at boot time, you could use the following commands:

```
[root@server1 ~]# firewall-cmd --add-service=postgresql
success
[root@server1 ~]# firewall-cmd --permanent --add-service=postgresql
success
[root@server1 ~]# _
```

You can instead define a firewall exception for traffic by port number. For example, to define a firewall exception for SSH (TCP port 22) in your default (current) zone and also ensure that this exception is loaded at boot time, you could use the following commands:

```
[root@server1 ~]# firewall-cmd --add-port=22/tcp
success
```

Network Zone	Type	Description
drop	Immutable	Deny all incoming connections; outgoing ones are accepted.
block	Immutable	Deny all incoming connections, with ICMP host-prohibited messages issued to the sender.
trusted	Immutable	Allow all network connections.
public	Mutable	Public areas, do not trust other computers.
external	Mutable	For computers with masquerading enabled, protecting a local network.
dmz	Mutable	For computers publicly accessible with restricted access.
work	Mutable	For trusted work areas.
home	Mutable	For trusted home network connections.
internal	Mutable	For internal network, restrict incoming connections.

Table 14-3   Common network zones

Option	Description
`--get-zones`	Displays all available network zones.
`--get-services`	Displays a list of names used by firewalld to identify network services.
`--get-default-zone`	Specifies the source port number for a rule.
`--set-default-zone=zone`	Specifies the destination port number for a rule.
`--get-active-zones`	Displays the network interfaces that are active for each network zone.
`--list-all-zones`	Displays the services that are enabled (allowed) for each network zone.
`--list-all`	Displays the services that are enabled (allowed) for the current network zone.
`--zone= zone` `--list-all`	Displays the services that are enabled (allowed) for the specified network zone (*zone*).
`--add-service=service`	Enable (allow) the specified *service* within the current network zone.
`--add-service=service` `--permanent`	Ensure that the specified *service* is enabled (allowed) within the current network zone at boot time.
`--add-port= port`	Enable (allow) the specified *port* within the current network zone.
`--add-port= port` `--permanent`	Ensure that the specified *port* is enabled (allowed) within the current network zone at boot time.
`--remove-service=service`	Disable (disallow) the specified *service* within the current network zone.
`--remove-service=service` `--permanent`	Ensure that the specified *service* is disabled (disallowed) within the current network zone at boot time.
`--remove-port=port`	Disable (disallow) the specified *port* within the current network zone.
`--remove-port=port` `--permanent`	Ensure that the specified *port* is disabled (disallowed) within the current network zone at boot time.
`--query-service=service`	Returns yes if the specified *service* is enabled (allowed) within the current network zone, and no if it is not.
`--query-port=port`	Returns yes if the specified *port* is enabled (allowed) within the current network zone, and no if it is not.

Table 14-4   Common firewall-cmd options

```
[root@server1 ~]# firewall-cmd --permanent --add-port=22/tcp
success
[root@server1 ~]# _
```

You used the `firewall-cmd` command in the hands-on projects in Chapter 13 to allow traffic destined to your Fedora Linux virtual machine by service name.

Many Linux distributions also provide a graphical firewall configuration utility that can be used to configure netfilter by service name or port. On Fedora 20, the **Firewall Configuration utility** shown in Figure 14-4 automatically creates netfilter rules based on your selections via firewalld. You can start the Firewall Configuration utility within the GNOME desktop by opening the Activites menu and navigating to Show Applications, Sundry, Firewall.

14

Figure 14-4 The Firewall Configuration utility

Configuring SELinux Security Enhanced Linux (SELinux) is a series of kernel patches and utilities created by the National Security Agency (NSA) that enforce role-based security on your system using security profiles and policies that prevent applications from being used to access resources and system components in insecure ways. Although it is enabled by default on Fedora 20, it is normally disabled on most Linux systems following installation.

NOTE To learn more about SELinux, visit *https://www.nsa.gov/research/ selinux/index.shtml.*

To enable SELinux, you can edit the /etc/selinux/config file and set one of the following SELINUX options:

- SELINUX = enforcing (policy settings are enforced by SELinux)
- SELINUX = permissive (SELinux generates warnings only and logs events)
- SELINUX = disabled (SELinux is disabled)

Next, you can select an SELINUX policy by configuring one of the following SELINUX-TYPE options within the /etc/selinux/config file:

- SELINUXTYPE = targeted (only targeted network daemons are protected)
- SELINUXTYPE = strict (all daemons are protected)

Most Linux systems that use SELinux have definitions for the targeted policy that protect the system from malicious applications that can damage system files or compromise security. After modifying the /etc/selinux/config file to enable SELinux, you must reboot to relabel the system for the changes to take effect. Once enabled, you can modify the SELinux-targeted policy settings by modifying the files within the /etc/selinux/targeted directory.

Recall from Chapter 3 that any important files on the filesystem that are monitored or managed by SELinux have a period (.) appended to their mode.

You can use the **sestatus** command to view your current SELinux status:

```
[root@server1 ~]# sestatus -v
SELinux status:             enabled
SELinuxfs mount:            /sys/fs/selinux
SELinux root directory:     /etc/selinux
Loaded policy name:         targeted
Current mode:               enforcing
Mode from config file:      enforcing
Policy MLS status:          enabled
Policy deny_unknown status: allowed
Max kernel policy version:  28

Process contexts:
Current context:            unconfined_u:unconfined_r:unconfined_t:
                            s0-s0:c0.c1023
Init context:               system_u:system_r:init_t:s0
/usr/sbin/sshd              system_u:system_r:sshd_t:s0-s0:c0.c1023

File contexts:
Controlling terminal:       unconfined_u:object_r:user_devpts_t:s0
/etc/passwd                 system_u:object_r:passwd_file_t:s0
/etc/shadow                 system_u:object_r:shadow_t:s0
/bin/bash                   system_u:object_r:shell_exec_t:s0
/bin/login                  system_u:object_r:login_exec_t:s0
/bin/sh                     system_u:object_r:bin_t:s0 -> system_u:
/sbin/agetty                system_u:object_r:getty_exec_t:s0
/sbin/init                  system_u:object_r:bin_t:s0 -> system_u:
/usr/sbin/sshd              system_u:object_r:sshd_exec_t:s0

[root@server1 ~]# _
```

Many Linux distributions provide a graphical utility that can be used to view any warnings or alerts generated by SELinux regarding unsafe application access, as well as identify and remedy problems in which SELinux prevents access to a desired application. For example, on Fedora 20 you can use the SELinux Troubleshooter utility, which can be started within the GNOME desktop by navigating to Activities, Show Applications, Sundry, SELinux Troubleshooter.

Configuring AppArmor AppArmor is an alternative to SELinux that provides a similar type of protection for applications and systems resources. It consists of a kernel module and a series of utilities that you can use to associate a set of restrictions for individual programs on a Linux system. Restrictions for each application are stored within text files named for the program under the /etc/apparmor.d directory; each text file is called an **AppArmor profile**. For example, the AppArmor profile for the CUPS daemon (/usr/sbin/cupsd) would be stored within the /etc/apparmor.d/usr.sbin.cupsd file.

To view the available settings that you can configure within an AppArmor profile, simply run the `man apparmor.d` command.

After modifying an AppArmor profile, you must reload the profile within the AppArmor kernel module. To reload the CUPS daemon AppArmor profile, you could use the `apparmor_parser -r /etc/apparmor.d/usr.bin.cupsd` command. Alternatively, to reload all AppArmor profiles, you could use the `/etc /init.d/apparmor reload` command.

AppArmor profiles can be enforced by AppArmor (called enforce mode) or simply used to generate warnings and log events (called complain mode). To view the AppArmor profiles configured for each mode, as well as the active processes on the system that are being managed by AppArmor, you can run the **apparmor_status** command, as shown here:

```
[root@server1 ~]# apparmor_status
apparmor module is loaded.
12 profiles are loaded.
12 profiles are in enforce mode.
   /sbin/dhclient
   /usr/lib/NetworkManager/nm-dhcp-client.action
   /usr/lib/connman/scripts/dhclient-script
   /usr/lib/cups/backend/cups-pdf
   /usr/lib/libvirt/virt-aa-helper
   /usr/sbin/cups-browsed
   /usr/sbin/cupsd
   /usr/sbin/libvirtd
   /usr/sbin/mysqld
   /usr/sbin/named
   /usr/sbin/ntpd
   /usr/sbin/tcpdump
0 profiles are in complain mode.
7 processes have profiles defined.
7 processes are in enforce mode.
   /sbin/dhclient (1900)
   /usr/sbin/cups-browsed (2284)
   /usr/sbin/cupsd (3195)
   /usr/sbin/libvirtd (2407)
   /usr/sbin/mysqld (2523)
   /usr/sbin/named (2276)
   /usr/sbin/ntpd (3274)
```

```
   0 processes are in complain mode.
   0 processes are unconfined but have a profile defined.
[root@server1 ~]# _
```

To switch an AppArmor profile to enforce mode, you can use the **aa-enforce** command. Alternatively, you can use the **aa-complain** command to switch an AppArmor profile to complain mode. For example, to switch the CUPS daemon (/usr/sbin/cupsd) to complain mode, you could run the following command:

```
[root@server1 ~]# aa-complain /usr/sbin/cupsd
Setting /usr/sbin/cupsd to complain mode.
[root@server1 ~]# _
```

Although AppArmor is installed by default on Ubuntu Server 14.04, you must install the apparmor-utils package from a software repository in order to use the `aa-complain` and `aa-enforce` commands.

To learn more about AppArmor, visit http://wiki.apparmor.net.

Using Encryption to Protect Network Data

Since network packets pass through many different computers and network devices, the data within them could easily be intercepted and read by hackers. To prevent this, many technologies use an encryption algorithm to protect the data before it is transmitted on the network. An encryption algorithm uses a series of mathematical steps in sequence to scramble data. Since the steps within encryption algorithms are widely known, nearly all encryption algorithms use a random component called a key to modify the steps within the algorithm.

Network technologies typically use **asymmetric encryption** to protect the data that travels across the network. Asymmetric encryption uses a pair of keys that are uniquely generated on each system: a **public key** and a **private key**. You can think of a public key as the opposite of a private key. If you encrypt data using a public key, that data can only be decrypted using the matching private key. Alternatively, if you encrypt data using a private key, that data can only be decrypted using the matching public key. Each system must contain at least one public/private key pair. The public key is freely distributed to any other host on the network, whereas the private key is used only by the system and never distributed.

Say, for example, that you wish to send an encrypted message from your computer (host A) to another computer (host B). Your computer would first obtain the public key from host B and use it to encrypt the message. Next, your computer will send the encrypted message across the network to host B, at which point host B uses its private key to decrypt the message. Since host B is the only computer on the network that possesses the private key that matches the public key that you used to encrypt the message, host B is the only computer on the network that can decrypt the message.

14

You can also use private keys to authenticate a message. If host A encrypts a message using its private key and sends that message to host B, host B (and any other host on the network) can easily obtain the matching public key from host A to decrypt the message. By successfully decrypting the message, host B has proved that it must have been encrypted using host A's private key. Since host A is the only computer on the network that possesses this private key, host B has proven that the message was sent by host A and not another computer that has impersonated the message.

A message that has been encrypted using a private key is called a **digital signature**.

The two most common technologies that provide asymmetric encryption on Linux systems are Secure Shell (SSH) and **GNU Privacy Guard (GPG)**.

Working with SSH Recall from Chapter 12 that SSH allows you to securely administer a remote Linux system by encrypting all traffic that passes between the two computers. By default, SSH uses the **Rivest Shamir Adleman (RSA)** asymmetric algorithm to encrypt data and the **Digital Signature Algorithm (DSA)** asymmetric algorithm to digitally sign data.

System-wide RSA and DSA public/private key pairs are generated the first time the SSH daemon is started. These key pairs are stored in the /etc/ssh directory for all future sessions:

- ssh_host_dsa_key contains the DSA private key
- ssh_host_rsa_key contains the RSA private key
- ssh_host_dsa_key.pub contains the DSA public key
- ssh_host_rsa_key.pub contains the RSA public key

For remote administration, the system-wide keys are sufficient, but SSH can also be used to protect the network traffic used by other network services by enclosing the network traffic within encrypted SSH packets (a process called **tunneling**). SSH tunnels are used by a wide variety of programs today.

The most basic type of SSH tunnel involves sending X Windows traffic over an SSH session, as was discussed in Chapter 12. By adding the −X option to the ssh command, any graphical utilities executed during the remote SSH session will be tunneled to X Windows on your computer.

Most programs that use SSH tunnels require that all users using the program have their own SSH key. Recall from Chapter 12 that the ssh-keygen command can generate or regenerate SSH keys. If you run the ssh-keygen −t rsa command, the following files will be created in the ~/.ssh directory:

- id_rsa contains the user's RSA private key
- id_rsa.pub contains the user's RSA public key

Passwords and Keys ×

File Edit Remote View Help

Passwords
   🔒 Login
Certificates
   📁 Gnome2 Key Storage
   📁 User Key Storage
   ⚙ System Trust
   ⚙ Default Trust
PGP Keys
   🔑 GnuPG keys
Secure Shell
   🔑 OpenSSH keys

Filter

Figure 14-5 The Passwords and Keys utility

Alternatively, if you run the `ssh-keygen -t dsa` command, the following files will be created in the ~/.ssh directory:

- id_dsa contains the user's DSA private key
- id_dsa.pub contains the user's DSA public key

The `ssh-keygen` command prompts you to choose an optional passphrase that protects the private key. If you set a passphrase, you will need to enter the passphrase each time that the private key is used.

These keys can then be used to secure communication to other computers. However, each user will need to authenticate to other computers before SSH is used to encrypt the data. Since private keys can also be used as a form of authentication, you can create an **SSH identity** (using the **ssh-add command**) for your user account and use the **SSH agent** (ssh-agent) to automatically authenticate to other computers using digital signatures. On systems that contain a desktop environment, an additional utility may provide for the SSH agent and SSH identities. For example, on Fedora 20, the SSH agent and SSH identities are provided by the GNOME keyring daemon (gnome-keyring-daemon) and managed by the Passwords and Keys utility shown in Figure 14-5. You can start this utility within the GNOME desktop environment by navigating to Activities, Show Applications, Utilities, Passwords and Keys.

Working with GPG GPG is an open source version of the Pretty Good Privacy (PGP) system that was popular in the 1990s for encrypting e-mail and e-mail attachments prior to sending them to other hosts on the Internet. Each GPG user has a public/private key pair, which is used for encryption as well as authentication. GPG authentication uses a trust model that involves users digitally signing other user's public keys with their private key. Say, for example, that UserA has digitally signed UserB's public key and vice versa. This allows UserA and UserB to send and receive e-mail without requiring authentication. If UserB digitally signs UserC's public key and vice versa, then UserA, UserB, and UserC can send and receive e-mail without requiring authentication.

Like SSH, GPG typically uses RSA and DSA key pairs for asymmetric encryption and digital signing, respectively. These keys and associated GPG configuration options are stored within the ~/.gnupg directory for each user.

14

Although you can manage keys, encrypt data, and digitally sign other user's public keys using the **gpg command**, it is much easier to use a graphical utility such as the Passwords and Keys utility within Fedora 20. Additionally, many graphical e-mail programs for Linux, such as Evolution, have built-in GPG management tools and wizards that allow you to easily configure GPG keys.

Detecting Intrusion

Although you can take many security precautions on your Linux computers, there is always the chance that someone will gain access to your system either locally or from across a network. Fortunately, log files contain information or irregularities that can indicate if an intrusion has indeed occurred. To get the full benefit of the information stored in log files, you should regularly analyze the contents of the journald database (if your system uses Systemd) as well as the log files in the /var/log directory associated with the network services that are run on your computer.

At minimum, you should review system events associated with authentication to detect whether unauthorized users have logged in to the system. Network applications that authenticate users typically do so via **Pluggable Authentication Modules (PAM)**. PAM logs information to the journald database on systems that use Systemd, or to a log file under the /var/log directory on other systems, such as /var/log/secure or /var/log/auth.log. You should also check the /var/log/wtmp log file, which lists users who logged in to the system and received a BASH shell. Because this file is in binary format, you must use the who /var/log/wtmp command to view it, as shown in the following output:

```
[root@server1 ~]# who /var/log/wtmp
user1              pts/0        2015-09-05 11:21 (:0.0)
root               pts/1        2015-09-05 11:40 (10.0.1.3)
root               pts/1        2015-09-05 16:41 (10.0.1.3)
root               pts/1        2015-09-06 09:19 (10.0.1.3)
root               tty2         2015-09-06 10:16
postgres           tty2         2015-09-06 10:17
user1              tty1         2015-09-06 15:11 (:0)
root               pts/0        2015-09-06 15:23 (10.0.1.3)
user1              pts/1        2015-09-06 17:21 (:0.0)
user1              tty1         2015-09-07 09:58 (:0)
root               pts/0        2015-09-07 09:58 (10.0.1.3)
root               tty2         2015-09-07 10:01
root               pts/0        2015-09-07 18:06 (10.0.1.3)
root               pts/0        2015-09-08 06:58 (10.0.1.3)
root               pts/0        2015-09-08 11:51 (10.0.1.3)
user1              tty1         2015-09-08 15:05 (:0)
root               pts/0        2015-09-08 15:08 (10.0.1.3)
user1              pts/1        2015-09-08 15:11 (:0.0)
user1              tty1         2015-09-08 15:22 (:0)
root               pts/0        2015-09-08 15:23 (10.0.1.3)
root               tty3         2015-09-08 15:25
user1              pts/1        2015-09-08 15:25 (:0.0)
[root@server1 ~]# _
```

If a hacker has gained access to your system, he has likely changed certain files on the hard disk to gain more access, modify sensitive data, or vandalize services. The **lsof** (**list open files) command** can be used to list files that are currently being edited by users and system processes. Thus, you could use the lsof | grep root command to list the files that are currently open on the system by the root user. If there are key configuration files listed in the output that you are not currently editing, a hacker may have compromised your system.

Hackers often use a buffer overrun exploit to attempt to create executable files within the filesystem that are owned by the root user and have the SUID bit set. This allows the executable program to be run as the root user and gain access to the entire Linux system. As a result, you should periodically search for files on the filesystem that have the SUID bit set using the find / -type f -perm +4000 command.

Not all exploits need be performed as the root user. For example, hackers may use a malicious program that a user downloads to create a .forward file in the user's home directory. Any e-mail that the user receives will then be forwarded to the e-mail address listed in the ~/.forward file, which is usually an e-mail server that contains a script that records the user's e-mail address and sends unwanted e-mail on that user's behalf. To prevent this type of attack, you can create an empty .forward file in each user's home directory that is owned by the root user and has a mode of 000 to prevent users from modifying it.

 If you create and run custom shell scripts to perform security checks, you can use the **logger command** to create system log entries that alert you to potential problems.

Since the list of potential files that hackers can modify on a system is large, many Linux administrators use a program, such as **tripwire**, to check the integrity of important files and directories. You can use tripwire to take a checksum of key system files and periodically check the checksums on those files to ensure that they have not been modified by an intruder. Because tripwire can be used to detect intruders on a Linux system, it is referred to as an **Intrusion Detection System (IDS)**. Several IDS programs are available for Linux that can be used to detect hackers who are trying to gain access to your system or have done so already. Table 14-5 lists some common IDS programs.

Name	Description
Advanced Intrusion Detection Environment (AIDE)	An alternative to tripwire that has added functionality for checking the integrity of files and directories.
Integrity Checking Utility (ICU)	A PERL-based program that is designed to work with AIDE to check the integrity of Linux computers remotely across a network.
PortSentry	An IDS that monitors traffic on ports and allows you to detect whether hackers are probing your ports using port scanning utilities such as nmap.
Snort / Airsnort	A complex IDS that can be used to capture and monitor network packets. It can be used to detect a wide range of network attacks and port probing.
Linux Intrusion Detection System (LIDS)	An IDS that involves modifying the Linux kernel to increase process and file security as well as detect security breaches.
Simple WATCHer (SWATCH)	An IDS that monitors log files and alerts administrators when an intrusion is detected.

Table 14-5   Common Linux Intrusion Detection Systems

14

Chapter Summary

- After installation, Linux administrators monitor the system, perform proactive and reactive maintenance, and document important system information.

- Common troubleshooting procedures involve collecting data to isolate and determine the cause of system problems as well as implementing and testing solutions that can be documented for future use.

- Invalid hardware settings, absence of device drivers, and hard disk failure are common hardware-related problems on Linux systems.

- Software-related problems can be further categorized as application-related or operating system-related.

- Absence of program dependencies or shared libraries as well as program limits are common application-related problems, whereas X Windows, boot failure, and filesystem corruption are common operating system-related problems.

- Users can use assistive technologies to modify their desktop experience to suit their needs.

- System performance is affected by a variety of hardware and software factors, including the amount of RAM, CPU speed, and process load.

- Using performance monitoring utilities to create a baseline is helpful when diagnosing performance problems in the future. The sysstat package contains many useful performance monitoring commands.

- Securing a Linux computer involves improving local and network security as well as monitoring to detect intruders.

- By restricting access to your Linux computer and using the root account only when required via the su and sudo commands, you greatly improve local Linux security.

- Reducing the number of network services, implementing firewalls, enabling SELinux or AppArmor, performing service updates, using encryption, preventing services from running as the root user, restricting permissions on key files, and using TCP wrappers can greatly reduce the chance of network attacks.

- Analyzing log files and key system files as well as running IDS applications such as tripwire can be used to detect intruders.

Key Terms

aa-complain command A command used to set an AppArmor profile to complain mode.

aa-enforce command A command used to set an AppArmor profile to enforce mode.

AppArmor A Linux kernel module and related software packages that prevent malicious software from executing on a Linux system.

AppArmor profile A text file within the /etc/apparmor.d directory that lists application-specific restrictions.

apparmor_status command A command used to view the status of AppArmor and AppArmor profiles.

assistive technologies Software programs that cater to specific user needs.

asymmetric encryption A type of encryption that uses a key pair to encrypt and decrypt data.

baseline A measure of normal system activity.

buffer overrun An attack in which a network service is altered in memory.

bus mastering The process by which peripheral components perform tasks normally executed by the CPU.

chains The components of a firewall that specify the general type of network traffic to which rules apply.

digital signature Information that has been encrypted using a private key.

Digital Signature Algorithm (DSA) A common asymmetric encryption algorithm that is primarily used for creating digital signatures.

documentation The system information that is stored in a log book for future reference.

file handles The connections that a program makes to files on a filesystem.

Firewall Configuration utility A graphical firewall configuration utility within Fedora 20.

firewall daemon (firewalld) A daemon used on some Linux systems to provide for easier configuration of netfilter via the `ipchains` command.

`firewall-cmd` **command** A command used to view and configure firewalld zones, services, and rules.

`free` **command** A command used to display memory and swap statistics.

GNU Privacy Guard (GPG) An open source asymmetric encryption technology that is primarily used by e-mail programs.

`gpg` **command** A command used to encrypt and digitally sign information using GPG.

Intrusion Detection System (IDS) A program that can be used to detect unauthorized access to a Linux system.

`iostat` **(input/output statistics) command** A command that displays Input/Output statistics for block devices.

`iptables` **command** A command used to configure IPv4 rules for a netfilter firewall.

`ip6tables` **command** A command used to configure IPv6 rules for a netfilter firewall.

jabbering The process by which failing hardware components send large amounts of information to the CPU.

key A unique piece of information that is used within an encryption algorithm.

Knoppix Linux A small Linux distribution often installed on removeable media.

`ldconfig` **command** A command that updates the /etc/ld.so.conf and /etc/ld.so.cache files.

`ldd` **command** A command used to display the shared libraries used by a certain program.

`logger` **command** A command that can be used to write system log events.

`lscpu` **command** A command that lists hardware details for CPUs on the system.

`lsof` **(list open files) command** A command that lists the files that are currently being viewed or modified by software programs and users.

14

`lspci` **command**   A command that lists the hardware devices that are currently attached to the PCI bus on the system.

`lsusb` **command**   A command that lists the USB devices that are currently plugged into the system.

monitoring   The process by which system areas are observed for problems or irregularities.

`mpstat` **(multiple processor statistics) command**   A command that displays CPU statistics.

netfilter   The Linux kernel component that provides firewall and NAT capability on modern Linux systems.

network zone   A component of firewalld that defines the level of trust for network connections.

`nmap` **(network mapper) command**   A command that can be used to scan ports on network computers.

`nohup` **command**   A command that prevents other commands from exiting when the parent process is killed.

Pluggable Authentication Modules (PAM)   The component that handles authentication requests by daemons on a Linux system.

private key   An asymmetric encryption key that is used to decrypt data and create digital signatures.

proactive maintenance   The measures taken to reduce future system problems.

public key   An asymmetric encryption key that is used to encrypt data and decrypt digital signatures.

reactive maintenance   The measures taken when system problems arise.

Rivest Shamir Adleman (RSA)   A common asymmetric encryption algorithm.

rules   The components of a firewall that match specific network traffic that is to be allowed or dropped.

`sar` **(system activity reporter) command**   A command that displays various system statistics.

Security Enhanced Linux (SELinux)   A set of Linux kernel components and related software packages that prevent malicious software from executing on a Linux system.

server closet   A secured room that stores servers within an organization.

`sestatus` **command**   A command that displays the current status and functionality of the SELinux subsystem.

`ssh-add` **command**   A command that can be used to add an SSH identity to a user account.

SSH agent   A software program that can be used to automatically authenticate users using their private key.

SSH identity   A unique configuration for a user account that is associated with user-specific SSH keys.

stateful packet filter   A packet filter that applies rules to related packets within the same network session.

`sudo` **command**   A command that is used to perform commands as another user via entries in the /etc/sudoers file.

System Statistics (sysstat) package   A software package that contains common performance-monitoring utilities, such as mpstat, iostat, and sar.

TCP wrapper   A program that can be used to run a network daemon with additional security via the /etc/hosts.allow and /etc/hosts.deny files.

tunneling   The process of embedding network packets within other network packets.

tripwire   A common IDS for Linux that monitors files and directories.

troubleshooting procedures   The tasks performed when solving system problems.

ulimit command   A command used to modify process limit parameters in the current shell.

Universal Access utility   A graphical utility within Fedora 20 used to configure assistive technologies.

vmstat command   A command used to display memory, CPU, and swap statistics.

xwininfo command   A command used to display status information about X Windows.

Review Questions

1. On which part of the maintenance cycle do Linux administrators spend the most time?
   a. monitoring
   b. proactive maintenance
   c. reactive maintenance
   d. documentation

2. Which of the following files is likely to be found in the /var/log/sa directory on a Fedora 20 system over time?
   a. 15
   b. sa39
   c. sa19
   d. 00

3. The lspci command can be used to isolate problems with X Windows. True or False?

4. Which of the following commands can be used to display memory statistics? (Choose all that apply.)
   a. free
   b. sar
   c. vmstat
   d. iostat

5. Which command indicates the shared libraries required by a certain executable program?
   a. ldconfig
   b. ldd
   c. rpm -V
   d. slconfig

14

6. RSA is a common symmetric encryption algorithm used by SSH and GPG. True or False?

7. What type of iptables chain targets traffic that is destined for the local computer?

   a. INPUT

   b. ROUTE

   c. FORWARD

   d. OUTPUT

8. Which of the following steps is not a common troubleshooting procedure?

   a. Test the solution.

   b. Isolate the problem.

   c. Delegate responsibility.

   d. Collect information.

9. Which of the following firewalld commands can be used to allow incoming SSH connections the next time the system is booted?

   a. `firewall-cmd --add-service ssh`

   b. `firewall-cmd --add-port 22/tcp`

   c. `firewall-cmd --add-port 22/udp`

   d. `firewall-cmd --add-service ssh --permanent`

10. Which file contains information regarding the users, computers, and commands used by the sudo command?

   a. /etc/sudo

   b. /etc/su.cfg

   c. /etc/sudo.cfg

   d. /etc/sudoers

11. Which command can increase the number of file handles that programs can open in a shell?

   a. `ldd`

   b. `ulimit`

   c. `lba32`

   d. `top`

12. The private key is used when creating a digital signature. True or False?

13. Which of the following actions should you first take to secure your Linux computer against network attacks?

   a. Change permissions on key system files.

   b. Ensure that only necessary services are running.

   c. Run a checksum for each file used by network services.

   d. Configure entries in the /etc/sudoers file.

14. What will the command `sar -W 3 50` do ?

    a. Take 3 swap statistics every 50 seconds.

    b. Take 50 swap statistics every 3 seconds.

    c. Take 3 CPU statistics every 50 seconds.

    d. Take 50 CPU statistics every 3 seconds.

15. Which of the following commands can be used to scan the available ports on computers within your organization?

    a. `traceroute`

    b. `tracert`

    c. `nmap`

    d. `sudo`

16. Which of the following are common assistive technologies? (Choose all that apply.)

    a. mouse keys

    b. high contrast

    c. sticky keys

    d. on-screen keyboard

17. Which of the following Linux Intrusion Detection Systems can be used to detect altered files and directories? (Choose all that apply.)

    a. AIDE

    b. SWATCH

    c. tripwire

    d. Snort

18. When the `fsck` command cannot repair a nonroot filesystem, you should immediately restore all data from tape backup. True or False?

19. When performing a `sar -u` command, you notice that %idle is consistently 10 percent. Is this good or bad?

    a. good, because the processor should be idle more than 5 percent of the time

    b. good, because the processor is idle 90 percent of the time

    c. bad, because the processor is idle 10 percent of the time and perhaps a faster CPU is required

    d. bad, because the processor is idle 10 percent of the time and perhaps a new hard disk is required

20. What are best practices for securing a Linux server? (Choose all that apply.)

    a. Lock the server in a server closet.

    b. Ensure that you are logged in as the root user to the server at all times.

    c. Ensure that SELinux or AppArmor is used to protect key services.

    d. Set the default run level to 1 (Single User Mode).

14

Hands-on Projects

These projects should be completed in the order given. The hands-on projects presented in this chapter should take a total of three hours to complete. The requirements for this lab include:

- A computer with Fedora Linux installed according to Hands-on Project 2-1 and Ubuntu Server Linux installed according to Hands-on Project 6-1.

Project 14-1

In this hands-on project, you detect modified package contents and observe shared libraries used by programs on your Fedora Linux virtual machine.

1. Boot your Fedora Linux virtual machine. After your Linux system has been loaded, switch to a command-line terminal (tty2) by pressing **Ctrl+Alt+F2** and log in to the terminal using the user name of **root** and the password of **LNXrocks!**.

2. At the command prompt, type **rpm -ql grep | less** and press **Enter** to view the file contents of the grep package on the system. When finished, press **q** to quit the less utility. Next, type **rpm -V grep** at the command prompt and press **Enter** to verify the existence of these files on the filesystem. Were any errors reported? Why?

3. At the command prompt, type **rm -f /usr/share/doc/grep/AUTHORS** and press **Enter** to remove a file that belongs to the grep package. Next, type **rpm -V grep** at the command prompt and press **Enter** to verify the existence of all files in the grep package. Were any errors reported? Why? If critical files were missing from this package, how could they be recovered?

4. Type **ldd /bin/grep** at the command prompt and press **Enter** to determine the shared libraries used by the grep command. Were any missing libraries reported in the output of the command? If libraries are missing, what should you do to regain them?

5. Type **exit** and press **Enter** to log out of your shell.

Project 14-2

In this hands-on project, you install the sysstat package on your Fedora Linux virtual machine and monitor system performance using the command-line utilities included within the package.

1. On your Fedora Linux virtual machine, switch to a command-line terminal (tty2) by pressing **Ctrl+Alt+F2** and log in to the terminal using the user name of **root** and the password of **LNXrocks!**.

2. At the command prompt, type **yum install sysstat** and press **Enter**. Press **y** when prompted to complete the installation of the sysstat package.

3. At the command prompt, type **mpstat** and press **Enter** to view average CPU statistics for your system since the last boot time. What is the value for %usr? Is this higher,

lower, or the same as %system? Why? What is the value for %idle? What should this value be over?

4. At the command prompt, type **mpstat 1 5** and press **Enter** to view five CPU statistic measurements, one per second. How do these values compare to the ones seen in the previous step? Why?

5. Switch to a graphical desktop by pressing **Ctrl+Alt+F1** and log into the GNOME desktop as **user1** with a password of **LNXrocks!**.

6. Open several applications of your choice.

7. Switch back to tty2 by pressing **Ctrl+Alt+F2**. Type **mpstat 1 5** at the command prompt and press **Enter** to view five CPU statistic measurements, one per second. How do these values compare to the ones seen in Step 4? Why?

8. Switch back to the GNOME desktop by pressing **Ctrl+Alt+F1** and close all programs.

9. Switch back to tty2 by pressing **Ctrl+Alt+F2**. Type **iostat** at the command prompt and press **Enter** to view average device I/O statistics since the last boot time. What devices are displayed? How many blocks were read and written to your hard disk since the last boot time, on average?

10. At the command prompt, type **iostat 1 5** and press **Enter** to view five I/O statistic measurements, one per second. How do these values compare to the ones seen in the previous step? Why?

11. Switch to the GNOME desktop by pressing **Ctrl+Alt+F1** and open several applications of your choice.

12. Switch back to tty2 by pressing **Ctrl+Alt+F2**, type **iostat 1 5** at the command prompt, and press **Enter** to view five I/O statistic measurements, one per second. How do these values compare to the ones seen in Step 10? Were there any significant changes? Why?

13. Switch to the GNOME desktop by pressing **Ctrl+Alt+F1** and close all programs.

14. Switch back to tty2 by pressing **Ctrl+Alt+F2**, type **sar** at the command prompt, and press **Enter**. What statistics are displayed by default? What times were the statistics taken?

15. At the command prompt, type **sar -q** and press **Enter** to view queue statistics. What times were the statistics taken? How does this compare to the output from the previous step? What is the queue size? What is the average load for the last minute? What is the average load for the last five minutes?

16. At the command prompt, type **sar -q 1 5** and press **Enter** to view five queue statistics, one per second. How do these values compare to those taken in the previous step? Why?

17. Switch to the GNOME desktop by pressing **Ctrl+Alt+F1** and open several applications of your choice.

18. Switch back to tty2 by pressing **Ctrl+Alt+F2**, type **sar -q 1 5** at the command prompt, and press **Enter** to view five queue statistic measurements, one per second. How do these values compare to the ones seen in Step 16? Why?

14

19. Switch to the GNOME desktop by pressing **Ctrl+Alt+F1** and close all programs.

20. Switch back to tty2 by pressing **Ctrl+Alt+F2**, type **sar -W** at the command prompt, and press **Enter**. How many pages were swapped to and from the swap partition today, on average?

21. At the command prompt, type **sar -W 1 5** and press **Enter** to view five swap statistics, one per second. How do these values compare to those taken in the previous step? Why?

22. Switch to the GNOME desktop by pressing **Ctrl+Alt+F1** and open several applications of your choice.

23. Switch back to tty2 by pressing **Ctrl+Alt+F2**, type **sar -W 1 5** at the command prompt, and press **Enter** to view five swap statistic measurements, one per second. How do these values compare to the ones seen in Step 21? Why?

24. Switch to the GNOME desktop by pressing **Ctrl+Alt+F1**. Close all programs and log out of the GNOME desktop.

25. Switch back to tty2 by pressing **Ctrl+Alt+F2**, type **exit**, and press **Enter** to log out of your shell.

Project 14-3

In this hands-on project, you monitor memory and swap performance using the top, free, and vmstat commands.

1. On your Fedora Linux virtual machine, switch to a command-line terminal (tty2) by pressing **Ctrl+Alt+F2** and log in to the terminal using the user name of **root** and the password of **LNXrocks!**.

2. At the command prompt, type **top** and press **Enter**. From the information displayed, write the answers to the following questions on a piece of paper:

   a. How many processes are currently running?

   b. How much memory does your system have in total?

   c. How much memory is being used?

   d. How much memory is used by buffers?

   e. How much swap memory does your system have in total?

   f. How much swap is being used?

3. Type **q** to quit the top utility.

4. At the command prompt, type **free** and press **Enter**. Does this utility give more or less information regarding memory and swap memory than the top utility? How do the values shown by the free command compare to those from Step 2?

5. At the command prompt, type **vmstat** and press **Enter**. Does this utility give more or less information regarding memory and swap memory than the top and free utilities? How do the values shown by the vmstat command compare to those from Step 2? What other information is provided by the vmstat command?

6. Type **exit** and press **Enter** to log out of your shell.

Project 14-4

In this hands-on project, you examine the services running on your Ubuntu Server Linux virtual machine using the nmap utility and /etc/services file.

1. Boot your Ubuntu Server Linux virtual machine and log into tty1 using the user name of **root** and the password of **LNXrocks!**.

2. At the command prompt, type **apt-get install nmap** and press **Enter**. Press **y** and press **Enter** when prompted to complete the installation of the nmap utility.

3. At the command prompt, type **service apache2 stop** and press **Enter**.

4. At the command prompt, type **service xinetd stop** and press **Enter**.

5. At the command prompt, type **nmap –sT 127.0.0.1** and press **Enter**. What ports are listed that you recognize? Are there any unknown ports? Where could you find information regarding the unknown ports? What is the service associated with port 631/tcp?

6. At the command prompt, type **grep 631 /etc/services** and press **Enter**. What is the full name for the service running on port 631?

7. At the command prompt, type **service apache2 start** and press **Enter**.

8. At the command prompt, type **service xinetd start** and press **Enter**.

9. At the command prompt, type **nmap –sT 127.0.0.1** and press **Enter**. What additional ports were opened by the Apache Web server and Extended Internet Super Daemon?

10. Type **exit** and press **Enter** to log out of your shell.

Project 14-5

In this hands-on project, you configure and use the sudo utility to gain root access on your Ubuntu Server Linux virtual machine.

1. On your Ubuntu Server Linux virtual machine, log into tty1 using the user name of **root** and the password of **LNXrocks!**.

2. At the command prompt, type **useradd –m dailyuser** and press **Enter**.

3. At the command prompt, type **passwd dailyuser** and press **Enter**. Supply the password **LNXrocks!** when prompted both times.

4. Run the command **vi /etc/sudoers**. Add the following line to the end of the file (where hostname is the hostname of your Ubuntu Server Linux virtual machine):

   dailyuser hostname = (root) /usr/bin/touch

   When finished, save your changes (you must use :w!) and quit the vi editor.

5. At the command prompt, type **su - dailyuser** and press **Enter**.

6. At the command prompt, type **touch /testfile** and press **Enter**. Were you able to create a file under the / directory?

7. At the command prompt, type **sudo touch /testfile** and press **Enter**, then enter the password **LNXrocks!** when prompted. Were you able to create a file under the / directory?

8. At the command prompt, type **ls –l /testfile** and press **Enter**. Who is the owner and group owner for this file? Why?

9. Type **exit** and press **Enter** to end your dailyuser session.

10. Type **exit** and press **Enter** to log out of your shell.

Project 14-6

In this hands-on project, you configure and test the netfilter firewall on your Ubuntu Server Linux virtual machine.

1. On your Ubuntu Server Linux virtual machine, log into tty1 using the user name of **root** and the password of **LNXrocks!**.

2. At the command prompt, type **iptables -L** and press **Enter**. What is the default action for the three chains?

3. At the command prompt, type **service apache2 start** and press **Enter** to ensure that the Apache Web server is running.

4. Open a Web browser on your Windows host and enter the IP address of your Ubuntu Server Linux virtual machine in the location dialog box. Is your Web page displayed?

5. On your Ubuntu Server Linux virtual machine, type **iptables –P INPUT DROP** at the command prompt and press **Enter**. What does this command do?

6. At the command prompt, type **iptables -L** and press **Enter**. What is the default action for the three chains?

7. Switch back to the Web browser on your Windows host and click the reload button. Does your page reload successfully?

8. On your Ubuntu Server Linux virtual machine, type **iptables –A INPUT –s IP –j ACCEPT** at the command prompt (where *IP* is the IP address of your Windows host) and press **Enter**. What does this command do?

9. At the command prompt, type **iptables -L** and press **Enter**. Do you see your rule underneath the INPUT chain?

10. Switch back to the Web browser on your Windows host and click the reload button. Does your page reload successfully?

11. On your Ubuntu Server Linux virtual machine, type **iptables -F** at the command prompt and press **Enter**. Next, type **iptables –P INPUT ACCEPT** at the command prompt and press **Enter**. What do these commands do? At the command prompt, type **iptables -L** and press **Enter** to verify that the default policies for all three chains have been restored (additional stateful rules will be re-added over time as traffic passes to your Ubuntu Server Linux virtual machine).

12. Type **exit** and press **Enter** to log out of your shell.

Project 14-7

In this hands-on project, you configure firewalld and test the results on your Fedora Linux virtual machine.

1. On your Fedora Linux virtual machine, switch to a command-line terminal (tty2) by pressing **Ctrl+Alt+F2** and log in to the terminal using the user name of **root** and the password of **LNXrocks!**.

2. At the command prompt, type **iptables -L | less** and press **Enter**. Can you tell that firewalld is configured to set netfilter rules on your system? Press **q** when finished to quit the less utility.

3. At the command prompt, type **firewall-cmd --get-zones** and press **Enter** to view the network zones on your system.

4. At the command prompt, type **firewall-cmd --get-default-zone** and press **Enter**. What is the default zone on your system?

5. At the command prompt, type **firewall-cmd --zone=public --list-all** and press **Enter**. What services are allowed in your firewall? Is the Apache Web server listed? Why not?

6. At the command prompt, type **systemctl start httpd** and press **Enter** to ensure that the Apache Web server is started.

7. Open a Web browser on your Windows host and enter the IP address of your Fedora Linux virtual machine in the location dialog box. Is your Web page displayed?

8. On your Fedora Linux virtual machine, type **firewall-cmd --add-service=http** at the command prompt and press **Enter** to allow the http service in your firewall. Next, type **firewall-cmd --add-service=http --permanent** and press **Enter** to ensure that the http service is allowed in the firewall after the next boot.

9. At the command prompt, type **firewall-cmd --zone=public --list-all** and press **Enter**. Is http listed?

10. Switch back to the Web browser on your Windows host and click the reload button. Did your page reload successfully?

11. On your Fedora Linux virtual machine, type **exit** and press **Enter** to log out of your shell.

Discovery Exercises

1. Given the following situations, list any log files or commands that you would use when collecting information during the troubleshooting process.

   a. A CD-ROM device that worked previously with Linux does not respond to the mount command.

   b. The system was unable to mount the /home filesystem (/dev/sda6).

   c. A new database application fails to start successfully.

   d. The Modem Manager utility that you have installed cannot recognize any modems on the system.

   e. You have installed a new sound card in the Linux system, but it is not listed within any sound utility.

2. For each problem in Exercise 1, list as many possible causes and solutions that you can think of, given the material presented throughout this book. Next, research other possible causes using resources such as the Internet, books, local HOWTOs, magazines, or LUGs.

14

3. You are the administrator of a Linux system that provides file and print services to over 100 clients in your company. The system uses several fast SSD hard disks and has a Xeon E5 processor with 16GB of RAM. Since its installation, you have installed database software that is used by only a few users. Unfortunately, you have rarely monitored and documented performance information of this system in the past. Recently, users complain that the performance of the server is very poor. What commands could you use to narrow down the problem? Are there any other troubleshooting methods that might be useful when solving this problem?

4. Briefly describe the purpose of a baseline. What areas of the system would you include in a baseline for your Linux system? Which commands would you use to obtain the information about these areas? Use these commands to generate baseline information for your system (for the current day only) and place this information in a system log book (small binder) for later use. Next, monitor the normal activity of your system for three consecutive days and compare the results to the baseline that you have printed. Are there any differences? Incorporate this new information into your baseline by averaging the results. Are these new values a more accurate indication of normal activity? Why or why not?

5. Use the Universal Access utility to explore the different assistive technologies available within Fedora 20. Note the ones that you find useful.

6. You are a network administrator for your organization and are required to plan and deploy a new file and print server that will service Windows, Linux, and Macintosh client computers. In addition, the server will provide DHCP services on the network and host a small Web site listing company information. In a brief document, draft the services that you plan to implement for this server and the methods that you will use to maximize the security of the system.

7. Use the Internet to research the installation and configuration process for the tripwire IDS on your Ubuntu Server Linux virtual machine. Next, install and configure the tripwire IDS on your Ubuntu Server Linux virtual machine using the default options. Following installation, use the `tripwire --init` command to create the tripwire database, and then use the `tripwire --check` command to analyze your system for possible security breaches based on file changes since the last tripwire database update.

8. Using the information provided in this chapter, explore the default configuration of SELinux on your Fedora Linux virtual machine. Next, explore the default configuration of AppArmor on your Ubuntu Linux virtual machine. Finally, use the Internet to research the strengths of SELinux and AppArmor and prepare a short memo comparing and contrasting them.

9. Many more security-related tools are available for Linux systems in addition to those discussed in this chapter. One example is Nessus, which can test for security vulnerabilities on your system. Use the Internet to research the installation, features and usage of the NESSUS tool and summarize your findings in a short memo.

Certification

As technology advances, so does the need for educated people to manage technology. One of the principal risks that companies face is hiring people to administer, use, or develop programs for Linux. To lower this risk, companies seek people who have demonstrated proficiency in certain technical areas. Although this proficiency can be demonstrated in the form of practical experience, practical experience alone is often not enough for companies when hiring for certain technical positions. Certification tests have become a standard benchmark of technical ability and are sought after by many companies. These tests can vary based on the technical certification, but they usually involve a multiple-choice computer test administered by an approved testing center. Hundreds of thousands of computer-related certification tests are written worldwide each year, and the certification process is likely to increase in importance in the future as technology advances.

 It is important to recognize that certification does not replace ability; rather, it demonstrates it. An employer might get 30 qualified applicants, and part of the hiring process will likely be a demonstration of ability. It is unlikely the employer will incur the cost and time it takes to test all 30. Rather, it is more likely the employer will look for benchmark certifications, which indicate a base ability and then test this smaller subgroup.

Furthermore, certifications are an internationally administered and recognized standard. Although an employer might not be familiar with the criteria involved in achieving a computer science degree from a particular university in Canada or a certain college in Texas, certification exam criteria are well published on Web sites and are, hence, well known. In addition, it does not matter in which country the certification exam is taken because the tests are standardized and administered by the same authenticating authority using common rules.

Certifications come in two broad categories: vendor-specific and vendor-neutral. Vendor-specific certifications are ones in which the vendor of a particular operating system or program sets the standards to be met and creates the exams. Obtaining one of these certifications demonstrates knowledge of, or on, a particular product or operating system. Microsoft, Novell, and Oracle, for example, all have vendor-specific certifications for their products. Vendor-neutral exams, such as those offered by CompTIA, demonstrate knowledge in a particular area but not on any specific product or brand of product. In either case, the organizations that create the certification exams and set the standards strive to ensure they are of the highest quality and integrity to be used as a true benchmark worldwide. One globally recognized and vendor-neutral Linux certification used by the industry is CompTIA's Linux+ Powered by LPI certification.

Linux+ Certification

Linux is a general category of operating system software that share a common operating system kernel and utilities. What differentiates one Linux distribution from another are the various accompanying software applications, which modify the look and feel of the operating system. Vendor-neutral certification suits Linux particularly well because there is no one specific vendor; Linux distributions can have different brands attached to them but essentially work in the same fashion. To certify on one particular distribution might well indicate the ability to port to and work well on another distribution, but with the varied number of distributions it is probably best to show proficiency on the most common features of Linux that the majority of distributions share. The CompTIA Linux+ Powered by LPI certification achieves this well and tests a wide body of knowledge on the various ways Linux is distributed and installed, as well as common commands, procedures, and user interfaces. Two exams comprise the ComptTIA Linux+ Powered by LPI certification: LX0-103 and LX0-104. Both exams can be taken at any participating VUE or Sylvan Prometric testing center worldwide, and each exam involves 60 questions to be answered within a 90-minute timeframe.

 To find out more about the Linux+ Powered by LPI certification exam and how to book one, visit the CompTIA Web site at *http://certification.comptia.org/getCertified/certifications/linux.aspx*.

Linux+ Certification Objectives

The following tables identify where the certification exam topics are covered in this book. Each table represents a separate domain, or skill set, measured by the exam. Domains 101 through 104 are tested on the LX0-103 certification exam, whereas domains 105 through 110 are tested on the LX0-104 certification exam.

Domain 101: System Architecture

Objective	Chapter
101.1 Determine and configure hardware settings	2, 5, 6, 12, 14
101.2 Boot the system	8
101.3 Change runlevels and shutdown or reboot system	8

Domain 102: Linux Installation and Package Management

Objective	Chapter
102.1 Design hard disk layout	2, 5, 6
102.2 Install a boot manager	2, 8
102.3 Manage shared libraries	14
102.4 Use Debian package management	11
102.5 Use RPM and YUM package management	11

Domain 103: GNU and UNIX Commands

Objective	Chapter
103.1 Work on the command line	2, 3, 7
103.2 Process text streams using filters	3, 7
103.3 Perform basic file management	4, 11
103.4 Use streams, pipes, and redirects	7
103.5 Create, monitor, and kill processes	9
103.6 Modify process execution priorities	9
103.7 Search text files using regular expressions	3, 7
103.8 Perform basic file-editing operations using vi	3

Domain 104: Devices, Linux Filesystems, Filesystem Hierarchy Standard

Objective	Chapter
104.1 Create partitions and filesystems	5
104.2 Maintain the integrity of filesystems	5
104.3 Control mounting and unmounting of filesystems	5
104.4 Manage disk quotas	5
104.5 Manage file permissions and ownership	4
104.6 Create and change hard and symbolic links	4
104.7 Find system files and place files in the correct location	4

Domain 105: Shells, Scripting, and Data Management

Objective	Chapter
105.1 Customize and use the shell environment	7
105.2 Customize or write simple scripts	7
105.3 SQL data management	13

Domain 106: User Interfaces and Desktops

Objective	Chapter
106.1 Install and configure X11	2, 6, 8, 14
106.2 Setup a display manager	8
106.3 Accessibility	14

Domain 107: Administrative Tasks

Objective	Chapter
107.1 Manage user and group accounts and related system files	10
107.2 Automate system administration tasks by scheduling jobs	9
107.3 Localization and internationalization	2, 13

Domain 108: Essential System Services

Objective	Chapter
108.1 Maintain system time	2, 13
108.2 System logging	10, 14
108.3 Mail Transfer Agent (MTA) basics	1, 13
108.4 Manage printers and printing	10

Domain 109: Networking Fundamentals

Objective	Chapter
109.1 Fundamentals of Internet protocols	12
109.2 Basic network configuration	12
109.3 Basic network troubleshooting	12
109.4 Configure client side DNS	12

Domain 110: Security

Objective	Chapter
110.1 Perform security administration tasks	4, 10, 12, 14
110.2 Set up host security	10, 12, 14
110.3 Securing data with encryption	12, 14

GNU Public License

A copy of the original GNU Public License referred to in Chapter 1 is shown in Figure B-1. This license and its revisions can be found at *www.gnu.org*.

GNU GENERAL PUBLIC LICENSE

Version 3, 29 June 2007

Copyright © 2007 Free Software Foundation, Inc. <*http://fsf.org/*>
Everyone is permitted to copy and distribute verbatim copies of
this license document, but changing it is not allowed.

Preamble

The GNU General Public License is a free, copyleft license for
software and other kinds of works.

The licenses for most software and other practical works are
designed to take away your freedom to share and change the works. By
contrast, the GNU General Public License is intended to guarantee
your freedom to share and change all versions of a program–to make
sure it remains free software for all its users. We, the Free
Software Foundation, use the GNU General Public License for most of
our software; it applies also to any other work released this way by
its authors. You can apply it to your programs, too.

When we speak of free software, we are referring to freedom, not
price. Our General Public Licenses are designed to make sure that
you have the freedom to distribute copies of free software (and
charge for them if you wish), that you receive source code or can
get it if you want it, that you can change the software or use
pieces of it in new free programs, and that you know you can do
these things.

To protect your rights, we need to prevent others from denying you
these rights or asking you to surrender the rights. Therefore, you
have certain responsibilities if you distribute copies of the
software, or if you modify it: responsibilities to respect the
freedom of others.

For example, if you distribute copies of such a program, whether
gratis or for a fee, you must pass on to the recipients the same
freedoms that you received. You must make sure that they, too,
receive or can get the source code. And you must show them these
terms so they know their rights.

Developers that use the GNU GPL protect your rights with two steps:
(1) assert copyright on the software, and (2) offer you this License
giving you legal permission to copy, distribute and/or modify it.

For the developers' and authors' protection, the GPL clearly
explains that there is no warranty for this free software. For both
users' and authors' sake, the GPL requires that modified versions be
marked as changed, so that their problems will not be attributed
erroneously to authors of previous versions.

Some devices are designed to deny users access to install or run
modified versions of the software inside them, although the
manufacturer can do so. This is fundamentally incompatible with the

Figure B-1 GNU Public License

aim of protecting users' freedom to change the software. The systematic pattern of such abuse occurs in the area of products for individuals to use, which is precisely where it is most unacceptable. Therefore, we have designed this version of the GPL to prohibit the practice for those products. If such problems arise substantially in other domains, we stand ready to extend this provision to those domains in future versions of the GPL, as needed to protect the freedom of users.

Finally, every program is threatened constantly by software patents. States should not allow patents to restrict development and use of software on general-purpose computers, but in those that do, we wish to avoid the special danger that patents applied to a free program could make it effectively proprietary. To prevent this, the GPL assures that patents cannot be used to render the program non-free.

The precise terms and conditions for copying, distribution and modification follow.

TERMS AND CONDITIONS

0. Definitions.

"This License" refers to version 3 of the GNU General Public License.

"Copyright" also means copyright-like laws that apply to other kinds of works, such as semiconductor masks.

"The Program" refers to any copyrightable work licensed under this License. Each licensee is addressed as "you". "Licensees" and "recipients" may be individuals or organizations.

To "modify" a work means to copy from or adapt all or part of the work in a fashion requiring copyright permission, other than the making of an exact copy. The resulting work is called a "modified version" of the earlier work or a work "based on" the earlier work.

A "covered work" means either the unmodified Program or a work based on the Program.

To "propagate" a work means to do anything with it that, without permission, would make you directly or secondarily liable for infringement under applicable copyright law, except executing it on a computer or modifying a private copy. Propagation includes copying, distribution (with or without modification), making available to the public, and in some countries other activities as well.

To "convey" a work means any kind of propagation that enables other parties to make or receive copies. Mere interaction with a user through a computer network, with no transfer of a copy, is not conveying.

An interactive user interface displays "Appropriate Legal Notices" to the extent that it includes a convenient and prominently

Figure B-1 GNU Public License (continued)

visible feature that (1) displays an appropriate copyright notice, and (2) tells the user that there is no warranty for the work (except to the extent that warranties are provided), that licensees may convey the work under this License, and how to view a copy of this License. If the interface presents a list of user commands or options, such as a menu, a prominent item in the list meets this criterion.

1. Source Code.

The "source code" for a work means the preferred form of the work for making modifications to it. "Object code" means any non-source form of a work.

A "Standard Interface" means an interface that either is an official standard defined by a recognized standards body, or, in the case of interfaces specified for a particular programming language, one that is widely used among developers working in that language.

The "System Libraries" of an executable work include anything, other than the work as a whole, that (a) is included in the normal form of packaging a Major Component, but which is not part of that Major Component, and (b) serves only to enable use of the work with that Major Component, or to implement a Standard Interface for which an implementation is available to the public in source code form. A "Major Component", in this context, means a major essential component (kernel, window system, and so on) of the specific operating system (if any) on which the executable work runs, or a compiler used to produce the work, or an object code interpreter used to run it.

The "Corresponding Source" for a work in object code form means all the source code needed to generate, install, and (for an executable work) run the object code and to modify the work, including scripts to control those activities. However, it does not include the work's System Libraries, or general-purpose tools or generally available free programs which are used unmodified in performing those activities but which are not part of the work. For example, Corresponding Source includes interface definition files associated with source files for the work, and the source code for shared libraries and dynamically linked subprograms that the work is specifically designed to require, such as by intimate data communication or control flow between those subprograms and other parts of the work.

The Corresponding Source need not include anything that users can regenerate automatically from other parts of the Corresponding Source.

The Corresponding Source for a work in source code form is that same work.

2. Basic Permissions.

All rights granted under this License are granted for the term of copyright on the Program, and are irrevocable provided the stated

Figure B-1 GNU Public License (continued)

conditions are met. This License explicitly affirms your unlimited permission to run the unmodified Program. The output from running a covered work is covered by this License only if the output, given its content, constitutes a covered work. This License acknowledges your rights of fair use or other equivalent, as provided by copyright law.

You may make, run and propagate covered works that you do not convey, without conditions so long as your license otherwise remains in force. You may convey covered works to others for the sole purpose of having them make modifications exclusively for you, or provide you with facilities for running those works, provided that you comply with the terms of this License in conveying all material for which you do not control copyright. Those thus making or running the covered works for you must do so exclusively on your behalf, under your direction and control, on terms that prohibit them from making any copies of your copyrighted material outside their relationship with you.

Conveying under any other circumstances is permitted solely under the conditions stated below. Sublicensing is not allowed; section 10 makes it unnecessary.

3. Protecting Users' Legal Rights From Anti-Circumvention Law.

No covered work shall be deemed part of an effective technological measure under any applicable law fulfilling obligations under article 11 of the WIPO copyright treaty adopted on 20 December 1996, or similar laws prohibiting or restricting circumvention of such measures.

When you convey a covered work, you waive any legal power to forbid circumvention of technological measures to the extent such circumvention is effected by exercising rights under this License with respect to the covered work, and you disclaim any intention to limit operation or modification of the work as a means of enforcing, against the work's users, your or third parties' legal rights to forbid circumvention of technological measures.

4. Conveying Verbatim Copies.

You may convey verbatim copies of the Program's source code as you receive it, in any medium, provided that you conspicuously and appropriately publish on each copy an appropriate copyright notice; keep intact all notices stating that this License and any non-permissive terms added in accord with section 7 apply to the code; keep intact all notices of the absence of any warranty; and give all recipients a copy of this License along with the Program.

You may charge any price or no price for each copy that you convey, and you may offer support or warranty protection for a fee.

5. Conveying Modified Source Versions.

You may convey a work based on the Program, or the modifications to produce it from the Program, in the form of source code under the

Figure B-1 GNU Public License (continued)

terms of section 4, provided that you also meet all of these conditions:

a) The work must carry prominent notices stating that you modified it, and giving a relevant date.

b) The work must carry prominent notices stating that it is released under this License and any conditions added under section 7. This requirement modifies the requirement in section 4 to "keep intact all notices".

c) You must license the entire work, as a whole, under this License to anyone who comes into possession of a copy. This License will therefore apply, along with any applicable section 7 additional terms, to the whole of the work, and all its parts, regardless of how they are packaged. This License gives no permission to license the work in any other way, but it does not invalidate such permission if you have separately received it.

d) If the work has interactive user interfaces, each must display Appropriate Legal Notices; however, if the Program has interactive interfaces that do not display Appropriate Legal Notices, your work need not make them do so.

A compilation of a covered work with other separate and independent works, which are not by their nature extensions of the covered work, and which are not combined with it such as to form a larger program, in or on a volume of a storage or distribution medium, is called an "aggregate" if the compilation and its resulting copyright are not used to limit the access or legal rights of the compilation's users beyond what the individual works permit. Inclusion of a covered work in an aggregate does not cause this License to apply to the other parts of the aggregate.

6. Conveying Non-Source Forms.

You may convey a covered work in object code form under the terms of sections 4 and 5, provided that you also convey the machine-readable Corresponding Source under the terms of this License, in one of these ways:

a) Convey the object code in, or embodied in, a physical product (including a physical distribution medium), accompanied by the Corresponding Source fixed on a durable physical medium customarily used for software interchange.

b) Convey the object code in, or embodied in, a physical product (including a physical distribution medium), accompanied by a written offer, valid for at least three years and valid for as long as you offer spare parts or customer support for that product model, to give anyone who possesses the object code either (1) a copy of the Corresponding Source for all the software in the product that is covered by this License, on a durable physical medium customarily used for software interchange, for a price no more than your

Figure B-1 GNU Public License (continued)

reasonable cost of physically performing this conveying of source, or (2) access to copy the Corresponding Source from a network server at no charge.

c) Convey individual copies of the object code with a copy of the written offer to provide the Corresponding Source. This alternative is allowed only occasionally and noncommercially, and only if you received the object code with such an offer, in accord with subsection 6b.

d) Convey the object code by offering access from a designated place (gratis or for a charge), and offer equivalent access to the Corresponding Source in the same way through the same place at no further charge. You need not require recipients to copy the Corresponding Source along with the object code. If the place to copy the object code is a network server, the Corresponding Source may be on a different server (operated by you or a third party) that supports equivalent copying facilities, provided you maintain clear directions next to the object code saying where to find the Corresponding Source. Regardless of what server hosts the Corresponding Source, you remain obligated to ensure that it is available for as long as needed to satisfy these requirements.

e) Convey the object code using peer-to-peer transmission, provided you inform other peers where the object code and Corresponding Source of the work are being offered to the general public at no charge under subsection 6d.

A separable portion of the object code, whose source code is excluded from the Corresponding Source as a System Library, need not be included in conveying the object code work.

A "User Product" is either (1) a "consumer product", which means any tangible personal property which is normally used for personal, family, or household purposes, or (2) anything designed or sold for incorporation into a dwelling. In determining whether a product is a consumer product, doubtful cases shall be resolved in favor of coverage. For a particular product received by a particular user, "normally used" refers to a typical or common use of that class of product, regardless of the status of the particular user or of the way in which the particular user actually uses, or expects or is expected to use, the product. A product is a consumer product regardless of whether the product has substantial commercial, industrial or non-consumer uses, unless such uses represent the only significant mode of use of the product.

"Installation Information" for a User Product means any methods, procedures, authorization keys, or other information required to install and execute modified versions of a covered work in that User Product from a modified version of its Corresponding Source. The information must suffice to ensure that the continued functioning of the modified object code is in no case prevented or interfered with solely because modification has been made.

Figure B-1 GNU Public License (continued)

If you convey an object code work under this section in, or with, or specifically for use in, a User Product, and the conveying occurs as part of a transaction in which the right of possession and use of the User Product is transferred to the recipient in perpetuity or for a fixed term (regardless of how the transaction is characterized), the Corresponding Source conveyed under this section must be accompanied by the Installation Information. But this requirement does not apply if neither you nor any third party retains the ability to install modified object code on the User Product (for example, the work has been installed in ROM).

The requirement to provide Installation Information does not include a requirement to continue to provide support service, warranty, or updates for a work that has been modified or installed by the recipient, or for the User Product in which it has been modified or installed. Access to a network may be denied when the modification itself materially and adversely affects the operation of the network or violates the rules and protocols for communication across the network.

Corresponding Source conveyed, and Installation Information provided, in accord with this section must be in a format that is publicly documented (and with an implementation available to the public in source code form), and must require no special password or key for unpacking, reading or copying.

7. Additional Terms.

"Additional permissions" are terms that supplement the terms of this License by making exceptions from one or more of its conditions. Additional permissions that are applicable to the entire Program shall be treated as though they were included in this License, to the extent that they are valid under applicable law. If additional permissions apply only to part of the Program, that part may be used separately under those permissions, but the entire Program remains governed by this License without regard to the additional permissions.

When you convey a copy of a covered work, you may at your option remove any additional permissions from that copy, or from any part of it. (Additional permissions may be written to require their own removal in certain cases when you modify the work.) You may place additional permissions on material, added by you to a covered work, for which you have or can give appropriate copyright permission.

Notwithstanding any other provision of this License, for material you add to a covered work, you may (if authorized by the copyright holders of that material) supplement the terms of this License with terms:

a) Disclaiming warranty or limiting liability differently from the terms of sections 15 and 16 of this License; or

b) Requiring preservation of specified reasonable legal notices or author attributions in that material or in the Appropriate Legal Notices displayed by works containing it; or

c) Prohibiting misrepresentation of the origin of that material, or requiring that modified versions of such material be marked in reasonable ways as different from the original version; or

d) Limiting the use for publicity purposes of names of licensors or authors of the material; or

e) Declining to grant rights under trademark law for use of some trade names, trademarks, or service marks; or

f) Requiring indemnification of licensors and authors of that material by anyone who conveys the material (or modified versions of it) with contractual assumptions of liability to the recipient, for any liability that these contractual assumptions directly impose on those licensors and authors.

All other non-permissive additional terms are considered "further restrictions" within the meaning of section 10. If the Program as you received it, or any part of it, contains a notice stating that it is governed by this License along with a term that is a further restriction, you may remove that term. If a license document contains a further restriction but permits relicensing or conveying under this License, you may add to a covered work material governed by the terms of that license document, provided that the further restriction does not survive such relicensing or conveying.

If you add terms to a covered work in accord with this section, you must place, in the relevant source files, a statement of the additional terms that apply to those files, or a notice indicating where to find the applicable terms.

Additional terms, permissive or non-permissive, may be stated in the form of a separately written license, or stated as exceptions; the above requirements apply either way.

8. Termination.

You may not propagate or modify a covered work except as expressly provided under this License. Any attempt otherwise to propagate or modify it is void, and will automatically terminate your rights under this License (including any patent licenses granted under the third paragraph of section 11).

However, if you cease all violation of this License, then your license from a particular copyright holder is reinstated (a) provisionally, unless and until the copyright holder explicitly and ?finally terminates your license, and (b) permanently, if the copyright holder fails to notify you of the violation by some reasonable means prior to 60 days after the cessation.

Figure B-1 GNU Public License (continued)

Moreover, your license from a particular copyright holder is reinstated permanently if the copyright holder notifies you of the violation by some reasonable means, this is the first time you have received notice of violation of this License (for any work) from that copyright holder, and you cure the violation prior to 30 days after your receipt of the notice.

Termination of your rights under this section does not terminate the licenses of parties who have received copies or rights from you under this License. If your rights have been terminated and not permanently reinstated, you do not qualify to receive new licenses for the same material under section 10.

9. Acceptance Not Required for Having Copies.

You are not required to accept this License in order to receive or run a copy of the Program. Ancillary propagation of a covered work occurring solely as a consequence of using peer-to-peer transmission to receive a copy likewise does not require acceptance. However, nothing other than this License grants you permission to propagate or modify any covered work. These actions infringe copyright if you do not accept this License. Therefore, by modifying or propagating a covered work, you indicate your acceptance of this License to do so.

10. Automatic Licensing of Downstream Recipients.

Each time you convey a covered work, the recipient automatically receives a license from the original licensors, to run, modify and propagate that work, subject to this License. You are not responsible for enforcing compliance by third parties with this License.

An "entity transaction" is a transaction transferring control of an organization, or substantially all assets of one, or subdividing an organization, or merging organizations. If propagation of a covered work results from an entity transaction, each party to that transaction who receives a copy of the work also receives whatever licenses to the work the party's predecessor in interest had or could give under the previous paragraph, plus a right to possession of the Corresponding Source of the work from the predecessor in interest, if the predecessor has it or can get it with reasonable efforts.

You may not impose any further restrictions on the exercise of the rights granted or affirmed under this License. For example, you may not impose a license fee, royalty, or other charge for exercise of rights granted under this License, and you may not initiate litigation (including a cross-claim or counterclaim in a lawsuit) alleging that any patent claim is infringed by making, using, selling, offering for sale, or importing the Program or any portion of it.

Figure B-1 GNU Public License (continued)

11. Patents.

A "contributor" is a copyright holder who authorizes use under this License of the Program or a work on which the Program is based. The work thus licensed is called the contributor's "contributor version".

A contributor's "essential patent claims" are all patent claims owned or controlled by the contributor, whether already acquired or hereafter acquired, that would be infringed by some manner, permitted by this License, of making, using, or selling its contributor version, but do not include claims that would be infringed only as a consequence of further modification of the contributor version. For purposes of this definition, "control" includes the right to grant patent sublicenses in a manner consistent with the requirements of this License.

Each contributor grants you a non-exclusive, worldwide, royalty-free patent license under the contributor's essential patent claims, to make, use, sell, offer for sale, import and otherwise run, modify and propagate the contents of its contributor version.

In the following three paragraphs, a "patent license" is any express agreement or commitment, however denominated, not to enforce a patent (such as an express permission to practice a patent or covenant not to sue for patent infringement). To "grant" such a patent license to a party means to make such an agreement or commitment not to enforce a patent against the party.

If you convey a covered work, knowingly relying on a patent license, and the Corresponding Source of the work is not available for anyone to copy, free of charge and under the terms of this License, through a publicly available network server or other readily accessible means, then you must either (1) cause the Corresponding Source to be so available, or (2) arrange to deprive yourself of the benefit of the patent license for this particular work, or (3) arrange, in a manner consistent with the requirements of this License, to extend the patent license to downstream recipients. "Knowingly relying" means you have actual knowledge that, but for the patent license, your conveying the covered work in a country, or your recipient's use of the covered work in a country, would infringe one or more identifiable patents in that country that you have reason to believe are valid.

If, pursuant to or in connection with a single transaction or arrangement, you convey, or propagate by procuring conveyance of, a covered work, and grant a patent license to some of the parties receiving the covered work authorizing them to use, propagate, modify or convey a specific copy of the covered work, then the patent license you grant is automatically extended to all recipients of the covered work and works based on it.

A patent license is "discriminatory" if it does not include within the scope of its coverage, prohibits the exercise of, or is conditioned on the non-exercise of one or more of the rights that are

Figure B-1 GNU Public License (continued)

specifically granted under this License. You may not convey a covered work if you are a party to an arrangement with a third party that is in the business of distributing software, under which you make payment to the third party based on the extent of your activity of conveying the work, and under which the third party grants, to any of the parties who would receive the covered work from you, a discriminatory patent license (a) in connection with copies of the covered work conveyed by you (or copies made from those copies), or (b) primarily for and in connection with specific products or compilations that contain the covered work, unless you entered into that arrangement, or that patent license was granted, prior to 28 March 2007.

Nothing in this License shall be construed as excluding or limiting any implied license or other defenses to infringement that may otherwise be available to you under applicable patent law.

12. No Surrender of Others' Freedom.

If conditions are imposed on you (whether by court order, agreement or otherwise) that contradict the conditions of this License, they do not excuse you from the conditions of this License. If you cannot convey a covered work so as to satisfy simultaneously your obligations under this License and any other pertinent obligations, then as a consequence you may not convey it at all. For example, if you agree to terms that obligate you to collect a royalty for further conveying from those to whom you convey the Program, the only way you could satisfy both those terms and this License would be to refrain entirely from conveying the Program.

13. Use with the GNU Affero General Public License.

Notwithstanding any other provision of this License, you have permission to link or combine any covered work with a work licensed under version 3 of the GNU Affero General Public License into a single combined work, and to convey the resulting work. The terms of this License will continue to apply to the part which is the covered work, but the special requirements of the GNU Affero General Public License, section 13, concerning interaction through a network will apply to the combination as such.

14. Revised Versions of this License.

The Free Software Foundation may publish revised and/or new versions of the GNU General Public License from time to time. Such new versions will be similar in spirit to the present version, but may differ in detail to address new problems or concerns.

Each version is given a distinguishing version number. If the Program specifies that a certain numbered version of the GNU General Public License "or any later version" applies to it, you have the option of following the terms and conditions either of that numbered version or of any later version published by the Free Software Foundation. If the Program does not specify a version number of the

Figure B-1 GNU Public License (continued)

GNU General Public License, you may choose any version ever published by the Free Software Foundation.

If the Program specifies that a proxy can decide which future versions of the GNU General Public License can be used, that proxy's public statement of acceptance of a version permanently authorizes you to choose that version for the Program.

Later license versions may give you additional or different permissions. However, no additional obligations are imposed on any author or copyright holder as a result of your choosing to follow a later version.

15. Disclaimer of Warranty.

THERE IS NO WARRANTY FOR THE PROGRAM, TO THE EXTENT PERMITTED BY APPLICABLE LAW. EXCEPT WHEN OTHERWISE STATED IN WRITING THE COPYRIGHT HOLDERS AND/OR OTHER PARTIES PROVIDE THE PROGRAM "AS IS" WITHOUT WARRANTY OF ANY KIND, EITHER EXPRESSED OR IMPLIED, INCLUDING, BUT NOT LIMITED TO, THE IMPLIED WARRANTIES OF MERCHANTABILITY AND FITNESS FOR A PARTICULAR PURPOSE. THE ENTIRE RISK AS TO THE QUALITY AND PERFORMANCE OF THE PROGRAM IS WITH YOU. SHOULD THE PROGRAM PROVE DEFECTIVE, YOU ASSUME THE COST OF ALL NECESSARY SERVICING, REPAIR OR CORRECTION.

16. Limitation of Liability.

IN NO EVENT UNLESS REQUIRED BY APPLICABLE LAW OR AGREED TO IN WRITING WILL ANY COPYRIGHT HOLDER, OR ANY OTHER PARTY WHO MODIFIES AND/OR CONVEYS THE PROGRAM AS PERMITTED ABOVE, BE LIABLE TO YOU FOR DAMAGES, INCLUDING ANY GENERAL, SPECIAL, INCIDENTAL OR CONSEQUENTIAL DAMAGES ARISING OUT OF THE USE OR INABILITY TO USE THE PROGRAM (INCLUDING BUT NOT LIMITED TO LOSS OF DATA OR DATA BEING RENDERED INACCURATE OR LOSSES SUSTAINED BY YOU OR THIRD PARTIES OR A FAILURE OF THE PROGRAM TO OPERATE WITH ANY OTHER PROGRAMS), EVEN IF SUCH HOLDER OR OTHER PARTY HAS BEEN ADVISED OF THE POSSIBILITY OF SUCH DAMAGES.

17. Interpretation of Sections 15 and 16.

If the disclaimer of warranty and limitation of liability provided above cannot be given local legal effect according to their terms, reviewing courts shall apply local law that most closely approximates an absolute waiver of all civil liability in connection with the Program, unless a warranty or assumption of liability accompanies a copy of the Program in return for a fee.

END OF TERMS AND CONDITIONS

How to Apply These Terms to Your New Programs

If you develop a new program, and you want it to be of the greatest possible use to the public, the best way to achieve this is to make it free software which everyone can redistribute and change under these terms.

Figure B-1 GNU Public License (continued)

To do so, attach the following notices to the program. It is safest to attach them to the start of each source file to most effectively state the exclusion of warranty; and each file should have at least the "copyright" line and a pointer to where the full notice is found.

<one line to give the program's name and a brief idea of what it does.> Copyright (C) <year> <name of author> This program is free software: you can redistribute it and/or modify it under the terms of the GNU General Public License as published by the Free Software Foundation, either version 3 of the License, or (at your option) any later version. This program is distributed in the hope that it will be useful, but WITHOUT ANY WARRANTY; without even the implied warranty of MERCHANTABILITY or FITNESS FOR A PARTICULAR PURPOSE. See the GNU General Public License for more details. You should have received a copy of the GNU General Public License along with this program. If not, see <*http://www.gnu.org/licenses/*>.

Also add information on how to contact you by electronic and paper mail.

If the program does terminal interaction, make it output a short notice like this when it starts in an interactive mode:

<program> Copyright (C) <year> <name of author> This program comes with ABSOLUTELY NO WARRANTY; for details type 'show w'. This is free software, and you are welcome to redistribute it under certain conditions; type 'show c' for details.

The hypothetical commands 'show w' and 'show c' should show the appropriate parts of the General Public License. Of course, your program's commands might be different; for a GUI interface, you would use an "about box".

You should also get your employer (if you work as a programmer) or school, if any, to sign a "copyright disclaimer" for the program, if necessary. For more information on this, and how to apply and follow the GNU GPL, see <*http://www.gnu.org/licenses/*>.

The GNU General Public License does not permit incorporating your program into proprietary programs. If your program is a subroutine library, you may consider it more useful to permit linking proprietary applications with the library. If this is what you want to do, use the GNU Lesser General Public License instead of this License. But first, please read <*http://www.gnu.org/philosophy/ why-not-lgpl.html*>.

Figure B-1 GNU Public License (continued)

appendix C

Finding Linux Resources on the Internet

Open source development has made Linux a powerful and versatile operating system; however, this development has also increased the complexity of Linux and Linux resources available on the Internet. Newcomers to Linux might find this bounty of resources intimidating, but there are some simple rules that make finding particular types of Linux resources easier. Understanding how to navigate the Internet to find these resources is a valuable skill to develop.

By far, the easiest way to locate resources on any topic is by using a search engine such as *www. google.com*. However, because a plethora of Linux-related Web sites are available on the Internet, a search of the word "Linux" yields thousands of results. You might find that you need to be more specific in your request to a search engine to obtain a list of Web sites that likely contain the information you desire. Thus, it is very important to approach Linux documentation by topic; otherwise, you might be searching for hours through several Web sites to find the resources you need.

Many Web sites describe the features of Linux and open source software. Many of these Web sites contain links to other Linux resources organized by topic and, hence, are a good place for people to start if they are new to Linux and desire some background or terminology. Unfortunately, many of the sites do not follow a common naming scheme; Table C-1 is a partial list of some valuable Web sites offering general Linux information.

Description	Web Site
Linux Online	*www.linux.org*
Linux International	*www.li.org*
Linux Jargon File (terminology)	*www.catb.org/jargon*
The Cathedral and the Bazaar (history of open source)	*www.catb.org/esr/writings/cathedral-bazaar*
The Free Software Foundation	*www.fsf.org*
The GNU OS	*www.gnu.org*

Table C-1 General Linux and open source Web sites

Other important sources of information, for inexperienced and expert Linux users alike, are Linux news sites. Some of these Web sites are hosted by organizations that publish trade magazines and, as a result, share the same name as the magazine with a .com suffix, making the Web site easier to find. One example is the Linux Journal, which can be found at *www.linuxjournal.com*. Often, these sites contain more than just Linux news; they also contain tutorials, FAQs (frequently asked questions), and links to other Linux resources. Table C-2 lists some common Linux news Web sites.

Description	Web Site
Linux Journal (magazine)	*www.linuxjournal.com*
Slashdot	*www.slashdot.org*
Linux Weekly News	*www.lwn.net*
Linux Focus	*www.linuxfocus.org*
Linux Magazine (magazine)	*www.linux-mag.com*

Table C-2 Common Linux news Web sites

Although many Web sites offer general information and news regarding Linux and open source software, the most important resources the Internet offers are help files and product documentation. These resources take many forms, including instructions for completing tasks (HOWTO documents), frequently asked questions (FAQs), supporting documentation (text files and HTML files), and newsgroup postings (Usenet). Almost every Web site containing Linux information of some type provides at least one of these resources; however, many centralized Web sites make finding this information easier. Table C-3 lists some common Web sites that make locating documentation and help files easier.

Description	Web Site
Linux Documentation Project (HOWTOs)	*www.tldp.org*
Linux Help Network	*www.linuxhelp.net*
Google Newsgroups (formerly Deja News)	*groups.google.com*

Table C-3 Common Linux documentation and help resources

In many cases, you can find help on a particular open source software component for Linux by visiting its development Web site. Most large open source software projects, such as the KDE project, have their own Web sites where information and news regarding the software is available and the latest release can be downloaded. These Web sites usually follow the naming convention *www.projectname.org*, where *projectname* is the name of the project; thus, they are easy to locate without the use of a search engine. Table C-4 is a partial list of common open source software project Web sites available on the Internet.

Description	Web Site
The Apache Web Server	*www.apache.org*
The KDE Desktop	*www.kde.org*
The GNOME Desktop	*www.gnome.org*
The Xfree86 Project (X Windows)	*www.xfree86.org*
The X.org Project (X Windows)	*www.x.org*
The Linux Kernel	*www.kernel.org*

Table C-4   Open source software project Web sites

Smaller open source software packages and projects rarely have Web sites hosting the development. Instead, they are listed on open source software repository Web sites, also known as open source software archives, which contain thousands of software packages available for download. Often, these Web sites offer several different distributions of Linux as well, conveniently saving a visit to a distribution Web site in order to obtain one. There are many repository Web sites available on the Internet that are searchable via a Linux command such as yum or apt-get (discussed in Chapter 11). You can also search for open source software using a Web browser by navigating to the SourceForge Web site at *www.sourceforge.net*.

Glossary

*sum commands Commands that can be used to verify the checksum on a file where * represents the checksum algorithm. For example, to verify a SHA1 checksum, you could use the sha1sum command.

/dev directory The directory off the root where device files are typically stored.

/etc/at.allow A file listing all users who can use the at command.

/etc/at.deny A file listing all users who cannot access the at command.

/etc/cron.allow A file listing all users who can use the cron command.

/etc/cron.d A directory that contains additional system cron tables.

/etc/cron.deny A file listing all users who cannot access the cron command.

/etc/crontab The default system cron table.

/etc/cups/cupsd.conf A file that holds daemon configuration for the cups daemon.

/etc/cups/printers.conf A file that holds printer configuration for the cups daemon.

/etc/default/useradd A file that contains default values for user creation.

/etc/dumpdates The file used to store information about incremental and full backups for use by the dump/restore utility.

/etc/fstab A file used to specify which filesystems to mount automatically at boot time and queried by the mount command if an insufficient number of arguments are specified.

/etc/group The file that contains group definitions and memberships.

/etc/login.defs A file that contains default values for user creation.

/etc/logrotate.conf The file used by the logrotate utility to specify rotation parameters for log files.

/etc/mtab A file that stores a list of currently mounted filesystems.

/etc/passwd The file that contains user account information.

/etc/rsyslog.conf The main configuration file for the System Log Daemon.

/etc/shadow The file that contains the encrypted password as well as password and account expiry parameters for each user account.

/etc/skel A directory that contains files that are copied to all new users' home directories upon creation.

/etc/systemd/journald.conf The configuration file for the Systemd Journal Daemon.

/proc/devices A file that contains currently used device information.

/var/log A directory that contains most log files on a Linux system.

/var/spool/at A directory that stores the information used to schedule commands using the at daemon on Fedora systems.

/var/spool/cron A directory that stores user cron tables on a Fedora system.

/var/spool/cron/atjobs A directory that stores the information used to schedule commands using the at daemon on Ubuntu systems.

/var/spool/cron/crontabs A directory that stores user cron tables on an Ubuntu system.

| A shell metacharacter used to pipe Standard Output from one command to the Standard Input of another command.

< A shell metacharacter used to obtain Standard Input from a file.

> A shell metacharacter used to redirect Standard Output and Standard Error to a file.

~ A shell metacharacter used to represent a user's home directory.

1U server A rackmount server that has a standard height of 1.75 inches.

aa-complain command A command used to set an AppArmor profile to complain mode.

aa-enforce command A command used to set an AppArmor profile to enforce mode.

ab (Apache benchmark) command A command that can be used to obtain performance benchmarks for a Web server such as Apache.

absolute pathname The full pathname to a certain file or directory starting from the root directory.

access control list (ACL) The section within an inode of a file or directory that lists the permissions assigned to users and groups on the file or directory.

active partition The partition searched for an operating system after the MBR/GPT.

add-apt-repository command A command used to add repository information to the database used by the apt-get command.

Advanced Technology Attachment (ATA) See *Parallel Advanced Technology Attachment*.

AIX A version of UNIX developed by IBM.

`alias` **command** A command used to create special variables that are shortcuts to longer command strings.

ANDing The process by which binary bits are compared to calculate the network and host IDs from an IP address and subnet mask.

Android A mobile Linux-based operating system currently developed by Google's Open Handset Alliance.

`apachectl` **command** A command that can be used to start, stop, and restart the Apache Web server as well as check for syntax errors within the Apache configuration file.

AppArmor A Linux kernel module and related software packages that prevent malicious software from executing on a Linux system.

AppArmor profile A text file within the /etc/apparmor.d directory that lists application-specific restrictions.

`apparmor_status` **command** A command used to view the status of AppArmor and AppArmor profiles.

application (app) The software that runs on an operating system and provides the user with specific functionality (such as word processing or financial calculation). Applications are commonly referred to as apps today.

`apt-cache` **command** A command used to search DPM repositories for package information.

`apt-get` **(Advanced Package Tool) command** A command used to install and upgrade DPM packages from software repositories, as well as manage and remove installed DPM packages.

Aptitude A utility that can be used to manage DPM packages using a graphical interface.

`aptitude` **command** The command used to start the Aptitude utility.

archive The location (file or device) that contains a copy of files; it is typically created by a back-up utility.

arguments The text that appears after a command name, does not start with a dash (the - character), and specifies information that the command requires to work properly.

artistic license An open source license that allows source code to be distributed freely but changed at the discretion of the original author.

assistive technologies Software programs that cater to specific user needs.

asymmetric encryption A type of encryption that uses a key pair to encrypt and decrypt data.

`at` **command** The command used to schedule commands and tasks to run at a preset time in the future.

at daemon (atd) The system daemon that executes tasks at a future time; it is configured with the `at` command.

authentication The process whereby each user must log in with a valid user name and password before gaining access to the user interface of a system.

Automatic Private IP Addressing (APIPA) A feature that automatically configures a network interface using an IPv4 address on the 169.254.0.0 network.

`background` **(bg) command** The command used to run a foreground process in the background.

background process A process that does not require the BASH shell to wait for its termination. Upon execution, the user receives the BASH shell prompt immediately.

bad blocks The areas of a storage medium unable to store data properly.

baseline A measure of normal system activity.

BASH shell Also known as the Bourne Again Shell, this is the default command-line interface in Linux.

Beowulf clustering A popular and widespread method of clustering computers together to perform useful tasks using Linux.

Berkeley Internet Name Domain (BIND) The standard that all DNS servers and DNS configuration files adhere to.

binary data file A file that contains machine language (binary 1s and 0s) and stores information (such as common functions and graphics) used by binary compiled programs.

BIND configuration utility A graphical utility that can be used to generate and modify the files that are used by the DNS name daemon.

BIOS (Basic Input/Output System) The part of a computer system that contains the programs used to initialize hardware components at boot time.

blade server See *rackmount server*.

block The unit of data commonly used by filesystem commands; a block can contain several sectors.

block devices The storage devices that transfer data to and from the system in chunks of many data bits by caching the information in RAM; they are represented by block device files.

boot loader A program used to load an operating system.

broadcast The TCP/IP communication destined for all computers on a network.

BSD (Berkeley Software Distribution) A version of UNIX developed out of the original UNIX source code and given free to the University of California, Berkeley by AT&T.

B-tree Filesystem (BTRFS) An experimental Linux filesystem that contains advanced features such as storage pools and filesystem snapshots.

btrfs command A command used to configure btrfs filesystem options and check btrfs filesystems for errors.

buffer overrun An attack in which a network service is altered in memory.

bunzip2 command A command used to decompress files compressed by the bzip2 command.

bus mastering The process by which peripheral components perform tasks normally executed by the CPU.

BusyBox DHCP daemon (udhcpd) A lightweight Linux daemon used to provide IPv4 addresses to other computers on the network.

bzcat command A command used to view the contents of an archive created with bzip2 to Standard Output.

bzip2 command A command used to compress files using a Burrows-Wheeler Block Sorting Huffman Coding compression algorithm.

bzless command A command used to view the contents of an archive created with bzip2 to Standard Output in a page-by-page fashion.

bzmore command A command used to view the contents of an archive created with bzip2 to Standard Output in a page-by-page fashion.

cancel command The command used to remove print jobs from the print queue in the CUPS print system.

cat command A Linux command used to display (or concatenate) the entire contents of a text file to the screen.

cd (change directory) command A Linux command used to change the current directory in the directory tree.

cfdisk command A command used to partition hard disks; displays a graphical interface in which the user can select partitioning options.

chage command The command used to modify password expiry information for user accounts.

chains The components of a firewall that specify the general type of network traffic to which rules apply.

character devices The storage devices that transfer data to and from the system one data bit at a time; they are represented by character device files.

chattr (change attributes) command The command used to change filesystem attributes for a Linux file.

checksum A calculated value that is unique to a file's size and contents.

chfn command The command used to change the GECOS for a user.

chgrp (change group) command The command used to change the group owner of a file or directory.

child process A process that was started by another process (parent process).

chkconfig command A command that can be used to configure UNIX SysV daemon startup by runlevel.

chmod (change mode) command The command used to change the mode (permissions) of a file or directory.

chown (change owner) command The command used to change the owner and group owner of a file or directory.

Chrony NTP daemon (chronyd) A daemon that provides fast time synchronization services on Linux computers.

chronyc command A command that can query the state of an NTP server or client as well as synchronize the system time with an NTP server.

chroot command A Linux command that can be used to change the root of one Linux system to another.

chsh command The command used to change a valid shell to an invalid shell.

classless interdomain routing (CIDR) notation A notation that is often used to represent an IP address and its subnet mask.

closed source software The software whose source code is not freely available from the original author; Windows 98 is an example.

cloud Another term for the Internet.

cloud platform A series of software components that are installed on servers distributed across the Internet and provide services to a large number of Internet users.

cluster A grouping of several smaller computers that function as one large supercomputer.

clustering The act of making a cluster; see also *cluster*.

command A program that exists on the filesystem and is executed when typed on the command line.

command mode One of the two modes in vi; it allows a user to perform any available text-editing task that is not related to inserting text into the document.

Common Unix Printing System (CUPS) The printing system commonly used on Linux computers.

Compiz Fusion A window manager that is often used alongside the KDE and GNOME desktops to provide advanced graphical effects.

compression The process in which files are reduced in size by a compression algorithm.

compress command A command used to compress files using a Lempel-Ziv compression algorithm.

compression algorithm The set of instructions used to reduce the contents of a file systematically.

compression ratio The amount of compression that occurred during compression.

concatenation The joining of text together to make one larger whole. In Linux, words and strings of text are joined together to form a displayed file.

counter variable A variable that is altered by loop constructs to ensure that commands are not executed indefinitely.

cp (copy) command The command used to create copies of files and directories.

cpio (copy in/out) command A command used to run a common back-up utility.

cracker A person who uses computer software maliciously for personal profit.

cron daemon (crond) The system daemon that executes tasks repetitively in the future and that is configured using cron tables.

cron table A file specifying tasks to be run by the cron daemon; there are user cron tables and system cron tables.

crontab command The command used to view and edit user cron tables.

CUPS daemon (cupsd) The daemon responsible for printing in the CUPS printing system.

CUPS Web administration tool A Web-based management tool for the CUPS printing system.

cupsaccept command The command used to allow a printer to accept jobs into the print queue.

cupsdisable command The command used to prevent print jobs from leaving the print queue.

cupsenable command The command used to allow print jobs to leave the print queue.

cupsreject command The command used to force a printer to reject jobs from entering the print queue.

curl command A command that can be used to obtain a Web page from a Web server.

cylinder A series of tracks on a hard disk that are written to simultaneously by the magnetic heads in a hard disk drive.

daemon A Linux system process that provides a system service.

daemon process A system process that is not associated with a terminal.

data blocks A filesystem allocation unit in which the data that makes up the contents of the file as well as the filename are stored.

database A file that contains data that is organized into tables.

Database Management System (DBMS) Software that manages databases.

Date & Time utility A graphical utility within Fedora 20 that can be used to set the date, time, and timezone information for a system.

Debian Package Manager (DPM) A package manager used on Debian and Debian-based Linux distributions, such as Ubuntu Server.

decision construct A special construct used in a shell script to alter the flow of the program based on the outcome of a command or contents of a variable. Common decision constructs include if, case, &&, and ||.

default gateway The IP address of the router on the network used to send packets to remote networks.

desktop environment The software that works with a window manager to provide a standard GUI environment that uses standard programs and development tools.

developmental kernel A Linux kernel whose minor number is odd and has been recently developed yet not thoroughly tested.

device driver A piece of software containing instructions that the kernel of an operating system uses to control and interact with a specific type of computer hardware.

device file A file used by Linux commands that represents a specific device on the system; these files do not have a data section and use major and minor numbers to reference the proper driver and specific device on the system, respectively.

df (disk free space) command A command that displays disk free space by filesystem.

DHCP daemon (dhcpd) The most common Linux daemon used to provide IPv4 and IPv6 addresses to other computers on the network.

digital signature Information that has been encrypted using a private key.

Digital Signature Algorithm (DSA) A common asymmetric encryption algorithm that is primarily used for creating digital signatures.

directive A line within a configuration file.

directory A special file on the filesystem used to organize other files into a logical tree structure.

disk mirroring A RAID configuration consisting of two identical hard disks to which identical data are written in parallel, thus ensuring fault tolerance. Also known as RAID 1.

disk striping A RAID configuration in which a single file is divided into sections, which are then written to different hard disks concurrently to speed up access time; this type of RAID is not fault tolerant. Also known as RAID 0.

disk striping with parity A RAID configuration that incorporates disk striping for faster file access, as well as parity information to ensure fault tolerance. Also known as RAID 5.

distribution A complete set of operating system software, including the Linux kernel, supporting function libraries, and a variety of OSS packages that can be downloaded from the Internet free of charge. These OSS packages are what differentiate the various distributions of Linux.

DNS cache file A file that contains the IP addresses of top-level DNS servers.

document root The directory on a Web server that stores Web content for distribution to Web browsers.

documentation The system information that is stored in a log book for future reference.

Domain Name Space (DNS) A hierarchical namespace used for host names.

dpkg command A command used to install, query, and remove DPM packages.

dpkg-query command A command used to query installed DPM packages.

du (directory usage) command A command that displays directory usage.

dump command A command used to create full and incremental backups.

dumpleases command A command that can be used to obtain current DHCP leases from the BusyBox DHCP daemon (udhcpd).

echo command A command used to display or echo output to the terminal screen. It might utilize escape sequences.

edquota command A command used to specify quota limits for users and groups.

egrep command A variant of the grep command used to search files for patterns, using extended regular expressions.

ELILO A boot loader used with computers that support Intel Extensible Firmware Interface (EFI) technology.

Emacs (Editor MACroS) editor A popular and widespread text editor more conducive to word processing than vi. It was originally developed by Richard Stallman.

env command A command used to display a list of exported variables present in the current shell, except special variables.

environment files The files used immediately after login to execute commands; they are typically used to load variables into memory.

environment variables The variables that store information commonly accessed by the system or programs executing on the system; together, these variables form the user environment.

escape sequences The character sequences that have special meaning inside the echo command. They are prefixed by the \ character.

Ethernet The most common media access method used in networks today.

executable program A file that can be executed by the Linux operating system to run in memory as a process and perform a useful function.

export command A command used to send variables to subshells.

exporting The process used to describe the sharing of a directory using NFS to other computers.

ext2 A nonjournaling Linux filesystem.

ext3 A journaling Linux filesystem.

ext4 An improved version of the ext3 filesystem, with an extended feature set and better performance.

Extended Internet Super Daemon (xinetd) A network daemon that is used to start other network daemons on demand.

extended partition A partition on a hard disk that can be further subdivided into components called logical drives.

facility The area of the system from which information is gathered when logging system events.

fault tolerant Term used to describe a device that exhibits a minimum of downtime in the event of a failure.

fdisk command A command used to create, delete, and manipulate partitions on hard disks.

fgrep command A variant of the grep command that does not allow the use of regular expressions.

field An attribute within a record in a database table.

file command A Linux command that displays the file type of a specified filename.

file descriptors The numeric labels used to define command input and command output.

file handles The connections that a program makes to files on a filesystem.

File Transfer Protocol (FTP) The most common protocol used to transfer files across networks such as the Internet.

filename The user-friendly identifier given to a file.

filename extension A series of identifiers following a dot (.) at the end of a filename, used to denote the type of the file; the filename extention .txt denotes a text file.

filesystem The organization imposed on a physical storage medium that is used to manage the storage and retrieval of data.

filesystem corruption The errors in a filesystem structure that prevent the retrieval of stored data.

Filesystem Hierarchy Standard (FHS) A standard outlining the location of set files and directories on a Linux system.

filter command A command that can take from Standard Input and send to Standard Output. In other words, a filter is a command that can exist in the middle of a pipe.

find command The command used to find files on the filesystem using various criteria.

Firewall Configuration utility A graphical firewall configuration utility within Fedora 20.

firewall daemon (firewalld) A daemon used on some Linux systems to provide for easier configuration of netfilter via the ipchains command.

firewall-cmd command A command used to view and configure firewalld zones, services, and rules.

firmware RAID A RAID system controlled by the computer's BIOS.

flavor A term that refers to a specific type of UNIX operating system. For example, Solaris and BSD are two different flavors of UNIX.

foreground (fg) command The command used to run a background process in the foreground.

foreground process A process for which the BASH shell that executed it must wait for its termination.

forking The act of creating a new BASH shell child process from a parent BASH shell process.

formatting The process in which a filesystem is placed on a device.

forward lookup A DNS name resolution request whereby a FQDN is resolved to an IP address.

free command A command used to display memory and swap statistics.

Free Software Foundation (FSF) An organization started by Richard Stallman that promotes and encourages the collaboration of software developers worldwide to allow the free sharing of source code and software programs.

freeware Software distributed by the developer at no cost to the user.

frequently asked questions (FAQs) An area on a Web site where answers to commonly posed questions can be found.

fsck (filesystem check) command A command used to check the integrity of a filesystem and repair damaged files.

ftp command A command-line FTP client program that is found in most operating systems.

full backup An archive of an entire filesystem.

fully qualified domain name (FQDN) A host name that follows DNS convention.

fuser command A command used to identify any users or processes using a particular file or directory.

gcc (GNU C Compiler) command The command used to compile source code written in the C programming language into binary programs.

gdisk (GPT fdisk) command A command used to create partitions on a GPT hard disk. It uses an interface that is very similar to fdisk.

gedit editor A common text editor used within GUI environments.

General Electric Comprehensive Operating System (GECOS) The field in the /etc/passwd file that contains a description of the user account.

getfacl (get file ACL) command The command used to list all ACL entries for a particular Linux file or directory.

GNOME Display Manager (gdm) A program that provides a graphical login screen.

GnomeBaker CD/DVD Writer A common disc burning software used on Linux systems.

GNU An acronym that stands for "GNU's Not Unix."

GNU General Public License (GPL) A software license, ensuring that the source code for any OSS will remain freely available to anyone who wants to examine, build on, or improve upon it.

GNU Network Object Model Environment (GNOME) The default desktop environment on most Linux systems; it was created in 1997.

GNU Privacy Guard (GPG) An open source asymmetric encryption technology that is primarily used by e-mail programs.

GNU Project A free operating system project started by Richard Stallman.

gpg command A command used to encrypt and digitally sign information using GPG.

GRand Unified Bootloader (GRUB) A boot loader used to boot a variety of different operating systems (including Linux) on a variety of different hardware platforms.

GRand Unified Bootloader version 2 (GRUB2) An enhanced version of the GRUB boot loader. It is the most common boot loader used on modern Linux systems.

graphical user interface (GUI) The component of an operating system that provides a user-friendly interface comprising graphics or icons to represent desired tasks. Users can point and click to execute a command rather than having to know and use proper command-line syntax.

grep command A Linux command that searches files for patterns of characters using regular expression metacharacters. The command name is short for "global regular expression print."

group When used in the mode of a certain file or directory, the collection of users who have ownership of that file or directory.

Group Identifier (GID) A unique number given to each group.

groupadd command The command used to add a group to the system.

groupdel command The command used to delete a group from the system.

groupmod command The command used to modify the name or GID of a group on the system.

groups command The command that lists group membership for a user.

GRUB root partition The partition containing the second stage of the GRUB boot loader and the GRUB configuration file.

grub2-install command The command used to install the GRUB2 boot loader.

grub2-mkconfig command The command used to build the GRUB2 configuration file from entries within the /etc/default/grub file and /etc/grub.d directory.

grubby command A command that can be used to configure the LILO, GRUB and GRUB2 boot loaders.

grub-install command The command used to install the GRUB boot loader.

GTK+ toolkit A development toolkit for C programming; it is used in the GNOME desktop and the GNU Image Manipulation Program (GIMP).

GUI environment A GUI core component such as X Windows, combined with a window manager and desktop environment that provides the look and feel of the GUI. Although functionality might be similar among GUI environments, users might prefer one environment to another due to its ease of use.

GUID Partition Table (GPT) The area of a large hard disk (> 2TB) outside a partition that stores partition information and boot loaders.

gunzip command A command used to decompress files compressed by the gzip command.

gzip (GNU zip) command A command used to compress files using a Lempel-Ziv compression algorithm.

hacker A person who explores computer science to gain knowledge—not to be confused with "cracker."

hard disk quotas The limits on the number of files, or total storage space on a hard disk drive, available to a user.

hard limit A hard disk quota that the user cannot be exceed.

hard link A file joined to other files on the same filesystem that shares the same inode.

hardware The tangible parts of a computer, such as the network boards, video card, hard disk drives, printers, and keyboards.

Hardware Compatibility List (HCL) A list of hardware components that have been tested and deemed compatible with a given operating system.

hardware platform A particular configuration and grouping of computer hardware, normally centered on and determined by processor type and architecture.

hardware RAID A RAID system controlled by hardware located on a disk controller card within the computer.

hashpling The first line in a shell script, which defines the shell that will be used to interpret the commands in the script file.

head command A Linux command that displays the first set of lines of a text file; by default, the head command displays the first 10 lines.

home directory A directory on the filesystem set aside for users to store personal files and information.

host ID The portion of an IP address that denotes the host.

host name A user-friendly name assigned to a computer.

hostname command A command used to display and change the host name of a computer.

hostnamectl command A command used to change the host name of a computer as well as ensure that the new host name is loaded at boot time.

hot fix A solution for a software bug made by a closed source vendor.

HOWTO A task-specific instruction guide to performing any of a wide variety of tasks; it is freely available from the Linux Documentation Project at www.linuxdoc.org.

HP-UX A version of UNIX developed by Hewlett-Packard.

hwclock command A command that can be used to view and modify the system clock within the computer BIOS.

id command The command that lists UIDs for a user and the GIDs for the groups that the same user belongs to.

ifconfig (interface configuration) command A command used to display and modify the TCP/IP configuration information for a network interface.

incremental backup An archive of a filesystem that contains only files that were modified since the last archive was created.

info pages A set of local, easy-to-read command syntax documentation available by typing the info command-line utility.

infrastructure services Services that provide TCP configuration, name resolution, time synchronization, or system configuration to other computers on a network.

init command A UNIX SysV command used to change the operating system from one runlevel to another.

initialize (init) daemon The first process started by the Linux kernel; it is responsible for starting and stopping other daemons.

initstate See *runlevel*.

inode The portion of a file that stores information on the file's attributes, access permissions, location, ownership, and file type.

inode table The collection of inodes for all files and directories on a filesystem.

insert mode One of the two modes in vi; it allows the user to insert text into the document but does not allow any other functionality.

insmod command A command used to insert a module into the Linux kernel.

installation log files The files created at installation to record actions that occurred or failed during the installation process.

Integrated Drive Electronics (IDE) See *Parallel Advanced Technology Attachment*.

interactive mode The mode that file management commands use when a file can be overwritten; the system interacts with a user asking for the user to confirm the action.

Internet Control Message Protocol version 6 (ICMPv6) A protocol used by computers to obtain an IPv6 configuration from a router on the network.

Internet Printing Protocol (IPP) A printing protocol that can be used to send print jobs across a TCP/IP network, such as the Internet, using HTTP or HTTPS.

Internet Protocol (IP) address A series of four 8-bit numbers that represent a computer on a network.

Internet SCSI (iSCSI) A SCSI technology that transfers data via TCP/IP networks.

Internet service provider (ISP) A company that provides Internet access.

Internet Super Daemon (inetd) A network daemon that is used to start other network daemons on demand.

Intrusion Detection System (IDS) A program that can be used to detect unauthorized access to a Linux system.

iOS A mobile version of UNIX developed by Apple for use on iPhone, iPod and iPad devices.

iostat (input/output statistics) command A command that displays Input/Output statistics for block devices.

ip command A command used to manipulate the route table.

IP forwarding The act of forwarding TCP/IP packets from one network to another. See also *routing*.

IP version 4 (IPv4) The most common version of IP used on the Internet. It uses a 32-bit addressing scheme organized into different classes.

IP version 6 (IPv6) A recent version of IP that is used by some hosts on the Internet. It uses a 128-bit addressing scheme.

ip6tables command A command used to configure IPv6 rules for a netfilter firewall.

iptables command A command used to configure IPv4 rules for a netfilter firewall.

iSCSI initiator A term that refers to the computer that connects to the iSCSI target within an iSCSI SAN.

iSCSI target A term that refers to a storage device within an iSCSI SAN.

ISO image A file that contains the content of a DVD. ISO images of Linux installation media can be downloaded from the Internet.

iterative query A DNS resolution request that was resolved without the use of top-level DNS servers.

jabbering The process by which failing hardware components send large amounts of information to the CPU.

jitter The difference between time measurements from several different NTP servers.

jobs command The command used to see the list of background processes running in the current shell.

journald A daemon used to record (or journal) system events on some Linux distributions, such as Fedora 20.

journalctl command The command used to query the database created by the Systemd Journal Daemon.

journaling A filesystem function that keeps track of the information that needs to be written to the hard disk or SSD in a journal; common Linux journaling filesystems include ext3, ext4, and REISER.

K Desktop Environment (KDE) A desktop environment created by Matthias Ettrich in 1996.

K Window Manager (kwin) The window manager that works under the KDE Desktop Environment.

KDE Display Manager (kdm) A graphical login screen for users that resembles the KDE desktop.

kernel The central, core program of the operating system. The shared commonality of the kernel is what defines Linux; the differing OSS applications that can interact with the common kernel are what differentiate Linux distributions.

key A unique piece of information that is used within an encryption algorithm.

kill command The command used to kill or terminate a process.

kill signal The type of signal sent to a process by the kill command; different kill signals affect processes in different ways.

killall command The command that kills all instances of a process by command name.

Knoppix Linux A small Linux distribution often installed on removeable media.

ldconfig command A command that updates the /etc/ld.so.conf and /etc/ld.so.cache files.

ldd command A command used to display the shared libraries used by a certain program.

less command A Linux command used to display a text file page-by-page on the terminal screen; users can then use the cursor keys to navigate the file.

lilo command The command used to reinstall the LILO boot loader based on the configuration information in /etc/lilo.conf.

Line Printer Daemon (LPD) A printing system typically used on legacy Linux computers.

link local The portion of an IPv6 address that refers to a unique computer. It is analogous to the host portion of an IPv4 address.

linked file The files that represent the same data as other files.

Linus Torvalds A Finnish graduate student who coded and created the first version of Linux and subsequently distributed it under the GNU Public License.

Linux A software operating system originated by Linus Torvalds. The common core, or kernel, continues to evolve and be revised. Differing OSS bundled with the Linux kernel is what defines the wide variety of distributions now available.

Linux Documentation Project (LDP) A large collection of Linux resources, information, and help files supplied free of charge and maintained by the Linux community.

Linux Loader (LILO) A common boot loader used on legacy Linux systems.

Linux server distribution A Linux distribution that contains packages that are useful for Linux servers.

Linux User Group (LUG) The open forums of Linux users who discuss and assist each other in using and modifying the Linux operating system and the OSS run on it. There are LUGs worldwide.

live media Linux installation media that provides a fully functional Linux operating system in RAM prior to installation on permanent storage.

ll command An alias for the ls -l command; it gives a long file listing.

ln (link) command The command used to create hard and symbolic links.

local area networks (LANs) Networks in which the computers are all in close physical proximity.

locate command The command used to locate files from a file database.

lock an account To make an account temporarily unusable by altering the password information for it stored on the system.

log file A file that contains past system events.

logger command A command that can be used to write system log events.

logical drives The smaller partitions contained within an extended partition on a hard disk.

Logical Unit Number (LUN) A unique identifier for each device attached to any given node in a SCSI chain.

Logical Volume (LV) A volume that is managed by the LVM and comprised of free space within a VG.

Logical Volume Manager (LVM) A set of software components within Linux that can be used to manage the storage of information across several different hard disks on a Linux system.

logrotate command The command used to rotate log files; typically uses the configuration information stored in /etc/logrotate.conf.

loop construct A special construct used in a shell script to execute commands repetitively. Common decision constructs include for and while.

lp command The command used to create print jobs in the print queue in the CUPS printing system.

lpadmin command The command used to perform printer administration in the CUPS printing system.

lpc command The command used to view the status of and control printers in the LPD printing system.

lpq command The command used to view the contents of print queues in the LPD printing system.

lpr command The command used to create print jobs in the print queue in the LPD printing system.

lprm command The command used to remove print jobs from the print queue in the LPD printing system.

lpstat command The command used to view the contents of print queues and printer information in the CUPS printing system.

ls command A Linux command used to list the files in a given directory.

lsattr (list attributes) command The command used to list filesystem attributes for a Linux file.

lscpu command A command that lists hardware details for CPUs on the system.

lshw command A command used to list details regarding hardware devices in a Linux system.

lsmod command A command used to list the modules that are currently used by the Linux kernel.

lsof (list open files) command A command that lists the files that are currently being viewed or modified by software programs and users.

lspci command A command that lists the hardware devices that are currently attached to the PCI bus on the system.

lsusb command A command that lists the USB devices that are currently plugged into the system.

lvcreate command A command used to create LVM logical volumes.

lvdisplay command A command used to view LVM logical volumes.

lvextend command A command used to add additional space from VGs to existing LVM logical volumes.

lvscan command A command used to view LVM logical volumes.

Macintosh OS X A version of UNIX developed by Apple for use on Apple desktop computers and servers.

mail command A common e-mail client on UNIX, Linux, and Macintosh systems.

Mail Delivery Agent (MDA) The service that downloads e-mail from a mail transfer agent.

Mail Transfer Agent (MTA) An e-mail server.

Mail User Agent (MUA) A program that allows e-mail to be read by a user.

major number When referring to device files, the major number is used by the kernel to identify which device driver to call to interact properly with a given category of hardware; hard disk drives, CDs, and video cards are all categories of hardware; similar devices share a common major number. When referring to kernel versions, the major number is the number preceding the first dot in the number used to identify a Linux kernel version.

man pages See *manual pages*.

manual pages The most common set of local command syntax documentation, available by typing the man command-line utility. Also known as man pages.

Master Boot Record (MBR) The area of a typical hard disk (< 2TB) outside a partition that stores partition information and boot loaders.

master DNS server See *primary DNS server*.

mdadm command A command used to configure software RAID on a Linux system.

media access method A system that defines how computers on a network share access to the physical medium.

memtest86 A common RAM-checking utility.

Message Passing Interface (MPI) A system that is used on Beowulf clusters to pass information to several separate computers in a parallel fashion.

metacharacters The key combinations that have special meaning in the Linux operating system.

MINIX Mini-UNIX created by Andrew Tannenbaum. Instructions on how to code the kernel for this version of the Unix operating system were publicly available. Using this as a starting point, Linus Torvalds improved this version of UNIX for the Intel platform and created the first version of Linux.

minor number When referring to device files, the minor number is used by the kernel to identify which specific hardware device, within a given category, to use a driver to communicate with. When referring to a Linux kernel, the minor number is the number following the first dot in the number used to identify a Linux kernel version, denoting a minor modification. If odd, it is a version under development and not yet fully tested. See also *developmental kernel* and *production kernel*.

mkdir (make directory) command The command used to create directories.

mkfs (make filesystem) command A command used to format or create filesystems.

mkisofs command A command used to create an ISO image from one or more files on the filesystem.

mknod command A command used to re-create a device file, provided the major number, minor number, and type (character or bock) are known.

mkswap command A command used to prepare newly created swap partitions for use by the Linux system.

mode The part of the inode that stores information on access permissions.

Modem Manager utility A graphical utility that can be used to configure modem settings on Linux systems.

modprobe command A command used to insert a module into the Linux kernel.

monitoring The process by which system areas are observed for problems or irregularities.

more command A Linux command used to display a text file page by page and line by line on the terminal screen.

mount command A command used to mount filesystems on devices to mount point directories.

mount point The directory in a file structure to which something is mounted.

mounting A process used to associate a device with a directory in the logical directory tree such that users can store data on that device.

mpstat (multiple processor statistics) command A command that displays CPU statistics.

multi boot A configuration in which two or more operating systems exist on the hard disk of a computer; the boot loader allows the user to choose which operating system to load at boot time.

multicast The TCP/IP communication destined for a certain group of computers.

multihomed hosts The computers that have more than one network interface.

Multiplexed Information and Computing Service (MULTICS) A prototype time-sharing operating system that was developed in the late-1960s by AT&T Bell Laboratories.

multitasking A type of operating system that is able to manage multiple tasks simultaneously.

multiuser A type of operating system that is able to provide access to multiple users simultaneously.

mutter window manager The default window manager for the GNOME Desktop Environment in Fedora 13.

mv (move) command The command used to move/rename files and directories.

named pipe file A temporary connection that sends information from one command or process in memory to another; it can also be represented by a file on the filesystem.

nano editor A user-friendly terminal text editor that uses Ctrl key combinations to perform basic functions.

NetBIOS A protocol used by Windows computers that adds a unique 15-character name to file- and printer-sharing traffic.

netfilter The Linux kernel component that provides firewall and NAT capability on modern Linux systems.

network Two or more computers joined together via network media and able to exchange information.

Network Address Translation (NAT) A technology used on routers that allows computers on a network to obtain Internet resources via a single network interface on the router itself.

Network Connections tool A graphical utility in Fedora 20 that can be used to configure DSL settings.

Network File System (NFS) A set of software components that can be used to share files natively between UNIX, Linux, and Macintosh computers on a network.

network ID The portion of an IP address that denotes the network.

Network Information Service (NIS) A set of software components that can be used to standardize the configuration files across several different Linux and UNIX computers.

network service A process that responds to network requests.

Network Time Protocol (NTP) A protocol that can be used to obtain time information from other computers on the Internet.

Network utility A graphical utility in Fedora 20 that can be used to configure network settings for the NICs on the system.

network zone A component of firewalld that defines the level of trust for network connections.

newaliases command A command that can be used to rebuild the e-mail alias database based on the entries within the /etc/aliases file.

newgrp command The command used to temporarily change the primary group of a user.

newsgroup An Internet protocol service accessed via an application program called a newsreader. This service allows access to postings (e-mails in a central place accessible by all newsgroup users) normally organized along specific themes. Users with questions on specific topics can post messages, which can be answered by other users.

nice command The command used to change the priority of a process as it is started.

nice value The value that indirectly represents the priority of a process; the higher the value, the lower the priority.

NIS client A computer in an NIS domain that receives its configuration from an NIS master server or NIS slave server.

NIS domain A group of computers that share the same NIS configuration.

NIS map A system configuration that is shared by the computers within an NIS domain.

NIS master server The computer in an NIS domain that contains the master copy of all NIS maps.

NIS slave server A computer in an NIS domain that receives a read-only copy of all NIS maps from an NIS master server.

nmap (network mapper) command A command that can be used to scan ports on network computers.

nmblookup command A command that can test NetBIOS name resolution on a Linux system.

nm-connection-editor command A command used to start the Network Connections tool on Fedora 20 systems.

nohup command A command that prevents other commands from exiting when the parent process is killed.

NTP daemon (ntpd) The most common daemon used to provide time synchronization services on Linux computers.

ntpdate command A command that can view the current system time as well as synchronize the system time with an NTP server.

ntpq command A command that can query the state of an NTP server or client.

octet A portion of an IP address that represents eight binary bits.

od command A Linux command used to display the contents of a file in octal format.

offset The difference in time between two computers that use the NTP protocol.

Open Source Software (OSS) The programs distributed and licensed so that the source code making up the program is freely available to anyone who wants to examine, utilize, or improve upon it.

OpenSUSE One of the most popular and prevalent distributions of Linux, originally developed in Europe.

operating system (OS) The software used to control and directly interact with the computer hardware components.

options The specific letters that start with a dash (the - character) or two and appear after the command name to alter the way the command works.

other When used in the mode of a certain file or directory, all the users on the Linux system.

overclocked Term used to describe a CPU that runs faster than the clock speed for which it has been rated.

owner The user whose name appears in a long listing of a file or directory and who has the ability to change permissions on that file or directory.

package dependencies A list of packages that are prerequisite to the current package being installed on the system.

package group A group of RPM packages that are commonly installed to provide a specific function on the system.

package manager The software used to install, maintain, and remove other software programs by storing all relevant software information in a central software database on the computer.

packets The packages of data formatted by a network protocol.

Parallel Advanced Technology Attachment (PATA) A legacy hard disk technology that uses ribbon cables to typically attach up to four hard disk devices to a single computer.

Parallel SCSI The traditional SCSI technology that transfers data across parallel cables.

parent directory The directory that is one level closer to the root directory in the directory tree relative to your current directory.

parent process A process that has started other processes (child processes).

parent process ID (PPID) The PID of the parent process that created the current process.

parted (GNU Parted) command A command used to create partitions on a GPT or MBR hard disk.

partition A section of a hard disk or SSD. Partitions can be primary or extended.

passwd command The command used to modify the password associated with a user account.

PATH variable A variable that stores a list of directories that will be searched in order when commands are executed without an absolute or relative pathname.

permissions A list that identifies who can access a file or folder and their level of access.

physical extent (PE) size The block size used by the LVM when storing data on a volume group.

Physical Volumes (PVs) A hard disk partition that is used by the LVM.

ping (Packet Internet Groper) command A command used to check TCP/IP connectivity on a network.

pipe A string of commands connected by | metacharacters.

Pluggable Authentication Modules (PAM) The component that handles authentication requests by daemons on a Linux system.

port A number that uniquely identifies a network service.

Postfix A common e-mail server daemon used on Linux systems.

PostgreSQL A common SQL server used on Linux computers.

PostgreSQL utility The program used to perform most database management on a PostgreSQL server.

Power On Self Test (POST) An initial series of tests run when a computer is powered on to ensure that hardware components are functional.

PPP over Ethernet (PPPoE) The protocol used by DSL to send PPP information over an Ethernet connection.

pppoeconf command A command used to configure a DSL connection on Ubuntu Server 14.04 systems.

pppoe-setup command A command used to configure a DSL connection on Fedora 20 systems.

primary DNS server The DNS server that contains a read/write copy of the zone.

primary group The group that is specified for a user in the /etc/passwd file and that is specified as group owner for all files created by a user.

primary partitions The separate divisions into which a hard disk or SSD can be divided (up to four are allowed per hard disk).

print job The information sent to a printer for printing.

print job ID A unique numeric identifier used to mark and distinguish each print job.

print queue A directory on the filesystem that holds print jobs that are waiting to be printed.

printer class A group of CUPS printers that are treated as a single unit for the purposes of printing and management.

Printers tool A graphical utility used to configure printers on a Fedora 20 system.

priority The importance of system information when logging system events.

private key An asymmetric encryption key that is used to decrypt data and create digital signatures.

proactive maintenance The measures taken to reduce future system problems.

process A program loaded into memory and running on the processor performing a specific task.

process ID (PID) A unique identifier assigned to every process as it begins.

process priority A number assigned to a process, used to determine how many time slices on the processor that process will receive; the higher the number, the lower the priority.

process state The current state of the process on the processor; most processes are in the sleeping or running state.

production kernel A Linux kernel whose minor number (the number after the dot in the version number) is even, therefore deemed stable for use through widespread testing.

program A structured set of commands stored in an executable file on a filesystem. A program can be executed to create a process.

programming language The syntax used for developing a program. Different programming languages use different syntaxes.

protocol A set of rules of communication used between computers on a network.

proxy server A server or hardware device that requests Internet resources on behalf of other computers.

ps command The command used to obtain information about processes currently running on the system.

psql command The command used to start the PostgreSQL utility.

pstree command A command that displays processes according to their lineage, starting from the init daemon.

public key An asymmetric encryption key that is used to encrypt data and decrypt digital signatures.

Putty A cross-platform SSH client.

pvcreate command A command used to create LVM physical volumes.

pvdisplay command A command used to view LVM physical volumes.

pvscan command A command used to view LVM physical volumes.

pwconv command The command used to enable the use of the /etc/shadow file.

pwd (print working directory) command A Linux command used to display the current directory in the directory tree.

pwunconv command The command used to disable the use of the /etc/shadow file.

Qt toolkit The software toolkit used with the K Desktop Environment.

queuing See *spooling*.

quota command A command used to view disk quotas imposed on a user.

quotaoff command A command used to deactivate disk quotas.

quotaon command A command used to activate disk quotas.

quotas The limits that can be imposed on users and groups for filesystem usage.

rackmount server A thin form factor used to house server hardware that is installed in a server rack.

RAID-Z An implementation of RAID level 5 using ZFS, which uses a variable stripe that provides for better performance and fault tolerance.

reactive maintenance The measures taken when system problems arise.

read command A command used to read Standard Input from a user into a variable.

record A line within a database table that represents a particular object.

recursive A term referring to itself and its own contents; a recursive search includes all subdirectories in a directory and their contents.

recursive query A DNS resolution request that was resolved with the use of top-level DNS servers.

Red Hat One of the most popular and prevalent distributions of Linux in North America, distributed and supported by Red Hat, Inc. Fedora is a Red Hat-based Linux distribution.

Red Hat Package Manager (RPM) The most commonly used package manager for Linux, and the default package manager used on Fedora Linux.

redirection The process of changing the default locations of Standard Input, Standard Output, and Standard Error.

Redundant Array of Inexpensive Disks (RAID) A type of storage that can be used to combine hard disks together for performance and/or fault tolerance.

regexp See *regular expressions*.

regular expressions The special metacharacters used to match patterns of text within text files; they are commonly used by text tool commands, including grep.

REISER A journaling filesystem used in Linux.

relational database A database that contains multiple tables that are linked by common fields.

relative pathname The pathname of a target directory relative to your current directory in the tree.

renice command The command used to alter the nice value of a process currently running on the system.

repquota command A command used to produce a report on quotas for a particular filesystem.

resource records The records within a zone on a DNS server that provide name resolution for individual computers.

restart command A command that can be used to manually restart an upstart daemon.

restore command A command used to extract archives created with the dump command.

reverse lookup A DNS name resolution request whereby an IP address is resolved to a FQDN.

revision number The number after the second dot in the version number of a Linux kernel that identifies the release number of a kernel.

Rivest Shamir Adleman (RSA) A common asymmetric encryption algorithm.

rm (remove) command The command used to remove files and directories.

rmdir (remove directory) command The command used to remove empty directories.

rmmod command A command used to remove a module from the Linux kernel.

rogue process A process that has become faulty in some way and continues to consume far more system resources than it should.

root filesystem The filesystem that contains most files that make up the operating system; it should have enough free space to prevent errors and slow performance.

route command A command used to manipulate the route table.

route table A table of information used to indicate which networks are connected to network interfaces.

router A computer running routing software or a special function hardware device that provides interconnection between networks; it contains information regarding the structure of the networks and sends information from one component network to another.

routing The act of forwarding data packets from one network to another.

rpm command A command used to install, query, and remove RPM packages.

rules The components of a firewall that match specific network traffic that is to be allowed or dropped.

runlevel A UNIX SysV term that defines a certain type and number of daemons on a Linux system.

runlevel command The command used to display the current and most recent (previous) runlevel.

runtime configuration (rc) scripts Scripts that are used during the system initialization process to start daemons and provide system functionality.

sar (system activity reporter) command A command that displays various system statistics.

scalability The capability of computers to increase workload as the number of processors increases.

SCSI ID A number that uniquely identifies and prioritizes devices attached to a SCSI controller.

search engine An Internet Web site, such as www.google.com, where you simply enter a phrase representing your search item and receive a list of Web sites that contain relevant material.

secondary DNS server A DNS server that contains a read-only copy of the zone.

sector The smallest unit of data storage on a hard disk; sectors are arranged into concentric circles called tracks and can be grouped into blocks for use by the system.

Secure Shell (SSH) A technology that can be used to run remote applications on a Linux computer; it encrypts all client-server traffic.

Security Enhanced Linux (SELinux) A set of Linux kernel components and related software packages that prevent malicious software from executing on a Linux system.

segmentation fault An error that software encounters when it cannot locate the information needed to complete its task.

Serial Advanced Technology Attachment (SATA) A technology that allows for fast data transfer along a serial cable for hard disks and SSDs. It is commonly used in newer workstation and server-class computers.

Serial Attached SCSI (SAS) A SCSI technology that transfers information in serial mode rather than the traditional parallel mode.

server A computer configured to allow other computers to connect to it from across a network.

server closet A secured room that stores servers within an organization.

Server Message Blocks (SMB) The protocol that Windows computers use to format file- and printer-sharing traffic on TCP/IP networks.

server services The services that are made available for other computers across a network.

service command A command that can be used to manually start, stop, and restart UNIX SysV daemons.

service unit A Systemd term that is used to describe a daemon.

sestatus command A command that displays the current status and functionality of the SELinux subsystem.

set command A command used to view all variables in the shell, except special variables.

setfacl (set file ACL) command The command used to modify ACL entries for a particular Linux file or directory.

shareware The programs developed and provided at minimal cost to the end user. These programs are initially free but require payment after a period of time or usage.

shell A user interface that accepts input from the user and passes the input to the kernel for processing.

shell scripts The text files that contain a list of commands or constructs for the shell to execute in order.

showmount command A command used to view NFS shared directories on a remote computer.

skeleton directory A directory that contains files that are copied to all new users' home directories upon creation; the default skeleton directory on Linux systems is /etc/skel.

slave DNS server See *secondary DNS server*.

Small Computer Systems Interface (SCSI) A high-performance hard disk technology that is commonly used in server-class computers.

smbclient command A command that can be used to connect to a remote Windows or Samba server and transfer files.

smbpasswd command A command used to generate a Samba password for a user.

socket file A named pipe connecting processes on two different computers; it can also be represented by a file on the filesystem.

soft limit A hard disk quota that the user can exceed for a certain period of time.

software The programs stored on a storage device in a computer, which provide a certain function when executed.

software mirrors Software repositories that host the same RPM or DPM packages as other software repositories for fault tolerance and load balancing of download requests.

software RAID A RAID system that is controlled by software running within the operating system.

software repositories Servers on the Internet that host RPM or DPM packages for download.

Software utility A program that can be used to install, update, and remove RPM packages within a desktop environment on Fedora 20.

Solaris A version of UNIX developed by Sun Microsystems from AT&T source code.

solid-state drive (SSD) A type of disk drive that functions within a computer like a hard disk drive but instead uses fast flash memory chips to store data.

source code The sets of organized instructions on how to function and perform tasks that define or constitute a program.

source file/directory The portion of a command that refers to the file or directory from which information is taken.

spanning A type of RAID level 0 that allows two or more devices to be represented as a single large volume.

special device file A file used to identify hardware devices such as hard disks and serial ports.

spooling The process of accepting a print job into a print queue.

SQL server A server service that gives other programs and computers the ability to access a database.

SSH agent A software program that can be used to automatically authenticate users using their private key.

ssh command A command that connects to a remote SSH daemon to perform remote administration.

SSH identity A unique configuration for a user account that is associated with user-specific SSH keys.

ssh-add command A command that can be used to add an SSH identity to a user account.

stand-alone daemons The daemons that configure themselves at boot time without assistance from inetd or xinetd.

Standard Error (stderr) A file descriptor that represents any error messages generated by a command.

Standard Input (stdin) A file descriptor that represents information input to a command during execution.

Standard Output (stdout) A file descriptor that represents the desired output from a command.

start command A command that can be used to manually start an upstart daemon.

stateful packet filter A packet filter that applies rules to related packets within the same network session.

stop command A command that can be used to manually stop an upstart daemon.

Storage Area Network (SAN) A group of computers that access the same storage device across a fast network.

strata The levels used within an NTP hierarchy that describe the relative position of a server to an original time source such as an atomic clock.

strings command A Linux command used to search for and display text characters in a binary file.

Structured Query Language (SQL) A language used by database servers to query, add, and modify the data within a database.

subdirectory A directory that resides within another directory in the directory tree.

subnet mask A series of four 8-bit numbers that determine the network and host portions of an IP address.

subnetting The process in which a single large network is subdivided into several smaller networks to control traffic flow.

subshell A shell started by the current shell.

sudo command A command that is used to perform commands as another user via entries in the /etc/sudoers file.

superblock The portion of a filesystem that stores critical information, such as the inode table and block size.

swap memory See *virtual memory*.

swapoff command A command used to disable a partition for use as virtual memory on the Linux system.

swapon command A command used to enable a partition for use as virtual memory on the Linux system.

symbolic link A pointer to another file on the same or another filesystem; commonly referred to as a shortcut.

syncing The process of writing data to the hard disk drive that was stored in RAM.

system backup The process whereby files are copied to an archive.

system initialization process The process that executes the daemons that provide for system services during boot time and bring the system to a useable state.

System Log Daemon (rsyslogd) The daemon that logs system events to various log files via information stored in /etc/rsyslog.conf and files within the /etc/rsyslog.d directory.

system rescue The process of using a live Linux OS to access and repair a damaged Linux installation.

system service The additional functionality provided by a program that has been incorporated into and started as part of the operating system.

System Statistics (sysstat) package A software package that contains common performance-monitoring utilities, such as mpstat, iostat, and sar.

system-config-keyboard command A command used on Fedora Linux systems to configure a keyboard for use by X Windows.

systemctl command A command that can be used to manually start, stop and restart Systemd daemons, as well as configure Systemd daemon startup during the system initialization process.

Systemd A relatively new software framework used on Linux systems that provides a system initialization process and system management functions.

Systemd Journal Daemon (journald) A Systemd component that logs system events to a journal database.

Tab-completion feature A feature of the BASH shell that fills in the remaining characters of a unique filename or directory name when the user presses the Tab key.

table A database structure that organizes data using records and fields.

tac command A Linux command that displays a file on the screen, beginning with the last line of the file and ending with the first line of the file.

tail command A Linux command used to display lines of text at the end of a file; by default, the tail command displays the last 10 lines of the file.

tar (tape archive) command The most common command used to create archives.

Tarball A gzip-compressed tar archive.

target See *target unit*.

target file/directory The portion of a command that refers to the file or directory to which information is directed.

target ID See *SCSI ID*.

target unit A Systemd term that is used to describe the number and type of daemons running on a Linux system. It is functionally equivalent to the UNIX SysV term *runlevel*.

TCP wrapper A program that can be used to run a network daemon with additional security via the /etc/hosts.allow and /etc/hosts.deny files.

tee command A command used to take from Standard Input and send to both Standard Output and a specified file.

telinit command A UNIX SysV command used to change the operating system from one runlevel to another.

telnet command A command used to run remote applications on a Linux computer.

terminal The channel that allows a certain user to log in and communicate with the kernel via a user interface.

terminator A device used to terminate an electrical conduction medium to absorb the transmitted signal and prevent signal bounce.

test statement A statement used to test a certain condition and generate a True/False value.

testparm command A command that can be used to check for syntax errors within the Samba configuration file as well as display the current Samba configuration.

text file A file that stores information in a readable text format.

text tools The programs that allow for the creation, modification, and searching of text files.

time slice The amount of time a process is given on a CPU in a multiprocessing operating system.

Time-To-Live (TTL) The amount of time that a computer is allowed to cache name resolution information obtained from a DNS server.

Token Ring A media access method commonly used by industrial networks.

top command The command used to give real-time information about the most active processes on the system; it can also be used to renice or kill processes.

total cost of ownership (TCO) The full sum of all accumulated costs, over and above the simple purchase price of utilizing a product. Includes training, maintenance, additional hardware, and downtime.

touch command The command used to create new files. It was originally used to update the time stamp on a file.

tr command A command used to transform or change characters received from Standard Input.

tracepath command A command used to trace the path an IPv4 packet takes through routers to a destination host.

tracepath6 command A command used to trace the path an IPv6 packet takes through routers to a destination host.

traceroute command A command used to trace the path an IPv4 packet takes through routers to a destination host.

traceroute6 command A command used to trace the path an IPv6 packet takes through routers to a destination host.

track The area on a hard disk that forms a concentric circle of sectors.

trapping The process of ignoring a kill signal.

tripwire A common IDS for Linux that monitors files and directories.

troubleshooting procedures The tasks performed when solving system problems.

tune2fs command A command used to modify ext2 and ext3 filesystem parameters.

tunnelling The process of embedding network packets within other network packets.

tzselect command A command that can be used to change the time zone of a Linux computer.

Ubuntu A major Linux distribution that is widely used in North America.

ulimit command A command used to modify process limit parameters in the current shell.

umask A special variable used to alter the permissions on all new files and directories by taking away select default file and directory permissions.

umask command The command used to view and change the umask variable.

umount command A command used to break the association between a device and a directory in the logical directory tree.

uncompress command A command used to decompress files compressed by the compress command.

unicast The TCP/IP communication destined for a single computer.

uninterruptible power supply (UPS) A device that contains battery storage and is used to supply power to computers in the event of a power outage.

Universal Access utility A graphical utility within Fedora 20 used to configure assistive technologies.

UNIX The first true multitasking, multiuser operating system, developed by Ken Thompson and Dennis Ritchie, and from which Linux was originated.

UNIX SysV A UNIX standard that is used to provide the structure of the system initialization process on Linux systems.

update-rc.d command A command that can be used to configure UNIX SysV daemon startup by runlevel on Ubuntu Linux systems.

upstart A recent version of the UNIX SysV system initialization process used on modern Linux distributions.

user A person who uses a computer.

user When used in the mode of a certain file or directory, the owner of that file or directory.

user account The information regarding a user that is stored in a system database (/etc/passwd and /etc/shadow), which can be used to log in to the system and gain access to system resources.

User Datagram Protocol/Internet Protocol (UDP/IP) A faster but unreliable version of TCP/IP.

User Identifier (UID) A unique number assigned to each user account.

user interface The interface the user sees and uses to interact with the operating system and application programs.

user process A process begun by a user and which runs on a terminal.

useradd command The command used to add a user account to the system.

user-defined variables The variables that are created by the user and are not used by the system. These variables are typically exported to subshells.

userdel command The command used to remove a user account from the system.

usermod command The command used to modify the properties of a user account on the system.

variable An area of memory used to store information. Variables are created from entries in environment files when the shell is first created after login and are destroyed when the shell is destroyed upon logout.

variable identifier The name of a variable.

Very Secure FTP daemon (vsftpd) The default FTP server program used in modern Linux distributions.

VFAT (Virtual File Allocation Table) A non-journaling file-system that might be used in Linux.

vgcreate command A command used to create LVM VG.

vgdisplay command A command used to view LVM VG.

vgextend command A command used to add additional physical volumes to an LVMVG.

vgscan command A command used to view LVM VGs.

vi editor A powerful command-line text editor available on most UNIX and Linux systems.

virtual machine An operating system that is running within virtualization software.

virtual machine host An operating system that runs virtualization software.

virtual memory An area on a hard disk or SSD (swap partition) that can be used to store information that normally resides in physical memory (RAM), if the physical memory is being used excessively.

Virtual Network Computer (VNC) A cross-platform technology that allows users to connect to a graphical desktop across a network.

virtualization software A set of programs that can be used to run an operating system within an existing operating system concurrently.

vmstat command A command used to display memory, CPU, and swap statistics.

VNC viewer A program used to connect to a VNC server and obtain a graphical desktop.

vncpasswd command A command used to set a VNC password for a user.

Volume Group (VG) A group of PVs that are used by the LVM.

Web page hit A single HTTP request that is sent from a Web browser to a Web server.

well-known ports Of the 65,535 possible ports, the ports from 0 to 1024, which are used by common networking services.

which command The command used to locate files that exist within directories listed in the PATH variable.

whois command A command used to obtain information about the organization that maintains a DNS domain.

wide area networks (WANs) Networks in which computers are separated geographically by large distances.

wildcard metacharacters The metacharacters used to match certain characters in a file or directory name; they are often used to specify multiple files.

window manager The GUI component that is responsible for determining the appearance of the windows drawn on the screen by X Windows.

Wireless-Fidelity (Wi-Fi) A LAN technology that uses Ethernet to transmit data over the air.

workstation A computer used to connect to services on a server.

workstation services The services that are used to access shared resources on a network server.

X client The component of X Windows that requests graphics to be drawn from the X server and displays them on the terminal screen.

X Display Manager (xdm) A graphical login screen.

X server The component of X Windows that draws graphics to windows on the terminal screen.

X Windows The component of the Linux GUI that displays graphics to windows on the terminal screen.

X.org A common implementation of X Windows used in Linux distributions.

XFree86 A common implementation of X Windows used in Linux distributions.

xvidtune A program used to fine-tune the vsync and hsync video card settings for use in X Windows.

xwininfo command A command used to display status information about X Windows.

yum (Yellowdog Updater Modified) command A command used to install and upgrade RPM packages from software

repositories, as well as manage and remove installed RPM packages.

zcat command A command used to view the contents of an archive created with compress or gzip to Standard Output.

Zettabyte File System (ZFS) A high-performance filesystem and volume management software that is often used to create volumes from multiple storage devices on Linux and UNIX systems.

zfs command A command used to configure ZFS filesystem features.

ZFS pool A series of storage devices that are managed by ZFS.

ZFS subfilesystem A subdirectory on a ZFS volume that can be managed as a separate unit by ZFS.

ZFS volume A volume created from space within a ZFS pool that contains a ZFS filesystem.

zless command A command used to view the contents of an archive created with compress or gzip to Standard Output in a page-by-page fashion.

zmore command A command used to view the contents of an archive created with compress or gzip to Standard Output in a page-by-page fashion.

zombie process A process that has finished executing but whose parent has not yet released its PID; the zombie still retains a spot in the kernel's process table.

zone A portion of the Domain Name Space that is administered by one or more DNS servers.

zone transfer The process of copying resource records for a zone from a master to a slave DNS server.

zpool command A command used to configure ZFS pools and volumes.

Index